GEORGE ANTON SCHAEFFER:
Arm Wrestling Kamehameha

BY:
LEE B. CROFT

SPHYNX PUBLICATIONS
Phoenix, Arizona, USA
MMXII

© Copyright Lee B. Croft, 2012

ALL RIGHTS RESERVED WORLDWIDE

No part of this book may be reproduced, stored in a retrieval system, or transmitted by any means without the written permission of the author.

This is the "Market Edition," having the ISBN: 978-0-9858908-1-0. There is also a "Presentation Edition" congener of variant title: "GEORGE ANTON SCHAEFFER: Arm Wrestling With Kamehameha." Both editions are available at www.lulu.com/LeeCroft

Sphynx Publications is located at 11622 S. Tusayan Ct., Phoenix, Arizona, 85044, USA. Telephone is 480-496-0229 (agent's cell is 480-567-4501). E-mail at Lbcroft@cox.net.

The author of this book, Lee B. Croft (1946--), is a teacher, scholar, and Professor Emeritus of the Russian Language and Culture at Arizona State University, where he taught and administered language programs for thirty-eight years. He is the author of thirteen books and over 200 scholarly articles, translations, and reviews. Many of these can be accessed, directly or indirectly, through www.lulu.com/LeeCroft.

Front Cover Art and Illustrations by BROOK KAPŪKUNIAHI PARKER

Introduction

The reader should know that this is a work of "faction," in the sense that every fact now known about a real individual, George Anton Schaeffer (1779-1836), is related in its chronological order. And George Anton Schaeffer's personal context—its geography, its politics, and its progression of a fascinating abundance of actual historical characters—is related as accurately as I could write it, so that well recorded history is not intentionally violated. But I have filled in the gaps between the known facts of George Anton Schaeffer's life with conjecture plausibly based upon the known facts and on Schaeffer's character as I've come to understand it. Since you, the reader, cannot be sure what of this "faction" is actual fact and what is plausible conjecture (fiction), you must presume this historical narrative in its totality to be a work of fiction, the creation of me, the author. I do hope that I've brought Schaeffer and his times back to life for you. Certainly I know him well by now.

This book, GEORGE ANTON SCHAEFFER: Arm Wrestling Kamehameha, is the second book of a trilogy—THREE books depicting Dr. Schaeffer's life and times. The first and preceding book takes him from his birth in Germany in 1779 to his involvement in Napoleon Bonaparte's invasion of Russia and a bit beyond to 1813. I am very pleased to have published this first book in the year 2012, the bicentennial of the historic 1812 Battle of Borodino for Moscow. This current and second book, GEORGE ANTON SCHAEFFER: Arm Wrestling Kamehameha, treats Dr. Schaeffer's circumnavigation of the globe, giving primary focus to his adventurous year and a half (November 1815 to July 1817) in the Hawai'ian islands. The third and final book of the trilogy, GEORGE ANTON SCHAEFFER: Shipping Germans to Brazil, views Dr. Schaeffer's return to Europe and to Brazil, from where he engaged in transporting thousands of German colonists and mercenary soldiers to Brazil for the benefit of Dom Pedro I. It includes a colorful chapter on his wife Barbara's activities in St. Petersburg during the five years she lived there waiting for her husband to return. Dr. Schaeffer died at Frankenthal, the colony he founded in the Bahia State of Brazil, in 1836.

I first decided to research the facts of George Anton Schaeffer's life when I realized for the first time, sometime in the early 1980s, that the man who was involved in a Russian plot to build a balloon to kill Napoleon in 1812, the man who was co-regent of the Hawai'ian island of Kaua'i for more than a year and built forts there that remain to this day, and the man called the "creator" of the German emigration to Brazil *was the same man*. Each of these THREE chapters of Schaeffer's astonishingly peripatetic life had individual scholars presenting it to our historical understanding. But each of these scholars, mainly because of language limitations, were limited in their knowledge of the other chapters. My advantage over even the most competent of these scholars—I'm thinking here primarily of Richard A. Pierce and Carlos Oberacker—is that I was for thirty-eight years a Professor of Foreign Languages in the academic department that is now Arizona State University's School of International Letters and Cultures.

Russian is my language of specialty, but finding help in the translation of sources and correspondence in German and Portuguese is less problematic for me. So I have been "working on" George Anton Schaeffer for more than twenty-five years...giving talks, writing papers, engaging others in correspondence and interviewing them.

Over the years I have tried to travel to every place George Anton Schaeffer traveled: Germany, Russia, Turkey, Australia, Alaska, Hawai'i, China, Brazil... I've tried to stand where he stood, touch what he touched, see what he saw. Following him around the world almost two hundred years after him has changed my life. My wife and I have now spent two decades of our summers in Hawai'i in places connected to George Schaeffer's activities there. Hawai'i's "mana" has captured me as it did him, and I actually wrote most of this text during my periods of residence in Hawai'i.

Lee B. Croft

Waikiki, July 18, 2009

ACKNOWLEDGMENTS

I have many, many people to thank for their contributions to this work. First among these is my wife, Dr. Lesley Hoyt Croft, who listened to me read every word of it to her many times, giving me her wisdom as a published scholar and a voracious reader in editing, suggesting changes...and for her emotional support. Others who have heard me read parts of it and gave me their thoughts include my son Hayden L. Croft, who is establishing himself as a film critic and writer, my brothers Jerry and Wayne Croft, my sister Nancy Jacobson, my now deceased father William S. "Bill" Croft, my wonderful mother Norma Croft, and Lesley's mother, Kathryn Hoyt. Then there are so many other friends and relatives: Wolfgang and Claudia Kasmayr of Dachau, Germany, who aided in finding German documents and Dr. Schaeffer's birth records and gave us their hospitality, Richard and Billie Hyde Watson, who have even stored written chapters in their house for reasons of security, George and Debby Morgan, who have shared our time in Hawai'i, Paul and Sara Muriello, and Eugene and Peggy Wedoff. All of these people have been encouraging to me.

The list of the scholarly "giants" on whose shoulders this work rests is also long. Please go through the bibliography that I provide and read my annotations. All these hundreds of people contributed something, sometimes substantial somethings. But I feel that I have to give first and special named mention to the late Richard A. Pierce (1918-2004), the leading previous scholar on Schaeffer and Russian America, for his large corpus of work and his helpful and encouraging personal correspondence and communication. Other personally contacted contributors include Stephen K. Batalden, Walter D. Wetzels, Patricia Polansky, Peter Horwath, John Alexander, Jane Mund, Clarice Deal, Charles Oelfke, Peter Littke, Delbert D. Phillips, Dwight Brown, Timur Guseynov, Tanya Domenico, Tatyana Dhaliwal, Don Livingston, Saule Moldabekova Robb, David Mashuri, Charles Winkler, Agnes Kefeli-Clay, William H. "Mick" Hawley, Mark Curran, Kenneth N. Owens, William Brumfield, Christopher W. Croft, and Sarah Gould. Also, I have been inspired by the maritime art and early contact history of Raymond Massey and the Hawai'ian cultural and historical art of Herb Kawainui Kane and Brook Kapūkuniahi Parker. They have carried on well the tradition of Hawaiian historic art exemplified by John Webber, Louis Choris, Jacques Arago, J. Alphonse Pellion, and others.

Lee B. Croft

A NOTE ON THE NAMES

I refer to my main character here as "George Anton Aloysius Schaeffer." Other spellings of his name abound in the research on him. Most problematical is his last name, which may have been spelled either "Schäfer" or "Schäffer" in his original time and place. There is evidence for both the single "f" spelling, and for the double "f" spelling. In present day Münnerstadt, Germany—George's birthplace-- there is a street named "Schäfergässchen" and there are people there to this day who spell their name "Schäfer" with only one "f." There were no people listed in the 2002 phone directory there who spelled their name with two "f's" as "Schäffer." On the hand-written German birth record, one simply cannot be sure…it might be either way. Militating for the double "f" is the spelling in Russian, which we have in George's own hand wherein he clearly transliterates his own name, signing letters and documents as "Шефферъ," that is, allowing for modernization (omission of terminal "yer"), "Sheffer" with *two* "f's," even though Russian generally has no geminate consonants in its native words or names. In Russian he is uniformly "Egor (translation of "George," pronounced "Ye-GOR") Nikolaevich (patronymic for "son of Nikolai (translation of Nicholas)) Sheffer." Also, in the 1960s, a Brazilian professor, Enrico Schaeffer, wrote genealogical works on his "collateral ancestor" and spelled the name with two "f's." And, most definitive, is the fact that J. F. Hammerich publishers of Altona (Hamburg) spelled his name "Ritter von Schäffer Dr." on the title page of the book Schaeffer wrote about Brazil in 1824. For all these reasons I spell his name with two "f's," but, of course, this does not mean that any number of "Schäfers" in the world are not possibly related to him.

Then there is the matter of the German umlaut…the "two dots." I am generally changing the name to "Schaeffer" instead of writing "Schäffer" because I desire to facilitate ease of English-language search-engine access to research concerning him, given that the majority of works on him to date use the English (also Portuguese) "Schaeffer." I do use the umlaut on other words, though perhaps not entirely uniformly. For example, I am writing "Münnerstadt" and "Nürnburg." But, because the English reader knows it better that way, I write the city name as a translated "Munich" instead of writing "München." My aim, of course, is to indulge the English reader's expectation while retaining a certain foreign flair.

So, my main subject character is either George or Georg or Egor or Yegor or Jorge. He is either Anton or Antonio. He is Aloysius or Alois. He is Schäfer or Schäffer or Sheffer or, as here, Schaeffer. It all depends on the source—German, English, French, Russian, or Portuguese—and the translation or transliteration therefrom. In Hawai'ian, he was "Kepa," but this was never written. Dr. Schaeffer was indeed an amazing polyglot with an oft-mentioned-by-others extraordinary ability to "pick up" and use even exotic languages. The list of languages he used in his life is long, including: German, French, Latin, Yiddish, Dutch, Czech, Slovak, Hungarian, Roma, Ukrainian/Galician, Russian, English, Brazilian Portuguese, Tlingit (Kolosh), Aleut, Hawai'ian, and Pataxo. He had passing contact also with Spanish, Chinese, and Latvian.

For Hawai'ian names and place names, mainly in the second book of the trilogy, GEORGE ANTON SCHAEFFER: Arm Wrestling Kamehameha, I try to be linguistically accurate, including the "'" ("okina" symbolized by the apostrophe in my work instead of the vertical hash for reasons of processing convenience) as a sign for the Hawai'ian consonantal glottal stop, writing, for example, "Hawai'i," "Kaua'i," "Ka'ahumanu" and "Kaumuali'i." Also, I try to render the Hawai'ian plural accurately...as in "kahuna=kāhuna" or "mu=mū." Citations of the sources are not, however, uniform in this and not all authorities agree on certain of the spellings. Schaeffer and other European contemporaries from the time of Captain James Cook's first contact with the Hawai'ians spelled the Hawai'ian places and names diversely as the words sounded to them. Schaeffer, who was reputed to speak and understand Hawai'ian better than other Europeans who had been there longer, apparently (evidenced from a transliteration of Schaeffer's written Russian equivalents) perceived and spoke Hawai'ian with more than *half* of Hawai'ian's stock of eight consonants replaced by his own native German or acquired Russian consonants. He, like many others, replaced Hawai'ian "p" with "b," "h" with "g," "k" with "t," "l" with "r," and "w" with "v."   Thus, an English transliteration of Schaeffer's Russian word for "Kamehameha" is "Tomi-omi," for "Honolulu" is "Gonerua," for "Oahu" is "Ovagu," for "Hanalei" is "Gonnarej," for "Kaumuali'i" is "Tomari," for "Lana'i" is "Rany," for "Ka'ahumanu" is "Kagumanu," for "Kaua'i" is sometimes "Atuvaj" and sometimes "Gauaj," for "Moloka'i" is "Maranaj," and for "Hawai'i" itself is "Ovagi." One might think that so many replacements of native sounds with foreign sounds would result in unintelligibility. But it did not, because the replacements, using only consonants that *Hawa'iian did not have* (such as Schaeffer's "g," "b," "t," "l," and "v"), caused there to be NO NEW PHONEMIC CONTRASTS in the speech perceived by the Hawai'ians, who understood Schaeffer easily and often praised his "mastery" of their language. Linguists know this phenomenon well. In his Things Hawaiian: A Pocket Guide to the Hawaiian Language (Island Heritage Publications, Aiea, Hawaii, 1998, pp. 10-11...notice here the lack of the okina) Albert J. Schultz writes: "At first, all these letters were used (to represent the Hawaiian sounds). But it really made no difference which sound or letter you used. For instance, whether you said 'tai' or 'kai,' the word still meant 'sea.' In the same way, you could use either 'lani' or 'rani' for 'heaven,' 'vai' or 'wai' for 'water.' And this held for any words containing these sounds." For the purposes of this book, however, I write the Hawai'ian names, places, and words in conformance to their modern usage (e.g. not referring to them in text as being in the "Sandwich Islands") and spellings as explained above, the picturesque variants of Schaeffer and his contemporaries notwithstanding. I do this for the modern reader's ease of reference to people and things currently Hawai'ian.

For Russian names and place names I follow the US Library of Congress system without diacritics (e.g. "Kondratii Ryleev," and "Sysoi Slobodchikov"), but the citations preserve the transliterations of others, often reflecting popular English spellings (e.g. "Tolstoy" instead of my transliterated "Tolstoi"). Occasionally I stray from my own convention in the interests of reducing English-language confusion (e.g. using "Semyon" instead of "Semen" to transliterate the common Russian name). Again, the criterion here is to aid others in English search-engine access. I have tried to be accurate in textual inclusions of the Portuguese names and places, writing with the diacritics "Antônio" and "São Paulo" and so on. The search engines generally will access these topics, however, with the diacritics omitted.

Russians frequently address each other by first name and patronymic. The patronymic, the apparent "middle name," is formed for males from the first name of their father plus the suffix –ovich or –evich; and for females from the first name of their father plus –ovna or –evna. Thus George Anton Schaeffer is called "Yegor Nikolaevich" (George, son of Nicholas) and Barbara Hindernacht Schaeffer is called "Varvara Vul'fgangovna" (Barbara, daughter of Wolfgang).

A NOTE ON RUSSIAN DATES

The Russians used the Julian Calendar in the eighteenth, nineteenth, and twentieth century until March of 1918, long after the countries of western Europe and most of the rest of the world had changed to the Gregorian Calendar. This means that the dates for events that transpired in Russia and the Russian Empire were basically eleven days behind the date commonly used elsewhere in the eighteenth century, twelve days behind in the nineteenth century, and thirteen days behind in the first eighteen years of the twentieth century. I give the "old style" date first, then the "new style" date when known and applicable when citing dates relevant to the Russian imperial period of history, which includes much of this trilogy. Thus, the date of the Battle of Borodino for Moscow is given as 26 August (Russian Calendar)/7 September (French Calendar), 1812, because of the twelve-day difference of dates in the nineteenth century. Russian birth and death dates are given in citation as those of "Mikhail Illarionovich Golenishchev-Kutuzov (5/16 September, 1745—16/28 April, 1813)," showing the eleven-day difference in the eighteenth century and the twelve-day difference in the nineteenth. Russian dates in the empire's North American territories (e.g. Alaska) were an additional day behind the Gregorian Calendar date because of the lack of an international global dateline convention. At www.calendarhome.com you can see that although the dates were different, the days of the week were the same.

TABLE OF CONTENTS

    Introduction…………………………………….page 3
    Acknowledgments...……………………………page 5
    A Note on the Names…………………………..page 6
    A Note on Russian Dates……………………….page 8
    Table of Contents.. page 9

CHAPTER SIX: To Novo-Arkhangelsk by Sea

    Life on the *Suvorov*...page 11
    London..page 16
    Becalmed..page 19
    Rio de Janeiro (Captain M. P. Lazarev/Slavery)........................page 23
    Dom João and *Boa Vista*……………………………………...page 30
    The Young Princes, Dona Carlota, Gen.Thomas Sumter...........page 37
    Meeting Drs. Langsdorff and Flach..page 41
    "I Shall Return"—With Capital…………………………….….page 44
    Unpleasant Words..page 46
    Guanabara Bay Expedition..page 49
    The Way to Port Jackson/Vehicles of the "Progeny"?...................page 50
    Action in the Rocks (Gov. Lachlan Macquarie).......................page 57
    Across the Pacific (Suvarov Island)..page 69
    First Days at Novo-Arkhangelsk (Gov. Aleksandr Baranov)….....page 79
    Guests of Governor Aleksandr Baranov………………….….....page 90
    Lazarev Leaves………………………………………………...page 99
    Life Stranded………………………………………………….page 101
    Letters from Barbara………………………………………….page 102
    Going to Hawai'i……………………………………………...page 105

CHAPTER SEVEN: Hawaii

    Kamehameha………………………………………………….page 108
    John Young, "Olohana"……………………………………….page 113
    Kailua—King and Queen (Ka'ahumanu)…..………………….page 117
    The Stay on Hawai'i…………………………………………...page 122
    Maui……………………………………………………………page 155
    Honolulu……………………………………………………….page 159
    The Nu'uanu Pali Battle Site………………………………….page 167
    Captain Isaiah Lewis…………………………………………..page 173
    The Ships Arrive………………………………………………page 176
    Back to Kailua…………………………………………………page 180
    Kaua'i (King Kaumuali'i)……………………………………..page 183
    The Agreement and the Ceremony……………………………page 191

The Celebration in Waimea……………………………………….page 199
The *Otkrytie* Departs……………………………………………..page 202
Touring Kaua'i with the Royal Party……………………………page 207
Kaumuali'i's Story…………………………………………………page 209
George's Explanation of the Story………………………………page 218
Treaties………………………………………………...…………..page 221
Buying Ships (Timofei Tarakanov's family)…………………….page 224
Building Forts……………………………………………………..page 238
The Ane'ekapuahi and Mare Amara……………………………page 243
More Land (Chief Hanalei/Mi'ikina)……………………………..page 250
The Hike Back to Waimea……………………………………….page 256
A Conversation with Kekaiha'akulou……………………………page 257
The Visit of James Wilcocks…………………………………….page 261
Storms (Timofei loses a man)…………………………………..page 269
Troubles in Waimea……………………………………………...page 291
The Stand at Hanalei…………………………………………….page 308
Crisis in Honolulu…………………………………………….…..page 313
Hiding on the Ship in Waimea…………………………………..page 321

BIBLIOGRAPHY………………………………………………...page 323

ILLUSTRATIONS LIST…………………………………………page 401

Chapter Six-- To Novo-Arkhangelsk by Sea

Life on the *Suvorov*:

George had imagined that a long sea voyage might become boring to him. But it never did. There seemed to be something to do every minute. And often, what needed to be done had to be done in a hurry. George found that the time passed surprisingly quickly.

A likeness of George Anton Schaeffer at age 34

In the first days after their departure, George struggled with seasickness. He was all right if he was up and walking about the deck of the ship, but, as soon as he sat down at his bunk below and folded down the desktop to read or write, the feeling of nausea and dizziness would overcome him and he would have to get up and make his way to the rail to empty his stomach over the side. He was not alone in this. Seasickness affected several of the others, including even some experienced sailors. They told George that "sooner or later" he would get the better of the seasickness. It usually struck them, they said, in the first two weeks after being in port, but, after that, it diminished.

George, as the ship *Suvorov*'s surgeon, with his own bunk and semi-private area near Captain Mikhail Petrovich Lazarev's cabin, quickly became a kind of intermediary between the crewmembers, whose names and personal situations he made a point of learning early on, and the ship's officers. Captain Lazarev remained relatively aloof from the rest of the ship's company, except for his second-in-command Lieutenant Semyon Yakovlevich Unkovskii, the "Shturman," Maxim Andreevich Samsonov, and his cadet apprentice from the Kronstadt Navigational School, Aleksei Ivanovich Rossiiskii, who were permitted into the Captain's cabin daily for navigational consultations and access to the charts. Captain Lazarev was a stocky young man of medium height. He had a round, clean-shaven face with a smooth complexion. His hair

Captain Mikhail Petrovich Lazarev (3/14 November, 1788—11/23 April, 1851), from: http://it.wikipedia.org/wiki/Michail_Petrovic_Lazarev. The likeness here shows him at an older age, perhaps 50.

was very dark brown and he kept it cut short except for a longer patch, which piled up on the top of his head. But he almost always wore a black three-cornered hat so the top of his head was rarely visible. He appeared on the deck only for short periods to give instructions to his subordinates. He took his meals alone in his cabin, except for selected times when he would invite other officers, the Russian-American Company supercargo Germann Nikolaevich Molvo, or George, to dine with him. Lieutenant Unkovskii took the visible lead on deck, interacting with the crew through his "Michman," Nikolai Ivanovich Bestuzhev, whose always capable demeanor quickly won the crew's respect.

It took the *Suvorov* almost two months to sail from Kronstadt near St. Petersburg to Portsmouth harbor in England. At Karlskrona, Sweden, a week away from Kronstadt, they had joined, for security's sake, a group of British merchant ships accompanied by several warships. The fall weather was cooperative and the sailing was pleasant until the convoy skirted Denmark and entered into the North Sea. Then they encountered their first storm. George was awakened in the night by the scream of the wind and the increased rocking motion of the ship. He dressed and went up on deck to find the entire crew trying to reduce sail in the icy nighttime blast. The froth-topped waves on either side of the ship were equal in height to the ship's side railing. Thick clouds just above the waves were scudding along with the ship, limiting visibility except during flashes of lightning that struck so close by that the resultant thunder was instantaneous and deafening. George was almost overcome by a feeling of awe and even terror at nature's power and the apparent prospect of the ship's foundering. But the crewmembers all seemed calm enough, even as they worked frantically to change the ship's posture. George was astounded at the sailors working aloft on the yardarms. They had climbed the rigging to fearsome heights in the gale and, their feet supported only by rope as they clung to the narrowing yards, had begun to haul and furl the stiff but terribly unruly sails. It didn't seem possible to George that such work could be required of a human being. It looked to him that at any second the howling wind would pluck these sailors, their ungloved fingers frozen beyond ability to grasp in rescue, their eyes squinted beyond sight by the icy rain and spume of sea, from their precipitous perches and throw them into the relentless raging waves so far below. But the sailors were intrepid and carried out their tasks efficiently and without mishap. In less than an hour, the *Suvorov*'s attitude in the storm was improved, and George felt secure again.

By the time they anchored in Portsmouth, George had managed to surmount the daily seasickness. Keeping constantly busy was the key to this, he thought. Staying on deck in his waking hours with his eyes on the horizon also helped. Interacting with the crewmembers, he learned a lot about diverse aspects of life on a sailing ship. He extracted, for example, many of the secrets of navigation from Shturman Samsonov and his cadet apprentice Rossiiskii. He learned where to find, if the clouds allowed, several constellations of stars in the night sky overhead. He had never taken the time to master these celestial "guideposts" before. From the gunners, Rodion Shushkov and Naum Semyonov, he learned the rudiments of loading, aiming, and firing the cannons. This was a skill entailing more complexity than George had previously imagined. There were several different types of loads available…balls, shot, chains…and the powder charges varied with the intended effect. For practice during periods of calm, the gunners floated flag-topped planks away from the ship, then fired at these improvised targets with the eight twelve-pound cannons or the six smaller falconets or "punt guns" which fired from side-rail mounts on deck. A dead strike elicited loud cheers from the watching crewmembers.

From several of the sailors George learned considerable knot craft. He learned to tie all manner of hitches, bends, and knots in the differing types of nautical line that connected all the working parts of the ship. The bowline knot, he learned, was the "king of knots." It could not be broken by any tension on the line. It was as strong as the line itself under any pull. And yet it could easily be untied by anyone who knew how. The sailors would jokingly compete to see who could tie a bowline the fastest, and George was constantly amazed at their dexterity in tying this knot. George even learned to make decorative knots…like the spherical "monkey's fist" which could be used as a belay between pins…and to splice the line. Out of a "tail" of three-strand jute line, he made, under the instruction of quartermaster Ivan Fokin, a two-meter rope having a "monkey's fist" at one end and a wrist-sized loop spliced into the other. With this he practiced and practiced until he could, like the other sailors, throw a slip knot over the "monkey's fist" by holding the looped end and making a whiplike gesture with his hand and wrist.

"If ye'r ever aloft and hangin' onto the mast, it's a skill that'll keep ye alive," advised Fokin, smiling. "Ye can keep hanging on with one arm and use the other to throw the knot around the yard end. Then ye can just lower ye'sef down to the deck. A landlubber wouldn't know what to do."

George tried to find opportunities to interact more with Captain Lazarev, seeking to earn the man's respect. Since they were initially headed for England, George decided to ask the Captain to be involved in teaching him some useful English phraseology. George's request would have been ample specification of the English consultant Joseph Desilvier's duty to teach the ship's surgeon and Company stockholder English. But George wanted to involve the Captain as well. He was aware that Captain Lazarev, like many Russian captains, had learned his profession in the British navy and that he spoke English well. To his delight, Captain Lazarev assented to meet with him and with Desilvier and occasionally Lieutenant Unkovskii also for an hour every day, during which time they would only speak in English. George's previous exposure to the English language was limited to a few words he had heard from Franz Leppich who had once worked in London, but he soon impressed both the Englishman Desilvier and Captain Lazarev with his ability to acquire communicative facility in the language.

"It's amazing how rapidly you are learning to understand and use English, Yegor Nikolaevich," Captain Lazarev said to him in English one day. "I've never seen anyone come to use a language so fast. You are truly gifted in this regard."

"I've always been able to learn other languages quickly," George responded. "I think it's because I was exposed to so many different languages in my youth…German, of course, and French, some Yiddish, some Roma, the languages of the Czechs and Slovaks, then Hungarian, then Russian. I always try to speak to whomever I meet in their own language as soon as I can."

George advised the ship's head cook, Pyotr Rychkov, on antiscorbutic aspects of diet. Scurvy was a constant threat to men at sea for long periods of time. Lacking fresh fruit, he suggested that Rychkov use potatoes in the sailors' fare at least twice a week. The cabbage, with which Rychkov made "shchi" soup, was also known to have antiscorbutic properties, but the cabbage could not be preserved as well as the potatoes. Before boarding, George had given some thought to issuing a ban on the smoking of tobacco aboard the *Suvorov*. But right away on board he encountered the fact that Captain Lazarev was a smoker, as was Quartermaster Fokin and Shturman Samsonov. So he decided upon an educational approach, initiating a campaign of denouncing the habit to one and all "in the interests of health and happiness." This caused some amusement, and later some friction, among the smoking sailors. But Captain Lazarev and the other officers simply ignored him, and never commented on his denunciation of the smoking habit.

Captain Lazarev was an avid chess player and a chess aficionado. At one of his dinners with George and several other officers, he told the story of Wolfgang von Kempelen's chess automaton, the "Turk," and how it had beaten Napoleon in a game. He was certain, he told his company, that he could defeat the Turk in

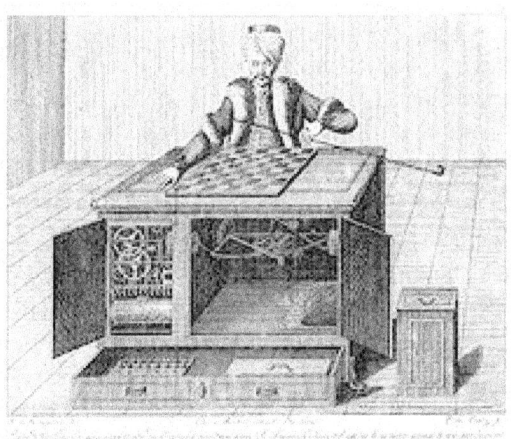

An engraving of Wolfgang von Kempelen's (1734-1804) chess automaton, "The Turk" from http://en.wikipedia.org/wiki/The_Turk.

a chess match. To show his skill, he challenged the officers and crew to a chess match. He would play them all at once, and pay them all with extra rations of vodka if they beat him. A game board with pegged pieces would be affixed to the rail near the aft toilets. The crew, playing white, could consult all they wanted, but they then had to make one move per day. He, playing black, would answer at the same rate. He had made the same challenge on several previous voyages, he said, and had never been defeated. He predicted victory for himself within thirty days.

The chess challenge gave the crewmembers something to talk about every day. The more experienced chess players among them, Lieutenants Unkovskii and Povalo-Shveikovskii, and Supercargo Molvo, took the lead in suggesting moves, but, by the time, three weeks out, when they harbored at Portsmouth, Captain Lazarev was at advantage by two pieces. George, who knew how to play chess but had not spent much time at it, took a real interest in the Captain's challenge. He understood that the challenge united the ship's company in a common endeavor of a non-seafaring nature, and he considered that positive for the ship's morale. But, responding personally to the challenge, he set about to play separate games with Unkovskii, Povalo-Shveikovskii and Molvo in order to improve his own skill at chess.

London:

While the *Suvorov* was anchored in Portsmouth harbor and the crew was adding provisions to its stores by dinghy and longboat, Captain Lazarev decided to allow the officers and Russian-American Company representatives a week's leave to visit London, which was located some fifty miles to the north. Of the officers, only Michman Bestuzhev would remain on board in surrogate command of the crewmembers who had to stay aboard. George was invited to join Captain Lazarev and Lieutenant Unkovskii, accompanied by the Englishman Desilvier, in the hiring of a separate special coach. The others would travel by ordinary coach and make their own arrangements when they reached London.

In the coach, the men talked of what they expected to find in the great city of London. They marveled at the reported population of the city…over a million inhabitants. Joseph Desilvier had been born in London and planned to visit relatives there, clearing up some personal matters before resuming his voyage to Australia. He had not been in England for several years and noted some changes in the road and in the buildings along the way. In talking with the coachmen, he had learned that a new theater, the Theatre Royal, had been constructed on Drury Lane in London. The new theater had three mezzanine levels and provided seating for an audience of two thousand people. He hoped to go there and see the play *Remorse* by Samuel Taylor Coleridge. He was an avid reader and wanted to buy Walter Scott's *Lady of the Lake* and Jane Austen's *Pride and Prejudice* to take with him on the ship. Lieutenant Unkovskii was interested in visiting London's architectural sites: the Tower of London, with its moat and menagerie, Westminster Abbey, and St. Paul's Cathedral. He had never seen a real tiger, he said, and he had been told that the Tower of London's menagerie had one.

Joseph Desilvier informed Unkovskii and the others that the English poet William Blake had seen a tiger at the Tower of London menagerie years before and been inspired to write one of the most famous poems in the English language about it. "I can still recite the first verse of it," he said. "I've forgotten the rest. It goes, 'Tyger, tyger, burning bright, In the forests of the night, What immortal hand or eye, Could frame thy fearful symmetry?…'."

Captain Lazarev asked George what he would most like to do in London. George answered that he would like to meet King George…or if not him personally, then some of the other British royalty.

"You'll have to make some inquiry about that with the Russian Embassy, I would say," commented Captain Lazarev. "I'm sure the staff there is aware of our mission. You could inform them that we have arrived safely in Portsmouth, and that we plan to continue our voyage by sailing for Brazil next week.

Perhaps they could send someone to Portsmouth before we leave in order to collect our mail. Otherwise we'll leave it with the port authorities in Portsmouth."

In London, the Captain's party stayed in a most luxurious hotel near the city center. The hotel was called "The Sphinx" and sported an Egyptian motif in its interior decoration. The wallpaper above dark wainscoting featured imitation ancient hieroglyphics like those discovered in the tombs of the pharaohs. The hotel was run by Egyptian personnel wearing thick white turbans and carrying golden daggers in wide red waist sashes. Their red shoes had toes, which curled upwards at the front. They served a delicate tea, pouring it already steeped from ornamented brass teapots into white porcelain cups on gold-rimmed saucers. And they kept coming back around to the guests seated in the lounge and to those in the hotel's restaurant, asking "More tea, Effendi?"

One of George's first impressions of London was the very unpleasant stench of the Thames River, into which the city poured its untreated sewage. The Sphinx Hotel addressed this problem by soaking its curtains in a solution of lime in order to remove the smell from the air coming in through the windows. "Something else will have to be done with the sewage," George thought.

George was pleased to find that his work to become facile in English was rewarded. The English people he met were very happy to listen to him and to try to understand him, especially when it was communicated to them that he was "Russian." The common effort against Napoleon had, of late, made Russians the bosom friends of all Englishmen, even those, the vast majority, who had never met a Russian. And George could see that saying he was a "Russian" in London at this time was much better than being identified as a "German." After touring around the city and taking in the sights, George decided he would try to make the acquaintance of King George III. At the Russian Embassy, however, he was told that audiences with King George were impossible at this time as the King was permanently "indisposed." Meetings with other members of the royal family would not be possible to schedule within the week. He would have to content himself with frequenting public places where royalty were known to appear on the chance that he could find a way to meet them.

At the Russian Embassy, George found out about recent political events. The European Allies had defeated Napoleon's forces at the Battle of the Nations at Leipzig. Both sides incurred terrible losses of life. The Allies suffered 54,000 casualties, and the French lost almost 75,000 men, including 30,000 taken prisoner and several thousand defectors. Forty-eight French officers of General's rank were lost to death or capture, including the valiant General Joseph-Antoine Poniatowski, who had, after being awarded his Marshal's baton in the field, drowned trying to escape capture by swimming the Elster River while wounded. The embassy staff expected that the Allies would now be able to dictate very advantageous peace terms to Napoleon. Prince Klemens von Metternich of Austria was being given the task. Hostilities between Britain and the United States were continuing in America, with the British losing their Native-American ally, the Shawnee Chief Tecumseh, at the Battle of the

Thames River, being forced to surrender the previously captured city of Detroit, and losing the naval Battle of Plattsburg on Lake Champlain. The British-allied Canadian Militia, however, had repelled an army of 7000 United States soldiers on the Chateaugay River, inflicting heavy losses. George remarked to the embassy officials that Russian Minister of Foreign Affairs, Nikolai Petrovich Rumiantsev, whom he "had worked with and knew well," was planning to mediate in the conflict between Great Britain and the United States through his acquaintance, the U.S. Ambassador to Russia, John Quincy Adams, the son of the second U.S. President. While at the Embassy, George made arrangements for the collection of the *Suvorov*'s mail as Captain Lazarev had suggested he do. He resolved to write a letter to Barbara about his visit to London and include it with the others he had already written. The Embassy would forward all of their mail to Russia with the next ship bound for St. Petersburg.

The next evening George encountered Captain Lazarev and Lieutenant Unkovskii in the hotel lobby. They were asking one of the turbaned staff members for directions to the location of a well-known bordello...and they asked George if he wanted to accompany them.

"No," said George. "I'm a married man."

"So am I," responded Lieutenant Unkovskii, "But that's in Russia. This is England. The women here are not baptized Orthodox...so fornication with them doesn't make me guilty of any sin."

"Whereas I am married only to the Russian Navy," said Captain Lazarev, chuckling. "So I can fornicate as I want and feel no guilt about it."

"Guilt is one thing...disease is another," said George. "If I were you, I'd avoid fornicating with women who make a business of it. You may wind up needing more than my dietary advice."

"Well, that's why you're here, isn't it?" grumbled Captain Lazarev. He and Lieutenant Unkovskii walked away and exited the hotel together, leaving George in the lobby with the turbaned staff member.

George turned to the staff member and asked, "Do you know any place where I might meet members of the royal family?"

"No," the man replied. "I don't."

On the way back to Portsmouth, the mood of the men in the coach was merry. They had all purchased bottles of liquor as souvenirs of their visit to London. Joseph Desilvier was partial to gin and insisted the others sample some. But George and the naval officers had purchased bottles of Scotch Whiskey of different sorts, which they also sampled, in order to compare. After their sampling, they began to joke with one another. Captain Lazarev related that in the bordello Lieutenant Unkovskii had naively exposed to the women occupants a thick wad of pound notes he had obtained in exchange for some gold coins he had appropriated in Turkey several years before. This immediately caused the women to rush him in a group and usher him away behind a dressing screen, from where neither he nor they emerged for more than an hour. "Well," said Unkovskii, "I got my money's worth." Then he started to sing an old Russian song about the Cossack river pirate, Stenka Razin…about how Stenka, dallying excessively with a captive princess in his river boat on the Volga, displeased his jealous men. To placate them, he "throws her over the side into the rushing waves."   When he got to the words "zabort yeyo brosaet," where Stenka Razin throws the captive princess overboard, Unkovskii made a grand sweeping gesture with his hand, accidentally knocking a bottle of gin from Desilvier's hands and onto the floor of the coach where it shattered on the heater grate, spilling its contents onto their feet. Desilvier was a bit irritated, but George and Captain Lazarev began to laugh. And George began to sing in Latin one of his favorite refrains from the Carmina Burana:

"Bibit pauper et egrotus,	The poor man drinks, the sick man drinks,
bibit exul et ignotus,	the exile drinks, and the stranger,
bibit puer, bibit canus,	the boy drinks, the old man drinks,
bibit presul et decanus	the bishop drinks, and the deacon,
bibit soror, bibit frater,	the sister drinks, the brother drinks,
bibit anus, bibit mater,	the old lady drinks, the mother drinks,
bibit ista, bibit ille,	this man drinks, that man drinks,
bibunt centum, bibunt mille.	A hundred drink, a thousand drink."

"You sing well, Yegor," exclaimed Captain Lazarev. "And what a fine melody! Let's sing it again together. What is it now…bibit pauper et ignotus, bibit soror…? My Latin is a bit too weak. But you can teach us how it goes."

George coached the men through the song again, then again and again until, laughing uproariously, they finally got through it together successfully. Only then did Lieutenant Unkovskii ask, "What does it mean?" So George explained the words to them and they laughed even louder. The merriment and frivolity of these hours together, they knew, were a prelude to a long and possibly arduous trial on the Atlantic Ocean as they sailed for Brazil the next day.

Becalmed:

Three days out of Portsmouth, George extracted a decayed and broken tooth from the back of Quartermaster Ivan Fokin's mouth using the tried-and-true dental pliers he had acquired years before in Wŭrzburg. Fokin expressed his gratitude to George strangely, rubbing his jaw and winking as he said, "Ah, now

I feel a whole lot more like I do now than I did a little while ago." George just shook his head and said, "Well, I hope so. That was a real bad tooth…surely very painful. And, it is my considered opinion that you would have less trouble with your teeth if you stopped smoking."

"Well, I'll take that under advisement…yes I will," said the Quartermaster with a wry smile.

On the tenth day out of Portsmouth, Captain Lazarev's chess acumen forced the crew to admit that their being checkmated was inevitable. They grumbled about losing the chance to get the extra ration of vodka and asked Michman Bestuzhev to propose to the Captain that he should give them another game for the same stakes. The Captain agreed, but wanted to play white this time.

They were between the Azores and Cape Verde in the central Atlantic at the turn of the year to 1814. Orthodox Christmas was approaching and George was reminded of the birthday of his daughter Inga, who would soon be two years old. But the men were too busy to celebrate. They had to fight their way through a strong gale which made their lives more difficult by its destruction of some of their food stores as waves washing over the deck managed to penetrate the hatches to pool itself below. "Seawash," it was called, and it ruined the stock of white crackers, dissolved much sugar, and clotted flour. The men, working tirelessly at all hours, pumped the seawash into buckets, then soaked up the remainder with sponges.

In January of 1814, nearing the equator, the wind reduced to a mere breeze, then ceased altogether, becalming the *Suvorov*. For nearly a month the ship did not perceptibly move, except that Captain Lazarev decided that the crew, working in shifts in the *Suvorov*'s four longboats, might pull the ship to wind with oars. This was an unpopular effort. It was very hot at this latitude…too hot to sleep well, except by extreme exhaustion. And the sun, high in the cloudless sky, burned the pale-skinned men mercilessly even through their hats and shirts. George ministered to them with his herbal salves until his supplies were endangered. After that, the men, who could not launder their clothing except in seawater, began to develop skin sores and uncomfortable rashes.

After two weeks of rowing, the crew was becoming surly. Michman Bestuzhev had to threaten to use the cat-o-nine-tails to flog anyone who refused to work his shift in the longboats. When the men were in the longboats they rowed only perfunctorily since the ship did not seem to be moving no matter how they put their backs into the job. But Michman Bestuzhev insisted that the ship *was* moving and that they would eventually find wind if they kept up the effort long enough. The men's only pleasure was that they could fish with line and bait from the longboats while they rowed. They then roasted the fish they caught on an on-deck grill and everyone enjoyed the fare. Quartermaster Fokin assured them that they still had plenty of drinking water available, and Captain Lazarev, even though he won the second chess challenge in even fewer moves than before, allowed the men an extra dram of vodka per day "until wind be found."

Michman Bestuzhev organized an arm-wrestling tournament among the men of the crew to determine who was strongest of arm.

"We're going to crown a 'King of the Right Arm' and a 'King of the Left Arm'," he announced. "And each king will be exempted from one shift of rowing."

This contest was well received. A makeshift table of the right height was set up on the deck amidships. The men began to bet among themselves on several candidates of apparent arm strength, and insisted on some refinements of the rules. No one should have to put his arm to the test more than once per hour, and thumb grip was mandated over palm grip. By the next day, after many a raucous contest, accompanied by partisan cheering and groaning, the kings were crowned—sailor Ivan Nikitin was "King of the Right Arm" and sailor Sagamit Bikulov was "King of the Left Arm."

"With these strong fellows exempted from a shift of rowing, the Suvorov will start to drift backwards," joked the men.

Michman Bestuzhev was left-handed and possessed very muscular arms. The men couldn't help speculating on the outcome of an arm-wrestling contest between him and Sagamit Bikulov, the "King of the Left Arm." Bikulov was eager to contest the matter with one of the ship's officers, but insisted that he get another shift's exemption from rowing if he won. Bestuzhev assented to his terms and the men set to it. At first, when Lieutenant Povalo-Shveikovskii gave the signal to start pulling, the arms didn't move at all. Both men's faces contorted with the extreme effort and both emitted strained grunting sounds as they tried to get an advantage. Both men leaned in closer to their hands, trying to get their shoulders behind the effort of their arms. Still, the arms did not move. Each tried to twist the other's hand to weaken the opposing wrist. But neither made any progress toward bending back the other's arm. In a minute or so of this, beads of sweat appeared on both foreheads. With a hissing sound, Bikulov started to drool from the side of his mouth.

"Come on, Sagamit!" shouted several of the men. "You can do it!"

"Aj-da, Michman!" shouted others, supporting Bestuzhev. "Turn him down! We need him at the oars."

At last, Michman Bestuzhev, squinting one eye shut and clenching his teeth, managed to start sailor Bikulov's arm declining toward the table. Bikulov mustered up a sudden wrenching movement of his arm, arresting the decline for a second, but then surrendered the contest, the back of his hand being flattened onto the table surface under Bestuzhev's meaty palm. "Hurrah!" the men shouted. "The King is dead. Long live the King!" Bikulov just shook his head and rubbed his left arm with his right hand. "You really are a strong one, old man," he said.

George, who had witnessed the contest with amusement, was struck by the sailor's reference to Michman Bestuzhev as "old man." Bestuzhev, he thought, was about thirty-five years of age…the same as he was. "Excuse me, Sagamit," he asked the vanquished sailor politely, "How old are you?"

Bikulov answered, "I'm twenty."

"Well, you're the strongest twenty-year-old on this ship," said George, trying to console the young man.

"You know, Doctor, you look like you might be pretty strong of arm yourself," said Bikulov. "Why don't you challenge Ivan…the "King of the Right Arm"…and see how you do?"

The men all shouted for the match. "Yes, go on and do it. Let's see who the real king is!"

Ivan Nikitin, the "King of the Right Arm," was leaning against the side rail smoking his pipe. But now he stepped forward to the table and put his arm into the ready position. "Give it a try," he said to George.

Nikitin was a stocky sailor only a year or two older than Bikulov. His rolled-up shirt exposed an arm of most daunting musculature. But George decided to try. He stepped up to the table, looked Nikitin straight in the eye and grasped his hand. Michman Bestuzhev put his hand on the top of the men's joined hands and adjusted their elbows into what he considered a fair starting position. Then he said "Start!" and released their hands.

Nikitin attacked immediately with his strongest effort, trying to burst through George's resistance at the onset of the struggle. But George's arm stiffened after only an inch or two of decline and withstood Nikitin's initial attack. He then took a breath and exerted himself with every ounce of energy he had. Nikitin's arm was forced back to the neutral starting posture. But that was all. The men were deadlocked. And so it continued for three minutes or more. Neither man could gain anything against the other no matter what they tried. George noticed that Nikitin's forehead was wet with sweat. A clear fluid was trickling out of his right nostril onto his upper lip. The men had ceased their shouting and were suffering vicariously along with the combatants in the struggle. They all had pained looks on their faces as they watched the agonizing standoff of arms.

When George was on the very verge of surrender, when his arm felt like it was about to break, when the air was about to burst from his seized lungs, he decided to try a mental ploy. Forcing a smile, he tried to look as fresh as if he had just begun the match and could easily continue it indefinitely. Then, he said to the similarly straining Nikitin in a calm voice, "Aha, I've got you now."

At his words, Nikitin's arm collapsed backwards, giving the contest to George. He shook his ailing arm almost violently, casting it downward toward the deck. "I can't believe it," he exclaimed. "You're even older than the Michman. How could you be so strong?"

"I live right," George answered so that all could hear, and, noting the quick return of Nikitin's pipe to his hand, he added, "And I don't smoke."

A few days after the arm-wrestling contest, George won further respect from the men by volunteering to serve a daylight shift as lookout. This required him to climb the ratlines clear to the crowsnest on the main mast—a position ninety feet above the deck. He had wanted to climb into this position since he came aboard, but had delayed attempting it because he was unsure if he would be able to conquer a fear of great height he had had since childhood. But now was a good time because the sea was so calm and there was no wind. The ship would be as stationary as if it were anchored in a calm bay. So he replaced a sailor named Dementei Biakov aloft as lookout. To his surprise, the middle stages of the climb were the most harrowing. After he passed the topsail's yardarm the height caused his perspective to change to that of an "exterior eye" like that of a bird. He didn't feel a connection, somehow, with the height and the possibility of falling. And he felt secure seated on the platform of the crowsnest, his legs hanging down and his torso surrounded by the round metal stays. He had brought along a ship's telescope tucked into the back of his pants. At the top he removed it and began to look through it at the various points of the horizon. There were no clouds in the sky at all, and no birds. And the iridescent blue sea showed no waves. No whitecaps could be seen no matter where he looked. At mid-day he at last spotted something of interest. It was a large pod of whales, less than a mile distant, showing an occasional fluke and blowing spurts of misty vapor through their blowholes. The day was very hot, and the blazing equatorial sun seemed to be just over George's head. He was glad that Dementei Biakov, the usual lookout, had suggested he cover his head with a large kerchief.

Rio de Janeiro:

In late February the *Suvorov* at last caught steady, though mild, winds out of the northeast and made headway toward the Brazilian coast. By mid March they were in periodic sight of land. The sea in this coastal region was alive with flying fish, skimming over the surface in great bunches so fast and with so little disruption of the water that one had to focus the eyes with great concentration to assure that the intermittent blurring of the sea was, in fact, visual flashes of winged fish. There were mobs of stinging jellyfish also, and, at one point, the sea around the ship appeared to turn red because of the dense swarms of some kind of tiny crab.

Quartermaster Fokin informed the crew that the Brazilian coast was rife with savage cannibals called the Waitacá who had roasted and eaten many a shipwrecked sailor. "We'll be wise," he said, "To run well avast of the coast in these parts. I've heer'd that the Waitacá will cut off a man's head and shrink it down to the size of an orange to use as a decoration in their lodges."

Along the coast, a favorable current, running to the south, added to their speed. On Tuesday, the 21st of April, 1814…3 May by the Brazilian calendar…, the *Suvorov* had, due to an early afternoon change in the wind, successfully entered the large protective Guanabara Bay, passing by the striking rock protuberance called by the Portuguese "Pão de Açúcar," the "Sugarloaf," which seemed to guard the entrance to the bay. George was most impressed by the spectacular site of Rio de Janeiro, a city named "River of January" because one of the early explorers, Amerigo Vespucci, wrongly concluded, in January, that the bay was the mouth of some huge river. The inhabitants of the city, recently swelled to sixty thousand residents by the infusion of European Portuguese accompanying their refugee royal house under Regent João of the Braganza family, built their homes along the coast adjacent to the south side of Guanabara Bay and extending southward along the Atlantic. Clean, moderately sloped, golden-sand beaches of great width were immediately backed by dense green jungle, limited very soon by verdant cliffs rising to inaccessible heights.

Early 19th century view of Rio de Janeiro from http://ebooks.adelaide.edu.au

There were many other ships anchored in the bay near the city's port. Captain Lazarev ordered the sails down, but did not let down the anchors, not knowing where the ship should be situated in the harbor. A boat rowed out to them then and a man in the boat who had four completely naked black children with him shouted out that he would lead them to the best spot for twelve milreis, an amount equal to ten Spanish piastres. Captain Lazarev threw that amount down to the man and ordered boats lowered to tow the *Suvorov* into the position the man indicated. It was indeed a fine spot, among several other anchored ships. When they let down the anchors, the depth beneath them turned out to be ten fathoms. Seeing the settlement from the anchored *Suvorov* on a sunny late-April day, George thought it difficult to imagine a more beautiful place for a city to be located.

The flags of the Russian-American Company and of Russia itself on the *Suvorov,* together with an eleven gun salute, brought a delegation of Portuguese port officials out to the ship in a dinghy. Captain Lazarev asked George to participate in the initial conference with them. His aim was to gain replenishment of water and stores as cheaply as possible from this "ally against Napoleon." And, he wanted permission to give the crew leave to visit the city. He told George it was his plan to stay in Rio de Janeiro for three or four weeks.

The Portuguese port officials had no one with them who could speak Russian, nor German, nor even English. After some frustration, they decided their best chance for adequate communication was to use French, the language of their mutual international adversary. One of the Portuguese port officials spoke French quite well, as did George. He explained that the ship's crew was to be checked for signs of disease by their medical inspector, and that a postal official would take from them any letters which were either intended for residents of Rio de Janeiro or to be forwarded to other destinations through Rio de Janeiro. But then, to George's surprise, the official wanted to know whether anyone of the ship's officers was a baptized Catholic. If there was not a baptized…and confirmed…Catholic among the officers—someone to take responsibility for the others, then their regulations prohibited fraternization…the crew could not enter the city. This was their law and they were committed to enforcing it. But George told them that he, an "officer of the ship's chartering company," was a baptized and confirmed Catholic and that he would stand responsible for the crew, most of whom were "Christian, but Orthodox." When they seemed to doubt him, George told them he had been educated in a Catholic school, that he knew the Latin liturgy by heart, and that his own sister was a Catholic nun.

"It was not a Jesuit school, was it?" the Portuguese official asked suspiciously in French.

"No, it was an Augustinian school," replied George. He had heard that the Jesuits had been expelled from Brazil after troubles with the Portuguese government.

"How devout is the Pope?" the official abruptly asked.

"Our Holy Father the Pope is seven times pious," answered George quickly, making the required pun on the name of Pope Pius VII.

"Let me hear you say the 'Lord's Prayer' in Latin," demanded the official.

George immediately commenced to recite: "Pater noster, qui es in caelis, sanctificetur nomen tuum. Adveniat regnum tuum. Fiat voluntas tua, sicut in caelo et in terra. Panem nostum quotidianum da nobis hodie, et dimitte nobis debita nostra sicut et nos dimittimus debitoribus nostris. Et ne nos inducas in tentationem, sed libera nos a malo. –Amen."

"Bien! Bien!" announced the official, who then turned to his companions with a smile and began conversing with them in rapid Portuguese.

George turned to Captain Lazarev and said, "I think we'll be all right now."

Once they were ashore, the *Suvorov*'s officers and crew found themselves the objects of much attention from the Portuguese and the native Brazilians in Rio de Janeiro. Cheap replenishment of the ship's stores and water was no problem at all. And housing was also no problem. The men were shown to a grand walled villa in the Laranjeiras quarter. They were told that it had been built at the cost of 40,000 French francs by the former Russian Minister to Brazil, Baron Tuil, who had returned to Russia in 1812 after news of Napoleon's invasion. George and the officers were all given individual rooms and told to order what they needed from the staff of servants. The crewmembers were housed two or three to a room in another wing, but had no access to servants. A central courtyard included a lush garden. George was amazed at the vegetation, realizing that the month of May, which they were in the middle of by the Portuguese calendar, was, in the southern hemisphere of the world, the end of the fall season. Winter was approaching, yet the weather was pleasantly warm and the vegetation was lush.

In the morning, in a large dining room with rough benches and tables, the officers and crew were served bread and cheese with very strong coffee and delicious fruits they didn't even recognize.

"What kind of fruit is this?" they asked the staff, pointing to each. The answers were unclear, but sounded to them like "a-ta" and "ja-bo-ti-caba."

"Ja-bo-ti-caba," they repeated. "What a strange name! But it tastes sweet enough."

Most of the men wanted to return to the port area of the city, seeking strong drink and female companionship. But George wanted to request an audience with "Dom João, the Regent" for himself and Captain Lazarev. He was told that his request would be considered.

Walking around the next day, George found that the city had been built on four hills. The houses were mostly made of brick or cut stones, and all the balconies were closed with shades. The streets were paved with stone and very wide. There were many large squares, each with a golden statue of a saint in the center. Each of the four hills was surmounted by the city's most magnificent buildings: the former Jesuit College, now a school for physicians, with its Cathedral of São Sebastian, the oldest church in the city surrounded by a citadel; the Benedictine Abbey; the Franciscan Monastery of São Antônio and the Capuchin Monastery on Mount Gloria; and the Women's Monastery on the eastern hill. There was in the city a wonderful new theater, equaling in its size and tasteful interior that of the San Carlos Theater in Lisbon. And on the large Theater Square was the grand Palace of the Baron de Rio Seco. On the Main Market Square was the city Palace of the Regent, marked by an obelisk facing the harbor, where the custom's office, the admiralty, the new stock exchange, and the most important trading houses had recently been constructed. George was reminded of the rich merchants' trading houses along the Bosporus in Constantinople. He walked through the "Passeio Publico," a public garden with shady alleys through Mango trees where the air was fragrant with blossoms of a great variety of trees and flowers. This garden was, George, thought, like Eden in the Bible…the fragrant air and the beautiful sights satisifying his every desire. George found that the hospitals of the pious brotherhoods were exquisitely equipped, and the public hospital, linked to a medical school, could serve as many as 3000 patients.

George marveled at the acqueduct, Carioca, built in 1747 by Viceroy Vasconcelos, from which the people of Rio de Janeiro called themselves "Cariocas." The acqueduct was made of large carved stone conduits atop eighty masonry arches that were at some points fifty feet high. This Carioca Acqueduct, which George termed a "Roman miracle structure," had survived well a strong earthquake that had taken place three years before in 1811. George followed it to find the source of the water--springs almost six miles away at the base of the Corcovado Mountain. With a mercury thermometer in his medical bag he measured the water temperature at 20 degrees Centigrade. It was clear and tasted pure.

On their third day in Rio de Janeiro, George, Captain Lazarev, Lieutenant Unkovskii, and Joseph Desilvier…companions from the London excursion…were together at the port surveying the wharves and the towers rigged for ship repair. The diversity of the people in the streets was striking. There were people in all shades of color and states of dress. The fine ladies, sometimes borne in shaded sedan-chair litters by teams of muscular black slaves, wore their hair piled up on top of their heads to remarkable heights. In the heat of mid-day the fish glue, which held the goatskin pads onto their tresses' iron frames liquefied and ran down into their eyes. Frequently these women attached pendants and other items of jewelry to their hair and even hung their house keys from their hair frame. Their expensive dresses, in bright colors, had broad round skirts, supported by circular hoop stays, which reached to the ground. But the bodices exposed to view the top portions of their breasts. Often they were accompanied by plainly dressed servants or slaves and had barefoot children running along behind them.

At one of the port's wharves, a dilapidated two-masted ship of squat appearance and shallow draft had been towed by rowboat alongside a dock for the unloading of a shipment of slaves from Africa. A party of men armed with muskets and pistols cautioned the Russians to stand well down the dock beyond the section needed for getting the slaves from the ship to shore. In a minute or two the slaves started coming up out of the hold of the ship, down a gangplank, and onto the dock's rough-planked surface. The men came out first. They were completely naked and slender, very black in color. They were drenched in sweat and immediately put their hands to their eyes to shield them from the bright sun. Several were befouled with their own feces and a terrible odor quickly reached the noses of George and his companions.

"My God," said Desilvier to George, commenting on the sight, "I've never seen black people before. Have you?"

George replied, "I saw some blacks in Constantinople when I visited there on a diplomatic mission in late 1811. A Turkish Pasha I met, Abdul Selim Hamid, had some black servants in his household. But they were all well covered in robes and turbans. These blacks are as naked as animals."

The women and children then began to emerge, also naked, gaunt to the point of emaciation, and black as coal. The armed party on the wharf goaded them roughly down the wharf and onto the street at the end of it. Soon the slaves, surrounded by the armed men, were all gathered on the dusty street near the entrances to several bars and mercantile establishments. There were close to four hundred of them. George and his companions found it difficult to believe they had all been transported across the Atlantic Ocean…a journey of two or three months…in such a small ship. They had to have been packed together below in extremely dense arrangement. But then, as they passed the ship's gangplank themselves on their way down the dock to the street, they saw the ship's crew stacking about twenty black bodies along the outer side-rail. The smell of vinegar, which was used as a disinfectant of the slaves and their hold, filled the air.

"Those are the ones who didn't survive the journey," observed George.

"What a horrible thing!" said Desilvier.

"Well, the entire economy here depends on slave labor from Africa," explained Captain Lazarev. "The slaves are needed to clear the land, plant the land, build the roads, the houses…everything. The native savages just can't be turned to such work…they're incapable of it. So, without the African slaves, the country can't develop into a fit place to live."

"England is a fit place to live," responded Desilvier. "And we've never had slaves."

On the street, several of the slaves were, of necessity, urinating and loosing diarrhea in plain sight of the crowd of bar patrons who had gathered. Two of these bar patrons came up to one of the armed men, talked with him briefly and put something into his hand. Then they walked over and grabbed one of the slave women, the least emaciated one they saw, and dragged her with them out of sight around a bar corner into an alley. One of the male slaves suddenly bolted past the armed men and ran toward the bar corner, apparently trying to rescue the abducted woman. But one of the armed guards just raised his pistol and fired—"BANG!" into the back of the male slave's neck, killing him instantly. Then, with hand gestures, he ordered two other male slaves, who were now cowering in fear, to drag the dead man's body back to the group.

George was shocked and began to step forward to say something in protest. But Captain Lazarev held him back, saying, "There's nothing we can do, Yegor. Stay out of it."

In a few minutes another party of citizens arrived. They were well dressed and had printed signs with them. The leader of this group, a huge and corpulent individual with a sweeping black mustache, loudly announced something in

Portuguese to the crowd. With a hammer he tacked one of the signs on the wall of a store building. Then he gave a signal and the guards began kicking slaves and directing them to start walking the street to some other location. Soon all the slaves and their guards were gone. But the body of the killed slave remained lying on the dusty street. A swarm of flies was rapidly gathering around it.

George stepped around the body, went up to the sign on the wall, and, standing among others from the crowd, managed to decipher it. "There will be an auction today of these slaves in some square nearby," he told his companions. "These are slaves from the Loruba tribe of Africa. The sign says they're top quality stock…men, women, and children. Minimum bid is three 'patacão'."

"How much is a 'patacão'?" they asked.

George managed to find someone in the crowd who spoke French and was able to explain to him what a "patacão" was. After some minutes of questions and answers with the French speaker, George told the others: "Regent Joao has ordered the removal of all the Spanish pesos of 8 reals' value…equaling 750 Brazilian 'réis…and restamped them with a new value of 960 'réis.' Then he's begun the minting of coins in this value called 'patacao.' So that means that 'three patacão' equals three inflated Spanish pesos or about three thousand Brazilian 'réis'."

"Then, if there are 120 Brazilian 'réis' to the actual Spanish peso," figured Lieutenant Unkovskii aloud, "And the Spanish peso is worth about the same as a Russian ruble in gold redemption, then 'three patacão'—the minimum bid on one of these slaves—is approximately 25 rubles. At that rate, you can see that it will take a rather wealthy man to buy any of these slaves, especially if the bidding runs up at all."

"And, of course, whoever buys them will have to feed and clothe and house them. And get them to work," commented Captain Lazarev.

"I imagine most experienced slave owners are interested in buying pairs of males and females so they can breed their own slaves," said Desilvier with evident disgust. "You only need to buy two to get started."

"Let's try to find where the auction is," proposed Lieutenant Unkovskii.

"I'd rather not," said George. "I've seen enough. I think I'll just walk back to the villa in Laranjeira. I'm sure I can make it by dinner. You all just go on and find the slave auction without me."

"I'll walk back to the villa with you," said Desilvier. "All this has made me feel quite ill."

As George and Desilvier started to step away in the direction of the villa, the two men who had taken the slave woman behind the bar roughly shoved her back into sight on the street. They had found a rope and tied it into a noose around her neck. Now they seemed intent on returning the naked woman to the group of slaves. Her gaze was blank and she apparently did not notice the body of her dead compatriot lying in the street. Pushing her ahead of them, the two men set off in the direction the group of slaves and their guards had taken.

"Come on, Lieutenant," said Captain Lazarev to Unkovskii, "We can follow them to find the auction."

The men parted company. George and Desilvier set off to return to the villa, and the two officers followed after the men who had apparently raped the slave woman and were now returning her to the group for sale. "She'll be worth more now," they shouted to some laughing friends along the way, "She's pregnant for sure."

Dom João and *Boa Vista*:

At the villa, George was told that his request for an audience with Dom João had been granted. He and Captain Lazarev were to attend a dinner at the Regent's residence the next day. A carriage would be sent to collect them at eleven o' clock in the morning.

The Regent's country palace, called *Boa Vista* or "Beautiful View," was the main house of a large plantation village called São Cristovão some distance from the center of Rio de Janeiro. The carriage took most of an hour to get there, negotiating near the end of the journey a road that cut through dense forest. The main house itself was built of stuccoed adobe blocks, similar in structure to the villa where George and the *Suvorov*'s officers and crew were accommodated. The interior of the house was extravagantly furnished with carved wooden furniture and colorful tapestries. But the walls were starkly whitewashed and largely unadorned by art. The ceilings were unfinished, with exposed log beams. The windows had no glass or oilcloth in them, but only slat shutters which opened like doors to the outside. The São Cristovão plantation and its main house appeared surprisingly dilapidated. But Captain Lazarev commented that he'd never seen such fine furnishings…not even in St. Petersburg.

George and Captain Lazarev were shown into an official reception room to await Dom João. The only chair in the room was that obviously intended for the Regent. It was an elaborately carved dark wooden chair, padded with red velvet seat, back, and arm cushions. Behind it was a thick gold-colored tapestry hanging from ceiling to floor. Apparently, George and Captain Lazarev were to stand as they waited for the arrival of their host.

In only two or three minutes, Dom João came into the room, accompanied by several other men. All were well dressed. Dom João, George noticed, wore especially fine black leather boots, but he was generally a man of unprepossessing appearance. He was in his late forties in age, short in height and quite corpulent with an especially large belly. His face, framed by a mane of long graying brown hair, appeared to George to be a bit swollen. At his approach, George and Captain Lazarev bowed in respect.

"Bom dia," said Dom João, nodding to the men. He was smiling and seemed friendly, but he did not offer his hand.

Dom João VI of Portugal (13 May, 1767-10 March, 1826), from: http://en.wikipedia.org/wiki/John_VI_of_Portugal.

One of the men with Dom João spoke up, saying in heavily accented Russian, "My name is João de Melho and I am Dom João's interpreter. I'm told that you don't understand Portuguese easily. My Russian is not very good, however, and I wonder if we might better speak in either French or English."

"English is best for us," said Captain Lazarev in English. "Doctor von Sheffer here spoke with the port authorities in French, but both he and I can communicate in English."

Another of the men with Dom João then said, "That's fine. I'm Percy Smythe— King George's Minister to Brazil from England. English is my native language and I can help Mr. de Melho interpret."

The man handed a printed card to Captain Lazarev, who looked it over and handed it to George. It was a calling card on which was written: "Sir Percy Clinton Sydney Smythe, 6th Viscount of Strangford and Penshurst."

"Thank you, my good sir," said George, taking notice of the man's impressive size and bearing, "How should we address you?"

"I'm officially 'Lord Strangford', but you can just call me Percy," he said.

Dom João began to address them. Interpreter de Melho listened to Dom João speak for a few moments, then translated, saying, "We welcome you, our Russian allies against Napoleon, to Rio de Janeiro. We will extend to you every courtesy here and we trust that you will report to your Tsar and his government that our treatment of you was most satisfactory."

Captain Lazarev responded, saying, "We are already most impressed with our treatment here, Your Excellency, and we are most grateful for your aid."

Dom João replied, "You will please address us as 'Your Majesty'." By "us" he meant only himself. He had become accustomed to refer to himself in the manner of ruling royalty as someone more than merely one…as "we." He then asked for a clarification of their mission. "What has brought you so far from Russia?"

Captain Lazarev frowned and, using no term of address, explained, "We are traveling around the world to replenish the stores of the Russian settlement of Novo-Arkhangelsk on the northwest coast of North America. In our country there is a large stock company, the Russian-American Company, which operates a fur-trading business there. This Company has chartered the Russian Navy ship *Suvorov* to transport provisions to Novo-Arkhangelsk. I am the Captain of the *Suvorov*, representing the Russian Navy, and Doctor Yegor von Sheffer here is our ship's surgeon and represents the interests of the Russian-American Company."

"So you will be delivering provisions and transporting furs back to Russia," concluded Dom João. "What is your route?"

Captain Lazarev continued, "We plan to sail eastward from here around the Cape of Good Hope and across the Indian Ocean to Australia. Then we'll head northeast across the Pacific to Novo-Arkhangelsk in Alaska. On the way back we'll come southward along the coast of the Americas to round Cape Horn back into the Atlantic, stopping here again on the way north to Europe."

"How long will that take?" asked Dom João.

"We plan to be back in St. Petersburg in about two years," Captain Lazarev answered.

"That's a long time to be at sea, Captain," Dom João remarked. "When we came here with a British fleet in 1807—we were on the flagship, the *Prince Royal*-- the journey from Lisbon to Bahia took only fifty-two days. Then it was another two weeks to get here to Rio de Janeiro. That was considered good time, but it seemed like hell to us. We went through several storms and we were seasick the entire time. All the ships were extremely crowded. There were thousands of us, after all. And our mother, Her Majesty the Queen Maria, was a real trial for us, running around the ship shouting 'Ai Jesus! Ai Jesus! Ai Jesus!'all the time. We had to watch her continually, fearing she'd jump overboard."

George and Captain Lazarev were discomfited by Dom João's continued royal reference to himself as "we." And they glanced at one another, not knowing how to respond to this story about Dom João's mother. They had heard that she was demented and that Dom João had become Regent in her stead in 1799.

The men followed Dom João and his retinue out of the reception room and through a hall into a large dining room. Rows of windows, the shutters turned outward, were open behind the chairs lining the table on both sides of the room, admitting a cooling breeze. Dom João took the large chair at the head of the table and invited the others to sit. Servants in white frocks with aprons scurried in and out. The tableware was particularly beautiful. The dishes were made of Chinese porcelain and inlaid with gold. The implements were elaborately cast silver. Each place had a selection of delicate glassware…tumblers for water, goblets for wine, and little glasses that looked like the Russian riumochki.

"The little glasses are provided to drink some vodka later," the Englishman Percy Smythe told George. "His Majesty wanted you to feel at home."

George decided to take the lead in continuing the former conversation. "What has become of your mother here, Your Majesty?" he asked, stressing loudly the proper title. "We certainly hope she is well."

"She is as well as can be expected. She lives in a Carmelite convent not far away," answered Dom João. "The nuns there are wonderful in their care for her."

George thought he would continue to ask about Dom João's family. Everyone liked to talk about their family, he thought. "And how are your children taking life here in Brazil, your Majesty? I understand you have two fine sons."

"They're doing very well here," answered Dom João. "They've almost forgotten Portugal, in fact. Pedro, who is now sixteen, is mostly interested in chasing after girls. And Miguel, who is twelve, thinks only of collecting things—butterflies, coins, knives…whatever raises his interest. Soon we'll be trying to find proper marriages for them. Does the Russian Tsar Aleksandr have any eligible daughters?"

George was delighted to provide this information, since he always made an effort to acquaint himself with the names and birthdates of the children of royalty.

"No, the Tsar has no eligible daughters, unfortunately," he explained. "He and Princess Elizaveta Fyodorovna have suffered the loss of two daughters in infancy…little Maria Aleksandrovna in June of 1800, and Elizaveta Aleksandrovna in May of 1808. He does, however, have an eligible sister…the Grand Duchess Anna Pavlovna, who is now nineteen years old."

"Is she betrothed to anyone?" asked Dom João.

"I don't think so," answered George. "But I'm sure the Tsar must be deciding upon candidates for her hand even now. Once, in 1809, Napoleon Bonaparte himself proposed marriage to her through his Ambassador to St. Petersburg, Count Caulaincourt. But the Tsar rejected this offer because he then considered his sister too young. But now she is no longer too young, and, since I am personally acquainted with the Tsar, I would be most happy to propose to him, if Your Majesty so desires, the candidacy of your son Pedro who is, after all, close in age to that of the Grand Duchess."

"Doctor von Schaeffer," said Dom João through interpreter de Melho's English speech, "That is a most welcome suggestion. You are hereby authorized to make such a proposal on our behalf. Of course you will not have an opportunity to make the proposal until you return to St. Petersburg, and that may not be for two years or more. But, if the opportunity still exists and the Grand Duchess is not betrothed to anyone else…then go ahead and propose the idea to the Tsar when first you see him. We tell you, however, that we are considering sending emissaries to Europe to make proposals for our son elsewhere as well. We are told that Austria's Emperor Franz Joseph I still has another eligible daughter after giving the eldest one, Marie-Louise, to Napoleon."

"Indeed he has three more daughters," informed George, displaying his command of aulic matters, "Leopoldina Josepha Caroline, who is now a bit older than Pedro at age seventeen, Maria Clementina who is the same age as Pedro at sixteen, and Marie Caroline Ferdinanda who just turned thirteen. But marrying any of them would make your son a brother-in-law to Napoleon."

"By that time, God willing, Napoleon will no longer be of concern to us," said Dom João. "The European allies will soon put an end to him and restore King Louis the Eighteenth to the throne of France."

"I would like to propose a toast to that idea," announced George, raising his wine glass. The others, including Dom João, immediately raised their own wine glasses in response and cheered the idea.

Thick slices of roast beef with potatoes and gravy were served. Then there was a green salad with mushroom slices and some vegetables George could not identify. After that a large bowl was placed in the center of the table and George could see that the cooks had gone to the effort to make Russian "pelmeni," the little balls of meat wrapped in pasta envelopes to be eaten with sour cream. The pelmeni were delicious. And then Dom João ordered the servants to bring in silver bowls full of water. He commenced a hand-washing ritual that he said he usually enjoyed as he ate together with his sons. He invited the other guests to join him in this. Then followed a delightful dessert of slices of banana with a covering of sweet cream sprinkled with gratings of nutmeg. After months at sea, such a meal was almost overwhelming to George and to Captain Lazarev. They both stated to Dom João and the others that they "had never before eaten such a fine meal."

The vodka was served last. The servants brought in two large bottles of it with Russian labels on their sides and poured some into each "riumochka."

George asked interpreter de Melho where they had obtained the Russian vodka and also the recipe for the Russian pelmeni.

"These are the benefits of having a member of the Russian Academy of Sciences resettle here a couple of years ago. He was also a visitor once to the Russian outpost in Alaska, and to Japan as well. His name is Dr. Georg Heinrich von Langsdorff and he's the official Russian Consul here after the departure of former Minister Tuil."

"Indeed," exclaimed George. "I know of him. He was on the first Russian-American Company circumnavigation with Company Director Nikolai Rezanov in 1806. He and I have much in common. Both of us are originally from Germany. Both are medical doctors. I'd very much like to meet him if that is possible. Where does he live?"

The interpreter shook his head positively. "You may be in luck," he said. "Dr. Langsdorff is said to be here in Rio de Janeiro provisioning for an expedition to explore the upper reaches of the Amazon. He's quite an accomplished naturalist and is interested in all kinds of trees, bushes, and plants. He purchased a plantation quite some distance from here where he now lives. He calls his estate 'Mandioca,' and he's trying to establish it as an agricultural experimentation station with the labor of twenty African slaves. His wife Fredericke will be directing the effort while he is gone. I will find him if I can and arrange for you to meet him."

"Thank you," said George. "I am most anxious to meet him. But I'm disappointed to hear that he, a fellow German and Doctor, would buy slaves," said George. "We saw a shipment of slaves from Africa unloaded at the port here yesterday, and it was not a pleasant thing to see."

Dom João heard George commenting on slavery, and addressed the issue to him, saying through de Melho, "We're just like the Russian Tsar Aleksandr as regards slavery. He would like to end serfdom in Russia. He feels great moral pressure to put an end to it. His powerful British allies have even demanded it of him, as they have of us. The British made the slave trade illegal in all their colonies back in 1807, you know. But we are not their colony, no matter that we depend upon their protection here."

When Dom João mentioned the British he turned toward Percy Smythe. Then he continued, "No doubt his Majesty Aleksandr thought he would end serfdom when he took the throne. But he learned in Russia, as we have here in Brazil, that the country's development depends upon slave labor. This is a simple fact, and we hear it every day from our plantation owners, our mine operators, and our manufacturers. And then there is the welfare of the serfs or slaves themselves to consider. They're not able to fend for themselves in freedom. They aren't ready for that. They need a strong hand to protect them and to guide them."

"Yes, Your Majesty," said Captain Lazarev, using the title "Your Majesty" for the first time since being requested to use it. "You are right. It was

Napoleon's idea to free the serfs precipitously, abruptly, all at once. He did it in Prussia and probably thought he would do it in Russia too…but he didn't get the chance. Napoleon gave no thought to the lives of the serfs in Prussia. The freedom he gave them has only been a hardship to them, to be sure. Their lot is worse now than it was. How are they to earn a living with no land, inappropriate skills, and no education?"

"There may be some," commented George, "who would rather starve in freedom than grow fat in slavery." Then, to divert attention from this comment, he asked Dom João, "How many African slaves are there in Brazil?"

"Our officials reckon that there are almost two million of them," Dom João answered. "Certainly they far outnumber the European population here. And that presents some real problems. At this very time we are experiencing some troublesome uprisings of slaves…rebellions against their owners and against our government. Our militia in Bahia has had to act decisively to quell two such uprisings so far this year."

Percy Smythe, sensing George's sympathy for the slaves—a sympathy he shared, turned to him alone and said, "The slave leaders were drawn and quartered in public as a lesson to the others." Then he turned to Captain Lazarev and said, "My good Captain, I have a request that I hope you will honor. You say that your route will take you to Port Jackson and the settlement of Sydney in Australia. Well, I wish to send a message to the British Governor there, the honorable Lachlan Macquarie. If I prepare such a message, will you deliver it to him for me?"

Captain Lazarev answered, "Of course, Lord Strangford. I will be very happy to meet the Governor there and transmit to him whatever you wish."

"Thank you," replied Percy Smythe. "I'll have the message delivered to your residence here before you leave."

After the meal, as a spectacular sunset was illuminating the western mountain tops visible over the enveloping trees, George asked Dom João if he could stay for a few days or more near the royal residence at the São Cristavão plantation so he could meet and become acquainted with Dom João's son Pedro. "I would be better able to describe him to the Tsar as a candidate for his sister's hand," he said. To his surprise, and to the surprise of Captain Lazarev, who clearly thought that George was being presumptious, Dom João told his servants to prepare a place on the plantation for George to stay. Captain Lazarev was driven back to Rio de Janeiro without him.

The Young Princes Pedro and Miguel:

The next morning George used a scalpel from his medical bag to trim around the edges of his beard and moustache and to shave his neck. He had only brought his medical bag with him to São Cristovão. He was able to use the water in a pitcher on a washstand near his bed to give himself a kind of standing bath. His shirt, he thought, had developed an unpleasant aroma, and he decided to wash it. He repeatedly soaked it with water from the pitcher and leaned out the window to wring it out. Then he hung it in the window to dry. Instead of the shirt, he put on a medical smock that he kept folded in his bag. Before he left his room he decided to wash his stockings as well. When they were hung alongside his shirt in the window, he put his shoes onto his bare feet and walked outside. His lower legs were also bare.

At the main house, George again met João de Melho the interpreter, who said he would accompany him to the São Cristovão stables to meet Dom João's son Pedro. Pedro was an avid horseman and spent almost every morning at the stables. When they had walked to the stables, which were obscured from the main house by trees at a distance of approximately two hundred meters, they found Pedro at the front corral. He was a handsome young man with curly black hair covering his ears and cascading down to his neck. Bushy dark eyebrows united over his nose and he had wispy dark hair just making its masculine presence known on his upper lip, cheeks, and chin. His prominent lips seemed pursed into a permanent pucker. He was taller than his father and a bit taller than George. He was slender, but seemed fit and athletic in physique, his movements vigorous and graceful. But he was using a carriage whip to train four small black children to dance in formation for his amusement. He was giving them instructions they didn't seem to understand, then snapping them harshly with the whip to punish them when they didn't step to the patterns he desired. He stopped this as George and João de Melho approached him. Laughing, he shouted to some adult blacks by the stable entrance to come and collect the children. One of these blacks brought out with him a magnificent black horse, bridled and saddled with the finest tack George had ever seen. As the children ran off with the others, the horse remained tied to the corral rail waiting for Pedro to mount and ride.

João de Melho introduced George to Pedro, telling him inaccurately that "Doctor von Schaeffer" was an agent of Tsar Aleksandr's government and that he might be presenting his candidacy for marriage to a Russian Grand Duchess. "But I don't want to marry any Rooshian Duchess," Pedro blurted out. Then, turning to George, he asked, "Why are you dressed so strangely? Without stockings the mosquitoes will eat your legs."

Through interpreter de Melho, George explained his circumstances. Pedro then turned to the interpreter and said, "Tell the servants to get this man some new clothes right away. When I come back from my ride I expect to find him properly dressed." Then he mounted up and rode off.

George spent the next three days getting to know Pedro and his brother Miguel. He found that Pedro, the heir apparent after the death of an older brother Antonio at the age of six, was very energetic and headstrong, though he was epileptic and had seizures almost monthly. He was, at sixteen, consumed with sexual debauchery involving known mistresses and slave girls as young as eight. He got this turn of character, George heard from one of the servants and from interpreter de Melho, from his mother, the Spanish Bourbon Princess Carlota Joaquina, who was a known sexual adventuress and lived with her three daughters away in the old Bobadela mansion, which the Portuguese Viceroy of Brazil, Count Arcos, had prepared as a palace for the arrival of the royal family six years before. Dona Carlota had been suspected of involvement in a plot to overthrow Dom João as Regent even before they left Portugal. But now Dona Carlota had become an embarrassment to Dom João for so indiscriminately bestowing her favors, and he had banished her, and the daughters with her, to Bobadela mansion and its environs. Pedro continued to live in the Boa Vista residence at São Cristovão with his father, but Miguel spent periods of time in the custody of his mother as well.

The Portrait "Dom João VI e Dona Carlota" (25 April, 1775-7 January, 1830) by Manuel Dias de Oliveira (1764-1837) from:
http://pt.wikipedia.org/wiki/Carlota_Joaquina_de_Bourbon.

Dona Carlota liked to impress her royalty on all she encountered, and especially men of apparent importance. She was obsessed with dominating them. She would ride around the Botafogo and Laranjeira districts of the city in her elaborate carriage with a mounted escort of six soldiers. When she saw any apparently important male from her carriage, she would order her coachman to stop and her soldiers to accost him. She shouted orders to the man to kneel in obeisance to her. If he were slow in doing this, the soldiers would dismount and assault him, beating him with their fists and the flat surfaces of their sword blades. When he could no longer stand on his own, she and her guards would leave to accost someone else.

Dona Carlota's penchant for domination and assault caused Dom João diplomatic troubles. In 1809, the Russian Minister, Baron Tuil, had personally abandoned the expensive villa he had had constructed as the Russian Embassy in the Laranjeira district because of several traumatic beatings from Dona Carlota's guards. He decided that his Embassy was simply too close to Dona Carlota's frequent haunts. The next year, the former United States Minister to Brazil, the renowned U.S. Revolutionary War hero, General Thomas Sumter, a man known as the "Gamecock" and seventy-six years of age, refused to kneel as Dona Carlota demanded.

1796 Portrait of Thomas Sumter (14 August, 1734-1 June, 1832) by Rembrandt Peale (1778-1860), from: http://en.wikipedia.org/wiki/Thomas_Sumter.

"A United States General does not kneel before European royalty," he loudly proclaimed.

When Dona Carlota ordered her guards to attack General Sumter, he swiftly drew two already cocked pistols from the back of his belt sash and pointed them at the guards. "I'll kill at least two of you right now if you come any closer," he told them.

Dona Carlota was incensed and screamed at her guards, "He's an old man. Attack him! I order you!"

But the guards, looking at General Sumter's steely-eyed look of determination and his rock steady hands on the pistols, hesitated. General Sumter, seeing them waver, stepped forward toward them, and they backed away. Dona Carlota, rabidly spewing insults and threats, was driven away. General Sumter returned to his South Carolina plantation and retired from a long career of military and public service in 1811.

Even Percy Smythe, the Lord Strangford, his Britannic Majesty's Minister Plenipotentiary, and a very large and formidable man, was once seriously assaulted by Dona Carlota and her guards. And so was his naval attaché, Commodore Bowles. But their complaints to Dom João finally caused the Regent to threaten his troubled consort Dona Carlota into less aggressive treatment of important men.

From Dom João's twelve-year-old son Miguel, George learned that no one had yet climbed to the top of the Sugarloaf. Here was a city, founded in the seventeenth century, of over sixty-thousand people living at the base of a spectacular mountain and no one had climbed it. It didn't surprise George to learn that no one had climbed the much higher mountain, called "Corcovado," which loomed so precipitously over the city at its rear. It was so obviously formidable. But Sugarloaf didn't seem all that high…probably less than 400 meters in altitude. And the approaches to the top appeared smooth and relatively easy to traverse.

"Why has no one climbed the Sugarloaf?" George asked Miguel. "It doesn't look that difficult to do."

"Why would anyone want to climb it?" Miguel asked in response. "Climbing it is too much work for too little reward. A person would undoubtedly get sore, scratched, and bitten. And there's the danger of falling and getting injured or killed."

"Aren't you curious about what you could see from the top?" asked George. "I would think the view to be most spectacular. And who knows what could be found at the top? Perhaps the ancient Indians made their way to the top and left relics behind. Maybe the top of the rock has some embedded gold or even diamonds waiting only for some adventurous soul to claim."

At this, young Miquel became infected with some of George's enthusiasm for climbing Sugarloaf. "Maybe I should climb it," he said, and then he suggested, "Maybe we could do it together."

George felt that he should demur, saying, "I don't think I'll be here in Rio de Janeiro long enough for us to carry out such an attempt. But if the Sugarloaf is still unclimbed when I come back here on our return journey, then you and I will be the first ones to accomplish it. Are you agreed?"

"I'm agreed," said Miguel.

Meeting Drs. Langsdorff and Flach:

On the third morning at São Cristovão, interpreter de Melho came to George's room and informed George that Dr. Georg Heinrich von Langsdorff, the distinguished physician and naturalist, member of the Russian Academy of Sciences and Honorary Russian Consul in Brazil, was waiting to meet him at breakfast.

In the dining room at Boa Vista, George was pleased to meet Dr. Langsdorff who had come to the royal residence to see him. Dr. Langsdorff was a slender man of unprepossessing appearance. He was slightly taller than George, clean-shaven and with short light-colored hair only slightly graying. George knew him to be five years older than he, but he looked younger to George. With Langsdorff was another man he introduced as "my colleague from Switzerland, Dr. João Martinho Flach." Dr. Flach appeared to be approximately the same age as Langsdorff, but he was shorter, and sturdy, with impeccably pressed clothes. Immediately upon their introduction all three men began an animated conversation in German.

"So we are countrymen, it seems, Dr. von Schaeffer," said Dr. Langsdorff. "How nice it is to find a fellow German speaker here, and to find one in the same capacity of ship's surgeon on a Russian round-the-world voyage that I once enjoyed. Tell me, how are things back in St. Petersburg? My wife will want to know, and if she finds out that I talked to someone fresh from St. Petersburg and did not find out all the facts…and all the rumors…about life there, then she will be angry with me."

George set about telling Drs. Langsdorff and Flach all about St. Petersburg. He told about the history of his laudanum factory—the commendation by the Grand Duke Konstantin. He told of his acquaintance with General Aleksandr Tormasov and of how General Tormasov, now a member of the Tsar's Military Council in St. Petersburg, had moved with his wife into George's new Nevskii Prospect mansion.

"A Nevskii Prospect mansion?" mused Dr. Langsdorff. "The laudanum factory must be very lucrative."

George Heinrich von Langsdorff (Grigorii Ivanovich Langsdorf, 8 April, 1774--9 June, 1852) from http://en.wikipedia.org/Grigory_Langsdorff.

"Indeed it is," answered George. "But I also earned a large sum of money for managing a military project for the Tsar…a project to construct an aerostat with which to kill Napoleon."

"Are you an aerostier too?" asked Dr. Langsdorff. "I have studied the making of balloons myself and once constructed a small one in Japan."

"I know of this," George told him. "I read of it in the memoirs of the first circumnavigation. These memoirs are very popular now in St. Petersburg…yours and Kruzenshtern's and Lisianskii's especially. So we have some experience in balloon construction in common also."

"But you didn't kill Napoleon," commented Dr. Flach. "Why not?"

"The project was extremely hurried by Napoleon's rapid advance toward Moscow," explained George. "We had both supply and construction problems that we were unable to solve before the decisive Battle of Borodino. And, after the French occupation of his city, Moscow Governor-General Rostopchin disavowed the project, causing the Tsar's financial support to be withdrawn. After a very tough winter in Nizhnii Novgorod, I resigned as project manager when it was moved to St. Petersburg. And now the entire project has been abandoned and balloon master Leppich has disappeared."

"But you're living in a Nevskii Prospect mansion," said Dr. Langsdorff. "I congratulate you."

After breakfast, Dr. Langsdorff proposed that he and Dr. Flach give George a personal tour on horseback of the city and its environs. George was delighted by this proposal and soon the men were riding horses from the royal stable out of the settlement of São Cristovão toward the north boundary of Rio de Janeiro.

As they rode, the men talked all day of many things and became friends. George was impressed by the two doctors' enthusiasm for Brazil. Every turn they took occasioned another explanation from Langsdorff or Flach about the advantages of settling in Brazil. The weather, the people, the incredible agricultural fertility, the vast wilderness with its territorial, timber, and mineral wealth waiting for development, the prospects for a constitutional monarchy independent of Europe…all were factors in Langsdorff's and Flach's acceptance of Brazil as an ideal place to reside.

"But what about the slavery?" abruptly asked George.

"I think it is inevitable that slavery will end here," answered Dr. Langsdorff. "And indeed I'm in favor of ending it sooner, rather than later. Economic reasons have forced me to purchase some slaves to construct my new plantation at Mandioca and to begin the farming of it. There is no way I could afford to pay laborers to help me, even if such laborers were available…and they're definitely not. But Fredericke and I have a plan for freeing our slaves, and even allotting some of the land to them individually if they want, after Mandioca is producing profitably. Meanwhile we treat them very well and they seem to respect us now."

"I have no slaves, and would not purchase any," said Dr. Flach. "But I am employed as an advisor to the Royal family and in that capacity have often taken advantage of their slaves' labor. Indeed they helped me build a house here that I could not have afforded without them."

At the end of their tour, George asked his new friends to accompany him to the Laranjeira residence to meet Captain Lazarev and the other officers of the *Suvorov*, but Langsdorff replied that he had a party of men ready to begin an expedition into the interior of the country. It was an expedition he had planned for some time and he did not feel that he could delay its departure another day. So he bade George farewell, saying he hoped they would meet again someday, and departed São Cristovão in a royal carriage back to the city. Dr. Flach left with Langsdorff, but agreed to come two days later to the Laranjeira residence to meet the others from the *Suvorov*. He asked George if he would like to accompany him on a short expedition by boat and by mule around the circumference of Guanabara Bay. He would show George the forts of São João, Santa Cruz, Nuestra Donna da Gloria, Villegagnan, São Domingo and São Jago that protected the bay as well as several attractive rural settlements. He thought the trip would take two or three days. George assented to accompany him.

"I Shall Return"—with Capital:

The next morning at São Cristovão, George walked to the front of the *Boa Vista* residence and heard organ music. When he entered the building he asked the servants to summon João de Melho, and he asked the interpreter in English who was playing the organ.

"Dom João is musically inclined," answered João de Melho. "He plays very well. And he also likes to chant."

"Chant?" inquired George.

"Yes," replied de Melho. "Religious chants. He has quite a repertoire."

"Will you go to him and tell him that I also like to chant?" requested George. "I know a fine chant from the Russian Orthodox mass and I would be most happy to teach it to him."

In truth, George did not really know any particular Russian Orthodox chant. He did know to utter "Gospodi pomilui!" or "Lord be merciful!" in varying tones, high and low, and in varying numbers of repetitions. He knew he would be using triple repetitions, chanting the whole phrase three times, then following this by very rapidly chanting the first word nine times and following, at last and in slowly protracted fashion, with the final word. He figured that's the way a real Russian would best do it…although he had never done it and didn't know if that was how it was done. But he thought this offer to teach Dom João a chant from a "heretical" religion might earn him some further conversational time with the Regent…and that was what was really important to him.

In a few minutes Dom João came waddling out of an inner room in his silken nightclothes. He was wearing a white cotton nightcap.

"My good fellow," he said to George through interpreter de Melho, "We understand that you are acquainted with a Russian religious chant. Be so good as to perform it for us."

George cleared his throat and explained that the chant, called "Lord have mercy," functioned, in its triplistic permutations of the phrase in three tones, as a symbol of the Christian religious trinity—Father, Son, and Holy Spirit; and of the three realms of the soul—Hell, Earth, and Heaven; and of the number of years Christ was on earth—33.

"Very good," exclaimed Dom Joao. "But I'm anxious now to hear it."

George cleared his throat again and began in a very low voice. "Gospodi pomilui. Gospodi pomilui. Gospodi pomilui." Then, accelerating rapidly and raising to a higher tone, he chanted "Gospodi, Gospodi, Gospodi, Gospodi, Gospodi, Gospodi, Gospodi, Gospodi, Gospodi…" counting the nine repetitions on his fingers behind his back. Then, dropping his voice to its lowest and stretching out the syllables, he finished—"Gooo-spa-deeee paa-meee-looo-u-eee!"

Dom João was thrilled and broke into applause. "You have an extraordinary voice, Doctor von Schaeffer," he said. "The chant was marvelous. And the Trinitarian doctrine is most apparent in it. Can you teach it to us? Just three repetitions and we should be able to learn it."

George laughed at Dom João's joke and replied, "Of course I would be most happy to teach it to you, Your Majesty. You might be interested to know that there are people in Russia called 'Old Believers' who don't accept the notion of a triune God. They still cross themselves with two fingers instead of three."

"And does the Tsar tolerate such heretics in his country?" asked Dom João.

"He lets the Church's Holy Synod take care of heretics," answered George. "But the Old Believers are often persecuted. One of their early leaders, Archpriest Avakum, who would not bend to the Church's insistence on the trinity, was burned at the stake during the reign of Tsar Aleksei the Quiet in the seventeenth century."

"And well he deserved it," stated Dom João authoritatively.

George soon had Dom João repeating his Russian chant until he mastered it. Dom João then asked de Melho to point out to George that each of the two words had three syllables, and George shook his head in feigned wonderment at this insight. Soon they were conversing about all manner of things, as George had desired.

George was excited to learn from Dom João of the possibility that he could, by contributing enough investment capital into Brazil--which could include the purchasing of a large tract of land for development and generation of tax revenue for the government-- be granted a position at court with a title and hereditary nobility. This was the kind of possibility he had dreamed of all his life. And he could see very clearly that Brazil was a land of great promise. It was almost as large as Russia, and had every kind of natural resource in abundance. Anything planted grew so vigorously that it shoved other things aside in its eagerness to flower. Even the diverse peoples of Brazil seemed to share this kind of eagerness to exceed their bounds, to "flower" and get the most out of life. It was, George thought, the sheer magnificence of the landscape—the azure sea below a clouded sky rushing in savage waves upon the wide golden beaches, the fresh-water lagoons and estuaries filled with fish still unclassified, the vast bays, surrounded by dense jungle filled with macaws and monkeys and unknown primitive tribes, offering protective harbor to ships both foreign and domestic, and the dark green cliffs stretching upward to dizzying heights below a sun at the very peak of the sky. It was the prevailing friendly weather, warm even in its winter and moderated by refreshing ocean breezes. It was this kind of constant natural beauty, which imparted into the people a special kind of enthusiasm for life. George could sense it. Every time he turned to face a new direction, the scenery made him gasp and marvel. The Brazilians, he was beginning to understand, from the royalty to the street beggars, had a kind of wildness about them, a lack of inhibition in dealing with others, and an infectious zeal for enjoying themselves in this natural paradise. Before he left São Cristovão and returned to the Laranjeira villa where the others from the *Suvorov* were staying, George decided that he would return here someday with enough investment capital to realize his dream…and he made sure he registered that intent with Dom João and with Prince Pedro.

"I am accustomed to being of service to the crown," he told Dom João. "In Moscow and St. Petersburg I directed military projects for Tsar Aleksandr for which he and his government rewarded me handsomely. I am a major stockholder in the Russian-American Company as well, and I am confident that I will someday be able to bring here enough investment capital to contribute significantly to Brazil's development and earn a titled position for myself in your court."

"If you have done that well for yourself in Russia, Doctor von Schaeffer," asked Dom João, "Why would you want to leave there? What causes you to consider uprooting yourself and your family to move here?" He was mystified, himself having been forced by Napoleon to move from Portugal to his colony in Brazil.

"All my life I've dreamed of finding a better place, a better situation for myself and my family," answered George. "That's why I've moved from place to place. I've been looking for a better place. Even though I've done well there, Russia is too cold for me. After my wife and daughter and I left Moscow before Napoleon occupied it and fled to Nizhnii Novgorod for the winter, we almost froze. Here it's much warmer. And my opinion is that this is, for many reasons, the best place I've seen. Certainly it's the most beautiful place."

"My own dream," said Dom João, suddenly abandoning the royal "we," "Is to leave Brazil and return to Portugal. I'm like a salmon, yearning to return to the stream where it was spawned. Can you understand this?"

"Yes, Your Majesty," George said, "I understand." But he did not. If he were Dom João, he thought, he would cease being his mother's exiled Regent of Portugal, Algarve, and Brazil. He would let Portugal and the Algarve suffer as they might and declare himself ruler of an independent Brazil. But he did not say this to Dom João.

Unpleasant Words:

When he returned to the villa, George had an unpleasant conversation with Captain Lazarev. It was apparent that Lazarev was angry about something, but George could not immediately discern what it was. It was apparently not just that Dr. Langsdorff, the Russian Consul, had chosen not to delay his planned expedition and so would not meet him. He expressed only slight irritation about this. It was something else.

"You should be careful, Yegor Nikolaevich, of what you say in the presence of a foreign ruler like Dom João," he told George. "You made some negative comments about slavery in his presence and I don't think you should have. He may well have taken serious offense. And if he thinks ill of us Russians, he may think ill of all Russians…and withdraw from them the hospitality he's granted to us."

"Well, he didn't seem to take offense," said George. "Surely he's heard many other criticisms of slavery. I thought he defended himself on the issue quite well."

"But he shouldn't have to defend himself on any issue…especially not in the presence of Russians who are his allies and have serfdom in their own country," Captain Lazarev responded, his voice growing louder.

"Perhaps you and I should not argue the matter of slavery, Captain Lazarev," said George, becoming somewhat annoyed at such a rebuke coming from a younger man. "It's apparent that you don't have as negative an opinion of slavery as I do."

"Perhaps that is because I am a Russian," said Captain Lazarev, "And you are a transplanted German. I understand that in Russia we can't just end serfdom in an instant. Too much of our lives depend upon it. And it's the same way here in Brazil."

"As I said," repeated George, "You and I should not argue the issue of slavery."

"All right," said Captain Lazarev, "But that isn't all. There is the other serious matter of your offer to propose marriage between Prince Pedro and the Tsar's sister. If that isn't preposterous I don't know what is. You don't know the Tsar…have no practical access to him at all. You've misrepresented your status in this regard to Dom João simply in order to ingratiate yourself to him. I tell you, I was embarrassed by your presumption and your deception. I now think that I should have spoken out in Dom João's presence to correct any misapprehensions you gave him. But I didn't, and now I'm complicit in them."

"You are mistaken," answered George, growing angry, "I *do* know the Tsar. He personally entrusted a major military project to me. I also know his brother, the Grand Duke Konstantin, who rewarded my service with an official commendation. If I were in St. Petersburg I would have little trouble to put such a proposal into the Tsar's consideration. Besides, Dom João apparently thought it was a fine idea, and so did Dr. Langsdorff."

"Well I think it's a ridiculous idea…only concocted to make yourself look important in the eyes of Dom João," said Captain Lazarev. "The very notion of a Russian Grand Duchess from the culture of St. Petersburg coming all the way here to the wilderness of Brazil to marry a young Braganza…well, it's hard to imagine. What does the Tsar care about gaining influence in Brazil…or Portugal, for that matter?"

"I don't know," said George. "But that would be for him…and his younger sister…to consider."

Captain Lazarev had calmed down some, having vented most of his anger and his ill feelings about George's actions at São Cristovão's Boa Vista. But in a sarcastic tone, he asked George, "Do you really think that Prince Pedro and Grand Duchess Anna Pavlovna could make a positive marriage?"

"After getting to know the Prince a bit, I think that any woman would have a very difficult time living as his consort. He will be hard to tolerate and impossible to tame. He's just too wild and unruly. But then, I don't know the Grand Duchess. And history teaches us that many royal marriages are successful in the political sense even though the couples themselves might be unhappy."

Captain Lazarev only smirked in answer to George's comment on royal marriages. But there were other matters on his mind.

"Lieutenant Unkovskii tells me that two of our sailors have run off to God knows where, giving up their shares and deserting the crew," complained the Captain. "They got drunk, were taken in by female companions, and decided to stay here in Rio de Janeiro…to become Brazilians for life and stay."

"Who are they?" asked George.

"Ilya Grigoriev and Ivan Nikitin…both young men with no real families waiting for them at home," was the answer.

"Nikitin!" said George with surprise. "That's the fellow I beat at arm wrestling when we were becalmed."

"That's him," agreed Captain Lazarev. "And now we're short-handed on the ship at a time when we need every man. I shouldn't have given the crew leave to come ashore here in Rio. It would have been better if you hadn't passed the 'Catholic' test and taken responsibility for us. We could have replenished by longboat and then sailed on. It's my fault for wanting to provide some rest and recreation to the crew. And it's your fault for being such a good Catholic." George could see that the Captain's anger was now gone. He was merely frustrated.

"What will we do now?" asked George.

"We'll get the men back aboard lest we lose anyone else," answered Captain Lazarev. "And we'll sail on as soon as we can get a couple of new hands from one of the port crew brokers."

"Crew brokers?"

"Most major ports have crew brokers," explained the Captain. "They are people who charge a commission for finding crew members for ships who've lost hands. Sometimes their methods of providing these crewmembers are pretty brutal. But, in our case, the brokers could attract them by offering them our defected sailors' profit shares. Only you would have to pay it to them early when we return them here on our way back home."

"I would pay them?" asked George.

"As the senior representative on board of the Russian-American Company, you would be responsible for paying them these shares in advance of the profits the rest of us will get in St. Petersburg," Captain Lazarev explained. "That's the way it works on a chartered navy ship."

"All right," agreed George. "I'll pay them."

Guanabara Bay Expedition:

Dr. Flach, whom George came to call "Martin," came to the villa to take George on the expedition around Guanabara Bay. George introduced Flach to Captain Lazarev, Lieutenants Unkovskii, Povalo-Shveikovskii, and several others, but the conversation was short. Captain Lazarev was not pleased that George's going on an expedition for several days might delay their departure from Rio de Janeiro. But George was firm in his resolve to go and he and Dr. Flach left.

At first the men traveled by boat across the broad bay, then they hired three mules and continued along narrow tracks through dense rain forest around the circumference of the bay. George was struck with the natural splendor of his surroundings. When they looked down on the bay behind them from a clear promontory, the sun that set to the west of the mountain crown painted the curling ocean waves in virgin pink and mildly illuminated the verdant bay islands, which reminded George of the Greek Archipelagos. Everywhere his eye turned, strangely formed flowers opened up in glowing color mixtures to inhale the cooling air, while, surrounded by shining hummingbirds and iridescent butterflies, the trees were full of life. Grotesque monkeys shook the stronger branches while making bizarre grimaces and ear-piercing shrieks. Birds of every imaginable shape and size chirped and cooed and broke noisily into flight above them. Wild turkeys and feral pigs raced ahead of them through the brush.

By the time they spent their second night outdoors near Porto d'Estrelha on their way back, George was more convinced than ever that this was the place he wanted to settle permanently with Barbara and Inga. The sheer magnificence encountered at every turn was overpowering. He could not resist its attraction. In the late evening around their campfire were swarms of brightly illuminating fireflies, which George had previously read about but had never before seen. When he looked at the mighty show of the southern sky he was sure that it counted many more stars of premiere size and brightness than the northern sky with which he had been familiar. He told Flach, who had become already a fast friend, "I'll be coming back here someday."

The Way to Port Jackson/Vehicles of the Progeny?:

When George returned to the villa in Rio de Janeiro, preparations were being made to depart. The crew brokers had supplied two young brothers, Esteban and Rodrigo Rodriguez, to the *Suvorov*. These brothers had been incarcerated in Rio de Janeiro for assaulting one of the members of Dom João's Portuguese retinue who had evicted their family from land they had worked for three generations. In their early twenties, both were handsome and strong and eager, by learning to become sailors on a Russian ship, to get out of the hellish conditions in Dom João's poorly run Aljube prison. The brothers' liberation had been accomplished by a bribe the crew brokers had arranged for Lieutenant Unkovskii to pay to a corrupt prison administrator.

The *Suvorov* sailed out of Guanabara Bay on the 18th of May, 1814, after its stay of almost a month. Since George was to pay the Rodriguez brothers' share of the ship's anticipated profits in advance, he felt a special responsibility for their performance as members of the ship's crew. Also, he let them know right away that part of their duties would be to spend several hours each week with him so that he could learn Portuguese from them. He continued to work with Joseph Desilvier and Lieutenants Unkovskii and Povalo-Shveikovskii in English as well, though Captain Lazarev had removed himself from this effort, saying that he was "too busy" to continue. George thought that this was because the Captain felt less friendly toward him after the surfacing of their disagreements attendant to their stay in Rio de Janeiro.

Joseph Desilvier was excited when George told him that he and Captain Lazarev had met Percy Clinton Sydney Smythe, the Lord Strangford, at Dom João's residence.

"He's a genuine literary personality, George," explained the erudite Desilvier. "He's the translator into English of a most popular collection of verse by the Brazilian poet, Luis de Camões. His English translations are extremely clever. They preserve the form of the original without sacrificing meaning. He's made Luís de Camões very popular in England, and in America too. And Lord Strangford is apparently quite a rake. Lord Byron satirizes him in an entire canto of his "English Bards and Scotch Reviewers" which was published in the Edinburgh Review. Indeed I know some of the canto by heart. It goes:

> 'Hibernian Strangford! With thine eyes of blue,
>
> And boasted locks of red or auburn hue
>
> Whose plaintive strain each love-sick Miss admires,
>
> And o'er harmonious fustian half expires
>
> ...
>
> Mend, Strangford! Mend thy morals and thy taste,
>
> Be warm, but pure; be amorous, but be chaste'."

"You have a real talent for poetry, my friend," said George. "And I wouldn't have known of Lord Strangford's poetic accomplishment without you. To me, he seemed sort of a pompous diplomat. I heard that he had been beaten once by the guards of Dom João's consort, Dona Carlota. She is apparently quite obsessed with having men kneel before her…and also with taking them to bed. And she doesn't tolerate refusal."

"Well, I don't doubt which behavior Lord Strangford refused," joked Desilvier. "But he's likely too able a diplomat to make trouble for himself by taking the Regent's wife to bed…surely. So either way, he probably refused."

"He's apparently a foe of slavery," George said. "And I admire him because of that."

"I also admire him," said Desilvier. "He's a close friend and supporter of our former Foreign Minister, George Canning, who fought a duel a few years ago with the incompetent War Minister, Lord Castlereagh, over a wrongful assignment of troops in the war against Napoleon. Canning, they say, gave Lord Castlereagh the first shot, which missed. Then, not wanting to kill the War Minister, he deliberately fired into the ground at Castlereagh's feet. Lord Castlereagh insisted that they had both inadvertently missed and demanded that they reload and fire again. Again he shot first and managed only to graze Canning in the thigh. Then, even though wounded, Canning again deliberately shot into the ground. As a result of the scandal, both men resigned from their positions. But Canning continues to advise the King and Prime Minister on foreign policy. It is his view, and the view of Lord Strangford as well, that the European powers should not continue to oppose constitutional movements in their colonies. You can imagine the contention that has raised, with such movements springing up all over the new world. Columbia is even now rebelling against Spain. And Portugal has already found that Brazil is not immune from the constitutional fever. Indeed, I think that the days of the absolute kings and emperors are numbered."

"I think that constitutional government is even better with the royalty retained," said George. "England is a good example. And, I think, the other European powers, including Russia, will eventually follow this example. What happened in France was a horror…the revolutionaries leading all the royalty and royalists to the guillotine. So the anti-royalist Napoleon came to power, and declared himself the new Emperor of France. If the constitutionalists prevail in Brazil, I hope that they retain their royalty, if only in the capacity of figureheads."

The Atlantic crossing to the southern tip of Africa was almost uneventful. The winds were steady and strong, and the *Suvorov* reached the settlement at the Cape of Good Hope on June 15th. A few days out of Rio de Janeiro, however, George had diagnosed a sailor's facial rash and fever as measles. This was because of some infectious contact the man had while in Rio de Janeiro. George decided to quarantine the sailor by putting him into one of the longboats and setting it in tow behind the ship. The sailor, a man named Marko Khrenev, and some of his friends objected to this, saying that the wind was too strong and that, as a result, the ride in the longboat behind the ship would be too severe. But George insisted and the ship's officers were firm in his support. Fortunately, the strategy worked well. Sailor Khrenev was put out in the longboat and it rode the waves without too much danger of swamping or capsizing. George had it pulled up to the ship twice a day so he could check on Khrenev's status and give him food and water. In ten days he was clearly better and George allowed him to be brought back aboard. No one else contracted measles.

The citizens of Cape Town, which had been called Kaapstad by its Dutch founders, were excited about becoming a British Colony. The Cape of Good Hope had been militarily annexed by the British in January of 1806 from the French-dominated Dutch as a way to guarantee a replenishment port for their ships bound for India. But now, in 1814, the Cape was to become a colony beginning in August.

Captain Lazarev decided, after the two defections in Rio de Janeiro, not to allow the crew ashore in Cape Town. But he and George and Lieutenant Unkovskii went ashore to arrange replenishment. There, they were informed that the army of the British Duke of Wellington had captured Bourdeaux, France, in March, and that, shortly after that, the allied armies had entered Paris, occupying the city. Napoleon had abdicated on April 11 and had been exiled to the island of Elba in the Tyrrhenian Sea between Corsica and the Italian mainland. Louis XVIII had been restored to the French throne in June. The Russians were exultant.

"At last, at last," exclaimed George. "The tyrant is no longer in power. Now there will be some positive changes in the world, to be sure. All Napoleon's puppets will be replaced as well, and I might even be able to return home without fear."

"Can you imagine the Russian armies being quartered in Paris, our Tsar riding his horse down the Champs Elysées and strolling into the Cathedral of Notre Dame?" asked Lieutenant Unkovskii in amazement. "It's like a dream…a dream we thought we'd never see realized. And now it has been realized. Thank God Almighty!"

Captain Lazarev commented that Dom João, at the Boa Vista dinner they had shared, had accurately predicted these events. "Yegor Nikolaevich," he asked, "Do you remember what Dom João told us? Now it has turned out that his prediction is correct. Now he can return to Portugal."

"Yes he can," said George. "He told me that such was his dream. And now he can realize it. Still, I think that Brazil should be separately ruled. All of the American colonies are separating from the European powers that claim them…and Brazil should do the same. They could become a constitutional monarchy even if Portugal does not. Perhaps young Pedro could remain in Brazil as a Regent when Dom João returns to Portugal. He has the needed 'Brazilian temperament,' if you know what I mean."

After celebrating the news with the British port officials, Captain Lazarev, Lieutenant Unkovskii, and George returned to the *Suvorov*. The replenishment was complete and Captain Lazarev wanted to take advantage of the continuing strong winds. The crew, rejuvenated by their vociferous toasting Napoleon's abdication and exile and the allied occupation of Paris with extra-ration drams of vodka, hoisted anchor and set full sail for Australia. The course was to follow the 35th south latitude across the Indian Ocean eastward, trying to strike land in the Great Australian Bight and then skirt the southern coast around to Port Jackson.

In the middle of the Indian Ocean, north of the French islands of Amsterdam and St. Paul, George was summoned to the front of the ship by Michman Bestuzhev. The sun was just setting into a cloudless horizon straightaway behind them. Bestuzhev was shouting through his "rouper," the copper megaphone he almost constantly carried, to the lookout Dementei Biakov, who was nearing the end of the day watch in the mainmast crowsnest.

"Put the glass to the fore," he was shouting to Biakov. "Directly in front of us! Five degrees above the line! What do you see?"

George hurried up to where Bestuzhev was standing, just at the base of the *Suvorov*'s bowsprit, which rose and fell, scribing a path perpendicular to the horizon.

"Doctor von Sheffer," requested Bestuzhev with urgency in his voice, "Look ahead of us there in the sky and tell me what you make of it!"

George looked to where Bestuzhev was pointing and easily saw a group of black objects in the sky. The objects were quite far away and visually small. But they were definitely objects of some substance. And they appeared to be stationary in the air about a hand's width, at the length of an extended arm, above the eastern horizon.

"Birds away!" shouted Biakov from the crowsnest. "Land birds, I'd say!"

"They don't look like birds to me," said Bestuzhev to George. "What do you think?"

George squinted his eyes and contemplated the strange sight. "No, I don't think they're birds at all," he said. "They're too uniform in size and shape and they appear to be hovering in some kind of formation. How many are there?"

"I see nine of them," came Biakov's call. "And they're not birds. They may be balloons."

The objects looked to George as if they were made by placing two shallow soup bowls together top-to-top to enclose their mutual contents. They appeared dark against the sky above the horizon. And they were moving strangely in a nine-point formation, with more of them at the top of the formation than at the bottom. In only a minute or two, however, the black objects began to glow as the sky behind them turned darker until they resembled dim stars, but larger, like miniature moons.

"They're not like any balloons I've ever seen or heard of," said George.

"I've certainly never seen anything like them," said Michman Bestuzhev. Then he turned away to yell down to several sailors on the deck amidships, "Get the Captain up here right now! Summon the Lieutenants!"

"They're flying away," came Biakov's call from above.

The nine objects, now brightly illuminated, suddenly ascended to forty-five degrees above the horizon and, in sudden silence, accelerated away to the south, vanishing completely from view in only two or three seconds.

"What hath God wrought?" Bestuzhev wondered aloud. George too, was astonished.

Sailor Rodion Shushkov, who had been polishing one of the punt guns on the forward rail, had also seen the objects. Rubbing his eyes, he came over to George and Michman Bestuzhev and asked, "What were those things?"

Captain Lazarev and Lieutenant Unkovskii promptly came up to the fore as they had been asked. The objects in the sky, however, were gone.

"What is it, Michman?" asked Captain Lazarev. "What's the matter?"

Michman Bestuzhev decided to defer to George. "You tell him, Doctor," he said.

George related, "We saw some strange objects in the air, Captain. There were nine of them…neither birds nor balloons in our judgment…and they hovered in formation at a distance of several kilometers or more. At first they appeared black, but then began to glow like a lamp of some kind. And then they rose up to great height together and flew off to the south with tremendous speed."

Captain Lazarev and Lieutenant Unkovskii looked at each other strangely. Lieutenant Unkovskii asked Michman Bestuzhev, "Did you also see the same thing?"

"Yes I did, Sir," responded Bestuzhev. "Doctor von Sheffer described it well."

"And I saw them too," interjected sailor Shushkov. "It was some kind of miracle, I think…something God doesn't usually allow mortals to see."

It was getting dark, and Dementei Biakov had come down from the crowsnest. So far from any recorded land, the Captain had ordered suspension of the night watch. But he asked Biakov, "What did you see through the telescope?"

"I saw what looked like nine flying lampshades," said Biakov. "At first they were dark, then they were lit up. As I was cleaning the front of the telescope, thinking they might be spots of some kind on the glass, I saw…with my naked eyes…all of them fly off to the south and out of sight in no time at all. I've never seen anything like it."

The Captain was puzzled and shook his head. Then, he said to George, "Yegor Nikolaevich, I want you to write me a report about this incident. Be as exact as you can in your description. Draw the objects if you can. And have the others who saw these objects sign that the report is accurate."

"I will do that right away," said George.

The next morning George took his report around to Michman Bestuzhev and sailors Biakov and Shushkov. In the report was his drawing of the objects and a likeness of their formation.

Each of the objects, according to George's report, looked like this:

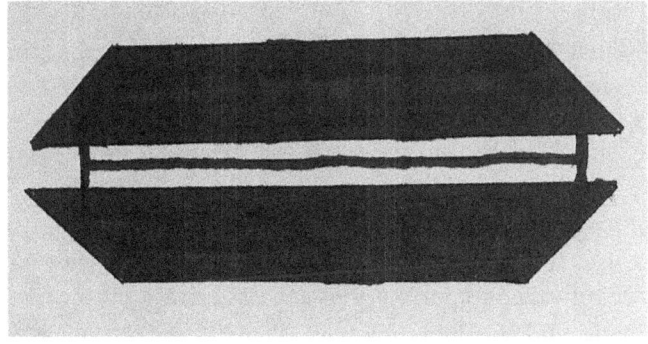

And the formation in which the objects hovered and flew, looked like this:

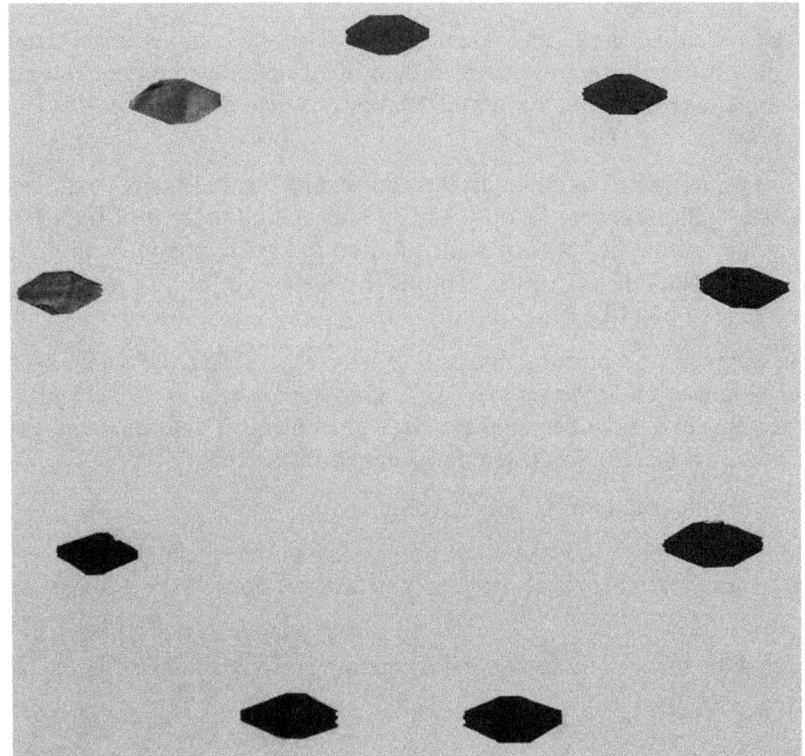

George discussed his report with the other witnesses, obtained their assent to it, and had them sign it. Since Dementei Biakov was illiterate, George wrote out the lookout's full name and then added his own initials to Biakov's primitively scribed letter "X." Then he took the report to Captain Lazarev.

"I'll add your report to the ship's log," Captain Lazarev told George. "I'll list the coordinates of the location and record that our michman, our surgeon, and two sailors witnessed the event mentioned in the attached report. But I don't know what further commentary to add. I don't want to stand before any Admiralty inquiry on something like this...which I didn't even see. I'll just let whoever reads it figure it out."

"You know, Captain," said George. "I've been thinking about the objects that we saw. And I think I know what they are."

"You do?" replied Captain Lazarev skeptically. "What are they?"

George decided to share with the Captain information that he had not shared with anyone other than his wife...information he had not mentioned in almost eight years.

"When I was a medical student in Würzburg and courting my wife," explained George, "A prominent scientist, now deceased, told me that he had been contacted by a man from the future who said that he was one of our mutual progeny. I have personal reasons to believe that this member of our progeny was genuine. He told this scientist that he had come here to visit in a vehicle that could move through vast distances and through time itself with great rapidity. My thought is that I have now seen a group of such vehicles."

Captain Lazarev was silent for a minute, then he said, "I think you have an imagination that is well beyond your own control. I've seen certain aspects of it already in my acquaintance with you...your stated relationship with the Tsar, for example, and your delusions about developing Brazil. Now you're telling me about an actual visit by a person from the future in a vehicle that travels in time? Well, you can wager I won't be entering that in the log."

"That's all right," agreed George. "But such is my opinion nevertheless. And I challenge you to find a more reasonable interpretation of what four of us saw in the sky yesterday evening."

"Oh, I think I can come up with any number of more reasonable interpretations," answered Captain Lazarev. "I have heard that when one person sees a mirage in the desert...evidence of water where there is none, for example...and announces this to his thirsty companions, then they too will report seeing the same mirage. It's some kind of infectious hysteria."

George just shook his head and left the Captain's cabin.

Action in the Rocks:

On the morning of the 13th day of August 1814, the 25th day by the Australian calendar, the *Suvorov* anchored at Port Jackson. The Harbor Captain, a man named John Piper, came out to give instructions on how the Russians should conduct themselves during their stay. His initial caution was changed to enthusiasm when he heard from Captain Lazarev the news of Napoleon's abdication and exile. He took this news with him back to shore and soon the *Suvorov* was exchanging cannon salutes with a shore battery that fired off a salvo of thirteen guns. By that afternoon, Harbor Captain Piper had returned to inform Captain Lazarev that the *Suvorov* would be allowed to move south and into Neutral Bay. This was done the next day, but that evening Captain Lazarev requested a general inspection of the ship and its rigging, stating his intention to repair any shortcomings and to give the ship a recaulking before it embarked upon its Pacific journey. This request resulted in his being allowed to move the ship to Sydney Cove closer to the center of the settlement and its ship repair facilities.

When the ship was anchored in Sydney Cove, Captain Lazarev ordered a twenty-one-gun salute. Gunners Rodion Shushkov and Naum Semyonov mustered several comrades and directed the effort. The noise was deafening and the smoke obscured everyone's sight of the harbor for several minutes. But then came the same response from the local fort. The men cheered loudly. They knew that they would be going ashore.

Captain Lazarev gave the crew a speech threatening to see any attempted defectors punished severely.

"The Englishmen here in Australia are our allies," he said, "And they'll help us enforce our policy on desertion. The settlement at Sydney is not so large that you can't be found. And there's nowhere out of it you can go where you won't quickly be recognized and arrested. So I am going to allow you leave here. But it's a tough place, populated by criminals, and I want you all to be on your best behavior. We will be sailing on as soon as the ship's fit and I want everyone healthy and in good shape. Are you all agreed?"

The men of the *Suvorov's* crew, assembled on the deck for the Captain's speech, in unison shouted, "Da, Da, Kapitan. My soglasny…We agree."

Joseph Desilvier had informed the officers of the facts of Australia's history. He told them that the Colony of New South Wales had been settled after 1788 by successive shiploads of English convicts. The settlement at Sydney Cove south of Port Jackson had grown to become the Colony's center. Captain William Bligh, famous for surviving a mutiny on his ship, *Bounty*, in the late 1780's, had endured another mutiny in 1808 as Governor of the New South Wales Colony for disrupting a monopoly on rum run by his own militia. The rum had become a kind of currency in the Colony and Governor Bligh knew that he had to control it. But his militia, led by Major George Johnston and incited by sheep-industry pioneer John Macarthur, rebelled and placed the overbearing Bligh under house arrest for some time, until aid arrived from England. Governor Bligh and Major Johnston were returned to England for the resultant court martial on the same ship, but, in the end, the mutineers were not severely punished and Bligh was replaced as Governor by Lieutenant Colonel Lachlan Macquarie.

Captain Lazarev, Lieutenant Unkovskii, and George soon found their way to Government House in Sydney to meet Governor Macquarie. Macquarie was a Scotsman from the family of a prominent clan. He was tall and fit at 53 years of age. He had dark hair, partially grey, which he wore short, and he was clean-shaven. He wore a red British military uniform with gold epaulets. He told them of his delight to hear the news about Napoleon's abdication and exile, and he promised all due aid in replenishing the *Suvorov*.

Captain Lazarev gave to Governor Macquarie the packet containing the communication, which Lord Strangford in Rio de Janeiro had asked him to transmit. Governor Macquarie was very glad to receive it.

Lachlan Macquarie (31 January, 1762-1 July, 1824), from
http://www.schools.nsw.edu.au/nswconstitution/html/3rd/bgr/gov/macquarie.

"Yes, Lord Strangford and I agree on many things," he said with a clear Scottish accent. "We both side with George Canning in his disputes with Lord Castelreagh, for example. But now, after their duel, all the colonial affairs are confused. The King is not in control and neither are the government. Our budget here is clearly insufficient and we have to make do on our own devices."

The Russians did not know how to respond to Governor Macquarie's complaint about the lack of funding from England. George, ever conscious of language nuances, took notice of Governor Macquarie's saying "the government…are," considering the "government" to be something plural. He had been translating such phrases in his mind from the Russian equivalent and saying in English "the government…is." And none of his English-speaking interlocutors, Joseph Desilvier, Captain Lazarev, Lieutenants Unkovskii or Povalo-Shveikovskii, had corrected him. And how had his English speech been regarded in Rio de Janeiro by Dom João's interpreter João de Melho or by Lord

Strangford? He would have to adjust this aspect of his English speech, he thought, if he were to speak with linguistic advantage to British gentlemen.

George changed the direction of the conversation by asking the Governor, "Have you ever encountered Russians before us?"

The Governor's enthusiasm immediately increased. "A Russian captain named Hagemeister," he related, "brought the navy ship *Neva* into Port Jackson in 1807, but he dealt with my predecessor, Governor Bligh. I was not here yet. But indeed I have met many Russians and have a high regard for them."

"Were you in military campaigns with Russians?" asked George.

"No," said Governor Macquarie. "My military career has taken me to America, to Egypt, and to India…but I haven't campaigned with any Russians. No, I met Russians in 1807 when I traveled overland through Russia on my way back to England from Bombay to get married to my present wife Elizabeth…my first wife Jane died in Macao some years ago. The trip back to England was quite an adventure. First, I almost drowned in the Persian Gulf before I took to land. Then, on land, I drove most of the way in a 'kibitka'—a two-wheeled covered cart pulled by a troika of horses. I had to sleep in it many a night. I traveled in it from Baghdad to Baku, then to Astrakhan, Tsaritsyn, Tambov, Riazan, Moscow, and finally St. Petersburg. I finally sailed back home from Kronstadt on His Majesty's Ship *Calypso*, managing to complete the entire journey in only seven months, despite all kinds of bureaucratic delays, two quarantines, and even a stint in jail. I found that Russians are the very friendliest of people…and endlessly helpful…as long as they are 'off duty.' In their work capacities they are just the opposite…obstinate and inefficient…especially the officials."

Captain Lazarev, who was quite proud of being a Russian, frowned when he heard Governor Macquarie say this. But he commented, "Russians are always helpful to those who help them. And that is why we love the English."

"I even learned to speak some Russian," continued Governor Macquarie. "And to you and your crew I say 'Dobro pozhalovat'… 'Welcome,' and I wish you 'vsevo khoroshevo'… 'all the best'!"

Macquarie continued to dominate the conversation. He told them that he had embarked on a public campaign to "civilize" the settlement: no more profanation of the Sabbath, all public houses were to be closed on Sunday for church services, the number of establishments licensed to serve spirited drink was being reduced, the proliferation of brothels was to be limited by increased taxation, and all manner of profligacy, dissipation, idleness, and rudeness were being punished by public flogging. He had issued a ban on the shameful cohabitation of unmarried couples. He had started a number of schools for the children as a way to keep them off the streets. He was even having a school built in Parramatta, the community where he was also building a personal residence for himself and his wife Elizabeth, which would teach reading and writing in English to the aboriginal children who could be attracted to it. He had sent explorers—one man's name mentioned was George Evans-- off into the hinterlands to chart the vast landmass away from the coast. And he had instituted a vigorous course of public improvements in the Colony—a hospital, better roads and bridges, and a new plan for the development of Sydney as a modern city.

"The rum," Governor Macquarie said at last, "and other spirited drinks are a terrible problem here. Our citizens are more than ordinarily desirous of it. And the natives will sell their children for it. That's why we had to be sure that none of your men try to sell any such drink. We will be searching your men as they come ashore. Only one bottle per man is allowed…and that for personal consumption or possible trade for hard goods. The sale of spirited drink for cash or other 'services' is not permitted. We are, I warn you, very serious about this here. The Honorable brothers Bent, Ellis and Jeffery, who are in charge of the courts here, are not men to trifle with."

"We hear you and will heed your wishes, Governor Macquarie," assured Captain Lazarev. We can only admire your campaign to civilize the Colony. How is the campaign working? I imagine there must be considerable resistance to such measures from people who came here as prisoners."

"The civilization campaign is going very well in most areas," said Macquarie. "Mostly we keep the people hard at some productive work. Hard work ennobles a person. And here there is no end of hard work. A good laborer can soon earn his freedom ticket here, and the work never ceases. But there is one bad area on the west side of Sydney Cove where all manner of our malcontents and troublemakers congregate. We call this area 'The Rocks.' There are miscreants there who continue to act as if they were not subject to government and law. You should tell your crew to stay away from this area. It's easy to get into trouble there."

As they left the Government House, Captain Lazarev asked Lieutenant Unkovskii if he knew to which part of the settlement of Sydney the crew had gone. "The Rocks, of course," was Unkovskii's answer.

Convict shipwrights set to work setting the *Suvorov* into top condition. Yardarms were reinforced with iron bands. New rope was spliced and strung. Hempen canvas sailcloth was purchased from the Sydney Harbor stores, cut, sewn, and fitted in. The outer hull was caulked with hot pitch above the waterline and the inner hull was caulked to the keel with a bituminous gum. The work went on all the daylight hours, but every day half of the crew would go ashore in rotation.

Prominent citizens of Sydney began entertaining the officers of the *Suvorov* and the ship's representatives of the Russian-American Company almost every evening. Captain Lazarev and officers Unkovskii, Povalo-Shveikovskii, navigators Samsonov and Rossiiskii, and even Michman Bestuzhev and Quartermaster Fokin…as well as Company representatives George, supercargo Molvo, and the clerk Krasilnikov… found themselves at dinners hosted by Governor Macquarie and his young wife Elizabeth, by Militia Colonels Erskine and Noelle, by beef rancher George Johnston, known as "the younger" to dissimilate him from the former head of the Militia under Governor Bligh, by ship provisioner Robert Campbell, and by Port Jackson Harbor Captain John Piper. At one of these dinners, the one hosted by Colonel John Erskine, over forty people sat at a table set with vintage crystal and silver implements. A large quantity of wine was consumed and endless toasts to King George and to Tsar Aleksandr were made. In the course of this entertainment several lasting friendships were made. George Johnston the younger and Lieutenant Semyon Unkovskii, for example, became fast friends and took several long walks together, visiting Sydney's windmills and inspecting the construction of a wooden bridge on the road to the very pleasant community of Parramatta. Later, with Lieutenant Povalo-Shveikovskii too, they rode horses to Parramatta and visited a Pastor Marsden who was the head of a mission to convert the natives of the Society Islands to Christianity. He had advocated ministering to the islanders in their own language of Tahitian, and that, he told them, had led to genuine success in the conversion effort. Now he was proposing to send a similar mission to New Zealand and was hosting, preparatory to that effort, two Maori kings and a large group of their relatives. Lieutenants Unkovskii and Povalo-Shveikovskii met these guests with real interest, although the Maoris' English language abilities were very limited. Also interesting was the fact that Pastor Marsden and his wife had eight young daughters…girls "delightful to the eyes and to the mind," in the description of George Johnston the younger.

On August 20th Podshturman Aleksei Rossiiskii, Joseph Desilvier, and ship's clerk Fyodor Krasilnikov obtained permission from Captain Lazarev to attend a public spectacle some distance out of Sydney in which two tribes of aborigines would be engaging in a fight. The fight, they said, was the result of the native custom of marriage by abduction. When a young man from one tribe forcibly abducted a young woman from another tribe to take as a wife, a fight between the men of the two tribes would ensue. The status of the marriage would not be altered by the fight. The abducted woman was not the issue. In the aboriginal language called Burra-Burra, the word for "wife" and the word for "slave" or "prize of war" were the same. The fight was a matter of tribal honor.

The next day Aleksei Rossiiskii regaled his crewmates with his tale of the aboriginal fight they had witnessed.

"One group of about twenty completely naked black men," he said, "attacked another group of similar size with spears and thick crooked clubs called 'sagays' made of ironwood. The natives were so quick and clever at dodging the spears and the blows of the sagays that few were actually struck full force. They had small shields made of bark, which partially protected them. But many were grazed and scraped by the weapons, and were pushed to the ground where they were trampled. No one was killed, but several had broken bones and there was a lot of blood spilled. The noise of the screaming and the moaning was upsetting to us. But the Englishmen there watching seemed to enjoy it. The worse the conflict got, the louder they laughed and urged the combatants on."

"Were there any women there?" several men of the crew wanted to know.

"Only a couple of native women," Rossiiskii answered. "But they didn't take part in the fight. They just watched. They were also completely naked and one had her body smeared with red, white and yellow paint of some kind. And there was a native chief there called 'Bongaree' of the tribe from Broken Bay. He also did not participate in the fight…probably too old. He spoke pretty well in English with some of the other spectators. He told Joseph Desilvier why his tribesmen were all missing their front teeth. They bashed them out against a rock or tree, he said, when they became men and eligible for marriage. That is their custom."

The work on the *Suvorov* was finished and the stores were replenished by the end of August. But George and Supercargo Germann Molvo were excited about the possibility of negotiating with Governor Macquarie a permanent waystation for Russian-American Company ships on the way to and from Novo-Arkhangelsk. The new "reverse" circumnavigation route, they told Captain Lazarev, was apparently successful and, in their view, should be even easier and faster for future ships if such a permanent anchorage could be negotiated. This, to Captain Lazarev's irritation, delayed the *Suvorov*'s departure. To make the situation of tension between the Russian Navy officers and the Russian-American Company representatives worse, the negotiations were unsuccessful because of Governor Macquarie's departure on an inland expedition. George was unable to find out when he would return, and so the delay continued. Captain Lazarev, in the meantime, had begun to spend his nights ashore, only coming back to the ship in the early afternoons.

George, wanting to talk with the Captains of some of the other ships in the harbor, found that, in order to do this, he had to visit the area known as "The Rocks." By going into the Rocks and spending time in the licensed drinking establishments, he managed to have conversations with Captain Savigny of the *Alligator* and Captain Raine of the *Surry*. These were two of the English ships anchored in Sydney Cove near the *Suvorov*. Another English ship, loaded with Chinese fabrics, was the *Broxbornebury*. And there was a New England whaling ship, the *Jefferson*, whose Captain Josiah Barnes somehow managed to avoid his ship's being seized as a matter of policy in Great Britain's war with the United States. He was exempted from seizure, he said, because his was a civilian ship, not a military one, and because he was personally acquainted with Governor Macquarie, who held him in high esteem. Captain Barnes told George that his crew had killed seventeen sperm whales off New Zealand already that year. He thought that his load of whale oil and of spermaceti would be worth a fortune when he returned home. Like Governor Macquarie, Captain Barnes had been in Russia, having sailed several times into the White Sea port of Arkhangel.

Another ship in the harbor, the British warship *Seretoptam*, had been captured in a sea battle by the United States frigate *Essex*. But the ship was retaken in the Marquesas Islands by seven of the original English crewmen who had been imprisoned on board. The seven crewmen, confining their American captors below decks, had then eluded the *Essex* and taken seven weeks to sail the *Seretoptam* to Port Jackson. These seven crewmen were regarded as heroes in Sydney and were the "toast of the Rocks."

Several of the *Suvorov*'s crewmembers mentioned to George that, to their surprise, they had encountered a man in a bar in the Rocks who spoke fluent Russian. His name was Josef Josefovich Awrowicz and, although he was born in Poland, he had been impressed in his teens into the Russian Navy. While ashore in London in August of 1812 he had been arrested for stealing a pair of stockings worth 14 shillings. His violent assault on the arresting policemen caused him to be sentenced to death initially, but then his sentence was commuted to penal servitude in Australia. He had arrived in Sydney the previous year. He was a big man in his late forties and the Rocks community of brigands called him "Aurora," because that was how his last name sounded to them and because he was known to show up for work irregularly and shine brightly…then disappear. George was anxious to meet this "Aurora," and so he accompanied several crewmembers on a tour of the Rocks bars in order to find him. In the party of crewmembers with George were the Rodriquez brothers, Rodrigo and Esteban, from Brazil, to whom he had grown close as a result of his study with them of the Portuguese language, Naum Semyonov the gunner, and Sagamit Bikulov, the crew's "King of the Left Arm."

On their way through the Rocks, the men saw a flogging stand and a pillory with seven traps, though no one was being pilloried at that time. There was also a public gallows not far away with a large tramped-down area around it where crowds would come to watch hangings. In many of the house doorways sat a woman, provocatively dressed, who was ready to take an inquiring sailor inside. A dark-haired little girl with dirty bare feet was ambling down the pathway on her own with no supervision at all. She looked so young that George could not help thinking of his own daughter Inga who was now the same age back in St. Petersburg. The little girl stopped when, on the street ahead, she saw a pack of dogs tearing into a pile of gory animal viscera. Apparently someone had butchered a sheep or goat there in the street and left the offal for the dogs and birds and insects to clean away. George walked over to the girl, thinking to pick her up into his arms protectively and then to see if he could find her parents. But, seeing George approach, the girl turned away and ran with surprising speed into a very narrow space between two buildings so that George could not follow. He shrugged his shoulders and continued onward with the other men. Naum Semyonov said sympathetically, "She's a fast one…you've got to give her that. She'll likely be all right."

"A girl that age shouldn't be out of her parents' sight for even a second," said George. "I've got a daughter that age, and I can tell you that her mother would never let her roam around the streets alone."

The sewage in the Rocks ran down open ditches into the harbor and contributed to a foul stench that was only intermittently relieved by the sea breeze. George unbuttoned his shirt collar and pulled the shirt up over his nose. But he gave up this strategy as they started looking into the drinking houses to find the Russian-speaking man. In a particularly disreputable drinking establishment, they found "Aurora" sitting by himself at a large table by the front window. On the table in front of him was a dark bottle of rum. Next to it was the cork…but there was no glass. Sagamit Bikulov, who had met Aurora previously, led the others over to him and introduced them. He told Aurora that George was the *Suvorov*'s ship's surgeon and that he represented the Russian-American Company, which had chartered the vessel.

"Ochen prijatno vas vstretit'…Very nice to meet you," Aurora said in Russian. "It's a fucking delight to be able to speak with someone in Russian again. I thought I might never see another Russian again."

George took notice of the man's coarse vocabulary. His language was the language of the Russian sailors, interspersing some obscenity into every sentence and even into the middle of some words. On the *Suvorov* the sailors spoke to George deferentially, trying to prune such items out of their vocabulary…a vocabulary that George didn't use. But Aurora saw no reason to alter his Russian for George's sake…or he could not.

Aurora was a big man, balding with reddish brown hair in evidence around his ears and the lower portion of his head. When he rose to meet George and the others he seemed hunched in posture, as if bending forward toward them, but, because of his great size, hulking over them. He did not embrace the Russians to hug them and exchange three perfunctory kisses in the native manner, but, instead, shook their hands like an Englishman would do. His hands were very thick and the force of his handshake was strong enough to be intimidating.

"How long have you been here," George asked him.

"I arrived here last October 9th on the *Earl Spencer*," Aurora answered. "So I've been here in this rat's nest a year now. The police and militia bastards keep trying to put me to work here, but I've gotten the best of them every time. I've managed to become a kind of boss here in the Rocks. The authorities have given up trying to find me, and no one tells me what to do anymore."

"How do you keep yourself housed and fed?" asked George.

"There's all kinds of ways to make a living here," Aurora replied. "You don't have to shovel shit in the sun all day. What I do is take a little commission for finding things…drink, women, whatever you want. And if you need someone persuaded to give you what you want…I'll get them persuaded for you. Also, I dispense information about people…whomever you want to know something about, I can tell you…for a few shillings, of course."

"I see," said George. "But it sounds like you could easily get into serious trouble with such activities."

"What more trouble am I going to get into?" asked Aurora. "I've already been sentenced to a lifetime here in 'bloody kangaroo land.' I figure I can only make the best of my situation here every day…and this is the way I do it."

"But someone could complain. The police could arrest you. You could be pilloried, flogged, or even hanged," said Sagamit Bikulov.

"I've already been pilloried and flogged," said Aurora. "I got twenty-one lashes for theft, when a man who'd been seen taking a ewe to wife only got fifteen. But the floggers didn't correct either one of us."

At this point Aurora broke into a coarse laughter, then continued, "Well, I don't really know about the other bloke. But I'm staying the same course. And as for hanging…I'd rather be hanged than work mindlessly every day like a damned draft mule."

George commented, "Governor Macquarie has a different view of work. Work, he says, ennobles a person."

"Aye," answered Aurora, "The work of us convicts is damn well ennobling him, the son-of-a-bitch."

Again Aurora laughed in a rough cackle. Then he went on, "Governor Macquarie has become a 'bolshaya shishka'…a 'big bump' by working to advance himself. And that's what I'm doing…working to advance myself. I consider him a model, in fact. But why should I work to put his ass over mine?"

George had no ready counter to Aurora's stated philosophy. The man was clearly drunk and no amount of reason was going to affect his views. The Rodriquez brothers, who did not understand all of the Russian conversation, had already wandered away from the table to the establishment's bar, where they began to drink. Now Naum Semyonov and Sagamit Bikulov also walked away from the table to join the Rodriquez brothers. But George stayed at the table to continue his conversation with the colorful Aurora.

Aurora picked up the bottle of rum and took a long drink from it. Then he continued to brag to George about his activities as a "boss" in the Rocks. To George's surprise, the man said he was already acquainted with Captain Lazarev.

"Your own Captain," said Aurora, "has earned me a nice commission or two. I arranged for him to spend his nights with a family here…a really interesting family, if you know what I mean. The man of the house—one of my drinking mates, Will Taggart, is still recovering from a harsh-regime flogging for offering his mere daughter to sailors. And the woman of the house, Annie Dalton, is an exceptionally wanton wench. I imagine that your Captain may be fucking both Annie and the daughter. Will doesn't care. All he wants is another bottle."

George, who immediately called to mind the little girl he had just seen on the streets…and his own daughter as well, was shocked to hear this, but then he realized that the "mere daughter" was likely to be quite a bit older, and he recalled the young Captain's statement in London that since he was "married only to the Russian navy," he could "fornicate as he wanted and not feel guilty about it." Still, it was hard for George to imagine Captain Lazarev in quite the scene of debauchery described by this Aurora.

"I don't think you even know our captain," George said firmly. "You must be mistaken."

"Oh, fucking well I know the bugger," insisted Aurora, his raised voice now slurring from the drink. "This very rum," he said, picking up the dark bottle from the table in front of him, "was poured from a hundred-gallon cask purchased off the *Suvorov* two fucking days ago. Four twenty-gallon kegs of the vodka were purchased as well. That's how your Captain is paying for the work on the ship. And it was none other than me that brokered the deal...made meself a pretty penny too."

At that moment a fight erupted at the bar. Several tough-looking men had gathered around the Rodriquez brothers and tried to grab them and take from them the purses they had tied to their belts. Naum Semyonov and Sagamit Bikulov instantly jumped to the Rodriguez brothers' defense, knocking two of the men to the floor. In a few seconds there was a large scrum of men tangled together, flailing away wildly with both arms and legs. Esteban Rodriquez was on the bottom, biting a man's ankle as he kicked upward at another man's crotch. The bartender began to shout at the top of his lungs "Rube! Hey Rube! Rube, I say! Hey Rube!" He came out from behind the bar with a cudgel and started swinging it at the outnumbered sailors. One of the first men he struck with the cudgel was Naum Semyonov. Semyonov cringed from the blow but instantly delivered a hard blow back to the middle of the paunchy bartender's stomach. The bartender dropped his arms, exhaling all his air with a "wwwhhoooooo" sound and crumpled to the floor. Sagamit Bikulov managed to pick one of his opponents up to shoulder height and slam him to the floor. Then he grabbed another by his neck and swung him violently around into the bar, kicking at him as he fell. Rodrigo Rodriquez got a man into a headlock and bit off his ear. But one of the man's friends, hearing his shriek, picked up a chair and, swinging it from over his head, smashed it on Rodrigo's back. Rodrigo fell to the floor unconscious.

George jumped up from the table and moved to help his shipmates. He pulled a man roughly from Sagamit Bikulov's back and tried to strike him with his right fist, but another man suddenly connected with a blow to George's right eye. George turned away from the blow to his left, shaking his head to clear his vision. What he saw then was a group of ten other men running into the bar from outside to help their friends who had assaulted the crewmembers. Also, he noticed that Aurora was already gone. He had fled the bar as George had joined the fight.

In very short order the men from outside the bar turned the fight to an overwhelming hometown advantage. George and the others were held and hit until they dropped. Their purses were all cut away and taken. Only the appearance of a lone policeman on the street outside the bar caused the attackers to skulk quickly away without doing further damage to the bodies of George and his companions huddled into tight curls on the bar floor. The policeman, seeing so many men exit the bar at the same time, entered it and, seeing the men on the floor, asked the bartender, "So what happened here this time?"

"I'm damned if I know," answered the bartender. "These men picked a fight with some of my customers. One of them bit a man's ear right off. And this one here hit me." As he said this he walked over and kicked Naum Semyonov in the side.

The policeman sat down on a chair and waited for the men on the floor to come around. George was the first to try to get up.

"Who are you?" asked the policeman.

"I am Dr. George Anton von Schaeffer, ship's surgeon on the Russian ship *Suvorov* presently anchored here in Sydney Cove," answered George in his best English. "And these are members of the *Suvorov*'s crew. We are here as special guests of Governor Macquarie, having brought to him an ambassadorial communication from Brazil and the news of Napoleon Bonaparte's abdication."

The policeman was obviously impressed with this explanation. "I have heard of this," he said. "So how did you get yourselves into such a brawl here the Rocks?"

"We came here looking to meet a man who speaks Russian," George answered. He noticed that the others were now picking themselves up off the floor. Only Rodrigo Rodriquez had to be helped to his feet by the others.

"That would be Aurora now, wouldn't it?" asked the policeman.

"Yes, that's right...Aurora," said George. "But he wasn't involved in the fight. He left as it began."

"He has a gift for that," said the policeman. "But sooner or later we'll catch him at something. You can be sure of that."

"They took our purses," complained George. "Is there any hope of getting them back?"

The policeman laughed and asked, "What do you think?"

George didn't answer, but only asked another question, "Can we go?"

"Aye, you can go," the policeman said, casting a glance in the bartender's direction. "I don't think there will be any charges from these quarters."

George and his four companions managed to walk unsteadily out the door. As they headed down the street toward the wharf at Sydney Cove they recovered some of their strength and accelerated their pace. In half an hour they were back on board the *Suvorov* tending to their wounds and telling the tale of the fight to the other crewmembers.

"It sounds like that fight I witnessed between the native tribes," exclaimed Aleksei Rossiiskii. "It was a ferocious melee in which everybody was hurt, but nobody was killed. And what was it all about? Tribal honor?"

"This was about robbing us of our money," said Naum Semyonov. "And I think the people who did it are even less 'civilized' than those natives."

"I agree," said George.

Across the Pacific:

On the 3rd of September 1814 by the Russian calendar, the *Suvorov* sailed away from Sydney and out into the Pacific Ocean heading directly east. George took a full week to recover from the beating he had taken in the Rocks' bar. And even after that he continued to sport a shining black right eye. He prescribed a week's convalescence also for seaman Rodrigo Rodriguez who had been knocked literally dizzy in the fight and had trouble for a time maintaining his balance when standing on the rolling deck.

Saying farewell to Joseph Desilvier had been difficult for George. Desilvier was a learned man and George liked to converse with him. He had come to appreciate Desilvier's enthusiastic relation of English literary works while he played chess with George. But Desilvier had signed on to the *Suvorov* so that he could get to Sydney. There, he said, was a new land, a land of opportunity, where he could find his fortune and leave a positive legacy to his progeny. But Desilvier had become attached to many of the men on the *Suvorov*. When the last crewmembers left the wharf at Sydney Cove in a longboat heading out to where the *Suvorov* was ready to raise its anchor and sail, they could see Desilvier on the dock waving them off and shouting "Godspeed and Good Luck!"

On the second day out of sight of land, another ship was sighted coming toward them from the north. It was a two-master of smaller size with no apparent gun ports and it was flying a green and white flag that none of the officers of the *Suvorov* could identify. For this reason, Captain Lazarev ordered that the guns be readied and brought to bear on the ship as it approached. Grim tales of pirates in the southern Pacific made such precautions necessary. But no hostile intent was perceived as the ship came closer and closer. Soon it was within hailing distance as it angled behind them across their wake. Lieutenant Povalo-Shveikovskii shouted at them in English through the rouper, "We are the Russian navy ship *Suvorov*. Captain Lazarev in command. Who are you?"

"The *Kanaka King* out of Kogerah," came the response. "Back from blackbirding in the Solomons. Where are you bound?"

"We're bound for Alaska," shouted Povalo-Shveikovskii. "What's your flag?"

The response shouted from the passing ship was lost in the wind and the rapidly increasing distance.

"They're not ones to gam about, are they," observed Lieutenant Unkovskii to George in English, referring to the whalers' term for dropping sail to stop and socialize.

"Where in the world is Kogerah?" Povalo-Shveikovskii asked the other officers gathered at the ship's control station.

"It's the native name for a bay in Sydney Harbor," said Lieutenant Unkovskii. "The Australians call it Rushcutter's Bay. I went there with my friend George Johnston the younger. It's only a short distance east of Sydney Cove where we were anchored."

"Maybe the ship was flying some kind of commercial flag," suggested Povalo-Shveikovskii. "What does 'blackbirding' mean?"

"It's a labor business… kind of like that of the crew brokers' enterprise," explained Unkovskii. "The 'blackbirders' sail up into the remote islands of the South Pacific and trade mirrors and hatchets and beads and other things to the native chiefs in exchange for young men and women to come back with them to Australia to work on the livestock stations and the plantations. The young natives are called 'blackbirds' or 'kanakas.' The ranchers and the plantation owners pay a healthy commission to the blackbirders for each able-bodied laborer they provide."

"It sounds like slavery to me," commented George, who was interested in the Lieutenants' discussion.

"It isn't really slavery," answered Unkovskii. "The young men and women are given a place to live. They're fed and they are paid…though not much. And they're free to return to their native islands if they can find a way…or to find a better circumstance in Australia if they can. They're not really bound to the land like our serfs or to their owners like the Brazilian slaves."

"It still sounds like slavery," commented George. "What real choice do they have?"

Captain Lazarev was also listening to the conversation around the wheel. He responded sarcastically to George's question, "Indeed what choice? They could choose to resist their chief's wishes, deprive their families of the valuable trade goods, and continue living the life of a poor benighted heathen cannibal on some God-forsaken island. I tell you, Yegor Nikolaevich, a year or two of experiencing even such civilization as there is in Australia will have them thanking the blackbirders for making such a choice for them."

"There are many forms of slavery," said George, turning away to descend the stairs to the lower mid deck. "And I think this is one of them."

On September 15th, while still dark in the very early morning, a watchman on deck heard the rushing of waves over a reef and called up to the crowsnest for the lookout to check the sea to the north of them with the telescope. The lookout called out "Land Ho! Off north a verst away!"

A kilometer to the north a low island could be seen as the dawn broke. There was brush on it and palm trees. And as they sailed past it, keeping well away to prevent scraping on the proximate protecting reef, they could see another low island to the north of the first one. Captain Lazarev ordered reduction of sail and the *Suvorov* steered to the northeast. The reefs and low islands were part of an atoll…a ring of islands, all part of the same underlying reef structure, encircling a large area of calmer lighter-colored water. As they rounded the north edge of the atoll, a higher island came into view. This island had a fine beach and dunes climbing back to low hills covered in dense vegetation. Tall palms swayed in the breeze. Captain Lazarev decided to haul in sail and anchor there while he researched the charts for such an atoll.

Lieutenant Unkovskii ordered that two longboats should be lowered and two squads of men would row in different directions around the atoll. The sea was calm and the men were eager to explore some of the larger islands in the group. Dementei Biakov, looking from the crowsnest with a telescope, estimated that the atoll was approximately 15 kilometers in diameter…appearing to be wider east-to-west than its north-south dimension. He said there was an apparent entrance to the inner lagoon just to the south of where they were anchored. A passage through the reef of deeper water penetrated into the lagoon immediately to the east of the largest island in the group.

George went along in the boat commanded by Lieutenant Povalo-Shveikovskii. Eight men steadily rowed their way eastward, then southward, then westward around the atoll. It was a beautiful day, sunny and warm, with a slight breeze out of the south. Only two or three high thin clouds were visible. The surf rushing over the reefs made a sound that George thought was somehow soothing and pleasant, "shushing" the screeching sea birds as if they were noisy children. Land, he thought…even the small amounts given by islands…called to sailors with a reassuring voice, distinguished from the eerie alien whistle and moan of the wind through the rigging of their ships' sails and the creaking of the masts and yards.

At noon the boat George was in caught sight of the boat commanded by Lieutenant Unkovskii coming from the other direction. Shortly the two boats, now surveying the southern edge of the atoll, were lashed together and the men conversed about what they had seen.

"I didn't see any signs of human life," said Lieutenant Unkovskii. "But there are certainly great numbers of birds, and plenty of sea turtles and crabs. We might pick an island to go ashore and gather up some. And there are coconuts. It looks like there are plenty of them. We came upon several floating in the water, but they're no good."

"It looked to us that the island nearest where the ship is anchored is the biggest island," said Lieutenant Povalo-Shveikovskii. "We could easily send a boat ashore there after we row back around."

By four o'clock in the afternoon the men were back aboard the *Suvorov*. George and the two Lieutenants had a conference with Captain Lazarev.

"I've been studying the charts and the logs all day, and I'm convinced we've discovered a new atoll," he said. "We are at 13 degrees 14 minutes South Latitude and 164 degrees 6 minutes West Longitude as I mark it. The nearest known islands are those some three hundred to four hundred versts to the northwest that were recorded by Captain James Cook. But this atoll is not on any chart or map."

"Can we claim it for Russia?" asked George.

"No," answered Captain Lazarev crisply. "We are not to claim any territory. Admiral Traversé was very specific about that. But we can register its existence in our log. That will assure its presence on future maps of the Pacific. And we can give it a name."

"A name?" asked George. "How will we do that?"

"We'll make up a permanent sign of some kind, saying that we were here on this day and that we have recorded this atoll's existence and given it a name. We'll stake the sign on the highest point of the largest island in the group."

"I think we should name the atoll after our ship and after its namesake, General Aleksandr Suvorov," said George. "What could be more appropriate than that?"

"There are plenty of things already named after him," said Captain Lazarev, scowling. "I think the atoll should be named after me. It is I, after all, who command the ship that came upon it, and I who reckon that we're the first here. Other islands are named after the captains of the ships that first encountered them. Indeed that's the custom. This atoll should be recorded as 'Lazarev Island' on the world's maps henceforth."

Lieutenant Unkovskii and Lieutenant Povalo-Shveikovskii looked at each other apprehensively, trying to see in each others' faces approval or disagreement. Indeed they weren't sure they were to have any voice in the matter anyway.

But George was firmly against this notion, and said so. "The custom is not for a captain to name a discovery after himself," he said. "That is immodesty...even an affront to the tradition of naming things. After you have discovered many places and have performed such meritorious service that others recognize your accomplishments in life...then *they* will name things after you in your honor. I can imagine that such a time will come in your life, Mikhail Petrovich, but now you are just beginning your career as a sea captain and you should be honoring those who have gone before you."

Captain Lazarev was stung by this rebuke. "You don't have any say in what our discoveries should be named," he spat out. "I'll just write it up as I decide. That's my right as captain of the ship."

"Your course, Captain, and your mission are determined by the Russian-American Company. Like it or not, you are in the Company's service, and I am the Company's leading representative on this ship," said George forcefully. "You will be well advised to do as I say in all matters not having to do with the sailing of the ship...and this is such a matter."

Both men's tempers were about to reach the point of physical action, when Lieutenant Unkovskii interrupted. "You are both getting inappropriately angry," he said. "It isn't that important a matter. Let's just drop the issue for now. We can think about it over night and decide in the morning."

Captain Lazarev frowned at Unkovskii, but said, "All right. We'll talk about it again in the morning."

Late that evening George, still perturbed at Captain Lazarev, decided to speak with Supercargo Molvo and his clerk Fyodor Krasilnikov about the status of the cargo.

"Germann Nikolaevich," he said to Molvo. "I know that when we were in Sydney Cove the cargo was moved around a great deal while the caulking of the inner hull was going on. Have you managed to get all of it put back into its proper place?"

"It was put back, but Fyodor Fyodorovich and I are still trying to get some things into place," answered Molvo. "We have to be most careful with the gunpowder. Fifty poods of it are enough to blow this ship and everyone on it to perdition."

"Is anything missing?" asked George.

"Like what?" asked Molvo defensively.

"Like one of the large casks of rum and four kegs of vodka," answered George.

Krasilnikov gave a noticeable start and exclaimed, "Indeed I haven't been able to account for precisely four kegs of vodka. I didn't say anything because I thought I would be blamed for it. I do have a reputation for liking vodka, you know."

"We know," said Molvo. "But you could have told me. I know you've never stolen any vodka, no matter how you might crave it."

"I was going to check through the cargo one more time," Krasilnikov said, "And if I was still short four kegs of vodka, I planned to tell you."

Molvo shook his head and asked George, "How did you know we might be missing four kegs of vodka?"

"Before the fight I got into in Sydney's Rocks, that Russian-speaking lout Aurora told me that he had arranged for Captain Lazarev to pay for the *Suvorov*'s repairs by selling a hundred-gallon cask of rum and four kegs of vodka…something strictly prohibited by Governor Macquarie."

"Gospodi pomilui…Lord have mercy!" said Molvo. "If such a sale had been discovered by the Australian authorities, we'd all be laboring there in penal servitude for years. And the diplomatic relations between Great Britain and Russia could have been damaged, and the reverse route to the Company's outposts compromised. This is a very serious matter."

"That's why I'd like to make sure it's true, Germann Nikolaevich," said George. "I myself heard Captain Lazarev tell Governor Macquarie that nobody on the *Suvorov* would sell spirits for money or services in Sydney."

"We'll go through all the cargo most carefully and let you know," said Molvo.

"Don't let the Captain or any of the other officers know why you're going through it," cautioned George. "Make it look like you're just rearranging it as before."

"We'll do as you say," said Molvo.

In the morning, Captain Lazarev proposed that he and George settle the disagreement about what to name the atoll by playing a game of chess.

"I know that you've been beating Lieutenants Unkovskii and Povalo-Shveikovskii, and Supercargo Molvo regularly now, Yegor Nikolaevich," he said. "And so you might think you have a good chance to beat me in a game. We can simply flip a coin…one of these piastres with the hole in them we picked up in Sydney will do nicely…and decide who will play white and who will play black. If you win the chess game, we'll name the atoll 'Suvorov Island,' as you propose, but if I win, we'll name the atoll 'Lazarev Island' after me. Do you agree?"

"I will agree," said George, thinking of a strategy that might turn the advantage his way, "If we have only one minute's time to make each move."

"That's fine with me," said Lazarev. "Let's get to it."

Captain Lazarev took out of his pocket a Spanish piaster that had been drilled and overstamped on one side with the inscription "New South Wales," and on the other with the value "Five Shillings." He flipped it high up in the air, caught it with his right hand, and slapped it down on the back of his left hand. With his right hand still covering the coin, he asked George to call it: "New South Wales," or "Five Shillings."

"New South Wales," said George.

Captain Lazarev removed his right hand and scowled, "New South Wales it is. What'll you play?"

"I'll play the white," answered George. "And I would like Lieutenant Unkovskii to keep the time and watch the play."

"Agreed," said Captain Lazarev.

In a few minutes the men had moved to the back rail where the pegged chess board was attached. Lieutenant Unkovskii had a fine silver-plated pocket watch with a second hand. It had been made by the renowned watchmaker Bruguet and he was proud of it. "Whenever you're ready," he said to George.

George moved the white king's pawn to the fourth row and began the game. Captain Lazarev countered in the standard way, trying to get his knights early into the fray. George played more cautiously from the white in the early game, aligning his pawns defensively, thinking that the Captain, unaccustomed to moving within a minute's time, would make a mistake. But every capture was countered by another equivalent capture. Into the middle game, at twenty moves each, there was no real advantage. George had captured a bishop, a knight, and three pawns. Captain Lazarev had both George's bishops and three pawns. Both queens were still shielded, holding only partial sway. George castled queenside, and Captain Lazarev moved his remaining black bishop forward to threaten George's queen. But George moved the queen to the strong side, checking Lazarev's king. When Lazarev moved the king, George's queen took Lazarev's remaining knight. This swung the advantage George's way.

Captain Lazarev clenched his teeth and moved his bishop back one space, threatening George's queen. But George then moved the queen into a position forking Lazarev's rook and a pawn. Lazarev, now on the defensive, moved the rook and watched George's queen capture the pawn. In the next series of moves, George brought his knights into action in support of his queen at mid-board, managing in the process to keep Lazarev's queen bottled up. He knew he had to keep the pressure on, not giving Lazarev even a single move's respite. By checking Lazarev's king again with one of the knights, he captured a rook with his queen. It was now clear that, unless he made some grievous mistake, George was going to win the game.

In a few more moves, Lazarev's queen fell to George's overlapping threats, and George was moving his rooks into place to capture the remaining pawns and pursue a checkmate. Lazarev had only his black bishop and a rook left to protect his king. But soon George forced a trade of one of his knights for the bishop and the rook was worked out of its guarding position by George's knight, two rooks, and queen. A few moves more and it was over.

"Checkmate!" George announced.

"You're damned lucky, Yegor Nikolaevich," said Captain Lazarev. "It was that delay in bringing your knights out. What kind of strategy is that, for God's sake?"

"I was trying to do something you hadn't seen before, that's all," said George.

"Well, I haven't been beaten at chess in a long time. But I'm a man of my word. 'Suvorov Island' it is then," Captain Lazarev said. "We'll have a metal sign made with the name on it in Russian and English." Then, turning to Lieutenant Unkovskii, he continued, "And you can take a squad ashore to explore this biggest part of land and place the sign. We'll weigh anchor tomorrow."

Lieutenant Unkovskii and his squad of rowers were soon on their way to the largest segment of land in the atoll. It looked to be about two kilometers long and a half kilometer across, rising to a height of twenty five or thirty meters at its highest elevation. It was covered with banyan trees and palms. The men were carrying a sign, made in haste by the blacksmith, Vlas Stepanov, which said, in both Russian and in English, "Suvarov Island…discovered Sept. 15, 1814 by the Ship *Suvarov*, Lieutenant Mikhail P. Lazarev, Captain, Russian Naval Fleet."

George was aghast that blacksmith Stepanov had misspelled the Russian name "Suvorov" as "Suvarov," putting an "a" in for the first "o" in both the name of the island and the name of the ship. The English letters were spelled strangely too, as "Suwarrow." He requested that another sign be made, but Captain Lazarev, chuckling at the semi-literate blacksmith's mistake, said there wasn't time to make another sign. This one would have to do, he said. To George's irritation, he then said, "At least he knew how to spell my name correctly. Maybe I'm more important to him than General Suvorov after all."

When Lieutenant Unkovskii and his men returned, they brought baskets of coconuts and crabs, and they related what they had seen. "There are wild pigs on the island," Unkovskii said. "We tried to shoot one to bring back for roasting, but missed. And, after that, we didn't see any more pigs. But there are rats too. That has to mean that someone brought them here. We aren't the first."

"It could have been natives in their outrigger canoes," said Captain Lazarev. "Or maybe it was Spanish conquistadors or even pirates. It's hard to know. But no matter who it was, they didn't record the place's existence…they left no record of it. Did you put up the sign?"

"Yes we did," said Unkovskii. "We nailed it to the trunk of a banyan tree at the top of the central hill."

"Then Suv-a-rov Island it is, for now and forever," Captain Lazarev asserted, emphasizing the misspelling, "And I'll record it just that way in the log."

The next day, September 18 on their calendar, the *Suvorov* weighed anchor and sailed away to the northeast. By mid-October they were in the middle of the Pacific, having crossed the equator, and sailing steadily toward Alaska. The climate was changing, growing steadily colder as they sailed northward.

Germann Nikolaevich Molvo came to George with a report from the careful inventory he and Fyodor Fyodorovich Krasilnikov had made of the Company's cargo.

"There are indeed four of the twenty-gallon kegs of vodka missing, Yegor Nikolaevich," said Molvo. "Both the hundred-gallon rum casks are there, but one of them is full of water."

"Water?" asked George.

"Yes, water…and, I'd say, seawater," answered Molvo. "Of course it still smells like rum. But it's water. Someone poured out the rum and replaced it with water…so we wouldn't notice the lack of a hundred-gallon cask."

"Well, I think we know what happened to the rum and the vodka then," said George. "Our Captain took it upon himself to sell Company property to pay for the ship's repairs…and he didn't want us to know about it. Maybe paying in that way makes it possible for him to keep some of his contingency allowance. He'll have receipts for having spent the money on repairs, but he'll put it in his pocket."

"And by doing it against the law in Sydney he endangered our entire mission," commented Molvo. "What are we going to do?"

"While we are at sea, Captain Lazarev definitely has the upper hand," said George. "But when we reach Novo-Arkhangelsk we can report him to Company Manager Baranov. He may be able to relieve Captain Lazarev of command and replace him with someone else."

"That would be just fine with me," said Molvo. "As Company Supercargo I will be the first to make such a report."

"I think we should be careful not to bring the matter into open conflict with Captain Lazarev while we are at sea under his command," said George. "I hope you agree and that you will impress the necessity of this upon Fyodor Fyodorovich as well. We don't want to start a dispute of this sort on the ship at this time. Lazarev is likely to take very unpleasant action if confronted…and we would clearly suffer."

"It will be as you say, Yegor Nikolaevich," said Molvo. "And I'll make sure Fyodor keeps his mouth shut."

But that was not possible. Fyodor Fyodorovich, learning from Captain Lazarev, began to work his own water-replacement strategy on some of the remaining kegs of vodka under his supervision. He got the water, in fact, from the ersatz cask of rum. After swigging away for several hours from the pilfered vodka, he went up on deck in a clearly drunken state and began shouting "The Captain is a criminal! He's a criminal! He's sold away half our rum and four kegs of our vodka to the Australians!"

Lieutenant Povalo-Shveikovskii had Michman Bestuzhev and two others subdued Krasilnikov physically and tied him with rope to the main mast. In this way, the Lieutenant said to George and to others who were watching, Krasilnikov was in no danger of falling overboard in his drunken condition. But Krasilnikov continued to shout "Half the rum is gone. A lot of vodka is gone too…sold by that criminal, our Captain!"

Captain Lazarev was summoned to the deck. When he got there it was clear that he had been told what was going on. He walked directly up to Krasilnikov and said, "You are drunk. You've obviously drunk more than your share of the spirits yourself."

Krasilnikov blurted out, "You are a criminal. You sold the rum and the vodka to the Australians!"

Captain Lazarev retorted, "Now you are being disrespectful to the Captain. You can be flogged for that."

"You are the one who should be flogged!" shouted Krasilnikov. "Selling spirits was against the law."

"Selling spirits is not against Russian law…and not against the law on this ship," said Captain Lazarev. "God knows we've got more spirits than anyone needs…especially you."

"You don't know what I need," shouted out Krasilnikov. "You're a criminal."

"I order you to stop saying that," commanded Captain Lazarev.

"You're a criminal, you're a criminal, you're a criminal," said Krasilnikov.

George and Supercargo Molvo, watching the scene from the starboard rail, cringed as Krasilnikov repeated his indictment of the Captain three times.

Captain Lazarev turned to Michman Bestuzhev and said, "Prepare this man for a flogging. He'll be given nineteen bites of the cat straight away."

Bestuzhev and two others grabbed Krasilnikov and held him while his ropes were untied. Then he was turned face-to-the-mast and retied, his shirt stripped to his waist exposing his bare back. The Captain walked away to his cabin and returned with the hempen cat-o'nine-tails. "Michman Bestuzhev," he said, putting the wooden handle of the weapon into Bestuzhev's hands, "I order you to administer nineteen hard bites of this instrument to clerk Krasilnikov's back…this for being disrespectful to the Captain before the ship's company."

Michman Bestuzhev did as he was ordered. He swung the woven ropes fiercely at the wincing clerk. "SSSSHHMAAAK!" went the cat-o'nine-tails on the clerk's exposed flesh. Then again, and again, and again. On the twelfth strike of the cat-o'nine-tails the skin on Krasilnikov's back began to shred away and blood soaked his girdling shirt. Krasilnikov screamed at every strike until the seventeenth, then lapsed into unconsciousness. Bestuzhev made the last two strikes somewhat lighter, seeing that Krasilnikov had already passed out and was silent.

"Splash him with the water," ordered Captain Lazarev.

One of the sailors who had helped tie Krasilnikov to the mast picked up a bucket of salty sea water and sloshed it onto Krasilnikov's bloodied back. Krasilnikov remained motionless and silent, held up against the mast only by the ropes.

"Untie him and carry him to his hammock below," said Lazarev.

The men untied the ropes holding Krasilnikov to the mast and carried him below.

Captain Lazarev also turned away to start toward his cabin, but George walked into his path and said, "I'd like to talk to you about this."

Captain Lazarev said, "I'll talk to you about it when I'm ready and not before. Now step aside."

George stepped aside and let the Captain pass. Since his own compartment was close by the Captain's cabin door, he remained on deck for a time, talking with Germann Molvo and several others about the flogging. Germann Molvo seemed angrier about it than any of the others, likely because he worked most closely with Krasilnikov and felt responsible for him in some way. The two lieutenants were insistent that Krasilnikov's behavior had left Captain Lazarev no choice but to order a flogging. Anything else, they said, would have been encouraging disrespect and insubordination.

First days at Novo-Arkhangelsk:

    The *Suvorov* came within sight of the American mainland still a week's sailing distance south of Novo-Arkhangelsk. The shoreline as the crew could see it was spectacular, heavily forested above jagged crags of rock, against which the sea dashed itself with a constant violence. High mountains seemed to be diving directly into the sea, resulting in most spectacular natural scenery. There were many forested islands, both large and small, and Captain Lazarev decided to sail outboard of them rather than negotiate through the channels between them. He told the officers to look for a particularly high volcano caldera…likely snow-covered. This would be Mount Edgecumbe, which marked the location of Norfolk harbor and the Novo-Arkhangelsk settlement. The settlement, he said, was on the ocean or "shee" side of a large island the Tlingit natives, called by the Russians "Kolosh," had named "atika." The contraction of these two Tlingit words, "shee" and "atika," resulted in the native name of the settlement's location—Sitka. It was to be found on the outboard coast at precisely 57 degrees, 4 minutes, and 48 seconds north latitude, marked by the white-topped volcano, Mount Edgecumbe.

    The weather was miserable, featuring a cold rain and thick fog until noon every day. And the daylight time was getting shorter, so there was some concern that the *Suvorov* might sail right past the Novo-Arkhangelsk settlement and not see it. Indeed for hours on end it was hard to see anything at all. Only the afternoons gave the men a clear view of the coastal mountains where they hoped to find their destination at last.

    The ocean along the coast teemed with sea creatures of diverse kinds—birds, fish, and sea mammals of various sizes. The most awesome of these creatures were the soaring and diving eagles overhead and the black and white killer whales, which glided through the water with the same apparent effortlessness as the eagles in the air around the *Suvorov* in groups as large as thirty. Once or twice, when the ship came closer to land in its journey northward, the crew watched as the killer whales attacked large numbers of seals who had ventured too far from the safety of the shoreline rocks. Seals were torn into bloody pieces as the whales cut through their number. A seal on the surface was devoured as a whale came up from under it at great velocity, its mouth wide open and showing its teeth. Another whale, using its powerful tail, batted a seal pup into the air higher than the *Suvorov*'s deck. It fell into the jaws of another whale coming up from behind its partner. The killer whales' rapacity was punctuated with playfulness. Their sleek power and the carnage they wrought among the seals made a deep impression on the crewmembers who witnessed their attacks. George shuddered as he watched and realized that it wasn't because of the bitter cold.

On the 17th of November, 1814, the *Suvorov,* having recognized Mount Edgecumbe on the horizon, and then catching sight of the smoke from the chimneys of a settlement on shore, sailed into the harbor of the Novo-Arkhangelsk settlement. Just offshore from the settlement was a smaller island formed from the approaches to Mount Edgecumbe. The port was very scenic, with a number of forested islands and the smoothly towering snow-covered volcano in the background. Several other ships were anchored in the harbor and large numbers of "baidarkas"…hide-covered kayaks…were paddled about by native hunters or were lined up in rows on the shore.

Before the *Suvorov* could announce its presence by the firing of its guns, a cannonade was heard from a fortification atop a promontory on shore. This was followed by rockets fired into the evening sky. They were being welcomed back to Russian territory by compatriots a world away from that they knew.

A delegation rowed out to the ship and several men were taken on board. One of these was a man named Bandar who invited the ship's officers and Company representatives and messengers to come ashore immediately to have dinner with "His Excellency, Governor Aleksandr Andreevich Baranov." Captain Lazarev accepted this invitation and ordered a longboat lowered to transport the company ashore. George and the others were on deck and warmly dressed, but they hurried below to find more ceremonial dress. In addition, George fetched his medical bag.

The longboat brought the *Suvorov*'s officers, Captain Lazarev, Lieutenants Unkovskii and Povalo-Shveikovskii, together with the Russian-American Company representatives, to shore. A large party of men in hooded parkas shouted at them and waved them to a wharf near the wooden building on a high steep outcropping of rock. It was a large wooden structure, part lodge and part fortress, with a fortified observation tower on the top of it. George thought it resembled an artist's conception of a medieval English castle, except that it was made of an amalgam of rough-sawn planks and interlocking logs. He could see that openings in a surrounding wall served as ports for cannon.

"Prikhodite na bereg! Dobro pozhalovat!" the men on shore were shouting, "Come ashore…Welcome!"

In a few minutes the men were out of the longboat and exchanging hugs and back-slaps with the greeting party of Russians and Aleuts, all wearing bird-skin parkas with hoods allowing only their faces to be visible. But they all were smiling and laughing and urging the sailors to come along into the fortress to meet Governor Baranov, who, they said, was preparing a welcome banquet for them.

In "Old Sitka," the Russian palisade atop "Castle Hill" surrounding the Governor's residence had three watchtowers armed with thirty-two cannons for defense against Tlingit (Kolosh) attack. From: http://en.wikipedia.org/wiki/Novo-Arkhangelsk.

They walked through the wooden palisade and up to the entrance of the central building on the promontory. The heavy wooden doors opened as they reached the entrance, thanks to an observation hatch in one of the doors through which a man's eyes could be seen watching their approach. George noticed that the doors were very heavy, but they were not very high. He could see that he would have to duck his head to clear the top of the doorframe. But then the doors were opened and there in the vestibule stood a small old man in a black silk dressing gown and cloth slippers. He was wearing a loose-fitting black wig and he seemed physically quite frail. George knew that this man had to be Governor Aleksandr Baranov.

"So you're here at last, my dear friends," the man said, addressing the group. "I am Aleksandr Baranov, the Company Manager here. And I can tell you that we are so happy that you've made it here to what we call the 'Paris of the Pacific.' Please, take off your coats and boots. We've got fur slippers for you to wear while you're in my palace here. When you're ready I'll show you around. Then we'll have dinner in the banquet hall."

The guests removed their coats and their boots and shoes, putting on the fur slippers. As George was adjusting his slippers, he noticed that Captain Lazarev and the two lieutenants were exchanging some satiric commentary about Governor Baranov's mention of his 'palace' in the 'Paris of the Pacific.' "Just look at that floor," said Lazarev to Lieutenant Unkovskii, pointing to the rough-hewn planked floor of the interior beyond the entry vestibule. "Does he really imagine we need to don fur slippers to protect it? Maybe we should put our boots back on to protect our feet from splinters."

Aleksandr Andreevich Baranov (1746-19 April, 1819), from: http://www.netstate.com/states/peop/ak_aab.htm.

A round of introductions followed, with each man saying his name and shaking Governor Baranov's hand. Baranov wanted to know if the Russian-American Company's special messengers, the servants of Company board member Mikhail Matveevich Buldakov and of the deceased Chief-Manager-designate Tertii Stepanovich Bornovolokov, were in their party. Captain Lazarev explained that these men were still aboard the *Suvorov* and that they would be coming later after accommodations were arranged.

Governor Baranov urged the men to follow him on a tour of the building. He launched into a narration about the history of the settlement. "We now call this settlement Novo-Arkhangelsk," he said. "There are more than a thousand people here. But I had real trouble establishing this place…wresting it away from the Kolosh. In 1800, I made a deal with the Kolosh Toion, Ska-out-lelt, to buy this place for iron and beads and other trade goods. At first, I called it Fort St. Mikhail, and by 1802 there were 29 Russians and over 200 Aleuts living and working here, and the fur hunting was good. But then the Kwan clan of Kolosh…most likely under Ska-out-lelt's nephew Kotlean, who became and is still the Kolosh Toion…attacked Fort St. Mikhail in great force and slaughtered almost everyone. Captains Ebbets and Barber who were the next traders to arrive reported that the Kolosh had severed scores of my men's heads and had them displayed on poles in front of the burnt fort. The word gruesome doesn't do the situation justice. Three Russians were taken alive to the Kolosh camp and tortured for days…only my man Timofei Tarakanov survived to tell of it."

"Did he escape?" asked Lieutenant Unkovskii.

"He was ransomed from the Kolosh by Captain Barber," replied Governor Baranov. "But then I had to ransom him from Captain Barber."

Governor Baranov interrupted his narration to point out the "palace reception hall." This was a very large room with a higher ceiling, from which hung a large, blazing candlefish chandelier. The candlefish were rich in oil, which gave off substantial light when burned. This also gave off an unpleasant odor. But there was also a cavernous stone fireplace with a roaring wood fire, which provided both light and heat in abundance. In the corner of the room was a fine pianoforte of polished black wood, which looked strikingly out of place. On the piano was a life-size bronze bust of Tsar Aleksandr.

"It was Nikolai Rezanov who transported the piano here when he came on the *Maria Magdalena* in August of 1805," said Baranov. "He also brought some of the art you will see on the walls, and many of the books in the library. I have more than a thousand volumes now, with books in ten languages."

In the library, which had full shelves of books along each wall, was an intricate scale model of a Russian warship, complete with accurate rigging and unfurled sails. After explaining that the model had been sent to him by Admiral Chichagov to congratulate him on the Tsar's granting him, born a simple "meshchanin" or tradesman, a rank of nobility in 1804 as a "Collegiate Councilor," Baranov returned to his history of the settlement. "After the terrible massacre here at Fort St. Mikhail," he said, "I desperately wanted to recapture the place and teach the Kolosh a lesson. But I simply didn't have the means to do it. The Kolosh had attacked other settlements as well, killing another hundred men at Frederick Sound and wiping out the serfs at the agricultural station at Yakutat Bay. So it was hard to recover from this and continue our operations along this part of the coast. But then the *Neva* under Captain Yurii Lisianskii arrived in fall of 1804. Nikolai Rezanov, having heard of our troubles from King Kamehameha's subordinates in Hawai'i, had directed Lisianskii to depart from the joint circumnavigation with Captain Kruzenshtern's *Nadezhda* and sail here directly while the *Nadezhda* with Rezanov aboard continued to Kamchatka and Japan. I knew that with the *Neva*'s guns I could retake this place from the Kolosh who had made a fort of their own on this very 'kekur' or promontory. But still it wasn't easy. In our first assault on their fort the Kolosh surprised us by attacking us directly out of the gates. Kotlean led this attack himself wielding a blacksmith's hammer he had stolen from us. In the battle we lost ten good men and I was wounded even though I was wearing my chain-mail vest."

Louis Glanzman's 1988 painting of the 1804 "Battle of Sitka," from http://en.wikipedia.org/wiki/Battle_of_Sitka. Notice the Kolosh Toion Kotlean with upraised smith's hammer charging the attacking Russians from the gates of Fort St. Mikhail.

"Did a ball penetrate the mail?" asked Lieutenant Povalo-Shveikovskii.

"No, I was shot through the arm, in the part uncovered by the mail," answered Governor Baranov. "But I certainly came to curse the renegade traders who sold the firearms and ammunition to the Kolosh. When our attempt to storm the fort failed, we decided to shell it from the bay with the *Neva*'s heavy cannon. We kept up the shelling from the bay for a day and a night. The Kolosh sent a party to ask my terms. I told them they would be allowed to live only if they agreed to leave the entire island of Sitka forever. They would not agree to this, and so we continued to shell them in the fort. The next night…all night after midnight…we heard some strange and eerie wailing coming from the

A model of the Russian sloop *Neva* from http://www.ship-modelers-assn.org/shipmodels/sloop-neva.html.

fort, and the sound of drums. The next morning we were able to walk into the fort unopposed. Kotlean and the Kwan clan were gone. But there had taken place some grisly ritual of abandonment in which they had killed their own children…cut their throats. Inside the fort were the bodies of five murdered children."

"Bozhe moi!…My God," exclaimed George, horrified. "Why did they do that?"

"It's always been a mystery to us," said Governor Baranov. "Lisianskii thought it might be because they needed to slip away in silence and the children's crying would have prevented that. But that was not it. They had been told that we would not harm them if they left and they did not need to sneak away. In my understanding of them, they were being forced to leave the land they had inhabited since the beginning of their reckoning of time. Their children were, in some way, part of their sense of contract and obligation to the land. Giving up the land meant giving up their future on the land—and along with it, giving up the children who would live in the future on that land…something like that."

Portrait of Yurii Fyodorovich Lisianskii (13 August, 1773-6 March, 1837) by Vladimir Borovikovsky (1757-1825) from: http://en.wikipedia.org/wiki/Yuri_Lisyansky.

"Where are these Kolosh now?" asked George.

"They're on the mainland, considered interlopers by the other clans of Kolosh…the Chilkats to the north, the Awks, and the Hootsnahoo," explained Baranov. "For five years we saw not a one of the Kolosh on Sitka. But then, gradually, we allowed some to come back temporarily to trade. There's an encampment of them even now at the edge of the settlement. They watch us, and we certainly watch them."

"So then you were able to construct this place," commented George, wanting to be complimentary. "It's very impressive."

"I chose the site," said Baranov. "I wanted to build a large fortified residence on this promontory to take advantage of its highest site. I wanted it to have an observation tower from which we could see and signal to ships as they passed by us in Norfolk Sound. But it was really my Assistant Manager Ivan Kuskov who did the construction. The building itself, the attached barracks, the walls, the wharf, shipyard, and warehouse…all are of his design and constructed at his direction. I had gone back to Kodiak Island and elsewhere in the meantime, but when I returned here after two years and saw it, I was most pleased."

"Where is Kuskov? Is he here?" asked Germann Molvo.

"No, I've sent him to start our southernmost outpost at Fort Ross on the border with Spanish California," answered Baranov. "He's been away for three years or more now. Brave Timofei Tarakanov is down there with him too…sailed on the *Ilmena* last year. He would have made a fine assistant, having had, in his time, to deal with all manner of dire tribulation. First he was held hostage by rival hunters, then he was taken by the Kolosh, who tortured to death everyone except him, and then he had to live for a year as the slave of savages in the coastal forests north of the Columbia River after the wreck of the *St. Nikolai* in 1808...yet he hasn't lost his spirit and still desires to serve me, the Company, and Mother Russia. But now he too is away. So I have no assistants from my former years. Now I'm assisted by my own nephew, Ivan Kuglinov, and other young men."

Governor Baranov then escorted the party into a large banquet hall lit with the candlefish in sconces on the walls. A long thick wooden table ran the entire length of the room, and there were more than forty men seated on benches along its sides. They were rough-dressed men and crude in appearance. Some were Aleuts and Kenaitse with bare tattooed faces, but many were bearded Russians. There were also officers from an English ship and from an American ship of John Jacob Astor's Pacific Fur Company...strange dinner fellows in a time of war between England and the United States, George thought.

When Baranov and his guests from Russia entered the banquet hall, the forty men rose in unison and lifted their glasses toward him in salute. The Russians began to sing at the top of their coarse voices a song, the "Baranovskaia pesnia," or "Baranov's Song."

"The spirit of hunters, the spirit of trade,

On these far shores a new Moscow has made,

In bleakness and hardship finding new wealth

To Russia we send it, for the Tsar's health.

Kremlin towers old Moscow adorn,

The bells ring at evening, the guns boom at morn,

But so far away is the glory of Ivan the Great—

Here we've only our own Alaskan estate.

Father Almighty we pray for thine aid

That Russian arms may be here obeyed,

That we may dwell here in friendship and peace,

The cold and the perils to give us release.

And Toion Baranov will lead us on far,

To hell and back we'll follow his star.

With many baidarkas and ships of our own,

We'll reap the rewards of our stern northern home."

"That's quite a song, Your Excellency," said George to Governor Baranov.

"I wrote it myself some time ago," said Baranov. "But the men added the verse about me. They keep changing it around. I never know how they're going to sing it next."

George noticed several Aleuts rapidly moving in and out of the hall with trays of drinks and food. There were several women among them, and some of these had bone labrets pierced through their lower lips making what George thought was a hideous and unattractive appearance.

Governor Baranov took his seat at the head of the long table, inviting the newly arrived Russians from the *Suvorov* to sit on the benches on both sides of the table nearest him, which had been vacated as they approached. George took the seat to Governor Baranov's immediate left.

The banquet went on all night. The food was not very appetizing. There was no bread at all…and only a few potatoes. There was one course of venison, but then came courses of boiled fish filet, fried whole fish, dried and salted fish, and a dessert of very tart wild cranberries in candlefish butter called yukola. To George the venison was tough and had a wild taste to it that was not to his liking. The fish courses were very bland, and so he reached for a small saucer of a dark red garnish. "What's this?" he asked Governor Baranov.

"It's 'ozhiga,' young man," Baranov said. "It's a sauce made from fermented peppers of the habanero plant that the *Juno* brought back from California. It's very lively stuff and will definitely cure whatever ails you."

George put a small dab of the red ozhiga relish on a piece of fish and put it into his mouth. He waited only a second or two to spit it back out into his hand…but he was too late. It felt like his mouth had exploded and his teeth were melting. In rising panic he reached for a cup of water, but Governor Baranov quickly stayed his arm and handed him a cup of kumys…fermented milk. "This is better," he said. "Water just spreads the fire." Then he started to laugh.

George took several swallows of the kumys, trying to rinse out his burning mouth and salve his stinging tongue. He should have known the relish might be hot, he thought, from the word "ozhiga." The root of the word "ozhiga," "zhig," means "ignite" in Russian.   And indeed the relish had ignited his mouth and ruined his taste for eating anything else. But that was all right, since the real fare of the banquet was not food at all, but alcoholic drinks. Wine and rum and vodka of the worst quality George had ever tasted flowed like a waterfall the entire time. And there was some kind of alcoholic punch of Governor Baranov's own recipe, which tasted like turpentine to George that the other men there praised and praised. Toast after toast after toast was drunk to everyone of anyone's mutual acquaintance or renown. By midnight, Governor Baranov had removed his wig to reveal a completely bald pate ringed by wisps of gray hair that George could see might once have been reddish brown. At about three o'clock in the morning, George felt that he could no longer tolerate the pressure on his bladder, and he asked Governor Baranov the way to the toilet.

"Right out there, my good man," said Baranov, pointing to a door behind where George was sitting. "Be careful, the path to the toilets is muddy. You've got to walk on the planks."

George excused himself and got up from the bench. When he did so, several others in his party, including Captain Lazarev and Germann Molvo, got up also. They followed George to the door and, when they got outside, followed George's lead in walking on the planks through the mud to the toilets, which were some distance away against the fortification walls. As George got to the first toilet and opened its door, he looked back and saw Captain Lazarev suddenly lose his balance and fall sideways, landing with a splash into a mud puddle. George and Germann Molvo broke out laughing. But Lazarev was angry. He sprang up quickly, rushed headlong at Molvo and shoved him, knocking him back into the mud as well. "See," he blurted out. "It isn't so funny, after all."

Molvo sat up in the mud to the side of the plank, but he didn't stand up. "There was no reason for you to push me into the mud as well, Captain Lazarev," he said. "You're a mean drunk."

Lazarev strode to the toilet next to George's, opened the door and went in, saying, "Yes, I am, and don't you forget it."

George didn't go into the toilet, but went over and helped Molvo to his feet.

"Germann," he whispered, "Don't do anything foolish. I think we'll be able to get Governor Baranov to remove Lazarev from command of the *Suvorov*. That will serve him right."

"All right, Yegor," said Molvo. "But I can hardly wait."

Late the next morning, Governor Baranov informed the men where they could "spend the night." After another long visit to the toilet, George retired to the bed he was shown during the short light of mid-day and didn't wake up until the light of the next day.

Guests of Governor Aleksandr Baranov:

The weather was terribly cold and the crew of the *Suvorov* was anxious to get ashore. But the work of unloading the cargo kept them busy on board for a week. They had to row everything ashore in the longboats and help the native dockworkers unload it into a dockside warehouse made of logs.

By the end of November, the *Suvorov* was unloaded and resting at anchor. The ship's crew was housed in a long wooden barracks building not far from the harbor and close to the settlement's central buildings where they could find food and spirited drink. Captain Lazarev and the other navy officers were in guest quarters attached to Manager Baranov's residence where they were attended to by a staff of Aleut servants. George, Supercargo Molvo, clerk Krasilnikov, and the Russian-American Company's two special messengers were able to stay in the residence itself. George, in fact, had a guest room to himself…this after he impressed Manager Baranov with two important facts—his personal acquaintance with Tsar Aleksandr, whom Baranov greatly admired, and his ownership of fifty shares of the Russian-American Company's closely held stock—more than the number of shares that Baranov himself owned.

Aleksandr Baranov was sixty-seven very hard years of age. He was a small man and appeared frail, as if worn out by the several dashed expectations that he would, as he had requested, be replaced. But he was, through the almost unimaginably persistent exercise of his great will, "Lord of Russian America," holding personal sway over thousands of miles of coastal territory-- from the western tip of the Aleutian Islands and the Pribylov Islands in the Bering Sea all the way down the western coast of the North American continent as far as California. He was respected by native and foreigner alike. Over the winter of 1814-5, George spent many hours in conversation with him and came to revere him, even though Baranov told George that he was not amenable to receiving formal complaints from him and Supercargo Molvo about Captain Lazarev and would not consider removing Lazarev from command of the *Suvorov*.

So far was Novo-Arkhangelsk and the other venues of Aleksandr Baranov's operations on behalf of the Russian-American Company from the happenings of Europe and of European Russia that he didn't seem to care when the *Suvorov's* officers jubilantly told him about the Russian occupation of Paris and the abdication of Napoleon Bonaparte. He was only a bit concerned about the war between the United States and England. He had heard that the British had burned the U.S. capital in Washington, D.C. in August of 1814 and that Baltimore had been besieged. He had felt the inconvenience of the British navy's campaign to destroy or confiscate all U.S. shipping in the Pacific, because it hampered his ability to conduct trade with the U.S. ship captains. He had arranged a scheme to circumvent the British blockade. He simply purchased the U.S. ships by arrangement with their skippers, who then continued trade as before under the Russian flag, since the Russians and the

British were allies. He traded with English merchant ships, like the notorious Captain Henry Barber's *Unicorn*, while the ships from the United States, like Captain William Heath Davis' *Isabella* operated by purchase arrangement under the Russian flag. English merchant captains and Yankee trader skippers were thus able to dine together at his table during time of war between their countries. In Baranov's remote north Pacific realm, trade was simply more important than politics.

The furs for trading…seal and sea otter, most desirably…were provided by native hunters in great phalanxes of baidarkas. All down the coast from the Aleutian islands to California each tribal chief would pledge so many baidarkas to Baranov's summer hunts in exchange for the metal implements, textiles, beads, and foodstuffs brought by the trading ships. Baranov did all he could to see that the natives did not receive firearms and ammunition. He announced as widely as he could that he would take action against any trader caught giving such weaponry to the natives. And he would confiscate the ship of any captain violating this policy. He had indeed begun shipyards where he was constructing his own ships out of native timber, and he had in twenty years of effort, and despite some severe losses, amassed a fleet of seven ships, including five of small frigate size and two schooners. All in all, he had become very successful, selling his furs to the traders, commissioning them to sell more furs for him in Canton, China, and sending back furs to Okhotsk and then Irkutsk, so that in twenty-four years he had contributed almost twenty million rubles to the Russian-American Company's accounts. By the second decade of the nineteenth century, he was exporting over 60,000 fur pelts per year, worth almost 700,000 rubles to the Company. Eighty percent of these pelts were fur seal, and five percent were the pelts of the sea otter, worth up to 300 rubles each.

The relationship between Governor Baranov and Captain Lazarev took its first negative turn when, only several days after the *Suvorov*'s arrival, Lazarev asked Baranov to provide him with a native woman to "warm his belly during the winter stay."

Governor Baranov's response was curt: "I'm not a procurer. You'll have to find a woman for yourself. And you'd better treat her well."

Baranov took the next opportunity at meal to lecture the *Suvorov*'s officers on how he had learned to treat the relationships between his Russian men and the native companions they inevitably found. "I make sure," he said, "That the native women are treated better by their Russian husbands than they would be by a native husband. In the tribes each husband may have several wives…but our Russians have only one. In the tribes, the husbands beat and can even kill their wives…but our Russians can't. I've had men flogged for beating their native wives. And I make sure the children are well taken care of by both parents. It turns out that the children are the reason why the Russians here renew their contracts and stay beyond their term. By the time, in either five or seven years, when their first contract is expired and they would be ready to leave, they typically have a native wife and creole children…and these children are not allowed to go back to Russia. They know this and they accept it…that's the law. So the men renew their contracts and stay. Without this, we wouldn't have anyone here worth keeping. And we educate the creole children, both boys and girls, teaching them to read and write Russian and to write their own languages in our Cyrillic alphabet. The Shelikhovs began a school on Kodiak Island thirty years ago. And they sent the monks here with the mission of not only Christianizing the savages, but educating them too. My own son Antipatr and my daughter Irina were educated in this way, by Elder Germann and the other monks on Kodiak Island. I always treated their mother, Anna Grigorievna, as if she were my church-married wife…although, as you may have heard, I already had a church-married wife back in Russia when Anna Grigorievna's father, the Kenaitse Toion we call Raskazchikov, the "Story Teller," gave her to me. But treating Anna Grigorievna right, and seeing to it that the Russians here treat their native women well, has been an important factor in the success of our efforts here…and, no matter what the monks might tell you, I require that any new Russians here abide by that same policy."

But Captain Lazarev was soon bringing a succession of different native women into his quarters. Some of them were from the encampment of Kolosh, purchased from their fathers and husbands with tobacco, coins or metal spikes. But one or two were Aleuts, the already claimed companions of contracted Russians, and this caused trouble. Complaints to Governor Baranov led him to ask Captain Lazarev to vacate the guest quarters and move back on board the *Suvorov*.

Another dispute had erupted between Governor Baranov and Captain Lazarev when Baranov asked the Captain to sail the *Suvorov* to the Pribylov Islands in the Bering sea north of the Aleutians to collect two seasons' worth of seal skins from his hunters there. Captain Lazarev resisted this request, citing the dangers of the Bering Sea in winter, and saying that such duty was not part of his ship's charter with the Russian-American Company. "We were engaged to come here to provision you and to take back home what you might send," Lazarev maintained. "We don't have to help you in your business while we're here."

Governor Baranov was quite irritated at this, and responded forcefully. "You are to be of whatever aid to me I require, and if you're not, I'll certainly make that fact known to your commanders in the Navy and to the Tsar himself. The *Suvorov* is by far the most seaworthy vessel here, and it's perfectly capable of sailing to the Pribylovs to get the hunters' harvest of sealskins. They're worth a great deal of money, but if I don't get them back here soon, they won't be fit to ship for sale. I order you to sail the *Suvorov* to the Pribylovs to collect the skins. If you refuse, I'll have you arrested and put in the guardhouse."

Captain Lazarev could see that Governor Baranov was not bluffing. "All right," he said, "I'll sail in three days, after the New Year's celebration. You'll have to give me someone who knows where to go and what to say to the hunters there."

George, Germann Molvo, Fyodor Krasilnikov, and the other Russian-American Company representatives stayed in their Novo-Arkhangelsk quarters and did not sail on the *Suvorov* when it departed for the Pribylov Islands just after the settlement's celebration of the New Year of 1815. But, in only three days, the *Suvorov* returned to port, anchoring again off Novo-Arkhangelsk. Captain Lazarev came ashore to explain that the ship "had sprung a leak," and that the voyage to the Pribylovs would not be possible until repairs were made. Governor Baranov did not believe Captain Lazarev and said that he would send his own shipwrights aboard to examine the leak with the intention of repairing it immediately. But Captain Lazarev insisted that, on board the *Suvorov*, he was in command and that he didn't trust Baranov's "incompetent shipwrights." He would have the ship repaired in his own way and in his own time.

Soon it became apparent that the *Suvorov*'s repairs were likely to drag on throughout the winter. Captain Lazarev set up a longboat shuttle to and from shore so that he could carry on as he desired with the native women of his choice. A crew of six men, in weeklong rotations, stayed on board with him and manned the longboat when he required. The Lieutenants Unkovskii and Povalo-Shveikovskii, Shturman Samsonov, Shturman-apprentice Rossiiskii, and Michman Bestuzhev were exempted from the rotations aboard, but quartermaster Fokin was not exempted. "It's not exactly a circus," he told George, "hauling firewood back to the ship so we don't all freeze on it. Sometimes the Captain brings an extra woman or two aboard just for us. Still, I prefer it in the barracks ashore."

George soon became aware of Antipatr Aleksandrovich, Governor Baranov's eighteen-year-old son, and Irina Aleksandrovna, his thirteen-year-old daughter from the absent Anna Grigorievna. In later conversations with Governor Baranov and from other people, George learned that Anna Grigorievna's father, the Kenaitse Toion Raskazchikov, had long been one of the most stalwart of Baranov's native allies, supplying great numbers of hunters and helping Baranov keep peace with other tribes. But Anna Grigorievna, torn between the values of two cultures, had had some episodes of instability, as when she once tried to sacrifice three-year-old Antipatr by throwing him off a cliff so she could embrace Christianity unencumbered by this link to her heathen past. In 1807, after Baranov received word that his Russian wife, whom he had not seen in almost thirty years, had died, he obtained for Anna Grigorievna an ukase from St. Petersburg which officially designated her a "Princess of Kenai." At last he allowed her to be baptized by Elder Germann into the Russian Orthodox Faith. And now she had become a zealous devotee of Elder Germann, calling him "Ap'a" or "Father," and would not leave him. Elder Germann had moved his flock from Kodiak to the small Spruce Island, where he called his new settlement "New Valaam." Elder Germann had become difficult for Baranov in other ways as well, advocating against his exploitation of native labor for commercial purposes and forbidding all sexual relations outside of church-sanctioned marriage.

George became friendlier with Governor Baranov as the winter wore on. The Governor's children, Antipatr and Irina, liked to listen to George's stories of his life in Europe, of his trip to Constantinople, of the attempt while he was in

Moscow to kill Napoleon from a balloon, of his visits to London, Rio de Janeiro, Capetown, and Sydney. He told them of seeing the nine strange flying objects in the South Indian Ocean and of the discovery of an uninhabited island in the South Pacific. He taught Antipatr how to tie the "monkey's fist" knot in jute line and how to play chess. Soon George noticed that when he talked with Governor Baranov at meals or in the fortress library, the Governor had already heard from his children something that George had told them and about which he was curious. And George too heard from Antipatr and Irina about how their father often related to them stories about his early life in Russia. He had, they said, witnessed the coronation parade of Catherine the Great in Moscow's Red Square as a teen-ager in 1762.

In February of 1815, Governor Baranov proposed to George that he begin accepting patients from the settlement community. "If you were good enough a physician to be consulted by the famous General Bagration," he told George, having heard of George's treating of the famous general from his children, "You're good enough to deal with the medical problems here."

"But General Bagration died," protested George. "And here I have only the most limited of supplies."

"Believe me, a person of your training and experience can make a big difference here," insisted Governor Baranov. "We have had other physicians here from time to time. Dr. von Langsdorff, who was here with Director Rezanov in 1805-6 helped us a great deal while he was here. We were having real trouble with scurvy at that time."

"Von Langsdorff, eh?" commented George. "I had heard much about him and read his memoirs. In St. Petersburg I was told that he had married and, having been appointed Honorary Consul to Brazil, had moved there. So I requested a meeting with him in Rio de Janeiro and was fortunate enough to make his acquaintance. He is doing very well there, having won the respect of the royal family and the entire population there. He and his wife Fredericke live on an estate called 'Mandioca.' When I left him he was planning to lead an expedition to the head waters of the Amazon River."

"I didn't know that," said Baranov. "And I'm happy to hear of his successes and happiness. But after he left, we benefited from the work of Dr. Karl Mordgorst of the *Neva,* which had returned here under Lieutenant Leontii Hagemeister in 1807. We had rescued a shipwrecked young Scottish sailor here at that time named Archibald Campbell whose feet had been frozen while in a lifeboat at sea and become rotten with gangrene. He would certainly have died, but Dr. Mordgorst was able to amputate his feet so that he survived. He's done so well since, even with no feet, that I sent him with Hagemeister to King Kamehameha in Honolulu. And even though Lieutenant Hagemeister did not impress the Hawai'ian King, apparently Archibald Campbell did…because he stayed on there, living at Waikīkī, working as a sail maker and advising the King until sailing back to England in 1810."

"That's amazing," said George. "How does he move around?"

"He has shoe-like pads for his stumps and he uses two crutches," answered Governor Baranov. "Before he left here he challenged me to a race from the fortress entrance to the shore. He was joking, but, considering how feeble I've gotten these days, he could probably beat me now."

"You still have considerable vigor, Your Excellency," said George. "But it was most considerate of you to obtain for your people here the medical services of such doctors as von Langsdorff and Mordgorst."

"Yes, they were learned men, and very able," said Baranov. "But they were only here temporarily. We had another physician too, a Brazilian named Juan Elliot de Castro. He had been in Hawai'i treating King Kamemeha and his retinue of Ali'i before he came here in 1812. But he didn't seem to be as able a physician as the others. He was quick to bleed people with leeches and didn't know what to prescribe against fevers. In January of last year, 1814, I sent him on the brig *Ilmena*…formerly the *Lydia*…with Captain William Wadsworth to California to negotiate trade with the Spaniards. But now I've heard that the Spaniards are holding him prisoner. Who knows if we'll ever see him again? And so, we have now been more than a year without competent medical services. That is why I suggest that you begin to practice here in the settlement."

"And I will do as you suggest," George agreed. "I'll transfer all my things off the *Suvorov* and set up an infirmary of some kind here in the settlement. I'm sure special messenger Larion Afanasievich Trifonov, who is a trained feldsher, will agree to help me."

The next day, George and Larion Afanasievich went on board the *Suvorov* to remove their personal trunks and medical supplies. George there encountered Captain Lazarev, who grumbled disapprovingly about Governor Baranov's use of his ship's medical staff to set up an infirmary in the settlement. And he complained also about Baranov's scheme to continue to trade with ships from the United States under a Russian flag.

"I've been talking with some of the Yankee skippers," he told George. "And he isn't really buying their ships. It's really just an agreement, paid for in trade goods, to rename the ships and put a Russian flag on them so he can keep trading with them here and use them to ship his furs to China and elsewhere. It's just a ruse, no doubt about it. I'm telling you…and you can tell him…that the *Suvorov* is an armed ship of the Russian Navy, and I, its Captain, don't like offering protection here to enemies of our British allies."

"The British merchant captains don't seem to mind," observed George. "Besides, we're so far from things out here that the war between the British and the Americans could be over and we'll not find out about it for another year. Governor Baranov told me that when France suddenly became our ally in 1808, making Great Britain our adversary, he didn't know it until 1810, and that, since there was practically no French shipping here, it didn't matter anyway. This is truly another reality here, separate in many ways from European politics. And here Aleksandr Andreevich Baranov has established himself not only as a

Company Manager and Governor…but even as a kind of Tsar. If I were you, I would start to show him a bit more respect."

"I am very happy that you are not me," replied Captain Lazarev. He turned his back on George and walked away.

It took five months for Captain Lazarev to repair the leak in the *Suvorov*'s hull that only he could find. In that time, George established an effective infirmary in the Novo-Arkhangelsk settlement, pulling bad teeth, lancing boils, applying poultices and bindings, stitching lacerations, and prescribing his herbal remedies for all manner of troublesome medical conditions. He delivered several children of both Russian and native women and all of these were successful births, a clear improvement over previous conditions. He and his assistant Trifonov won the respect of the Novo-Arkhangelsk community, Russians, Aleuts, Kenaitse, and even the Kolosh. In this they were different than the other officers and crewmembers of the *Suvorov*, whose prolonged presence seemed to irritate the permanent members of the settlement. Much of the problem concerned the competition among the men for the native women. The visitors, the community members felt, did not sufficiently respect the relationships they had with the native women. Several times the competition flared into physical combat, requiring George to treat the damages to both parties.

One morning in the spring of 1815 George encountered Governor Baranov in the fortress library. Baranov told George that, to his surprise, Captain Lazarev had ordered his crew aboard the *Suvorov* to sail to the Pribylov Islands to retrieve the crop of sealskins. He had sent Lazarev, he said, a formal written order and this order, apparently, had brought about the desired action at last.

"He doesn't need me on that mission," said George. "I'll stay here."

"Apparently he didn't ask you," replied Baranov. "He's sailing off this morning."

"He's a brash young man," said George. "I haven't gotten along well with him. And it isn't merely the old Company-Navy conflict, which has troubled other expeditions here…though no doubt that is present as well. It's my opinion that he does not possess the sound judgment necessary for command of a ship of the *Suvorov*'s stature…and that he should be relieved of command. You will remember that I asked you shortly after we came here to consider taking formal complaints from me and from Germann Molvo so as to remove him."

"Yes, I remember. But what precisely has led you to such an opinion, Yegor Nikolaevich?" asked Baranov.

"He was upset at the way I talked to the Regent, Dom João, in Rio de Janeiro about slavery and about my offer to make a proposal on behalf of Dom João's son Pedro for the hand of our Tsar's sister, the Grand Duchess Anna Pavlovna," explained George. "Then he violated the New South Wales Governor Lachlan Macquarie's strict ban on selling spirits in Sydney in order to pay for ship repairs…this after I heard him tell Governor Macquarie that he would obey the ban. He wanted to name an island we found in the South Pacific after himself, and only agreed to name it in honor of General Suvorov after I beat him in a game of chess. He had the Company clerk Krasilnikov flogged when the man, who had gotten drunk, called him a criminal for selling the spirits in Sydney."

"Is there anything else?" asked Baranov.

"Well, I think he is basically unscrupulous…an immoral man…who sets a bad example for others," George went on. "He defends slavery, even while witnessing its horrors. He's an ardent and indiscriminate womanizer…as you know. And, I think, he's only interested in advancing himself in both power and money. His claim to represent the interests of the Russian Empire or of the Russian Navy is false. It's personal prestige, and the control of more and more others, that he really seeks."

"Is he really so different, then, from me?" mused Baranov. "I've spent most of my days hammering a profitable enterprise out of this harsh wilderness for the sake of a title and a little recognition and respect. I was marooned the first year on an Aleutian island when the ship that was bringing me here foundered. I almost starved…and almost froze. After that, many of my attempts to establish settlements failed and many good men, both Russian and native, died trying to carry out my orders. And when at long last and despite the terrible opposition of the Kolosh, I established a tolerable community here in Novo-Arkhangelsk, a cabal of rebels calling themselves the "Order of Ermak" thanked me by rising up against me and plotting my assassination and the murder of my children Antipatr and Irina. They wrote documents proclaiming their plan to abscound with a bunch of the settlement's women on a Company ship and start a "free republic" on Easter Island…of all the implausible schemes. But I found out about the scheme, seized the ringleaders and sent them back to Siberia in irons. All these trials I have endured…and why? For money or heavenly reward? No. I did it to earn others' respect."

"I hadn't heard about all of this," George commiserated. "Life here has been extremely difficult for you. But you have triumphed in life by now as I see it. The people here that I have met esteem you highly. You can already pass on satisfied, knowing that you will be well remembered, and leaving a positive legacy from which your children will benefit."

"I had a family back in Russia…a wife and three daughters," continued Baranov morosely. "My wife there has died, and I send money to my brother for my daughters' support, but essentially I have forsaken them. What legacy have I left them? How will they remember me?"

"They will tell people that their father was 'Lord of all Russian America' and that he tried all his life to help what people he could. That's what they'll say," said George.

"You're very kind to say that, Yegor Nikolaevich," said Governor Baranov. "I sincerely hope you will not be distanced from your family as long as I have been distanced from mine. In time I had to find what companionship I could. In the 1790s I was given a captive Inuit girl by an Eskimo Toion from Bristol Bay. I liked her because she had no lip labret and her facial tattoos were confined to stitch marks from her mouth down over her chin. She was a fine compliant companion when I was there in the settlement we made on Kodiak Island called St. Paul, but I was away too much of the time…and when I was away she was a fine compliant companion to others as well. So I set her aside. When the Kenaitse Toion we call Grigorii Raskazchikov wanted to give me Anna Grigorievna, I resisted. I refused the gift of his daughter and offended the Toion. But he persisted and eventually I took her to myself and treated her as a wife, even though I could not marry her and would not allow her to be baptized into my faith. She is not with me any longer, but she has given me Antipatr and Irina…and in them I take great pride. In my will, I have specified that they are to be my major beneficiaries."

"I understand," said George. "And I am resolved not to be distanced from my wife and daughter for such a long time as you were. I want to go back to St. Petersburg and get them and take them with me to Brazil. It's very beautiful there, temperate and warm. Clouds of brilliant blue butterflies cover the trees, the fruits from which drop right into your hands. Macaws and monkeys screech in the jungle just to greet you. And the people are vibrant with the joy of life. There, I can buy a large amount of land, settle down at last and grow great crops and earn titled nobility from the royal family. I've already spoken to Dom João about this possibility."

"It sounds like a wonderful place, Yegor," said Baranov. "Your description makes it sound like the descriptions I've heard of the Hawai'ian Islands…so beautiful, so warm and wild. I'd like to go to Hawai'i myself some day and meet King Kamehameha. But I doubt if I ever will. Once, after we had exchanged gifts by ship and he had sent us supplies during a period of near starvation after the Kolosh massacred Fort St. Mikhail, he told one of my shipmasters that he would come here and visit me. But he didn't."

"What do you have in common with him?" George wanted to know.

"That's a good question, Yegor Nikolaevich," answered Baranov. "One would think that as the King of a native people now beset with European and American foreigners whose influence is so demanding of changes in their way of life, that he would sympathize not with me, the Russian Governor, but with the native Kolosh Toions like Ska-out-lelt and Kotlean. But, when he heard of what Kotlean's Kolosh had done to my men here, he sent us aid, asking nothing in return. Once, before that, he sent me a grand feather cap, gold and red, made with such handiwork as is hard to imagine. I used to display the cap on the bust of Tsar Aleksandr on the piano in the reception hall, but it got dusty and I had it wrapped and put into storage. I have heard that Kamehameha has long struggled to consolidate all the Hawai'ian Islands into his rule…that he has fought war after war with a succession of rival kings. And now, like me, he's getting old and wondering about the worth of what he's done and what benefits it will bestow…and on whom. That indeed we have in common. That, and the fact that we've run parallel courses of survival for so many years, facing challenge after challenge. I've heard about him all my days here, and he's heard about me. Yet I'm afraid we're fated never to meet…and that's a pity."

Lazarev Leaves:

The *Suvorov* was away from Novo-Arkhangelsk almost two months. During this time several ships arrived in the harbor to take up trading for the summer's fur crop. Already in the harbor since January was Captain Wilson P. Hunt's brig, *Pedlar*. This ship, owned by New York magnate John Jacob Astor's Pacific Fur Company, which had been forced by the British blockade to give up its Astoria outpost at the mouth of the Columbia River, had been "adopted" by Governor Baranov the preceding year and sent under Russian flag to New Albion in California to trade for foodstuffs. But the trip had been troubled by the Spanish seizure of the ship for some time and it had returned without much food. Captain Hunt had spent the winter allowing his crew to engage in petty trade with the Kolosh around the Novo-Arkhangelsk settlement. But now another of John Jacob Astor's ships, Captain William Pigot's *Forester*, had arrived from California. The *Forester* had been masquerading as a British merchantman under a false flag, but was now seeking the kind of "arrangement" with Governor Baranov that her sister ship had. The *Isabella,* a previously adopted ship under Captain William Heath Davis returned from its voyage to the Philippines. Also arrived were the *Albatross* and the *O'Cain* under Captains William Smith and Robert MacNeil. These ships, owned by the Winship family in New England, had been blockaded in the Hawai'ian Islands for over two years, but had escaped. They also were seeking an arrangement from Governor Baranov. On the *Albatross* with Captain Smith was Captain James Bennett of the previously adopted *Bering* and many of his crew.

Captain Bennett's *Bering* had previously been the Boston trader *Atahualpa*, but Baranov had renamed it the previous year and sent it down the coast to obtain sealskins for trade in Hawai'i for foodstuffs. Bennett had traded throughout the islands there, but wound up off the village of Waimea on the island of Kaua'i trading not the sealskins, but muskets, powder, fabrics, and alcohol stills to King Kaumuali'i for pigs, taro, dried fruit, and coconut fiber for cordage. King Kaumuali'i offered to buy the *Bering* itself for a large quantity of the highly desired sandalwood, for which the Chinese paid dearly, and a document of offer was made to Governor Baranov. But then a January storm came up and blew the *Bering* ashore, where it listed badly in the shallow surf. Kaumuali'i ordered two thousand of his men to try to right the ship by pulling on ropes tied to its side, but they could not. After that, his men helped the crew unload all of the *Bering*'s cargo before the surf broke the foundered ship into pieces. But then Kaumuali'i claimed the cargo as salvage, saying also that it was the price of his continued hosting of the stranded sailors. After six months, Captain Bennett and his men had now found their way back to Novo-Arkhangelsk on the *Albatross* and were advocating that Governor Baranov send several shiploads of armed men to Kaua'i to "teach this arrogant King Kaumuali'i a lesson."

When the *Suvorov* returned to Novo-Arkhangelsk heavily loaded with the sealskins in early July, Captain Lazarev refused to allow the skins to be unloaded into the settlement's warehouses. He told Governor Baranov that it was the ship's mission to transport a load of furs back home to St. Petersburg and that the present load of sealskins would constitute his cargo. It made no sense to him, he said, to unload the skins and then to reload the ship with other furs. Governor Baranov tried to explain to him the relative values of the different types of fur, the different states of preservation of the furs, and so on. But Captain Lazarev would not order his men to unload the sealskins. He further irritated Baranov by meddling in the agreement Baranov was trying to negotiate to "purchase" the *Forester* for furs instead of hard currency. The result of this was that Captain Pigot, badly misinformed by Lazarev, precipitously sailed the *Forester* out of Novo-Arkhangelsk mistakenly thinking he would be able to work the hard currency deal with other ports of the Russian-American Company in Kamchatka or Okhotsk. Baranov's deal was squelched and a ship endangered.

The next week a deputation of Governor Baranov's aides seized some Kolosh men in the act of assaulting Russian women who were on a harbor-island berry-picking excursion. These natives turned out to be in possession of firearms and powder the Russians knew to have been previously on board the *Pedler*. Confessions were quickly tricked out of the Kolosh. They had obtained the arms from Captain Hunt and his men from the *Pedler*. Trading firearms and powder to the Kolosh was Governor Baranov's strictest taboo, and there was no doubt that Captain Hunt knew it. Yet here he had violated Baranov's sternest rule right under the fortress windows. Baranov had no choice but to act against Captain Hunt immediately and forcefully. After a confrontation about the matter with Captain Hunt on August 7th, Governor Baranov ordered Captain Lazarev to have his men board the *Pedler* and seize the man. But Captain Lazarev refused to do this, and before Baranov could mobilize a force of 70 hunters in skiffs and baidarkas to seize the *Pedler* by force himself, Captain Hunt had escaped to Captain Robert MacNeil's *O'Cain*. Severely angered by Captain Lazarev's refusal, Baranov ordered the guns of his fortress aimed at the *Suvorov,* and Captain Lazarev opened the ship's gunports and trained his cannon on the fortress. The conflict between the two men was very near to causing a battle between the *Suvorov* and the Novo-Arkhangelsk settlement it had come to provision.

After boarding the *Pedler*, confiscating its arms and powder, spiking its guns, and hauling down its flag, Baranov ordered the second-in-command, Captain Samuel Northrup, to transport all but a watchman ashore. Then he had himself rowed to the *O'Cain*. His demand that Captain MacNeil give up

Captain Hunt was refused on the grounds of naval sanctuary. So he made Captain MacNeil responsible for Captain Hunt's conduct, saying that his fortress guns would fire on them if the *O'Cain* tried to sail and banning Captain Hunt from coming ashore. He would, he said, find a new captain and crew for the *Pedler*.

That evening at meal Governor Baranov related the events of the day to George, telling him how the limits of his patience had been reached by both Captain Hunt and Captain Lazarev. He said he would settle affairs with Lazarev the next day. But early in the morning on the next day, August 8th, 1815, Captain Lazarev sent supercargo Germann Molvo to shore with invoices as if he planned to unload the ship's sealskins. But then he hoisted sail and steered the *Suvorov* away from Novo-Arkhangelsk as fast as he could. Baranov, seeing this, ordered his cannon fired, but it was too late. He then ordered as many men as he could muster to be armed with muskets and to give chase in baidarkas. But this was futile. The *Suvorov* was soon out of sight. And left behind were Dr. George Schaeffer, Larion Trifonov, and Germann Molvo. They were stranded.

Life Stranded:

The day after the *Suvorov*'s departure, Governor Baranov invited George and Germann Molvo into the fortress library for a conference. He told them he planned to send formal complaints about Captain Lazarev's actions to St. Petersburg on the next ship headed for Kamchatka. He asked them to detail their own complaints against Lazarev, being as accurate and specific as possible, in letters that he would include with his own documents. He reckoned that he could get these complaints to St. Petersburg and into the hands of the Russian-American Company directors and of the Russian Admiralty before Captain Lazarev and the *Suvorov* could arrive there.

"But what if Lazarev comes back here?" Molvo asked.

"If he comes back here, I'll have him clapped in irons," Baranov responded.

George and Molvo spent the rest of that day composing their letters, and on September 15, 1815, Baranov put the packet containing their formal charges against Captain Lazarev onto the Company brig *Maria* bound for Kamchatka and Okhotsk. Germann Molvo went with it, but George, at Baranov's request, did not go.

For the next two months George worked in the infirmary with Larion Trifonov. He helped Governor Baranov with the design of scrip monetary tokens he planned to have printed on a bark parchment paper. Baranov had determined to issue his own scrip in amounts of twenty-five, ten, five, and one ruble…and also in fifty, twenty-five, and ten-kopeck amounts. He planned this because money from Russia was always in short supply and it took too long to get. George suggested that Baranov might want to have his own portrait on the notes, but Baranov demurred, saying that he had never had a portrait done and didn't think he should first see his own likeness on a ruble bill. So George scribed some designs for him to consider. His attempts to draw likenesses of various Tsars and military heroes were displeasing to him, even when he traced some likenesses from the few illustrated books in the fortress library. So he sketched instead a copy of the Russian Royal Seal with its two-headed eagle and cross-surmounted crown, writing on it the label for a twenty-five kopeck bill, writing "Russian-American Company Press" under the seal and surrounding it with the abbreviations of the words "Subject to His Highest Imperial Majesty, Tsar Aleksandr I." Governor Baranov seemed pleased with George's design and said he would be issuing something very similar.

In late September a Company ship arrived from Kamchatka with the news that the war between Great Britain and the United States had ended. The Treaty of Ghent ending the war had been signed in late December of 1814, but word had not reached the United States until February of 1815, a month after the Battle of New Orleans. The news of the war's end soon brought a message from Captain Hunt on the *O'Cain* requesting that he be allowed to repurchase the *Pedler* which had not left port. He promised to leave his entire cargo as payment and leave. Thinking of his relationship with John Jacob Astor and the Pacific Fur Company, whose efforts would no doubt be revived by the cessation of hostilities between the U.S. and Great Britain, Baranov assented. When the *Pedler* left port, he refused it even one keg of gunpowder, which Captain Hunt had requested for defense purposes.

Letters From Barbara:

The ship that had brought the news of the end of the war between the United States and Great Britain also brought disturbing news that, in March, Napoleon Bonaparte had returned to power in France from his exile on the Island of Elba. His former Marshal Michel Ney, who had been sent to capture him, had instead defected to his cause and swelled his army. King Louis XVIII had fled Paris. The Russian, Prussian, and English allies were raising armies again to deal with the threat.

"What will it take to put a final end to Napoleon?" exclaimed George to Governor Baranov in exasperation. But Baranov was strangely unconcerned with Napoleon and his campaigns in Europe. "God will see that he gets what he deserves," was all he said.

Baranov had better news for George. He put into George's hands a packet of letters from his wife Barbara in St. Petersburg…letters that had come across all of vast Russia, through Krasnoyarsk and Irkutsk…to Okhotsk and to Petropavlovsk on the Kamchatka Peninsula…then by ship through the Aleutians to Novo-Arkhangelsk. There were ten letters, all written and sent on different dates. But because of the long processing of the mail along the route, with each letter waiting a month or more to move on to the next station on its way, the letters all arrived together in this packet. George was thrilled. He couldn't wait to read them.

The letters were in both German and in Russian, and Barbara's handwriting, its every feminine flourish so familiar to George, conveying to him a strange kind of personal assurance that she was really still there, at home and thinking about him. The Russian parts of the letters were general items of news and the German parts were Barbara's more personal professions of love for George. The letters informed George that Barbara had reestablished mail contact with her parents. The letters were full of news of daughter Inga, who was walking and talking in both Russian and German, and of life in St. Petersburg. The financial arrangements with Doctor Volkov and with Vasilii Shelikhov were working well. And so was home life in the Nevskii Prospect mansion with the Tormasovs. Nadia had given birth to a healthy baby girl in February of 1814, and she had recovered very quickly from the childbirth, which Barbara had attended. Nadia and Aleksandr had decided to name the baby "Varvara Aleksandrovna Tormasova" in honor of Barbara. Baby Varvara, whom they called "Varochka" was thriving, with both parents doting on her daily. The Karamzins, Nikolai and Ekaterina, had returned with their children to the Vyazemsky's Ostafievo estate near Moscow, where Nikolai, who had lost most of his library and documents during the great fire, was working on his eighth volume of the <u>History of the Russian State.</u> He was planning to move to St. Petersburg when it was ready for publication. He and Ekaterina had had another son in 1814 whom they named "Andrei" as they had planned after the death of their first son by that name in Nizhnii Novgorod in 1813. And Ekaterina was again pregnant and coping well with the four children. Now fourteen years old, their precocious daughter Sofia had found further piano instruction with someone else. There had been no word at all about Franz Leppich, and Governor-General Rostopchin was back in Moscow engaged in reorganizing the city's administration, though on August 30 of 1814 General Aleksandr Tormasov had been designated by the Tsar to replace him as Governor-General of Moscow in order to accelerate the reconstruction. Aleksandr was traveling back and forth between St. Petersburg and Moscow, planning to move Nadia and Varochka to their Moscow house when renovations of it were ready in late January of 1815…an eventuality Barbara dreaded.

The most recent letter was dated January 10, 1815.

"Darling George,

I am sorry to begin this letter to you with bad news. My father has died in Würzburg. Mother wrote that he had a terrible heart attack and died very quickly thereafter on August 1 of 1814 by their calendar. God bless him and keep his soul in peace! He was such a good father and a good man, as you know. There was a large funeral at St. Burkard's Church where we were married. It was attended by much of the city's population and he was buried in the cemetery there. Mother writes that she is doing well and that she doesn't need anything. But I am worried about her and how she will live there alone without father. She is 55 years old now and has only the rental income from the apartments she has now inherited…and in which she lives. Father had managed to sell the large house on the Main, but he didn't get as much for it as he should have and most of that money is now gone. Archduke Ferdinand is said to be leaving to return to Tuscany now that Napoleon is no longer in power, but that blessing will not help my mother's situation very much. I would like to find some way to get my mother moved here to St. Petersburg. Perhaps Aleksandr will be able to think of a way.

It's very cold here in St. Petersburg just now. We just celebrated little Inga's third birthday. Lara has been very useful to us as a nanny…she is such a dear. Nadia and I played a birthday duet and Aleksandr declared it to be 'marvelous.' George, you would be so proud of Inga. How lively and bright she is! She runs around the house singing 'la, la, la, la, la' and shouting 'Ishchi menia' that she wants to play hide-and-seek. Aleksandr bought her a large wooden 'Vanka vstanka'…a round doll almost her size with a weighted bottom that pops back upright when you push it over. Inga just loves it.

Aleksandr has been such a blessing, George. He told me that before he and Nadia leave permanently for Moscow he will find an opportunity to speak with Prince Nikolai Grigorievich Repnin-Volkonskii about those matters concerning Anton Demidov and Leppich and you. He thinks that with the Prince's assent he can get the police to drop the investigation. He wants to show the Prince the letter you wrote about the matter and I have given him permission to do so. There is no doubt that we can trust him, George, and that he has only your best interests in his intentions. He retains still a firm resolve to find Leppich in his own way and to deal with him as you can imagine. Nadia tells me that he's never mentioned the fellow to her since before you left…not even a single word.

We have had to buy some new horses and a new and very fancy carriage. Aleksandr and Nadia and I drove in the new carriage to the New Year's Ball in the Winter Palace. Aleksandr got us invited. It was a simply fabulous experience. The Tsar was not there, but many others of the royal family were there. The building is the most spectacular place I've ever been in. The Residenz in Würzburg, though grand, does not compare. The dancing took place in the St. George's Hall on the second floor with a wonderful buffet served in the adjacent Armorial Hall. George, how I wish you could have experienced this event with me. Many people paid me compliments on my appearance and on my dress. One count from a prominent family came to sign my dance card and request a dance with me, but I declined and only danced one dance with Aleksandr who was acting as a chaperone for me, a 'ciscisbeo,' he terms it.

We have bought some fine works of art for our walls…very expensive but very beautiful. One artist from England has proposed to paint a portrait of Aleksandr in his general's uniform and Nadia is most enthusiastic to see this done, though now it will have to be done in Moscow. It reminds me of how little Inga has no likeness of you to remind her of the existence of her father. I know that you may have no possibility of engaging an artist to make a likeness of you. But I would like to request that you make a silhouette and send it to us in your next letter. Just stand in a dark room between a lamp and the wall, then have someone trace your shadow on a piece of paper and cut it out. Try to make it life-size. Then you can fold it into the letter and when I read it to Inga, I can show her what her papa looks like. Please try to do this for us. And, of course, keep writing to us. We have received only four letters from you in the entire year and a half you have been gone.

My Dear and Darling George, we all miss you and I miss you the most of all. Please keep yourself safe and come back as soon as you can. I truly think that all will be well here for you when you return. I hug and kiss you. With love,

Barbara.

P.S. I traced Inga's hand on the back of this letter for you. Underneath her hand is her own letter to you."

On the back of the second page of the letter was the tracing of Inga's small right hand. And underneath was a scrawl of ink, scratched in several directions, that represented his three-year-old daughter's attempt to send him her love. George carefully folded the letter back into its envelope and put it with the others into his trunk. But then, several times in the next weeks, he took it back out again and reread it.

Going to Hawai'i:

In early October of 1815, the American Captain Charles Tyler had made an offer to buy back the *Isabella* and Governor Baranov had accepted the offer. The *Isabella*'s former captain, William Heath Davis, had sailed for Boston on September 9th on the Yankee trader *Packet*. Baranov wanted to send a mission to Hawai'i to try to ask King Kamehameha to prevail upon his tributary King Kaumuali'i of Kaua'i for the return of the wrecked *Bering*'s cargo and for whatever further settlement might be possible. More important, however, was his desire to try again to establish a permanent outpost of some kind on Hawai'i from which provisions could regularly be sent to Novo-Arkhangelsk. So, he required Captain Tyler to sail the *Isabella* first to Hawai'i on such a mission as part of the purchase terms. Captain James Bennett of the *Bering* would be going along, as would Baranov's son Antipatr, who had been urging his father to give him experience on the sailing ships. And, Baranov wanted George to head this mission.

"I think you're the right man for this job, Yegor Nikolaevich," Baranov said, speaking in his characteristic measured way. "Captain Bennett wants us to move by force to get the cargo back, but that is not our primary aim. To get what we most desire—a permanent provisioning outpost there--we have to move carefully, by stealth even. Around Kamehameha are English and American advisors who are already committed against us. It will be difficult to obtain access to the King and to gain his confidence with these advisors already in place there. Indeed you will need to see one of them first, the Englishman John Young, in order to gain an audience with Kamehameha. Archibald Campbell, the footless young Scotsman I told you about, spoke well of us to King Kamehameha and did much to advance our cause in the King's estimation. Unfortunately, I've recently heard that he is no longer there. The only person I know of upon whom you might rely as a liaison or interpreter is an Aleut girl we named Barbara whom Captain Joseph O'Cain took aboard the *O'Cain* back in 1806 and then left at Honolulu when Kamehameha was ruling from there. She became some kind of companion to Kamehameha's wives and accompanied them to Kailua when the royal settlement was moved there in 1812. She's been part of Kamehameha's retinue now for almost nine years and is reportedly very sympathetic to us as employers of many of her people. Antipatr, who speaks Aleut well, or any of the Aleuts themselves can help you speak with her. As I recall, she doesn't speak Russian all that well."

Governor Baranov stopped speaking for a minute, but George understood that he had not completed expressing his plan and remained quiet. Clearing his throat, Baranov continued, "Kamehameha will have to oppose any outright moves of force against any of his subordinate kings…that's for sure. That is why force should be used only as a last resort. That is very important, Yegor. Do not forget this. Kamehameha should be convinced that our intentions are to benefit both him and us. You are to present yourself as a representative of the Russian-American Company who wants only some place where you can grow things to feed us here in our less temperate outpost. Be sure to mention that I, Governor Baranov, am desirous of this and that I will find whatever ways I can to repay him for this. Only if you do succeed in gaining Kamehameha's confidence are you to press forward with him our claims concerning the *Bering*'s cargo. Do not let Captain Bennett interfere in these priorities. He is only with you to help in communicating with King Kaumuali'i of Kaua'i, whom he now knows, in case you are able to advance the claim. He tells me that Kaumuali'i speaks English well, however, and you may not even need Captain Bennett to deal with him."

George, ever subject to mercenary considerations, asked, "What recompense will I receive for heading such a mission for you?"

"That's hard to say just now, Yegor," replied Baranov. "If you are successful you will become the Russian-American Company's Manager in the Hawai'ian Islands. Once you see the place, you might decide to settle there with your family instead of settling in Brazil. Certainly I will give you whatever support you need."

"What kind of support?" asked George.

"You will have a sizeable detachment of both Russians and Aleuts along at your command. Antipatr can help you direct the Aleuts and serve as your interpreter to them, though several of them speak Russian well," Baranov explained. "But I will have other Company ships coming there after you in support, and you will be empowered to direct their efforts. The *Otkrytie,* the *Ilmena*, and the *Kadiak* will all be directed your way. And there is reported to be another navy ship en route from St. Petersburg. It will also make a stop in Hawai'i and you can avail yourself of its support. I will send a large amount of money in silver with you. But if you need to make larger purchases on the Company's accounts, you will just write them up and send the bills to me. Tell whomever you buy things from to apply to me here in Novo-Arkhangelsk for payment. I'll negotiate later with them about the terms of the payment. As you know, my captains have purchased even ships in this way."

"How will I ever get back to St. Petersburg?" asked George.

"Hawai'i is closer to Cape Horn than we are on any ship you sail on, Yegor," Baranov answered. "You can leave the mission at any time you think it's secure. I know that you, a major stockholder in the Company, would only act in its best interests and not leave the mission until it was safe to do so. I will write up a formal version of my commission to you and you can take it with you to show whomever the situation requires."

"I see," said George, pondering the matter. "I'll do it. When do I sail?"

"Captain Tyler thinks he'll be ready next week. You'd better make arrangements with Larion Trifonov to take over the infirmary. I understand that he's found a companion here and that she's expecting a child. He'll be staying."

On October 6th, 1815 by the Russian calendar, the *Isabella* under Captain Tyler sailed away from Sitka Island bound for Hawai'i. On board in addition to the Captain and crew were Dr. George Schaeffer, Captain James Bennett, Governor Baranov's son Antipatr Alexandrovich, fifteen Russians and twenty-five Aleuts.

Chapter Seven-- Hawai'i

Kamehameha:

It took the *Isabella* under Captain Charles Tyler only eighteen days to reach the western coast of the easternmost and largest Hawai'ian island, the island of Hawai'i. This relatively short trip was occasioned by the strong fall tradewinds out of the northeast that blew clear the haze of volcanic dust from the April 1815 eruption of Mount Tambora on Sumbawa Island in Indonesia which intermittently covered the entire Pacific sky at that time, dramatically coloring sunrises and sunsets and even cooling the world's weather so that the entire next year became known as far away as New England as the "year without summer." The north Pacific tradewinds in the fall of 1815, however, were capable of clearing the air and, gusting mightily, they pushed the *Isabella* rapidly to the southwest toward its destination.

It was in a village called Kokoiki, on the northern-most Upolu Point in the Kohala district of this "Big Island" of Hawai'i, and near the important holy place called Mo'okini Heiau, that King Kamehameha had been born to the Ali'i or noble maiden Keku'iapoiwa, legendarily during the visibility of Halley's Comet in 1758, but, in many contemporaries' opinions, before that…perhaps, as some implausibly maintain, as early as 1736. After his birth he was, like baby Jesus in the time of Herod, taken away from his birthplace and hidden in the eastern Kohala village of 'Āwini by relatives, notably his mother's cousin Kaha'ōpulani and his childhood "kahu" or tutor Nae'ole, in order to avoid possible extermination by the King Alapa'inui, whose priests had prophesied a threat to his rule from such a child. Called in childhood Pai'ea, he was nurtured apart from other Ali'i children in his 'Āwini hideaway, a boy fated to greatness and aware of it from his earliest days. When, at the age of five years, he was returned to his parents, King Alapa'inui, no longer seeking to kill him, gave him the name Kamehameha, meaning "The Lonely One."

After much intrigue and violent conflict following the death of his adolescent mentor, Hawai'ian King Kalani'ōpu'u, in 1782, Kamehameha, in the next ten years, overcame several rivals among his kin for power on Hawai'i and, with the aid of captured or purchased western weapons and European advisors, he began a campaign to subjugate and place under his absolute rule the populations of all the other Hawai'ian Islands to the west of him.

Historic battles for Maui…off-shore in the boat-to-boat "Battle of the Red-mouthed Gun" and on land at the Battle of Kapaniwai, the "Damming of the Waters" in the Īao Valley… resulted in Kamehameha's control of that island and its neighbor islands of Kaho'olawe, Molokini, Lana'i, and Moloka'i of the formidable former King Kahekili's Maui Federation by 1795. And the terrible Battle of Nu'uanu Pali on O'ahu in 1795, during which the retreating warriors of the defector Chief Ka'iana and O'ahu Chief Kalanikūpule, the deceased King Kahekili's son, were forced over a 1200-foot cliff, brought him control of that island as well.

In 1801, a few years after he put down a rebellion on Hawai'i led by Ka'iana's brother Namakeha, whom he captured and sacrificed, Kamehameha's reaction to the destructive lava flow from erupting Mount Hualālai onto the north Kona coast of Hawai'i gave him a true God-like reputation among his subject population. After all the efforts of the priests to appease the volcano goddess Pele with human sacrifices had failed, and Pele's lava was covering fishponds and burning villages, Kamehameha had himself paddled in a canoe to the spot at Mahi'ula where the lava flow was entering the sea with roaring clouds of steam. There he cut off a large lock of his hair, wrapped it in a ti leaf and threw it into the lava as it entered the water. This was giving to Pele the gift of a part of himself and his powerful mana. The lava flow stopped as did the eruption of Mount Hualālai. After this he had no rivals for power on his home island of Hawai'i.

Twice Kamehameha had tried to invade and conquer the easternmost inhabited islands of Kaua'i and Ni'ihau. In 1796 a sudden storm in the perilous Kaua'i Channel swamped many of his boats and drowned many men, forcing him to order a return to O'ahu. And in 1804 a force of over 7000 men that he had gathered on O'ahu for an invasion of Kaua'i became afflicted with a serious cholera-like disease, killing a great number of them, their bodies immediately turning black by accounts of witnesses. Kamehameha was himself afflicted, but survived to call off the planned invasion.

In 1810, however, King Kaumuali'i, who had gained control of Kaua'i and Ni'ihau before the 1804 attempted invasion, decided begrudgingly to negotiate with Kamehameha in order to avoid what he saw as the inevitable forced subjugation of his islands…and what would mean the deaths of himself and his family in the subsequent executions and ritual sacrifice. In a historic personal meeting on the *Albatross,* then captained by Nathan Winship, in Honolulu harbor on the island of O'ahu, Kaumuali'i consented to rule Kaua'i and Ni'ihau as a subordinate and tributary to Kamehameha, surrendering the rights of his own heirs to rule these islands after his death.

Kamehameha had ruled his subject islands from settlements established on more than one of them, but in 1812 he moved the seat of his rule from Honolulu back to Kailua on the Kona coast of his home island of Hawai'i. It was there that George Schaeffer hoped to meet him and gain his confidence.

Kamehameha's rule, George had learned from discussions with Governor Baranov, Captain Tyler and other captains previously, was based on his claim, as a member of the elite "Ali'i" or ruling class of Hawai'ians, to a direct genealogical connection to the Gods that created the universe and the Hawai'ian world in it. This connection was spiritual in nature embodying an unseen force called "mana." The more pure and direct the lineage to the Gods that these Ali'i could evidence, the more powerful was their "mana." The evidence for their possession of this "mana" was a long and elaborate chant called the "mele inoa," learned from childhood, which described their particular connection to the Gods by tracing their genealogy back for many generations.

Kamehameha, it was claimed by his kahunas who knew an abbreviated version of it, could chant his genealogy back to the Gods, specifying 289 relational connections through more than fifty generations. The 289 relationships in his chant was said to be, accordingly, the precise number of human teeth he had ordered to have embedded into his calabash "ipu lepu" or refuse bowl…the repository of his spittle after consuming the intoxicating "'awa" drink made by fermenting saliva from chewing parts of a pepper plant, and of his trimmed whiskers, hair, or fingernails, and of his feces. The King's servants would follow him around with the teeth-embedded bowl and, after he contributed the products of his bodily processes to it, they would carefully dispose of the contents in a secret place so that enemies of the king could not seize it and thereby defile his mana.

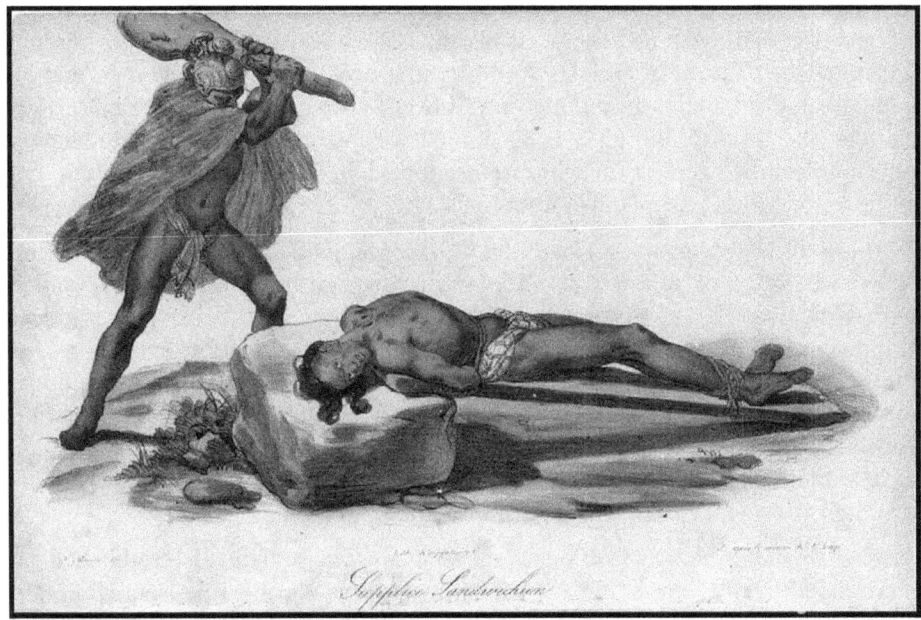

The execution of a "prostration kapu" violator, by Jacques Arago, from: http://en.wikipedia.org/wiki/Jacques_Arago to media commons site.

Mana was protected by an elaborate system of "kapus," sacred laws forbidding offensive behaviors. If so little as a commoner's shadow fell upon a ruling Ali'i or "Ali'i-nui's" person, or his clothing, his food, or his water, the crucial mana…the mana the entire population believed protected them all from looming natural disaster and human woe… would be diminished or destroyed. So the servants hurried in advance of the King, warning any commoners they approached with the shout "Kapu, Kapu-a-moe, Ka mo'ī!" so that these commoners should prostrate themselves on the ground at the sight of the King in order not to risk casting a shadow upon him and harming his mana. If they did not prostrate themselves, they were subject to immediate execution—by clubbing on the head, rope strangulation or, in the case of the worst transgressions, by being burned alive--by the King's bodyguards, strong young men called "Mu," or "black legs" for their having one leg tattooed in a dark pattern from hip to ankle.

Execution of a Kapu violator by strangling by Jacques Arago (1790-1855), from: http://www.grosvenorprints.com in the advertisement for Arago's <u>Maniere d'etranger un coupable aux iles Sandwich.</u>

The purity of the Ali'is' mana was maintained by encouraging marriage and procreation by close relatives. Brothers married sisters and cousins in order to keep the mana pure. The offspring of sons and daughters who were twins, belonging to the high and sacred caste called "ni'aupi'o," was considered to produce the purest mana of all. For this reason, King Kamehameha had more than twenty wives, many of whom were his relatives. From these wives he sired twenty-four children who survived infancy, but he sired another forty or more from women who were not his wives…this since the Hawai'ian culture encouraged sexual interaction with very little social inhibition. Legend has it that Kamehameha's first sexual partner was twenty-nine-year-old Kānekapōlei, one of the wives of King Kalani'ōpu'u. He was likely fifteen years old then, and he sired with her a son, Ka'ōleiokū, called "Pauli" who became a warrior of Kamehameha's Hawai'i rival and cousin Keōua Kūahu'ula. Kamehameha's son Liholiho, however, the oldest from sacred wife Keōpuōlani who was born in 1796, was considered to be Kamehameha's heir because Keōpuōlani, whom Kamehameha had taken into his household at age eleven and married when she was sixteen, came from a family, also related to Kamehameha, which was considered to possess the purest mana.

Kamehameha was not only a man of powerful spiritual mana who could evidence by chant his genealogical connection to the Gods. His power did not rest entirely upon the strength of his mana. Indeed he did not by birth belong to the highest possible caste of mana…the "pi'o" caste, and he felt a certain insecurity about this all his days. He belonged instead to the fourth Ali'i caste, that of "wohi," because Keku'iapoiwa, his mother, and Keōua Kalani, his putative father, were not brother and sister, but only cousins as had been one set of his grandparents. But he succeeded in becoming a great ruler despite this genealogical limitation, this limitation to his mana, because he was also a man of extraordinarily powerful will in an extraordinarily powerful body.

In his teens, Kamehameha grew to four or five inches above six feet in height. As an adult he weighed approximately 245 English pounds. He was well formed and athletic of build…quick, adept, and very, very strong. In his youth he trained for years under the tutelage of the most formidable warrior on Hawai'i, Kekūhaupi'o. He had qualified for this training by overturning the fabled Naha Rock at Hilo, reputed to weigh over two tons. Kekūhaupi'o had then trained him until he excelled at swimming and surfing, but also at "hākōkō" wrestling, the sport of boxing they called "mokomoku," and at dodging or catching spears thrown at him in bunches from different directions. He became an astonishing master of the stone sling, the shark-toothed warclub, and the heavy pololū spear. He became a master of the martial art called "lua" wherein he could lift an opponent over his head and slam him fatally onto one of his knees, breaking the man's back or neck. He was fearless on the kilometer-long steep "hōlua" slide into the ocean on a bed of pandanus leaves and pili grass made slick with the oil of the kukui nut. When other brave Ali'i youth so feared the velocity of the koa-runnered sled as it approached the embankment above the waves that they would, in panic, throw themselves off to the side, Kamehameha would, no matter the velocity and the vibration, remain atop the speeding sled and dive gracefully into the waves below, neatly parting from the sled as it plunged over the embankment at the bottom of the run.

Kamehameha had a fearsome visage…a look to him that frightened people, even the brave. This was recorded by several of the crew members of ships that he had come aboard, first among these Captain James Cook's *Resolution* that he boarded on the 30th of November 1778 with the party of Hawai'ian King Kalani'ōpu'u who was then warring with Maui King Kahekili, who had come aboard the *Discovery* to gift Cook's second-in-command, Captain Charles Clerke, with a red feather cloak only three days previously. About Kamehameha as a young member of Kalani'ōpu'u's retinue, Cook's executive officer, Lieutenant James King of the *Resolution,* wrote in his diary that: "He had as savage a looking face as I ever saw." Kamehameha bore himself with the confidence of a man who had never been bested in any physical confrontation.

John Young, "Olohana":

From the deck of the *Isabella*, anchored off the northwest shore of the island of Hawai'i at Kawaihae on the early morning of 23 October, 1815, George surveyed the island with awe. They had come to Kawaihae to meet first with Kamehameha's long-time foreign advisor, John Young, who had built his residence there, several hours' sail north of Kailua where King Kamehameha's ruling settlement was. Without the assent of John Young and his introduction, foreign visitors could not be assured of the opportunity to see King Kamehameha at all.

The small village of Kawaihae, composed of thatched huts the color of dry straw, had behind it, high up on a hill, a most impressive construction of lava rocks. It was a wide three-tiered platform of immense size surmounted by a high and very thick tapering back wall, which enclosed several thatched houses, a mat-covered tower, and a profusion of what appeared to be Kolosh totem poles. This, George later learned, was the Pu'ukoholā Heiau, a holy place that Kamehameha had ordered constructed in 1790 and dedicated to his war god Kūkā'ilimoku. Human sacrifices were made there.

After the *Isabella* was anchored among a swarm of natives in canoes, George went below deck to prepare his appearance and collect the letter that Governor Baranov had given him for King Kamehameha and some gifts. While he was doing this, Captain Tyler ordered away the longboat carrying Captain James Bennett and several others to shore. George was surprised at this and displeased, wanting to be among the first to come ashore and meet John Young. But Captain Tyler, trying to make amends, quickly arranged for George to be rowed ashore by a husky young Hawai'ian in a canoe.

As George sat in the front of the dugout canoe, he tried to count the number of outrigger canoes assembled on the beach, but there were too many to count easily as the Hawai'ian young man behind him vigorously paddled the canoe through the mild morning waves. He noticed also numerous medium-sized dogs that ran in packs along the shore. He could hear them barking from the canoe.

George was pleased to notice that his canoe was overtaking the longboat and that both craft would reach shore at the same time. George was wearing his best white shirt and dark formal jacket. He had brought a parcel of Russian coins as his initial gifts, and he wondered if John Young would recommend that he present them personally to Kamehameha and his chiefs.

On the beach, standing on an outcropping of lava rock, was a greeting delegation. Most of the men of the delegation were almost naked, wearing only "malo," or kilt-like wraps of pounded-bark kapa fabric, which covered them from the waist to the knees. They were large and muscular men with dark brown skin. Their heads were partially shaved, with effusions of hair on the tops of their heads, and they wore numerous bead and feather necklaces and other decorations. They were armed. Some carried native warclubs and spears, and others held heavy flintlock muskets of the "Brown Bess" type. But one man in the delegation was visibly different. He was quite an old man, clean-shaven with white hair, and he was wearing European breeches and shoes, with a factory-made white shirt, and a gray jacket. As George got out of the canoe and the others, only a few yards away, climbed over the front of their longboat onto the beach, this man came up and said, "Welcome, Russian friends. I am John Young, called by the natives here 'Olohana.' Do any of you speak English?"

Captain James Bennett, who had gotten out of the longboat first, stepped forward and said, "Mr. Young, don't you recognize me? We met only a year ago when I was trading here on the Russian-American Company ship *Bering*."

John Young adjusted his gaze to focus directly on Captain Bennett. "Ah yes, I remember you," he said. "You're the one who sold arms to Kaumuali'i on Kaua'i and then let your ship wash ashore there. I'm surprised you would come back here."

"I've come back to get my ship's cargo," answered Captain Bennett with clear irritation at Young's characterization of him "…and to teach Kaumuali'i a lesson if I have to."

George was not pleased at the way this initial contact was going between John Young and Captain Bennett. Bennett had already, in his first conversation on Hawai'i, brought to the fore the very issue which George intended to delay mentioning.

"Mr. Young," George said in English, stepping ahead of Captain Bennett, "I am Dr. George von Schaeffer and I am in charge of this mission, sent from the Russian community of Novo-Arkhangelsk on Sitka Island by Governor Aleksandr Andreevich Baranov. Governor Baranov wants me to assure you and King Kamehameha of our good will and of our intentions to pursue only mutually beneficial projects."

"What kind of mutually beneficial projects?" asked Young.

"Agricultural experimentation, for one thing," answered George. "I have with me a number of different types of crop seeds…a new kind of cotton, for example, and a new tobacco…and I want to see how they will grow here. Also, I would like to investigate your native crops and other plants in order to develop a food supply for our outposts on the northern American coast and on the Aleutian Islands. Whatever we grow here, we would, of course, pay for with what we produce…furs and timber, glass and ships, and, perhaps later, smelted iron. All we need is an allotment of land somewhere here in your King's domain. The results of our agricultural experiments would also be of benefit to your own people because we would be willing to share our knowledge with them."

Sketch of John Young (1742-17 December, 1835) by Jacques Arago (1790-1855) from http://en.wikipedia.org/wiki/John_Young (Hawaii).

"So you plan to stay here in the islands for some time then?" asked Young, saying what immediately sprang to his mind.

"I would stay here with a party of about forty men…fifteen Russians and twenty five Aleuts," George replied. "This young man here," he said, directing Young's attention to the handsome dark-haired youth at his side, "Is Antipatr Aleksandrovich Baranov—Governor Baranov's only son. He will be staying here with me. And so will Captain Bennett. Captain Tyler and the *Isabella* will be sailing on without us…assuming, of course, that your King allows us to stay. Will we be able to speak with him soon? I have some gifts for him, and for you, from Governor Baranov. Also, I have a letter to the King from Governor Baranov."

"Give the letter to me and I'll give it to the King and explain it to him," said Young curtly. "Is it in English?"

"No, it's in Russian," said George. "It simply introduces me and tells the King why my men and I have come here, as I've told you. It does mention that Governor Baranov desires the recovery of the *Bering's* cargo from Kaua'i."

"All right. Give me the letter then. I'll tell the King what it says."

George handed him the letter. John Young turned to look at the burly Hawai'ians surrounding him. He said something to them in Hawai'ian, then, returning to English and omitting the "von" from the way George had introduced himself, he said, "Dr. Schaeffer, I have to tell you that agricultural experiments are not new to us. There is a clever Spaniard on O'ahu named Don Francisco de Paula Marin who has been experimenting with all kinds of crops and plants for several years. He will tell you that anything planted will grow well here and yield more than it will anywhere else. He even has a vineyard from which he makes a very delicious wine. So I doubt that you will be able to acquaint us with any new crops. Any fool can grow anything here just by putting it into the fertile ground. So we don't really need any instruction in agricultural methods. Moreover, I can only doubt that agricultural experimentation is your primary intention here. It's hard for me to imagine a man like Captain Bennett coming here to spend his time planting seeds and harvesting crops."

Young waited a moment to assess the reaction to his skepticism about George's intentions. But George did not respond, so he continued. "I also have to tell you that we are not now inclined to allow the settlement on our territory of organized groups of foreigners. The King has put out some kapus preventing this. No foreigners, for example, will be allowed to build a European-style stone structure of any kind. No one will be allowed to fly a foreign flag above our land."

"I assure you," said George, "that if we are allowed to stay here and cultivate some plot of land to send food back to our northern outposts, then we will endeavor in all ways to benefit you with what we have in return. We will abide by your King's kapus and cause no trouble. I can't imagine that the King would not want to make such arrangements with the Russians who are, after all, his closest neighbors here in the Pacific. The future of Russian-Hawai'ian trade is surely a bright one, and it could begin right here and now. Do you not esteem positive relations with your neighbors? Do you not esteem Russians?"

"Some Russians we like…others we don't," tersely commented Young. "Captain Lisianskii, when he was here in 1804, we liked. He had the good sense to stay out of our conflict with King Kaumuali'i of Kaua'i. But Captain Hagemeister, who came here in 1807, we found to be arrogant and even threatening. We don't want any foreign power to dominate us in any way. I'm advising King Kamehameha that if we give to any foreign government an inch, it will likely take a mile. We don't intend to become some foreign government's colony here. We'll stay our own course."

"Well, will we be allowed to see King Kamehameha and ask him for ourselves if we can stay?" asked George.

"I will sail with you to Kailua," replied John Young. "The Makahiki festival is beginning and I want to go there for that reason. We will be there this afternoon. You and young Baranov can stay ashore there tonight. I will go to the King and try to arrange a meeting for you tomorrow. The rest of your party, including Captain Bennett, can visit in the village of Kailua while it is light, but they must return to your ship by nightfall. We can't allow any group of foreigners who have arms into the village where the King lives…at least not without his permission."

Kailua—King and Queen:

On the ship as it sailed southward to Kailua, George conversed with John Young, but perceived that the former Englishman was not well disposed toward George's stated purposes for the visit. Young had apparently given credence to negative assessments of Russian intentions by the American ship captains he had met. He seemed inalterably opposed to Governor Baranov's plan for George to establish a provisioning outpost on the islands.

As they drew nearer to Kailua the grand height of the island became more apparent. Behind the village was a smoothly ascending mountain called Mauna Kea, which was so high that the white snowy peak of it was obscured by a wide horizontal mantle of clouds it had attracted to itself as a man would pick up an umbrella. The mountainside was not as green in color as George had imagined the island would be. There were patches of green, even some near the shore, which appeared to be fields of cultivated crops of some kind. And farther up some forests were visible. But the overall color was that of the light dry grasses, which covered the lower slope of the mountain. And there were jagged fields of black lava rock to be seen, both to the left and the right of the village, with pathways of the lava winding up into the mountain draws and canyons. To the far south he could make out, rising from behind another immense mountain called Mauna Loa, huge cumulus-like clouds of light gray ash boiling up into the sky. It was, he knew, an actively venting volcano.

When the *Isabella* had anchored in the harbor at Kailua, and George was being rowed ashore with Captain Bennett, Antipatr Baranov and John Young, fleets of canoes, paddled by hardy young men and carrying older men, women, dogs, and even some pigs, came out to surround the ship. "As you can see," said John Young, "many of our people have already reached your ship by canoe and are meeting with the crew. I trust that the crew will treat them with respect."

"I am certain that they will be treated well aboard the *Isabella*," said George. "Captain Tyler is a fine man and will not tolerate the ill treatment of his guests. I can only hope that King Kamehameha is the same."

That night, before sleeping on woven mats in a grass-thatched hut in Kailua, George and Antipatr Baranov discussed the day's events and the strategy to be employed in meeting King Kamehameha the next day. They both agreed that the initial meeting with John Young, Kamehameha's primary European advisor, had not gone well.

The next morning a group of armed warriors led by a young Hawai'ian Chief who spoke enough English to give his name as "Cox," came to escort George and Antipatr to the royal residence compound called Kamakahonu. This compound was located on a portion of shore which extended westward a short distance into the larger bay and then curved southward forming a small cove. The outer point of the cove's encircling shore had been built up with lava rocks to form a platform area elevated about a sazhen…more than a fathom at seven feet…above the sea level. On the sea edge of this platform was a holy place, called the 'Ahu'ena Heiau, consisting of a large thatched building in the shape of a triangular prism where Kamehameha and his priests could consult the Gods in quietude and perform sacred rituals, a smaller similar building which served as a kind of priory for the priests or "kahunas," and a four-sided oracle tower of about three sazhens of height, the observation stand of which was obscured by kapa material hung from the thatched roof. All around the heiau were "ki'i," images painted and carved into wooden posts representing the Gods Kū, Hina, Kāne, Kanaloa, Haumea, Pele, Lono, and Kūkā'ilimoku. The pole to Kūkā'ilimoku the War God was the tallest at nearly thirty feet because of this God's special place in Kamehameha's spiritual makeup.

Behind the 'Ahu'ena Heiau, on the makai or ocean side, was a sazhen-high wall of lava rock which attached to the lava base platform and extended northward then eastward and back southward in a wide circle, completely enclosing the royal Kamakahonu compound and obscuring its insides from any exterior view. The only obvious path into the compound was at the very mauka or inland side of the small cove where one could walk between the end of the wall and the water just at a rocky outcropping between strips of pahoehoe...cooled and congealed lava. Inside the wall were, at first away from the entrance, three large thatched houses with three doors each. These were the "hale Mua" or "house for the male bodyguards," the women's house for the wives of the bodyguards, and the sleeping house in the middle. Further on, toward the center of the compound was a stone house of European style, built by a foreigner named Antonio Ferreira whom the natives called Aikona and adjoined by an additional thatched storehouse for gifts to the King. Near the stone house was the food preparation area. Then came Queen Ka'ahumanu's house, two thatched houses for the other wives, a "hale pe'a" or "house of the 'haumia' or unclean" for isolating the chiefesses during their menstrual periods, and then a small pond. On the other side of the pond, not far from the northernmost track of the encircling lava wall were three thatched houses, two small and one large, which constituted the residence of Kamehameha.

George noticed that the people in the King's compound were wearing toga-like garments of pattern-stamped kapa over their shoulders and that two or three apparent dignitaries were adorned with brilliantly colored feather capes and caps. There were several women there, some wearing the over-shoulder garments and others wearing nothing but necklaces above the waist. These women were beautiful of shape and had long black hair flowing down their deep brown backs. George was reminded of his wife Barbara's long black hair and how it looked on her bare back.

On a flat spot of leaf matting just to the south of Kamehameha's large thatched house and across the pond from the chiefesses' residences, Chief Cox asked George and Antipatr to sit and wait. Then he departed, leaving the escort of formidable-looking warriors standing around the edges of the leaf matting where George and Antipatr sat. At the corners of the mat and on the sides of the King's door were tall feather-topped standards called kahilis. A half hour went by. Several women walked past, and one of these was most striking in her appearance. She was very large…over six feet in height and very ample of hips, stomach, and bosom. Her face was especially pleasing to George, with highly arched eyebrows and a narrow, almost European, nose, and she bore herself up in a regal posture as she walked, attended by several much smaller women who trailed behind her. Her hair was long but pulled tight over her head and knotted over the back of her neck. It was extremely thick and streaked reddish with some kind of powder or dye. On her head was a brightly colored tiara-like adornment made of feathers. George wondered who she could be.

Suddenly one of the attendants of the large woman walked over to where George and Antipatr were sitting and exclaimed something to Antipatr in a language George did not understand. In an instant he realized that this woman was that "Barbara" whom Governor Baranov had mentioned to him and that she had recognized Antipatr. She was speaking to Antipatr in Aleut, saying, "Son Antipatr, do you not recognize me? I knew your family when you lived on Kodiak. My father was a huntsman for your father when you were small. I also studied with Elder Germann there, only a few years ahead of you."

Antipatr spoke back reassuringly to the woman, small and dark and squat of build, telling her that he did remember her, and that he was glad to meet her again here in Hawai'i. But then he whispered to George in Russian that he did not remember her well and would never have recognized her. He introduced George to her, saying "This is Dr. Yegor von Sheffer. He is a famous physician from Germany and Russia. And he is my father's official representative to King Kamehameha. I have accompanied him here on an important mission to find a source of food for our people in the north."

Barbara was able to say "Ochen' priiatno…Very pleased to meet you" to George in Russian. She then explained that her Russian was somewhat limited, especially because she had not heard or spoken it for a long time. "Moe imia bylo…my name was 'Chunagak'," she said. "A potom menia zvali…and then I was called 'Barbara'…i teper menia zovut…and now I am called 'Palapala'. I left Kodiak with Captain O'Cain almost ten years ago, but he became tired of me and left me in Honolulu. It was very difficult for me until I was adopted by my lady Queen Ka'ahumanu. She has been very good to me."

So the large woman was Queen Ka'ahumanu, Kamehameha's favorite and most influential wife. Only she and Keōpuōlani were regularly referred to as "queens," the other wives being called chiefesses. George looked at Ka'ahumanu as her maid Barbara continued to speak to him and to Antipatr, and the Queen, who loomed hugely over him and Antipatr in their still seated positions, smiled down at him. She then interrupted Barbara and spoke with her at some length in Hawai'ian. After this, Queen Ka'ahumanu motioned for George and Antipatr to get to their feet. "Kepa," she said, gesturing toward George, and "Hanikapa," gesturing toward Antipatr. These words, George surmised, were to be their names in Hawai'ian.

During the conversation with Queen Ka'ahumanu and her maid Palapala, George noticed that the Queen had several warts on the fingers and back of her right hand. In Russian he told Palapala that he had a medicament, an acidic ointment that would remove these warts with little pain and without leaving a scar. Palapala told this to Queen Ka'ahumanu and she seemed very pleased to hear it.

At this time a curtain was pulled aside from the King's residence door and John Young came out followed by Kamehameha himself. The King was a very large man, even taller than Ka'ahumanu though likely not as heavy. He was dressed in the western fashion but very colorfully, with loose blue trousers and a white shirt, with a red silk vest and yellow silk tie under a green jacket that resembled a Russian military uniform. He was barefoot, however, and George noticed the impressive size and the roughness of his feet. He had a lined face and appeared to be a man between sixty and seventy years of age. He was clean-shaven because the martial art lua taught that a man's beard made him vulnerable to be grabbed by an enemy. Masters of lua and other warriors shaved themselves with honed shark's teeth. George estimated that Kamehameha was a few years younger, however, than the also clean-shaven John Young. His short curly hair was thickly tinged with grey and his neck exposed wrinkles of skin below his chin. He had a slight thickness to his waist, but overall retained a muscular appearance, connoting great physical strength, and he moved gracefully like a younger man. As he approached them, John Young motioned for George and Antipatr to get down into a sitting position as Chief Cox had instructed them. They quickly did so. But then, as Ka'ahumanu had done a few minutes before, King Kamehameha gestured grandly with his arms, motioning for them to stand back up. He then approached Ka'ahumanu, who was still standing close by, briefly rubbed noses with her, and spoke to her for a minute or two. Then he directed his speech to George and Antipatr. The first thing he said was "Aloha," but after that George could ken nothing. George noticed that he had a deep and resonant voice and that his words resounded in the air like a distant thunder. Among his words, George tried to pick out mention of Governor Baranov, of his name or that of Antipatr, but he could not. At last he did notice that the King referred to John Young as "Olohana." The name "Olohana" had been given to Young because of his frequent boatswain's call to "all hands" in his training of the Hawai'ian "kōa" or warriors.

Sketch of Kamehameha I ("The Great") (1758?-8 May, 1819) by Louis Choris (1795-1828) in 1816, from:
http://www.nps.gov/puhe/historyculture/Kamehameha.htm, also from: http://en.wikipedia.org/wiki/Kamehameha_I.

John Young began to interpret Kamehameha's words into English. "The King says that he is happy to welcome Governor Baranov's son and representative here. He has long felt that he and Governor Baranov, even though they have not met, are like brothers traveling similar difficult paths in life. He says that you and your men may stay here in the Kailua settlement as his guests after your ship departs. But Captain James Bennett cannot stay. He has angered Kamehameha by selling weapons to Kaumuali'i. If he comes ashore here again, he will be killed. He must leave on the *Isabella.* You and the rest of the group will be given houses to live in, mats to sleep on, and you will be given food. You will all be treated with respect. He wants to become better acquainted with you, Doctor Schaeffer, and he invites you to come speak further with him in the coming days, be they weeks or months. When he feels that he knows you better, he will decide whether you will be given what you want."

"That is right and fair," said George, putting several Russian coins into John Young's hands as he spoke. "Ask him to accept these coins as our gifts. Each coin is stamped with the likeness of our great ruler, the Russian Tsar Aleksandr. Please tell him that we are very grateful for his hospitality and that I will try to learn his language as quickly as I can so that he and I can speak together without an interpreter."

George noticed that John Young seemed a bit disconcerted to interpret the last part of this statement, but King Kamehameha seemed pleased by the response. He smiled, nodded to George and Antipatr, and said, "You will be happy to know that I have learned some English from Olohana and others. It is important that different people learn each others' languages. He who gains a language adds a soul to his life and increases his mana. In Russian I know only 'Da' and 'Nyet,' but perhaps I will learn more from you." Then he walked back into his residence.

The Stay on Hawai'i:

In the next month, George and Antipatr learned much about Hawai'ian life. Through John Young, George requested that Queen Ka'ahumanu loan Palapala to him and to Antipatr as a servant so they could interact with her in order to advance their facility in Hawai'ian. This request was granted and Palapala came every morning to the house where George and Antipatr were and stayed with one or both of them all day, accompanying them wherever they went and leaving them only at sundown. Aided by her ability to explain Hawai'ian terms in both Aleut and Russian, George and Antipatr made rapid progress.

George was characteristically curious about the royal family. He wanted to know the names of all Kamehameha's wives and all of his children. He wanted to know the circumstances of each marriage and the relationships of power and affection among the wives. Palapala was well acquainted with several of the wives. She best knew Hana- Maui-born Ka'ahumanu, who was Kamehameha's third wife in marriage order, but clearly first in favor and power. "The Gods," Palapala explained, "had decided that Ka'ahumanu would remain childless so that she could fulfill other important functions in Kamehameha's life." Ka'ahumanu's brother, Kuakini, was one of Kamehameha's close advisors. Kuakini, who had features of appearance and manner considered feminine and was therefore, strangely, said to be very attractive to women, had indulged a kind of fashion among the Hawai'ian nobility of adopting the name of American or European political figures. Kuakini was called "John Adams." His half brother Kahekili Ke'eaumoku, the chief who had first led George and Antipatr to see Kamehameha, had been named after Kahekili, the prominent former ruler of the Maui Federation, and his own father, and that of Ka'ahumanu, Ke'eaumoku. Perhaps to distinguish himself from these more prominent namesakes, he chose the English name "Cox." Kamehameha's closest advisor, prime minister, and war chief Kalanimoku was called "Billy Pitt." His younger brother, also close to Kamehameha's court was called "Boki," which Hawai'ians thought was the English term for "boss." Other Ali'i had such names tattooed on their arms, middle, or legs. George noticed tattoos of the names "Thom. Jefferson" and "Napoleon Bonapart" on Ali'i arms. George had chuckled at the tattooer's misspelling of Napoleon's last name. "No doubt," he joked to Antipatr, "the man's arm was too skinny and the tattooer ran out of room to scribe in the final 'e'. He should have tattooed it on the man's butt instead."

Palapala knew the quiet and beautiful Keōpūolani, the most sacred wife and mother of the heir, Liholiho, who lived across the cove in another European-style stone house built for him by Francisco de Paula Marin who had come from O'ahu to complete the task. Just this past year, Keōpūolani had given birth to her third surviving child with Kamehameha, the daughter Nahi'ena'ena, called "the pride of Hawai'i." In her nineteen years with Kamehameha, Keōpūolani had had fourteen pregnancies from which only three children, sons Liholiho and Kauikeaouli and daughter Nahi'ena'ena, survived. Keōpūolani's aunt Peleuli was also one of Kamehameha's wives and was known to Palapala. She knew the Chiefess Kaheiheimālie, and also Kahukauha'akoi, the very portly Nāmāhana, and the slender Kalākua, all of whom were Ka'ahumanu's younger sisters. She knew the currently pregnant wife Manono. But, she related, the Chiefess Kekauluohi, the daughter of Kaheiheimālie and Kamehameha's favorite younger brother Keli'imaika'i who died in 1809, was the favored wife of the season. She had been specially secluded for Kamehameha's access until pregnancy resulted and had one of the two chiefesses' houses to herself and her servants.

Palapala was also acquainted with several prominent Ali'i women who were not Kamehameha's wives. One of these was Kapi'olani, who lived in Ka'awaloa in the south of the Kona district near Kealakekua Bay with her husband Naihe. Kapi'olani had been born in Hilo and had come to support Kamehameha in the struggle for power on Hawai'i after the death of the Hilo King Keawema'uhili. She was a chiefess of the most powerful mana and was widely respected. She and her husband had been with Kamehameha on O'ahu during the "'ōku'u" or great sickness in 1804. They survived, although she was so ill that all her hair had fallen out.

At a gathering in the royal compound during the second week of George and Antipatr's stay in Kailua, they witnessed a session of native dances, accompanied by drums. The sensual hula dancing was most impressive to them, but there was also a male dancer, Pua'aiki, called Bartimeus according to the English-naming fashion, who had gone completely blind in his youth, but was supported by the community as a kind of cultural resource. When Bartimeus danced in the hula ensemble, the top of his body moved in such a way as to give symbolic messages to the audience and his feet stamped in rhythm to the "pāhu"...the hula drums. On his feet were anklets called "kūpe'e niho 'īlio" made of the strung-together canine fangs of five hundred dogs. These dog-teeth anklets made a surprisingly audible rattle at each stamp of his feet in accompaniment of the drums. And there was the subtle accompaniment as well by a man playing a stringed instrument called the "ūkēkē." This was a simple stick about two feet long with three woven strings stretched across its length that was held to the player's mouth as he strummed it to add resonation to his oral vocalizations, which reminded George of Tyrolean yodeling, only softer in tone.

Kamehameha had a local ruling council of advisors who lived permanently in Kailua near him. He met with them in the compound almost every evening, unless the day was a holiday or declared kapu for some reason. These advisors included Kaikio'ewa, who had married Kamehameha's sister Kalanikaulikiwakama, genealogist and chanter Kalaikuahulu, sailing masters Nahili and Keaweopu, Haleino, Kaioea, and Kuhia. Son Liholiho, aged nineteen, sometimes joined the group as did Hewahewa, the senior priest or kahuna, but each of the regular council members were men who had their own network of administrators out in the different ahupua'a or districts of the islands and they were responsible for collecting tax goods from the population, for arranging celebrations, and enforcing kapu's. Kamehameha's closest advisors, Hoapili, Kalanimoku or "Billy Pitt," and Kuakini or "John Adams, did not reside permanently in Kailua, but commuted back and forth as summoned from their posts on other islands. Together with the designated successor to Kamehameha in the keeping of the ki'i or image of the War God Kūkā'ilimoku, Kekuaokalani, the son of Kamehameha's deceased younger brother Keli'imaika'i, these men had high military positions and were responsible for advising the king on political matters in the islands, including trade with foreign nations, quelling internal rebellions, and dealing with perceived threats of all kinds.

Kamehameha and the closer advisors depended on advice from 'Olohana, John Young, who lived where George had first visited him, in a compound of European-style buildings on his own ahupua'a in Kawaihae some thirty five miles north of Kailua near the massive Pu'ukoholā Heiau that Kamehameha had ordered built when he was still trying to overcome his rival Keōua Kūahu'ula for control of his home island. This Keōua, whose army had been caught in the violent 1790 eruption of the Kīlauea Volcano, leaving its footprints in the hardened lava, had been killed by one of Kamehameha's chiefs, Ka'ahumanu's father Ke'eaumoku, when he came to Kawaihae for an invited parlay. He was then sacrificed to the war god at the Pu'ukoholā Heiau. John Young had chosen this spiritually powerful area for the residence where he lived with his second wife Kaoanaeha, whom he called "Kuamo'o." She was a niece of Kamehameha's, and their four children were son John, Jr. (Keoni Ana) and three daughters, Fanny (Pane) Kakelaokalani, Grace Kamaikui, and Jane (Gini or Kini) Lahilahi. Young's first wife, Namokuelua, died in 1804 after giving birth to two sons, Robert and James Kanehoa. Robert had been sent away to Boston for education, and James Kanehoa, who called himself "Jim," was planning to follow his brother soon.

John Young had come with George and the others on the *Isabella* to Kailua, he said, to take part in the start of the long Makahiki holiday, which coincided with the lunar cycle beginning a new year after the fall harvest. The Makahiki was an important festival in Hawai'ian life, being dedicated to the God Lono, who was a God of peace and agricultural fertility, and opposed in purpose to the God Kū who controlled the outcome of war. War and conflict were prohibited during the Makahiki and the people engaged in all kinds of merry-making and cultural celebration—sports, music, hula, and feasting. But George sensed that Young had made the trip for another purpose as well…to assess the intentions of George's mission and to evaluate George personally. George thought that he had very likely given a skeptical report to Kamehameha about him and his mission, but that he had approved the audience with Kamehameha because he knew of Kamehameha's esteem for Governor Aleksandr Baranov. After three days, John Young returned to his home in Kawaihae. But whenever Kamehameha needed John Young's advice he sent a detachment of his most powerful outrigger canoists to Kawaihae to fetch "'Olohana," and in a half day John Young would be at his side. Very little happened in the King's affairs of which Young did not know.

One day George was able to have a conversation with Kamehameha's "Prime Minister" and native second-in-command, Ulumaheihei, called "the friend" or "Hoapili," who spoke English passably. Hoapili was the son of a royal twin of the Maui line, an Ali'i of exceptionally strong mana, Kame'eiamoku. George determined that Hoapili was three years older than he was, having been born in 1776 on the Fourth of July by the Americans' reckoning according to their calendar. After he was told the significance of the date, Hoapili sanctioned thereafter fireworks from the United States ships in the harbor on their July 4th as a tribute to his birth. He had several servants around him at all times. One servant, named Mo'o or "Lizard," who also spoke English and claimed to be able to read and write it, was Hoapili's fly swatter and pipe lighter. He followed after Hoapili with a long cord-like slow match, lit in the fire in the morning, and wound around his neck so that it smoldered off a bit of smoke behind his neck. As for the flies, which were not really a bother, George had been told, and was now able to see for himself that many insect pests had not yet been able to reach Hawai'i. There were flies, moths, butterflies, and fleas, but no termites, roaches, scorpions, bees, or even mosquitoes. And there were no snakes.

In mid December of 1815, George met a man called John Marshall, who told George that he was a nephew of the prominent New York fur entrepreneur John Jacob Astor. His mother Mary Marshall, John Jacob Astor's cousin, had emigrated from the Astors' hometown in Germany to New York City, where he had settled after living for some years in England. John Marshall's native language was German, and he surprised George by engaging him in German conversation. This is because he spoke American English, which he had learned while very young, without a trace of German accent. George would never have guessed that he was, in fact, a German compatriot by birth. He related that he had been the second officer on one of Astor's ships, the *Lark*, when it had wrecked off Kahoʻolawe in 1814. He had been rescued and brought to Kailua the previous summer. Since then he had been trying to arrange passage back to the east coast of the United States with another ship, but had been unsuccessful in finding a position on a ship headed directly that way. He had been engaged by Queen Keōpūolani to teach her son, the heir Liholiho, English and other subjects. George liked John Marshall immediately. Marshall did not seem to share the American captains' negative opinions about the Russians. He told George, in fact, that some of these captains' opinions were clearly false and motivated purely by a desire to exclude Russians from trading in Hawaiʻi. As an example, he mentioned Captain Wilson Price Hunt of the *Pedler*, who had visited Kailua earlier that very month. Even though his former Captain and friend, Samuel Northrup, of the wrecked *Lark* had become Captain Hunt's second-in-command aboard the *Pedler*, and even though the *Pedler* had been one of John Jacob Astor's trading vessels, he told George that he was embarrassed to hear of Hunt's calumnies to John Young and to Kamehameha and his native advisors about Governor Baranov, the Russian Tsar, and Russians in general.

"I met Captain Hunt and Captain Northrup too when I was in Novo-Arkhangelsk," George told John Marshall. "I got along well enough with both of them then. They were there in Governor Baranov's protection from the British. But Captain Hunt blatantly violated Governor Baranov's rules by trading guns and powder to the hostile Kolosh. So Governor Baranov seized the *Pedler* and only allowed Captain Hunt to sail it away without trade cargo when he heard that the war between Great Britain and the United States was over. That's the reason why Hunt slanders Governor Baranov and the Russians."

"I'm not surprised," said Marshall. "Hunt is a bad man to cross. He was even urging the chiefs here to have you killed."

"To have me killed?!" said George with surprise.

"Yes, when he found out you were here with a group of Russians and Aleuts on a mission from Governor Baranov, he went straight to Kawaihae to see John Young. He then got his friend Captain Ebbets the Elder of the *Enterprise* to warn Kamehameha and Chief Kalanimoku about your intention to take the islands by force of arms. He and Ebbets both claimed that the Hawaiʻians should simply eliminate you and your group right now, before any more Russians arrive. Only the honorable Englishman, Captain John Jennings, of the schooner *Columbia* told Kamehameha and his chiefs that, in his opinion, your efforts are worthy of support."

"Thank you for telling me this, John," said George. "I'll have to do all I can to convince Kamehameha and all his advisors that we Russians do not intend to take any territory by force of arms. But I will also tell my men to stay always in armed groups while we are here in Kailua."

"I would do the same," replied Marshall.

In the next few weeks George and Antipatr were able to witness many of the Hawai'ians' forms of amusement. They played a board game similar to checkers called "kōnane," at which Kamehameha was said to be a great master. Boys and girls were seen playing with toys called "pala'ie," a loop-ended stick onto which a round rock had been tied with cord. They tried to swing the rock upward and downward so as to make it land in the stick's end loop. George was unable to resist trying to master the pala'ie and to show the Hawai'ian boys and girls the sailor's trick he had learned of flinging a slip knot over the knotted head of a piece of line. The Hawai'ians had a game similar to the Russian "gorodki" in which sticks were thrown at formations of upright stakes in an attempt to knock them down in a certain order. And there was a bowling game called "'ulu maika" in which boys cast stone disks, trying to make them roll between two upright sticks quite a long distance away. One physical contest had young men leaning forward to touch foreheads and then trying to straighten back up without bending their knees or backs. Another called "kula'i wāwae" had seated opponents trying to push each other away, feet-to-feet. Arm-wrestling or "uma" was popular among the men and boys as was "loulou," the pulling of hooked fingers. But most of the Hawai'ians' amusements revolved around the sea. Canoe races were events of importance to the entire community. They loved the sport of "he'e nalu," or surfing on great boards in the waves, and they loved "'au," or swimming. The Hawai'ians were wonderful swimmers, able to stroke rapidly to make progress on the surface or to submerge and stay below the surface for extraordinary lengths of time...and to see things underwater. Once George thought he would demonstrate to some Hawai'ians how he could swim in a stream near the houses where he and the other men were staying. He stripped down to his underclothes to wade out into the water and swim. But the Hawai'ians laughed at him for swimming in a stream that was only as deep as his waist. They couldn't understand why he would want to swim in such a context at all. And they were amused by his pale skin which contrasted so dramatically with his sunburned neck, face, and bald pate.

One day George and Antipatr hiked north of the royal compound along the shore to watch some Hawai'ian men rope a shark from an outrigger canoe. At this place there was a deep cut in the shore between giant plates of rock, which extended quite far out into the sea. The cut provided a narrow avenue for sharks to swim to large chunks of fish bait the men had suspended from a pole. When a small shark went for the bait, the men pulled the bait up out of the water. But when a suitably large shark swam down the cut toward the bait, the men suddenly pulled tight around the shark a loop of strong rope that had been arranged beforehand surrounding the shark's avenue of swim. The shark then panicked and swam wildly forward further down the narrow cut, pulling the trailing canoe at increasing velocity until either the rope broke, the canoe swamped, or the men let the rope go, exhausted by the thrill of the ride and their raucous laughter. George and Antipatr watched this happen from shore three times in one afternoon. Other men there watching told them that sharks could be caught to pull boats in the open sea by a similar method, and that after the shark was exhausted the men would paddle and pull the shark backward through the water, drowning it.

One of the first problems George faced after the *Isabella* left for Canton in late November, taking the disgruntled Captain James Bennett with it as a passenger, was that of the many Hawai'ian women and girls who turned up at the guest residences seeking sexual relations with the men. Some were after some kind of recompense, asking for coins, beads, or cloth from the men. But many were merely curious or were just expressing themselves in friendly fashion as the royal guests' sexual hostesses. When they came around, they left no doubt about what they wanted to do. They would simply approach a target male…they seemed to prefer the Russians to the Aleuts, the young to the old…and try to rub their bare bodies on his, signaling their offers with graphic gestures of their hips, hands, and fingers. Scenes on the mats of the sleeping quarters even in the middle of the day became so embarrassing for George and for some of the others that he had to call a meeting to address the problem.

"Men," he addressed them, "We've got to do something about all this fornication."

A young Russian named Stepan Likhachev, who had been one of the most active and even exhibitionistic fornicators, loudly asked, "Why?"

George had an answer for him. "Because you'll never get anything done if you spend all day every day mounting these wahines, that's why."

But Likhachev was not done. "Just what else is it that we should be doing? So far we're just waiting around for you to make some deal with the King. We've been here more than a month now. Without the women, I'd be bored to death. Also, the food isn't entirely to my liking. The fish is good, as is the pork and even the dog, but the poi tastes like shit."

Most of the men, even including Antipatr, laughed in agreement.

"Well, you're being served the food like wealthy gentlemen," reminded George. "You don't have to catch the fish or pound the taro root or anything else. You are guests here. And I don't want to anger our hosts in any way. It's important for the success of our mission."

Then Stepan Nikiforov, a middle-aged military veteran, spoke up. "But the Hawai'ian men are not angry at us for fornicating with their wives and daughters. Many of the women were sent to us by their fathers and husbands. Some of the fathers and husbands have even come to watch. Indeed they seem to want the creation of babies from us. We will most likely be long gone before any pregnancies could come to birth, and the children here all seem to be everyone's responsibility in any case."

"Pravil'no, pravil'no, pravil'no…right, right, right!" said most of the men, coming to Nikiforov's support.

George could see that he was making no headway in his effort to persuade the men that some restrictions would have to be adopted. "Men," he said,

"There is another important reason why you should cease this fornication. It's a medical reason. These women may have contracted venereal diseases from all the other sailors that have visited these shores. Indeed I have seen sores indicative of this on many of them, and on their fathers and husbands too. I don't want to see any of you get such disease. Not only that, but, heaven forbid, any of you who already have such disease from elsewhere…and I suspect there may be some…will be spreading it to the women here…and the fathers and husbands may well get very angry about that. Even if none of us are the carriers of disease, we will likely be blamed for any disease that does occur. It's always easiest to blame the outsider. It would be far better for us to comport ourselves in an exemplary, chaste way. Then we would stay out of numerous possible troubles."

Stepan Likhachev decided to make the resistance personal. "Your real problem, Dr. Sheffer, is that, being old, grey-bearded and bald, none of the women here want to have sex with you. So you, not being offered any yourself, want to deprive us of it."

The men were quiet. George, disgruntled about being termed "old" at thirty-seven years of age and being described as sexually unattractive because of his grey beard and bald head, did not directly answer Likhachev's personal charge, but, exasperated and embarrassed, he decided that some compromise was in order. "I am going to propose that each man limit himself to one partner. Every man will have to choose one and stay with that one. Then, we will keep one of the houses vacant, dedicated to the purposes of fornication if fornication must take place. That way those of us who aren't involved in fornication won't have to endure the thrashing and the grunting of those who are. Are you agreed?"

The men were still quiet. At last Likhachev spoke up to ask, "How about one per week?" The others seemed to agree with him.

"All right, one per week," said George. "But in a separate place. Are you agreed?"

"Soglasno…agreed!" said the men.

"All right, we'll start this tomorrow then," said George. "You men in the small house will have to move into the larger ones with us. The small house is now the fornication place. And if anybody comes up with any sores or rashes, come see me immediately."

In Hawai'ian society it was kapu for men and women to eat together. The Hawai'ians had separate dining areas for each gender. And there were many food items that women were not allowed to eat…pork, bananas, and coconuts, for example. A recent addition to the diet of both sexes, however, was beef. For many years, cattle, the descendents of the five cattle, two with calf, which had been brought to Kealakekua Bay on Hawai'i by Captain George Vancouver from Monterey, California during his second voyage in February, 1793, had been protected from slaughter by Kamehameha's kapu. But their population had grown large and become troublesome so that Kamehameha had removed the kapu of cattle protection and even engaged a young sailor from Newton, Massachusetts, named John Palmer Parker to hunt them in the Waimea forests with the intention of eating and salting their beef and trading their hides. Sheep, having been brought to Kaua'i by Captain James Colnett on the *Argonaut* in 1791 and to Kawaihae on Hawai'i by Captain Vancouver during his 1793 voyage, were now becoming plentiful enough on all the inhabited islands to supply mutton and wool.

Horses had been brought to the islands first at Maui in 1803 by Captain William Shaler and his partner R. J. Cleveland on the *Lelia Byrd*. The horses or "lio," termed "long-eared dogs" at first by the natives, caused much initial excitement. Great crowds of natives would gather to watch Europeans give riding exhibitions, "kau lio." And, in only a little over a decade, there were small populations of horses on Kaua'i, O'ahu, and Hawai'i as well. Kamehameha, when on O'ahu, had foreigners break horses there for riding and then fearlessly rode the horses in the Waikīkī surf for enjoyment and relaxation, soon impressing his retinue and the foreigners as well with his riding skill. But the horses at this time were not commonly used in draft, nor were they eaten.

One day in January of 1816 strong winds aloft swept the almost perpetual mantle of clouds away from the towering summit of Mauna Kea far above the Kailua village and revealed it to be covered, as was the almost equally high Mauna Loa to the south of it, with a gleaming shroud of snow. The previous November, soon after the group's arrival at Kailua, George had gotten the urge to make an exploratory hike up Mauna Kea, but had soon become discouraged trying to make his way through thorny brush on the south flanks of Hualālai Volcano which was between him and the main rise of Mauna Kea. But now George resolved again to climb Mauna Kea, at least to the snow line, in order to survey the rest of the island from its upper reaches. He could see that the volcanic activity at Kīlauea to the far southeast, causing clouds of ash to boil up into the heavens, was happening on the other side of Mauna Loa from him, and he realized that he might well view more of this volcanic activity from high up on Mauna Kea's south flank. He wrote a letter in English to Kamehameha reminding the King of his existence and his mutually beneficial purposes and requesting permission to make an exploratory excursion to Mauna Kea. But after several days, he had received no response.

George also wanted to visit Kealakekua Bay on the coast to the south. This was where Captain James Cook had been killed in February of 1779 after being regarded as the God Lono by the locals who first encountered him and his ship, *Resolution*. So, through Palapala, he requested that Queen Ka'ahumanu, whose hand warts his medicament had successfully removed and whose recent fever his yew-bark powder had eased, give him and Antipatr and John Marshall, who wanted to come along and hunt, a native guide to hike with them and show them the way…both to Kealakekua Bay and up to the summit of Mauna Kea. He felt that his and Antipatr's skill in Hawai'ian was now sufficient to interact with the guide without Palapala's help. She did not appear to be physically able to hike and climb to such heights with them. Ka'ahumanu immediately assented to this request.

1775 portrait of Captain James Cook (7 November, 1728-14 February, 1779) by Nathaniel Dance-Holland (1735-1811) from: http://en.wikipedia.org/wiki/James_Cook.

The guide, a very well-formed young man called "Pahu," meaning "the drum," with a dark pattern tattooed over most of his right leg signifying his status as a royal bodyguard, was able to carry a large rope-net bag of supplies as he led George, John Marshall, and Antipatr on the well-worn path southward to Kealekekua Bay. It was a bit difficult for George and his companions to stay with Pahu's pace of walking, so forcefully did he stride a few steps ahead of them, only rarely turning around to check to see if they were still with him. But they persisted and in less than four hours they were walking on the high steep bluff above Kealekekua Bay. It was a particularly beautiful bay, and George could see a population of porpoises below, cavorting in graceful leaps above the deep blue water. Pahu explained that they would be circling back inland to get to the actual shore. The cliffs below them were filled with hidden caves in the rock where the bones of dead Ali'i were interred and it was kapu to climb directly down to the water. In another hour, George and the others were shown the exact spot on the shore where Captain Cook had been killed. It was directly across the bay from the Hikiau Heiau where he had previously been venerated as the God Lono. Angered over the theft of one of the *Resolution*'s cutters, Cook had intended to take the Hawai'ian King Kalani'ōpu'u hostage for its return. But violence had broken out and he was stabbed and killed in the ensuing fight. Not all of his body had been returned to his second-in-command, Charles Clerke, who had commenced cannon fire on the Ka'awaloa settlement until the Hawai'ian chief gave up the remains. Captain Cook's body had already been

Unfinished 1795 painting by Johann Zoffany (1733-1818) of "The Death of Captain James Cook, 14 February, 1779" at Kealakekua Bay on the big island of Hawai'i's west coast. From: http://en.wikipedia.org/wiki/James_Cook.

dismembered and parts of him distributed to several chiefs for ritual consumption. Kamehameha, who was reported to have been active in the fight and wounded in the resultant bombardment, was then rumored to have claimed some of Captain Cook's hair for his war banner. What was subsequently returned, in a grisly parcel, was given into the waters of Kealekekua Bay from an on-ship ceremony on February 21, 1779. George was reminded that this was close to his own birthdate, almost 37 years before. Since that date, his own short lifetime ago, hundreds of other Europeans had sailed on the long routes first traveled by Cook to Hawai'i and caused great changes to transpire in the Hawai'ian peoples' lives. And now here he was among them, standing also in the final footsteps of Captain Cook.

That evening, after leading his charges through the village of Ka'awaloa to pay respect to Chiefess Kapi'olani and her husband Naihe, Pahu set up a camp in a forest clearing by lighting a fire of twigs and dead branches from small coals he carried in a shell container in his supply bag. He gathered grasses and made cushions for them under the woven mats he spread out where they were to sleep. The four men ate a meal of dried fish and poi, washed down with swallows of water from gourd containers. The sky was clear and the moon was merely a "muku" sliver as darkness enveloped them. The stars gleamed and twinkled above them in amazing abundance and brightness. It was profoundly quiet. From where they were camped they could no longer hear the surf. No yellow 'ō'ō or mamo birds, nor red 'i'iwi birds called, and there were no frogs or toads. Pahu took out of his bag a hollow yellow gourd with some holes drilled into it and began to breathe into one of the holes through his left nostril. He called this nose flute a "hōkiokio" and it sounded like an ocarina…with an eerie low-resonance whistle which Pahu modulated by contorting his face as he blew air into it through his nose. The melody he then performed was surprisingly pleasing to George, who had never heard anything like it. Later, as they were preparing to retire for the night, George complimented Pahu on the concert he had given them.

By noon the next day, the men were climbing Mauna Kea and had reached the end of the worn path. From here upward they would be making their own trail. Turning to look back toward the shore to the west provided them with a most impressive panorama. They could see almost the entire western shoreline of the island. They had traversed the slope's forested section already and were passing through a zone of low and hostile vegetation, which caused barefoot Pahu to stop now and then to remove thorns from his feet. At last he removed some kama'a sandals made of woven strips of hau bark from his net bag and put them onto his feet George and John Marshall, who carried an unwieldy musket loaded with shot, were breathing more and more heavily until they began to sweat profusely even though the temperature had become quite cool, even chilly. Young Antipatr fared a bit better with the effort of the climb. They stopped at last to eat a few bites of fish and poi. Pahu told them that they would find a stream of water ahead, melted from the snows at the top of the mountain. George noticed that he had a headache and felt a bit giddy. He asked Antipatr if he felt the same, and Antipatr answered that he did. "The air is thinner up this high," George told him. "Mountaineers in Switzerland report that it's difficult even to breathe at all on top of the mountains there. I would think that we are now three or four thousand meters above the sea."

By late afternoon they reached the snowline. It was cold and George worried about Pahu who did not have any protective clothing, but just his malo and a kapa drape for his shoulders. But the lower fringes of the snow were soft enough that George could make a snowball and throw it down the mountain. Antipatr, John Marshall and Pahu did the same thing. George noticed that Pahu could throw a snowball much further than either he or John or Antipatr.

"Are we going to spend the night up here, or start down?" he asked Pahu in Hawai'ian.

"There is a cave near here," said Pahu. "We will find it and stay the night in it. We have fire and will stay warm. In the morning we can start to descend."

The cave was a mere slot between boulders covered by a flat outcropping of rocks. The fire was welcome and warming, but, even though the climb had been very strenuous and the men were very tired, none of them could sleep. Pahu played again on his nose flute and something in the melody of it reminded George of Ludwig van Beethoven's "Für Elise." He remembered his wife Barbara being excited about this musical piece of Beethoven's. She had obtained the music for it and played it many times on the pianos they had in Moscow and in St. Petersburg. George began to whistle the tune, warbling smoothly through the first strains of it, and immediately he noticed that both Pahu and Antipatr were surprised to hear him whistle a melody. Antipatr said, "Egor Nikolaevich, I have heard you sing. But I did not know you could whistle so beautifully."

"I can make a sailor's whistle," said John, putting two of his fingers to his mouth and blasting out a loud harsh whistle. "But I can't whistle any songs."

"I've always been a whistler," said George. "My father taught me to whistle when I was a small boy and I became very good at it. I can whistle either through my lips or through my teeth. Often I whistle almost quietly to myself when I'm doing other things. I find it's a nice way to keep music in my life. It's like having an instrument you don't have to carry. Of course, it's not like the piano that my wife and your sister Irina play. It has the limitation that you can't simultaneously whistle and sing."

But Pahu was even more impressed than Antipatr. He told George and the others that he had never heard such whistling before. Some Hawai'ians of his acquaintance could make a whistling sound to imitate birds. But no one whistled melodies like he had just heard George whistle. He was amazed and wanted George to whistle more. So George did whistle more, and they talked all night.

In English so Pahu could not understand, John Marshall expressed his opinions of the Hawai'an culture. "It's the location and the land that really determine the culture," he opined. "One might point out that the Hawai'ians are primitive because they have no objects made of metal. But here on these volcanic islands there is no ore to smelt. One might notice that their only beasts of burden are the human commoners and they have not the wheel. But, with no draft animals, why would they need to invent the wheel? They have no writing system to record things. But they remember everything in chants. They have no written calendar, but they know the seasons from the stars, and they can navigate at sea by the stars as well. Their architecture is a bit primitive…all pili grass shacks and the occasional pile of lava rocks to make a heiau. But then, the weather is usually such that no other architecture is needed. When hurricanes do come, they simply rebuild…and they can do it in a hurry. The island continually threatens them with destruction by flow of lava and periodic tidal waves…but it nurtures them with its soil's astounding fertility and surrounding sea creatures in such abundance that catching them is not difficult. Indeed life here for everyone would be like that in those fabled Elysian Fields if it were not for the constant warfare and oppression of the population by these Ali'i and their taxes and their kapus and..."

"But the population believes that it is the Ali'i's spiritual mana which protects them from the lava, the hurricanes, and the tidal waves," George interrupted. "That's why they give their lives in support of these Ali'i. They believe they are protecting themselves and their families."

"Ay, but just see what they have to put up with," observed Marshall.

"I can certainly agree with that," replied George. "Even Ivan the Terrible did not inflict such terror on his subjects as Kamehameha does. I wonder if it is the same on Kaua'i where Kaumuali'i is king."

"I hear it's not so oppressive there," answered Marshall. "People have been known to flee there from O'ahu even though the channel makes the voyage a peril to them."

George was curious to know more about John Marshall's uncle, John Jacob Astor, the New York fur baron. Changing his speech to German, he asked Marshall, "Is your uncle, John Jacob Astor, really from Heidelberg in Germany?"

"He was born in the village of Walldorf in Baden Baden. It is actually south of Heidelberg between Pforzheim and Strasbourg. He still speaks English with a German accent, even though he has lived in New York City for years," answered Marshall.

"You now know that I am also from Germany," said George. "I was born in Münnerstadt in Franconia. But I speak English, I'm afraid, with a Russian accent. I lived for several years in Russia and learned my English largely from people who also speak Russian."

"You are right, George," responded Marshall. "I wouldn't have guessed right away from your English that you are also from Germany."

"I've read that your uncle is the richest man in America, John," said George. "How did he manage to accumulate such wealth?"

"He worked hard for years trading American furs for European musical instruments, earning constant profits on both," said John Marshall. "He and his wife Sarah organized firms and partnerships with family members and others. He's a partner in several businesses. He's on the board of banks. And he uses his savings to buy land in New York City. Many people there rent their homes and their places of business from him, and he is an exacting landlord."

"What kind of a man is he, then?" asked George.

"He's a frugal and very careful man," answered Marshall. "He never forgets anything. He doesn't seem friendly, but he strongly values his relationships with other powerful men—business leaders and politicians—and they wind up in his debt somehow and become his helpers. President Thomas Jefferson, Cabinet member Albert Gallatin, and Governor George Clinton and his nephew, the politician Dewitt Clinton, all helped him gain advantages over his competitors."

"I understand this," said George. "I also have managed to benefit from my contacts with powerful men. In Russia I was quite successful in gaining their confidence. I joined the freemasons there, in fact, in order to socialize with the powerful…to engage in common positive efforts with them."

"Uncle John Jacob is also a mason," commented John Marshall. "He's even been the Master of the Holland 8 Lodge in New York City. Many of his lodge brothers have become business associates of his or political supporters. He's managed to induct so many émigré acquaintances of his into the lodge that they sometimes conduct their rituals in German. And, even though he is a mason, he's active in the German Reformed Church. The congregation has even had services in his house."

"What lead him to get into the fur business?" asked George.

"I don't really know," answered Marshall. "But it doesn't really matter. I don't think he has any particular love of fur. I doubt if he's ever skinned an animal. It's being successful in business, finding profit in an enterprise, that matters to him. He's involved in all kinds of business ventures, and he isn't afraid to try daring new things. When I left him he was planning to purchase great quantities of opium in Turkey and ship it to Canton. The Chinese have outlawed opium because so many of their people are rendered unproductive by it, but the British and others keep shipping it in there anyway. I have no doubt he'll make a fortune in the opium business just like he has in the fur business and in real estate. He's just destined to be wealthy, and that's all there is to it."

"Mein Gott," exclaimed George, "Do you know that I also once founded an enterprise to buy opium poppies in Turkey and ship them to Russia to produce laudanum for the army?"

"That's interesting. So you're both Germans, both masons, and both opium dealers," observed Marshall in a jocular tone. "Are you also wealthy?"

"Indeed I am wealthy," replied George. "At least many would consider me so. In addition to the laudanum income, I have stock in the Russian-American Company, and my wife and daughter live in a stone mansion on Nevsky Prospekt in St. Petersburg. But there are many wealthier men in the world, and I have no doubt that John Jacob Astor is one of them."

"But he isn't a doctor, and he can't whistle Beethoven," joked John Marshall.

Antipatr asked George in Russian what he and Marshall were talking about. When George told him that they had been discussing John Jacob Astor, Antipatr mentioned that his father had always been very interested in Astor's ventures, particularly his attempt to found a fur-trading settlement called Astoria near the mouth of the Columbia River. This was part, he said, of a greater plan to connect by fur trade the American coast with China through the Hawai'ian islands.

George asked John Marshall if he knew anything about the effort to found Astoria.

"What really scuttled the effort at Astoria," related John Marshall, changing now to English in the hope that Antipatr might understand some of what he said, "was the war between the U.S. and Great Britain. But even before that there were difficulties."

"What kind of difficulties?" asked George.

"The same kind of difficulties that we have here in the islands," answered Marshall. "The difficulties are largely those of our captains dealing unscrupulously and even cruelly with the native populations. Each captain finds that the natives act in accordance with the way they were treated by the last captain…and that wasn't good. So the natives become harder and harder to deal with. They even become dangerous."

Marshall stretched and leaned his body back away from the fire, resting his head against a boulder. Then he continued to relate: "I had a friend named John Anderson. He was the Boatswain on Uncle John Jacob's ship *Tonquin*, which was sent out from New York under Captain Jonathan Thorn to aid in the settlement of Astoria at the mouth of the Columbia River. He found Captain Thorn to be an intolerable bastard and jumped ship here on Hawai'i in February of 1811. Others have said that he was beaten unconscious by the Captain and thrown overboard to be rescued by Hawai'ians. Either way, it turned out to be a lucky thing for him. Captain Thorn and all of his crew who had stayed with the ship after its stay at Astoria were later killed by savages the Captain had cheated and angered south of Nootka Island on the American coast. The *Tonquin*'s store of gunpowder was exploded by fuse as the last measure of the desperate escaping gunner, Stephen Weeks, blowing up the entire ship and two hundred savages with it."

"My word," exclaimed George. "I hadn't heard of that. When did it happen?"

"Sometime later in 1811, I think," answered Marshall. "It might have been 1812. My friend and I didn't hear about it until two years after that. Some savage chief named Lamazee who was aboard and was taken as a slave before the explosion, lived to tell the tale to Captain Hunt and others. My friend John Anderson later joined Hunt's crew. He might have been aboard when the *Pedler* was at Novo-Arkhangelsk."

"If he was there I did not meet him," said George. "But what happened to gunner Weeks?" asked George.

"He was seen with the ship's clerk, James Lewis, and a couple others getting away from the ship in a boat before the explosion," replied Marshall, "but after that, no one knows. Neither he nor anyone else has been heard from since."

Antipatr Baranov had been listening to John Marshall as he spoke to George, but his English was not good enough to enable him to understand everything the man had said. George related to Antipatr in Russian that their companion John Marshall had told a story about the killing by savages of the Captain and crew of the Pacific Fur Company's ship *Tonquin* and the destruction by explosion of the ship.

Antipatr was struck by the story, observing in Russian to George, "That's why my father treats the natives well. They are not fools and they can certainly be dangerous to those who mistreat them."

By morning, George's headache had become worse and he was eager to descend. The men walked around the slope of the upper reaches of Mauna Kea far enough to see the eastern shore and the turbulent caldera of Kīlauea Volcano to the south. The scene was a powerful one, the tremendous ash cloud soaring up above them and obscuring the background of blue sky and azure sea. Below them also was the mantle of clouds, which almost always blanketed the slopes below the snowline. They would be descending back through these clouds on their way down.

"Have you ever heard of any other 'haoles' climbing this mountain?" George asked Pahu.

"'A'ole...No," was Pahu's reply.

"Then, Antipatr, my young friend," declared George. "We are the first non-Hawai'ians on the top of Mauna Kea."

"We haven't really gotten completely to the top," said Antipatr.

"We have gotten close enough, Antipatr," said George. "And no other haole has ever been up this far. We should be proud of ourselves. I hope you will boast of it some day to your father. Surely this mountain is higher than Mount Edgecumbe in Sitka where you have lived. Do you know of anyone who has climbed to the top of Mount Edgecumbe?"

"No," answered Antipatr.

"Well you could look down on the top of it from here if it were closer to us," said George. "Of that you can be sure."

When they arrived back in Kailua two days later, they found that the village was mourning a prominent Ali'i, the aged Chief Kamanawa, who had died while visiting Kailua from his northern district. The relatives and friends of the man had struck their faces onto rocks to break out teeth as a sign of their great sadness. On a low block of lava rock near the center of the royal compound, the dead Ali'i's body was prepared for its eternal interment. The kahunas and their assistants carved the flesh from his bones with shell knives. The flesh would be taken out in canoes and given to the sea. Then they boiled the remaining skull and bones and wrapped them into a parcel called a "ka'ai." The deceased man's closest friends in life took this parcel to the cliffs above Kealakekua Bay, where George and Antipatr had recently been. There they had two "maka'āinana" or commoners lowered by rope, carrying the parcel, in order to deposit it into one of the rock caves there. These commoners were then seized and taken back to the royal compound where they were sacrificed by strangulation. Only the Kealakekua Bay birds knew where the bones of Chief Kamanawa were interred, and the souls of the strangled assistants were commissioned in the sacrifice ceremony to guard the Chief's mana, preserving its influence for his posterity.

George was at last invited to speak with Kamehameha starting in December of 1815, and he had several sessions with him on the mats outside his residence throughout the next three months. Once they went on a walk together. George had worked hard to learn the Hawai'ian language, thinking that it was even more difficult than the Hungarian he had learned in Debrecen eight or nine years before. But, speaking with Palapala and others in Hawai'ian several hours per day, and writing down lists of Hawai'ian words and phrases in English and Russian letters, then memorizing them every evening by the light of kukui nut torches, George was soon able to express his thoughts in such Hawai'ian as the natives could understand. And, as George's facility in Hawai'ian improved, he gained a positive assessment of Kamehameha's intelligence and his awareness of his place in the history and politics of his people. In one session, shortly after George's expedition to climb Mauna Kea, Kamehameha told of his long relationship with the recently deceased Chief Kamanawa and George was able to understand it well, as Kamehameha spoke slowly and deliberately, repeating himself at times. The story also demonstrated to George how Kamehameha had understood, even as a young Chief, the vital importance of taking western advisors and adopting some of the foreign ways.

"Chief Kamanawa was one of a number of half-brothers of King Kahekili of Maui," Kamehameha related. "He and his twin brother Kame'eiamoku, my friend Hoapili's father, were the ones who hid Kahekili's bones after his death. But later I made both of these twin brothers Chiefs of my northern districts here on Hawai'i. It was Kame'eiamoku who captured for us our first foreign sailing ship, the *Fair American,* which is out in the bay even now."

"How did that come about?" asked George.

"A very harsh American captain named Simon Metcalfe had come to the islands to trade in his ship, *Eleanora,* when Kahekili was still king of Maui and I had control only of part of this island. Simon Metcalfe's son, Thomas Humphrey Metcalfe, who was the age my son Liholiho is now…and the age, nineteen of your years, of Governor Baranov's son Antipatr who is with you, accompanied his father as commander of a much smaller vessel, the *Fair American*, which had a crew of only six men. The two ships became separated in a storm between Japan and here, but they had agreed, in case of separation, to meet at Kealakekua Bay on our island. At Olawalu Bay on Maui, where the *Eleanora* anchored on its way here, Captain Metcalfe became angry with Kahekili's subjects for stealing a boat and killing one of his crewmen. He then lured a large party of the Olawalu villagers alongside his ship and fired his cannons loaded with shot and scrap upon them by surprise, killing more than a hundred of them and wounding many more. The water in Olawalu Bay was turned red with blood."

George expressed his horror at hearing of this massacre for the first time. "Bozhe moi...My God!" he exclaimed, crossing himself. "A hundred dead? It reminds me of another story I heard recently about the fate of the ship *Tonquin*, on which two hundred natives were blown up after they killed the Captain and most of his crew. That Captain too had insulted them in some way. Did Captain Metcalfe get his boat returned?"

"'A'ole...no, he did not," answered Kamehameha, "And King Kahekili's Chief who had ordered the boat stolen was not among those who were killed. But Captain Metcalfe then sailed from Maui to our island of Hawai'i, thinking to meet with his son's ship. Off the northern village of Kaupulehu he took aboard my Chief Kame'eiamoku and a party of villagers to trade. But he became angry with Kame'eiamoku for some reason and struck him with the end of a rope in front of his retinue. Kame'eiamoku left the ship *Eleanora* sorely insulted and swore he would revenge himself on the next ship he saw. That ship was Thomas Metcalfe's *Fair American*. The son had sailed north from Kealekekua Bay looking for his father, but had not seen him. Kame'eiamoku's warriors came aboard the little ship pretending to be interested in trade, but they attacked young Metcalfe and his crew, killing all but one, the first mate Isaac Davis, whom they took captive. Very soon after that, Simon Metcalfe's *Eleanora* came into Kealakekua Bay where his son had only recently been, hoping to find there the *Fair American*. I had already been told that Kame'eiamoku had captured the son's vessel and killed the son. I was afraid of what Captain Simon Metcalfe would do if he or any of his men heard about it. I declared the *Eleanora* kapu and would not allow any trade or contact with it. But Captain Metcalfe's able boatswain was John Young, the man we now call 'Olohana,' and he had already rowed ashore. So I took him and kept him prisoner until Metcalfe was at last convinced he would not be returning to the ship and departed without him."

"So father and son never saw each other again, even though they were in the same place only days apart," commented George. "In some way, even though Captain Metcalfe was a bad man, that is a sad thing."

"I also think that, Kepa," said Kamehameha, using George's Hawai'ian name. "But I then took John Young north with me to claim the *Fair American* and its captive mate, Isaac Davis, from my Chief Kame'eiamoku, whom I chastised severely even though I was grateful for the results of his actions. These men, John Young and Isaac Davis, in time became the closest of friends. Once they planned to escape my care together, but I found out about it and persuaded them to stay. They became my closest of advisors. They taught us many things. And they fought bravely with us in our most important battles. At the Battle of the Red-mouthed Gun off Maui they fired the little cannon called 'lopaka' from the deck of the *Fair American*, which became a kind of warship for us. The enemy had a foreign advisor too...an experienced cannonier named Mare Amara...but our men fought more bravely under their direction. Before the Battle of Kapaniwai on Maui, I had them both, Olohana and Aikake, as we came to call them, carried to the fore on warriors' backs so they could direct the cannon and musket fire. And they fought well in the battles on O'ahu also. In time they both took Hawai'ian wives and had children, and I treated them as important chiefs, granting them land."

"Where is Isaac Davis now?" asked George.

"He and Kamanawa are in the same place," answered Kamehameha with sadness in his eyes. "It is said that some of my chiefs poisoned Aikake for warning Kaua'i's King Kaumuali'i in O'ahu about their plan to poison him. I do not know if that is true. I did not order the poisoning of Kaumuali'i and would not have assented to such a plan. But Aikake got very sick and died soon after that, having helped me for twenty of your years. Now Olohana is taking care of his wife and three children."

On another occasion, Kamehameha told George of some stories told among his people of other foreign men who had come to the islands on sailing ships long before Captain Cook. He now understood that these men might have been Spaniards, voyaging between Mexico and Manila in the Philippines. They left behind some objects made of "hao hemaiti" or iron, which the islanders preserved and venerated. They probably left behind also the disease of syphilis, which Captain Cook observed traces of among diverse populations of the islands within too short a time for it to have been propagated by his own sailors. It was even said that some of these long previous foreign men, having been shipwrecked on Hawai'i, were progenitors of some of the island's Ali'i who had recorded their Hawai'ian names into their genealogical chants.

Kamehameha was curious about George's knowledge as a physician and about what progress was being made against disease. George mentioned the progess being made against the terrible scourge of smallpox by Edward Jenner's process of injecting cowpox effluvium into the skin as a preventative measure. To his surprise, Kamehameha had heard of this already.

"I have a son by Peleuli named Keōua'opio after my father," explained Kamehameha. "In your year of 1801, when he was the age of Governor Baranov's son Antipatr, he decided to leave here on American Captain Amasa Delano's ship *Perseverance* which was visiting then in Kealakekua Bay. He wanted to learn to be a sailor of the foreign kind, and to be educated in the English language. He had already begun to call himself, as is our custom, 'Alexander Stewart' after the master of the British trader *Jackal* who had impressed him ten years before. Captain Delano assured me that he would treat Keōua'opio as if he were his own son. And so, my son, and several other young kanakas as well, left here on the *Perseverance*."

"Have any of them returned here?" asked George.

"No, none have returned," answered Kamehameha. "And that is why others of my sons who have also wanted to go on the foreign ships have not been allowed to go. But only last year 'Olohana read to me a letter he received from

Captain Delano in Boston. Captain Delano wrote that, fearing smallpox in Canton, China, he had had his ship's surgeon protect my son and his companions from it by scraping what he called 'kinepox serum' into their arms. Later, he wrote, my son decided to transfer himself to a British ship of the East India Company. And so, instead of going to the United States to be educated, he wound up in London. Captain Delano wrote that he was entertained there as my son by the British Ali'i."

Captain Amasa Delano (1763-1823) of the *Perseverance* (Duxbury, Massachusetts), from: http://drewarchives.org/2010/03/31/amasa-delano-and-benito-cereno.

"So this absent son of yours may well be the first Hawai'ian inoculated against smallpox," said George, marveling at the thought. "I certainly hope he stays well in England, and that he is able to return here some day."

"I also hope this, Kepa," said Kamehameha.

Some members of his bodyguards who knew Pahu had told Kamehameha about George's ability to whistle and at one meeting he requested a whistling concert from George, who complied with Beethoven's "Für Elise" again and two other tunes he could remember. Kamehameha told George that he had been given a great gift by the Gods. George tried to explain that the gift of the Gods had been not to him, the whistler of the tune, but to Beethoven, the composer of the tune, but Kamehameha only smiled at this explanation, seeming not to understand it. George showed Kamehameha how he could whistle both through his lips and through his teeth. George's whistling through his teeth led Kamehameha to show George that his own eyeteeth were missing. He had knocked one out as a sign of sorrow over the death in a training accident of his revered battle tutor Kekuhaupi'o and the other as a sign of respect for deceased Kalola, the wife of former King Kalani'ōpu'u, who died on Moloka'i while Kamehameha was there asking for her sanction in the taking of several high-ranking wives, including Keōpūolani.

Kamehameha also wanted to know George's opinion of Napoleon Bonaparte, the French ruler about whom he had heard so Much.

"Foreigners say that I am like him, Kepa," said Kamehameha. "They say this because of my desire to rule all of the islands. They say that I am 'Napoleon of the Pacific'. What do you think?"

George could understand the comparison, but, flattering Kamehameha, he said, "You want to be a father to everyone in your family. The people in these islands are all your family. You have no wish to be the father of the people of Japan, or of China, or of the United States, Great Britain, Austria, Prussia, or Russia. These people are not of your family. But Napoleon wants to be everyone's father. He wants to rule people in other families also. If he is not stopped, he will even come here and try to rule your family. The Russians know this. The English know it. And even the Americans know it."

"Will he be stopped?" asked Kamehameha, appearing quite worried at what George had said. "I have heard that he is a most powerful leader and that he has great armies and navies at his command."

"He does have great armies," answered George. "In many of the battles under his command he has had more men killed than there are people on this entire island of Hawai'i. But I believe he will be stopped. The Russian Tsar Aleksandr and his generals forced him out of our country and captured his capital city of Paris. The European allies sent him to a small island, hoping to put an end to his campaigns against them. But now he has come back to France, raised a new army, and is again threatening to force his rule upon these other countries. I think that the alliance of Russia, Great Britain, and Prussia, however, will be too much for him now and he will fail in his efforts. Then you won't have to worry about becoming a possession of the French."

"I don't want these islands to be anyone's possession but mine," said Kamehameha resolutely. "I was born to rule them. I have fought all my life to rule them. And now I do rule them and no one is going to take them away from me."

"You are correct, Great King," said George. "Surely, not even Napoleon can take these islands from you."

Kamehameha then asked, "What kind of a man is Napoleon? Does he look like me? Does he do things for the same reasons I do them?"

"I have not met nor seen the Emperor Napoleon, Great King," said George. "But, from descriptions I have heard and read, he is an 'ōpae'…a shrimp of a man, whereas you are 'palaoa'… a sperm whale. He does not look at all like you. He is, however, said to be very brave. Like you, he thinks that he was born to rule…and, because of that, he does rule."

"I understand this," said Kamehameha. "Once I considered naming one of my daughters 'Napoleoni,' but now, after speaking with you, I am happy that I did not."

George also had several opportunities to speak with Queen Ka'ahumanu. For her too he whistled "Für Elise." And on one occasion she had been drinking haole liquor together with Palapala and had become quite loquacious.

"I think some of the ancient kapus should be forgotten," Ka'ahumanu told George and Palapala. "We women should be able to eat pork or bananas or whatever we want. And we should be able to eat with the men whenever we want. The eating kapus are simply relics of past days. Haole women eat what they want, and they eat with their men…and nothing unfortunate happens to either them or their men as a result. We could do the same and no harm would come to us. I must confess that I once ate together with a haole man, a Lieutenant Thomas Manby who was here with Captain Vancouver and showed to me his tattoos, and nothing happened to me."

"The men would be upset if you came into their eating hall and sat down to eat with them," protested Palapala. "They are not ready for such a change."

"Kepa," asked Ka'ahumanu, turning to George. "Does your wife eat together with you and with other men?"

"Yes, she does," answered George. "But we live in a place that is not subject to your nobles' mana. It is the mana, as I understand it, that requires the kapus."

"But my own mana is very strong," said Ka'ahumanu. "My father was the great Chief Ke'eaumoku, younger brother of the royal twins Kame'eiamoku and Kamanawa. It was he, my father, who slew Kalani'ōpu'u's sons and named successors for Kamehameha. He slew Kiwala'ō in a desperate battle at Ke'ei in which he was almost killed himself, and then he slew Keōua Kūahu'ula whom Kamehameha sacrificed at Pu'ukohalā. Very few have stronger mana than I do. And Queen Keōpuōlani has very strong mana also. She is the granddaughter of the great Maui King Kekaulike, Kahekili's father, and the daughter of Kiwala'ō, whom my father killed. And both she and I agree that the eating kapu should be forgotten. Whose mana could overcome ours if we were to eat with the men?"

George thought that he should change the topic back to family matters. So he asked Ka'ahumanu, "Is your father still alive?"

"'A'ole…No," answered Ka'ahumanu. "He died of the great sickness that struck Kamehameha, his chiefs, and his 'koa' or warriors when they were on O'ahu preparing the great fleet of 'peleleu' or double-hulled canoes rigged with European-style sails to cross over the channel and invade Kaua'i. I loved my father very much and have kept the ka'ai of his bones with me since his death. But it was when my father died of the sickness that Kamehameha, who was very sick himself, knew that he had to order a stop to the invasion. It was in that same year that my father's half-brother, my uncle Kame'eiamoku, the royal twin, died also. That was when we were at Lahaina on Maui. I had a red brick house there. I remember how Kamehameha was so upset because, when Kame'eiamoku was dying, he told Kamehameha that Kahekili, who had died ten years before, had confided in him that he, Kahekili, was really Kamehameha's father."

Sketch of Ka'ahumanu (1768-5 June, 1832) by Louis Choris (1795-1828) in 1816, from: http://en.wikipedia.org/wiki/Louis_Choris.

"But I thought that Keōua Kalani was Kamehameha's father," said George.

"The truth is that either Keōua Kalani or Kahekili could have been Kamehameha's father," answered Ka'ahumanu. "Keku'iapoiwa had been with both men at the time Kamehameha was conceived."

"So Kamehameha spent much of his life campaigning against a man who might have been his own father?" asked George.

"'Ae…Yes," said Ka'ahumanu. "And he was upset at this thought, thinking of all the men who had died in the wars between him and Kahekili and then Kahekili's son Kalanikūpule on O'ahu. If Kahekili sired Kamehameha with Keku'iapoiwa as he told Kame'eiamoku, then Kamehameha and Kalanikūpule were half brothers. And Kamehameha sacrificed the body of Kalanikūpule after the Battle of Nu'uanu Pali on O'ahu. His bones were buried beneath the red brick house that Kamehameha had the foreigners Mela and Keaka build for me in Lahaina."

"Gospodi…Lord," exclaimed George in Russian. But then he collected his thoughts and continued in Hawai'ian. "All the Hawai'ian nobility are related to each other in some way. Whenever one goes to war, he is fighting against a relative, it seems."

"That is so," agreed Ka'ahumanu. "But the different families have different connections to the Gods, and different mana. Kamehameha did not know which mana to claim. He had learned from childhood his connection through Keōua. His family was of the 'wohi' class of royalty and its 'aumakua or totem was the honu or sea turtle. With such mana an ordinary chief would not have become a king. But Kahekili's family is of the highest 'pi'o' caste and its 'aumakua is the 'mo'o,' a great long lizard with ridged back and a fierce mouth full of teeth. This mana is more the mana of a great warrior, a guardian of the image of Kūkā'ilimoku, like Kamehameha."

"The mo'o lizard you describe does not sound like the lizards here on Hawai'i," said George. "The lizards here are small with smooth backs and have no fierce teeth. Where did Hawai'ians conceive of such a ferocious lizard, with ridged back and threatening teeth?"

"Our legends tell of such mo'o," said Ka'ahumanu. "They were larger and more ferocious in former days and ate people whole."

"That description fits better the alligator," observed George. "I have never seen a real one, but I have seen one depicted on a mural painting by the artist Giovanni Tiepolo as a symbol of America in the royal Residenz in Würzburg in Germany where I went to medical school. But the alligator and the similar crocodile are only found in the Americas, Africa, Asia, and Australia. How could you Hawai'ians have such a conception in your legends?"

"Perhaps before the days our legends tell, our ancestors were in those places where such large mo'o lived," Ka'ahumanu tried to explain. "And they told about these mo'o to their descendents. There is no doubt that such ferocious mo'o are part of our ancestral experience."

George did not mean to discuss lizards and alligators. He was too curious about Kamehameha's choice of fathers. So he brought the conversation back to that.

"So what did Kamehameha do?" asked George. "Did he acknowledge that Kahekili was his father to claim the stronger mana and the more ferocious 'aumakua?"

"After speaking much with me and with his closest advisors on the matter," explained Ka'ahumanu, "He decided not to acknowledge Kahekili as his father. He did this because then Kahekili's other heirs would have had as strong a claim to rule after him as his current heir Liholiho. Both Keōpuōlani and I were against this. We want Liholiho to be recognized by everyone as Kamehameha's successor. That is why Kamehameha has made me his 'kuhina nui' or 'exalted regent,' so that I might help Liholiho rule in the proper spirit."

"Why did Kamehameha not make Keōpuōlani, Liholiho's mother, the 'kuhina nui'?" George wanted to know.

"Keōpuōlani is a very spiritual person...a quiet person, and shy," explained Ka'ahumanu. "Both she and Kamehameha know that I would be the better ruler."

George was very positively impressed with Ka'ahumanu. And Ka'ahumanu seemed to be positively impressed with him. She told George that she would try to persuade Kamehameha to permit him the requested allotment of land for his agricultural experiments and for provisioning Governor Baranov's outposts in northern America. She also agreed that Kamehameha should order Kaumuali'i of Kaua'i to settle the matter of the *Bering's* cargo.

Later that same afternoon, when alone with Palapala, George asked her, "It seems to me that Kamehameha and Ka'ahumanu are truly in love with each other. Is that also your opinion?"

Palapala told George that she agreed with that opinion. "I have heard Kamehameha chant to others his tribute to Ka'ahumanu, saying 'she is all things; she is undefeatable. Strong in times of crisis, she can ride the waves like a bird. She is as lovely as a lauhala blossom'. And Ka'ahumanu, though she has paid attention to other men, always thinks of Kamehameha first. She says about him that he is 'Pāpale 'ai 'āina, ku'u aloha,' the 'Head covering the land, her beloved'."

"You can tell me," suggested George to the still inebriated Palapala. "To whom has Ka'ahumanu paid attention. What other man would dare pay such attention to her, Kamehameha's favorite wife?"

"It was long ago...before my time here, but I can tell you that it was Chief Ka'iana," revealed Palapala. "Ka'iana was a half-brother of Kahekili. He was as tall as Kamehameha himself, very strong and very handsome. He traveled to India and China with Captain John Meares on the *Nootka* six or seven years before Kahekili died. He sailed back with Captain William Douglas on the *Iphigenia*. He had learned English well and he knew how to use the foreigners' weapons. He was one of the first chiefs to advocate adopting the white man's tactics in war. He even tried to steal Captain Douglas' ship for that purpose, but failed. He became an important ally of Kamehameha's in the war against Keōua Kūahu'ula on Hawai'i. And he fought alongside Kamehameha on Maui. They became close friends, so that Ka'iana even called Kamehameha by his childhood name of Pai'ea. And he was widely respected. It was then that he paid attention to Ka'ahumanu. He and she were seen rubbing noses and playing the kissing game."

"What did Kamehameha do about that?" asked George.

"He became angry at Ka'ahumanu and would not speak with her," said Palapala. "And Ka'ahumanu was very regretful about this. She thought that Kamehameha was going to put her aside or give her to someone beneath her. But Captain George Vancouver, who was here at that time, counseled

Kamehameha and Ka'ahumanu also. It is said that he requested them to rub noses in his presence. He told Kamehameha that only small men are jealous men. And he told Ka'ahumanu to shun all other men's attention from that day on. They have almost always been happy since."

"But what happened to Chief Ka'iana?" George asked.

"After Kahekili's death, Chief Ka'iana continued to fight at Kamehameha's side. But somehow he came to think that Kamehameha was planning to have him killed in the battles to come on O'ahu," explained Palapala. "So just before the Battle of Nu'uanu Pali he deserted Kamehameha and with many of his warriors joined the forces of Kalanikūpule, who was his nephew. He was then killed in the battle. Olohana tells that he was run through with an ihe spear. Afterwards his head was cut off his body and placed on a stake at the Papa'ena'ena Heiau on Lē'ahi. Kamehameha took his feather cape and cap as prizes of war."

"I see," said George. "So Kamehameha was jealous of Ka'ahumanu and did not want other men to pay attention to her. In that, he is like a haole man, and not the Hawai'ian Ali'i. Is that not so?"

Palapala replied, "I think that is so...at least with regard to her. She is the only wife to whom he assigned a chastity guard. For the early years of her marriage she had this chastity guard, a hump-backed boy, who went with her whenever she left her royal residences out of Kamehameha's presence. If she became too friendly with any Ali'i or foreigner, this hump-backed boy would whine out a warning to this man and then report the occurrence to Kamehameha's servants. This was said to be because Kamehameha wanted a successor to be born with Ka'ahumanu and he wanted to make certain that if Ka'ahumanu had a child, the child would certainly be his and no one else's. A few years ago in Honolulu the hump-backed boy reported to Luheluhe, a guard of the sleeping house, that Kamehameha's own nephew, Kanihonui, had been with Ka'ahumanu. When Kamehameha heard this, he had his nephew put to death and offered to the Gods at the Papa'ena'ena Heiau on Lē'ahi...the same place where Ka'iana's head was placed on a stake. This caused Ka'ahumanu to become angry and she threatened Kamehameha. But by now it is known that Ka'ahumanu will not have children. And so she is able to go out on her own with only her Mū and servants...and no chastity guard. It is rumored that she had the hump-backed boy killed. I have never seen him here on Hawai'i. But even so, I think that Kamehameha is jealous of her in a way he is not jealous of his other wives and Ka'ahumanu is proud of his jealousy about her paying attention to other men. Kamehameha and Ka'ahumanu are like a haole husband and wife in that way."

George was pleasantly surprised to hear somewhat later that Queen Keōpuōlani wished to speak with him. He was told that she would visit his guest residence after sundown. This was because of her consideration that there be no risk of anyone's shadow falling upon her and causing her Mū to have to execute the offender. On the evening she was expected, George heard the Mū's warning cries outside his residence and went out to meet the Queen. When she arrived, George was immediately struck by the similarity of her appearance to that of his wife Barbara in St. Petersburg a world away. Keōpuōlani was the same size and comely shape. She had Barbara's rich long hair, dark as coal. She was darker of skin, and she was missing some of her teeth so that even if she had deigned to smile, she would have lacked the white radiance of Barbara's straight teeth. But she moved lithely, like Barbara, in her pattern-stamped toga-like robe, staying within reach of two dark-tattooed Mū who accompanied her. She wore a lei niho palaoa...a necklace emblematic of her high Ali'i status. The pendant, suspended on a thick necklace of woven human hair, was a hook-shaped object carved from a sperm whale's tooth. It was similar to one George had seen Kamehameha wear. He bowed low as she came close enough to speak.

Keōpuōlani (1778-16 September, 1823), Kamehameha's "sacred queen," by an unknown artist, from http://es.wikipedia.org/wiki/keopuolani.

"Aloha, Your Excellency," he said in a Hawai'ian and Russian mix.

"My son Liholiho's kahu, Mr. Marshall," she said. "tells me that you are a good man and that you and your Russians mean no harm here. Is this true?"

"'Ae...yes, this is true," answered George. He was struck also by how much her voice resembled Barbara's. The similarity, which penetrated through the language difference, unnerved him. It was as if he were speaking with Barbara.

"Captains Ebbets and Hunt and Chief Kalanimoku told Kamehameha that he should have you and all your men killed before any more armed Russians in ships can join you. And Olohana is against you also. But Kamehameha does not fear you and wishes to please his friend, Governor Baranov. So you are allowed to stay here. But I warn you that you and your men are in danger of being poisoned at the order of Kalanimoku or other chiefs. You should eat only food that you prepare yourselves from now on. That is what I have come here to tell you."

"Spasibo…Thank you, Your Majesty," stammered George in Russian. Then he asked in Hawai'ian, "Is there anything I can do to convince Olohana and the chiefs that my intentions are only peaceful ones?"

"You should come to visit Kamehameha when he is training his warriors in a camp near the village of Waikoloa," suggested Keōpuōlani. "I will send the guide Pahu to accompany you there for the visit. You will sleep in my hale lole there."

The invitation from the sacred Queen Keōpuōlani that he should sleep in her tent while visiting her husband King Kamehameha took George aback. He didn't know what to say. He looked at the faces of the tattooed Mū standing on either side of her. Either of these muscular men, he knew, could easily pick him up overhead and, in a practiced move of the martial art called lua, smash him down onto a knee, fatally breaking his back. Both were staring at him coldheartedly without a glimmer of emotion.

"You can then go to nearby Kawaihae and speak alone with 'Olohana," Keōpuōlani added.

George reckoned that Keōpuōlani would not make these suggestions to him if she thought they would bring him harm. The uncanny resemblance to Barbara had already convinced him in some irrational way that she was sincere.

"I will follow Pahu to the camp and speak with Kamehameha," he told her. "And I will go to Kawaihae to speak with 'Olohana. I thank you for your help."

Keōpuōlani gracefully turned and left, accompanied at each step by her Mū. George realized that he was breathing heavily as if he had just been running. He felt his forehead with his hand and went inside.

Two days later in the morning, the guide Pahu appeared at the guest residence and told George they would be hiking northward for a distance of about fifteen versts. The hike would take them until afternoon. Right after Keōpuōlani's visit, George had told Antipatr and Petr Kicherev that the men were to eat only food they were sure was not poisoned from that time on. He repeated this warning to them three times, stressing its seriousness. As the word spread, the rest of his men became discontented and agitated for him to make some arrangements to leave the island on one of the ships in the harbor. George explained to them that he would be speaking to King Kamehameha about their situation and that he felt confident that Kamehameha would assure their safety. It was with this thought in mind that he left with Pahu.

The training camp was in a field of pili grass surrounded by ridges of lava flow. On the lava stones near this camp were many stick figures and animal shapes called "ki'i pōhaku" scraped into the rocky surface like messages from the ancients…which Pahu assured George they were. Some of these figures in the lava rock, Pahu explained, marked the place of a child's birth. The umbilical cord or "piko" was placed under a rock after the child's birth, enabling the child to be imbued with the rock's mana. If a dog or pig came and found the piko and ate it, the child was destined to become a thief...and thieves were most cruelly punished by the Ali'i chiefs. Their flesh was stripped slowly from their bodies until they died in a process called "holehole."

At the training ground above Waikoloa, Kamehameha was standing on a high stone table and speaking to an assembly of more than a thousand young men. He made a most colorful appearance. He was wearing a tall mahi'ole cap of red 'ie'ie feathers surmounted with a golden ridge of underfeathers from the mamo bird. This very cap, which reminded George of a Spanish conquistador's helmet, had once belonged to Kalani'ōpu'u. Its central wide ridge projecting forward reminded George of the comb of a rooster. But Kamehameha was wearing as well his full golden 'ahu'ula cape as well. This was truly magnificent apparel, the visible sign of his supreme rank in Hawai'ian society. The cape had taken an entire village dedicated to the purpose two generations to make. It was composed of more than a half million tiny iridescent feathers from over 60,000 'ō'ō birds, caught by net and by an adhesive strategy, woven minutely into olonā cordage. Under the open front of Kamehameha's glorious golden cape, George could see the bright "ka 'ei kapu" feathered sash that signified his position of military command. Around his neck also was his lei niho palaoa of whale tooth and human hair. In his hand was a long and slender spear with three rows of barbs carved into it. This was the "laumeki," usually signifying a condition of war. He used it as a kind of baton, signaling movements and actions required of the men.

The men were also an impressive lot. They were large young men and very muscular and fit in appearance. Many of them carried long pololū spears and leiomanō shark-toothed clubs, but several organized squads of them had flintlock muskets of several types mostly of poor quality. Others had wooden sticks in their hands, which were meant to simulate muskets. The goal of the instruction was apparently to teach the warriors to load and fire their "muskets" in alternating ranks like European soldiers. But in each rotation was inserted a squad to throw the spears and attack with the clubs. These rushes of warriors were attended by horrendous screaming and by gourd rattles attached to their lower legs. The strategy was a strange mix of the native and the European. The musket volleys were ably done, with targets resembling Dutch scarecrows falling in abundance at thirty sazhens of distance and the reloading time allowing four ranks of musketeers, with the alternating attacks of the screaming warriors with spears and clubs, to keep up an almost continuous barrage of shot and ball. The noise level was such that George, witnessing it all from behind a lava-ridge barrier with Pahu and a few of the foreign ships' captains, held his hands over his ears.

When he saw this large training exercise, with young men assembled in such number and armed with so many of the precious muskets and using up so much powder and shot, George could not help but wonder at its purpose. For several years, Kamehameha had been in firm control of all the Hawai'ian islands and he had no effective opponents, no further armies to face. There had been no organized battles for almost two decades. So, against whom was Kamehameha training this army of young men to fight? But then the thought struck him that this entire exercise might have been staged just so he and the others would see it and be impressed by it. Perhaps the stories of the American captains about how he and his Russians were planning to take over the islands by force of arms had worried Kamehameha after all and motivated him to make this show of great force for George as a deterrent to that intention. It was Kamehameha's way of saying, "You might have forty armed men here and another hundred or so on the way, but with such force as I can muster you will have no chance of victory."

That evening George had the opportunity to speak to Kamehameha and Keōpuōlani together before they separated to eat. Several times he repeated to Kamehameha that his only intentions were to found a provisioning outpost for Governor Baranov's Russian-American Company settlements in Alaska and to gain restoration of value for the lost cargo of the *Bering*. Keōpuōlani spoke to Kamehameha also on his behalf, and, at the end of the conversation, he thought that Kamehameha had been convinced. Keōpuōlani then left, and he and Kamehameha supped together, waited on by several servants. When they finished their meal, Kamehameha went to the door and motioned into the hale a group of about fifteen chiefs and warriors who had apparently assembled outside. These were all impressive physical specimens of formidable appearance. Several were tattoed with patterns covering parts of their faces and bodies. George couldn't help feeling a sense of fear among such an assembly, but Kamehameha was calm and smiled at him in assurance of peace. He then took off his cap, cape, and sash, stripping himself bare to the waist. George wondered what he had planned.

"You might think, Kepa," said Kamehameha, "that I have gotten old and that I am not the strong man I once was."

"I do not think that at all, Great King," vigorously protested George, looking at the group that was now sitting in a row along one wall of the hale. "Your strength of both body and will are legendary among your people and also mine. I am sure that you are as strong as you ever were."

"Do you know our game of 'uma', Kepa?" asked Kamehameha.

"'Ae, Great King. I know it. We call it arm wrestling." George recalled his victory over the strong young "King of the Right Arm" on board the *Suvorov* almost two years before. He recalled that his name was Ivan Nikitin and he had defected from the ship in Rio de Janeiro.

"I want you to try to put down my arm, Kepa," said Kamehameha.

"But, Great King, I am sure that you are much stronger than I am. And I fear even to touch you. If I touch you, will I not harm your mana?"

"You will not harm my mana, Kepa," replied Kamehameha confidently. "I ask you to lie down facing me on this mat and join hands with me in the uma. Try with all your strength to put down my arm."

Kamehameha got down onto the mat on his belly facing George. George did as he was told. He grabbed Kamehameha's upstretched hand, interlocking thumbs with his above elbows planted about a foot apart. Immediately he sensed from the contact with Kamehameha's large and thick hand that he had no chance at all.

"Mākaukau…Ready…Ho'omaka…Begin," said Kamehameha. The group of spectators suddenly took deep breaths in unison and held them in silence.

George gave a mighty wrench and pressed his shoulder in behind his hand with all the force he had. His legs spread out and he exhaled…then he managed to increase the pressure even a bit more. But Kamehameha's arm, which felt to George like it was made of stone, did not budge.

"Hana hou…Once more!" insisted Kamehameha, and George almost popped an eyeball with the strain, but then slowly and without apparent effort Kamehameha pressed George's hand to the mat, rolling over his entire body as he did so. Obviously, Kamehameha even in his advanced age had strength far beyond anyone with whom George had ever grappled. The spectators let out their breath at once. "'Ae," some said, and others exclaimed "Maika'i!"

"You did not have to show me, Great King," said George, rolling back onto his belly. "I knew you were a man of great strength."

"Kepa, you are also a man of strength. But you would not want to fight with me, is that true?" Kamehameha looked at him with a slight smile.

"'Ae. That is true," said George, glancing around at the others in the hale. "I would not fight with you."

"Maika'i…Good," said Kamehameha with an air of finality. He stood up and so did the others. With a hand he motioned them out, and they quickly and silently departed. All were smiling.

"Great King," George then said as he stood up, deliberately not mentioning Keōpuōlani, "I have heard that some of your chiefs will try to poison me and my men as it is said they poisoned Isaac Davis. This is because they think that I will order my men against you. But I know that I could never beat you and therefore I will not oppose you. Can you stop them from doing this?"

"I can stop them," said Kamehameha. Then he repeated the statement, "I can stop them."

That night George slept in Keōpuōlani's hale lole...her dressing tent, but she was not there. All night he thought of Barbara…and of his little daughter Inga…in St. Petersburg.

The next day George and Pahu were paddled in a large outrigger canoe north to Kawaihae. On the way they encountered the brig *Forester,* which George remembered from Novo-Arkhangelsk, making its way southward along the coast toward Kailua. It lowered sail as the outrigger approached it and soon the brig was in hailing distance. From the deck Richard Ebbets, the thirteen-years-younger brother of Captain John Ebbets, yelled that they had sailed from

Kamchatka. The voyage there had, despite Captain Mikhail Petrovich Lazarev's advice, been a futile one. Captain Pigot had left the ship to travel overland to St. Petersburg to try to obtain payment for its furs. Young Ebbets said that he was now in charge of the *Forester*. To this, George could only shout in English, "Good Luck."

At Kawaihae, George found John Young tending a large garden. A young girl he called Betty was watching him work. She was his deceased friend Isaac Davis's daughter, whom Young had adopted. George asked politely for a conversation, and Young responded positively, inviting George to dine with him, his son Jim of approximately Antipatr Baranov's age, and his six-year-old son John, called Keoni Ana. The meal was roast dog, and afterwards George and John Young and Jim drank some rum and ratafia, a native fermentation, becoming quite drunk. Young Jim, the most affected by the drink, started to brag about the lengths to which his father had gone to please Kamehameha. He said that his father had had the bodies of discarded children cut up for Kamehameha to use as bait while fishing. This caused John Young, also quite inebriated, to become angry. He shouted at young Jim, "Damn it, son! Who told you such lies? How could you believe that?" And to George, he claimed, "That isn't true. I would never do something like that."

George assured John Young that he didn't believe what Jim had said. "Young people these days hear all sorts of things about their elders," he said. "And they don't know what to believe."

Jim did not retract his story nor apologize for telling it, but he became silent and morose thereafter, at last falling asleep while still seated at the eating mat. George and John Young continued to converse, talking about George's mission and the possible threat the Russians posed to Kamehameha's unified island government. George was his most persuasive in maintaining that the Russians posed no threat at all, and John Young, after an hour of George's presentation of this case, began to nod affirmatively at whatever George said. To George it seemed that 'Olohana too had at last been convinced that his intentions were peaceful.

One day in late March of 1816 when George arrived in the royal compound to meet Kamehameha as he had before, on the kahili-surrounded mats outside the residence, Kamehameha's servants came out and urged him into the house. Kamehameha was still lying on his sleeping mat in the center of the floor. He told George that he had been experiencing severe pain in the joint of his right big toe. It was swollen and red and it hurt so badly that he could not allow it even to touch the sleeping mat at night without stifling a scream of pain. This pain had bothered him for a week or more and his kahunas could not do anything to ease his plight. Even the juice of the ko'oko'olau leaves and buds had had no effect. He was afraid that he would not be able to walk any more.

"We call this condition 'gout'," George told him. "It happens to people sometimes when they become old…and even sometimes before that."

"Is there anything you can do for it, Kepa?" asked Kamehameha. "It is said that you are a wise physician and know how to make pain go away. When I was sick before with sneezing and my nose running, your medicines helped me to feel better. Can you help me now?"

"I have a medicine for your gout called colchicine," explained George, mixing his Hawai'ian with substantial doses of English and speaking very slowly. "It's a yellow powder made by grinding the corms and seeds of the *Colchicum autumnale*. These are the Latin words given in the classification system of Linnaeus to a lily-like flowering plant called the crocus or meadow saffron. The plant grows wild in central Europe. The colchicine powder, however, is a poison, and in the wrong amounts can make you get very sick and die like Isaac Davis did."

Kamehameha asked, "Can you give me the right amount of this medicine and take away the pain in my toe?"

"'Ae…yes," answered George. "I know how to use the colchicine medicine. I will go back to my guesthouse and return with the medicine. You must drink a tea I will make of the powder later today, and then again tomorrow. On the next day your toe will not hurt."

George was pleased to find that the colchicine tea he made for Kamehameha eased the pain in his toe within the first day. When he came to administer the second dose, Kamehameha was very happy to see him. "Kepa," he said, "I am giving you the name 'Papa'a,' which is the name of a healer who secures good health. You have delivered me from great pain. You have enabled me to walk again. You have prolonged my life and my rule. I am ready now to grant your requests for a land allotment and the return of the Russian cargo on Kaua'i. 'Olohana and Kalanimoku advise me strongly against this and you will have to earn their trust if you can. Also, the American captains say I should not allow any Russians here. But Ka'ahumanu has land in the mōku of Kona and Waialua on O'ahu she will grant to you, and her brother Kuakini will grant a portion of his land there to you also at her request. You will have to pay for these allotments out of what you produce on them. The amounts will be decided later. Do you agree to this?"

"Yes, I agree. That is very good of you, Great King," said George. "Your friend Governor Baranov will be very pleased."

George's men were also pleased when he told them they would be sailing for O'ahu in the next few days.

Maui:

George, Antipatr, John Marshall and several other Russians were transported to Honolulu on the southern shore of the island of O'ahu, the "gathering place," aboard British Captain Samuel B. Edes' *Beverly*. Kamehameha had refused

Captain Edes' initial request for sandalwood, but Edes' thought he might make the request again, raising his offer to nine Spanish piastres or American dollars after doing Kamehameha the favor of transporting the party to O'ahu. The other Russians and Aleuts of George's mission group were to follow in several days by peleleu canoes with sails.

The *Beverly*'s arrival in Kailua had brought the news that Napoleon Bonaparte and his army had been defeated at the Battle of Waterloo by the allied armies of Britain, Prussia, and Russia, and that, as a result, Napoleon was being exiled again…but this time to the remote south Atlantic island of St. Helena. On the 24th of March, 1816, in the company of Captain Edes at Chief Cox's house, a celebration was begun. This was also the anniversary of Tsar Aleksandr's accession to the Russian throne, and George sent messages to Kamehameha and several chiefs that it would be an insult to the Russian Tsar not to attend the celebration. To George's disappointment, Kamehameha did not attend, though Hoapili and Cox's brother Kuakini did. At noon three flags…the British, the Hawaiian, a crude white flag with a blue "X" in the upper staff corner with three blue stripes framing it in a color-red-deficient imitation of the British union jack combined with the American stars and stripes...used since the time of Captain Vancouver..., and the Russian… were raised over the *Beverly* and a cannon salute of 21 shots was fired.

Ka'ahumanu , Palapala, and another female servant sailed with George and the others on the *Beverly*, together with a giant Hawai'ian Mu as a guard, who got up onto the prow with his kapu stave and called out the "Kapu-moe!" warning even to the waves that an Ali'i-nui was coming toward them. Ka'ahumanu wanted to see the house she called "Kapapoko," where she had lived while Kamehameha had ruled from Honolulu until 1812.

The *Beverly* was quite crowded, and because of this the intermediate stop for two days in Lahaina, Maui, was quite welcome. George and Antipatr walked around the village and surveyed the large pond there with a small island in it called Moku'ula from where the ancient Maui kings had ruled the island. They saw the prominent brick palace that Kamehameha had built for Ka'ahumanu when his court was resident in Lahaina before the attempted invasion of Kaua'i in 1804. George was told that the two foreigners, Mela and Keaka, who had supervised the building's construction, burying beneath it the bones of the killed O'ahu King Kalanikūpule, were Australians who had once been convicts in Sydney. Their English names were Mr. Miller and "Black Jack."

Around the village of Lahaina were many taro fields, fishponds, and rock walls, and the high verdant mountains behind the village were most beautiful. The daily afternoon rains had stopped and the clouds above these mountains had partially cleared. Full arches of sun-brightened rainbows graced the sight of George and Antipatr as they looked upward, and George couldn't help marveling at what a truly beautiful place these islands were. Due to its greater rainfall, Maui was greener in its visual character than the island of Hawai'i, and much smaller, although its dominant volcano, Haleakalā, the "house of the sun," was of an elevation almost equal to those on the bigger island, making for a striking sense of vertical relief. As they had sailed along the southern shore of Maui as they approached Lahaina, they had seen the outlying smaller islands of Kaho'olawe and the tiny crater remnant of Molokini, and now, behind them and to the west, they could see the islands of Lana'i and Moloka'i. When George asked Ka'ahumanu, who had been born in Maui's eastern district of Hana, what she thought of Maui, she answered, "Maui—nō ka 'oi," meaning "Maui—there is no better."

The next day, early in the morning after a breakfast of roe and poi, George asked Antipatr and John Marshall if they wanted to hike from Lahaina to the west along the shore to the daunting "leina a ka 'uhane" or "soul's leap" from the crags of "pu'u keka'a," the "rumbling black bluff" from which King Kahekili had once jumped into the surf when he was reputed to be over eighty years of age. Ka'ahumanu had described the area to George previously. "We might even try to jump into the ocean from that same place ourselves," said George, exhilarated by his sense of sudden daring.

Antipatr, infected immediately with George's enthusiasm, said, "Let's go," but John Marshall responded with, "No thanks…you two go on without me. I'll stay here."

Three hours later, George and Antipatr and one of the young Aleuts who had long been Antipatr's friend, having walked along the shore rocks and the alternating wide beaches of light golden sand, were nearing a large black lava-rock promontory along the beach in an area known as Ka'anapali. Near here, in the days before the rule of Kahekili, known fully as "Kahekilinui-Ahu-Manu" the "Feather-Cloaked Mighty Thunderer," there had been a decisive battle called "koko o na moku" or "bloodshed of the islands" for control of Maui between the armies of brother Chiefs Kamehamehanui, who was victorious, and Kauhi'aimokuakama, who died. The blood of the killed warriors was reputed still to color the waters of the local spring.

The black rock promontory was about ten meters above the level of the surf, but a jagged outcropping of lava stuck out into the sea, tapering sharply at a lower level into it. It was just as Ka'ahumanu had described it. Surging along the edge of the projecting lava was a high surf which dashed itself, wave after foam-crested wave, onto a broad and gradually sloping beach. At one place about forty feet above the passing waves, sticking up from a rocky platform, was a support pole intended to hold a torch. This was to mark the spot visually at night. But it was now still well before noon, and the torch support only served to mark the spot from which Kahekili and generations of other warriors of Maui had leaped into the surf below as a demonstration of their bravery. Looking at the height of the small foot platform and the voluminous surging of the surf, Antipatr said to George, "You know I can't swim, don't you?"

Pu'u Keka'a (Black Rock) on Maui's Ka'anapali Beach, from: http://www.to-hawaii.com/maui/ancientsites/puukekaa.php.

"You can't swim?" asked George.

"No, I can't swim," repeated Antipatr. "It's very cold where I grew up, as you know, and I learned to move through the water only in a baidarka."

"So why did you agree to come with me here?" asked George.

"I wanted to see the place, and to see if you would really leap off such a height into the waves," Antipatr answered. His Aleut friend merely shrugged his shoulders. It was clear that he also would not be swimming.

George stripped down to his underwear and waded out into the waves. The water was only slightly cooler than his body temperature and it felt very pleasing to him. He swam out through several of the large waves to a point beyond where they were breaking and then made his way over to the end of the lava projection. When he started climbing up onto it he realized what tender feet he had as a consequence of always wearing shoes. Each step onto the sharp lava crags with his bare feet was surprisingly painful to him. But he persisted, pulling himself gradually upward over the crag by grabbing handholds and using the strength of his arms to relieve the pressure on the bottoms of his feet. When at last he got near the top he noticed that several natives had come onto the beach below to stand with Antipatr and watch him. From his vantage point at the top near the leaping platform the height of it appeared to be at least twice what it had appeared to be from the beach when he was looking up at it. He fought to overcome his fear of height, imagining King Kahekili as a very old man, but still a "pahupū" warrior, with the entire right half of his once fearsome body tattooed from head to toe a dark bluish black, placing his much tougher feet onto the platform and looking first down and then upward toward the sea, and then leaping out away from the black rock. He had survived it, George thought. But the place seemed awfully high to him now, and the rushing waves below not at all welcoming, but threatening.

"Why have I done this?" he said to himself as he stepped onto the platform and crossed himself. "Can I really make such a leap?" But then he steeled himself as he saw a large wave approaching below, took a deep breath and sprang out into space. He was falling, it seemed to him, long enough to say the Lord's Prayer on the way down, but then he hit the water feet-first with a great splash, smacking his outstretched forearms painfully as he entered the wave. Down, down into the water he went, then, at last, he started to rise back up because of the air in his lungs. But he was quickly running out of air and needed to take a breath and he was still rising. Just as he was about to expire, he broke back above the surface of the water. He looked around and saw Antipatr, the Aleut youth, and the natives on the shore. They were waving and yelling encouragements to him. He was proud of himself and felt that he was surely at the very acme of his life at that very minute on Mau'i.

When they had started back to Lahaina on the broad beach, George promised Antipatr and his friend that he would teach them to swim as soon as they got to Honolulu. At just that moment, off the shore to their right and only five hundred feet away from them, a huge "koholā"...a humpbacked whale...breached the surface of the water and soared into the air, exposing its light underbody, its flukes, and its tail as it splashed with a rushing roar back into the sea.

"Gott im Himmel!" exclaimed George in his native German. "What a sight!"

In Lahaina, Antipatr, who had seen many more whales breach than George, bragged of George's leap, first to John Marshall and then later to Ka'ahumanu, who told George that he was a "koa nui"...a "real hero." Before they left Lahaina the next morning on the *Beverly*, George asked Ka'ahumanu why Kamehameha had moved the seat of his rule from island to island over the years—Hawai'i, Maui, O'ahu, and then back to Hawai'i. She explained, "Kamehameha wants his people to love him. He says that he will be loved where he is known. But now, as he is old, he desires to be home."

Honolulu:

When the *Beverly* reached Honolulu harbor at the end of its third day of travel, George observed that there were many more foreign sailing vessels there than he had seen elsewhere. One ship he recognized to his displeasure...Captain Wilson Price Hunt's *Pedler*. He hoped that Hunt's enmity toward Governor Baranov would not cause him continued troubles in carrying out Governor Baranov's mission.

O'ahu had a very high and green mountain ridge, the spectacular Ko'olau Range, running to divide its north from its south on its entire eastern half. As a spine to the western half ran the Wa'ianee Range. A broad flat expanse, fringed at the sea side by a beautiful beach was delimited on the southeastern leeward edge of the island by "Lē'ahi," the rugged volcanic caldera foreigners, having found diamond-like mineral crystals there, called "Diamond Head." On shore was a central settlement not far from the mouth of a prominent river called the Pearl River because of the many pearls collected from the oysters there. The Pu'uloa estuary at the Pearl River's mouth was where several of the foreign ships were anchored. It was to the east of this area in the Honolulu ahupua'a that the smaller allotment of land from Kuakini was located. But the *Beverly*, having taken aboard an Englishman named John Harbottle, who functioned in the port of Honolulu as a pilot, anchored even further east, on the other side of an extrusion of land into the harbor. The area on shore at this location was called Waikīkī, meaning "spouting water." A protective reef and shallow water kept the *Beverly* quite far off the beach so that rowing ashore was a formidable task. But this was where Ka'ahumanu's primary grant of land was to be found.

Kamehameha had explained to George the terms of his allotment. The land he was being given by Ka'ahumanu was part of the ahupua'a of Waikīkī. It was an area particularly valued by the Ali'i and their ancestors. King Kahekili had ruled his Maui Federation from there at the height of his powers and had died there. It was there that Kahekili's son Kalanikūpule had, as a ruse to satisfy Captain George Vancouver, who demanded the execution of the culprits who had killed three of the crew members of his ship *Daedalus*, instead executed in Vancouver's presence with flintlock pistols borrowed for that purpose three innocent maka'āinana rather than give up three of his Chief Kamohomoho's elite fighters, the totally tattooed "pahupū" who had really committed the murder. But then, after his death following the Battle of Nu'uanu Pali, Kalanikūpule's body was stuffed, together with some of his live chiefs, into Waikīkī's largest imu, the Kuna oven. And Kamehameha, after he had conquered O'ahu in 1795, had first ruled from Waikīkī also, before moving to the better harbor at Honolulu three versts to the west. In the far past an O'ahu King named Kakuhihewa had planted a large number of niu...coconut trees...there and the tall slender ancestors of those trees formed a grove along the beach called Helumoa. Two streams, 'Apuakehau and Ku'ekaunahi, ran through the allotment, which comprised a broad strip almost two versts wide. It was centered on the location of four large gray boulders near the beach that legends said were imbued with the healing power of four wizards named Kapa'emāhū, Kahāloa, Kapuni, and Kinohi who had, many years before, returned to their native land of Tahiti. It extended north from the sea mauka across a swamp and up seven versts into the long steep valleys, Mānoa, Palolo, Nu'uanu, and Kalihi, leading up to the ridge of the Ko'olau mountains, and it had several types of terrain evident in it. There were forty families or more of maka'āinana living on it with flocks of sheep and goats. There were fishponds on it and the maka'āinana were also cultivating taro in irrigated muddy plots called lo'i.

George could instruct these commoners to help him and the members of his party as laborers in planting and harvesting his crops, in hunting and fishing, and in doing whatever he thought necessary to send provisions to Governor Baranov in Novo-Arkhangelsk on the Russian-American Company ships which George had told Kamehameha were coming. He could use Kuakini's allotment of land nearer to the Pearl River and the center of the Honolulu settlement and its port facilities as a warehouse for his outgoing produce. But Kamehameha was explicit that George was to construct no stone buildings. He was a foreigner and that was now kapu. He was not to fly a foreign flag over the land. That was kapu. And he was not to cut any growing sandalwood and ship it away for sale. That was kapu. Also, Kamehameha promised to send an emissary to King Kaumuali'i on Kaua'i strongly requesting him to settle with George on the matter of the wrecked *Bering*'s cargo. After that, George had heard to his distress from Captain Samuel Hill of the *Ophelia* that Captain John Ebbets had already taken delivery of some of the *Bering*'s cargo on Kaua'i, using the ruse with Kaumuali'i that he was returning it to Governor Baranov at Kamehameha's order. Captain Edes told George that he had been told that Ebbets' ship, the *Enterprise*, had nearly been washed ashore while it was off Waimea during a terrible storm that tore it away from all but one of its anchors, but that King Kaumuali'i had kindly sent out a boat with one of the *Bering's* anchors to help Ebbets save the ship.

Ka'ahumanu's other allotment of land was a large part of the ahupua'a of Kamananui in the Waialua moku on the northwest coast of O'ahu. Since this land was relatively remote from the port at Honolulu and he had only a limited number of men with him at the time, George, after a two-day trip there to inspect it, made the decision to postpone settling it until he was better established on the south shore. He returned to Honolulu and described the Waialua allotment as a region fertile for growing taro and with many ponds filled with fish. He noted that there was a small island offshore there to the north where ships might anchor. But he told Ka'ahumanu that he would not be placing any men there at this time. Ka'ahumanu reminded him that even if he produced nothing on this larger plot of land, he would still have to pay lease rent in trade goods for it. George agreed to this, thinking that he could arrange payment through letters of debt sent to Governor Baranov in Alaska.

Ka'ahumanu introduced the Russians to Kamehameha's Governor of O'ahu, the American from Plymouth, Massachusetts, Oliver Holmes, called "Homa." Homa had been one of the very first foreigners to live in Hawai'i, coming on the ship *Margaret* in 1793 and deciding to stay permanently. He had entered the service of King Kalanikūpule as a military advisor, and survived the Battle of Nu'uanu Pali to join the service of the victorious Kamehameha and help him rule on O'ahu. He took Mahi Kalani, a daughter of a killed Ko'olau District chief, as his wife, and despite his high position, resided in a native-style grass-thatched residence at the center of the Honolulu village near the large thatched house Ka'ahumanu called Kapapoko. It was at Kapapoko that George and the others were also introduced to the versatile Spaniard, Don Francisco de Paula Marin, who had come to O'ahu even before Governor Homa and lived not far away in Honolulu's outstanding personal residence, a large white stone house with a red roof in the waterfront area called "Kapu'ukolo" from which he entertained both native and foreign visitors, even charging ships' captains for rooms ashore in it as if it were a hotel. Marin, whom the natives called "Manini," meaning also the surgeon fish, a strikingly blue inhabitant of the reefs off shore which had a reputation for industriousness and for hoarding objects, had a very young native wife, a chiefess named Kaualua whom he married in 1813. Kaualua, a child herself, had not yet given him children, but she had adopted his daughter Lahilahi by his former wife, the High Chiefess Haiamaui who had died as a result of the childbirth in 1811. Five-year-old Lahilahi was also the object of affection and care of Governor Homa's two teen-aged daughters Maria and Hannah. These young women liked to swim and to ride the waves on surfing boards. Their father tried to enforce their wearing long drape-like garments for this purpose in the interests of modesty, but as soon as they were out of his sight, they shed the drapes to swim and surf bare-breasted in only a malo bottom. George asked them to help him teach Antipatr to swim, and they were eager to do so.

Don Marin was a handsome man of medium height. At forty-two, he was five years older than George, but he looked younger. His pale skin contrasted markedly with his still black hair and a heavy dark moustache. He was a multi-talented man who served the royal family as a Spanish interpreter, as a gardener extraordinaire, and even as a physician, though he had no real training in

Don Francisco de Paula Marin ("Manini") (28 November, 1774-30 October, 1837) by artist Louis-Jules Masselot (1815-1879), from: http://en.wikipedia.org/wiki/Don_Francisco_de_Paula_Marin.

medicine. Marin was also a devout Catholic, and this gave George some common ground of understanding with him. He told George that whenever he was asked to ease the plight of dying Hawai'ians he would secretly baptize them into the Catholic faith so that they would be welcomed into heaven.

"If a person is baptized into the faith, but doesn't know it," George observed, "they may not get to heaven."

"I pray for them too," said Marin. "Prayer is more powerful than you might think. The Hawai'ians know this. The Kahunas are said to pray a person they don't like to death with their 'ka pule 'ana'ana.' Or, they can cure people of illness by detecting who it is that is praying them to death and killing that person."

"But these are not really prayers in the Christian sense," said George. "They do not call upon the power of our Lord, and they are not positive in nature, but malicious, like some sorcerer's evil spell or incantation."

Don Marin said that he agreed, but then added, " Do you know that I have translated the Lord's Prayer into Hawai'ian?"

"You have?" asked George, thinking that Marin's Hawai'ian abilities after so many years there and with native wives must far exceed his own. "How does it go?"

Marin began to recite it from his memory, but quietly and only to George as if his saying it in Hawai'ian might be dangerous to him in some way. "E ko makou makua iloko o ka lani, E ho ano'ia kou inoa...E hiki mai kou aupuni...E malama'ia kou makemake ma ka honua nei...I like me ia i malama'ia ma ka lani la. E ha'awi mai ia makou i keia la, i 'ai na makou no neia la. E kala mai ho'i ia makou i ka makou lawehala ana, Me makou e kala nei i ka po'e i lawehala i ka makou. Mai ho'oku'u 'oe ia makou i ka ho'owalewale 'ia mai, E ho'opakele no na'e ia makou i ka 'ino. No ka mea, nou ke aupuni, A me ka mana, me ka ho'onani'ia, a mau loa, aku. Amene."

George was very impressed and repeated, also quietly and just to Marin, "Amene."

Two days later the remainder of George's party of Russians and Aleuts arrived by peleleu boats. This was, they reported, quite an adventure. Petr Kicherev and Aleksei Odnoriadkin were very impressed with the native captains' seamanship, saying that the double-hulled peleleus were "faster than our ships at full sail, to be sure." They told George, however, that many of their supplies and trade goods had been left at Kailua, including George's own large trunk. They made the judgment, given the limited cargo space and the continued threat from the natives, to bring the tools and arms instead. When the Russian-American Company ships arrived as promised, they would be able to return to Kailua and fetch what remained there.

Ka'ahumanu, accompanied by Palapala and the giant Mu, who carried a long round-topped kapu stave as a warning to commoners of Ka'ahumanu's status, took George around to the maka'āinana villages to inform the people there that they were to do George's bidding until she told them otherwise. They accepted this edict without question, having prostrated themselves appropriately at the approach of her and her Mu. Then she took George to the four stones near the beach.

"These stones hold the mana of four ancient wizards who came here from Moa'ulanuiakea village on the island of Raiatea near Tahiti and healed our people," she explained. "They lived here in a place called Ulukou and people came to them for healing. They were powerful wizards because they were men who did not seek the company of women. When they had become old and wanted to return to their native Tahiti, they had the people bring these great stones here from the Kaimukī hills east of here, closer to Lē'ahi. It took thousands of people to move the heavy stones. Two were placed by the wizards' house, which is no longer here, and two by their nearby swimming place where they are sometimes washed by the waves. There was a great celebration on the night of Kāne. A high-ranking and virtuous young chiefess was sacrificed and buried under them. The wizards then put their hands onto the rocks and transferred their healing mana to the stones. Then they sailed away forever. But the stones still have their healing power. Many who have come here and touched them have been cured. So do not allow anyone to move them or keep the people from them."

"We will respect the stones," George assured her.

When it was time for Ka'ahumanu and her retinue to sail back to the island of Hawai'i, George found it difficult to say farewell. He had come to respect Ka'ahumanu highly and he had a genuine affection for her. And he had to say farewell also to Palapala who had been so helpful to him in learning the Hawai'ian language and in acquainting him with Hawai'ian customs. Without her, he knew, he would have had much more difficulty in gaining the confidence of both Kamehameha and Ka'ahumanu. As she and Ka'ahumanu and the Mu were rowed out to the anchored *Beverly*, now ready to return to Kailua, George, standing with Antipatr, waved his arm and shouted, "Aloha…Proshchaite, vernye druzia…Farewell, true friends."

The month of April, 1816, and half of its following month of May was a time of very hard work for George, his party, and the maka'āinana.   From Francisco de Paula Marin, George bought many seeds and seedling plants to add to the stock of those he had.   On his Waikīkī allotment of land, there was a fine beach with "hukilau" or group net fishing. George made sure that the fishing was done every day, and that each day's catch was processed by drying, smoking, or salting. There was plenty of salt, obtained by evaporation from a salt pond on Kaua'i called nomilū and sent to O'ahu in jute bags, which George purchased from Francisco Marin. But a short distance back from the beach was a large fetid swamp of no agricultural use. George reckoned that a canal could be built to drain it westward into the Pearl River estuary, but he did not have sufficient labor for a project of that size. Instead he planted the land higher up at the base of the foothills, widening a path they would later use to transport the harvested crops to the storehouse they were building on the other plot of land nearer to the Honolulu port. He planned to add pumpkins, squash, potatoes, onions, cabbage, carrots, turnips, and radishes to the already cultivated taro. He began a citrus orchard with young trees purchased from Marin to whom he gave most of his sack of cottonseed in exchange. Marin was excited about the prospect of planting cotton. George planted tobacco too for trade purposes. And he planted sugar cane and grapes. Reckoning that Hawai'ian kukui nuts provided a source of light when burned superior to the candlefish used in Sitka, he began harvesting them and set the maka'āinana stringing them onto slivers of bamboo to make great numbers of the small illuminative torches he had used while in Kailua to read his notes of Hawai'ian words and phrases at night.

The Russian party built for itself with native aid a separate village of thatched houses on a pleasant spot just east of the four wizards' stones. From there it was a little more than an hour's walk along the scenic and pleasant "Waikīkī Road" to the center of the Honolulu settlement where the men could socialize with the constantly changing cadres of ships' officers and crews who visited the islands' busiest port. But for almost two months George kept the men working so vigorously and continuously that they did not have much opportunity to socialize.

"Diamond Head from Waikiki" in the early 19th century, by Enoch Wood Perry, Jr. (31 July, 1831-14 December, 1915), from:
http://fr.wikipedia.org/wiki/Fichier:'Diamond_Head_from_Waikiki',_oil_on_canvas_painting_by_Enoch_Wood_Perry,_Jr.,_c._1865.jpg.

The weather at Waikīkī was a constant blessing. The very air, in a constant state of motion, seemed to caress the men and bring to them the scent of flowers or of pork roasting in a distant imu. It rained almost every day off and on, but the rain, coming from rapidly shifting cumulus clouds that formed spectacularly over the Ko'olau Range, seemed to be coming from only a few feet above, striking the men as a cooling mist so that they welcomed it. Then the sun would emerge to both brighten and warm, and bring into view astonishing "ānuenue," or rainbows. As they worked, the men shed their clothes because they were not needed. They became lean and tanned as they labored in an environment they found constantly exhilarating. One of the men's natural leaders, Petr Kicharev, would sweep his arms around, pointing out the natural splendor, and ask the other men loudly, "Who would ever leave here, brothers?" Antipatr Baranov, who had grown up in Alaska, appreciating both the magnificence and the hostility of the environment there, commented to Kicharev and the others, "Yes, it really is a paradise here. There is no freezing cold or lurking bears to kill you without warning. A man, without working for it, is given food and warmth by nature itself."

George immediately committed himself to making supportive acquaintances of Don Marin and Governor Homa. Governor Homa assented to George's suggestion that they call each other by their English names, "Oliver" and "George." But harmonious relations were made more difficult than they otherwise would have been by the influence of the American ships' captains, like Wilson Hunt of the *Pedler*, William Smith of the *Albatross,* John Ebbets of the *Enterprise,* and Henry Gyzelaar of the *Lydia*. These men, together with other captains, continually agitated Governor Homa with the warning that "the Russians are trying to take over the place." George was very careful to refute at every opportunity the perception that the Russians and their Aleut comrades, constituting the largest group of foreigners on O'ahu, and being well armed, and with armed ships coming to help them, were a threat to the islands' political *status quo.*

Don Francisco Marin introduced George to the pineapple. Three years before, in January of 1813, he had taken delivery of some pineapple cuttings from a Spanish ship that had brought them from Paraguay. Christopher Columbus had discovered this strange and wondrous fruit on his second voyage to the Americas in 1493. It was a fruit that grew up out of the ground, supported when ripe after eighteen to twenty months by its spike-like leaves, instead of hanging down from the branches of trees like the breadfruit, which took much longer to grow. And each fruit was large in comparison to apples, oranges, or grapes. So Marin had been growing pineapples in his gardens and making plans to grow larger crops of them, since the exotic plant thrived in the warm volcanic soil and in the abundant rainfall. He had cooled several ripe pineapples from his second crop of the fruit in a stream that ran near his house. He cut them up into square pale yellow sections and served them to George, Antipatr, and John Marshall in bowls. At the first bite, George became almost ecstatic at the taste of this luscious fruit.

"My word!" he exclaimed to the others. "It's like making love for the first time, I swear. I've never tasted anything like it...so juicy, so cool, so tart, and yet sweet. It's got to be sinful. I think the tasting organs in my mouth are trying to jump out my ears."

John Marshall and Antipatr agreed. They had never tasted a fruit as lush and delicious as the pineapple. Antipatr said, "I've got to find a way to get one to Sitka and serve it to my father."

"What a juice this fruit would make," said Marshall. "Does it ferment?"

"I plan to find out," said Don Francisco. "I think it's heaven's finest fruit…the most flavorful in all the world. I can imagine the day when fields of them here will stretch for as far as the eye can see."

"Why do they call it a 'pineapple'?" asked Antipatr. "It doesn't taste like either pine or an apple."

"It's only a 'pineapple' in English, my friends. And that might be a matter of the plant's appearance," explained Marin. "It looks like a large pine cone, but it's a fruit like an apple…so that's why it's a 'pineapple'. But the Guarani word used in Paraguay, is 'ananás.' And that's what the French captains call it too. I think that ananás is a better word for it somehow than the English 'pineapple,' to be sure."

George responded in English, saying, "It's going to be ananás to me henceforth in Russian too."

The Nu'uanu Pali Battle Site:

On one occasion, George accompanied Governor Homa and two of his daughters on a two-day hike up to the site of the Battle of Nu'uanu Pali, in which Holmes had been a participant twenty-one years before. Holmes' teen-aged daughters Maria and Hannah had never been to the site and he thought they were now old enough to be acquainted with it. Antipatr Baranov went along, having become smitten with the sixteen-year-old Hannah while she helped teach him to swim at Waikīkī Beach. On the way up the steep valley into the mountains, Governor Homa showed George where large stands of the 'iliahi or sandalwood had been cut and carried away to be sold to the Chinese in Canton.

"I know the Chinese pay dearly for this wood," said George. "I've been told that a single pikul of the wood…or the 137-pound weight a strong man can carry…will bring ten Spanish piastres or American dollars worth of goods in Canton. But what do the Chinese do with it?"

"They grind the wood into a powder and squeeze the oil out of it," answered Homa. His English sounded strange to George, different by accent from what he had heard before because of the man's New England origin. "They burn the powder like incense for its aroma, especially in their religious rituals. And they make a perfume out of the oil."

"So why has Kamehameha made the cutting of growing sandalwood kapu?" asked George.

"For two reasons," Homa replied. "First, he desires to protect the 'iliahi trees that are left. Our people have been cutting them and carrying them into foreigners' ships for almost twenty years now. For a time Kamehameha allowed the Winships and other American captains exclusive rights to our 'iliahi wood. But he took away these rights during the hostilities between the Americans and the British when the American ships were blockaded here. This was because the 'iliahi trees here on O'ahu are getting fewer and harder to find. But also, he wants to reserve this business for himself as a way to get the money to have European-style sailing ships built for his growing fleet. Governor Lachlan Macquarie of Australia is even now having a ship built to Kamehameha's order in Sydney. The kapu keeps anyone but Kamehameha's men from cutting the 'iliahi."

George looked at the stumps of a multitude of the sandalwood trees that had been cut down in the past, realizing that they were still within the boundaries of his allotment of land. All around the stumps were piles of branches and brush that had been chopped from the main trunks of the trees as the laborers prepared to transport the wood down out of the foothills to the beach. An idea struck George. He could have all these branches and other remnential sandalwood foliage collected and ground into powder in the maka'āinanas' poi mortars. Then he could send the powder for sale to China. In doing this, he could demand an increased price from the Chinese, since the grinding of the wood into powder would already have been accomplished and they would not have to do it. And such a plan did not call for him to cut any growing sandalwood at all. His men would only be cleaning the forests of the remains of what had been cut long ago.

The trail to the pali cliffs dividing the south of eastern O'ahu from its northern windward side was steep and physically challenging. At times the trail merged into the streambed, since this was the only opening through the trees, bushes, vines, and ferns which grew in such abundance as to block their way. But they persisted at Governor Homa's direction and before sunset the group had ascended through the dense foliage to a verdant saddle between sharp vine-covered peaks where the wind, funneled through the gap in the mountains, grew to a fierce gale intensity. Governor Homa commented as he led them to the edge of the saddle's sharply precipitous cliff edge, "There are ghosts here."

As they came to the edge of the cliff, the entire north shore of O'ahu sprang suddenly up into their view. Clouds were below them. The deep teal color of shallow Kane'ohe Bay, mottled with light green reefs, seemed to change shades as they watched. There were a number of small offshore islands, the edges of which showed the white of the waves crashing onto their rocks. Seaside village roofs could be discerned in the hazy distance as the shadow of the mountain range they stood atop gradually darkened them and removed them from view. As high as they were, there were yet higher peaks to the right and to the left of them, towering close overhead and darkening also from green to black with every minute. Behind them was the sunset's orange glow, made more than usually colorful by the haze of volcanic ash in the air. George and the others were struck silent at the spectacular sight. The wailing wind blasted onto their faces so hard that they were forced to squint.

"You can still hear the screams of the fallen in the wind," shouted Governor Homa so he could be heard. "This is where Kamehameha's warriors forced our men…and even some of our women too…over the edge. The locals call the battle 'Kaleleka'ane,' the 'leaping fish'. Hundreds died here. Their bones were left below.

Nu'uanu Pali Battle Site, from: http://squidoo.com/haunted-hawaii.

"How did you survive, Governor Homa?" asked Antipatr.

Homa pointed to a clearing above them on the steep bare outcropping to the right. "I was up there with a few of Kalanikūpule's remaining chiefs. My friends Miller and Black Jack and I were advising them in directing the retreat. From there we saw the slaughter, heard the screaming. In my dreams I still see it, still hear it."

Homa's daughters were quiet, struck by their father's relation of his battlefield experience. But George, remembering Palapala's story about Chief Ka'iana, asked "Was Ka'iana with you also?"

"No," answered Homa. "He had already been killed in the ferocious fighting below at Laimi. Near there too, Kalanikūpule had been wounded and was carried off to 'Ewa. Miller, Black Jack and I with six others climbed down the other side of that peak and hid for a month or more in the villages and forests on the north shore and in Ewa west of the Pearl River where we were briefly reunited with Kalanikūpule. But frightened villagers in 'Ewa told Kamehameha's men where we were and they came to capture us, killing Kalanikūpule and a couple others in the struggle. He knew better than to be taken alive. They brought the rest of us, together with Kalanikūpule's body, back before Kamehameha in Waikīkī near the place where your men have built your settlement. Only we foreigners, Miller, Black Jack, and I, were spared. Kalanikūpule's four chiefs were cooked alive, together with Kalanikūpule's body, in a large imu there called the Kuna oven. Their remains were taken elsewhere for sacrificial ceremonies and display. One of these chiefs was my wife's father...Maria and Hannah's grandfather."

At this relation, Maria and Hannah, who had not previously heard this, gasped and clasped each other's hands. Homa went to them and put his arms around them, saying, "It is a sad thing. But I did not know your mother then, and your grandfather was a very savage man."

Homa cleared his throat and continued. "Kalanikūpule's bones were saved and buried under the brick house that Miller and Black Jack later built for Ka'ahumanu in Lahaina on Maui. It is the Hawai'ian Ali'is' custom, you know, to bury a sacrificed body under any structure of prominence they build."

"The chiefs were cooked alive?" Antipatr asked Homa, still thinking about the horror of it. "Did you witness this?"

"Yes, I witnessed this, young man," answered Homa. "And it's a very hard thing to forget."

George was curious as to how this American, Oliver Holmes, born in Massachusetts, had become Kamehameha's Governor of O'ahu after being captured among Kamehameha's enemies. "How did you then rise in Kamehameha's esteem high enough to become his Governor?" George asked.

"John Young and Isaac Davis convinced Kamehameha that I could be of use to him as an advisor," replied Homa. "And indeed I did become useful as an advisor. Eventually, like Young and Davis, I took a Hawai'ian wife. 'Olohana, 'Aikake, Manini, Homa...we were four of a kind. And soon I had these daughters and realized that I would never leave here as Miller and Black Jack...Mela and Keake... eventually did. All I can do now is strive to make Hawai'i the best possible place to live...for me, my family, and all the Hawai'ians too. And, in the long course of time, I've come to believe that the best way to accomplish this is to support King Kamehameha. He's not the same man he was when he ordered the cooking alive of Kalanikūpule's chiefs. He's mellowed with age and gotten wiser…and he's thinking more and more about what is good for his Hawai'ian people."

"What do you think caused him to change?" asked George.

"Contact with us foreigners is the main thing, of course. All of us advisors have had a role in this, as have the ships' captains. But, in addition, I think the key event was the 'ōku'u, the great illness that struck him in 1804 when he was preparing to invade Kaua'i," explained Homa. "For the first time in his life he felt powerless. He was so sick that he could only think that he would die as so many others around him did. He had to contemplate his mortality and his legacy. After he miraculously survived this illness, he seemed to lose his appetite for war and conquest. He allowed King Kaumuali'i of Kaua'i and Ni'ihau to continue to rule his islands as a vassal king…and refused to have him killed when he could have. So now we have had years of peace in these islands where previously was unending bloody war…chief against chief."

"But what has he done for the Hawai'ian people?" asked George.

"Have you heard of Kamehameha's 'Law of the Broken Paddle'?" asked Homa.

"Yes, I have," answered George. "It has to do with a fisherman he confronted who, not knowing who he was, broke a paddle over his head in self-defense."

"That's right," said Homa. "And he didn't have the fisherman executed for striking him…that's the point. He thought about the situation from the fisherman's point of view. He empathized with the man's need to defend himself and his position as a fisherman. When his chiefs protested his not taking the fisherman's life, he told them that they too were to begin considering their subjects' welfare in the way they rule under him. He told them he wanted anyone in his kingdom, Ali'i or commoner, to be able to lie down and sleep along the road in safety without fear of harm from any other man. When he gave this instruction to them, he became a different kind of King…no more an absolute ruler feeling entitled to squander his subjects' lives for his merest of purposes. He became a benevolent monarch, acting to better his subjects' lives."

"But his kapus are still enforced by death," said George. "It's as if he is not a King at all, but a God. And indeed all the Hawai'ian people are treated as his slaves. His guards extract from them much of all they produce, so that they see no worthwhile purpose in industry at all. And he makes impossible demands of them. Our maka'āinana have been told that they must pay a tax of a metal nail per family while they work for us. The only access to metal nails they have is to steal them from us. If we catch them in this, we flog them, but if they submit no nails to Kamehameha's tax collectors, they are killed. If they flee, their families are killed. Their treatment is, in fact, worse than that of the Russian serfs or the African slaves in Brazil. These at least are not sacrificed in order to dedicate a building. They aren't cut up into bait so the King can fish, as I've heard happens here. And they aren't generally executed for failing to fall to the ground in the Ali'i's presence."

"But the Hawai'ians have no awareness of mistreatment," replied Homa. "It's always been this way for them. Kamehameha is trying to keep most of the old ways in effect during his lifetime. He knows that his successors will likely forsake the old ways and become rulers in the mold of the European royals we all tell him about. Even now he's thinking of sending his son Liholiho to England to see how King George governs the country where John Young was born. He tells Liholiho that he already has a brother Keōua there in London calling himself Alexander Stewart whom he should seek. Kamehameha is interested in other governments, but he doesn't think the United States' conception of having the men there choose a temporary president is a good idea. He thinks that President Madison is himself controlled by his congress of advisors."

"When I spoke with him, he was most curious about Napoleon Bonaparte," George said. "I'm glad he isn't thinking of sending Liholiho to France. His son should instead travel to St. Petersburg and meet Tsar Aleksandr. He's a fine model of a benevolent monarch in my opinion. Do you think that John Young is the reason Kamehameha favors the model of England?"

"Yes, I do," answered Homa. "'Olohana has become the most influential of Kamehameha's advisors…and the most powerful. He was the Governor of O'ahu when Kamehameha ruled from here, and it was he who suggested to Kamehameha that I succeed him in that post. But now I answer primarily to him."

"But what about Hoapili, Kalanimoku and Kuakini…the native advisors?" inquired George.

"They are a very sly bunch, and treacherous," said Homa. "I deal with them very carefully. One day they are your hoaloha or friend, and the next they're trying to have you killed. Power is all they truly understand…and he who is in Kamehameha's greatest favor has the most power."

Homa directed the group away from the area of the cliff to make a camp for the night. They didn't start a fire even though it started to rain lightly, but only spread out sleeping mats in two separate areas under broad-leafed trees, two for the girls on one side, and three for Homa, George, and Antipatr on the other. Before retiring, they ate some dried fruit they had carried with them and drank some stream water from half-gourd containers. At Antipatr's request, George whistled some melodies he remembered from his youth and sang some humorous verses from the <u>Carmina Burana</u> in Latin. The girls were entranced during his performance, but, tired from their long day's ascent to the Nu'uanu Pali site, they afterwards quickly fell asleep.

The next morning before starting back down, George and the others returned to the windy edge of the cliff between the green spires and looked out over the spectacular vista in the morning sun. "I have traveled widely in this world and seen many beautiful sights," George told the others. "But this is the single most beautiful place I've ever seen."

"It is a beautiful place," said Governor Homa. "But it's a place accursed. Let's go."

Captain Isaiah Lewis:

George ordered the collection and grinding of the sandalwood branches and brush, and soon he had amassed fifty pikul-weight bags of aromatic powder. He began construction of a large storehouse on the Kuakini allotment to keep the sandalwood and the provisions safe until they could be transferred to ships in the harbor. Kamehameha had had a thatched storehouse there previously and had agreed to George's use of it. But George wanted something more substantial. The construction method he chose for the new storehouse was that of post and lintel, with the posts held stable in ditches packed with lava rock. The posts themselves were the trunks of sizeable trees—more than a foot in diameter each--that had to be rolled for almost a mile from where they were cut. The maka'āinana, who had initially hid when asked to work on the storehouse, were useful in this construction labor after George repeatedly assured them that no one would be sacrificed to hallow the building. Crossing poles were laid into cuts made in the adzed lintels, with a pitched roof of thatch above that. The storehouse walls were made of two layers of woven makaloa matting, one attached to the inside of the support posts and the other to the outside. Unfortunately for George, the foundation of lava rock supporting the posts extended more than two feet above ground level, causing the troublesome congregation of American ships' captains to complain to Governor Homa that "Doctor Schaeffer and his Russians and Aleuts had, contrary to Kamehameha's kapu, built a stone house of impressive size within steps of the harbor." They threatened that if George was not forced to tear down this affront to prevailing order they would tear it down themselves.

When Governor Homa presented George with the captains' view, George protested that the storehouse was in no way a "stone house," and was therefore not in violation of Kamehameha's kapu.

"Take a look at the structure yourself, Oliver," implored George. "It is made of wood and matting, just like many other structures here. It has a thatched roof. Only its foundation is made of lava rock...and without mortar. Surely it does not violate the kapu."

"I have seen the storehouse, George," answered Homa. "And I agree with you that it is not, strictly speaking, a 'stone house.' But it is not really a native structure either, and I worry about what John Young and Kamehameha's native advisors will think when they hear about the storehouse from these captains. I will send a letter to John describing it to him in detail, hoping that he does not consider it a violation of the spirit of the kapu."

"That is fine, Oliver, and I'm grateful to you," said George. "But it would only take one torch in the hands of one of these American captains or their crewmembers to destroy the storehouse and everything we have in it. I ask that you place armed guards at the storehouse to protect it. If it is destroyed, our mission here to supply provisions to Governor Baranov in Alaska will be severely hampered."

"I can't order my Hawai'ians to guard a Russian enterprise," answered Homa to George's consternation. "You'll have to guard the place yourself."

George chose a strong young half-Russian half-Aleut named Filip Osipov to lead a detachment of four armed guards for the storehouse. Osipov and the others took up residence in a corner of the building and made themselves visible with their muskets at all four corners of it day and night. This measure further incensed the American captains, who complained about this "threat to common safety."

On the 19th of April, 1816, John Marshall and his host, Don Francisco Marin, came to the Russian settlement to find George. They were accompanied by a man whose face was wrapped in a long towel. They were leading him like a blind man, and he staggered as he walked like a drunk.

"This is Captain Isaiah Lewis of the *Panther*," announced Marshall. "He's got a bad tooth and a bad ear…so bad that Don Francisco can't help him. We were wondering if you might be able to do him some good."

Francisco Marin put in, "It's some kind of abscess in his ear, I think. And the tooth needs pulling. But it's way in the back and broken into parts already. He's drunk a lot of rum and seems beyond most of the pain…but I just can't get hold of the tooth parts and don't know what to do about the ear."

Captain Lewis suddenly tore off the towel covering his head. He was a big man with a tousled head of sandy hair and a short full beard. The entire left side of his face was swollen and his left eye was bloodshot. "I'm in a bad way," he grunted in American-accented English. "Can't do a damned thing with this ear and tooth hurting so. Can you help me?"

"Yes, I can help you," answered George with authority. "I'll have to lance the eardrum, try to drain it, and irrigate the ear canal using a clyster. But first let me have a look at the bad tooth. Open your mouth as wide as you can and show it to me."

Captain Lewis winced as he opened his mouth as widely as he could. George turned him to face the sunlight and looked into his mouth. The left bottom wisdom tooth was broken into four parts and the surrounding gum tissue was bleeding.

George took his trusty dental pliers out of his medical bag and reached it into Captain Lewis' mouth. "Be still now," he said, clamping the bent-nosed pliers onto the largest shard of wisdom tooth. "Steady…" Then he pulled sharply and twisted out the shard. Captain Lewis looked as if he might faint.

"Good," George said. "I got the root of that one at once. Now again…open up."

Captain Lewis opened his mouth again and George extracted another shard and root. After this, Captain Lewis had to sit down. John Marshall and Francisco Marin held his shoulders and head steady as George pulled out the remaining shards and roots. Then George soaked a piece of cotton in rum from a bottle John Marshall had in his pocket and stuffed it into the hole in the back of Captain Lewis' mouth.

"When we get done, you'll have to keep the sore place moist with rum-soaked cotton for a week or more," said George. "I doubt if you'll be eating much, but if you do, be sure to chew on the other side."

"It's already been roe and poi for two weeks now, Doc," groaned Lewis, slurring his words. "I guess I can stay alive on that until I can chew again."

George pointed to a sturdy platform of wood he had been using as a desk and a table, and said to Captain Lewis, "Now I want you to lie down on that table on your left side with your head hanging over the edge of it. John and Don Francisco will help you."

When Captain Lewis was properly situated on the table so that his affected ear was pointed downward toward the dirt floor, George removed from his bag a long thin copper tube with a sharp beveled end. It was a siphon tube of the thinnest diameter, much finer than the one he had devised to drain the lung cavity of little Andriushka Karamzin in Nizhny Novgorod three years before. It was made to drain suppurating ears.

George got down on his back and scrunched himself into position below Captain Lewis' ear. "Now this is going to hurt some," he said.

"What's it been doing?" groused Captain Lewis sardonically. "Go ahead and do it."

George pushed the tube into Captain Lewis' ear…deeper and deeper until he felt it push through what seemed a minor barrier, Lewis' eardrum. Lewis screamed in a high-pitched yell as he felt the tube break through. Then George put his mouth to the tube and began to suck on it, soon spitting out onto the floor a mouthful, then two, then three, of pus from Captain Lewis' inner ear. Lewis was now screaming "Aaaahhh! Aaaahh! Aaaahhh!" He tried to put his hands to his ear in order to pull the tube out, but John Marshall and Francisco Marin held his hands and would not allow this.

At last George carefully pulled out the copper tube. He got up from the floor, asked Marshall for the rum, took a mouthful, washed it around in his mouth, and spat it all out onto the dirt floor. Then he took out of his medical bag another tube, slightly larger in diameter than the copper ear siphon. Out of the bag also came a flexible pouch made of a chicken's bladder. Quickly he poured into it a mixture of drinking water and John Marshall's rum. Then he inserted the tube into the fluid-filled bladder and tightly wound the connection between them with string.

Turning onto his back on the table, Captain Lewis knew that George was now going to irrigate his ear. "Will this hurt?" he asked.

"Not nearly as bad as the siphoning," said George. "Some people say the irrigation is a relief to them."

George inserted the clyster tube into Captain Lewis' ear until he felt the resistance of the pierced eardrum. Then he squeezed the chicken bladder's fluid through the tube and into the ear. Soon a stream of fluid exited the ear from around the tube. It carried out of the ear globs of yellowish mucous and blood. When George removed the clyster, he turned Captain Lewis back onto his left side so the ear could optimally drain itself and told him to remain in that position for a half hour. But in a half hour Captain Lewis was fast asleep on the table.

"I think you've saved a good man here, Doctor von Sheffer," said Francisco Marin in Spanish-accented English. "I've seen men die from tooth and ear infections like that. And few things are as painful. Now he's sleeping as peacefully as a baby. When he wakes up I think he will be most grateful to you."

"I hope so," said George. "I could use a friend among the American captains."

The Ships Arrive:

In late April of 1816, the *Forester,* which had been purchased by Kamehameha for sandalwood and renamed the *Ka'ahumanu,* arrived under its retained Captain Alexander Adams from Hawai'i. It turned out that Richard Ebbets, who had called to George from the ship off Kawaihae claiming to be the master of the *Forester* after Captain Pigot left the ship in Kamchatka, was in fact functioning only as the ship's clerk. From Captain Adams, George heard the news that the Russian-American Company ship *Otkrytie,* meaning "Discovery," under Fleet Lieutenant of the Russian Navy Iakov Anikievich Podushkin had arrived in Kailua having stopped first in Kawaihae to see John Young. George had heard of Podushkin before. He had been the Captain of the *Neva* when it had wrecked in a storm off Mt. Edgecumbe near Sitka in January of 1813. Over thirty of the men aboard had perished, including the man, Vladimir Grigorievich Bornovolokov, who was coming to Novo-Arkhangelsk to replace Governor Aleksandr Baranov. But Captain Podushkin and the others in his longboat had managed to survive. George was immensely pleased by the news that

Podushkin was in Kailua. He knew that the *Otkrytie* would soon come to Honolulu. "Now I'll have a full crew of good men, a good Captain, and a good ship to support my mission here," he thought.

On May 3 by the Russian calendar, the *Otkrytie,* a 300-ton frigate that had been built at Sitka in Governor Baranov's shipyard, sailed into sight of Waikíkí and then anchored just outside of Honolulu harbor. George went along in the pilot's boat with John Harbottle to meet Captain Podushkin.

When George and Pilot Harbottle came on board, Captain Podushkin greeted them warmly. He was a tall and slender man with a carefully trimmed goatee beard wearing a black felt tri-cornered hat.

"So you're the commissioner, then," he said, giving to George a title he had not previously heard. "I've heard good things about you, and I trust that I will be of good service to you here. Governor Aleksandr Andreevich Baranov sends his regards to you. I have letters from him to you and to his son Antipatr."

George, speaking Russian, introduced John Harbottle and volunteered to interpret for Captain Podushkin. But Podushkin stated that his English was good enough to understand Harbottle without an interpreter. He understood clearly when Harbottle informed them of the necessary harbor fee of eighty dollars or equivalent.

Captain Podushkin told George and Pilot Harbottle that the *Otkrytie* was suffering from a leak just below its water line. He thought that if they could be anchored alongside a heavier ship they could use blocks and tackle to careen the *Otkrytie* far enough over to address the leak adequately. Harbottle said that this could easily be done and directed Podushkin on the proper heading to enter the harbor. Inside the harbor they had teams of natives in double-hulled canoes tow them into position beside Captain Isaac Whittemore's Boston-based 350-ton *Avon.* Harbottle was rowed over to the *Avon* to make arrangements to tilt the *Otkrytie* over so it could be repaired.

While repairs on the side of the *Otkrytie* were proceeding, George stayed aboard, even though it was difficult to stand on the decks while the ship was careened, and made the acquaintance of the Russian-American Company Supercargo, Pavel Verkhovinskii. Verkhovinskii was a short obese man with unpleasantly distracting bumps on his nose and cheeks. He was most deferential in his manner toward George, assuring George of his long relationship with the Company and his loyalty to Governor Baranov, who had sent in his care a large shipment of assorted furs and trade goods for George's use in dealing with the Hawai'ian chiefs and the foreign ships' captains as well.

Captain Podushkin told George about his visit to Kawaihae and Kailua in Hawai'i. He said that he had gotten along superbly with both John Young and King Kamehameha, who had entertained him and his officers royally. The King and his chiefs were particularly delighted when a number of the Aleuts he had aboard showed the Hawai'ians their native dances, featuring athletic leaping and stamping of their feet. He also told of hauling a "edinorog" howitzer onto shore in Kailua at Kamehameha's request. Captain Podushkin gave the King a demonstration of how the heavy gun could fire grenades, which exploded at a great distance. Kamehameha was so delighted at seeing the distant explosions that he offered to purchase the howitzer immediately. But Captain Podushkin had steadfastly refused to sell Kamehameha the howitzer, saying that he needed the permission of his Commissioner...meaning George...to sell the weapon.

George could not help thinking that the warm welcome and entertainment given Captain Podushkin and the crew of the *Otkrytie* by John Young and Kamehameha reflected a deceit on the Hawai'ians' part. He knew that Young had no warm feelings for other foreigners in general, and that Kamehameha was too fearful of Russian intentions to be unwary. The matter of the howitzer was disturbing to him also. Now when he returned to Kailua to get the rest of his belongings Kamehameha would want him to sell the howitzer.

In the next two days the crew of the *Otkrytie* mingled with the Russians and Aleuts under George's command in the settlement at Waikīkī. They were enchanted by the beauty of the place...the majestic clouds in a steady parade overhead, the constantly caressing trade winds, the surprising misty rains and the resultant rainbows, the welcoming warmth of both air and sea, the cool fresh streams running down from spectacular mountain vistas. It was indeed the natural paradise of which they had long heard. And they were among friends. Some members of the crew were already long acquainted with the men who had previously come on the *Isabella* with George. Indeed the meeting reunited two Russian cousins and two sets of Aleut brothers. Inasmuch as Captain Podushkin and Supercargo Verkhovinskii clearly acknowledged George as their superior by Governor Baranov's instructions, George had now ninety men at his command...as well as an armed ship.

George made plans with Captain Podushkin to sail back to Kailua on Hawai'i to retrieve the things left there and to request an official letter from King Kamehameha to King Kaumuali'i of Kaua'i regarding the settling of accounts in the matter of the *Bering*'s cargo. George wanted to sail to Kaua'i to gain foodstuffs and trade goods from Kaumuali'i in exchange for items of cargo that may already have been given mistakenly to Captain Ebbets. But as they were discussing the completion of the *Otkrytie*'s preparations to sail, a messenger from Pilot Harbottle arrived to inform them that another Russian-American Company ship, the brig *Ilmena* under American Captain William Wadsworth, had arrived in Honolulu harbor after a twenty-day journey from California. The *Ilmena,* Harbottle's messenger said, had stopped for a single day's visit with King Kamehameha in Kailua, and, like the *Otkrytie*, had leak problems.

At Don Francisco Marin's house near the port, George, Captain Podushkin, and Supercargo Verkhovinskii met Captain Wadsworth, his American first mate Verol Madson, and the *Ilmena*'s Supercargo, Dmitrii Toropogritskii. They told of their problems with the Spaniards in California, and of their problems with the ship. George told them that they should remain anchored in Honolulu harbor. They were to unload the ship into the warehouse and repair it before taking on a cargo of foodstuffs and the ground sandalwood. The men of the crew, numbering another fifteen Russians and thirty Aleuts, could stay in their settlement at Waikīkī. George would sail with Captain Podushkin on the *Otkrytie* first to Kailua and then to Kaua'i, taking 36 men with him. This would leave a contingent on O'ahu numbering one hundred men. According to the suggestion of Governor Baranov, written to him in a letter conveyed by Captain Podushkin, he proposed to leave Supercargo Pavel Verkhovinskii in charge of the Company's operations on O'ahu while he was away.

But Pavel Verkhovinskii did not want to take command of the O'ahu operations in George's stead. At first he asked George to write out a lengthy instruction to him, specifying every action to be taken in every imaginable situation. Then, seeing the instruction, he refused to accept the position. This caused George some consternation, and led him to consider other choices. One of those choices was the senior hunter Petr Kicherev.

On the *Ilmena* was another senior hunter of whom George had heard much. This was Timofei Osipovich Tarakanov, whose three periods of trial in captivity had been described to him by Governor Baranov himself. Tarakanov had come aboard the *Ilmena* after poaching for seals along the California coast. He was well acquainted with Ivan Kuskov, Governor Baranov's manager of the Fort Ross outpost, and had many stories to tell of his career with both Baranov and Kuskov in the Russian-American Company's employ. He was a man of medium size, with a handsome clean-shaven face, but with particularly dark skin. George estimated his age at forty years, though his weathered face and hands made this estimate suspect. It was clear that the men on the *Ilmena* liked and respected Tarakanov, and George gave some brief thought to appointing him to head the remaining contingent, but decided that he had only just met Tarakanov and did not sufficiently know the man to trust him with such a responsibility. Kicherev, he thought, was the better choice, and so he made the appointment.

Not all of the original crew of the *Otkrytie* was to sail on the voyage to Kailua and to Kaua'i. Eleven men, including Supercargo Verkhovinskii, stayed with the unloaded cargo and the produced material at the warehouse in Honolulu, moving into it together with the guard detachment. Filip Osipov, who had headed the guard, asked that he and his friend Aleksei Odnoriadkin be allowed to sail on the *Otkrytie* and George granted the request. He delegated Antipatr Baranov to head the guard detachment…an appointment, which pleased everyone. The *Ilmena's* Supercargo Toropogritskii stayed in Honolulu too and caused George further consternation by asking for a detailed bill of lading in advance for the items to be transported to Sitka on the *Ilmena* after it was repaired. His insistence on the bill of lading finally angered George, who drafted a cursory bill specifying "Everything in the warehouse that will fit into the hold of the ship *Ilmena*."

"I trust you to take back with you whatever you think is most needed in Sitka," said George to Toropogritskii in the presence of Captain Wadsworth and several other men. "I haven't got the time to make a detailed list of it all for you. Look it over and make your own list. I'll attest to it."

Timofei Tarakanov, who was among the men witnessing this exchange, volunteered to write up the bill of lading for George. "I'll write down whatever we take," he said.

George was surprised to hear Tarakanov volunteer to take on a writing task. He had supposed the man to be illiterate, but this was obviously not the case. "Very good," he said. "I thank you for accepting this responsibility. You are now the mission clerk and will be given additional pay as such."

Before George's departure on the *Otkrytie* for Kailua and Kaua'i, Governor Homa came to George to express his concern about the size and nature of the "Russian force." The American captains, after the arrival of the *Otkrytie* and its crew, had told Governor Homa that the "Russian force" presented a danger both to Kamehameha's government and to their continued commerce. But when the *Ilmena* showed up as well and its crew swelled the number of the "Russian force" to almost 140 men, they demanded that the Russians be expelled, and when Governor Homa told them he would not confront the Russians, they said they would send their own emissaries to John Young and to Kamehameha urging them to act forcefully against the Russian "interlopers."

Back to Kailua:

When George and Captain Podushkin arrived in Kailua, they were greeted most warmly by King Kamehameha, whose guards escorted them into the royal settlement of Kamakahonu to meet with him. In fact, he waved his Mū aside to embrace and hug both George and Captain Podushkin in the Russian fashion, exclaiming to George, "Aloha, Papa'a. It is good to see you again. I am still well and have had no more illness. I have ordered the construction of a new heiau to honor you and other healers like you."

"I am honored, Great King," responded George. Then he added, "I trust that no one will be sacrificed at this heiau in order to honor healers."

"'Aole...no," answered Kamehameha. "We have two kinds of heiau, you know...the luakini heiaus dedicated to Kū, the God of War, and the ho'oulu'ai heiaus dedicated to Lono and the other Gods of peace and fertility. People are only sacrificed at luakini heiaus...for they are the wages of war. At the ho'oulu'ai heiaus we sacrifice animals, plants and objects that are dear to us. The heiau I have ordered built for you is a ho'oulu'ai heiau and no people will be sacrificed."

"That is a good thing, Great King," said George. "In civilized societies people are not sacrificed at all, and I think they should not be. A ruler should value highly the life of every one of his subjects and never sacrifice them."

"Sometimes the Gods demand that a ruler sacrifice his subjects, Kepa," answered Kamehameha, changing his form of address back to George's Hawai'ian name. "The order of things in our world depends upon this."

"The order of things in your world...and in the rest of the world too...is changing rapidly," said George. "And I hope that in the future people are never sacrificed by some ruler's command. Our duty is to preserve every human life."

"That is your duty as a healer, Kepa," replied Kamehameha. "My position as a ruler gives me other duties."

At this, Kamehameha turned away from George and Captain Podushkin and walked off the conversation mat back into his residence. The guards then motioned for George and Captain Podushkin to leave the royal compound. As they walked together to the guest residences where George and the others had spent several months of the past year, Captain Podushkin asked George, "Do you think you should have spoken so directly to the King about human sacrifice? I think he was quite perturbed by such discussion and that we may now expect some trouble."

"It's hard to determine what Kamehameha is really thinking," answered George. "But every step we take here is because of his grace. If he wanted us dead, we would already be dead. Did you notice that he didn't even mention the howitzer?"

At the guest residence the next day, Chief Cox and Ka'ahumanu, accompanied by two other of Kamehameha's wives George did not know, came to visit. Ka'ahumanu was friendly, especially after George congratulated her on Kamehameha's naming his new ship in her honor, but she told George that Kamehameha would not speak with him again. She did not mention the discussion of human sacrifice as a reason at all, but instead said that Kamehameha was angry about the number of Russians under George's command now on his islands. His feelings of friendship for Governor Baranov did not extend to allowing a threat to his government, and the three shiploads of Russians constituted such a threat. Chief Cox added that 'Olohana and the other chiefs had heard from the American captains in Honolulu about his Russians there, about how they had harvested sandalwood in violation of Kamehameha's kapu, built a non-native structure in violation of Kamehameha's kapu, and had posted armed guards in the structure who threatened the peace of the Honolulu community. The only kapu they had not violated was the one about flying the Russian flag above Hawai'ian land.

Both George and Captain Podushkin spoke quickly and vehemently to refute all these charges. George explained that no growing sandalwood had been cut, that the warehouse had only a stone foundation and no more, and that the American captains were lying about his activities in order to eliminate Governor Baranov's Russian-American Company as a trade competitor. He asked Ka'ahumanu to get him another audience with Kamehameha, but she refused.

"Kamehameha will be kapu until you leave, Kepa," she said. "And you should depart before the chiefs, seeing that you have lost Kamehameha's favor, decide to act against you on their own."

The next day Chief Cox returned to the guest residence as George and Captain Podushkin were supervising a detachment of the crew in the removal of all the remaining supplies, including George's personal trunk, to the *Otkrytie*. He offered to send a letter to Kaumuali'i, with whom he was acquainted, informing the Kaua'i King of Captain John Ebbets' ruse and suggesting that Kaumuali'i settle accounts on the cargo of the *Bering* and promising to visit him soon on the *Ka'ahumanu*. He discussed the wording of this letter with Captain Podushkin, who drafted it in English, which he was told King Kaumuali'i understood. As he wrote, he asked for grammatical advice from George. When the letter was complete, he signed it, spelling out in English the name "Kahekili Ke'eaumoku" and adding after it "Chief Cox." Chief Cox then took the quill and scrawled onto the page his emblematic likeness of a "mo'o" lizard similar to some of those on the messages George had seen scratched into the lava rocks near Waikaloa. The mo'o was the 'aumakua of Chief Cox as he was a descendent of the Maui line of Ali'i as he knew King Kaumuali'i of Kaua'i to be also. George also signed the letter as a witness.

When George and Captain Podushkin were back on board the *Otkrytie* and ready to sail away, they noticed the approach of a number of large double-hulled canoes filled with warriors. On the lead canoe, which was armed with a swivel gun, stood 'Olohana. In short order the *Otkrytie* was surrounded. John Young had heard of their presence in Kailua and had come from Kawaihae to visit with them. When he came aboard, George greeted him warmly, reintroduced him to Captain Podushkin, and asked him if he would like to have a drink or two to celebrate the successful establishment on O'ahu of the Russian-American Company's provisioning outpost.

"You know that I'll not drink to that," said Young forthrightly. "But I'll drink to your leaving here whole and to your heeding my warning about how to deal with King Kaumuali'i on Kaua'i."

"All right," said George. "Let's drink to that."

George went below to get a bottle of rum and a bottle of the native ratafia he had collected from Kailua. He brought three glass goblets up as well from the Captain's cabin. Back on deck, he poured drinks for himself, for Captain Podushkin, and for John Young. In a few minutes he poured another round.

"Do you know that I am not the one who is agitating King Kamehameha against you?" John Young asked. "It's the captains...Adams, Ebbets, Winship, Hunt, Smith, Gyzelaar and the others. I received a letter from Oliver Holmes reassuring me that you have been acting peaceably and not breaking the kapus...though you have been dancing a mite close to the line on those. My advice to the King was to leave you be, at least for now. Are you able now, after the arrival of the two ships, to make any payments on your allotments of land?"

"Yes," answered George. "I am able to make some payment in furs and glass and iron. It's all stored in the Honolulu warehouse. You could have it transported back here on the *Ka'ahumanu* easily enough after I get back to Honolulu to release it to you."

"My advice to you is make your visit to Kaua'i as brief as possible so as to return to Honolulu in less than two weeks," said Young. "We don't want you meddling in our complex relationship with King Kaumuali'i. That's the most important thing. Remember that above all else. Your life depends upon it. But we can't wait for even two weeks for some payment on the allotments. We have to have something now. The King says that he would take the howitzer and grenades."

John Young reached for the bottle of ratafia and poured himself another goblet of the strong drink. As he did so, he looked straight into George's eyes with a steely unblinking gaze. Captain Podushkin was also looking at George with a serious expression on his face. He glanced off the ship as well to the surrounding canoes filled with warriors.

"So be it," said George, perceiving that he had no other reasonable choice. "We'll send ashore the howitzer and its grenades."

Captain Podushkin ordered the howitzer and twenty of the ship's grenades to be loaded into a longboat and rowed ashore. This took several hours, during which John Young remained aboard the *Otkrytie* drinking himself into a stupor so that he had to be bodily lifted over the side to be deposited into the waiting double-hulled canoe. After that, the *Otkrytie* lifted its anchor, set its sails, and let the wind blow it away to the west on course toward Kaua'i.

Kaua'i:

During the three-day trip to Kaua'i, George expressed his anger at John Young to Captain Podushkin. With Podushkin he spoke Russian.

"I tell you, Iakov Anikievich," he said. "Old Young has the mind of a usurer, an extortionist, and worse. He's a damned thief...a natural born criminal. And he's found a real paradise for himself in Kamehameha's kingdom, that's for sure. Here he can take what he wants as long as he gives the King what he's due."

George also fomented against Kamehameha, saying, "King Kamehameha is a terrible tyrant...worse than Bonaparte ever thought to be. He takes everything his people have, including their lives, just to increase his mana. He's cruelly exterminated all his rivals and their families, taken their women to wife and had his own children with them. He wants his line to be the only ali'i line left alive...that's his real goal. Kaumuali'i is the only other possible ruler of these islands left, and Kamehameha has him on his knees in fear."

Captain Podushkin could only nod in agreement as George ranted against Kamehameha and John Young. But he ranted on his own against the American Captains.

"Vy sovershenno pravy...You're correct, Yegor Nikolaevich," he contributed, "but those lying unscrupulous American captains are a big part of the problem here. They take advantage of Kamehameha's abuse of his people to fatten their purses. I wonder why our allies the English have not enforced the claims on the islands made by Captains Cook and Vancouver and thrown the Americans out. Things were better for us when the English and Americans were fighting."

"They say that King George is seriously addled," said George. "So he hasn't been able to approve any claims made by the English captains. And his ministers have been too busy with Napoleon in Europe to concern themselves with affairs out here in the Pacific. I tell you, Iakov, there is now a clear opportunity for our Tsar Aleksandr to claim all of the Hawai'ian islands as a colony. Just think of what a valuable addition to his realm that would be."

"That's a large thought, Yegor," observed Podushkin, nodding his head affirmatively, "...a large thought indeed."

On the afternoon of the third day of the voyage, the coast of Kaua'i came into view to the west. They steered to the south and sailed into Nāwiliwili Bay near the southeast corner of the island. This was a beautifully protected small bay with high bluffs ringing it on the north and east and great green mountains to the south. To the east above the Hule'ia Stream was the massive Ha'upu Mountain, topped by its own dark mantle of clouds. To the north of the bay was the fine level sand of Kalapaki Beach, cut by the Nāwiliwili Stream, from where a small village sent out several canoes to greet them. Captain Podushkin did not allow the natives to board the *Otkrytie*, but bargained with them to tow the ship back out beyond the southern edge of the bay so they could pick up wind to make their way along the southern shore. In exchange for several hatchets and mirrors, the natives organized eight teams of strong paddlers to tow the *Otkrytie* back out to sea.

"That's quite a pleasant place," observed Captain Podushkin as he waved off the canoes and set sail southward. "But there isn't much room to maneuver a sailing ship of this size in it."

Along the southern shore they saw several fine beaches...Maha'ulepu and Poipu among them...but found no good place to anchor. They knew that they were retracing the route followed by Captain James Cook's ships at first landfall in the islands in 1778, and, like Cook, they would find an anchorage further west at Waimea. That was where they hoped to meet King Kaumuali'i.

"I've heard that Kaua'i is the rainiest of the Hawai'ian islands," said George. "But this southern shore seems dry enough and we've plenty of sunshine."

"Still, the place seems greener than the others to me," said Captain Podushkin. "And the clouds over the central mountains seem darker."

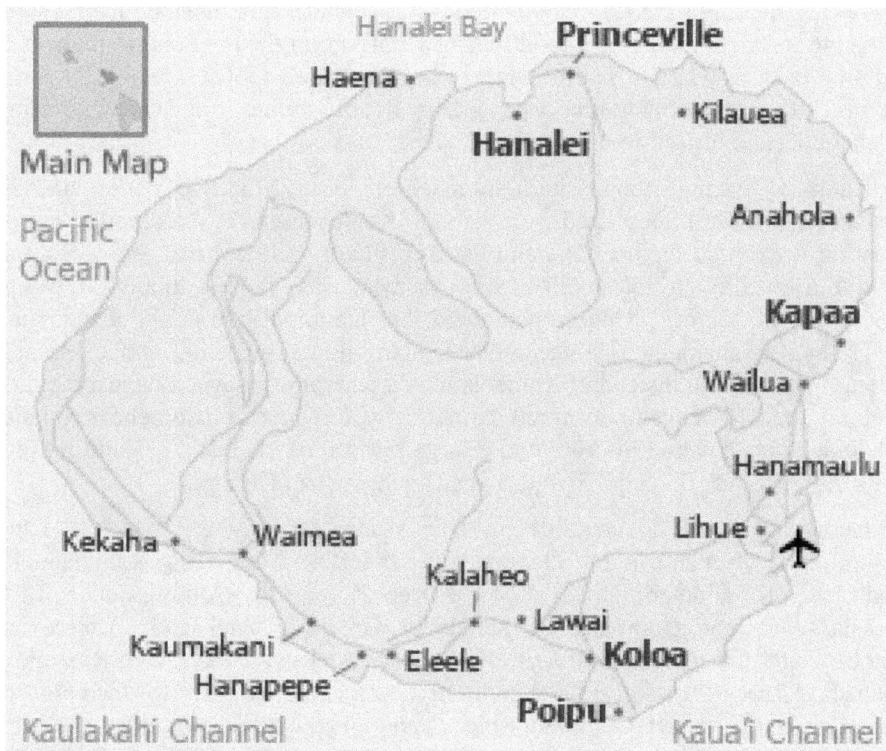

This modern map of Kaua'i, from www.tripadvisor.com, shows the relative locations of Nawiliwili (see airplane symbol), Poipu, Koloa, Hanapepe, and Waimea (all on Southern shore), Wailua on the east, and Hanalei Bay on the north shore…all places mentioned in this book. Kaua'i is very roughly a circle thirty-five miles in diameter, peak altitude near the center at around 5200 ' of elevation. Na Pali coast of steep cliffs is on the northwest.

Late in the evening of May 16th, 1816, they reached Waimea. A large village on the shore was easily visible, its abundance of thatched houses scattered unsystematically from the beach up into the surrounding hills. There was a heiau visible also, on a high hill above the center of the village. A river ran out of the mountains and into the ocean in the middle of the settled area. When its water met the ocean waves, a bore was created which made a constant rushing sound, louder than that of the ordinary surf, which could be heard all the way to the ship. Scores of canoes came out through the surf and surrounded the *Otkrytie*. In one canoe was a chief wearing a gold and red feather cape and a mahi'ole cap. George shouted to him in Hawai'ian, "Are you Kaumuali'i? We want to see King Kaumuali'i."

The chief waved his arms and shouted, "'A'ole...I am not Kaumuali'i. But he will come to visit you tomorrow."

During the night the *Otkrytie* drifted out a considerable distance from shore, dragging its anchor, so that it took the crew until noon the next day to maneuver the ship back to where it had previously been. At this spot was waiting a large flotilla of canoes, including one grand double-hulled one carrying King Kaumuali'i and his retinue.

Kaumuali'i came aboard with three chiefs, four Mū, two wives, and an extraordinarily tall teen-aged son named Keali'iahonui. Kaumuali'i was wearing a splendid feather cape and hat of brilliant gold and red. He was a tall man himself, though not as tall as his son, who was, George thought, close to seven feet in height. George estimated that Kaumuali'i was about the same height as Kamehameha. He was a leaner man, though muscular and apparently strong. But he had, instead of Kamehameha's fearsome visage, a handsome face with an almost European nose and dark eyes which appeared somehow Asiatic. His black hair covered his ears and a large portion of his neck. There was no grey in it. He was 36 years of age, a year younger than George.

George greeted Kaumuali'i in Hawai'ian by saying, "Aloha, King Kaumuali'i. My name is Dr. George von Schaeffer. Here King Kamehameha and Queen Ka'ahumanu have called me 'Kepa.' I am the Commissioner of the Russian-American Company on behalf of Governor Aleksandr Andreevich Baranov and the representative of His Majesty Aleksandr Pavlovich Romanov, the ruling Tsar of Russia. I have come here to receive payment for the cargo of the Russian-American Company ship *Bering* which you kept after the ship wrecked here in the month of January of last year, 1815. I have a letter in English written to you by King Kamehameha's Chief Cox, which explains how Captain John Ebbets deceived you into giving him payment for this cargo and why you should now give me payment for it."

George had trouble saying this in Hawai'ian, and, as he struggled, Kaumuali'i interrupted him and said in English, "I have learned to understand English. I can speak it also, but with some difficulties. I cannot read it well. But if you Russians know English, we might speak to each other better in that language."

"I had heard that you understand English," replied George. "That is why we helped Chief Cox to write you an English letter. Let me read it to you."

George took out the letter and showed it to Kaumuali'i. Kaumuali'i pointed out Chief Cox's mo'o lizard signature to one of his chiefs and they smiled at each other and appeared pleased. George read the letter aloud, slowly, in English. When he finished, Kaumuali'i said, "I will pay you for the cargo in sandalwood so that you will be pleased. But I wish to talk with you about other things. Can you come ashore to eat with me?"

George shot a glance at Captain Podushkin, asking with his eyes, "Do you think it's safe to do so?" Podushkin thought a second and then nodded affirmatively.

"I will come ashore to eat with you, Great King," George agreed.

By early evening George had been transported ashore and was taken to King Kaumuali'i's royal residence on a hill above the Waimea River and the village near its mouth. The heiau that had been visible from the ship was nearby. George had decided to leave Captain Podushkin on the *Otkrytie* and was accompanied by two crewmembers, the Russian-literate Englishman Charles Fox-Bennick to function as a kind of recording secretary and Grigorii Terentev, the ship's senior Russian-American Company hunter as an assistant and bodyguard.

A Heiau (or holy place) in Waimea, by Captain Cook's artist, John Webber, from:
http://commons.wikimedia.org/wiki/File:Heiau_at_Waimea_by_John_Webber.

The meal was served on a woven mat outside Kaumuali'i's residence. Kahili staffs bordered the mat and guards with tattooed legs stood to the sides. On the mat were numerous things to eat: yams and fruit, shellfish, fish, and pork. Gourds of water and 'awa were provided as well. Kaumuali'i, wearing still his feather cape, was accompanied by several of his chiefs and by his tall son

Keali'iahonui. He directed his guests to sit and eat. But no one ate as he began to speak.

Artist John Webber's "Inland View of Atooi (Kaua'i)" ca. 1785, from http://commons.wikimedia.org/wiki/File:An_Inland_View_in_Atooi

"When I was learning to speak English," Kaumuali'i began, directing his comments at George, "I took the name George in honor of the English King and the American President, George Washington, who once gave a meal in New York to one of my former native interpreters. I also named one of my sons…Humehume that I had with a commoner…George. I sent him to America with a Captain James Rowan to be educated and I hope he will return here someday wise in the ways of your world. But I think that since I have taken the English name George and you have the English name George, we should be friends and help each other. Do you agree to this?"

George could only agree. "'Ae…yes, King George, I agree," he replied.

"I have an English letter for you written by the American Captain John Ebbets, who is a friend of mine and did not, as Chief Cox wrote, deceive me," said Kaumuali'i. "Through Ebbets I sent an English letter about this to Governor Baranov also."

Kaumuali'i motioned with his hand and his son Keali'iahonui brought out a sealed envelope and gave it to him. He handed it to George.

George opened the envelope and read the letter:

"Kaua'i, 5th February, 1816

To the Commander of any Russian ship that may arrive at Kaua'i

Sir,

At the desire of Kaumuali'i, King of this island, I have left with him these few lines to inform you that the King has delivered me on account of Governor Baranov what furs were in the Russian ship *Bering* at the time she was lost—and has promised to give up what property he has in his possession that was saved from the wreck and for that lost to pay for in the produce of the island. This offer, I hope, will prevent any measures that may lead to hostilities from being adopted. The King assures me of his sincere desire to be in peace with your nation and to carry on a friendly commerce with Governor Baranov.

Yours, John Ebbets,

Commander of the ship *Enterprise*."

To his companions, Fox-Bennick and Terentev, George remarked in Russian so that Kaumuali'i and the others could not understand him, "It appears that Captain Ebbets has taken the *Bering's* furs away. Perhaps he has even delivered them back to Governor Baranov, though I doubt if the furs, after a year on this island, could still have been marketable. But from what he says we should be able to gain payment for what else was lost. And, on the ship, the King said he would pay us in sandalwood."

Fox-Bennick and Terentev nodded positively and said, in unison, "Khorosho…Good."

George then said to Kaumuali'i in English, "Captain Ebbets writes that he has taken the furs. I do not know if Governor Baranov has received them. But Captain Ebbets writes that you will pay for the lost cargo with the produce of the islands and that you want to have a friendly relationship with us Russians. Is that true?"

"'Ae…that is true," responded Kaumuali'i. "I will order that your ship be filled with whatever we have that you want."

"We want to send yams, taro, and fruit to Sitka," said George. "But we also desire sandalwood that Governor Baranov could send on ships to China to receive money and other goods there to pay him for what was lost."

"We will give you the sandalwood," agreed Kaumuali'i. "But I want to talk with you about something more important. I think you know that I have agreed to rule my islands of Kaua'i and Ni'ihau, and also the uninhabited Lehua and Kaula, as a tributary King to Kamehameha. When I die, my tall and splendid son Keali'iahonui who is sitting here with us will not succeed me as King, as I desire. Instead, Kamehameha, his son Liholiho, and his successors will rule all of the Hawai'ian islands, including mine. I agreed to this in order to spare the lives of my people, whom Kamehameha threatens. But the agreement is not good. It is not just. In truth I have a nobler ancestry than Kamehameha. I have a more direct connection to the Gods…a stronger mana. I, and not he, should be the King of all the islands. But he has more warriors, more ships, and more foreign help. Twice he tried to conquer my islands, and he would have kept trying until he did so if I had not agreed to serve him as a tributary king. I had to agree or die together with my family and many of my people."

"I have been told all this," said George. "And I do not like the rule of King Kamehameha as you do not."

"When the Americans were at war with the English," continued Kaumuali'i, "I gave sanctuary to American ships here on Kaua'i and I allowed the American captains to store their trade goods here. To the displeasure of my chiefs and my people I allowed them to cut and sell sandalwood. King Kamehameha favored the English captains and made trouble for me with their help. Some of my chiefs opposed me in his favor, so that I sacrificed two of them to the Gods. I made no more payments of tribute to him and still he did not attack me because he feared my American friends. But after the war ended and I refused to give the American captains any more sandalwood, the American captains became friends again with King Kamehameha, and I have been fearful of him again. But now I have you, a friend with my same name of George, who represents 'Ali'i Lukini nui,' the Great Russian Tsar. And this Tsar has many warriors and many ships, so that he could protect me here in my islands against the possibility of an attack by Kamehameha and perhaps he could even help me to become the King of all the islands instead of Kamehameha. Is this possible?"

George looked at Charles Fox-Bennick whose native English enabled him to understand Kaumauali'i more easily than Grigorii Terentev who knew only a few English phrases. Fox-Bennick clearly had no suggestion about how George should respond.

George thought for only a few seconds, then answered Kaumuali'i, "'Ae…this is possible. If you will provide the Russian-American Company with land where we can grow crops and hunt and fish to provision the Company's outposts in Alaska, then we could, in exchange, provide you the protection of the Russian Tsar Aleksandr's soldiers and ships. Indeed he already protects the Russian-American Company's enterprises in Alaska. I see no reason why he would not also protect its provisioning outpost in Hawai'i. Under such an agreement…the allotment of land in exchange for the Tsar's protection…I could move our operations on O'ahu here. There we have to make payments through old John Young to Kamehameha and his chiefs, and the American captains make continual trouble for us. Here on your island of Kaua'i we would expect no payments and no troubles. Is this possible?"

"'Ae…this is possible," answered Kaumuali'i, smiling. George noticed that the King apparently had all his teeth and that his smile was bright and attractive.

"Let's drink a toast to our agreement," proposed George.

Kaumuali'i poured some of the 'awa into several half gourds and handed the gourds to George, to Charles Fox-Bennick, and to Grigorii Terentev. George knew that the 'awa was a kind of tea made from the fermented saliva of young men and women who had chewed the leaves of a native pepper plant. Drinking the 'awa was most unappealing to him, but he took a drink of it with the others as Kaumuali'i raised his gourd to his mouth. It was very foul and bitter in taste, so that George wondered how the Hawai'ian Ali'i could desire it and order its preparation. He saw his companions stifle their gagging reflex.

"We shall smoke a pipe of tobacco together as well," announced Kaumuali'i. One of his chiefs produced a ceremonial pipe and tamped into it some chopped tobacco that he shook out of a woven bag.

George thought about how his wife Barbara would have reacted to the prospect of his smoking tobacco to confirm an agreement with a Hawai'ian King. No doubt she would protest this, he thought, and try to educate the King on the harm of inhaling the tobacco smoke. But he, also an ardent foe of tobacco smoking, could not now refuse. When Kaumuali'i lit the pipe, put it to his mouth and inhaled deeply from it, he passed it to George. George took a shallow draw from it, blew out the smoke and passed it to Terentev. "We are agreed, then," he said. "But we should have a written agreement...an actual document of contract written in Russian that I can show to Governor Baranov and to Tsar Aleksandr. Both you and I can think about the terms of this agreement for several days. But then we should have a formal ceremony on board the *Otkrytie* during which you and I will both sign the written agreement for all to witness. Then we'll have a cannon salute and a big celebration."

"You are right, Friend George," agreed Kaumuali'i. "I will summon all my chiefs and consult all my kāhuna. We will come to an agreement about everything. Then I will come to your ship."

"Maika'i...Good," said George.

The Agreement and the Ceremony:

When George returned to the *Otkrytie*, he had several discussions at length with Captain Podushkin. Podushkin agreed that moving the provisioning outpost to Kaua'i was a good idea, except for the very real possibility that Kamehameha might move by force to expel them from the islands altogether.

"We will not just suddenly abandon the O'ahu operations," suggested George. "We will continue them as before, paying Kamehameha as he expects. But gradually we will transfer more and more of our men here to Kaua'i. And while we do this, we will increase the level of our military capability to the point where we could not only repel an invasion, but aid Kaumuali'i in taking the other islands."

"That could take years, Yegor," said Captain Podushkin. "And it would require the substantial commitment of men and ships from the Russian navy. Company resources would clearly not be enough. Kamehameha can muster ten thousand men, put them in five hundred peleleu canoes, and be here in less than a month."

"I think we could get the commitment of the Russian navy as soon as I get back to St. Petersburg to present the case. These islands would certainly be of great value to Russia as a colony or even as a protectorate or exclusive ally. And wouldn't I enjoy dictating trade terms to those American captains?"

"That would be fine," agreed Podushkin. "But can we establish a sufficiently formidable position here long enough to allow Russian navy ships to sail here to support us? It would take you a year to get to St. Petersburg. And, even if you were immediately persuasive and the Tsar decided to annex the Hawai'ian islands as a colony, the ships would take another year to get back here. That's a minimum of two years' time. And what do you think Kamehameha will be doing during those two years?"

"He'll be wondering just what we are doing," answered George. "He may be angry when he at last perceives that we've abandoned O'ahu and taken up permanent residence on Kaua'i. But by then we'll have many more men and ships here. The Company ship *Kadiak* is due here very soon, as you know, and there is another ship…the Russian navy ship *Riurik*… reported to be on its way here from St. Petersburg. Also, we don't have to wait until ships come from Russia. We can purchase them here for notes on Governor Baranov's account and place them under our command. We'll have our own navy before Kamehameha and the American captains realize it. We'll help train Kaumuali'i's warriors into a more formidable force, we'll fortify the bays where European ships might anchor, and have our cannons trained upon all who approach. In fact, I would have all these measures completed before I left here for St. Petersburg. Even with ten thousand warriors, Kamehameha would not dare attack."

"You have an admirable sense of confidence that you can count upon the support of others," commented Captain Podushkin, stroking his goatee. "I would not be so sure even of Governor Baranov's support, no less the Tsar's. And without them you haven't got the strength you'll need to make such a venture work."

"When I explain the situation to them, they will understand," insisted George. "And if they understand, they will support us with all the needed force. In the case of Governor Baranov, I will be sending him a letter with you, since you are likely to be the next to see him when you sail back to Sitka. And I trust that you will be additionally persuasive on our behalf."

"Indeed, I will," said Captain Podushkin. "But it's a risky matter, in my opinion."

George worked on the agreement document for the next several days. Kaumuali'i came on board once during that time to discuss the terms. He brought with him his newest and favorite wife, the beautiful Kekaiha'akulou, whom he had husbanded after her first menstrual period. She now appeared to be in her teen years. Her coconut-sized bare breasts on an otherwise lithe figure attracted the lascivious attention of most of the crew. She was very vivacious in manner and enthusiastically smiled back at the leering men as she waited for Kaumuali'i to finish his business aboard. Next to her, however, dissuading the men from any closer approach, was her giant Mu guard, a man whose massive chest was scarred with the jagged marks of a shark-toothed club. He was holding a long kapu stave in an outstretched arm and his face seemed twisted into a constant scowl.

On May 19th, 1816, George went ashore to visit Kaumuali'i and was well received. But the next day Captain Podushkin was informed by a chief in a canoe that Kaumuali'i had declared Waimea kapu. He nevertheless had himself rowed ashore to invite the King to the formal ceremony on the *Otkrytie,* which was to take place the next day at eleven o'clock in the morning. It was, he explained, the birthday of His Highness, the Russian Grand Duke Konstantin Pavlovich, and they had chosen to sign the formal agreement on this auspicious day. On May 21st, 1816, at ten o'clock in the morning, the Captain sent a boat with twenty men ashore to bring King Kaumuali'i out to the ship. He instructed three of the men to stay ashore and to raise a flagpole in the center of the Waimea village. But when the boat came back to the ship, Kaumuali'i was not in it. He had sent two messengers instead who carried with them bottles of rum as a gift. These men said that Kaumuali'i had retreated into the heiau and was asking the Gods for their approval of his intentions to sign a written agreement with the Russians. George was upset about this apparent wavering of Kaumuali'i's resolve. But Captain Podushkin sent the messengers back with the return message that the King's absence at the ceremony was an insult to the Russian Grand Duke and to his brother, the Russian Tsar Aleksandr. For two hours he and George commiserated with each other about the apparent futility of their efforts.

At one o'clock in the afternoon a longboat that Captain Podushkin had sent ashore to bring back the three men who erected the flagpole came back to the ship with Kaumuali'i in it. He was alone, unaccompanied by other natives, but wearing yet another, and even more strikingly magnificent, gold-and-red-feathered 'ahu'ula cape and mahi'ole cap. Around his torso under the cape he wore a brilliantly colored feather sash similar to one George had seen Kamehameha wearing at the Waikoloa warriors' exercise. The sash, George noticed, was festooned in its end tassles with a large number of human molars. When Kaumuali'i stepped on deck and noticed that George was admiring his grand attire, he told George that all this regalia—the cap, cape, and sash-- had been given to him by Kamehameha in 1810 when he agreed to become

Kamehameha's tributary king. The sash, called "ka 'ei kapu o Liloa," dated back to a sixteenth-century predecessor of Kamehameha's on the island of Hawaii. The molars were taken from enemies either killed in battle or captured and sacrificed to the war god Kūkā'ilimoku.

A Portrait of <u>KAUMUALI'I</u> (c.1780—26 May, 1824), last King of Kaua'i, by BROOK KAPŪKUNIAHI PARKER, July 2012.

"Well, your days as a tributary king are over," George told him. "You will become a true king again very soon. We have some documents here for you to sign. And then we want you to announce these agreements to all your chiefs and to your people as well. Are you agreed to sign?"

"Yes, I do agree to sign," said Kaumuali'i.

"Then let us do things in the following order," George suggested. "First, we have an Act of Allegiance to Emperor Aleksandr I of Russia, our Tsar. Signing this agreement means that the Tsar becomes your protector. Do you understand this?"

"I understand," replied Kaumuali'i.

"Then I will read it in Russian and endeavor to translate its words into your language for you," said George. He held the document up to his gaze and began to read:

"Act of Allegiance of King Kaumuali'i to Emperor Aleksandr I of Russia

May 21, 1816

Copy—

His Majesty, Kaumuali'i, the King of the Hawai'ian Islands in the North Pacific Ocean, Kaua'i and Ni'ihau, and hereditary prince of the islands of O'ahu, Lana'i, and Mau'i, asks his Majesty, Sovereign Emperor Aleksandr Pavlovich, Autocrat of All the Russias, etc., etc., etc., to accept under his protection the above-mentioned islands. He (Kaumuali'i), for himself and for his successor, wishes to profess loyalty to the Russian scepter. As a sign of his faithfulness and devotion, he (Kaumuali'i) accepts the Russian flag from the ship *Otkrytie*, which belongs to the Russian-American Company.

    Sign of the king: X_____ Kaumuali'i

Translated into the Hawai'ian language and announced by the King himself to the inhabitants of the islands Kaua'i and Ni'ihau.

   Russian Imperial Collegiate Assessor,

   Commissioner of the Russian-American Company,

   Doctor of Medicine and Surgery,

          Yegor von Sheffer

Read on the ship *Otkrytie* in the presence of the total crew—thirty-eight men.

   Naval Lieutenant and Cavalier,

         Iakov Anikievich Podushkin."

After George had read the Act in Russian and explained the words of it as best he could in Hawai'ian, stopping occasionally to answer Kaumuali'i's questions in both English and Hawai'ian, he handed Kaumuali'i the ink-daubed quill. Kaumuali'i took the quill a bit awkwardly into his right hand, turned it around carefully, and then scribed a mo'o lizard glyph similar to the one Chief Cox had used onto the line after the "X."

George turned to the crew and exclaimed, "After me now, men…Ura!"

The men as one loudly yelled "Ura," then another "Ura," then another, after George…three in all. Kaumuali'i seemed impressed by this and smiled.

"Now we have an Award of Honorary Rank in the Tsar's Navy," explained George. "By signing this document you will become an officer…a leading warrior…in the Russian navy. Do you understand this?"

"I understand," answered Kaumuali'i.

"Before you sign this document, we wish to present you with a Russian naval officer's uniform…and we want you to wear it. Do not worry about your cape and cap. We will transport them ashore with you in a boat after the ceremony."

George and Captain Podushkin led Kaumuali'i below decks to the Captain's quarters. There they helped dress Kaumuali'i in one of Captain Podushkin's dress uniforms complete with its plumed hat and gold-braided epaulets.

"It's fortunate that you are so tall, Iakov," said George to Captain Podushkin, referring to Kaumuali'i's height. "Otherwise it wouldn't fit."

Their attempt to put Kaumuali'i in a pair of Captain Podushkin's dress boots, however, was futile. Kaumuali'i's feet were obviously too large and, besides, he was very reluctant to put them on. As they walked back onto the deck, the crew, seeing Kaumuali'i in the bright uniform, made another cheer of encouragement, shouting "Ura!"

George read the Award of Honorary Rank in Russian, again explaining in Hawai'ian to Kaumuali'i what each phrase meant. The Award read:

"Award of Honorary Naval Rank to King Kaumuali'i

May 21, 1816

According to the voluntary alliance of Kaumuali'i, King of the Hawai'ian islands of Kaua'i and Ni'ihau, with Aleksandr Pavlovich, the Sovereign Emperor, Autocrat of All the Russias, etc., etc., etc., on the occasions of visits by foreigners who come to these islands, as well as on any other occasions, King Kaumuali'i is to be given all honors which belong to the rank of a line-officer of His Imperial Majesty's Navy.

        Signed: Russian Commissioners

                           Yegor von Sheffer

                           Grigorii Terentev."

George and Grigorii Terentev had already signed two copies of this document. George explained to Kaumuali'i that he was to keep one copy while George would keep the other. The actual investiture of rank, however, came when Captain Podushkin, already a commissioned officer in the Russian navy, presented to him his officer's dirk.

Captain Podushkin came forward with a Russian officer's dirk. It had a white bone handle with a silver hilt, and the blade was encased in a polished silver scabbard wrapped in a long purple sash. Kaumuali'i's face brightened perceptibly when he saw it. Captain Podushkin placed the dirk into Kaumuali'i's hands, saying, "You are now an honorary officer in the Russian navy. I present to you this officer's dirk. Wear it well."

George urged the crew into another round of three cheers, after him, of "Ura," "Ura," "Ura!" Kaumuali'i turned the dirk this way and that, admiring it and smiling.

"We have prepared as well a medal for your son, the Prince," said George. "It's a silver cross of St. Vladimir to be worn on all ceremonial occasions and at the visits of Russian and foreign ships to this island."

He handed the large medal on its ribbon to Kaumuali'i.

"Now there is the official contract between you and me as representative of Governor Aleksandr Baranov and the Russian-American Company," said George. "This is a written statement of your promises to me and my promises to you. If you sign this, it means that you must do what you promise. Do you understand this?"

"I understand," answered Kaumuali'i.

George held the contract up and read it as he had read the other documents. The document read:

"Contract between King Kaumuali'i and Dr. Yegor von Sheffer

May 21, 1816

Copy No. 3

The undersigned has concluded the following contract:

1. King Kaumuali'i will deliver to the Russian-American Company whatever cargo of the wrecked ship *Bering* he was able to salvage.

2. King Kaumuali'i promises to trade exclusively with the Russian-American Company. In the case of American ships, he is to sell them only provisions.

3. The King will allow the Company to establish factories everywhere in his possessions and he will aid with his men in the erection of buildings and in the development of plantations.

4. The King will furnish provisions to any Russian vessel. For a small payment to the Russian-American Company the King will receive as much goods from the cargo as he needs, and besides he will receive from the cargo of the *Otkrytie* as much goods as will cover the year's delivery of sandalwood. I, myself (Dr. Egor von Sheffer), will judge how much sandalwood can be loaded on the *Otkrytie*. In six months the cargo should be ready and the Company undertakes to supply the King with a fully armed ship, and, in return, the King will again deliver as much sandalwood as the *Otkrytie* or a similar ship can carry. This

delivery should be ready a year after the first one has been made. The next load should be ready in eighteen months, and for every stipulated delivery of sandalwood the King will receive whatever goods he is pleased to take. The Company will leave the vessel at the Hawai'ian islands until the Kings harvests his crop of taro roots, which the King will deliver free. The Company will immediately send a messenger to St. Petersburg to make a report to the Emperor and to deliver the King's request for protection. The King gives permission for preparations here of mineralogical, botanical, and zoological collections.

Signed:_____   Russian Staff Officer and Commissioner of the Russian-American Company,

Dr. Yegor von Sheffer

X_____   King Kaumuali'i

On the island of Kaua'i, Port of Waimea, on the ship *Otkrytie*."

To three copies of this document, both George and Kaumuali'i signed, each in their own way. George gave one copy to the King. Captain Podushkin poured a dram of vodka for each member of the crew within his reach from a small keg, then he gave the keg to Filip Osipov and Aleksei Odnoriadkin to pour for the others. Soon another three cheers rang out.

At five o'clock King Kaumuali'i was ready to go ashore. Captain Podushkin ordered the longboat lowered and Kaumuali'i agilely climbed down into it and sat in its bow seat. The rowboat crew then climbed aboard. Captain Podushkin handed down Kaumuali'i's feathered cap and cape, and also handed him a folded Russian flag.

"When you get ashore, see that this flag is raised on the pole we've erected in the village," he said. "When we see it, we'll fire a fourteen-gun salute."

After the boat had left the ship for shore, Captain Podushkin asked George, "Don't you think it strange that he came out here to the ship all alone? I've never heard of any Hawai'ian chief doing that before…no wives, no guards, no chiefs…just him. Either he's very brave or he doesn't want any of his people to know what he's done."

"That's why at the big celebration tomorrow we'll ask him to make an announcement of the agreement to everyone in attendance," said George.

In a half hour the men on the *Otkrytie* watched the Russian flag raised over Waimea.

Captain Podushkin ordered a fourteen-gun salute, which echoed shot by shot back from the mountains behind the village. The agreement was now in effect.

The Celebration in Waimea:

The day after the shipboard signing of the agreement documents, George, Captain Podushkin, and most of the crew of the *Otkrytie* came ashore to participate in a banquet and celebration given by King Kaumuali'i. The banquet took place at the King's residence on the hill above the village. The food was arrayed on a great square table constructed of planks from the wrecked *Bering*. This was Kaumuali'i's concession to the foreigners who, he knew, were accustomed to eating from a table as opposed to a woven mat on the ground. The main fare was roast dog, and there were twenty or thirty of those, just taken up out of the cooking imus an hour before. There was also pork and a wide variety of boiled shellfish: oysters, mussels, clams, crayfish, crabs, and lobster. Clusters of bananas were at every table position in front of a low stool. Bottles of rum and glass tumblers were in position also. George counted the banquet places and recorded the detail that there were sixty-two stools and one high-backed chair for the King. King Kaumuali'i was wearing his Russian naval officer's uniform.

The weather was balmy that day and warmer than usual, with alternating clouds and sun. The feather tops of the King's kahili staffs were continually fluttering in the blustery wind. Thirty guards surrounded the banquet venue, each armed with a musket and a shark-toothed club. In attendance were several of Kaumuali'i's chiefs from different areas of Kaua'i. George had difficulty in memorizing their names when he was introduced to them, but several of them he did remember. There was the King's nephew Kamaholelani who had helped negotiate with Kamehameha and his ministers in 1810. Also there was Chief Kaloha'aki of Hanalei and Chief Ko'upikea of Hanapepe. George was introduced to Chief Ni'au who was described as "the chanter." He also met Chiefs Kaela, Lu'iawa, and Kahekili Haupu, also called Kaiawa, the father of Kaumuali'i's favorite wife Kekaiha'akolou. Other wives were also in attendance, including the senior wives Kawalu, Kapua'amohu and Namahana, the regal Monalau, and Kaininoa or "Naoa." Kawalu, Kapua'amohu and Naoa were also Kaumuali'i's half sisters. The tall son Keali'iahonui was there, as was a younger son by Namahana, Kahekili, who was about ten years old, and a still younger daughter by Naoa who was called "Princess Kapo," who was named after a sister of Kaumuali'i's, another Kapi'olani, who was over six feet tall and was surely, George thought, close to four hundred pounds in weight. George resolved to address all of King Kaumuali'i's wives with the title "Queen." When he asked "King George" how many wives he had, the King said only that he had "many." And to George's question about the number of his children, Kaumuali'i answered that he could not say, but that he had also "many."

Before the guests were asked to seat themselves at the table, the crowd from the Waimea village continued to grow until there were more than a thousand people surrounding the guarded table on the square in front of King

Kaumuali'i's residence on the hill. At one o'clock in the afternoon, Kaumuali'i stepped up onto the table and began to speak to the crowd. As George listened, he made the required announcement to his chiefs, wives, children, and people that he had concluded an agreement for their protection by the Tsar of Russia and secured their future in exclusive trade with the Russian-American Company, which the King's "Friend George" represented. He told them the agreement was "nui nui maika'i…very, very good" for all of them and that they should give their support to George and his men in building houses and developing the commerce and defense of their island home. He finished his announcement with the word "Aloha." George was positively impressed.

Kaumuali'i stepped down from the table and invited the guests to be seated. Thirty of the seats, every other one at Kaumuali'i's instruction, were taken by the men from the *Otkrytie*. The intermediate seats were then taken by his chiefs and other male dignitaries, including his son Keali'iahonui. Kaumuali'i's wives and all the rest of the women vanished suddenly from the banquet, slipping away to eat together at another site on the riverbank below. Their meal, also prepared by Kaumuali'i's staff of male cooks, did not include bananas, coconuts, or pork, which were kapu to them. George seated himself to Kaumuali'i's immediate right, between him and Chief Kamaholelani. As the servants carved the roasted dogs with bamboo knives, George reached for a bottle of rum and offered to pour some into the glasses of Kaumuali'i and Kamaholelani. They both declined with waves of their hands, and so George poured some rum into his own glass, noticing how spotlessly clean it was.

"Your glass came here years ago with Captain Vancouver," said Kaumuali'i, anticipating George's question. "Some of the other glasses come from Italy and still others come from France. I have a quite large collection of them and use them only for important occasions."

"And indeed this is an important occasion," said George. "I think we will have a bright future for our mutual endeavors."

"I have ordered that a luakini heiau be built to honor our agreement," said Kaumuali'i, matter-of-factly. "It will be located on the other bank of the river where you will be given land. Last night we sacrificed two 'kauwā' outcasts to be placed beneath it. As is our custom, their left eyeballs were cut out for me to consume…but I only pretend to eat them, as we are not cannibals. It is part of the ritual of commissioning the sacrifices…giving them duties to perform for us in the spirit world. One of them is to act in the spirit world to help you, and the other is to help me…against the martial spirit of Kamehameha."

George was upset to hear that humans had been sacrificed to bless his endeavors with Kaumuali'i on Kaua'i. Somehow he had expected that Kaumuali'i would not be as savage in his practice of the Hawai'ian religion as Kamehameha was, but that, obviously, was not the case. He decided he would try to convert Kaumuali'i to his own views, which would prohibit human sacrifice for any purpose. But he would first have to win Kaumuali'i's trust and confidence…and that would take time.

To start the banquet, Kaumuali'i stood up and proposed a toast to His Imperial Majesty, Tsar Aleksandr I of Russia. When he put his glass up to his lips, a salute of musket fire erupted from the shore below where he had stationed several warriors. The guards surrounding them broke into a triple cheer of "Ura," mimicking the cheers George had organized on the *Otkrytie* the day before. George was impressed, wondering how Kaumuali'i had coordinated the toast, the distant musket salute, and the cheer. But then he recalled that Kaumuali'i had refused his offer to pour rum into his glass. What was in it then? When Kaumauli'i sat back down, George glanced over into the glass and saw that it was filled with 'awa. Kaumuali'i obviously preferred the 'awa to foreign rum and had already had the glass filled with it before he came to the table.

A group of Hawai'ian musicians and dancers then performed for the Russian guests. Captain Podushkin responded to this by asking several of the Aleut crew members to perform a dance of their own. This the Aleuts willingly did, accompanied by one of the Russian crew members who played as loudly as he could in a RAZ-dva-tri, RAZ-dva-tri, RAZ-dva-tri beat on a borrowed large Hawai'ian pahu drum. The Chiefs seemed delighted by the Aleut dance, during which the Aleuts leaped about crazily in unison and screamed out a cadence with grunts and exhalations.

At a signal from Kaumuali'i several horses were suddenly led into view. Each of the horses was a different color, but all appeared strong and spirited.

"These are riding horses...paū kau lio," announced Kaumuali'i, and, at his words, a fit young man sprang to one of the horse's back. At the horse's mouth were reins attached to a rope halter without a bit. The young man goaded the horse into a trot and adroitly steered it into a circle around the banquet area. At one point he slid down into a position to hang onto the horse's side so that the people seated at the banquet table could not see him. Yet the horse continued to trot around the spectators, still under the young man's command. When the rider then righted himself, he kicked the horse's flanks and started the horse into a rapid gallop, headed first away down the hill, then, wheeling suddenly around, back up toward the banquet. As he reached the vicinity of the table, he stopped the horse, reared it onto its hind legs for a moment, then hopped off to the horse's side and bowed. All the spectators, Russian and Hawai'ian, burst into cheers.

The horseback riding demonstration was followed by a close-order drill of Kaumuali'i's guardsmen, who handed around their heavy muskets as if they were mere sticks as they marched in complex patterns in time to a beating drum. George was reminded of the similar drill he had seen by the Tsar's guards at the award ceremony for General Tormasov in St. Petersburg almost three years before, but whereas the Tsar's guard team had been comprised of nine men, Kaumuali'i's group...wearing the native mālo and little else...included thirty.

As they continued to eat and drink after the entertainment, Kaumuali'i told George and Captain Podushkin that they could begin unloading their things from the *Otkrytie* the next day. He would see that they had houses to store things in until they could settle onto land near the village. He would also order the remaining things from the *Bering* and the sandalwood to be brought to the shore for loading onto the *Otkrytie* once it was emptied. Captain Podushkin estimated that this process would take ten days time.

The *Otkrytie* Departs:

By May 29th, 1816, the *Otkrytie* had been emptied of its cargo of furs, arms, tools, and trade goods and filled with yams, taro, dried fruit and sandalwood.

The unloading of ten of the ship's fourteen cannon had been exciting. When the first cannon approached the shore, tied together with its carriage across the center of the longboat's middle seats, a large crowd of Kaumuali'i's warriors clammered into the surf to help lift it out of the boat and carry it onto the beach. In their excitement to come into contact with the cannon, they stopped the longboat in water still as deep as their necks. The longboat crew tried to restrain them, but a group of them pulled so hard on the side of the cannon's carriage that they capsized the longboat, turning the cannon and carriage underneath it. As the crewmembers found their feet in the water and struggled to get ashore, Aleksei Odnoriadkin, who had been in charge of the longboat, managed with his hunting knife to cut the ropes holding the cannon to the boat so that the boat might be righted. But the cannon and carriage fell onto one warrior who was apparently swimming under the boat after it had capsized. He was smashed into the bottom and trapped by the heavy falling cannon and carriage. For a minute or more, Aleksei and a group of the warriors wrenched violently on the submerged cannon to roll it off the man. At last they managed to do so and pulled the man up out of the water. His lower right leg had been badly mangled, so that the water was red with his blood. His shin was broken midway between his foot and knee so that the lower portion was dangling by a shred of skin. When his fellow warriors carried him ashore, Captain Podushkin, who had been watching from the beach, sent a man running to summon George who was supervising the construction of a warehouse on the bank above the river where the villagers had begun building their grass houses.

George sprinted to the beach with his medical bag. He made a tourniquet out of a sailor's belt and clamped off the warrior's leg. Using a scalpel from his bag, he cut away the man's dangling right foot and ankle.

"Get the man some rum," he shouted. "I need to dress up the stump and tie the veins. You'll have to hold him down."

In a half hour George had completed the amputation and the injured warrior was unconscious. King Kaumuali'i had come down to the beach to watch the operation and he was very impressed by George's skill.

"Will he live?" Kaumuali'i asked George.

"He's young and strong," said George. "I think he will live. When he wakes up, I want him to drink some tea that I will make for him. He should drink only this tea several times a day for three days…then he can eat if he wants. He will need to rest for a long time. When his stump heals, we can make for him a wooden leg. Meanwhile he will need a crutch."

"Maika'i," said Kaumuali'i. He turned away and commanded his men to go out into the surf and haul the cannon and its carriage ashore. "Let's see how it works," he said to Captain Podushkin.

After the cargo and the cannons were all ashore, Captain Podushkin gave a demonstration to Kaumuali'i and several of his chiefs of the cannon's operation. He discharged a grenade by fuse, then fired a ball, some grapeshot, and another grenade at the opposite bank of the Waimea River. Kaumuali'i, like Kamehameha, was most impressed at the result of the fired grenade, which exploded over 250 sazhens away. Captain Podushkin told him that with such a grenade they could drive even large ships out of their harbor and that with a charge of fired grapeshot they could kill many warriors well beyond spear range with a single shot. He warned Kaumuali'i to take great care in the storage of the barrels of gunpowder he was leaving with the cannons. "One spark in the wrong place," he said, "and you'll all be buried in the same thimble." Kaumuali'i did not seem to understand this figure of speech, but he agreed to keep the gunpowder well sheltered from the rain and away from any source of fire.

George decided that he would leave several men behind and sail back to O'ahu on the *Otkrytie*, taking with him fifty of Kaumuali'i's kanakas as workers. His plan was to send Captain Podushkin and the *Otkrytie* on to Sitka with the provisions and sandalwood for Governor Baranov, to whom he had written a long letter. Then he would return on one or more of the other ships, bringing back to Kaua'i as many of his Russians and Aleuts as he could sneak away from the Waikīkī outpost, replacing them with the Kaua'ian kanakas. He would still need, he knew, a strong workforce at Waikīkī to harvest and process the crops he had planted there.

George left Grigorii Terentev, Charles Fox-Bennick and an Unalaska Chieftain named Grigorii Iskakov with King Kaumuali'i at Waimea on Kaua'i while he sailed to O'ahu to retrieve other ships and more men. The *Otkrytie* sailed away from Waimea on May 31st.

Only a few hours away from Waimea the weather suddenly changed. Huge ominous clouds formed overhead and lightning flashed all around them with tremendous booming thunder. A great squall of rain drenched them and the wind kept increasing and increasing with a wild howling sound. The waves heightened to the level of the lower yards, and at two o'clock Captain Podushkin sent the men aloft to reef the topsails. A few hours later he reduced sail further and steered the ship into the wind as a protective measure, so strong was the blast and so high the waves. George came up on deck to watch the men's gallant efforts in the furious tempest. All that night and into the next day the storm raged with increasing strength. The Kaua'ians aboard huddled together aft in fear, thinking the ship would be torn apart. Most of the chickens they had brought aboard with them had been blown over the side, and they feared that they would soon follow.

The next afternoon, the main mast shattered at its midpoint above the deck and came crashing down in a tangle of rigging and furled sail. The men raced to cut the yards free, hacking like wild men with their knives at the ropes. Their object was to try to keep the top part of the mast from falling overboard and being washed away, but they failed. And just then the mizzenmast also broke, and close to the deck. Heroic efforts managed to salvage the fallen mast and yards, but the ship was now little more than flotsam on the churning surface of the sea. To make matters even worse, the ship sprang serious leaks below decks requiring the crew to man the pumps. The leakage and the seawash had ruined much of the crew's food.

"If we get a break in the storm, we can make it to Ni'ihau," Captain Podushkin shouted to George and several others. "There we can reprovision and do some makeshift repairs…raise false masts and such. But I'm afraid we'll have to head from there directly home to Sitka. Sailing to O'ahu is out of the question now."

After the trauma of the fallen masts and the damage to the ship and its stores, George did not object to Captain Podushkin's change of plans. Survival was now their first concern. In a few more hours the storm began to abate. Captain Podushkin put up what sail he could in an effort to reach Ni'ihau. "Kaumuali'i is King there too," he said, "And his men who are with us can help us get what we need from the natives there. We'll be all right."

Captain Podushkin's calm demeanor in these most frightful moments reassured both George and the crew. In a few hours, even though visibility was not good, Ni'ihau came into view. The *Otkrytie* found a place of nine sazhens depth near the steep shore where they could lower anchor. But a native canoe came out and the men aboard would not listen to any of the Kaua'ians aboard, no matter their professions of distress and their invocation of Kaumuali'i's name. This place was, they said, 'kapu' and the ship must leave. Help would be given to them further north toward Lehua, they said. There was nothing for it but to raise anchor and make their way further north.

In the night as they sailed north, the lookouts spied a large bonfire on shore in a small sheltering cove. Captain Podushkin's sounding measured a depth of twelve sazhens and he ordered the anchor dropped. The *Otkrytie*'s acute peril was over. The next morning a chief named Makawalao came out in a canoe and offered his aid to the ship. He acknowledged that he was a subject of King

Kaumuali'i and wished to have George report to Kaumuali'i that he had given whatever assistance was needed.

In six days the men of the *Otkrytie* had taken aboard fresh yams, taro, pumpkins, and watermelon. They restored their water supply. There were not many trees on Ni'ihau, but they did find one tree tall and straight enough to extend the main mast stub upwards sufficient to bear one yardarm for sail, and they fastened the broken mizzen mast back onto its stub, off-center and weak, but able to bear sail in a mild wind. The leaks were not stopped, but were reduced, so that Captain Podushkin felt ready to sail for Sitka. George offered the Kaua'ians the choice of leaving the ship and staying on Ni'ihau until they could be returned home to Waimea later or sailing on the *Otkrytie* for Sitka. To his surprise, three of the kanakas chose to remain on the ship bound for Sitka. The others, forty-seven in number, decided to stay at the village on Ni'ihau.

As the weather cleared, George devised a plan that would return him to Waimea. Filip Osipov and Aleksei Odnoriadkin, both half-Russian, half-Aleut, and very experienced in a seal-hide baidarka, told George they thought they could make the crossing back across the Kaulakahi Channel to Kaua'i in the largest baidarka they had aboard. It was an open-topped baidarka with places for four paddlers. It was the very craft that had first brought King Kaumuali'i aboard the *Otkrytie*.

"Do you really think we can make it?" George asked Filip Osipov. "It's probably much further than it looks. It could be thirty miles from here to Waimea."

"We've paddled thirty miles in a day before, Yegor Nikolaevich," answered Filip. "It really depends on the weather. But even if it gets rough, I think we'll be all right in the baidarka."

"Let's do it then," said George.

Saying farewell to the competent Captain Podushkin was difficult. George had come to appreciate him as a confidant with good insight into every situation. At their parting, he hugged Podushkin, telling him that he would commend his performance to Governor Baranov when he saw him next. "You are an outstanding Captain and leader of men, Iakov Anikievich," he said, "And I wish you 'schastlivogo puti'…a fortunate journey."

"Spasibo…Thank you, Yegor," responded Captain Podushkin. "And I wish the same for you." Then he smiled and joked, "I hope that you become the ruler of all these islands. The people here would be the better for it."

Three Aleuts paddling in a baidarka, from http://skinboatjournal.blogspot.com/2011/04_01_archive.html, attributed there to George Dyson's Baidarka: The Kayak, Alaska Northwest Books, 1986, ISBN 0-88240-315-X.

On the morning of June 9, 1816, George, Filip Osipov, and Aleksei Odnoriadkin watched the *Otkrytie* sail away to the north. Looking across the fearsome channel toward the island of Kaua'i they felt suddenly as if they had been orphaned. They sat down for a time according to the Russian superstition, and then they shoved off and set to work with the paddles, two at a time in shifts, and in a few hours the baidarka was making progress toward Kaua'i. A school of porpoises chose to circle them and amuse them with their graceful spinning leaps into the air. But then a strong wind came up into their faces and impeded their progress. The waves grew until they were rising and falling several sazhens of height as they slid down the faces of each one. Aleksei, who was sitting in the rear, steered a course diagonally across the top of the waves so that they would not be upset. But their course seemed to be changing to the south and the apparent distance to the Kaua'i shore did not diminish no matter how all three of them put their arms and shoulders into the paddles. This exhausting work continued the entire afternoon and into the evening, but as it got dark they could see that they were at last coming closer to the Kaua'i shore. But where?

"At this point I'd rather walk along the shore to Waimea than try to paddle there," said George. "Let's just beach the baidarka and leave it on foot."

The surf was rough and the baidarka accelerated rapidly down the face of a large wave as they rode into shore. At last the bottom of the craft struck sand and they jumped out and dragged it onto a wide beach. They collapsed onto the sand from the exhaustion of the day's effort and fell asleep.

In the morning they found some birds eggs in the dunes behind the beach. They ate the eggs raw and drank some of their water, before starting to hike to the east along the shore. In three hours they came within sight of Waimea.

"Slava Bogu...Thank God," said George. "We've made it. You boys were right. I congratulate you and commend you."

Filip and Aleksei laughed at George's calling them "malchiki" or "boys," and, joking, replied, "We'd have made it sooner if we didn't have such an old 'starik' paddling with us. Do you think the King will be happy to see us?"

"I think so," said George.

Touring Kaua'i with the Royal Party:

Indeed King Kaumuali'i was most pleased at the surprising return of George and his two companions. The storm that had damaged the *Otkrytie* had also destroyed many houses in the Waimea village and had flooded some of the taro fields. He expressed to George his concern that having only six Russians in Waimea would not be enough to be of aid to him in the event of an attack by Kamehameha's forces, but he accepted George's reassurance that the Russian flag flying above the island would dissuade all other foreigners from aggression. Besides, George explained, other Russian ships and men would be coming soon. All they could do was to wait.

George began his agricultural efforts by directing a native workforce in the planting of potatoes, carrots, cabbage, onions, pumpkins, squash, and turnips on the property called Hīpō he had been given on the east bluff of the Waimea River. He also planted some cuttings of pineapple from Don Francisco Marin on O'ahu, a few seeds of the new cotton, and some wheat. In short order he had almost twenty acres under cultivation, worrying only about how the planting in June was late according to farming conventions he was accustomed to in Europe. But, he thought, the climate here was not subject to European seasons.

The chiefs from other districts who had come for the signing of the agreement and for the celebration thereafter were now leaving Waimea to return to their residences. The chiefs who resided in the villages to the immediate east would be traveling by land. Kaumuali'i decided to accompany a few of them on their way in order to give George a guided tour of the island of Kaua'i. This was after he had already taken George on a hike up the Waimea River to show him the stone-lined Menehune Ditch or "Kīkīaola," the work of the legendary disappeared "little people" who had inhabited the islands in the long past. He told George about the Menuhune Chief, Papa'ena'ena, who designed and built the irrigation system for the taro fields, demanding only equal rations of food for his workers from the King. Papa'ena'ena was the name he gave to his current residence, said Kaumuali'i, in honor of this ancient Menehune chief. They visited also a spectacular waterfall up the slopes of the long extinct Pu'u Ka Pele volcano. Near there was the village of Kaumuali'i's canoe makers. For generations the "kāhuna ka lai wa'a," or "priests of the canoes" had manufactured the best canoes in the islands from this well forested region. The 'elepaio bird, a type of woodpecker, was used by the kāhuna to judge which trees were ideal for canoe construction. They could tell by the sound of the birds' pecking if the tree was sound, and if the birds lingered too long on any tree they knew that it was likely wormy and not worth cutting as a potential canoe. And they made a hike to a vantage point above the vast red and orange and brown Waimea Canyon, which awed George with its grandeur, backed by Mount Wai'ale'ale, the highest point on the island and the rainiest, whose numerous shades of green contrasted vividly with those of the deep dry canyon rift which had been carved from it by the river.

The royal party, including George and Grigorii Terentev, his "Assistant Commissioner," headed eastward from Waimea along an inland trail. In a short while they reached the village of Hanapēpē, which Kaumuali'i chose to enter in an open-topped palanquin carried by four strong guards. Ahead of him marched the Mū with their shouts of "Kapu-moi!" and their kapu staves, followed by the "pa'akāhili" or kāhili bearers. Behind him trekked his "iwikuamo'o" or masseuse, his "aipu'upu'u" or cape steward, and his "ipukuha," the spittoon bearer. In Hanapēpē they said farewell to one of the chiefs and continued the expedition to the villages of Kalāheo and Lāwa'i. Near there they surveyed the salt pond adjacent to the ocean called "nōmilu." Kaumuali'i showed George and Grigorii Terentev that this pond, from which salt was produced by evaporation so that it could be collected by hand or gourd, had a submarine connection to the ocean. The level of it rose and fell with the tide. After spending the night on the mauka edge of this salt pond, the royal party continued the next day to Kōloa, stopping first in the morning at "puhi," the "spouting horn" where the sea, intruding into a narrowing crevice of lava beneath the level of the surf, spouts through a tiny surface vent spectacularly up into the air above the shore with every large wave. George and Grigorii marveled at the spout's height and its rushing noise.

Kōloa and its surroundings were significant historically, Kaumuali'i related, because of the invasions of Kaua'i that had been repelled there. To the east of Kōloa's Poipu Beach, with its mild and fish-filled waters, there was, a mile or two further on, where the sheer ascent of the giant dark Mount Ha'upu ended the coastal flatlands, a beach called Māhā'ulepū. Kaumuali'i planned to spend the next night there, saying that he would tell the story in English of the invasions to George and to Grigorii.

Kaumuali'i's Story:

The next morning after eating dried fruit and poi on woven mats under the shade of fiery orange-blossomed wiliwili trees, George and Grigorii Terentev were told to prepare themselves for Kaumuali'i's narration. The King was, his steward said, in his tent praying for the Gods' guidance in telling the story. The weather was beautiful, and George could only admire the scenery around them. Māhā'ulepū beach was within sight of the camp and its eating mats. In George's immediate view were the red plumes of the kāhili overhead. In his ears was the rushing sound of the undulating surf. And in his nose was the scent of the fragrant pīkake buds in the air. Days like this in a man's life, he thought, were rare indeed.

Kaumuali'i soon came out of his tent and came over to the mat. He folded his legs under him as he sat down near George and Grigorii and began to speak.

"At this location twenty of your years ago was an invasion of our island by the warriors of Kamehameha," Kaumuali'i said. "It was Kamehameha's first attempt to conquer Kaua'i. At that time I was but sixteen of your years old and my kahu, old 'Inamo'o, was the regent in my place. 'Inamo'o was told by refugee O'ahu chiefs that Kamehameha had more than twice-four of your thousands of men with him on many hundreds of canoes in a fleet he had increased after his conquest of O'ahu. He had sacrificed hundreds of the O'ahu prisoners to his war god Kūka'ilimoku at several heiaus to assure the success of his campaign, which he called 'Ka'ie'iewaho,' or 'Crossing the Channel.' But despite all his sacrifices, Kamehameha did not gain the favor of the wind god La'amaomao, who sent his son, the strong blast called Kulepe to swamp his canoes in the sea between O'ahu and here. Because of the strong wind, Kamehameha was forced to give the order to return to O'ahu after many of his men had drowned. Back on O'ahu he heard of the revolt of Ka'iana's brother, the sun-shunner Namakeha, and so he took his warriors back to Hawai'i to deal with the rebellion. But more than a thousand of the warriors in Kamehameha's war canoes did not hear his order to turn back. Kulepe's wind was too loud and they could not see the command canoe over the high waves. And so these warriors in their canoes continued their journey with great difficulty and came ashore here at Māhā'ulepū Beach. Regent 'Inamo'o had managed to gather about three times their number to oppose them, however, and they were slaughtered, almost to the last man. For many days our warriors pursued those who fled the battle, captured them, and sacrificed them. Only three of them managed to reach the 'puhonua' or sanctuary at Piha ke kua, the 'Place full of Gods.' This is a small crater very near the shore at Poipu, the first place the fire goddess Pele stepped when she came to create our island. All things in this crater are safe...from storms and from human retribution. Since these three of Kamehameha's warriors had reached this sanctuary, 'Inamo'o could not have them killed or captured, and eventually they returned to Hawai'i to tell Kamehameha of the fate of his men."

Kaumuali'i looked for reaction to his story from George and Grigorii. They both seemed most interested, and so he continued.

"Later, in your year of 1810, some years after Kamehameha's second attempt to conquer us was defeated by the great 'ōku'u sickness, when I was on Captain Winship's vessel in Honolulu harbor, and Kamehameha came aboard, I was worried that he would remember the fate of his warriors on Kaua'i," Kaumuali'i related. "But he attributed their deaths to Regent 'Inamo'o, who was long dead, so that when I asked him if my fate was to be 'face up or face down,' meaning 'alive or dead,' he told me that I would continue to rule my islands as his tributary, but that I would pass them on to his successors' rule."

"So it was twice that Kamehameha tried and failed to conquer Kaua'i?" Grigorii Terentev asked. Terentev's English skills were not as good as George's and he strained to understand as Kaumuali'i spoke.

"That is true," answered Kaumuali'i, "but I want to tell you of another invasion that took place here…one that took place a very long time ago. My mele inoa chant reveals that it was more than half way back to the time of the ancient high priest Pā'ao, who voyaged to these islands from Tahiti, gave our people new gods, created the Ali'i and the kapus, and brought the legendary King Pili, my long-ago ancestor, to the island of Hawai'i. My estimate of the time in your terms would be that this invasion happened in approximately your year of 1480. The King of Kaua'i then was Kukona, the fourth in descent from the great King La'amaikahiki. He was known to be a very tall man like my son Keali'iahonui who is descended from him."

"Many great rulers were tall men," observed George. "Peter the Great of Russia was said to be nearly seven French feet in height."

"Who were the invaders?" asked Grigorii.

"Events of today are often echoes of the events of the past," Kaumuali'i answered. "The invaders in the past were the same as those who threaten us now. They were the warriors of the King of the island of Hawai'i, an ancestor of Kamehameha's. This was the storied Kalaunui, grandson of Kalapana, whose father Kanipahu the hunchback had helped him take back the island from Kamaiole the usurper. This Kalaunui had a powerful wife, Queen Kaheka, and a renowned 'kāula' or prophetess, the owl-woman Wa'ahia. Wa'ahia lived in an isolated hut near Waipio on which owls were wont to perch. She was an old woman with white hair who walked with the aid of a stick topped with the head of an owl. Waipio villagers said that she consorted with a mysterious stranger from the spirit world who told her of future events, and her predictions were always accurate."

George's curiosity was instantly piqued, and so he interrupted Kaumauali'i, urging him, "Please tell us more about this Wa'ahia and her mysterious stranger from the spirit world."

"Tradition records that the stranger was only rarely seen by the villagers," responded Kaumuali'i, "and that he had a pale ghostly appearance. He visited Wa'ahia most often at night, and, when he did so, her hut was lit up by some kind of lamp that did not flicker."

Kaumauli'i took a drink of 'awa that was served to him by his steward. He then spat several times into his refuse bowl, and continued, "Wa'ahia had taken in an orphaned Ali'i of the wohi caste named Kualu. Kualu grew up to be the most formidable warrior in Kalaunui's kingdom. With the spears he had no equal. He lived in Kalaunui's hale mūa as the Captain of the King's guard and he fell in love with the beautiful Kapapa, the daughter of Kalaunui and Queen Kaheka. But Queen Kaheka had Kapapa closely watched and would allow no offers for her hand in marriage from anyone not of the highest ni'aupi'o caste of Ali'i...and this did not include Kualu."

Kaumuali'i took another sip of the 'awa, spat again, and continued. "Once, Wa'ahia questioned her ward Kualu about his love for Kapapa. He admitted to her that he had been thinking of Kapapa, and so Wa'ahia cautioned him, saying 'it is not good for you to try to gather berries from the clouds...only the ni'aupi'o can reach that fruit.' But Kualu answered her by saying that 'the flying spear will bring down what the hand cannot reach.' So Wa'ahia, admiring his dauntless spirit, told Kualu that she would try to foresee his future and tell it to him in three days."

"Likely she had to consult the mysterious stranger from the spirit world, is that not true?" interrupted George.

"We do not know this," answered Kaumuali'i. "But in three days Wa'ahia told Kualu that his future was bright. His star, she said, would shine brighter than that of Kalaunui. And, she told Kualu that his future was related to events involving a race of pale-skinned people from foreign shores. When Kualu asked about his future relationship with the Princess Kapapa, the kāula said that she could not foresee this."

"Do you know how the 'race of pale-skinned people' was involved in Kualu's future?" asked George.

"Yes, I do know," said Kaumuali'i. "And I will tell you. But first I must relate that the ambitious King Kalaunui was making plans to conquer all the other Hawai'ian islands and bring them under his rule, just as Kamehameha has now tried all his life to accomplish. He sent out messengers to all his chiefs ordering them to contribute men and war canoes, and soon amassed a force of three times four thousand warriors. As the fleet was being readied to depart in an attack on the closest island of Mau'i, Kalaunui requested a prediction concerning the success of his campaign from his kāula Wa'ahia. In three days time she gave him her prediction, saying 'a good beginning...a bad end.' But Kaluanui announced to all that this message meant that it would be bad to put an end to such a good beginning, and he ordered his fleet to sea. Commanding the fleet himself, he left the government of Hawai'i in the hands of his young son Kuaiwa with Queen Kaheka as regent. Wa'ahia, concerned about the role her ward Kualu was expected to play in the invasion, got on board one of the followers' canoes and accompanied the warriors to Mau'i."

"Who was then the King of Mau'i?" asked Grigorii.

"The King of Mau'i was Kamoluohua, seventh in descent from Paumakua," answered Kaumuali'i. "His cousin Wakalana was Chief of the Wailuku District on the northern shore. And it is this Chief Wakalana who first came into contact with the 'race of pale-skinned people' foreseen in Kualu's future by Wa'ahia. Two years before Kalaunui's fleet set off to invade Mau'i, Wakalana had been summoned by excited fishermen to the rocky shore near Wailuku where a large vessel of an unknown kind was being washed ashore. The vessel was already severely damaged and Wakalana could see that it would be completely wrecked as the waves threw it onto the rocks. So he paddled out in a large canoe and rescued five people from the water as the vessel was destroyed. There were three men and two women of pale skin and different bright dark eyes who could not speak our language. But Wakalana saw the metal bracelets and rings on the women, and he saw on the belt of one of the men a strange object, which, because it was beyond his experience, intrigued him. It was a metal sword. He ordered that these people should be given two houses of their own in Wailuku and given food in abundance. And when his own people became frightened when they saw that the foreigners ate their food together, both men and women, he explained to his people that these foreigners were not subject to the wrath of our Gods. In time, as these foreigners learned to speak a few words of our language, Wakalana learned that they were from a far-away place called Japan. Wakalana gave them all Hawai'ian names. The man with the sword, who had been the Captain of the wrecked ship, was given the name Kaluiki-a-mano. The other men were called Hika and Ha'akoa. The women were Neleike and Malaea, and both were sisters of Kaluiki. In more time, all these foreigners married with Wakalana's people, the women taken as wives by prominent Ali'i in his court. Some of them are ancestors of today's Mau'i Ali'i."

"But what about the Captain's sword?" asked George. "What did Wakalana and his chiefs think of that?"

"It was a great marvel to them," explained Kaumauli'i. "They had never seen nor dreamed of any object as hard and strong as it was. All the implements they had ever experienced had been made of wood, bone, or stone. And this metal sword in Kaluiki's hands easily sliced through leather or wooden shields, chopped daggers and spears in half, and cut the heads off chickens, dogs, and pigs with a single swipe. It gleamed so brightly in the sun that Kaluiki could use it to shine signals to warriors at great distances. When a person looked closely at the sword's blade, he could see himself reflected on its surface...and more accurately than when one looked into a still pond. Wakalana and his chiefs were awed by the weapon, thinking it a unique gift to Kaluiki of the God Lono. Soon King Kamoluohua heard about Kaluiki and his sword of Lono and he ordered Chief Wakalana to bring them to Ka'anapali where he was so he could see them. A demonstration by Kaluiki there, during which he quickly killed three armed prisoners in an arranged combat, caused Kamoluohua to offer

Kaluiki a high position in his army, but Kaluiki, grateful to Wakalana for saving his life two years before, declined this offer, saying that he would remain in the service of Wakalana. It was in Wakalana's army that he encountered the warrior Kualu when King Kalaunui and his fleet invaded Mau'i from Hawai'i."

"How did the battle go?" asked Grigorii.

"King Kalaunui's great fleet landed at Lahaina and quickly took command of the village there, killing all its defenders," said Kaumuali'i. "Kamoluohua, who had had only a day's warning of the attack, sent orders to Wakalana to bring his forces overland from Wailuku to join with his larger army from Ka'anapali in opposing Kalaunui's advance toward Olowalu. A bloody battle was soon fought between Lahaina and Olowalu. Kalaunui had many more men in the battle, but he was attacked at the same time from two directions. Wakalana's warriors, with Kaluiki at their head, cut a large swath through Kalaunui's advancing army, and Kualu, who was near the front of King Kalaunui's lines, saw that Kaluiki was using to frightful advantage his shining metal sword, the likes of which Kualu had never seen. Bravely he hewed his way through the swarm of battle in Kaluiki's direction and soon confronted him directly, brandishing his spear and a stone battle-axe. Kaluiki swung his sword, cutting deeply into Kualu's heavy pololū spear. But the sword did not cut its way through, but became stuck for a moment in the wood of the spear. Like lightning, Kualu hammered down with all his strength on the blade of the sword with his battle-axe, knocking it from Kaluiki's grasp onto the ground. Kualu stepped upon the sword and swung the axe again, striking Kaluiki on the side of his head. Kaluiki fell onto the ground, and, seeing this, his battling companions fled back up the hill beyond a low lava wall."

"So Kualu captured the sword, then?" asked George. "What did he do with it?"

"He remained standing upon it until the tide of battle had swept away from him. Then he pushed it up to its hilt in the ground and, while separated from his men, covered it with dirt near the lava wall, being careful to mark the place," Kaumuali'i responded. "Later, after the victory of Kalaunui's invading army and the capture of King Kamoluohua, he went back to the lava wall at night and dug it up. Guarding it was the fallen body of one of Wakalana's chiefs. But Kaluiki had not died. He survived to serve Wakalana in other battles, but without the sword, which was lost to him."

"Did Kualu then use the sword in other battles for King Kalaunui?" asked George.

"No, he did not," was Kaumuali'i's answer. "He told Wa'ahia about the sword and she instructed him to give it to her, lest King Kalaunui hear of it and claim it from him. When Kalaunui's war fleet then attacked the realm of King Kahokuohua of Moloka'i and captured him also, she hid the sword in a cliff at Kalaupapa. She left it hidden there and followed the war fleet to O'ahu, where Kalaunui was again successful, overcoming and sacrificing the warriors of the highest Ali'i, Huapouleilei, who was Chief of Wainae and Ewa. Huapouleilei, like Kahokuohua and Kamoluohua before him, became Kalaunui's prisoner."

"How remarkable that before Kalaunui came here to invade Kaua'i with his war fleet, he had captured three other kings and took them along as prisoners," observed Grigorii Terentev. "He must have been a most formidable warrior. Did he prevail in his invasion here?"

"No, he did not," answered Kaumuali'i. "King Kukona proved too clever for him. When Kalaunui's fleet came ashore here at Māhā'ulepū, they saw no opposing forces at all at first. Only after they sent scouts inland toward Kōloa village did they encounter groups of Kukona's warriors, but these were always just a short distance away, visible on a hilltop or in a far-off clearing. Kalaunui decided to leave Kualu in charge of a force of three thousand warriors on the beach, guarding the canoes and forming a reserve. Kalaunui himself took the largest part of the army, almost two fours of your thousands of men, in pursuit of Kukona's warriors that his scouts had observed. But Kukona deliberately had his men retreat just out of contact with Kalaunui's advancing force until this force was far from the ocean, strung out across miles of hills, valleys, and streams. Then he began to attack sections of Kalaunui's now thin army from both sides with close-packed concentrations of men."

George couldn't restrain himself from commenting, "That's the same strategy that General Barclay de Tolly used against Napoleon in Russia."

Kaumuali'i nodded to George, acknowledging the comment without understanding it, and then continued, "For a day and a night many battles raged. Soon messengers came back to Kualu on the beach that Kalaunui's large army had been decimated and was retreating in pieces back toward the ocean. But Kualu could not move his reserve force to help cover Kalaunui's retreat, because, at this moment, he noticed that he was himself being attacked from the sea by a fleet of canoes Kukona had sent out from Waimea to destroy them. Kualu ordered his men into the surf to fight the warriors of Kukona's attacking fleet before they could beach their canoes. Ferocious hand-to-hand combat took place in hip-deep water, which soon turned red from the gore. All morning the fight continued until, at last, the warriors of Kukona's fleet were all slain. But only three hundred of Kualu's three thousand men were left. All the rest were dead, their bodies washing into piles on the beach, blocking the canoes."

"That must have been a tremendous battle," said George, looking down off the mat toward Māhā'ulepū Beach to his right. "I can almost see it occur as you tell the story at the place where it happened. You are a wonderful narrator, King George. Please continue."

Kaumuali'i drank a bit more 'awa, stretched back into a reclining position on the mat, and ordered his steward to provide him with a sunshade. Then he continued his story.

"Kualu ordered the few men he had left inland to help Kalaunui's retreating warriors, but they would not follow him. Instead they began moving bodies from behind the canoes so they could paddle out to sea. As they did this they looked up on the rise above the beach and saw King Kukona's army encircling a last pocket of Kalaunui's men, the group that he himself commanded. If they did not now flee, even the women and children in the followers' canoes were in great danger. So Kualu, seeing what he had to do, ordered the now cleared canoes shoved out into the surf and paddled swiftly away. Six days later the followers' canoes, accompanied by less than a hundred men, Kualu among them, returned to Waipio on Hawai'i. It was a day of great wailing there."

"Was King Kalaunui killed?" asked Grigorii. "And what about the captive kings of Mau'i, Moloka'i, and O'ahu?"

"Kalaunui was taken alive despite his efforts to die fighting," answered Kaumuali'i. "And the other kings were taken too, found bound together in a hut near the beach without guards. King Kukona treated all four of these captive kings with respect. He gave them a tour of Kaua'i much like the one I am giving you. Only was he angered when Kalaunui tried at one camp to get the other captive kings to join him in an attempt on Kukona's life and escape. Kukona could easily have sent his warriors back to these kings' islands to enforce his dominion over them. In a way, he was truly in command of all the islands at that time. But he chose to send each of the first three to their homes with his good will: Huapouleilei to O'ahu, Kahokuohua to Moloka'i, and Kamoluohua to Mau'i. These kings agreed to live at peace with Kukona for the rest of his days. But Kukona decided to keep King Kalaunui of Hawai'i a prisoner, demanding a ransom for him from Queen Kaheka in Waipio."

"What happened to Kualu and Wa'ahia?" asked George.

"Queen Kaheka was angry about Kalaunui's defeat and she blamed Kualu for it, saying that he had acted in a cowardly fashion in the battle for Kaua'i. Kualu would have confronted with force any man who said that against him, but he could not confront Queen Kaheka. After seeing his reputation suffer, he left Hawai'i and sailed to Moloka'i where he became a recluse in exile. He lived there near the place where the poisonous grove of Kalaipahoa trees once grew, so that no other life could survive there…no plants grew and even birds flying overhead fell dead."

"There is such a place on Moloka'i?" asked Grigorii.

"Yes, there is such a place," answered Kaumuali'i. "The poisonous trees are long gone now, but the cutting of them took many lives. The workers had to protect their bodies and their faces with kapa. Kamehameha is said to possess the only two fragments of the deadly wood left, but he keeps them a secret."

"Did Queen Kaheka manage to ransom King Kalaunui?" asked George.

"She and her son and her council of chiefs made an offer every year for three years by official emissary," Kaumuali'i said. "The first was for canoes, spears, and war materials…but Kukona refused. The second was for twenty royal feather cloaks, a canoe-load of ivory and whalebone, and a thousand of the fine Hawai'ian stone battle-axes like the one used so well by Kualu…but Kukona refused. The third offer showed how serious Queen Kaheka was about gaining the return of her husband. She offered her daughter Kapapa in marriage, either to Kukona or to his son Manokalanipo, and an agreement for perpetual peace between their two islands…but again Kukona refused. At last, at the suggestion of her chiefs, she turned to the old kāula Wa'ahia, asking her for help. Wa'ahia demanded to speak to Queen Kaheka's entire council of chiefs. Appearing before them with her white hair and bent over on her stick with the owl's head top, she told them that she could gain Kalaunui's return. But she asked them to agree to enforce any conditions she made Kalaunui agree to as the terms for his release. Then, accompanied by her ghostly stranger consort, who has remained unnamed to this day, she traveled to Kaua'i and found an audience with King Kukona. On three successive days she chanted the wonders of the sword of Lono to Kukona, a weapon that could elevate the military power of an entire kingdom, telling him that she could bring this much-to-be-desired object to him. Kukona, who had heard of this magical weapon from King Kamoluohua of Mau'i when he was in captivity, became consumed with desire to obtain it. After each of the first two audiences with Wa'ahia, he ordered his retainers to follow her to see if they could find the sword with her and take it by force from her. But, according to his retainers, Wa'ahia was impossible to follow. They said that she met another, a man of strange appearance, and just vanished with him into the air. They pointed to her footsteps in the sand, which came to an end without any sight of her."

"They vanished into the air?" exclaimed Grigorii. "How is that possible?"

George calmed Grigorii with his hand and said to him, "I think I know. But let's allow King George to continue."

Kaumuali'i coughed and continued to speak. "During the third audience, Kukona agreed to give his captive King Kalaunui of Hawai'i, of whom he was quite tired after three years of keeping him in lava-wall incarceration, the conditions for his release which were specified by Wa'ahia. There were three conditions. He was to announce to Queen Kaheka, to his son Kuaiwa, and to all his chiefs that the Captain of his guards Kualu, whom he had entrusted with a large command on Kaua'i, had performed bravely and wisely. He was to reward Kualu by making him a chief in control of an entire ahupua'a of land. And he was to give Kaulu the hand of his daughter Kapapa in marriage."

"What did Kalaunui think when these three conditions were presented to him?" asked Grigorii.

"He was very confused," answered Kaumuali'i. "He could not decide what advantage these conditions gave to his captor, King Kukona. But, as he was desperate to be released, he agreed. Kukona had him freed and taken to a canoe to be paddled back to Hawai'i with a retinue of Kaua'ian chiefs and warriors to make certain that he got there safely. As he was getting into the canoe to depart, Kalaunui saw, to his surprise, his old kāula, the crone Wa'ahia, standing by herself, leaning on her stick at the side of the beach. She waved to him as he was paddled away. Kukona saw her there also. But just afterwards she disappeared."

"Did Kukona get the sword?" asked George.

"Yes, he got the sword," said Kaumuali'i. "Three days later the sword appeared inside the door of his royal residence, just as Wa'ahia had told him it would. How it got there no one ever discovered. And, even stranger is the fact that when King Kalaunui arrived back in Waipio, Wa'ahia was already there ahead of him in Queen Kaheka's greeting party."

"No…" protested Grigorii. "That couldn't be."

"It could not be, and yet it was so," insisted Kaumuali'i. "Wa'ahia then accompanied Kalaunui's retainers when they voyaged to Moloka'i to ask Kualu to return to Waipio. When they were too fearful to cross the area of the poison kalaipahoa grove to approach Kualu's exile hut, Wa'ahia walked across it without harm and talked with her former ward. She told him that his 'flying spear had indeed brought down what his hand could not reach,' and that Kapapa's hand in marriage was awaiting him in Waipio. He was overjoyed and returned to Waipio with Wa'ahia and Kalaunui's retainers. He and Kapapa lived there together, enjoying his new lands and his position for the rest of their lives. They had many children and some of them are the ancestors of the leading Hawai'ian Ali'i today."

"What happened to Wa'ahia?" asked George.

"Soon after this she disappeared," said Kaumuali'i. "She was seen to enter her owl-perch hut after dark one night. The hut then burst into flames by Pele's will and was very rapidly consumed. But Wa'ahia's body was not found within its ashes. She was not there. In years of retelling, the narrators fixed the blame on King Kalaunui and his jealous Queen Kaheka, who, they said, had ordered her burned to death. But this is not true. She just vanished as she had before here on Kaua'i."

"It's a story like a Russian 'skazka'," said George. "A veritable fairy tale. But what did Kukona do with the sword?"

"He kept it closely guarded and passed it on to his son Manokalanipo," answered Kaumuali'i. "And Manokalanipo passed it on to his successors. Every King of Kaua'i since Kukona has been in possession of the sword of Lono, which originally came to Mau'i from Japan in Kaluiki's belt. My older brother Keawe inherited it from our mother Kamakaheilei, and I took it from him when he died. I have it still."

"You do?" said George. "Can we see it?"

"Yes, you can see it," said Kaumuali'i. "It is now broken and almost rusted away. But I will show it to you when we return to Waimea. It is an important relic of our past and serves as a sign of the King's power. I think that my possession of it is a reason why Kamehameha, like Kalaunui generations before, was unsuccessful in his attempts to conquer Kaua'i. Of course there are other reasons."

"I'm sure we'll learn them too as we get to know you better, King George," said George.

George's Explanation of the Story:

When George returned with the King's party to Waimea, he set to work with Grigorii Terentev, Charles Fox-Bennick, Grigorii Iskakov, Filip Osipov, and Aleksei Odnoriadkin expanding the fields and planting crops on the east bank of the Waimea River. Kanakas designated to George's command by King Kaumuali'i provided the labor, and much was accomplished. For the entire month of June, 1816, however, George heard nothing from O'ahu.

One evening when the six Company men were together in the house of Charles Fox-Bennick, Grigorii Terentev asked George about how the prophetess Wa'ahia and her mysterious consort in Kaumuali'i's story about King Kukona and the Japanese sword had managed to disappear without a trace.

"You told me at the time that you thought you knew how this happened," said Terentev. "I'd like to know what you think."

George and Terentev had shared Kaumuali'i's fascinating story with the others, so they knew what Terentev wanted to discuss.

But George began by talking about something seemingly unrelated.

"In 1806, when I was in medical school in Würzburg, I received a most interesting letter from the renowned scientist, Professor Johann Wilhelm Ritter," related George. "Ritter, in case you don't know who he was…he died in 1810, was the discoverer of light we can't even see, the inventor of the process by which metal can be electrically plated with another metal, and a pioneer in the generation of electricity for medical uses. I had met him in Munich some years before when I was training to become a pharmacist. But, at any rate, to continue…Ritter was coming at my request to Würzburg to give a lecture on electric shock therapy for the agitated insane. And, in his letter, he asked me to make the acquaintance of a family of his relatives in Würzburg, the Hindernachts. He was most insistent in his letter that I do this, and so I sought them out and contrived to meet them. And the meeting turned out to be a most fortuitous one for me…for it was there that I met the Hindernachts' daughter, Barbara, who became my wife. While I was courting her, Johann Ritter arrived in Würzburg to give his lecture. He told Barbara and me that he had insisted that I make the acquaintance of her family because he already knew that she and

I would meet. He also knew, he said, that we would marry and have offspring who would, in generations to come, be related to his offspring."

"How could he have known this?" asked Grigorii Iskakov.

"He told us that he had received a visit from one of his own progeny, one of his children's children's children…that is, from a man who came to him from his own, and our, future," related George. "This man had told him about Barbara and me."

"A man from the future?" exclaimed Charles Fox-Bennick in disbelief.

"You can imagine that I, a medical doctor and a man of science, also had trouble believing this, my friends," said George. "But Herr Professor Ritter was a man of great intelligence and apparent sincerity. And he had received the benefit of this man of his progeny's advice and had great faith in what this man told him."

"Did you ever see or meet the man?" asked Filip Osipov.

"No, I didn't," said George. "And Ritter only saw the man for a short time on one occasion. He said that the man looked vaguely familiar to him, but was pale in appearance. He said that the man was quite old, but looked younger. Ritter told Barbara and me that other people throughout human history have received such visits from their progeny as well, but that these visits are not often recognized for what they are. He said that these progeny from our future come to visit us only rarely and for purposes which are mysterious to us. And, he said that they come here in vehicles which move through both space and time at speeds we can't imagine."

"So what proof of such visits is there?" asked Fox-Bennick.

"I had a sort of proof made to me by events," answered George. "While Ritter was in Würzburg, I was challenged to a duel over Barbara's hand by a most formidable soldier, the Captain of the Archduke's guards. This man was a combat veteran who had killed several men in duels, whereas I had to that date never held a pistol in my hand. Yet I could not refuse to duel this man, even though I was sure that my death would be the result. But Ritter agreed to be my second, saying confidently that my victory was assured, since he already knew that I would survive to marry Barbara and to have children whose further offspring would intermingle with his. The duel was therefore a test of his assurance…a kind of proof, if you will. And, of course, I was not killed in the duel, but, to my great surprise, I killed the formidable Captain of the Archduke's guards instead, receiving only the loss of this part of my left ear. Afterwards, I married Barbara and together we have a daughter, Inga."

The other five men were silent for a time. Then Charles Fox-Bennick made a recapitulation of what they had heard.

"So people are sometimes visited by members of their own progeny who travel back in time in vehicles to visit them and give them advice," he said. "And this fellow Ritter got such a visit and shared information from it with you…information which enabled you to face a duel with unexpected confidence. Is that it?"

"That's it," replied George. "But that isn't all. In 1814, in the middle of the Indian Ocean on the *Suvorov*, I…and others as well…saw in the sky what I can only reckon to be some of the progeny's vehicles. There were nine dark objects hovering in the evening sky without wings…they then began to glow like lamps, vanishing from sight across a great distance in only a second or two."

"My heavens," exclaimed Fox-Bennick. "What a thing to see!"

"Aha!" exclaimed Grigorii Terentev. "Now I understand. You think that Wa'ahia, King Kalaunui's prophetess, was receiving visits from one of her future progeny…the mysterious ghostly consort sometimes seen by the Waipio villagers…and that he helped her vanish in his vehicle. That's what you think, isn't it."

"Yes, that's it," said George. "I think it was he who made her such an accurate prophetess. He already knew the future and he told some of it to her. It was he who transported her from Kaua'i back to Hawai'i ahead of the King's delegation. It was he who somehow enabled her to evade King Kukona's retainers by vanishing from their view. And it was he who finally came to carry her away in his vehicle, incinerating her house as he did so. That's indeed what I think."

"It reminds me of the story of Iliia in the *Bibliia's* Books of the Kingdoms," said Terentev, who had been raised in Russian Orthodoxy. "Iliia was a prophet who had been helped by an angel of the Lord to bring fire down on two groups of fifty soldiers that King Akhav sent to capture him. He at last accompanied a third group of fifty soldiers who had begged him for mercy back to Samaria to see King Akhav, who had consulted the false god of Akkaron, Veelzevul, about whether he would survive an injury that he had sustained in a fall from an upper window. Iliia told King Akhav that since he had consulted Veelzevul instead of consulting the true God Almighty, he would soon die…and King Akhav did soon die just as Iliia predicted. Then, after Iliia's friend Elisei three times in three different places refused to leave him, Iliia was swept up into heaven by an angel of the Lord in a fiery chariot as Elisei and others watched."

"In my Catholic *Bible*, this is the story of the prophet we call Elijah," said George. "And it's easy to see that the 'angel of the Lord' might really have been one of his progeny. The people who witnessed this event, who then told it, then wrote it…saw it as a manifestation of divinity…as a work of God. But it could have been a manifestation of future science. There are other stories in the *Bible* that can also be interpreted in this way. And, even further, Jesus Christ may have been one of our progeny who came back to instruct us how to live."

"Bozhe moi…My God!" burst out Grigorii Iskakov. "I don't even want to think such thoughts. We could just as easily be swept off to Hell by a fiery chariot too…and spending an eternity in fire and brimstone isn't something I'd enjoy."

"It certainly might give a man pause for thought, though," observed Charles Fox-Binnick. Then he joked, "I'd like to meet one of my own future progeny just before I sit down at the gambling table. He could tell me what cards to play and I'd win a fortune. Then I wouldn't have to work day and night with you fellows. I'd just have a castle built in the uplands near the Wales border and retire there until the fiery chariot comes for me."

"That's not a bad idea," said George. "But I think we may be building a castle right here on Kaua'i."

In the days after this evening meeting at Charles Fox-Bennick's house, the men often discussed Johann Wilhelm Ritter, the flying vehicles, Kaumuali'i's story of the prophetess Wa'ahia's mysterious consort, and biblical characters who may have been progeny. Why would these future people choose to visit Elijah, Wa'ahia, and Johann Ritter? Was it because these were "prophets" already, or were they "prophets" because of the progeny visits? Why would the progeny not visit political leaders like the Tsar or Napoleon and give their knowledge to them for the future benefit of all? Or had the Tsar and Napoleon had such visits and kept them secret? It was all so mysterious.

Treaties:

George and Kaumuali'i conversed often in the royal residence of Papa'ena'ena and the house under the Russian flag in Waimea village. Kaumuali'i was mostly concerned about Kamehameha. He feared Kamehameha greatly, but George's assurances of Russian support emboldened him into defiant plans. He raised with George the possibility of taking back from Kamehameha the islands that he considered properly his by right of higher nobility: O'ahu, Mau'i, Lana'i, and Moloka'i. George told Kaumuali'i that these islands could be taken by the force of Russian arms in the hands of his men on O'ahu and five hundred warriors that Kaumuali'i could supply. He described his settlement at Waikīkī and his warehouse in Honolulu as constituting a Russian "fort" on O'ahu. His thought was that once O'ahu was freed by force from Kamehameha's tyranny, the native population there would join their united forces in campaigns against the other islands…each one supplying more and more men as Kamehameha's warriors were defeated. They would then be able to move on Kamehameha's final stronghold on Hawai'i, he said, and, in only three years time, Kaumuali'i would be in control of all the islands and the sole possessor of the islands' most powerful mana.

On July 1st, 1816, after a long discussion, George and King Kaumuali'i signed a document of agreement, which was intended to remain a secret between them. It read:

"Secret Treaty,

Concluded and Ratified between His Majesty Kaumuali'i, King of Kau'i, etc., etc.

And Doctor von Sheffer, Collegiate Assessor of the Russian Empire

Port of Waimea, Island of Kaua'i

July 1, 1816

His Majesty, King Kaumuali'i sends his army to those Hawai'ian Islands that formerly belonged to him and were taken away by force, namely O'ahu, Lana'i, Mau'i, Moloka'i, etc. The King asks Dr. Sheffer to reconquer them, entrusting the command of the expedition to do so to Dr. Sheffer.

The King demands from Dr. Sheffer the delivery of necessary ammunition and clothing for the army. For transportation of troops, the king demands from Dr. Sheffer a sufficient number of ships to be at his disposal in the Hawai'ian Islands.

The King proffers and offers all the islands in his possession to his Majesty the Tsar, Aleksandr Pavlovich of Russia. Dr. Sheffer, through the Russian-American Company, is to use every effort to enable King Kaumuali'i and his successors to enjoy peaceful possession of the above-mentioned islands.

The King will at first put on the field five hundred men and will supply his own men as well as the Russian ships with necessary food.

The King will give full authority to Dr. Sheffer in regard to this expedition. He will also give aid for constructing a Russian fort on every island. These forts are to placed in charge of Russian commanders, as has already been done in the case of the fort in the port of Honolulu on the island of O'ahu.

On behalf of himself and his successors, the King cedes one-half of the island of O'ahu, with everything found there, to the Russian-American Company, which is to choose the half it wishes.

King Kaumuali'i cedes to the Russians forever all the sandalwood on the island of O'ahu.

King Kaumuali'i promises to pay in sandalwood from the island of Kaua'i for arms, ammunition, a brig or schooners, whether already received or to be received. He will also refuse to trade with the citizens of the United States.

King Kaumuali'i promises to give permission to the Russian-American Company for the establishment of factories on all his islands. In addition to one-half of the island of O'ahu, the Company is to receive a strip of land (an ahupua'a) on each of the King's other islands.

King Kaumuali'i promises to sell sandalwood to no one but the Russians.

In ten years, King Kaumuali'i is to establish on the newly acquired islands an army of two thousand warriors and Dr. Sheffer will undertake to bring a supply of fish from Russian North America. Dr. Sheffer is to arrange for the islanders sent by the King to Sitka to cut as much lumber as the King needs and Dr. Sheffer will take care that Russian ships bring most of this lumber to Kaua'i.

Dr. Sheffer undertakes to build factories on the Hawai'ian Islands and to introduce a better economy, which will make the natives educated and wealthy.

Graciously approved by His Majesty and signed by His Honor, Doctor von Sheffer.

    Signed: King Kaumuali'i (Lizard glyph)

    Russian Imperial Collegiate Assessor, Doctor Yegor von Sheffer."

Later that same day, after enjoying together thoughts of controlling all the Hawai'ian Islands, George suggested that King Kaumuali'i, now that he had been made an honorary officer in the Russian navy, might grant in return to Governor Baranov in Novo-Arkhangelsk the title of honorary chief of his realm. George drafted a Russian document of such appointment for Kaumuali'i to sign which read:

"Award of Chief's Rank to Aleksandr Baranov

by King Kaumuali'i

July 1, 1816

We, by the grace of God and the protection of His Imperial Majesty, the Emperor of Russia, Kaumuali'i, King of the Hawai'ian Islands, etc., etc., elevate His Honor, the Russian Imperial Collegiate Councilor and Cavalier Aleksandr Andreevich Baranov to the rank of first chief of the Hawai'ian Islands, as a token of our great appreciation of the protection of His Majesty Aleksandr Pavlovich, Emperor of Russia. This is done for the special service rendered by Baranov to the subjects of Kaumuali'i and to the islands. We also grant to him and his family, free from taxes for all time, a royal village at the port in the area of Honolulu.

    Signed: King Kaumuali'i (Lizard glyph)

Given in our capital

Waimea on Kaua'i

July 1, 1816."

George was very pleased with himself. He considered that he had now accomplished even more than he set about to do in Hawai'i. He had arranged more than adequate recompense for the cargo of the wrecked ship *Bering*. He had obtained agreements guaranteeing provisioning outposts for the Russian-American Company in the more temperate Hawai'ian Islands. He had sent much of this recompense and many foodstuffs to Sitka on the damaged *Otkrytie*.

And he had sent a healthy cargo of valuable sandalwood as well. But, more than that, he had given Russia itself a real opportunity to acquire a vital territorial stronghold in the middle of the Pacific Ocean. The consequences of this could alter the politics of the entire world for generations. All this he had accomplished…and, moreover, he was in a position to improve the lives of the islanders themselves. Not only would he heal their wounds and cure their diseases. He looked forward to helping them cast off their irrational superstitions, discard the Ali'i and the kapus, learn to read and write, accept Christianity, and adopt modern forms of government, technology and commerce. This really will be, he thought, a paradise. And his place in it now seemed superior to that of even the highest European nobility. Only the rulers themselves had more power. It was clear to him that this was the situation in life of which he had long dreamed. His plans to settle in Brazil were now in the past. This was an even better place, more beautiful, more advantageous. He could bring Barbara and Inga here and they would all live sublime lives indeed.

Buying Ships:

The first week of August 1816 passed without any word from O'ahu. George had been expecting the *Ilmena*, thinking that Captain Wadsworth of the *Ilmena* should have completed his repairs and come to Kaua'i on his way to Alaska with the wares from Honolulu by this time. On August 10th, the 260-ton ship *Atala* arrived at Waimea from the island of Hawai'i. This was one of the Winships' traders from Boston, temporarily captained by a Mr. Eric Lannert. Mr. Lannert disregarded the Russian flag over the village and requested an audience with King Kaumuali'i about buying provisions. He explained to Kaumuali'i that John Young had told him that shortages of food stores on Hawai'i made provisioning him there impossible. And Young had not allowed him to see King Kamehameha. But Kaumuali'i told Mr. Lannert that his ship would be kapu to his villagers and that he would have to deal for his provisions with his "Friend George, the Russian Dr. Sheffer."

George was pleased to see that Kaumuali'i, in conformance with his agreements, would not trade with this United States ship or even grant it provisions without clearance from him. This gave him the same kind of power in Kaua'i that John Young had in the rest of the islands. He decided to be magnanimous with Mr. Lannert, telling him and his clerk, Mr. Prince, that they could have taro, yams, pigs, and whatever else was needed.

For the next few days while the provisions were obtained and loaded, Mr. Lannert and Mr. Prince stayed on shore in guesthouses enjoying the company of Waimea women and girls. They heard much during this time from both the natives and the Russians about how King Kaumuali'i's domain was now a protectorateship of the Russian Tsar, and about how George was now the plenipotentiary of Kaumuali'i's "first chief," Governor Baranov.

Mr. Lannert told George that he planned to sail the *Atala* to Novo-Arkhangelsk before heading south toward Cape Horn on his way back to Boston. He thought he would be seeing Governor Baranov before December, he said. So George wrote Governor Baranov a long letter, asking Mr. Lannert to deliver it. And he told Mr. Lannert that his ship's provisions would be free if he would only agree to transport to Governor Baranov as well a large shipment of assorted fruit.

Three days after the *Atala* sailed, Captain Henry Gyzelaar arrived on the schooner *Lydia*. This fine two-masted ship with fore-and-aft-rigged sails had been built in Philadelphia and was owned by the New York Wilcocks family whose senior member, Benjamin Chew Wilcocks, was the American Consul in Canton, China. Its master, Captain Gyzelaar, was a voyage-hardened New Yorker and a patriotic American who, upon coming ashore into the Waimea village, tried personally to lower the Russian flag there. When he and his men were restrained from doing this by several native guards, he began to shout that he wanted to see Dr. Schaeffer immediately. George was summoned and a confrontation began.

"I knew in Honolulu that you were a trouble-maker, Dr. Schaeffer," Captain Gyzelaar exclaimed. "You know damned well that King Kamehameha does not allow the flying of foreign flags over his territories. And now here's this double-headed Russian eagle flying over Waimea. It'll be the end of trade and the beginning of war if you don't take it down."

George spoke in a calm voice, "Kamehameha is not the King here, Captain. Kaumuali'i is the King. And he has signed his islands into the protection of the Russian Tsar and his navy. That is why the Russian flag flies here, and I will not take it down."

"Foreign powers have no claim on these Hawai'ian Islands, Dr. Schaeffer," insisted Captain Gyzelaar. "An Englishman discovered them, but his claim was not approved by the English King. Even the Englishman John Young knows this…and flies no Union Jack over Hawai'ian territory. And, you may have noticed that the colors of the United States do not fly over the land here either."

"Young may have been born an Englishman," said George, "But he's really a pirate, taking power for himself in Kamehameha's name. He has no allegiance to any flag. And you United States' captains only care about keeping all the Hawai'ian trade for yourselves. You don't care about flags…only trade, sandalwood, and money. I've already seen how, during the war with Great Britain and its pursuit of United States vessels, you just sold your ships to the Russian-American Company to keep on trading."

Captain Gyzelaar was stung by George's depiction of his fellow captains' motives. And he could see that George was not going to be swayed by his bluster. He decided to take a more conciliatory tack.

"Listen, Dr. Schaeffer, it makes no sense for you to come here and stir up old hostilities by flying the Russian flag under Kamehameha's nose," he said. "You can have your provisioning outpost here and do all the trade here you want. We captains will leave you alone and urge John Young and Kamehameha to do the same. We don't want to see a return to the old bloody wars. It's bad for business…not only our business, but your business too. You don't need to fly any flag at all. It's just a provocation…that's all…a nonsensical provocation. I ask you in all respect to consider taking it down before all trade here ceases and lives are lost."

"You have already stated that no other foreign power has claimed these islands," responded George. "That means that Russia has a perfect right to claim them, especially since there are now so many Russians here on them. And now Russia is supporting King Kaumuali'i with its protection. If Kamehameha's warriors or any other powers move against Kaumuali'i, they will have to wage war against Russia and all the forces it can bring here."

"Do you really think the Russian Tsar would send ships and soldiers here to support you in such a situation as you seem to want to create? Why would he?"

"The Russian Tsar, His Majesty Aleksandr Pavlovich, understands the necessity of opposing tyranny wherever it may be," answered George. "That is why he has vanquished Napoleon Bonaparte, and why he would support Kaumuali'i against Kamehameha. Besides, there are the obvious commercial reasons. Hawai'i is in the center of the Pacific between his Siberian territories and Alaska."

"You are a zealot, Dr. Schaeffer," declared Captain Gyzelaar, exasperated. "And zealots are always dangerous."

As the argument between George and Captain Gyzelaar continued in Waimea village, King Kaumuali'i and his retinue unexpectedly appeared. George became aware of this when all the villagers in his sight quickly fell to their stomachs on the ground. Several Mū then came into view, followed by King Kaumuali'i, who was wearing his red and gold-feathered cape. Behind him walked the tall son Keali'iahonui, Queens Namahana, Naoa and Kekaiha'akulou and a large party of attendants. When Kaumuali'i saw George and Captain Gyzelaar and several others gathered near the flagpole, he walked regally over to them, waiting for them all to bow or get to their knees in obeisance before speaking.

"Who do we have here, Friend George?" asked Kaumuali'i in English.

"This is Captain Henry Gyzelaar of the schooner *Lydia* which is anchored offshore," answered George.

"Aloha, Captain Gyzelaar," said Kaumuali'i. "I can see your ship anchored offshore from my residence. It looks to be a fine craft. I decided to come down to the village to see whose ship it is. Where are you from and why do you come here?"

"I am from New York," answered Captain Gyzelaar, standing up at Kaumuali'i's hand gesture of permission and removing his hat respectfully. "And I've come here from Honolulu to bring you news and a proposal from your friend Captain John Ebbets."

"Do you know that you will have to speak with my Russian friend George?" said Kaumuali'i. "He will take your news and hear your proposal."

"King Kaumuali'i," said Captain Gyzelaar sharply, "you are making a mistake to trust this man. Russia cannot protect you from Kamehameha. You should take down the Russian flag before Kamehameha hears of it."

George looked at Kaumuali'i, wondering what the King would say. He knew that Kaumuali'i was very fearful of Kamehameha, and that he knew little of Russia's power in the world. It was a tense moment for George.

"We do not fear Kamehameha here," Kaumuali'i told Captain Gyzelaar with apparent confidence. "We will not lower the Russian flag."

Kaumuali'i then turned back toward the hill where his royal residence, Papa'ena'ena, was located. He took a few steps and paused to wait for all of his large party to get into order behind him, and then he strode away. In a few moments the villagers got back to their feet and returned to their normal activities.

George breathed a sigh of relief, and said to Gyzelaar, "What news do you bring, then, and what proposal?"

"The news is in a letter to you from Timofei Tarakanov and the proposal is in a letter to the King from John Ebbets," said Captain Gyzelaar. He took both letters from his coat pocket and handed them to George. "Tarakanov's letter is in Russian and I can't read it, but Ebbets is proposing that King Kaumuali'i purchase the *Lydia*."

"If John Ebbets is back in Honolulu, I wonder if he delivered the furs from the *Bering* to Governor Baranov in Novo-Arkhangelsk," said George.

"I don't know," said Captain Gyzelaar. "But if that's what he said he was going to do, then I would have every confidence that he's done it."

"I'm sure he wouldn't do it for nothing," replied George. "And why would he propose that Kaumuali'i purchase the *Lydia?* Who owns the *Lydia?*"

"The *Lydia* is owned by the Wilcocks family of Philadelphia," answered Gyzelaar. "But I am the master of the ship and I can sell it for them."

"How do you know they want to sell it?" asked George.

"Ebbets got word of this from Benjamin Chew Wilcocks when he was in Canton. Wilcocks is the American Consul there. If the price is right, I can sell it. Ebbets and I will earn a commission on it."

George thought for a time. "You stay here on the *Lydia* tonight, and I will come out to the ship tomorrow and tell you."

"All right," agreed Captain Gyzelaar.

In an hour, Captain Gyzelaar was back aboard the *Lydia*, and George was speaking with Kaumuali'i at Papa'ena'ena. The letter from Timofei Tarakanov had informed George that the Russian-American Company ship *Kadiak* had arrived in Honolulu under American Captain George Young with a company of 60 men. Like the *Otkrytie* and the *Ilmena*, the *Kadiak* was leaking and needed repairs. George communicated this news to Kaumuali'i, depicting it as the arrival of substantial reinforcements. Then he told Kaumuali'i that he would buy for him the schooner *Lydia*, using sandalwood from that owed by the treaty to the Russian-American Company as partial payment. Now, he told Kaumuali'i, their "navy" in the islands would increase to three European-style ships, the *Ilmena*, the *Kadiak*, and the *Lydia*, with others on the way…whereas Kamehameha had only the tiny *Fair American*, the *Beretania*, which had been built in the islands, and the *Ka'ahumanu*…and their contingent of armed Russians and Aleuts would number more than 150 men. This was, George said, only a harbinger of greater things to come.

The next morning, George had Filip Osipov and several natives row him out to the *Lydia* in the *Bering's* restored cutter. He told Osipov to keep his hands close to his pistol, the butt of which protruded from his belt. But Captain Gyzelaar and his crew were not antagonistic as they had seemed the day before. They even seemed to be friendly now.

The negotiations did not take long. George agreed to pay nine thousand dollars for the *Lydia*. Captain Gyzelaar had wanted ten thousand dollars, but he agreed to accept nine thousand dollars if George would pay half the price in sandalwood. Kamehameha, as was revealed to George during the discussion, had earlier been offered the ship, but had not had sufficient cash and had refused to part with any sandalwood in the bargain. This fact encouraged George to complete the sale. He negotiated the worth of the sandalwood, which he would have Kaumuali'i obtain for him, at ten dollars a pikul. This meant that George was to give Captain Gyzelaar 4500 dollars in silver from the money Governor Baranov had given him and 450 pikuls of sandalwood…137 lbs. per pikul…which had to be cut, transported and loaded into the schooner's hold before it left Waimea. This took an army of Kaumuali'i's kanakas six days to complete. The completion of the sale, however, was to take place in Honolulu, where George's silver was stored in the guarded warehouse and where other American captains could sign as witnesses to the terms. This would also return Captain Gyzelaar and his crew to their familiar port. Sailing back to O'ahu on the loaded *Lydia* suited George's purposes well, since he wanted an opportunity to reunite with his men at Honolulu and at Waikīkī. He intended to move as many of them as he could to Kaua'i.

George took only Filip Osipov and Aleksei Odnoriadkin with him on the *Lydia* to Honolulu. The reunion there with his men was a joyous occasion. It was especially nice to see Antipatr Baranov again. Antipatr's competence in diverse areas of the warehouse's operation had earned him the men's respect. The Honolulu contingent ate a large meal together at the warehouse, toasting their success innumerable times with vodka. George commiserated with Pavel Verkhovinsky, the supercargo from the *Otkrytie*, who had been stranded when Captain Podushkin decided to sail directly from the emergency damage repairs on Ni'ihau back to Sitka without returning to Honolulu. But Verkhovinsky, George found out, had made himself unpopular with the rest of the Honolulu contingent, as had Dmitrii Toropogritskii, the supercargo of the *Ilmena*. These supercargoes, Antipatr reported, had spent much of their time drinking the stores of vodka and rum, and offering these drinks to foreign sailors for cash. Both Governor Homa and Don Francisco Marin had complained to Antipatr and to Petr Kicherev about this, but the supercargoes would not cease this troublesome behavior.

At Waikīkī, George found that Petr Kicherev had done a fine job in charge of the O'ahu operations during his absence. The warehouse in Honolulu was almost filled to capacity with foodstuffs and sacks of powdered sandalwood. The crops in the new fields north of Waikīkī's swamps were all growing well, devoid of any weeds, which had been pulled up by hand. Timofei Tarakanov, having become irritated at the supercargoes in Honolulu to the point where he didn't trust himself in their presence, had moved to Waikīkī to be of aid to Kicherev. This was partly because Tarakanov struggled within himself to abstain from drinking the vodka and rum, which the supercargoes made available. Kicherev related that Tarakanov had a gift for interacting with the natives. He was alternately stern with them, and then kind. Sometimes he would simply amuse them by singing and performing a sailor's hornpipe dance. But soon they would do whatever he urged them to do without shirking.

Petr Kicherev and Timofei Tarakanov took George on a hike around the Waikīkī environs to survey the progress they had made in their operations. Following a stream into the hills they came to Mānoa Falls, a high thin cascade George had not previously seen. Near there he noted an area of previously harvested sandalwood where they might gather still more of the cast-aside branches for the powdering process. As it was a hot day and they had been hiking uphill through dense foliage for an hour or two to get there, the three men stripped to their underwear and waded into the pool at the base of Mānoa Falls. The water was delightfully cool and the spray of the falls wet their faces as they looked upwards to the rocks from whence the torrent poured down onto them.

Sitting in the refreshing water, Timofei Tarakanov observed to the others, "In many of the places I've spent my life I couldn't have imagined that such a place as this existed. Here there's no frost at all. A man doesn't really need a coat, nor even clothes, except for purposes of modesty…and the natives have very little of that. There are no land animals to fear. There are no leeches, for example, to hide in the water and suck your blood. And there are no mosquitoes. Can anyone who has lived in Alaska imagine a place where there are no mosquitoes? And no roaches either. Here I am a 'Tarakanov' in a land with no roaches."

Tarakanov was making a pun on the fact that his name, "Tarakanov," included within it the Russian word, "tarakan," which meant "roach."

"Well, you have to admit that you've lived in some tough places," suggested George. "Any warm peaceful place might seem a paradise to a man who spent his days hunting seals through the ice floes in a baidarka. There it isn't only the terrible frost that can kill a man, it's the killer whales, the sharks, and the polar bears. Leeches, mosquitoes and roaches are a mere bother compared to them, I'm sure."

"You are right about that, Yegor Nikolaevich," said Tarakanov. "And even California is not free of such dangers as that. I never saw more dangerous sharks in my life than when I was poaching for seals in the Farallon Islands off the California coast near the Spanish settlement at San Francisco. The sharks there were the great whites, and they seemed to hunt in family packs like the killer whales. A giant one…three sazhens or more…would rise up under a baidarka and just take a huge bite out it, capsizing it. Then three or four others of the same size would devour the swimming paddlers like 'zakuski' snacks before we could rescue them. During just three days there we lost seven Aleuts to the damned sharks. And one fellow had his leg bitten off clean…looked the monster in his coal-black eye as he heard the teeth crunch through his knee like a pelmena. Now he stumps around on a wooden peg. The great number of seals there in the Farallons kept us trying, but the sharks soon chased us out."

"Here the most dangerous beings are people," offered Kicherev. "The Hawai'ian Ali'i have no respect for their subjects' lives and squander them for nothing. And the American captains are a troublesome lot. They'd kill you to make a bargain."

"My thought is that we could change all that on Kaua'i at least," said George, who had already explained to them his intention of moving most of their operations to Kaua'i. "There we have an opportunity to build a real paradise. All we have to do is keep Kamehameha from invading it. He's an old man now and cannot live forever. His son Liholiho will not be as forceful, I'm sure of it. We can control and educate Kaua'i's younger King Kaumuali'i so that he treats his people better…the way we think he should treat them. We can control trade and commerce there, keeping the Americans out. And we can live like kings ourselves while we do it. And eventually we may come to control the other islands as well."

"I'm aboard such an effort," said Tarakanov. "You can count on me. I'll write a letter to Ivan Kuskov at Fort Ross and request support from him as well. He can send furs directly to Kaua'i instead of to Novo-Arkhangelsk or Honolulu."

"And me too," put in Petr Kicherev. "But you had better be careful of William Wadsworth, the Captain of the *Ilmena*. He's an American to the core…worrying all the time about what money he'll make. He's a heavy drinker and he stays a bit too close to the other American captains in Honolulu. We can't trust him. And his mate, Verol Madson, is little better, though he's taken a native wife."

"What about the captain of the *Kadiak*?" asked George.

"He's an American also, of course," said Kicherev. "But he appears to be quite trustworthy. Did you notice that he stays at the warehouse when he's ashore and keeps quite apart from the other Americans? Also, his Russian is very good…almost native. He has a Kenai wife in Novo-Arkhangelsk, and for that reason has great respect for Governor Baranov. He's loyal to the Company and the men like him."

"I plan to have a ceremony at the warehouse when the terms of the *Lydia's* sale are complete," said George. "We'll invite Governor Homa, Don Francisco Marin, and all the American captains to it. We will continue to act as if our O'ahu operations are of the utmost importance to us. We'll ask the captains to transport forty sacks of the powdered sandalwood to Kamehameha as a payment for our allotments of O'ahu land. This will allay any suspicions Kamehameha might have about our activities. But then we'll secretly load everything from the warehouse we can on the three ships and sail to Kaua'i, leaving only those men who want to stay. They will tell Governor Homa and the others that we have gone to Kaua'i on a trading expedition and will return soon."

"I can tell you that quite a number of men will want to stay here," said Tarakanov. "They've become involved with the natives on a personal level, if you know what I mean. As for me, I'd want to bring a woman and two children with me to Kaua'i."

Petr Kicherev nodded understandingly, but George was surprised to hear this. "Have you taken a native wife?" he asked.

"I guess you could say that," answered Tarakanov. "I took in a kauwā woman and her two children after the maka'āinana stoned her husband to death."

George's face expressed his wonderment at Tarakanov's statement, causing Tarakanov to explain further. "The kauwā are a class of outcasts, subject to persecution by the maka'āinana and to sacrifice by the Ali'i, who sometimes mark the kauwā males with a tattooed spot in the center of their foreheads. They are a darker-skinned breed of Hawai'ian…like I am thought to be a darker-skinned kind of Russian. They have no permanent settlements, but travel from province to province in extended family groups, like the gypsies in Europe and Russia. In order to survive, they sometimes steal from the settled villagers, taking away chicken, dogs, and pigs. For that reason, the villagers chase them away or persecute them."

"That's just the way the constable in my home town treated the gypsies," observed George.

Tarakanov continued, "My wife's first husband was caught trying to steal a pig from the Waikīkī village to where I moved two months ago. The men there chased after him when he ran and threw rocks at him. One of the rocks hit him in the head and killed him. Later they found his wife and children hiding nearby. They brought them into the village, planning to kill her too and give the children to others, but I stopped them. Somehow she appealed to me. I know what it's like to be a captive…completely subject to someone else's will, your very life hanging by the merest thread of someone else's mercy."

"I've heard of your captivities," said George. "Indeed you must have feared for your life."

"Yes indeed, Yegor Nikolaevich," said Tarakanov. "First the rival hunters of the Lebedev-Lastochkin Company had me, then the Kolosh took me and tortured me so that I thought I was going to die. And later, after the wreck of the *St. Nikolai* in November of 1808, I spent two years starving in the lands of the Koliuzbi savages. We who survived devoured our own dog, then ate our leather belts and shoes. At last our Captain, Nikolai Isaakovich Bulygin went mad after his wife Anna Petrovna chose Koliuzbi captivity over freedom in hardship with him. And I wound up the slave of a savage chief named Yutraniaki who took pity upon me and treated me well. At last, in May of 1810, Yutraniaki sold me to Captain Thomas Brown of the *Lydia*…the very ship that is now the *Ilmena*…for blankets, cloth, knives, mirrors, some gunpowder and shot."

"So, knowing what it's like to be in fear of your life in others' hands, you took pity on the poor kauwā woman and her children," said George.

"I took her and the children to live in my house in the village," Tarakanov continued to relate. "I'm only now able to speak a few words to her. Her name is Lawaholua, or something like that…but I call her 'Lara.' The son, who is about seven years old, I call 'Koli,' and the little daughter, who is perhaps four, I call 'Nina' or 'Ninochka.' I'm already so fond of them that I've given them my patronymic, calling them 'Koli Timofeevich' and 'Nina Timofeevna.' I sense that Lara is grateful to me and she works hard to please me. We are getting along well. But the villagers, although they apparently respect me, will not speak to her, and this is hard for her, especially since she can't well speak to me yet either. My thought is that on Kaua'i she would, because of her position with me, not be considered a kauwā. That is why I want to go there with you."

"That's all right," answered George. "Lara and the children can certainly travel with you. I can only imagine that the experience of sailing in a large European-style ship to another island might be overwhelming to them. But we will treat them as your wife and children if you want, even though the marriage is not sanctioned by God in the Church."

"That is what I want," said Tarakanov. "They'll be living with me there on Kaua'i too, no doubt about it."

"Any men, on the other hand, who want to remain here on O'ahu," said George, directing his comments to Petr Kicherev, "can stay. They can harvest the crops here and plant more, and continue to use the warehouse to store things. Hopefully they can stay out of trouble with the American captains and with John Young. But you'll have to find out right away who will go and who will stay. Those who are going will have to be ready to depart on a moment's notice…and soon. And all this has to happen secretly, without a word to anyone outside our group."

"It will be done," assured Petr Kicherev. "We'll begin arrangements as soon as we get back to the village."

In Honolulu, the schooner *Lydia*'s cargo of sandalwood was transferred to Captain John Ebbets' *Albatross,* and George's payment of 4500 dollars in silver was delivered to Captain Henry Gyzelaar at Don Francisco Marin's house. The signing over of the ship's title was to take place at the celebratory gathering at the Russian warehouse on the evening of August 24th, 1816. This event went smoothly at first, with Governor Homa, Don Francisco Marin and the Captains John and Richard Ebbets, Nathan Winship, Isaac Whittemore, William Smith, and Isaiah Lewis in attendance to participate in the banquet and to sign as witnesses to the transaction. George's friend John Marshall was there also, and he told George that he had signed onto the *Panther* as Captain Lewis' mate. But then, as the guests were starting to leave, a native ran into the warehouse and approached Governor Homa, saying a few words to him.

"John Young has arrived from Hawai'i and he is coming to the warehouse," Governor Homa announced.

As he said this, John Young appeared at the door. The old man was very drunk, and he fell, tripping as he crossed the threshold. Two native warriors who were following entered behind him, stacked their muskets against the doorframe and bent to pick him up off the dirt floor. Two Russian guards stacked their muskets as well and rushed over to help them. In a moment they all had John Young standing back on his feet.

Young was enraged. "What the hell is going on here?" he shouted. "There's a Russian flag flying over this building. And here there are armed Russian guards inside it. What do you think this is—the Tsar's palace?"

He flew at George, pointing his finger at him. "You tell these guards to surrender their arms right now," he said threateningly. "And you take down the flag or I'll take it down for you."

"Mr. Young," George said in as calm a voice as he could manage, "you are mistaken. There is no Russian flag flying over this building. And I need the guards to protect the valuable goods in this warehouse from actions threatened by some of the captains here. I asked Governor Homa for his assistance in the matter, but I was left to my own devices."

"By God, these old eyes can still see," insisted Young. "And I see a Russian flag flying over this building…something you know to be kapu."

"If there is a Russian flag flying over the land anywhere on O'ahu," maintained George with all sincerity, "then I don't know about it. Let's go outside together and you can show me this flag. If it is there, then I will remove it."

"All right. Let's go," said Young, and he led a march of guests out the door to show them the Russian flag. "There it is, right there," he said, pointing up to a pole above the warehouse roof on which a slender red ribbon had been attached as a wind vane.

"It's dark, Mr. Young, but I don't think anyone can claim that to be a Russian flag," said George. "It's merely a wind vane."

"It's a fucking flag put above a Russian building by a Russian," said Young, slurring his words. "And that makes it a fucking Russian flag. You have it struck down right now."

Filip Osipov and Aleksei Odnoriadkin rushed to George's aid. Aleksei made a stirrup out of his hands and boosted Filip up onto the warehouse roof. Filip scampered agilely up to the peak and grabbed the wind-vane pole with both hands, breaking it off at the roofline and throwing it to the ground below.

"Now are you satisfied?" George asked John Young, picking up the ribbon-topped pole and offering it to him.

"No, I'm not satisfied," said Young. "I know what you're up to, God damn it. I told you to stay only a short time on Kaua'i and not to meddle in our affairs with Kaumuali'i. But you stayed there almost three months and now I hear from the younger Ebbets here about how Mr. Lannert and Mr. Prince on the *Atala* told him that you've got a Russian flag flying there on Kaua'i too. And now you're buying ships with the sandalwood we told you was kapu."

The *Atala* had obviously not sailed directly from Waimea to Novo-Arkhangelsk as Mr. Lannert had told George, but had likely stopped in Honolulu before sailing north. George thought about how he should respond.

"You told me that cutting growing sandalwood was kapu," said George, looking to the others for moral support. "And Governor Homa can tell you that I have not had any growing sandalwood cut here. Only have we made a powder out of the branches, which the previous cutters left behind. And I did this so that I could pay Kamehameha, Ka'ahumanu, and Kuakini for their allotments of land here. Indeed I am prepared to give you forty sacks of this sandalwood powder out of this very warehouse. I trust that you will see that it is properly delivered. In China it will bring a fortune."

John Young lost some of his anger. He looked around at the captains. None of them wanted to mention to him that the *Lydia* had been offered to Kaumuali'i and that it was Kaua'ian sandalwood that had paid for it. He glared at Governor Homa, remembering the Governor's letter to him on George's behalf. And he darted his gaze toward the two Russian guards, who were standing nearby without their muskets.

"Let's have a drink," he said, entering the warehouse more carefully this time.

After the encounter was over, John Young and his guards went to stay at Kapapoko, Ka'ahumanu's O'ahu residence. The next day Young made arrangements for George to have the sacks of sandalwood left in the care of Francisco Marin until the *Ka'ahumanu* could be sent for them from Kailua. The day after that they left from Waikīkī on a double-hulled canoe for Hawai'i, but not before Young sought out George in the nearby village and warned him that meddling in Kaua'i was kapu.

"If I have to deal with you again in any way at all," Young told George. "It will not be to your liking. Do you understand me?"

"I understand," said George.

The next day George had trouble engaging a new crew for the *Lydia*. The obvious candidate to be the new captain was Verol Madson, Captain Wadsworth's first mate. He was a competent navigator but claimed to be incapable of taking over the sailing of a fore-and-aft-rigged schooner. George realized that he would have to be trained to the position, and he asked Captain Gyzelaar to train him. Gyzelaar agreed to stay with the *Lydia* until Madson felt competent to take over, but he wanted ten sacks of the powdered sandalwood in exchange for this task. George agreed, but stipulated that Gyzelaar pay several of his former crewmembers to stay aboard as well to train other sailors that George would designate from his men. The problem with this arrangement was that Captain Gyzelaar would have to sail the *Lydia* back to Waimea on Kaua'i as part of an exodus of the O'ahu Russians of which he was not supposed to be aware. George reckoned that this would be possible as long as the *Lydia* was the first to depart. Gyzelaar would only find out about the movement of most of the Russian company to Kaua'i after he was already in Waimea. He could then be kept there if need be, George thought.

After the *Lydia* had sailed with thirty of his men aboard, George was approached by Captain Isaac Whittemore who was the owner of the *Avon*. Captain Whittemore was elderly and had been in poor health. He said he wanted to sell the *Avon* for hard money and return to New England as a passenger. The price was astronomical—200,000 Spanish piastres. But the *Avon* was, at 350 tons, one of the largest and finest trading ships in the Pacific. It was well armed with twenty-two cannon of several types and was reputed to be easy to sail. George had no doubt that adding it to Kaumuali'i's fleet on Kaua'i would contribute much to swinging the balance of power in the islands his way. He could only imagine with enthusiasm what Kaumuali'i would think when he saw it. So he decided to use his credit arrangement with Governor Baranov to buy it for the Russian-American Company, writing a document of sale agreement and a letter to Governor Baranov with that purpose in mind. Captain Whittemore agreed to transport George to Kaua'i so that Kaumuali'i could see the ship, and then sail to Sitka to deliver the document and letter in order to receive the arranged payment from Governor Baranov. One of Baranov's captains could then sail the *Avon* back to Kaua'i and Captain Whittemore could sail as a passenger on the next ship out of Sitka for New England.

On September 1st, 1816, the *Ilmena* and the *Kadiak* sailed out of Honolulu harbor for Kaua'i. On board the *Ilmena* were thirty men, Russians and Aleuts, including Timofei Tarakanov with his wife and children, and Antipatr Baranov. And on the *Kadiak* were fifty more, including Filip Osipov and Aleksei Odnoriadkin. Petr Kicherev stayed on O'ahu at Waikīkī with the remaining forty men, saying that he would follow later. The Russian-American Company supercargoes Pavel Verkhovinskii and Dmitrii Toropogritskii stayed for the time being in the now unguarded and quite empty warehouse in Honolulu.

George himself left Honolulu on the next day aboard the *Avon*. It sailed north through the channel between O'ahu and Kaua'i and proceeded to Kaua'i's north shore. Captain Whittemore wanted to circle the island to show George the sailing abilities of the *Avon*. Anchoring for a day in Hanalei Bay gave George the opportunity to go ashore and survey the territory. He was mightily impressed. The tranquil bay was ringed by high bluffs and distant green mountains with silvery slivers of waterfalls adorning them. The beach was wide and bare of dune grass or even driftwood. A river which entered the bay below a steep bluff appeared to be navigable for small boats. And inland fields were planted in taro so that a view from a hill made the landscape appear like a checkerboard of alternating light and dark green squares. The experience of surveying the area was like George's earlier experiences in viewing many other parts of the Hawai'ian Islands—at every turn each new scene seemed to outstrip the former scene in beauty and magnificence. Again and again, confronted with a breathtaking vista, he wanted to exclaim, "I've never seen a more beautiful place."

The *Avon* then sailed southward along the jagged and spectacular Na Pali cliffs. Here too George was impressed with the scene…such severity, such grandeur. At one point the ship passed through a vast flotilla of jellyfish, their sail-like gelatinous protuberances appearing like myriad pox on the skin of the sea. A sailor extended down a long-handled net and scooped up several of them. He held one up for George to view, pinching its top portion carefully between his fingers. "The slender tentacles hanging down below it are the dangerous part," he said. "They give you a most painful sting upon the slightest touch. And some kinds of these jellyfish can even kill you."

The Na Pali coast of Kaua'i, from http://www.absolutevisit.com/blog/na-pali-coast-cathedral-kauai-hawaii-usa/

When the *Avon* reached Waimea, Captain Whittemore explained to George that Waimea was a difficult anchorage. Ships anchored there tended to drift away from their anchors. Several, like the *Bering*, had been washed ashore and wrecked on the beach. "Here we'll put both anchors down," said the Captain.

George could see that the *Lydia*, the *Ilmena,* and the *Kadiak* were already anchored nearby, and that each of them was held by more than one anchor. As he prepared to be rowed in, a cannon salute of eleven shots was fired from the shore. The Russian flag was proudly waving to him in the breeze.

The next day, August 29th, 1816, George arranged a meeting, in which Captains Whittemore, Wadsworth, Young, and Gyzelaar, with Gyzelaar's friend and fellow sailing tutor William Smith, ex-Captain of the *Albatross*, and the pupil Verol Madson, witnessed his presentation of the *Lydia*'s papers to King Kaumuali'i "as a gift of the Russian-American Company." Kaumuali'i was clearly pleased with this gift and with the increased number of Russian ships offshore. But his pleasure increased to delight when George invited him to come aboard the grand *Avon* and view this latest addition to "their fleet." George made sure in a signed affidavit that Kaumuali'i would be reimbursing the Russian-American Company more than 200,000 Spanish piastres worth of sandalwood, payable in yearly installments across the next five years.

When Kaumuali'i came onto the *Avon* he was accompanied by his son Keali'iahonui and by another younger son, a boy of about twelve years of age. This was Kaumuali'i's son by Queen Namahana, named Kahekili to honor the great former ruler of the Mau'i Federation, Kaumuali'i's paternal uncle. As George and Captain Whittemore showed Kaumuali'i around the ship,

Keali'iahonui and Kahekili were seen to be looking and pointing up to the main mast's crow's nest, the lookout post well over a hundred feet above the deck. Keali'iahonui had apparently dared Kahekili to climb to the lookout's lofty perch. The boy scampered onto the ratlines and made his way upward with impressive haste, and apparently without fear. In a minute or two he was ensconced in the lookout's safety staves and shouting for his father's attention. Kaumuali'i looked up at him, beaming with fatherly pride, and waved, shouting "Maika'i, maika'i nui!"

In a later private meeting with Kaumuali'i, George asked that parcels of land on Kaua'i be given to him personally by signed deed, so that he could look forward to residing there permanently and to passing his lands on legally to his successors. In particular, George said, he wanted to own the province of Hanalei on the north shore. Kaumuali'i did not object to this idea at all, but embraced it with enthusiasm.

Hanalei Valley on Kaua'i's north shore, showing the Hanalei River and taro fields, from http://en.wikipedia.org/wiki/Hanalei,_Hawaii.

"That area is administered by a chief named Kaloha'aki for my minister of war Kupikēapio," Kaumuali'i said. "I will tell Kupikēapio that Hanalei is now yours. It will be up to you to write the documents about this and have Kupikēapio and Kaloha'aki sign them. I think you should give Russian names to all the places there. The names are part of the spirit of the places, you know."

George had not thought of this, but, pleased by the ease of his acquisition, he said, "Yes, I know."

Building Forts:

George decided that Antipatr Baranov could most advantageously be sent home at this time on the *Avon*. He knew that Antipatr would be the most persuasive of all possible voices in convincing his father to support George and his endeavors in the Hawai'ian Islands by paying for the *Avon* and sending him whatever further aid he needed. He discussed this with Antipatr, and Antipatr agreed that it was time for him to return to Novo-Arkhangelsk. He missed his father and his sister. He had been away long enough. On September 6th, 1816, the *Avon,* filled to the gunwales with foodstuffs and powdered sandalwood, left for Alaska with Antipatr and about twenty other passengers aboard. It was difficult for George to say farewell to him, such a fine asset to the mission the young man had been. George made sure that Antipatr had copies with him of all the documents of agreement as well as a long letter he had written to his father, Governor Baranov. Kaumuali'i's appointment of Governor Baranov as Chief was accompanied by the gift of a glorious red and gold-feathered cape.

Now that most of his men, numbering more than eighty, were on Kaua'i to stay, it seemed important to George that he set about to fortify the main sea approaches to the island. He told Kaumuali'i that forts should be constructed to control all harbors and river entries. The first fort should be constructed, he said, right there at Waimea, on the bluff at Hīpo overlooking the river's entry into the ocean and able to pour cannon fire on any ships at anchor offshore or on any fleets of canoes that might attack Kaumuali'i's capital. Kaumuali'i was pleased with the location, saying that the place was very propitious, the location of two heiaus in former times called Pā'ula'ula o Hipo. George proposed to direct the construction of this fort personally, which was to be made of lava rocks from the former heiau and from the riverbanks. The rocks would be overlaid on groundworks to a height of more than two sazhens…eighteen feet. The walls would be wide enough at the top to walk upon easily and to fire cannon placed upon them. The overall shape of the fort was to be like that of a starfish…with guns placed on the points able to fire back into the gaps in the event of assault by warriors on foot.

"It will be a construction project as great as that of Kamehameha's Pu'ukoholā Heiau," George assured Kaumuali'i. "Just the sight of it will give invaders a feeling of despair."

Kaumuali'i sent for his chiefs. He required each of them to contribute laborers to work on the construction of the fort. George took the opportunity of the chiefs' presence to draft a document of deed to Hanalei and have it signed by Kaumuali'i and witnessed by more than thirty of his chiefs, including Kupikēapio and Kaloha'aki. He decided to give these two chiefs, with whom he would have to deal, his own special names. Kupikēapio he named "Ovana Platov" in honor of the Cossack General Platov he had once met. Kaloha'aki he would call "Hanalei" after the name of the area he was ceding to George's ownership. The area of Hanalei itself would now be known as "Shefferthal." The name of the Russian family "Vorontsov" was given to another northern Chief, Kaela. The Russian text of the deed, recorded in two copies, includes these terms:

"Deed of Hanalei Province to Ye. von Sheffer by King Kaumuali'i

September 21, 1816

By the Grace of God and by the protection of the great Russian Emperor Aleksandr Pavlovich, we, Kaumuali'i, King of Kaua'i and Ni'ihau, Prince of O'ahu, Lana'i, Mau'i, and etc., etc., etc., declare the following:

According to the contract which I concluded with the Commissioner of the Russian-American Company, Dr. Yegor von Sheffer, on May 21 of this year on the ship *Otkrytie*, I, King Kaumuali'i, have ordered my Chief Kupikēapio to hand over to the Commissioner, Dr. Sheffer, my province which is located on the northern side of the island of Kaua'i, in the place called Hanalei where Sheffer has acquired rights I granted to him as representative of the Russian-American Company, including my sovereign rights to rule there, my property, my land, and my peasants. I renounce the above-mentioned part of the island of Kaua'i in Sheffer's favor or in favor of whomever he wishes to rule there or of his successors who may do there whatever they please. I renounce this land also in the name of my own successors who will not have any right to claim as their own this land, its rivers, ports, sea, peasants or any other former possessions of mine.

This, my order and act with regard to this province, was made public through my Chief Kupikēapio and through the Commissioner and witnessed by the chief of this province and handed to the Commissioner and his secretary, Mr. Charles Fox-Bennick.

The witnesses present include: Chief Kaloha'aki of Hanalei, and also 33 others named below.

For the sake of greater security, this act was made in two copies with my name and sign. One copy is given to the Commissioner, Dr. Sheffer, and the other is to be placed in our archives.

Signed:_____ Kaumuali'i (lizard glyph)

Recorded September 24, 1816 on the Island of Kaua'i."

By the end of September, close to a thousand workers were toiling daily on the construction of the first fort at Waimea. George had insisted that no one be sacrificed to hallow the ground of the fort, and Kaumuali'i agreed. One of the most important factors enabling the monumental task of moving and piling the base mounds of earth and then surmounting this base with thousands and thousands of lava rocks… "any rock bigger than your head that you can pick up," was the workers' instruction…was George's innovation of directing the manufacture of a hundred wheelbarrows. These wheelbarrows were made of sturdy wooden planks from the wrecked *Bering* and from some lumber that had been unloaded from the *Avon,* which had also been stripped of more than half its cannon. The wheelbarrows' wheels were also made of wood, but the wheels had metal bands as edges and they rotated on metal axles, which George had ordered forged on the *Kadiak*.

By November the interior of the fort was nearing completion. The work to elevate the level of the rampart walls would continue for some time. Only a few days had been declared kapu so that work ceased. The natives clearly were taking pride in the fort's construction. Everyone wanted to be involved. One day George noticed that a large number of women had joined in the rock brigades, passing rocks up the banks to the men who were loading the wheelbarrows. Several of these women, with swollen nipples and grotesquely distended stomachs, were obviously due to deliver babies within days. He demanded that they be sent home. At the place where the rocks were being piled onto the ramparts, he saw Queen Naoa lifting rocks out of a wheelbarrow and placing them onto the edge of the east side wall. The laborers were crouching below in obeisance, waiting for her to withdraw so they could retrieve the wheelbarrow to refill it.

This likeness of the star-shaped Fort Elizaveta on the east shore bluff above the mouth of the Waimea River shows the fort as it looked shortly after its construction in fall of 1816, from: http://garysreflections.blogspot.com from the June 21, 2010 blog.

George walked over to Queen Naoa, bent briefly to one knee and removed his tricornered hat. She motioned for him to rise and said to him in Hawai'ian "Aloha, Friend Kepa. The building goes well. My brother the King thinks that this fort should have a Russian name. And he wants you to construct a new residence for him near it. The residence should also be constructed of lava rock. He will move to it and give it the old residence's name of Papa'ena'ena."

"That will be done, Queen Naoa," answered George. "The new Papa'ena'ena will be a grand residence."

It was only after the walls of the new residence were reaching ceiling height that George learned that two native men... reputed to have been spies from O'ahu...had been killed in the heiau near the old residence by Kaumuali'i's kahunas and buried under the corner of the new building's foundation. These sacrifices were intended to guard the mana of the new Papa'ena'ena.

The formal dedication of the fort at Waimea, which George decided to call "Fort Elizaveta" after the name of Tsar Aleksandr's consort, coincided with the beginning of the Makahiki festival. The highlight of the day was the twenty-one-gun salute from the fort's walls in the evening, followed by a show of fireworks, which Captain Young's sailors fired into the air from both the fort and the *Kadiak* offshore. The next day, George moved into the fort's commander's residence along the inside of the seaside wall. On the central flagpole he raised the Russian flag. Others who decided to make the fort their residence included Grigorii Terentev, Charles Fox-Bennick, Aleksei Odnoriadkin, and Filip Osipov. Crewmembers from the *Lydia,* the *Ilmena,* and the *Kadiak* visited there daily.

The Russians put the finishing touches on Kaumuali'i's new residence since native labor was kapu during the Makahiki holiday. The building had windows with shutters, and was furnished with European-style tables and chairs. It had a grand kitchen with a huge rock stove and a raised sink, which drained to the slope of the bluff outside. Water filled the sink from a fifty-gallon metal-lined cistern on the roof, which Kaumuali'i's servants would replenish by bucket every day. There was a banquet room and a reception room, on the wall of which a portrait of Kaumuali'i was hung. This portrait, Kaumuali'i's first artificial likeness, was painted on sailcloth using a limited number of oil-based colors by Aleksei Odnoriadkin, who surprised everyone with his artistic talent.

Before the construction of Fort Elizaveta was completed, George began construction also of two forts at Hanalei. These were smaller earthwork fortifications, built with the labor of Chief Kaloha'aki's people, including even some of his Mū. George used the *Lydia* to sail back and forth to Hanalei, giving Verol Madson an opportunity to command the ship. Captain Gyzelaar and his friend Captain Smith wanted to return to O'ahu and George thought that this would be now be possible.

George called the earthwork fort on top of the bluff overlooking the place where the Hanalei River entered the ocean "Fort Aleksandr" after the Russian Tsar. The river itself George renamed the "Volga." From the promontory of the fort he had a magnificent view of the entire bay to the southwest and its spectacular environs. From there also he could see far down the northern shore. It was a wonderful vantage point not only because of its scenery, but from the military point of view. He placed three cannon there, including a twelve-pounder, which could reach half way across the bay with a ball, chain, or shot. Twenty men would be permanently stationed there. The other fort, across the Hanalei River mouth on the lower shore near the beach, he called "Fort Barclay" after the Russian General Barclay de Tolly, whose heroism at the Battle of Borodino four years previously had so inspired him. This fort was not far from the largest native settlement in the province where Chief Kaloha'aki lived. George placed a swivel gun there and selected a detachment of twelve men to be stationed there.

George's plan was to fortify also the bay at Nāwiliwili on the southeastern shore, likely from the bluff just above Kalapaki Beach and its village, and also the approach to the Wailua River on the eastern shore, but for the remaining month of 1816 he was content to consolidate his gains and reap the benefits of his hard work.

The Ane'ekapuahi and Mare Amara:

In many conversations with Kaumuali'i, George found out about his life. His mother, Kamakahelei, had been the ruling Queen of Kaua'i. She was the daughter of Pelieioholani, an Ali'i Aimoku of Oahu. Although she was described by others who encountered her as a sturdy and unattractive woman of forceful personality, her genealogical mana was powerful enough to make her a highly desired mate for the highest ali'i of other islands. Her first husband, whom she married in her early teens, was Kina, a high chief of Ni'ihau. With

This likeness of Chiefess Kamakahelei (1755-1794) as a young woman is from http://www.guide2womenleaders.com/womeninpower/Womeninpower1770.htm

him she had two daughters, Lelemahoalani and Kapua'amohu, whom Kaumuali'i later took as a wife. By 1776 Kamakahelei had replaced her husband Kina with O'ahu ali'i Kaneoneo. Kina returned to Ni'ihau, pledging to return to reclaim Kamakahelei, but was killed in battle there. With Kaneoneo, who was killed fighting together with Ka'iana in a campaign against King Kahekili of Mau'i, she had a daughter Kawalu and a son, Keawe. But even before the death of Kaneoneo, Kamakahelei had taken yet another husband, a physically attractive and formidable Prince of the Mau'i line, Ka'eokulani, and had started having children with him. Ka'eokulani, called Ka'eo, was the son of the great Mau'i King Kekaulike and his wife Holau. He was a younger half brother of the Mau'i Federation King Kahekili. Ka'eo was Kamakahelei's husband during the visit in January of 1778 of Captain James Cook's ships *Resolution* and *Discovery*. A story long circulated among the Hawai'ian natives that Ka'eo and Kamakahelei offered Kamakahelei's daughter Lelemahoalani to Captain Cook as a sexual partner, so as to ascertain whether he was human or divine. The fact that Kamakahelei's next birth was that of son Kaumuali'i gave rise also to rumors that Kaumuali'i, who had facial features similar to those of the European visitors, was possibly the child of Captain Cook with the reputedly lusty Kamakahelei herself. But Kaumuali'i clearly considered Ka'eo to be his father. With Ka'eo, Kamakahelei also had two daughters, including the extremely large Kapi'olani or "Kapo" and Kaininoa or "Naoa," the younger full sister whom Kaumuali'i also later took as a wife. All of Kamakahelei's birthings likely took place at the Holoholokū Heiau on the north bank of the Wailua River on Kaua'i's eastern shore. This heiau is on a hill only a short distance above the ocean. There is a group of four stones there on which the highest Ali'i women of Kaua'i crouched to give birth, protected by a rectangular kapu stone under which a sacrificed dog was buried. Nearby is a pīko rock where the placentas were buried and large "bell rocks" to announce the birth. It was here that Kaumuali'i was born, most likely in the year 1780. The name he was given, Kaumuali'i, means "the oven of the nobles."

As the husband of Kamakahelei, Ka'eo became the *de facto* King of Kaua'i. But he did not spend much time there, being almost constantly involved in military campaigns on the other islands. His second-in-command, Chief Opunui, was thought to be Kaua'i's King by the early British captains who visited Kaua'i in the 1780s. But Ka'eo was a most imposing combatant in the island campaigns and an effective military organizer. He was both tall and large, and physically very strong. He practiced a kind of constant psychological warfare on anticipated enemies, striding around with a brace of two large "maneating" dogs on a short leash. He engaged some of the most formidable masters of lua as his military aides, including the legendary Ki'ikikī, who was said to knock over trees and throw pig-sized boulders great distances. And he had able foreign advisors, including the expert armorer and cannonier, Mare Amara, who had first come to Kaua'i, Kaumuali'i related, with "the Great Liar Captain, John Meares…either on the *Nootka* or perhaps later on the *Felice*."

"Kamehameha mentioned this man Amara to me once," said George to Kaumuali'i after the King mentioned Mare Amara.

"Yes, I know that Kamehameha knew who he was," said Kaumuali'i. "Amara fought against his warriors at the Battle of the Red-mouthed Gun off Mau'i and elsewhere. He fought for my father and for Chief Kalanikūpule of O'ahu. But he left my father when my father warred against Kalanikūpule and fought with Kalanikūpule's foreigners against my father. He killed one of my father's foreign advisors at Pu'unahawele on O'ahu with a musket shot, braced by an espontoon, at a distance of a half-mile. And later it was he who directed the cannon fire from British Captain William Brown's ship *Jackal* that caused the deaths of my father, my mother, and several of our most important chiefs. This was at the Battle of Kuki'iahu at Kalauao near 'Ewa in December of 1794."

"So this man Amara was responsible for the deaths of both your father and your mother?" asked George.

"'Ae…yes," said Kaumuali'i. "And I was then too young to rule. That is why Regent Inamo'o ruled for a time. It was he who had Kamehameha's first invaders killed, but he died soon after. And then the ruler was my brother Keawe, who kept me under guard and closely watched. Once he told me that he had made a spirit leap from between the two parts of Wailua Falls near our

Kaumuali'i's "Spirit Leap" from the top of 173-foot Wailua Falls, by BROOK KAPŪKUNIAHI PARKER, July 2012.

mutual birthplace, and that his mana had protected him in this leap, proving that he was chosen by the gods to rule instead of me. So I made this most dangerous leap myself, and, with him watching, I survived. But then, Ki'ikiki told me that Keawe had lied about making this leap. He had stood atop the falls, but feared the height and did not leap. He knew his lie would induce me to make the leap, and he thought I would die doing it. But my mana was stronger than his, and when he saw my leap he realized this."

"It was during the time of Inamo'o and Keawe that I first learned to speak your English language," Kaumuali'i continued. "Captain John Kendrick of the *Lady Washington* left three sailors here in 1791 to collect sandalwood. But Captain Kendrick did not return to get them. Their names were John Rowbottom, James Coleman and John Williams. They helped Captain George Vancouver, when he was here, to speak with Regent Inamo'o. I spoke English with them as often as I could, but later I found out from the American John Gowan who came later from Boston that the English they taught me was not proper to speak with captains or kings. So John Gowan became my English interpreter for about five years and I learned much from him. He left here several years ago, taking one of my wives with him. But I don't need an English interpreter anymore anyway."

"What happened to Keawe?" George wanted to know.

"Ki'ikikī shot and killed him at Kapa'a," answered Kaumuali'i. "Ki'ikikī and his brother Kāne'ekau, who was the Chief of Hanapepe then, were Keawe's supporters. But Ki'ikikī was very desirous of my sister Kapua'amohu, whom even Ka'iana had once courted. By that time Kapua'amohu, though much older than I, was my wife and I promised Ki'ikikī that I would send her to lie with him if he would kill Keawe."

"Did he then lie with Kapua'amohu?" inquired George, astonished to hear the King relate without any compunction the prostituting of his sister-wife to bring about the murder of his brother.

"Yes he did lie with Kapua'amohu," said Kaumuali'i. "And she did not like this, because Ki'ikikī was a very large and brutal man…like an animal, she said. He continued to lie with her every night for almost a month. I wanted to stop him from lying with her, but I had promised, and, besides, Ki'ikikī had stolen Keawe's store of foreign weapons, and I could do nothing to him. At last he and his brother were surfing at Makaweli, so that they left the calabashes of guns on the beach. My Mū, who were following them everywhere, stole the guns and brought them to me. Seeing this, Ki'ikikī and Kāne'ekau fled in a canoe to O'ahu. Later I heard where they were and sent my Mū to kill them."

"My God," exhaled George. "What did you do about the man, Mare Amara, who killed your parents?"

"I prayed him to death with the Ane'ekapuahi," answered Kaumuali'i. "He was burned up in a terrible consuming fire sent by Pele at my pule 'ana'ana."

"What?" asked George incredulously. "He just caught fire and burned up on his own because you prayed for this to happen to him?"

"My mother Kamakahelei taught me the Ane'ekapuahi prayer, known only to her in her generation, and now only to me in mine," explained Kaumuali'i. "As soon as I heard how my parents had died, and by whose hand, I prepared to pray the Ane'ekapuahi to cause Mare Amara to be consumed by fire. At the start of your year 1795, I was prepared to make the prayer, and I did make the prayer. For three days I spoke the prayer. Then I knew I could stop praying. I knew that he had been consumed by fire."

"Where was he when this happened to him?"

"I found out later that he was still on the ship *Jackal*," responded Kaumauli'i. "The *Jackal* was a Brig under Captain Alexander Stewart which started wintering in the islands in 1792 with the smaller sloop *Prince Lee Boo* under Captain Daniel Gordon and the British flagship, the 390-ton Frigate *Butterworth,* under the fleet commander, Captain William Brown. In 1793 the *Butterworth* returned to England, and Captain Brown took over the *Jackal,* with the former master, Alexander Stewart, taking his first mate's position. In the winter of 1794 Kalanikūpule offered Captain Brown 400 hogs in exchange for his help in the battle on O'ahu against my father, Ka'eo, and his warriors. Captain Brown's *Jackal* and Captain Gordon's *Prince Lee Boo* were powerful in the effort against my father, firing their cannons at him and his men from the sea. But they weren't all. The American Captain John Kendrick on the *Lady Washington* fired his cannons at my father's warriors also."

"Two British ships and an American ship…all firing at your father," asked George. "How do you know it was Mare Amara on the *Jackal* who fired the fatal shots?"

"Amara was given my father's 'ahu'ula cape and mahiole cap as trophies," said Kaumuali'i. "But he did not keep them long. They were taken off the *Jackal* after his death by Kalanikūpule, and now they are in Kamehameha's hands."

"How did this happen?"

"Pele was angry about the way my parents were faring in the battle," related Kaumuali'i. "First she caused Captain Brown on the British *Jackal* to fire a cannon salute at the *Lady Washington* to celebrate its participation in the battle. But Captain Brown's gunners fired the wrong cannons…ones loaded with ball instead of only with powder. This salute penetrated the *Lady Washington's* hull in Pearl Harbor and killed the American Captain Kendrick and four others of his officers and crew. This happened on the 7th of December, 1794, just five days before my parents were killed. But even worse was what happened to Mare Amara, because of my Ane'ekapuahi."

"What was that?"

"After the battle was over and my parents were dead, Mare Amara aided Kalanikūpule and his warriors to attack the British officers who had helped them in the fight. In this act of treachery they killed the *Jackal's* Captain Brown and also the *Prince Lee Boo's* Captain Gordon and most of their officers."

"Why did they do that?" asked George.

Kaumuali'i continued: "Kalanikūpule did not want to part with the 400 hogs he had promised Captain Brown. And he thought that Mare Amara would help him sail the two British ships against Kamehameha. After most of the officers on the two ships had been treacherously killed and Kalanikūpule and his men had come aboard them, Amara tried to convince the ships' mates, Alexander Stewart, Mr. Lamport, Mr. Bonallack and their fellow crew members, who were being held below the decks, that they should submit to his becoming their commander in an attack on Kamehameha. Indeed they were already sailing in the direction of Hawai'i, fully loaded with all the weapons they had gathered from my father's fallen warriors and accompanied by hundreds of war canoes. But Pele, answering my Ane'ekapuahi, prevailed upon her cousin La'amaomao, the wind God, to stir the winter waves. And shortly Kalanikūpule and his chiefs became very very seasick, being unaccustomed to such waves aboard an unfamiliar type of craft. Kalanikūpule, against Mare Amara's advice, ordered a return to Honolulu so that he and his men could recover their strength. In the calm of Honolulu's harbor most of Kalanikūpule's men left the ships, leaving too few of them to guard the crewmembers below decks, who, under the leadership of Alexander Stewart and mates Lamport and Bonallack, rushed their sick captors and overcame them. They then sailed the *Jackal* and the *Prince Lee Boo* away again, with Kalanikūpule and Mare Amara as their prisoners. The chiefs who had gone ashore and all the men in the returned canoes looked at the ships leaving and did not know what to think."

"The English have a saying," said George. "That the 'tables are turned.' The captors suddenly became the captives. But I know that Kalanikūpule lived to lose his life later after the Battle of Nu'uanu Pali? Did he then escape?"

"'Aole...no, Friend George," answered Kaumuali'i. "My Ane'ekapuahi did not include him, and so Alexander Stewart commanded that he be put into a boat and allowed to row himself back to O'ahu just off Le'ahi. But this was only after he was made to witness the burning of the traitor Mare Amara in a pan of gunpowder. Amara was burned to death and thrown to the sharks. Then the ships sailed to Hawai'i where the former mates, now captains, informed Kamehameha of Kalanikūpule's intent to attack him, giving him all the gathered weapons as well. Kamehameha's men used these weapons to kill Kalanikūpule's warriors later that year in Kamehameha's taking of O'ahu. And, of course, Kalanikūpule was later killed."

"So Amara was burned up in a pan of gunpowder?" observed George. "What a horrible way to die."

"It was Pele's way of putting an end, at my request, to a man who had used gunpowder to kill others for years," said Kaumuali'i dryly. "When I heard this, I thought it was a very appropriate thing for Pele to do."

"Why did the men of the *Jackal* and the *Prince Lee Boo* execute Mare Amara instead of Kalanikūpule? Why didn't they kill them both? Why did they consider Mare Amara a traitor?" George was full of questions for Kaumuali'i about his story.

"They wanted to teach Kalanikūpule a lesson, yet keep him as a possible partner for future trading," answered Kaumuali'i. "And they considered Mare Amara a traitor to his kind, even though he was not British, but was an Italian…from a city called Firenze in Tuscany. He was said to be some kind of Ali'i there."

"He was from Tuscany?" said George with surprise.

"Yes, Friend George," replied Kaumuali'i. "Here he was called Mare Amara, but his real name was 'Marius' in Latin or 'Mario' in Italian, and his family was named 'Amare'."

"My God," exclaimed George. "His name was 'AMARE'?!" He then repeated again, "AMARE'?!"

"Yes, his family name was Amare, Friend George. What is so surprising to you about that?" asked the King.

"Ten years ago this very month," said George, shaking his head in wonderment, "I killed a man named Lorenzo Amare in a pistol duel in Würzburg, Franconia, in Germany. He was also from Firenze, which the English call 'Florence,' and was related to an Austrian Grand Duke. And, he was a soldier and an expert at arms."

"Do you think the man you killed and the man I killed were brothers?" asked Kaumuali'i.

"They had to have been related, I would say," said George. "How old was your man Amara in 1795?"

"He was about the same age we are now," replied the King, recognizing the apparent equality of his and George's age. "Perhaps he was a bit younger. He was a tall man and strong, with hair as black as mine. He wore a beard."

"I would say there is little doubt that they were brothers," said George. "What an astonishing coincidence that is. We are connected, you and I, King George, despite the great distances between our birthplaces and our stations in life. We have killed men who were brothers. I suppose that makes us brothers of a kind…in some strange way."

"I agree with that, Friend George," said Kaumuali'i. "I also feel that we are brothers, at least in spirit. Let us have a drink of 'awa together to celebrate this feeling."

"Indeed, let's drink," agreed George, hiding his reluctance to swallow any of the foul 'awa. And then, as he drank, he had the thought that Kaumuali'i's other brother, Keawe, had not fared too well in the world for it.

More Land:

In the fall months of 1816, impressed by the construction and arming of Fort Elizaveta in Waimea and by the three Russian ships in port, King Kaumuali'i and his queens and chiefs made gifts of land to the Russian-American Company, to George, and even to some of George's men whom they favored. George was careful to record each gift by a formal deed, signed by as many and as prominent a group of witnesses as he could muster, and celebrated by banquets with endless toasts and cannon salutes.

First, Kaumuali'i gave the Russian-American Company the entire uninhabited islet of Lehua to the north of Ni'ihau, which George ordered stocked with sheep and goats. Then, Queen Naoa gave the Company a village on the east bank of the Waimea River with fourteen families of maka'āinana to provide labor. George named this tract "Gamaleia" after his Masonic mentor, Semyon Ivanovich Gamaleia. Naoa also granted the Company a tract of land with thirteen families in Makaweli, and an entire uninhabited valley in the hills northeast of Waimea. Queen Monalau gave to George personally a plot of land, fifteen versts wide and nine deep, along the coast between Waimea and Hanapepe. It was possible to gather salt there. The land included a fifteen-family settlement in a valley near the shore called Kaunakio, which George renamed and recorded in the deed as the "George Valley." Chief Kamaholelani gave the Company large plots of land on both banks of the Waimea, with twenty families to help build warehouses and tend vegetable gardens. The deed for this gift read:

"Declaration of Friendship and Deed of Land,

Chief Kamaholelani to Dr. Yegor Sheffer,

October 1, 1816

Contrary to false rumors coming from many seamen and other citizens of the United States of America, I assure His Honor, Doctor, and Collegiate Assessor of the Russian Empire, Commissioner of the Russian-American Company Yegor von Sheffer that myself and King Kaumuali'i never wished anything but friendship with the Russians and especially with the Russian-American Company. From the Russians, we never heard anything that was not good. From the Americans we have heard much that is evil. As evidence of my friendship, I am making to Dr. von Sheffer for the Company's factory a gift of two strips of land, one in his harbor on the right bank of the Waimea River, with twenty families of peasants, at the place called Waikali. This is given permanently. I assure all of my service to the Great Russian Tsar and shall do for the Russians here all I can.

    Signed:_____ Kamaholelani, Minister (X)

    _____ Kaumuali'i, King of Kaua'i, Ni'ihau, etc.

                   (lizard glyph)"

Only Chief Kupikēapio or "Ovana Platov" seemed not pleased to be giving land to George and his compatriots. He was cooperative initially in the giving over to George, through his subordinate Chief Kahola'aki, the large grant of land in Hanalei, but after that he obviously wanted to give no more land or power to the Russians. To George, he seemed jealous and potentially dangerous.

Timofei Tarakanov was also given land. He had positively impressed Kaumuali'i, not only with his able leadership in the construction of Fort Elizaveta, but with his native family. Also, because of his family, he was able to speak Hawai'ian as well as George, and he communicated his desire to have a separate place in which to live. Kaumuali'i deeded him a village with eleven families on the east bank of the Hanapepe River, which George renamed on the deed as the "Don," after the historic river flowing through eastern Ukraine. Tarakanov agreed to Kaumuali'i's request that he take in the King's young son Kahekili in order to teach him Russian. This arrangement, successful from its first days, did much to contribute to positive relations between Kaumuali'i and Tarakanov.

The *Lydia* made two trips back to Honolulu under Verol Madson, leaving there Captains Gyzelaar and Smith and bringing back to Kaua'i more of the Waikīkī Russians and Aleuts, including Petr Kicherev. The Americans Madson and Captain Wadsworth of the *Ilmena* were not, in George's opinion, entirely reliable, but he was dependent upon their sailing and navigation skills. Captain Young's *Kadiak* had continuing problems with leaks so close to the keel that the careening strategy employed to fix the *Ilmena* after its arrival in Honolulu was not feasible. The ship had to be pumped constantly, and the crew was irritated about this. Captain Wadsworth wanted to "make a run to Sitka" in the *Ilmena*, but George would not let him, not wanting to decrease his contingent in the islands at this time. He did, however, agree to allow the *Ilmena* to sail back to Honolulu, instructing Captain Wadsworth to return to Waimea within a month's time.

George wanted to spend as much time as he could at his personal domain of Shefferthal, the name he now called the former Hanalei on the north shore. On one trip there on the *Lydia*, he took Timofei Tarakanov, Grigorii Terentev and Petr Kicherev with him. At the settlement near Fort Barclay, they met Chief Kaloha'aki, whom George called "Chief Hanalei of Shefferthal." Kaloha'aki invited the four men to accompany him on a tour of the area.

A large party under Kaloha'aki's leadership set out to the east along the shore of Hanalei Bay. With Kaloha'aki was one of his senior wives, the Chiefess Mi'ikina, a massive and very garrulous woman of about fifty years of age who openly flirted with the smaller Timofei Tarakanov, walking near him and stroking his head and neck…much to his concealed annoyance. The scenery was most spectacular. The gentle surf from protecting offshore reefs washed onto fine golden beaches backed by dense jungle foliage and sheer mountain cliffs of dark green. These cliffs were bejeweled with an array of sparkling silver waterfalls of great height. Timofei Tarakanov remarked to George that he'd "never seen such a beautiful place."

After several hours of hiking, the group came to an area where the beach was narrowing and the distance to the rising frame of cliffs was only a hundred meters or so. Kaloha'aki led the party via a jungle path toward the cliffs and climbed up over several bare rocks, which had fallen from above, resulting in a jagged slope. At just the place where the slope met the cliff face was a wide crevice. As they surmounted the slope and looked down into the crevice, the men could see that it opened below them into a cavern filled with water.

"This area is called Hā'ena," explained Kaloha'aki. "And this is one of the 'wet-and-dry caverns,' which serve as a place of test and sacrifice. Near here is Kē'ē Beach, the last beach before the Na Pali. There are many hōnu turtles living at Kē'ē Beach, and, above it on a terrace in the cliffs of the great Makana Mountain, is a heiau built by the Menehune in honor of Kaulu Paoa, an ancient master of the hula. There too is our 'hālau hula'…a place to train our people's dancers and chanters in the ways of the Goddess Laka. Every twelve moons on the night of Kāne we have a ceremony when the new dancers and chanters are ready to be sent away to villages in all the other parts of Kaua'i. We have men climb to the top of the cliffs and wait until it is dark. Then they set fire to torches and throw them down, like lightning from the sky. At that signal the dancers and chanters are released from a kapu, which prohibits them from sexual relations during their long period of study. It is a wonderful celebration for everyone there."

"But it is not a good time for those who fail the tests," said Mi'ikina, addressing her addition to her husband's explanation primarily to Timofei Tarakanov, whose back she was rubbing. George was translating what Kaloha'aki had said into Russian for the others.

Timofei moved away from Mi'ikina toward Kaloha'aki and asked him in Hawai'ian, "What kind of tests do you give the dancers and chanters?"

Chief Kaloha'aki answered, "There are three tests. The first is the test of knowledge. This test is given by the kāhunas to see that they have mastered the dances and the chants of the Ali'i in the districts they will serve. They are to be the masters who will teach the dances and chants to others. There can be no mistakes. A single misstep or wrongly spoken word is punished by death. Then is the test of courage. They are made to swim out beyond the reef to the place where many sharks are known to gather. If they make their way safely back to Kē'ē Beach, they are brought here for the final test…the test of faith."

Kaloha'aki gestured below them to the water-filled cave. "Sometimes this cavern is wet, and sometimes it is dry," he said. "We test the dancers and chanters only when it is wet. When it is wet, the cavern appears to end at the wall in the back of the chamber you see below. But dry periods reveal that it does not end there. The cavern continues quite some distance behind the wall, so that a swimmer, with severe effort, can swim under the wall and reach an air-filled chamber behind it. Only swimmers of great faith can reach it. A swimmer whose lungs are bursting and who turns back to the certain air of the entry chamber is considered to have failed the test of faith and is sacrificed. Successful swimmers are those who disappear under the rear wall and don't come back for ten or more of your minutes, meaning that they have reached the air-filled chamber, having faith in our assurance that it is there."

"Those tests seem awfully severe," said Timofei.

"Making good dancers and chanters is very important to us. They are not merely entertainers. They preserve our history…and give evidence of our mana," responded Kaloha'aki.

"Will we see any of these dancers and chanters?" asked Timofei.

"'Ae…yes, you will see them," said Kaloha'aki.

In a half hour, the party was looking down on Kē'ē Beach from the terrace where the Kaulu Paoa Heiau was located. From there they made their way to the Keahu-a-Laka Hālau Hula, where a meal and a performance had been arranged. Their vantage point was a dizzying one, perched on a flat terrace far above the waves crashing onto the rocks below and with the starkly carved green cliffs soaring so high above them.

George looked around and thought to himself that this was again one of those "most beautiful places he had ever seen." Catching Kaloha'aki's attention and gesturing widely with his right arm downward off the high terrace toward Kē'ē Beach and beyond, he asked the Chief, "Do I own all this…all the way to Fort Aleksandr and further?"

"'Ae…yes," replied Kaloha'aki. "All the Hanalei District is yours to rule…from the mountains north to the sea for as far as a man can walk in half a day…the land and every living thing on it."

"And how long will I own it?" asked George, seeking reassurance of such a heady reality.

"Until you die," answered Kaloha'aki. "And then the successor you choose will own it. King Kaumuali'i has ordered this. And I am to serve you here. Your life is my life, your mana is my mana."

George noticed that Timofei Tarakanov had apparently heard Kaloha'aki's answers to his questions concerning the extent of his ownership of the Hanalei District, but he couldn't restrain himself from asking the man in Russian, "Timofei, did you hear what the Chief said?"

"Da, ia slyshal…yes, I heard," Timofei said.

After the meal, which they ate on mats spread out on the ground, the Chief's party arranged themselves to sit in a semicircle at the seaside edge of the terrace. The women of the party, including Chiefess Mi'ikina, rejoined the men after separating from them to eat. Kaloha'aki, after speaking with the kāhunas, explained that the most outstanding chanter would perform a chant in his honor.

This was, he said, a "mele ma'i," a chant, which celebrated the size and power of his genital organs and their reproductive fertility. All his wives and children were to be named in the chant. This chanter had been selected to stay, after his term of training, to take a position with Kaloha'aki in the Hanalei District. Kaloha'aki was obviously pleased with him.

The young chanter, who had a high sharp voice, was accompanied by several drummers who enforced a rapid staccato rhythm of the chant by their beating of sticks on gourd drums. The rhythm seemed to be more important than the words themselves, even though the words were pronounced very carefully. Both George and Timofei had difficulty understanding the chant and explaining its meaning to the others. The words seemed disconnected to them somehow, related to each other as much by rhyme as by logic. But the words describing Kaloha'aki's hālala penis and testicles were clear…stretching out metaphorically in their fertility as far as the horizon and erecting to the sky… as was the name Mi'ikina and the names of many other women and children. George gained only a kind of filigree or mosaic of the total sense of the chant, which went on for approximately twenty minutes. At the end of it, George and the others applauded politely in the European fashion. Kaloha'aki and Mi'ikina rubbed noses and smiled proudly.

The first dances were performed by a large group of men, each coming forward singly at the direction of a leader called the "kumu hula." Flutes joined the drum accompaniment, and the men had dog-teeth rattles on their ankles making a noise as arresting as that of a poisonous snake's warning. The motions of the dancers' hips and buttocks mimicked sexual actions, which excited the women members of the Chief's party so that they tittered discretely among themselves as each dancer came before them. A group of women also danced, their bare breasts and swaying hips exciting the men. When the dancing ended, it was almost dark. It appeared that the party was to spend the night on the elevated terrace in front of the Hālau Hula.

Before the members of the party could rise, Chiefess Mi'ikina sprang to her feet and proposed that the group participate in a native game called "'ume." George did not understand the term when Mi'ikina said it, and thought initially that she wanted the group to engage in arm-wrestling, the similar word for which was "uma." But Kaloha'aki explained that 'ume was a game of "making aloha." George had an intuition of uncomfortability and declined to participate, telling Mi'ikina that he would merely watch the game, but he urged the others to take part.

One of the kāhunas directed the building of a bonfire in the middle of the terrace yard. The members of Chief Kaloha'aki's party, of whom there were about twenty five, including Grigorii Terentev, Petr Kicherev, and Timofei Tarakanov, were directed to sit in a wide circle around the fire. Three gourds of 'awa were passed around. Sitting among the men were Chiefess Mi'ikina and seven or eight other women, several of whom were her attendants. As the game began, Kaloha'aki, who had been standing with George at a more distant vantage point, left George and sat down in the circle to participate.

One of the most agile of the male dancers leaped forth and began to gyrate around the roaring fire. He was holding in each hand a small feather-topped kahili about the length of an arm and pointing them at various people as he sprang to and fro. From behind the group a clattering cadence was pounded out on the drums. But suddenly the drums stopped, and the dancer instantly ceased his wild motions, standing as still as a statue. The dancer's two kāhili were focused in their direction upon two people: a robust girl who was an attendant of Mi'ikina, and Chief Kaloha'aki. The natives in the game burst out laughing. But Chief Kaloha'aki got up and walked around the bonfire to the girl, who looked to George as if she could have been Kaloha'aki's granddaughter. She kept her eyes pointed at the ground as he approached. But when he motioned for her to get up and follow him away from the fire, she did so. George noticed that Chiefess Mi'ikina was smiling broadly. She was missing her front teeth.

The drums began again. The dancer with the kāhili sprang back into action, leaping around the fire and pointing out various candidates for the love game of 'ume. When the drums stopped, the dancer found himself pointing out two men: one of Kaloha'aki's Mū, and Grigorii Terentev. The natives burst into raucous laughter. Grigorii looked quite disturbed, but then, at a voiced command from the supervising kahuna, the drums and the dancer continued. When they stopped again the designated lovers were the same Mu as before and a middle-aged woman attendant of Mi'ikina's with very flat sagging breasts. In a minute, the large young Mu and the woman attendant left the terrace together. At this point the kahuna made some remark to the group, which George did not understand. The natives fell very quiet and listened for sounds of the love-making activities of the first two couples. They did not hear anything, but one of the men made some kind of joke, causing the others to laugh uproariously. Mi'ikina called out to her husband, "My Chief, are you enjoying the game?" Out of the darkness came the answer, "'Ae."

Three other couples were selected by the stopping of the drums, with two more unsuitable pairings of same-sex pairs. Petr Kicherev led away a most comely young woman with long braided hair. Chief Kaloha'aki and the girl attendant returned to the circle. George noticed that both of their faces were flushed. But then the kāhili fell on Timofei Tarakanov and Mi'ikina.

"I think this was arranged," Timofei protested in Russian. "Yegor Nikolaevich, dare I refuse?"

George did not hesitate to tell him, "It's too late now. I think you should not refuse, Timofei."

Timofei got up and walked over to Chiefess Mi'ikina. He extended his hand to help her get to her feet. When she took hold of his hand, the remaining natives, including her husband, gasped with excitement. Timofei led her away into the darkness. Soon the group could hear Mi'ikina giggling and moaning loudly.

The next day, at Fort Barclay, Timofei was the object of mirth among his fellow Russians who, having heard the story from George and the others, had difficulty imagining him in the sex act with a woman of Mi'ikina's physical size. "Give us the report, Timo," they demanded. "Were you on top or was she?"

Timofei growled at them and threatened them with grave harm if they mentioned his adventure with Mi'ikina to anyone on the other side of the island. "If I hear of it again over there on the Waimea side, comrades, I'll start shooting people," he said.

The Hike Back to Waimea:

With the construction of Forts Aleksandr and Barclay well advanced on the north shore in Shefferthal, the former Hanalei District, George decided to send the *Lydia* back to Waimea. He told Verol Madson, however, that he would not be aboard. He wanted to explore the territory between Shefferthal and Waimea by hiking back to Waimea on foot. He had asked Chief Kaloha'aki to assign to him a native guide. The young Russian Ivan Larionov would accompany him.

The hike was an obviously formidable undertaking. Both Chief Kaloha'aki and George's own men attempted to dissuade him from this course of action, viewing the height of the precipitous cliffs and the green, cloud-shrouded mountains that separated them from the southern part of the island. But George was resolute, saying "When I was young I climbed many a mountain. All you have to do is keep putting one foot in front of the other. It can't be more than forty versts in total distance. I've hiked that many times."

"But there are terrible cliffs, ravines, and waterfalls," injected Verol Madson. "What if you fall and break an ankle? You'd surely starve before Ivan Larionov and any native guide could carry you out."

"I'll watch my step, as I always do," said George. Then he joked, "I'll likely be back in Waimea before the *Lydia* gets there."

But that was not the case. The trip took three days. George and Ivan Larionov, led by a spry teen-aged native named Kealohiwai, hiked to Hanakapiai Falls up a stream-path strewn with rotten fruit, then to the Kalalau Valley with its terraces and steep moss-encrusted walls. The path, alternately winding upward and then downward, was unabatingly steep and torturous, winding abruptly and scattered with sharp rocks. George's legs began to pain him from the heels through the shins, knees, thighs, and hips, all taking the unaccustomed strain in their own unique ways.

They spent the first night in a village in the Kalalau Valley populated by people who had never heard of Russia or of England or of America. Then, the next day, they climbed a track upward over the cliff tops and up toward the summit of Mount Waialeale, which they could not see. Rivulets of water from a constant rain flowed past them with each step they took, and they were themselves completely saturated with the water of the rain and the mist. The water, before it poured over the cliffs and fell down into the sea, inhabited a high flat area of land called Alaka'i causing it to become a swamp, infested with strange dense weeds. The broken track meandered through this swamp by following ridges of moss-covered lava, which protruded above the weeds. Every step here presented George with the possibility of turning or breaking an ankle, and he thought to himself that he should be extra careful to avoid making Verol Madson's warning into a reality. The climb up into the swamp had been extremely exhausting and he noticed that he was the "slaboe zveno" or "weak link" among his companions, the one who had to call for pauses to catch his breath and rest, and this fact perturbed him. The magnificence of the view from the cliff path the day before had dissipated into a constant visual apprehension of the mountain's gray clouds through mist-befogged eyes. As the men stopped and sat to eat dried fruit and meat from their net bags, George admitted to Ivan Larionov that the hike was significantly more difficult than he had anticipated.

"Are you going to make it?" asked Ivan Larionov. "If not, you could stay here and rest and I could go on ahead and bring back help to carry you out."

George was a bit startled to hear his companion say this. Could he appear to be that exhausted and debilitated?

"Don't worry about me," he said, getting up to continue, "I'll make it all right."

At the end of the second day's hike, the men had descended out of the clouds into drier territory at the top of the spectacular Waimea Canyon, which spread itself out deeply before them, revealing in the sunset the glorious red, orange, and gold layers of rock and soil through which the Waimea River had taken eons to cut its meandering way to the ocean. The land here was heavily forested, with many straight trees of great height, which would make fine masts for ships. There were also large stands of untouched sandalwood. The way back to Waimea Village was now clear to George and he knew that, after a night's rest, he would make it back to his quarters in Fort Elizaveta before the next afternoon. He decided to himself, however, that he would not attempt such a hike again.

A Conversation with Kekaiha'akulou:

In Waimea, George spoke very well with Kaumuali'i's wives. He had conversations often with queens Namahana, Kapua'amohu, Monalau, and Naoa. Kekaiha'akulou, the youngest and favorite queen, however, he saw considerably less often. But one day in mid-November she came into Fort Elizaveta with two of her most formidable Mū and three attendants, and George had an opportunity to talk with her. She appeared, he thought, to be about twenty years of age. In only the course of the several months since he had first seen her on the *Otkrytie*, she had filled out physically, becoming a bit heavier in her middle and in her hips. Although she was, to European standards, clearly Kaumuali'i's most attractive queen, George could imagine that she would, in her older years, take on an appearance similar to that of Mi'ikina. She still had the vivacity of youth, appearing even child-like in her facial features, but certain nuances of plumpness elsewhere foreshadowed future obesity.

"What brings you here to the fort today, My Queen," George asked her.

"I have come to ask you about Kamehameha's Queen Ka'ahumanu, Friend George," she said. "Kaumuali'i has told me that you have often spoken with her, that you cured her of illness, and that she gave you land on O'ahu. I want you to tell me what you think of her."

"She is a woman more than twice your age," began George. "She is a very large woman, and taller than I am. And she is very forceful in her personality. She is very proud of her strong mana. I am certain that she has as much power in Kamehameha's kingdom as anyone except the King himself...even more, I would say, than Kalanimoku, Hoapili, or Kuakini, and more even than John Young. She is the 'kuhina nui' to be sure. When Liholiho succeeds Kamehameha, it is my opinion that Ka'ahumanu will be the real power."

"I would like to be like Ka'ahumanu, Friend George," said Kekaiha'akulou. "I would have her place if Kaumuali'i becomes the ruler of all the islands."

"Yes, you would, My Queen," George assured her. "And in the meanwhile you can learn from her. When I spoke with her she told me that she does not really believe in the kapus...that she would violate them and eat together with the men."

"She said that?" asked Kekaiha'akulou, astonished. "What about the punishment of the Gods?"

"I think she no longer believes in your old Gods," answered George. "She told me that she once ate with a man and that your Gods did not punish her. She has seen that foreigners who violate your kapus are not punished by the Gods, nor even by the Ali'i. She thinks that men are ruled only by other men...and that it is time they were ruled by a woman."

"Such thought is beyond my understanding," said Kekaiha'akulou. "I think Kuamuali'i would be angry just to hear of such thought. He believes in the Gods most strongly. And the Gods give him great power. His prayers can kill people."

"He has told me of his Ane'ekapuahi prayer and how he used it to cause the burning to death of the man, Mare Amara, who killed his mother and father," related George. "But someone else might say that English sailors killed Mare Amara, and not Kaumuali'i's Ane'ekapuahi."

"It only seems that way because the Gods like Pele cause men to carry out the actions requested by the Ane'ekapuahi," explained Kekaiha'akulou. "The Gods can also control other forces of nature…the animals, for example. On Hawai'i it is said that one of King Kalani'ōpu'u's kāhunas prayed his enemy Nu'uanupa'ahu to death by causing sharks to attack him while he was surfing. Nu'uanupa'ahu was brave and tore the gills out of two of the attacking sharks, but he was so injured that he later died. This was because of the God Kanaloa, who heeded the kahuna's pule 'ana'ana and caused the sharks to attack Nu'uanupa'ahu."

"I think that the kahuna only said he had prayed for sharks to attack Nu'uanupa'ahu after he learned that Nu'uanupa'ahu was already dead," maintained George. "I don't believe that sharks can be controlled by any prayer."

"Yes, they can," insisted Kekaiha'akulou.

George could tell that doubt was creeping into Kekaiha'akulou's mind even though she was insistent. He glanced at her two giant Mū, who seemed to lean a bit closer to their conversation. They were holding their kapu staves at the ready.

"Why has Kaumuali'i not used the Ane'ekapuahi against Kamehameha?" he asked. "Kamehameha has twice tried to invade this island. If he had conquered it, he would have had Kaumuali'i and you too killed or sacrificed. It seems to me that if Kaumuali'i could just say a prayer and cause Kamehameha to burn up, he would have done it already. Why hasn't he?"

Kekaiha'akulou was clearly disconcerted by this question. She paused before answering. "I can say that I do not know this," she said. "It could be that Kamehameha has too strong a mana for Kaumuali'i to overcome. Or it could be that the Ane'ekapuahi can only be used once…and he used it already to kill the foreigner Amara. But Kamehameha does not know this either. And he fears Kaumuali'i's Ane'ekapuahi. Aikake told Kaumuali'i this in Honolulu after he agreed to Kamehameha's terms of rule. I was there and I know this."

"Kamehameha might fear the Ane'ekapuahi," said George. "But he is a man who believes in your Gods. I do not believe in your Gods, and so I do not fear the Ane'ekapuahi."

"Which Gods do you believe?" asked Kekaiha'akulou.

"I believe in only one God…the Father Almighty, maker of Heaven and Earth," said George, paraphrasing the creed he had learned in his Catholic upbringing. "This God has a Holy Spirit…a mana, if you will, more powerful than any imagined among your Gods …and he sent to us his Son, Jesus Christ our Lord, to show us how to live here on earth and how to continue to live in Heaven with God after our earthly lives are done."

"How does this God say we are to live? Does he have kapus?"

"He does have kapus," answered George. "But they are righteous and just kapus…commandments that we should respect only Him as a God, respect our parents, not kill each other, or steal from each other, or covet what others have. The most important thing, taught to us by his Son, is that we should love each other as brothers and sisters and do unto others only what we would have them do to us. If we live this way, we will live forever in Heaven with him. If we do not, we will burn in Hell."

"Where is Heaven, and where is Hell?" asked Kekaiha'akulou innocently.

"Heaven is a paradise like this island would be without the Ali'i and their unjust and oppressive kapus," explained George. "It's a place where everyone is as happy as they can be forever and ever. But Hell is the worst place anyone can imagine. It's where people who violated God's kapus are tortured horribly throughout all time."

"How would our lives change if we believed in your God?" asked Kekaiha'akulou.

"You would be ruled by fair and kind kings," said George. "Your people would not be the slaves of cruel and capricious Ali'i, but would be paid for their work. For this reason they would take joy in their work and become more productive in it. Soon they would develop a more modern industry, which would enable them to produce more than they need so that they could enjoy time without the constant need to work in order to survive. Their children would be taught to measure and to cipher with numbers and to read and to write, not only Russian or English or Spanish, but their own languages as well. They would be instructed by men and women of the Church to live in harmony with each other and be happy in their lives."

"Is that how the people live where you come from?" asked Kekaiha'akulou.

"Some of them live this way," answered George. "But not all. We still have many conflicts about how we are to be ruled."

"I have heard this, Friend George," said Kekaiha'akulou. "But you foreigners are powerful people. And I think this means that you have a powerful God."

"Indeed we do," said George.

Kekaiha'akulou turned to leave, ending her conversation with George. Her Mū strode ahead of her to the Fort's entrance, brandishing their kapu staves and shouting out the warning that she was coming out. But just then she turned and walked quickly back to George, approaching more closely than before and asking him, "Do you want to rub noses with me?" The two Mū, seeing that she was not leaving George just yet, quickly returned to her side.

George shot a glance at the Mū and her attendants and was unsure. But he said "'Ae," and extended his face downward toward hers. They briefly rubbed noses, sharing a breath.

"Your beard feels like an urchin on my chin," she said. Then she said "Aloha" and motioned for her Mū to lead the way back out of Fort Elizaveta's main gate.

BROOK KAPŪKUNIAHI PARKER'S July 2012 sketch of Kaumuali'i's Queen Kekaiha'akulou rubbing noses ("Hone") with George Anton Schaeffer at Fort Elizaveta, Waimea, in November, 1816. Note the Mū with their kapu staves.

The Visit of James Wilcocks:

In the last days of November, 1816, George was in Hanapepe inspecting the lands that had been given to the Russian-American Company, to him personally, and to Timofei Tarakanov. He found that there were many taro fields there, and he ordered the dry land planted in cotton, tobacco, corn, and some chayote squash from Mexico he had gotten from Don Francisco Marin. He had several small orange, lemon and olive trees transplanted onto the Company plot, and gave the maka'āinana workers there several brood sows to begin producing swine. Two of the older Aleuts were stationed on George's land to supervise the production of salt from it. George suggested that they find native wives and live in the village there instead of making separate houses. Tarakanov, thinking it important to establish a presence in Hanapepe, moved his wife Lara, his son Koli and daughter Ninochka to the village which bordered his land, telling them that he would be able to spend more time with them there and build a new house for them on the land after matters in Waimea and on the north shore became more settled. He was obligated also to teach Russian to Kaumauli'i's son Kahekili and he felt that he could not permanently move away from Waimea just yet for that reason. He was pleased that the Hanapepe villagers did not object to his moving his wife and children, formerly of the kauwā, among them. They seemed, in fact, to welcome them as relatives of the "New Luakini (Russian) Chief." Tarakanov reckoned that he would be able to spend three days in every ten there.

On the 2nd of December, George returned to Waimea and found anchored offshore the schooner *Traveller*. This schooner was flying the American flag and Kaumuali'i would not allow its officers ashore until George arrived to deal with them. It turned out that the *Traveller's* master was James Smith Wilcocks, the brother of the American Consul in Canton, Benjamin Chew Wilcocks, who had directed the elder Captain Ebbets to sell the *Lydia*. When George was paddled out to the *Traveller* and met James Wilcocks, Wilcocks told him that he and his mate, William Gaul, were both ill and in need of his medical skills. They had been at both Kailua and Honolulu before sailing to Kaua'i to find him.

"So what is your problem?" George inquired in English.

"It's a persistent fever, Dr. Schaeffer," Wilcocks said. "We've both got it and it won't go away. At Kailua we got some leeches from Dr. Elliot de Castro, and we've been covering each other with them ever since, but we keep getting weaker and weaker. The bad humours just won't leave us in the blood."

"Did you say you got the leeches from a Dr. Elliot?" asked George.

"That's right," answered William Gaul. "He's there in Kailua on the Russian navy ship *Riurik*. Captain Kotsebue…Otto is his first name…brought him on board in California."

"So Kotsebue is in Kailua with Kamehameha, eh?" mused George. "That's interesting. How long has he been there?"

"We don't know," said Wilcocks. "But his Dr. Elliot didn't help us any, we can tell you that. In Honolulu, Governor Holmes and Don Francisco Marin told us that you might be able to cure us. Do you think you can?"

"If I can't, no one else in these islands can," said George. "Of that you may be sure."

"Well, let's get started," urged Wilcocks. "Will you allow us to come ashore?"

"Yes, you and William will come ashore and stay in my apartment in the fort," said George. "I have some medicine I think will end the fever. You can throw Dr. Elliot's leeches overboard right now. You won't be needing them anymore."

"What do you want for your services, Doctor Schaeffer?" asked Wilcocks.

"Just honest conversation with you about matters in Kailua and Honolulu will suffice," said George.

While James Wilcocks and William Gaul stayed with George in his Fort Elizaveta quarters for a week, their health improved markedly, thanks to George's yew-bark tea and the cessation of the bleeding by leeches. They were grateful to George for this and shared with him many interesting bits of news. They gave him some old newspapers, including copies of the *Independence Chronicle* from Philadelphia, which they had been carrying with them for three years, and George was delighted to read them, finding information about American life from politics to agriculture most fascinating.

James Wilcocks told George that he had delivered to Kamehameha three important letters that he had received from Governor Lachlan Macquarie in Sydney.

"I have met Governor Macquarie," said George. "We got along quite well. He told me that he had once traveled across Russia."

"He's now thinking of declaring 'Australia' to be the official name of his colony," said Wilcocks. "The others names, like 'New Holland' and whatever, just don't please him. Australia has been gaining in usage, and he now favors making it official."

"What kind of letters did he send Kamehameha?" asked George.

"Two of the letters were from London…one from Lord Liverpool and the other from Lord Bathurst…answering an inquiry Kamehameha had sent to King George about five years ago," explained Wilcocks. "These two answering letters were both written in 1812. One tells Kamehameha that his inquiry was not able to be presented to King George because of the King's illness. But it assures Kamehameha that all commanders of the British fleet have been ordered to respect his small vessels in Hawai'ian waters. The other thanks Kamehameha for his provisioning of the English military sloop *Cherub* and informs him that his request to have a small vessel of the European style built for his use will be granted. It says that Governor Macquarie has been ordered to have such a vessel constructed in Sydney for Kamehameha."

"I have already heard of this from Kamehameha himself," observed George. "He must have found out from other sources already that the ship was being built for him in Sydney."

"That is likely, given the length of time this letter took to get to him," replied Wilcocks. "He makes the request in his inquiry of 1810 or 1811, the Lords Liverpool and Bathurst answer on behalf of King George in 1812, and now he's finally gotten the letters in 1816 after they were in Macquarie's hands. The third letter, from just this past summer, is from Macquarie himself, telling Kamehameha that the vessel of forty tons will be ready to sail to Hawai'i in about four months. He also sent Kamehameha a British navy captain's uniform."

"That's interesting," mused George. "Macquarie makes Kamehameha a British navy captain, and I've made Kaumuali'i a Russian navy captain. Fortunately, the British and the Russians are allies…no?"

Wilcocks chuckled at this and continued. "I had our ship's secretary make several apographs of these letters. Governor Macquarie specifically instructed me to do this, in the interests of security. So I can give you copies of the three letters if you desire them."

"Indeed I would like to see them," said George.

"Although there is nothing really secret in them, I don't think Kamehameha would like it if he knew that letters addressed to him were being read by you," said Wilcocks. "So I would ask you to keep your possession of these copies very confidential. Also, I would ask that, in exchange for the copies, you order that our ship *Traveller* be given some more provisions for its journey to the Spanish coast of America. The Spaniards are not generally willing to give us provisions, and we might want to go north to Sitka before heading back south around Cape Horn and home. We are not without supplies, but we could use yams, dried fruit and meat. And, some of that fine cotton you've had picked would be nice too. Cotton of that quality will bring a pretty penny in Philadelphia. Too bad you don't have more of it."

George could see that James Wilcocks was a born trader and bargainer, always trying to get what he could out of the other man. He chuckled and agreed to provision the *Traveller* without cost in exchange for the copies of the letters to Kamehameha. "You know," he told Wilcocks later, after receiving the copies, "I would have provisioned your ship for free even without these letters to Kamehameha. But tell me, how did Kamehameha regard them?"

Wilcocks replied, "Kamehameha seemed very pleased by the letters from London and by Governor Macquarie's letter and gift. But he told John Young to tell us that he was disappointed that there was no news about his son, who Boston Captain Amasa Delano had written was in London."

"So you met John Young too, eh?" asked George.

"Yes, he introduced us to Kamehameha and served as our interpreter," said Wilcocks. "He's quite a sly old Englishman. And I think it fair to tell you that he doesn't favor you much."

"I know this only too well," said George.

"We are loyal Americans, you know," said Wilcocks, smiling seriously and glancing at his friend William Gaul. "And we think that John Young's point of view is a correct one. We can only oppose the idea of you Russians taking over the island of Kaua'i or any of the other islands here. Of course we think that the Hawai'ian Islands should someday be American territory, but that's in the far-away future. For now we favor a hands-off policy, like John Young does…with no nation interfering in matters of Hawai'ian governance. And, from what Russian navy Captain Kotsebue was telling Kamehameha when we were there, he thinks the same. He told Kamehameha and his advisors that Russia and its Tsar do not want to take control of any part of these islands, and that you are acting on your own as a kind of rogue commissioner of a private company."

"I'm acting here on behalf of Governor Aleksandr Andreevich Baranov and the Russian-American Company, which has the exclusive charter of the Russian government and His Imperial Majesty, Tsar Aleksandr…with whom I am personally acquainted," said George, angered. "And I can tell you that my actions here only stand to benefit not only the Russian Tsar and people…by providing them a trading base in the central Pacific which is rich in both soil and population…but also the Hawai'ian people. They are better off rid of rapacious Ali'i like Kamehameha and their oppressive kapus and constant outrageous demands. They may not know it, but they require the kind of freedom you Americans enjoy. They need to be converted to Christianity, educated to read and write, and paid properly for their abundant resources and their labor. And if I get my way here as a representative of the Tsar's government and its chartered Company, they will be, and soon."

"But what about Captain Kotsebue and the *Riurik?*" asked William Gaul.

"I'll straighten him out when he gets here to Kaua'i," said George. "He can't be expected to understand the entire situation in the Hawai'ian Islands in only a brief visit to Kamehameha. When he comes here I'll educate him and he'll become a powerful and vigorous advocate of my viewpoint, you'll see."

James Wilcocks and William Gaul looked at each other in doubt.

George paused a moment and then asked, "Did you get any sense of when Captain Kotsebue might be sailing for Kaua'i?"

"No, we didn't," answered Wilcocks. "Kamehameha told him that he would send his advisor Kalanimoku, the one called 'Billy Pitt,' here on the *Ka'ahumanu* to visit King Kaumuali'i. Kalanimoku would then, Captain Kotsebue said, 'straighten out' Kaumuali'i and you would have to strike the Russian flag and leave the islands. I don't think Kotsebue was inclined to interfere in this. He may not be coming here at all."

"What?!," growled George. "Of course he'll come here. He has a duty to support me here. I'll get letters to him immediately reminding him of this."

Despite their differences, George came to think of James Wilcocks and William Gaul not only as patients, but as friends. On December 3[rd,] the second day of their visit, George had designated them "special guests" of the celebration, in the Fort Elizaveta inspection square, of Governor Baranov's name day, during which a twenty-seven-gun cannonade was fired from the seaside ramparts as the Russians and Aleuts saluted the Fort's Russian flag.

Later, after he knew the men better and had conversed with them for many hours as they recovered, George gave to James Wilcocks some letters he had written to Governor Baranov in Sitka, to Ivan Kuskov at Fort Ross in California, and to his wife Barbara in St. Petersburg. It was anticipated that Wilcocks would be delivering Kuskov's letter personally, and then, if he decided for reasons of weather or other reasons not to continue north to Sitka, he would leave with Kuskov the letter to Baranov for transmittal by other Russian-American Company ships. He would keep the letter to Barbara with him until he returned to Philadelphia and forward it to Russia from there.

The letter to Governor Baranov, written in Russian, read as follows:

"December 5, 1816,

Island of Kaua'i.

Your Honor, My Dear Sir,

Aleksandr Andreevich,

I suppose that the ship *Avon* with Antipatr Aleksandrovich on board has by now arrived safely at Novo-Arkhangelsk. You must excuse me for bargaining with Captain Whittemore. Circumstances here required that; all the American captains were set against us, and when I accomplished this bargain with Whittemore, I ceased to be afraid of them. However, everything here is well. All the sandalwood on this island belongs to the Company. As soon as I receive information and orders from you, I think I will send the brig *Ilmena* for such goods as the King might require. In five days I expect the Russian ship *Riurik* which is now on its way to me from Hawai'i, likely through Honolulu on O'ahu. I know about it from some American guests here who were in Kailua, Hawai'i when it arrived. It is the same ship about which I told you two years ago, the one which His Excellency the Foreign Minister, Count Nikolai Petrovich Rumiantsev, wanted to send around the world. The name of the captain of this ship is Otto Avgustovich von Kotsebue. He is the son of the great and famous Estonian writer and Russian Collegiate Councilor and diplomat August von Kotsebue, whose German-language journals Die Biene and Die Grille ridiculed Napoleon in 1812. ...On the *Riurik* Captain Kotsebue has aboard the famous German author of Peter Schlemihl, Adelbert von Chamisso, who is working as the ship's botanist, and a talented artist named Ludwig Choris, who was reported to me to be painting portraits of Kamehameha for the first time. Kotsebue had previously visited the port of San Francisco and he met your Commissioner Ivan Kuskov. He settled former hostilities between the Russians and the Spaniards, liberating even some Russian prisoners. Among them, he liberated the former commissioner on the *Ilmena*, Dr. John Elliot de Castro, who at present is also on the *Riurik*, and whom I intend to bring here to Kaua'i. In sum, I am confident that Captain Kotsebue and the people aboard the *Riurik* will be of great aid to me in our cause when they get here, and I will provision them and send them on to Sitka to meet with you when our cause is advanced.

I wrote a short letter to Mr. Kuskov describing my progress here, the agreements signed with King Kaumuali'i and etc., and my plans to advance the interests of Russia and the Russian-American Company. To you I am writing that I have almost ready here one fortress of stone—named Fort Elizaveta after our Tsar's lovely consort--and two fortifications of earth, with palisades—Forts Aleksandr and Barclay. I am now waiting for more men from Sitka; only do not send such men as Verkhovinskii and Toropogritskii, who have done nothing but disgrace themselves by their incompetence. I must also report that we absolutely must have RUSSIAN captains for the Company ships, which are to be assigned here. English and American captains will not do. They are too treacherous. Also send me a man who can take care of the office work here, and send some paper because otherwise we shall not have anything to write on. Mr. James Smith Wilcocks, brother of the American Consul in Canton, who reported to me about the visit of the *Riurik* to Hawai'i, promised to forward this letter on to you if he does not deliver it to you personally. I think you should consider establishing a friendly relationship with him if you do meet him, because through him we could carry on a rich business in Canton. According to a letter of which I have a copy, even Governor Macquarie of Australia has paid him high honors and given him commissions to accomplish. Wilcocks, though he is an American, is entirely different in his character from other Americans here. The King and I supplied him with provisions, giving him taro root and swine without any charge. You will see for yourself how honest he is. I do not think that there ever was in Sitka an American captain as honest as he is. Cavalier Anders Ljungstedt, the Swedish Consul in Macau, whose letters Wilcocks will see that you receive, is also his friend. I did manage to sell Wilcocks a few trifles: 15 female and 10 young seal pelts and 77 sea bears, both females and young. These were all sold at the same price (500 U.S. dollars, which I will retain to our purposes here) because the largest of the skins were spoiled by worms. The drunkard Toropogritskii left them with me and I did not want to use them for trade purposes at all, but Timofei Tarakanov asked me to sell them before they were altogether ruined by the worms.

I plan to send the ship *Kadiak* to Sitka also…or to some other place. It is leaking very badly. While it is in port here, the crew has to pump out of it 24 feet of water every day. At the first opportunity send here horses, cows, and about ten silver medals for distribution among the prominent natives who are serving us faithfully in the provinces, which now belong to us. A major amassing of sandalwood, 24,000 logs, is ready for shipment from Waimea. I am only awaiting reliable ships to send it to Canton, where, according to Mr. Wilcocks, his friend Cavalier Ljungstedt, who lives in nearby Macau, can help us gain a great deal of money for it. Please communicate to me your policies on this.

On December 3rd, I celebrated your Slava with a 27-gun salute at Fort Elizaveta in Waimea. More than a hundred people were there to toast your health and wish you a long life with continued success. With admirers you are many times blessed.

Your Honor's obedient servant,

Yegor Nikolaevich Sheffer."

The letter to Barbara in St. Petersburg, written in German, read as follows:

"December 5, 1816

Fort Elizaveta, Waimea, Island of Kaua'i.

Darling Wife Barbara and Daughter Inga,

I hope you know how much I love you both and how much I miss you. I am very busy and every day is a challenge to me, but I think of you both continually. How I long to embrace you. Barbara, my dear sweet wife, I dream of the time when we will be together again, and I implore you to be lavish in your praise and support of our darling child Inga. Hug her and kiss her and tell her that her father, who loves her, has requested that you do so. It is such a torture to me to think of how, in a month and three days, she will be five years of age, and to think that she has spent most of her young life with me away from her.

I am sorry to write that I have now been gone from you for more than three years. By now the *Suvorov* on which I left you is likely to have returned to St. Petersburg without me. Perhaps you have heard through Vasilii Grigorievich Shelikhov or others that the Governor of Russian America, Aleksandr Andreevich Baranov, the *Suvorov's* supercargo, Germann Nikolaevich Molvo, and I have sent official complaints to be charged against Captain Mikhail Petrovich Lazarev, who angered us with his irresponsible behavior as captain of the ship and violated the policies of the Russian-American Company as established by Governor Baranov. In my opinion, Lazarev should be stripped of his command and reduced to the ranks. But do not worry about me, my darlings. Lazarev stranded me in Novo-Arkhangelsk on Sitka with Governor Baranov, but now I am doing very well here on the island of Kaua'i in the Hawai'ian Islands in the middle of the vast Pacific Ocean. The King here on Kaua'i…whose name is Kaumuali'i…has granted land, not only, thanks to my efforts, to the Russian-American Company as a base for provisioning and trade, but to me personally, who now speaks his language and understands his people. I am now the liege lord, in fact, of such a fertile and beautiful portion of paradise that you will have difficulty imagining the size and splendor of it…and also of the numerous people who are my subjects living in it. This is the place of our dreams, a veritable Eden, where the natives wear no clothes and find daily sustenance within easy reach. I can't wait to bring you Barbara, and you, little Inga, to this wonderful and spectacular garden island. It is December now and I can imagine you walking together down dreary Nevskii Prospekt and shivering in the bitter St. Petersburg cold, while I remain shirtless outside in the warm sun, hatless in the fine refreshing sprinkles of rain, and enjoy the colorful rainbows in the sky almost every day. Soon you will experience all this for yourselves, for I am coming there to get you as soon as I can leave here with the assurance that I may return safely to the same situation I have here now.

Barbara, I fervently pray that all is going well with you and Inga. I'm sure it must be difficult for you there. By now the Tormasovs must be permanently occupied in Moscow and you are managing everything alone. I trust that the Shelikhovs are helping you and that you have steady income at your disposal from Dr. Volkov's laudanum factory. I send letters to you on every ship that comes to our port, hoping that they will eventually be transmitted to you. I know that you are also sending letters to me…although I have received only three in this now-ending-itself 1816 year. Thank you for assuring me that it is now safe for me to return there to St. Petersburg, that I need not fear any unpleasant consequences from my administration of Leppich's balloon project or from any other of Leppich's actions. Of course I am curious about whether Leppich has been found, and I would like to know about our dear friends, the Tormasovs and the Karamzins. Any news from you is a tonic to me, I assure you. Please hug Inga for me and tell her nice things about me. I still cherish the tracing of her little hand, which you sent me. It gives me such joy to know that she is speaking both German and Russian and learning to play the piano at such a young age. I'm sure she will be a musical prodigy like Mozart was. I love you. I hug you. I kiss you.

Your faithful husband,

George."

When, in the second week of December, 1816, James Wilcocks and William Gaul rejoined their anxious crew on the schooner *Traveller* and sailed away with George's letters, they thanked George for doctoring them and wished him "all the best of luck."

Storms:

In mid-December of 1816 George decided to organize his closest compatriots into a cadre of defined administrative responsibilities. He desired to spend more time on his own land of Shefferthal on the north shore in order to cope with the rivalries among the chiefs there. He had stationed a number of Russians and Aleuts there at Forts Aleksandr and Barclay, lead by Petr Kicherev. The Shefferthal resident Chief Kaloha'aki, whom George called "Chief Hanalei," was very friendly and supportive, as was his forceful senior wife, Mi'ikina. But the Chief of the northeastern shore, Kaela, whom George called "Chief Vorontsov," was inimical and even sent warriors into Chief Hanalei's territory to threaten and harass George's men at Forts Aleksandr and Barclay. They stole pigs and chickens, and killed several dogs. George was disturbed that Chief

Vorontsov's warriors were armed with muskets. He asked Chief Kamaholelani, who was Kaumuali'i's highest minister, to order Kaela, his subordinate, to cease his hostile actions, but Kamaholalani refused to do so. George thought that he would deal more effectively with Chief Vorontsov if he were there in Shefferthal himself. He designated Charles Fox-Bennick to stay in Waimea and represent him there because Fox-Bennick's native facility in English enabled him to communicate to advantage with Kaumuali'i. Timofei Tarakanov wanted to spend more time in Hanapepe with his wife and children, so George named him the Company's representative there. Hanapepe's native Chief Kupikēapio, whom George called "Chief Platov," was respectful of the Russians, but remained distant after his initial grant of land. Timofei retained his obligation to teach Russian to Kaumuali'i's son Kahekili, however, and this necessitated an almost constant state of travel between Waimea and Hanapepe. The native chiefs of other districts seemed to be waiting for the resolution of the issues between Chiefs Kaloha'aki and Kaela, deciding to determine their stance toward the Russians by aligning themselves with whichever chief became dominant in the conflict of policies. Kaumuali'i himself had recently become more aloof and less communicative with George. Many days were declared "kapu" and he was inaccessible even at George's urgent request. George attributed this to the Makahiki holiday and Kaumuali'i's taste for 'awa, but it bothered him.

On December 27th the brig *Ilmena* arrived back from O'ahu. George had himself rowed out to the ship before anyone had come ashore, wanting to find out from Captain William Wadsworth if he knew anything about the Russian navy ship *Riurik* and its presence in the islands. When would Captain Kotsebue be coming to Kaua'i? But Captain Wadsworth was drunk and had trouble answering George's inquiries. He said he had heard that Captain Kotsebue and the *Riurik* were at Kailua on Hawai'i, but he knew nothing more. He got surly at George's irritation with him, and, with slurred words, told George that the American captains in Honolulu were full of news that the United States, having been victorious in the struggle with England, was now embarking on a course of hostilities against Russia. "The United States," he said, "is going to clear the Pacific of all Russians."

"Who told you such nonsense as that?" George demanded to know. "The United States has no fight with Russia."

"You're wrong about that, Gospodin Manager," slurred Captain Wadsworth. "In Honolulu it's already well known that the Americans want the Pacific for themselves. The captains there think that Secretary of State James Monroe will be elected president and that he'll declare war on Russia. He's known to be very protective of the United States' foreign interests."

"Any U.S. president would be very foolish to declare war on the Russian Tsar and his European allies," said George. "The Tsar and his allies will prevail over Napoleon's return to power in France, and they would have no trouble defeating the upstart United States if disagreements led to war."

"Well, you are right about Napoleon," Wadsworth admitted. "His armies were defeated by the Duke of Wellington and Marshal Blücher at Waterloo in Belgium last year. He abdicated again and was exiled to St. Helena Island in the far South Atlantic Ocean. Louis XVIII is back on the throne of France, and Napoleon's marshals are either in prison or dead. They court-martialled Murat and tried Ney for high treason. Both were shot."

"Mein Gott!" exclaimed George, struck by this news. "When did you hear this?"

"It's also common knowledge in Honolulu, brought back from the mainland by more than one captain there. Napoleon is all through. You would know this, but you've been out of touch here on Kaua'i for some time."

George looked at Captain Wadsworth, squinting his eyes with skepticism. The Captain was a large man, but he had a strange shape, large at the waist and small at the shoulders. His head seemed to sit directly on his shoulders without a visible neck. George knew that he was regarded to be a discerning and clever man, but treacherous. He wondered what to make of the man's statements about hostilities between the United States and Russia. He decided to continue to assail this possibility, saying, "So you see, Russia and its allies have now disposed of the threat from Napoleon's France. What chance would the United States have against them?"

"I don't know," answered Captain Wadsworth, seating himself by the rail and rubbing his forehead. "I don't know. But here in the Pacific the American ships outnumber the Russian ships ten or more to one. And, as you know, many of the captains of the Russian ships are Americans, like I am. And I tell you right now, I won't raise my hand against a fellow American…Russian Company 'managers' be damned."

"I didn't know you were such a patriot, Captain Wadsworth," retorted George. "You've had no trouble accepting a Russian captaincy and receiving Russian pay. You are a Russian Company's employee and you owe it at least some of your loyalty."

"I don't owe it anything," replied Captain Wadsworth. "And I'll do as I think fit."

"Well, I trust that you will supervise the unloading of the ship's cargo here and await further orders from me," said George. "And as you do so, try to get sober and stay that way. I don't employ drunkard captains of any nationality."

Without waiting for a response, George turned and climbed over the rail and down to his waiting canoe. The native paddler took him quickly away toward shore. As he looked back at the *Ilmena* from the canoe, George noticed in the distance a dark gray wall of low clouds that seemed to be approaching with some rapidity. A wind came up and George's paddler turned and pointed at the cloud wall, saying something to him that he did not understand. On the *Ilmena* George could see Captain Wadsworth moving about animatedly, goading his men into rapid action to raise the anchors and hoist some sail to tack further from shore, lest the coming storm push the ship onto the beach.

Within an hour the storm hit Waimea and its nearby shoreline with a ferocious intensity, driving tremendous waves up into the river, swelling it ten feet above normal levels, submerging the ferry lines and swamping the crossing boats. The wind screamed and tore in at such a pace that many of the native houses were blown apart. A violent rain came down almost horizontally with such force that the fields, both wet and dry, were flooded out in less than three hours. George, secure within the commander's apartment in Fort Elizaveta, marveled at the power of the raging storm. It was, he knew without being told, an "uragan," a hurricane, about which he had heard. He had never experienced anything like it.

In the next two days, many of the people in the Waimea area, especially those who lived east of the river, came into Fort Elizaveta for shelter. George directed his men to prepare hot tea in great amounts to be served to the storm's refugees. He walked among them, speaking soothingly to them when great booms of thunder scared them into tight huddles of humanity. He noticed that none of the Ali'i were there…all were commoners. One man there he recognized in particular. It was the man, now walking on a whalebone stump with the aid of a cane, whose leg he had amputated six months before. He asked the man how he was getting along, and the man answered with a smile, "mai-kai." George smiled back at the man and moved on. He wondered how Kaumuali'i and his queens and chiefs were weathering the storm.

When the hurricane abated, George was relieved to see that the *Ilmena,* further out than normal due to Captain Wadsworth's hurried efforts, was intact. It was entertaining canoe delegations of women from shore in addition to the cargo haulers. The leaky *Kadiak* under Captain George Young was in Hanalei Bay on the north shore and George hoped that this position had sheltered it from the hurricane's ferocity. The schooner *Lydia* under Verol Madson was in Honolulu. Kaumuali'i and his retinue, who had taken refuge from the storm in the heiau on the hill above the village instead of in the King's new stone house on the east bank of the river, had come down into the Waimea village to direct the clean-up and the rebuilding of houses. George, looking down from the bluff across the river through a telescope, could see several of the queens with him, including Naoa and Kekaiha'akulou. The Ali'i had obviously survived unharmed.

George had let his awareness of the calendar date lapse in the course of his daily activities. But now he realized that he had allowed Tsar Aleksandr's name day, December 24th, to pass uncelebrated. This was partly because he had been using the European calendar in his own diary for some time. And so he informed Kaumuali'i that he would, as a tribute to the Tsar, as a gesture of victory over the storm, and as a celebration of the belated news about the European allies' victory over Napoleon, be firing a cannon salute. He decided to make it a cannonade of unprecedented size…a cannonade to rival the hurricane's thunder and force…fifty-one shots…each of all seventeen twelve-pounders firing three times in rapid succession. George took joy in giving the command to fire, and when the booming cannonade was over, he was pleased to hear that Kaumuali'i had ordered an answering salute of seven guns to be fired from their positions above the village. All seemed well to George, and he thought that even Tsar Aleksandr would have been impressed to witness such a booming celebration.

Later the same day, December 29th, the *Kadiak* sailed into view and anchored off Waimea. Captain George Young came ashore with the bad news that one of the Aleuts had been killed by natives near Fort Barclay just before the storm. He gave George a letter that he and some of the other Russians had written. He also reported that the *Ilmena* had stopped at Hanalei before it came to Waimea—a fact new to George--, and that Captain Wadsworth had been a problem for him there, demanding casks of the wine and vodka they made there and running the *Ilmena* briefly aground when he was asked to depart, requiring Captain Young's aid."

"He showed up here drunk," commented George. "But he had the sense to take the ship further out when he saw the storm coming."

George then read the letter:

"Your Honor, Dear Sir, Yegor Nikolaevich,

We, your humble and obedient servants, take the liberty of asking you to extend your protection to us as your children because we are placed here at your orders. We depend on you and expect you to defend us, for there have been grave happenings in the place called Shefferthal. As you will learn from this letter, an Aleut was murdered here on the twenty sixth of December. According to Mr. Young and others, you should investigate it. The boat with your messenger Fyodor Leshchinskii was ready, as was the boat loaded with chalk and clay. Mr. George Young was then on the beach about to send a letter to you. The natives left their houses and went somewhere near our buildings, which include the winery by the lake, with casks and masses of calabashes. They took two butts of wine and a large quantity of the roots used in making alcohol. We decided that we needed a watchman so no one would dare steal or rob us of anything. We thought we could avoid trouble that way, but just as we were handing Mr. Leshchinskii the sealed envelope, we heard a gunshot. [We ran to investigate and were told by others that the watchman was dead] and the building was burning on all sides. There was not a single islander to be seen. In ten minutes this unusual fire was over. The grass was burned out and we could see the watchman's dead body. Using water brought from the lake in calabashes we put out the rest of the fire. We examined the body of the dead man in the presence of a large crowd and found the cause of death—a large wound in the chest and two more in the back. We brought the body to the fort and summoned the Chief Hanalei. He came together with Chief Platov, who was visiting Hanalei to receive care for his injured foot. Chief Platov said that he would use all his influence in our favor and asked us all to begin carrying guns. He offered us armed kanakas to aid us in catching the north-shore kanakas who did this, and, if the latter refused to surrender, to shoot them. He asked to be allowed to subdue them all by force of arms so that in the future they would not dare to provoke the Russian Empire, but we hesitated to begin the conquest of the savages without Your Honor's command. Even Chief Hanalei himself, with tears in his eyes, requested us to conquer the savages, so that the latter would feel the might of the Russian people.

Signed: George Young,

    This statement is correct—Ivan Bologov

    This statement is correct—Ivan Felenin

    This statement is correct—signed in person by Nikolai Ponomarev

    This statement is true—Petr Kicherev

December 29, 1816"

As he finished reading, George had a frown on his face.

"So you must have brought Kicherev and the others back here with you, then," he said. "I notice that the letter is dated today."

"Yes, they're on board," answered Captain Young. "We had a tough passage back around the Pali. We had contrary winds and the waves are still high from the storm. Also, we're pumping out a lot of leakage and the ship is heavy."

"But who then is in charge at the northern forts?" George wanted to know.

Captain Young continued, "Leshchinskii decided to stay there. He is not afraid. He told us that you planned to go there soon yourself, and that you would be able to deal with Chief Vorontsov…that is, Kaela and his savages. The Aleuts want you to bring Grigorii Iskakov back with you. They think of him as their leader, as you know. And I have to tell you that, after the murder of their fellow, their mood is to leave these islands and return to Sitka. They hope that Grigorii will represent them in this and request it of you. They are not so happy here as we are, Yegor. Weather isn't everything, they say."

George's frown deepened and expanded into a scowl. "There's nowhere you can live without some problems to overcome," he said. "And we can overcome these problems of conflicts among the chiefs. I have to admit I'm surprised that Chief Vorontsov is not more respectful of the other chiefs…Hanalei and Platov. Of course, he likely did not know that Chief Platov was there to witness his deeds. And now Platov, who is Chief Hanalei's superior, appears to be on our side in the matter. Previous to this, I would have thought him to be an ally of Vorontsov's against us. I have already asked High Chief Kamaholelani to order Vorontsov to cease his hostilities toward us, but Kamaholelani will not help us in this. I will have to take up the matter with the King himself. And if he refuses to help us, we will have to find a way to subdue Vorontsov ourselves. But don't worry, we can do this."

The next week, George had several occasions to be angered by Captain Wadsworth's behavior both on the ship and off it. After one of these occasions, the *Ilmena*'s clerk, the previously troublesome Stepan Nikiforov who had been with George during the stay in Kailua, told George that Captain Wadsworth had requested an individual audience with King Kuamuali'i and had spoken with him. This irritated George as a breech of accepted protocol…only he could speak directly to the King on the Company's behalf. But he assumed it was because he had expelled five Hawai'ian women, on whom Wadsworth had designs, from the *Ilmena* and reprimanded Wadsworth in the presence of his crew for trading away essential cooking implements and decorative drapery. No doubt the Captain was complaining about such treatment to the King. Such complaint would, he was sure, avail the man naught. But then Timofei Tarakanov, reporting a conversation with Kaumuali'i's son Kahekili, told him that Wadsworth had told Kaumuali'i that the Americans and Russians were at war, and that George and the other Russians planned to take over his island for themselves and hand him over to Kamehameha. This was very dangerous treason, in George's opinion, and he had to do something about it.

When Captain Wadsworth next visited the storehouse to take receipt for his cargo from Honolulu, George was waiting for him with an armed party.

"Captain William Wadsworth, you are under arrest," he announced.

"What for?" asked the Captain.

"For treachery damaging to our cause here," answered George. "You've gone on your own and without my permission to King Kaumauli'i and told him stories designed to subvert his trust in us. You are a rumor-mongerer and a traitor."

Captain Wadsworth looked at the armed men with George. There was clearly no point to resistance. "What are you going to do with me?" he asked.

"I'm confining you to quarters aboard the *Kadiak*. You are to have no visitors…and no spirits to drink. Captain Young will see that you are well fed and well treated. Verol Madson will become the Captain of the *Ilmena* in your place when he gets back here from Honolulu. There are others who could be master of the *Lydia*. Timofei Tarakanov could sail it easily."

"Madson might be more loyal to me than you think. He's also an American, you know. And the *Kadiak* is pumping out thirty feet a day. It could sink at any time. How long am I to be confined aboard her?"

"Until I say otherwise," answered George. "And if you try to escape, I'll have you put in iron shackles. Do you understand this?"

Captain Wadsworth did not answer. George's men escorted him to the beach and rowed him out to the *Kadiak*. Then George sought an audience of his own with Kaumuali'i, thinking to undo the damage done by Wadsworth's stories and to request the King's help in dealing with Chief Vorontsov on the north shore.

In the meeting with Kaumuali'i, George began by going over all their mutual agreements in detail, asking Kaumuali'i to affirm his commitment to them. He then told Kaumauali'i that there was no evidence of any hostilities between the United States and Russia, and that rumors to that effect were no doubt the malicious concoctions of John Young, the American captains, or of Kamehameha himself, designed to frighten Kaumuali'i into further submission. "Besides," he added, "our military strength on this island is now most formidable. We have three substantial well-armed fortifications in strategic locations. We have four Russian Company ships here now, with another, Captain Whittemore's *Avon*, being purchased in Sitka for return here, and a Russian navy man-of-war, the *Riurik*, on its way here from Kailua in support. We have accomplished all this in only six months time. In another six months we will not feel threatened at all by either Kamehameha or the Americans. They will feel threatened by us, and not only because of our military strength. They will feel threatened as well when their people begin to flee them and their oppressive regime and come to the better place we will build together."

"What do you mean by that?" asked Kaumuali'i.

"I mean that your people are, because of your beneficence to them, happier than Kamehameha's people," George explained. "That is why they work harder and achieve more…so that the fewer number of them can serve notice of threat to the greater number of Kamehameha's people. That's what I mean, King George. And the more beneficent you can be to your people, the more powerful they will become with you at their head."

"You talked with my Queen Kekaiha'akulou about such things, and she reported them to me, Friend George," Kaumuali'i replied. "I am King because of our Gods. Our Gods gave me my place to rule, and they gave my people their places below me to be ruled. The Gods have not told me that being kind to a man will make him powerful."

George thought before answering. "Yet you have been kinder to your people than Kamehameha is to his people. You demand less of what they work to create, and you punish them less for transgressions of law and custom. For this reason, your people are more powerful than Kamehameha's people. He is powerful only because he has so many people, and you have a lesser number. Together we will change this. His people will come to you when they see how kind you can be…when they see people paid for their work, when they see children learning to cipher, read, and write…"

"And when they see an end to the Ali'i and the kāpus…is that it?" inserted Kaumuali'i.

George realized he may have gone too far, but he decided to see the thought through. "Yes, that's it," he said. "It is the same all over the world. The nobility and their oppressive restrictions on people's actions are created NOT by Gods, but by men. We're finding this out in Europe and in South America. They've acted upon this in the United States. It's time to act upon it here."

"Everything I have done in my life has been in response to my Gods' instructions," said Kaumuali'i. "I can not now do differently. I would have to give up my belief in the Gods who created me."

"Can you not change to a different, a kinder, system of government, without giving up your Gods?" asked George.

"I think I cannot, Friend George."

"Then you might consider changing your beliefs to mine. My beliefs would not prohibit a kinder form of government, but would require it."

"I will speak with you later about your beliefs, Friend George," said Kaumuali'i. "For I am very curious about them. But for now I will continue to do as I have been doing. For now I will honor my commitments to you and to the Russians, hoping that we do not come to woe because of this. But you should know this—that I will change as conditions change in order to remain as ruler of my islands and to have any chance of passing this rule on to my son. If I see that you are not able to bring such Russian power to bear on my behalf that causes Kamehameha and the American captains to tremble, then I will seek other ways to stay as I am or improve my situation. And this is because my situation is also the situation of my people. As I rise or fall, so do they."

"So be it," declared George, satisfied that the conversation had gone far enough. "And we will remain friends…is that not so?"

"That is so," said Kaumuali'i.

"Then I wish that you and your chiefs would sign another document of agreement affirming this. I will write this document very soon."

"I will sign the document, Friend George," assured Kaumuali'i. "And I will have Chief Kamaholelani sign it also. I have ordered him to have Chief Kaela sacrifice the men who killed your man at Hanalei. Their eyes will be brought to you. And Chief Kaela will give you no more trouble there. All of Hanalei is now kapu to him and to his people."

"So you already know of what happened there?" asked George in surprise.

"'Ae, I know it," answered Kaumuali'i.

On the 1st day of January, 1817, by George's European calendar, he and Timofei Tarakanov witnessed Kaumuali'i's and Kamaholelani's signing of the new agreement George had written in Russian:

"Agreement Between Friends:

By the grace of God and under the protection of the Tsar of all the Russias, Aleksandr I, we, Kaumuali'i, King of Kaua'i, Ni'ihau, etc. etc. etc., and Dr. Yegor Nikolaevich Sheffer, Russian Collegiate Assessor and Commissioner of the Russian-American Company, agree to conduct our mutual operations under the following terms:

1. King Kaumuali'i and his chiefs shall not trade in any articles with any foreigners but the Russians, unless he has the consent of Dr. Yegor Nikolaevich Sheffer or his successor. He also agrees that only the Russian flag will fly over Kaua'i as a sign of its protection.

2. King Kaumuali'i agrees to cede to the Russians all of the sandalwood, whether cut or uncut and growing, on the island of Kaua'i. The Russians will be responsible for cutting, gathering, and shipping this sandalwood and they will not be impeded in this by any subject of King Kaumuali'i no matter where the sandalwood is found. In addition, King Kaumuali'i agrees to have his men cut and gather sandalwood for the Russian ships in the amount of two ship cargoes per year.

3. King Kaumuali'i will provide the Russians on the island of Kaua'i with food for their sustenance—pigs, dogs, salt, yams, fruits, taro-roots and other foods in amounts needed to nourish them. He will provide Dr. Sheffer with 400 peasants in addition to the population of the region of Hanalei already ceded to him to be used as labor in such projects of agriculture or construction that Dr. Sheffer specifies. In exchange Dr. Sheffer undertakes to provide King Kaumuali'i with whatever items of import he desires—iron, firearms and gunpowder, tools and implements, cut lumber, furs, etc. etc. etc in amounts equal in their cost to 12,000 rubles per year or less.

4. King Kaumuali'i shall do all in his power to protect Dr. Sheffer and his men in the conduct of their operations on Kaua'i or elsewhere in his dominions. He agrees that he shall not allow his Ministers and Chiefs to bring harm to Dr. Sheffer or any of his men. In exchange, Dr. Sheffer agrees to continue his efforts to fortify and strengthen Kaua'i in all ways compatible with its protection under Tsar Aleksandr I of Russia against invasion by the forces of Kamehameha or anyone else.

5. King Kaumuali'i and Dr. Sheffer agree to remain friends and to speak with each other first and exclusively in trust about any matters of difficulty that may arise.

        King Kaumuali'i X_____(lizard glyph)

        Minister Kamaholelani X_____

        Yegor Sheffer_____

        Timofei Tarakanov_____

Signed at Waimea, Island of Kaua'i

January 1, 1817"

After the signing, Timofei Tarakanov remarked to George, "It sure seems like you've gotten the best of them in this latest agreement, spelling out the numbers of peasants, the whole sum of their sandalwood, the food supplies, and everything else…and in exchange for 12,000 rubles or less worth of unspecified goods."

"Every time I have them sign another document, I add more and more specificity to it," smiled George. "I want to make sure everything in it is understood."

Timofei nodded his assent, but said, "I'm just not so sure these people have the same sense of a contract as we do. Kamaholelani, in my opinion, didn't understand what the document meant. He was only doing what he thought his King wanted him to do. And I think the King's commitment too may be doubtful. Just because he speaks English pretty well and says he is your friend because you're both named George doesn't mean that he holds his agreement with you sacred. Our sense of honor and his sense of mana are not the same."

"What matters most is the King's perception that we provide him with security from Kamehameha and the hope that he and his successors will rule not only Kaua'i and Ni'ihau, but the other islands as well," explained George. "As long as Kaumuali'i has that perception, we will prosper here and these islands will become as valuable to Russia as India or Gibraltar is to the English. Kamaholelani's perception doesn't matter. You're right when you say that he will do whatever the King wants."

Three days later Chief Kamaholelani came into Fort Elizaveta with his Mū and a retinue of warriors and delivered to George a carved wooden box with four human eyeballs in it. George accepted this token of justice without comment. He knew that Chief Kaela could well have executed any commoners he could find and extracted their eyeballs in order to satisfy the orders of his superior. He had heard of a similar ploy used two decades before by O'ahu Chief Kalanikūpule and his subchief Kamohomoho to protect their warrior Koi from the justice demanded by the British Captain George Vancouver, two of whose men from the ship *Daedalus* had been killed for their guns by Koi and his pahūpu. But George knew too that his showing the gory eyeballs to his men, and especially to his Aleuts, would reassure them that he was indeed capable of bringing about justice for them through his influence on the Kaua'ian King and chiefs.

On the 10th the *Lydia* returned to Waimea from Honolulu with the news that the *Riurik* was in port there. Verol Madson told George that he had been refused a meeting with Captain Kotsebue on board the *Riurik*, but he had met Dr. John Elliot de Castro at the house of Don Francisco Marin. Dr. Elliot de Castro had written a letter to George in English while Madson was in his presence. It seemed strange to Madson that the Doctor would write the letter in English, since he was a native Portuguese who had spent considerable time in Russian and Spanish-speaking territories. But Elliot de Castro was, he said, drunk when he wrote it.

"Maybe he was just being polite to you, an American," speculated George. "He didn't want to write a letter for you to deliver that you couldn't read."

"Or maybe he thought that his writing it in English would prevent me from showing it to any Russians," said Madson. "I never told him that you could read English. As I say, it just seems strange to me."

George read the letter:

"O'ahu, January 7th, 1817

To Dr. Schaeffer,

Dear Friend,

You will think it strange that at last I am arrived here—after having been twice through California and to St. Blas, the city of Tepic and as far as Acapulco. I received my liberty when I was at St. Blas and from thence I had to go in the Spanish brig of war *St. Carlos* to Acapulco and from there to Monterey. From Monterey I went on board the Russian brig *Riurik*. Captain Kotsebue, who is on a mission of discovery, landed me here on these islands. I should be happy if you would land all my things here with me and receive my letter for Governor Baranov. In case you cannot, I shall be obliged to proceed in the first vessel bound for Sitka. I do not wish to go at present as I have the venereal upon me and the cold there would be too much for my weak constitution. After being thirteen months a prisoner and at St. Blas it has brought me down exceedingly.

In case I cannot go to the North I shall write to Governor Baranov for all my things and my pay. I should like very much to see you. They inform me that Antipatr is gone with Whittemore to Sitka. Give my best love to all my friends who may be with you and let me see you here as soon as possible. I hope in God that Governor Baranov is well. The people who were taken with me are now at Monterey. Mr. Kuskov was at San Francisco, but I did not see him. I shall let you know everything when I meet you, which I hope will be before long. So God bless you and keep you in good health—that is the sincere wish of your true friend.

John Elliot de Castro"

"So when will the *Riurik* be sailing here to Kaua'i?" asked George in English.

"From what I've heard, I don't think it will be coming here, Dr. Schaeffer," answered Madson. "Dr. Elliot de Castro said that Captain Kotsebue and others of the *Riurik's* company had become very friendly with Kamehameha and his chiefs while they were in Kailua. Kotsebue told Kamehameha that the Russian government will not make any claims upon the Hawai'ian Islands, and that he, as a Russian navy captain representing the Tsar's military, would not come to Kaua'i and would not help you in any way. That's obviously why he refused to allow me aboard the *Riurik* to meet with him. The American captains in port told me it was because I am an American and the Russian Captain Kotsebue was reacting to the United States' new hostilities toward Russia…and that I, an

American working for a Russian Company, am some kind of traitor in his eyes. That's all they wanted to talk about with me."

"And why Dr. Elliot de Castro thinks I should come there to Honolulu instead," George put in. "But I can't leave here just now. It's vital that the *Riurik* at least make an appearance here. I will write the Doctor a letter, and another letter to Captain Kotsebue. You will depart tomorrow and deliver them the next day."

"But I won't have the *Lydia* unloaded," said Madson.

"Someone else will do that," George informed him. "There have been a few changes while you were gone. I arrested Captain Wadsworth for treacherous actions against our cause here and had him confined without possibility of contact on the *Kadiak*. I'm appointing you Captain of his ship in his place. You can sail back to Honolulu immediately on the *Ilmena*."

"I appreciate your trust in me, Dr. Schaeffer," responded Madson after a moment or two of disconcert at the news, "but you put me in a difficult position. William Wadsworth has been like a father to me. And in Honolulu I'm a traitor to both the Americans and the Russians now that hostilities between the two countries are beginning."

"There are no such hostilities, Mr. Madson," said George firmly. "That is a rumor, most likely concocted by that old devil John Young and cleverly spread by those American captains to frighten King Kaumuali'i here on Kaua'i into expelling us 'Russians.' And Captain Kotsebue's stance on the matter is precisely to their liking. If the United States has commenced hostilities against Russia, then why is the Russian navy ship *Riurik* sitting unmolested in Honolulu harbor surrounded by American ships? Believe me, if there is any sense at all in all of Russia, its Tsar will recognize the tremendous value of these Hawai'ian Islands and make what claims upon them he can…especially inasmuch as no other country…not England, not France, not Spain, and not the United States…has formally made such a claim. My letter will make this obvious to Captain Kotsebue and he will change his mind and sail here in support of what we're doing. Future tsars of Russia will then thank him, Governor Baranov, me, and you for what we've all done. And, by the way, did I mention that your new captaincy involves a higher share and higher rate of pay?"

"I'll sail on the *Ilmena* tomorrow," said Madson.

George reckoned January 13th to be the first day of the Russian New Year of 1817. Usually the Russian calendar was 12 days behind the European calendar. But George had lost an additional day to the European calendar when he had traveled around the world west-to-east on the *Suvorov*. The Russian colonies in America were not 12 days behind, but 13 days behind most of the rest of the world. While he was on the island of Hawai'i, George had abided by the Russian calendar without conflict, but on O'ahu, with the increased contact with American and English captains and crews, dates had been confusing. On Kaua'i, especially in his own diary, he began using the European dates.

George wrote two letters that he described in his diary as "most persuasive"—one in Russian, taking up seven sheets of his precious writing paper, to Captain Kotsebue of the *Riurik* and one of a single sheet in English to Dr. Elliot de Castro. The letters forthrightly stated that Russia would profit immensely if it would claim the Hawai'ian islands as its territory, expanding upon the protectorateship he had already arranged on the island of Kaua'i with King Kaumuali'i. He denounced Kamehameha as a tyrant "worse than Napoleon and unworthy of the Tsar's support." He characterized the American captains as "evil traders," and repeated the malicious rumor that John Young was such a vile monster that he had butchered children to provide Kamehameha with fishing bait. After sealing the letters into their envelopes, he instructed Verol Madson to return to him from Honolulu not to Waimea, but to Hanalei on the north shore. This was where he planned to reside for a time, in his own territory of Shefferthal. He told Madson to wait for only one more day until Timofei Tarakanov came from Hanapepe back to Waimea. He wanted Tarakanov to accompany Madson to Honolulu. But Madson sailed precipitously without Tarakanov. This irritated George, but, knowing how the two men did not get along, he did not tell Tarakanov about it. He sailed for the north shore the next day, leaving Grigorii Terentev and Charles Fox-Bennick in charge at Fort Elizaveta.

At Fort Aleksandr, high on a bluff overlooking scenic Hanalei Bay, George was happy, distanced from the concerns, which afflicted him in Waimea. He was accompanied by some of the men who had left there previously, after the murder of the Aleut. These included Petr Kicherev and Ivan Bologov. The young Russian Aleuts Filip Osipov and Aleksei Odnoriadkin came along. And with him also was Grigorii Iskakov, the Aleut Prince and leader of the Aleut contingent. To all these men, and also to those, like Fyodor Leshchinskii, who had stayed in Shefferthal after the killing, George had shown the eyeballs given to him by Chief Kamaholalani and assured them that justice had been done to the murderers. He told them also that they could expect no more trouble from Chief Vorontsov and his warriors. All his territory was now "kapu" to Chief Vorontsov and his men. Chief Hanalei and his people would be friendly and peaceable, he was sure.

For almost a month, George involved himself in agricultural pursuits and in the continued construction of the forts and their surrounding warehouses and factories. The winery was rebuilt and pens for chickens put up. George began to work shirtless in the sun and soon became, the men said, "as brown as any kanaka." He began work on the design of a stone house for himself and his family. The location was to be on the bluff just east of Fort Aleksandr near a path down through the incline to a small wave-enriched pool in the shore rocks the natives considered a natural bath. The house would be a veritable palace, with column-lined galleries on two floor levels and wide covered verandas facing both north to the sea and south to the waterfall-bejewelled green mountains in the distance. "When Barbara sees this place," he thought to himself as he surveyed the spectacular site, "she'll never want to leave."

In late January, another severe storm came up suddenly and blew down some of the chicken pens and some of the winery's new walls. The men at Fort Barclay near the exit of the Hanalei River into the sea found themselves in a pool. The fort's embankment walls provided no exit for the torrents of rainwater so that it filled the fort to a depth of six inches. The sea waves backed up the river so that it overflowed its banks and surrounded Fort Barclay, inundating the outbuildings. A dead humpbacked whale washed up surprisingly high onto the beach nearby, soon causing a stench so bad that George ordered Fort Barclay temporarily abandoned, allowing the men there to cross the river and climb up the bluff to reside at Fort Aleksandr which had remained relatively dry.

On February 6th of 1817, the *Ilmena* sailed into Hanalei Harbor. Verol Madson rowed ashore and reported to George that the *Riurik* had departed from Honolulu before he could deliver George's letter to its Captain Kotsebue. Dr. Elliot de Castro, however, had not continued on with the *Riurik*, but had stayed in Honolulu. Madson had given Dr. Elliot de Castro the letter meant for him and had received an answer in return. He handed it to George.

"I gave the letter you wrote to Captain Kotsebue to Captain Caleb Brintnell of the *Zephyr* to take to Governor Baranov in Sitka," said Madson. "Governor Baranov can then forward it through Petropavlovsk and Siberia to Kotsebue in St. Petersburg. It could be waiting for him there when he returns home."

"What?!" exclaimed George in disbelief and outrage. "You gave my letter to Captain Kotsebue to some American Captain?"

"Brintnell is an American, from Boston. But he isn't like Ebbets and the others," said Madson. "He told me he would take the letter to Sitka and see that it was forwarded to Captain Kotsebue…and I believe him."

George was upset. "Damn it, Mr. Madson, he'll probably open the letter straight away and find someone who can read it to the other American captains, who will then report on it to John Young and Kamehameha. Then our troubles here will be immeasurably increased. You should have brought the letter back here to me."

"You didn't tell me what to do with it in case the *Riurik* had already sailed," said Madson. "I figured I'd get it forwarded as soon as possible to the Captain anyway. What's wrong with that?"

George looked Madson straight into his eyes and came to the judgment that the man, though foolish, was sincere. He shook his head in consternation, repeating, "You should have brought the letter back to me. Now that the *Riurik* is gone from here, it doesn't matter whether Captain Kotsebue receives it or not."

"I have to tell you also that I had to bring back here to Kaua'i almost all the men left at Waikīkī and Honolulu," said Madson. "The Americans, all excited about going to war with Russia, began harassing them and threatening them so that they didn't want to stay there anymore. Captain Brintnell had offered some of them passage back to Sitka and they were inclined to leave with him, but I talked them out of it. The English Captain Jennings also proposed to transport them, saying he'd remove them from the coming hostilities with the Americans."

George was upset at this news. "Damn it," he exclaimed, "They let the Americans chase them out with unfounded rumors. There is no hostility between the United States and Russia, I tell you. All they had to do was stand up to the Americans' intimidation. But they couldn't do it. Damn it!"

Then George asked, "Who's looking after the storehouse in Honolulu and all our goods."

"The supercargoes, Verkhovinskii and Toropogritskii, are still in Honolulu, living in the warehouse with a couple of the Aleuts," Madson answered. "The Americans for some reason treat them more kindly. But they say that you should figure out how to transfer all the goods from there to here as soon as possible."

"The Americans are probably helping themselves to our stores there, paying off those two drunken cowards," snapped George. "Damn it, damn it, damn it!"

It took until the *Ilmena* was unloaded for George's anger to subside. The men who had abandoned O'ahu walked sheepishly past him, guided off the beach toward Fort Barclay where places would be found for them. Standing at the inland edge of the beach with Verol Madson, he gave much thought to what he would tell Kaumuali'i about the promised *Riurik's* passing them by. "The Tsar has many ships in his navy, Great King," he would explain. "We will see others here in support of our agreements soon." What else could he say?

George realized he was still holding the letter Madson had given him from Dr. John Elliot de Castro. He opened it and read:

"Most Illustrious Sir,

I rec'd your kind letter inviting me to come to the island of Kaua'i. I am, Dear Sir, at present in a bad state of health, but in case I am better, I shall proceed to Sitka this summer. I have been unable to send a letter to Governor Baranov requesting that the things I previously left aboard the *Ilmena*...my clothes, my writing desk, and my wages...be returned to me. Another thing is that I do not wish to forfeit the friendship of King Kamehameha by going there to Kaua'i. So when I leave here it will be in an American vessel.

The Russian-American Company owes me for my commission upwards of two thousand dollars and, as I am now very short of everything, I must concern myself with getting to Sitka to receive what I am owed. In the meantime I would be most grateful if you, as a commissioner of the Company, could send me some money. Three thousand piastres should suffice.

I am, Dear Doctor, Your Humble and Devoted Friend,

John Elliot de Castro

Insula O'ahu

3 February, 1817"

When George read Dr. Elliot de Castro's letter, he crumpled it in his hands in front of Verol Madson and said, "We don't need him here anyway." Then he asked Madson, "Are any of Elliot de Castro's things still aboard the *Ilmena*?"

"Not that I could find," answered Madson, indicating that he already knew of Elliot de Castro's complaint.

In mid-March Timofei Tarakanov, Ivan Larionov and three natives from Hanapepe walked into Fort Aleksandr. They had hiked on foot around the island's eastern shore, passing through the territory controlled by Chief Vorontsov. Timofei was upset that he had lost a man, a young Russian named Ivan Krivoshein.

"How did that happen?" asked George.

"When we passed Nāwiliwili Bay we saw the *Ka'ahumanu* anchored there," Timofei said. "The natives there told us that Kamehameha's Minister Kalanimoku had come on it and that he had sent secret messengers to Kaumuali'i summoning him to a meeting at the Poli'ahu Heiau in Wailua. I sent the two Ivans to try to get closer to the ship, instructing them to stay out of sight. But some villagers caught sight of them and chased them. Ivan Larionov got away, but Ivan Krivoshein did not. Later, we decided to go into the village and try to retrieve Ivan. But the villagers told us that they had already taken him out to the *Ka'ahumanu* and turned him over to its Captain."

"That would be Alexander Adams," said George. "He would be doing Kalanimoku's bidding, but might not want to see Ivan hurt. Perhaps we'll get him back. What else happened on your way here?"

Timofei continued, "We stayed well clear of the sacred area on our journey here, but I would guess that a conference between Kalanimoku and Kaumuali'i was going on there as we passed by. The natives in Chief Kaela's territory saw us, but we weren't bothered. Kaumuali'i's kapu apparently protected us."

"The conference between Kaumuali'i and Kalanimoku is bad news for us," said George. "We'll have to return to Waimea in short order to counteract whatever influence Kalanimoku may have had on the King."

The men at the Hanalei forts were glad to see Timofei and Ivan. They poked fun at Timofei, telling him they supposed he had hiked to the north shore so that he could reestablish amatory contact with Queen Mi'ikina, who had often asked about him.

George was curious about affairs in Waimea, and he asked Timofei, "Have you been in Waimea recently? How are things there?"

"I was there a week ago, giving Kahekili Russian lessons," answered Timofei. "I did not see King Kaumuali'i there, but I did not think to ask his son about him. He may have been gone already to Wailua, I don't know. Captain George Young on the *Kadiak* told me that Captain Wadsworth has been a troublesome prisoner, constantly complaining and agitating the crew by telling them that their constant pumping is futile and they're doomed to sink with the ship if it remains at Waimea. You really should replace much of the crew with fresh men."

"When we get back there, I'll explain to Captain Young just what my instruction 'with no possibility of contact' means," said George with irritation. "I don't want Wadsworth talking to the crew. Young should have him isolated…even if it means giving up his own cabin to do it."

"Well, it's tough to keep him completely isolated aboard a ship in such a situation," said Timofei. "Captain Young has stayed aboard continuously himself ever since you arrested Wadsworth and incarcerated him there. He doesn't feel like he can leave the ship with Wadsworth aboard it, lest Wadsworth somehow take command and sail it away. The crew is very tired of the pumping and Wadsworth uses their dissatisfaction to his advantage, telling them that they should sail back to Sitka immediately and put the ship into the yard for repairs."

"Did you see Terentev and Fox-Bennick?" asked George.

"Yes, I saw them at Fort Elizaveta and in the village," said Timofei. "They are doing well. They report that the remaining construction projects on the Fort and on the King's residence are essentially completed and that the crops are growing very well. Fox-Bennick has gotten quite friendly, if you know what I mean, with one of the queens."

"Which queen?" asked George.

"Kekaiha'akulou," answered Timofei.

"Wouldn't you know it?" scowled George. "That's definitely not good. If there is any one of the queens Kaumuali'i is jealous of, it's Kekaiha'akulou. What does Charles think he's doing?"

"He says that he is only teaching her English at her request so that she can understand the language her King also speaks, but everyone assumes that more is going on. I think the relationship might turn out to be dangerous for us and that you should caution him."

"Don't worry, I'll caution him all right," threatened George.

As they made preparations to sail on the *Ilmena* back to Waimea, a storm blew in from the north to delay their departure. The temperature turned surprisingly cold and the rain, driven by the fierce wind, stung the skin as it fell on the men's bare bodies. Fort Barclay again filled with water and everyone there forded the dangerously swollen river and hiked up to Fort Aleksandr on the blufftop where they huddled together under the thatched roofs. Attempts to build a bonfire in the middle of the enclosure failed, and only the smaller bucket fires under the shelters provided precious heat. George was reminded for the first time in almost two years of the human need for clothing and body warmth. "It feels like Sitka is sending us a message, men," he shouted over the blast. "But at least there's no ice in it!"

It was a week before the weather relented and the *Ilmena* could sail. But as preparations to sail were being completed, the grand ship *Avon* sailed into Hanalei Bay. The sight of the large three-masted *Avon*, with its clean white sails, its gunports, eleven to a side, and its brightly painted trim, was a tonic to George. It was at last, he thought, a positive event sure to interrupt the recent string of negative developments with which he had been beset—the rivalries of the native chiefs and the death of one of his men, the pressing desire of his Aleuts to return to Sitka, the rumors spread by John Young and the American captains in Honolulu about American-Russian hostilities, the wholesale abandonment of the O'ahu mission, the disheartening disavowal to Kamehameha of his efforts by Russian Navy Captain Kotsebue of the *Riurik*, the irritation with Dr. Elliot de Castro, Captain Wadsworth's treachery, the leaky *Kadiak* and its crew's dissatisfaction, the news that Kamehameha's intimidating Minister Kalanimoku may have come to visit King Kaumuali'i, his deputy Charles Fox-Bennick's troubling dalliance with Queen Kekaiha'akulou…it was all mounting up ominously in his mind. But as he was rowed out toward the *Avon*, George was certain that his luck had finally turned around. Governor Baranov had no doubt purchased the ship as he had requested and sent it back to him filled with cargo valuable to his efforts. King Kaumuali'i was sure to be impressed with the addition of such a fine vessel to help in their mutual endeavors.

When George came aboard the *Avon,* old Captain Isaac Whittemore had more bad news for him. Governor Baranov, despite the arguments of both Whittemore and his son Antipatr, had refused to give the money for the purchase of the ship. The price of 200,000 piastres was too much, even if he believed in George's assurance of repayment from Kaua'i's sandalwood. But Baranov's main objection was that George was, contrary to his instruction, supporting Kaumauli'i instead of Kamehameha, with whom he had a long-time special relationship. He had given Captain Whittemore a packet of letters to deliver to George and his men. The letter to George read:

"Novo-Arkhangelsk, Sitka

February 25, 1817

My Dear Dr. Sheffer,

First, I want to thank you for taking such good care of my son Antipatr while he was in your company. He speaks very well of you and strongly recommends your plans there in the Hawai'ian Islands. He tells his sister Irina and me many tales of his adventures with you and how you entrusted him with important responsibilities. He relates about the climbing of a great volcano, about seeing huge sharks harnessed to native canoes, about seeing you leap from a tall cliff into the sea, and about falling in love with the O'ahu Governor's daughter while learning to swim. I daresay that in his time with you he became more of a man than a boy. He now desires to travel someday to St. Petersburg and become a sea captain and a commander of important missions on behalf of the Russian Tsar 'like Dr. Sheffer.'

I also inform you that Captain Mikhail Petrovich Lazarev of the *Suvorov* arrived back in St. Petersburg in July of 1816. His villainy apparently did not end here in Novo-Arkhangelsk when he abandoned you and supercargo Molvo. While in Peru on his way south toward Cape Horn, he exchanged most of the seal pelts he retrieved for me from the Pribylov Islands for baubles and artifacts useless to the Company. He is to be tried by a naval court for his violation of the Company's charter and for his many offenses. Our charges arrived in St. Petersburg in time to be taken into account and I am confident that his days as a commander of Russian Navy ships are numbered. I await word of his fate.

I thank you also for all the goods and gifts you sent. These are much appreciated, especially the wonderful feather cape, for which I trust you will convey my thanks to King Kaumuali'i. I congratulate you on your leadership there and on the victories you have achieved, BUT I have read all the documents you sent and considered them carefully, discussing the agreements they represent with several people here whose judgment I trust. I have listened carefully to the voices of my son and of Captain Whittemore, who wishes to cease his Pacific trading and return to his homeland to spend his final years…something I have myself long desired. But all my experience here in the Pacific tells me NOT to sanction your attempt to transfer our Company's long relationship of alliance with King Kamehameha to his Kaua'ian tributary, Kaumuali'i. I know that Kamehameha is the greater man. He has the greater power there and he will triumph in the struggle of wills. He is, I know, buying for himself all the sailing ships he can, so that the addition of the *Avon* to Kaumuali'i's fleet will inevitably be of consequence only to our pocketbook. That is why I will not allow your purchase of it. I can only hope that you have not by now so aggravated Kamehameha by your support of his tributary that he becomes hardened against us, either as a Russian company or as a Russian nation. Personally I do not feel aggrieved. Kamehameha has separately communicated to me that he considers you to have overstepped your instructions from me—which is true, and that he does not blame me in this. And indeed I forgive you for overstepping your instructions, having heard the story of your time there from people who know it well. My sincere advice to you is to leave Kaua'i as soon as you receive this letter, avoiding any contact with Kamehameha or his chiefs or his American trading partners. If God allows, I will later send other commissioners to redress the damage your mission has done there, hopefully to provide for us here permanently as you have done temporarily.

As you know, I am now an old man and my days may not be long here. I would be most glad to see you again here in Novo-Arkhangelsk, arriving with all the ships and men before the summer season. But if this is not to be, I wish you well on whatever course you may next attempt, expressing to you my gratitude for our acquaintance in this life.

Sincerely and with all best wishes,

(signed)

Russian-American Company Manager Aleksandr A. Baranov,

    Collegiate Councillor of the Russian Empire."

George ground his teeth as he read Governor Baranov's letter. He was angered by it, feeling insulted. "He doesn't know the situation here," he snarled to Captain Whittemore. "He's making his decisions about it on the basis of John Young's lies and the other American captains' treachery. He won't even listen to his own son. But I'll buy the *Avon* anyway. We now have more than enough sandalwood ready to ship to Canton. All you have to do is take it there, get the money, and bring the ship back here. Then you can find your way back home as a rich man."

"I'll be selling my ship to someone else," said Captain Whittemore firmly, his entire face hardened. "Selling sandalwood to the Chinese in Canton is not as easy as you think. My days of such trial and adventure are over. I'm not a healthy man, and I want to go home."

"It would only take you a couple of months," insisted George. "And I could pay even more than 200,000 piastres."

"No," said Whittemore. "I won't sell you my ship, and that's my final word. Your country and mine are about to go to war and I don't want you to have it."

George looked at Captain Whittemore in frustration. The man was spouting that same troublesome rumor about hostilities between America and Russia. Where could he have heard this? "It's John Young, isn't it?" he asked. "You sailed to Kailua first, and John Young got to you, didn't he? He's filled your head with nonsense about the United States and Russia going to war, promised you Kamehameha's money for your ship and threatened you if you sold it to me. And it's he who then sends you here, isn't it? It's that damned John Young, isn't it?"

Captain Whittemore did not answer George's ranted questions, but replied only, "I ask you to leave the ship. I'll have our goods for you unloaded as quickly as possible. Then I'm sailing for Waimea and Honolulu."

George thought for a moment about asking Captain Whittemore not to sail to Waimea, but then thought better of the notion. He would have to beg the man, he could see, and, in any case, this would not prevent Kaumuali'i from finding out that the *Avon* would not be added to his fleet of European-style ships. George was sure that the American captains would see to that. He gritted his teeth and climbed over the rail to leave the ship.

On shore, George ordered an additional twenty men to accompany him on the *Ilmena* to Waimea. He wanted to arrive there as soon after the *Avon* as he could, so as to seek an immediate audience with Kaumuali'i. It was paramount that he explain all these recent negative developments to the King in his terms so that the King's confidence in him be retained, if not strengthened. He urged Verol Madson to set sail immediately.

On the *Ilmena*, while sailing parallel to the towering Na Pali cliffs, George could see the sails of the *Avon* in the distance ahead. It was clearly moving faster than the *Ilmena* and was gradually disappearing into the southern horizon. Timofei Tarakanov hopped up onto the elevated foredeck and approached George.

"Yegor, I've got something I want to talk with you about," Timofei said.

"What is it?" asked George.

"Likely you noticed that there was a letter for me from Governor Baranov in the packet you brought back off the *Avon*," answered Timofei. "Well, I've read the letter and find some of it disturbing. We'll not have the use of the *Avon* at all, will we?"

"No, we won't," said George. "Governor Baranov refused the purchase in Novo-Arkhangelsk, and Captain Whittemore won't now sell it to us for any price. He's either been fooled by the rumors of war between the United States and Russia, or he has another customer for the *Avon*, or both."

"So this means that Kaumuali'i will soon find out that we are here alone…on our own, without the support of the Russian Tsar and his navy, and even without the support of Governor Baranov and the Russian-American Company. He will think that he is essentially alone then also…at a time when Kalanimoku reminds him of Kamehameha's increasing power and the Americans are chasing out all Russians because of this coming war."

"There is no coming war," George burst out angrily.

"Kaumuali'i may not be as sure of that as you are," said Timofei. "He may well see sacrificing all of us as a way to restore the agreement he had with Kamehameha and the profits he had in trading with the American captains. He'll have some chief of his give them our eyeballs."

"No he won't," said George with a confident smile. "He will not act against us. I understand him. He is my friend and he will listen to me. Our situation is still strong here. With further persuasion of our own kind, we can prevail in time. I can convince him of this and he will remain on our side."

"Yegor, you are fooling yourself and this is dangerous…not just to you, but to me and all the rest of us," said Timofei. "Governor Baranov thinks we should leave Kaua'i immediately, and I agree. He wrote to me that he would rather see me a live hunter on Sitka, than a dead farmer on Kaua'i. I ask you—when we get to Waimea, let's give it up and get out. We can use the *Kadiak* and the *Lydia* too, taking away all hands, sailing back to Hanalei and picking up the rest. Then we can make for Sitka."

George frowned and thought for several moments. Then he took a deep breath and said, "Timofei, listen to me now very carefully. I forbid you to repeat any of these thoughts to the other men. We will not be quitting in Waimea. There I will restore the King's confidence in us despite these negative mishaps…and we will persevere. This island will become not only a provisioning post for Russians, but a paradise for Russians and Hawai'ians alike."

"Now you're dreaming, Yegor," said Timofei.

"If you do not solemnly promise me that you will not relate any of your defeatist thoughts to the other men, I will be forced to write of your insubordination to Governor Baranov and to the Tsar himself," George stated.

Timofei looked George in the eyes and thought for a time. A deep frown wrinkled his dark brow. "I am not without respect for you, Yegor. You have been a very clever and resourceful leader. And even though I think you are mistaken in this, I will promise to say nothing to the men about what Governor Baranov's letter has brought to my mind and to follow your orders as long as they appear to offer any hope at all for us. I hope you will henceforth, however, pardon my return to the drinking of hard spirits. I feel one of my dark times coming on me, and I'll need the spirits to stay the course with you."

George was struck by Timofei's response. "How curious," he thought, "…the man's talking about his 'dark times' and his 'return…to spirits.'" But he knew that the man had experienced travail and trauma in his life such as he could not fathom. "I pardon you, Timofei," he said. "You can have all the spirits you want."

Troubles in Waimea:

On the morning of April 9, 1817, the *Ilmena* anchored off Waimea near the *Avon*, which had arrived the previous evening, the schooner *Lydia*, and the leaky *Kadiak*. There also was the English Captain John Jennings' 185-ton schooner *Columbia*. George and Verol Madson went ashore in the first boat, George to seek an immediate meeting with Kaumuali'i and Madson to supervise the unloading of his ship. The men he had brought from O'ahu were to be accommodated temporarily in the central yard of Fort Elizaveta. George had gotten the majority of them to agree to replace the crew of the *Kadiak* in the onerous job of pumping.

George was pleased that Kaumuali'i was now residing in the stone house he called Papa'ena'ena that had been built for him adjacent to the Fort on its east side. George had heard that Kaumuali'i had ordered the ornately carved sea trunk in which he kept important relics, including the nearly rusted-away sword of Lono that had been passed down to him from his ancestor Kukona, transported to the stone house. This surely meant that the King now regarded the stone house to be his permanent residence. George walked to the door and asked one of the guarding Mū to announce his presence to the King. In a few minutes Kaumuali'i, wearing a gold-and-red-feathered cape and his lei niho palaoa of whale tooth and hair, came out to meet George. Through the open door, on an inner wall, George caught sight of the portrait of Kaumuali'i that Aleksei Odnoriadkin had painted. It was a fine likeness. All the natives within sight except the Mū instantly fell to their faces on the ground. With a broad upward sweep of his arm Kaumuali'i allowed them to rise. He greeted George with a smile, saying, "Aloha, Friend George. I have much to speak to you about."

George asked, "What is it, Great King?"

"Kamehameha's ship *Ka'ahumanu* came here," Kaumuali'i began. "Kamehameha's Chief Kalanimoku…the man foreigners call 'Billy Pitt'…was aboard and he spoke very angrily to me, saying that if he ever had to see me again I would no longer be the ruler of Kaua'i. If we had not been at a sacred heiau near my birthplace in Wailua, I would have had him killed for his disrespect. He told me that the Russian Navy Captain Kotsebue of the *Riurik* had become Kamehameha's friend and supporter and that he agreed not to come here to help you. He told Kamehameha that the Russian Tsar will not protect us here on Kaua'i."

"It is true that Captain Kotsebue will not help us, Great King," replied George. "He was apparently deceived by John Young and Kamehameha when he was in Kailua and by the American captains when he was in Honolulu. But he does not speak for the Russian Tsar and his government. He could not have received any instruction from the Tsar on the matter. We are so far away from the Tsar's capital that he is only just now being informed of our agreements from last year. I am sure that he will decide to enforce these agreements against Kamehameha."

"But we will not be safe here until the Tsar's forces can arrive," complained Kaumuali'i. "Captain Whittemore has told me that your Governor Baranov refused to buy the ship *Avon* and that he would not sell it to you because of the war between his country and yours. I think he plans to sell the *Avon* to Kamehameha. Captain Jennings, who once wanted to sell his ship to me for sandalwood, tells me that he has agreed to sell his ship, the *Columbia*, to Kamehameha instead. And we know that Kamehameha has yet another ship coming from Governor Macquarie in Australia. Kalanimoku says that Kamehameha will soon have a fleet of three-times-four warships with cannon that can carry and lead here many, many warriors. We have only the *Ilmena,* the leaky *Kadiak*, and the lightly armed schooner *Lydia.* What would we do if Kamehameha decides to make a third attempt at invading this island?"

"We would fight them from our forts with our cannon and our firearms and your warriors, Great King," answered George firmly. "And we would win."

Kaumuali'i did not change his expression in response to George's assurance. His look remained serious.

George added, "We may receive help at any time from other Russian-American Company ships. Captain Podushkin's *Otkrytie* is likely to be repaired by now and could arrive back here at any time."

"Kamehameha is now not the only worry, Friend George," said Kaumuali'i. "I have heard that the Americans and the Russians are at war, and the Americans on the other islands have, because of this, chased all your Russians here to Kaua'i. The Americans have many more ships and men here than you Russians. Even the captains of your Russian ships here are Americans. I know that you are holding Captain Wadsworth captive on the *Kadiak* because he opposes you Russians and my agreements with you. Other American captains like him may soon sail here on their ships to kill you and your men and then I will have no hope of protection at all."

George was nonplussed to discover all that Kaumuali'i knew. "How did he find out about Wadsworth?" he thought. But he continued, "The American captains are lying about there being a war between America and Russia at the instruction of John Young," said George assuredly. "There is no such war now, and there will be no such war. This is a lie. The Americans here are merchants and are interested in profit. They all know they would have much less profit if they could not trade with us Russians. They would never sail here to attack me and my men."

Kaumuali'i thought for a while, rubbing his forehead with his right hand. Then he declared, "You are my friend and I want to believe you when you tell me that there is no war between America and Russia. But how could you know this? The American captains have sailed away to far places and come back with this news. Several of them have said this at different times and coming from different places. And Kalanimoku tells me that there is war."

"All of these people want you to give up your agreements with us Russians and force us to leave, Great King," explained George. "Then the captains would trade here and make more profit, and Kamehameha and his successors would inherit your island. That is why they tell you this."

"But Captain John Jennings is not an American, and he tells me also about the war," said Kaumuali'i. "He is from England, and England is Russia's friend, is it not?"

George was surprised to hear that Captain Jennings too was repeating the rumor of war between the United States and Russia. But, in a few seconds, he said, "Yes, England is Russia's friend and ally. Together they conquered the world's major villain, Napoleon Bonaparte. But Captain Jennings has already, you said, refused to sell you his ship and agreed to sell it to Kamehameha. That means that he is closer to Kamehameha than to you. That is why he repeats the story that favors Kamehameha."

"I tell you, Friend George," said Kaumuali'i, "that I have refused to take down the Russian flag over the Waimea village, even when Captain Alexander Adams and Kamehameha's Chief Minister Kalanimoku demanded that I take it down. Just yesterday Captain Jennings and Captain Whittemore said that I should take it down, and again I refused. But I do not agree with some of the plans that you have, Friend George, for my island and my people. You speak of changing our belief in the Gods, putting a kapu on the Ali'i, teaching our children to read and write Russian, paying our maka'ainana for their work, and other disturbing things. In some ways, these notions are as threatening to us as Kamehameha and his warriors. How am I to rule when faced with such a threat of strange and foreign ideas?"

"For the sake of your son Keali'iahonui and the future people of your kingdom, you should continue to abide by your agreements with me, the Russian-American Company, and the Great Russian Tsar," instructed George. "In fact, I would like you to sign a new agreement, affirming your commitment to the ones we signed last year. If I draw up such a new agreement, will you sign it? Will we smoke a pipe and drink 'awa about it as we once did?"

Kaumuali'i thought for a long time and did not answer. But then, just as George exhaled loudly preparing to turn away, he said, "I will sign it."

In writing the new agreement, George relied heavily on the content of the agreement from January 1st. The text specified signature places for King Kaumuali'i, Chief Kamaholelani, Timofei Tarakanov, and himself. He would have to arrange to have these same people sign again, but that, he thought, would be no great problem.

But King Kaumuali'i stalled for two weeks, saying that Chief Kamaholelani was away. And Timofei Tarakanov resented waiting in Waimea just so that he could sign another agreement. He wanted to go to Hanapepe and be with his family. He drank steadily in a gloomy mood and was not fit to return to giving Kaumuali'i's son Kahekili any more Russian lessons, even though young Kahekili was avidly requesting that he do so. Two weeks passed in this way.

The signing of the new agreement took place on April 23rd. The text of the document read:

"Trade Agreement

By the grace of God and the protection of the Great Sovereign of all the Russias, Aleksandr Pavlovich, we, Kaumuali'i, King of Kaua'i, Ni'ihau, etc. etc. etc., enter into the following contract with the Russian Collegiate Assessor, Commissioner of the Russian-American Company, Dr. Yegor Nikolaevich von Sheffer.

1. King Kaumuali'i shall not trade in any articles with anybody but the Russians, unless he has the consent of Dr. Sheffer or his successor.

2. Every year King Kaumuali'i is to provide the Russian factory on the island of Kaua'i with one hundred pigs, five hundred poods of salt, about 15,000 dry taro-roots, bast fibers, coconuts in whatever amount the King is able to have

gathered, and also other products and fruits growing on this island—yam roots, etc. In exchange Dr. Sheffer undertakes in the name of the Company to provide King Kaumuali'i with such articles and goods as His Majesty, King Kaumuali'i, may demand, provided the value thereof will not be in excess of 12,000 rubles. If there are none of the required goods in the factory, then Dr. Sheffer will obtain them with all possible speed from Sitka.

3. King Kaumuali'i gives away forever all the sandalwood, whether cut or still growing in the forests, on the whole island of Kaua'i, and he and his people undertake to prepare every year two cargoes for ships such as the *Otkrytie* and the *Kadiak*. In case the Company requires more than two cargoes, then the cutting of the wood is to be done by the Company's own men. For the wood, land, and the port of Hanalei, for the four hundred peasants ceded permanently to the Company, for the food supplies delivered by the King and those still to be delivered until May 21 of 1817, the King has been paid in full and does not demand anything further. Likewise, for the food supplies delivered and to be delivered until May 21, 1817, for the Company's ships, the King does not claim any payment. Both sides mutually reassure each other in the friendships established by agreements from May 21, 1816.

        King Kaumuali'i X_____(lizard glyph)

        Minister Kamaholelani X_____

        Yegor Sheffer_____

        Timofei Tarakanov_____

Signed at Waimea, Island of Kaua'i

April 23, 1817"

After the signing ceremony, George and Timofei puffed on a long pipe passed to them by Chief Kamaholelani. King Kaumuali'i also smoked from the pipe, and commented that the smoke from his mouth was mingled in the air with the smoke from their mouths, signifying that their "mana" was mingled with his. All four men drank 'awa and George proposed a toast with the drink "to their friendship," and then another "to their health." Afterwards George found an opportunity to ask the Chiefs if they knew what had happened to the young Russian, Ivan Krivoshein, who had been taken aboard the *Ka'ahumanu*. Kaumuali'i stated that Captain Adams had made no mention to him of having a Russian aboard when he had seen him.

In the meantime the *Columbia* sailed away, and the crew of the *Kadiak* was reinforced with fresh men. The *Avon* remained anchored where it had been, but Captain Whittemore had come ashore. He was reported to have taken ill, yet he did not seek consultation with George and his whereabouts were unclear. Captain George Young came ashore to reside in Fort Elizaveta's commander's quarters with George, Timofei, Grigorii Terentev, and Charles Fox-Bennick, with whom George had pointed words regarding his reported conduct with Queen Kekaiha'akulou.

"Charles," he said, "You're a smart and handsome man, and you can fornicate here with any woman you want, God knows. But fornicating with Kekaiha'akulou is dangerous. She's the King's favorite queen and he's jealous of her."

"I have absolutely not fornicated with Queen Kekaiha'akulou," insisted Fox-Bennick. "I'm speaking with her and trying to teach her English at her request. The other men think that I've been fornicating with her because they saw me rub noses with her. But she is merely being friendly to me. If I were to make any further advance upon her, she would have her Mū strangle me immediately."

From his own experience with Kekaiha'akulou, George believed the man. "But Kaumuali'i might have heard about your rubbing noses with his queen," he said, "And he could be as jealous about the affection she feels for you as he would be about your fornicating with her. I think it better that you avoid her from now on."

Charles Fox-Bennick did not really reply, but only grunted in apparent assent. George let the subject drop. He had agreed to accompany the besotted Timofei Tarakanov to Hanapepe and he wanted to leave Fox-Bennick in command at Fort Elizaveta. Further disagreement with the man would not be useful to him.

George and Timofei Tarakanov, accompanied by a group of natives, made the hike to Hanapepe on the 1st of May, 1817, passing through the tract of land George had named Gamaleia. They visited Chief Ko'upikea, presenting him with the gift of a commemorative medal imprinted with the likeness of Russian Tsar Peter the Great. Governor Baranov had sent a bag of such medals on the *Avon.* When Timofei was reunited with his wife Lara and his children, his demeanor changed. He stopped his steady drinking and spoke amicably with George again. During the next week, George enjoyed Timofei's children, the boy Koli and especially the little girl, Ninochka. Ninochka was dark of skin and hair, and pitifully skinny, but her age was close to that of his own daughter Inga, whom he had not seen in almost four years, and this similarity of age ignited his imagining that he and Inga might also be reunited and live together in this paradisical place. On the morning of the 8th of May, George was holding Ninochka on his lap and showing her some clever manipulations of his fingers he had learned as a child, making a "church" of the interlocked digits of his two hands, then popping up a "steeple" with his two forefingers, then turning out and upward his interlocked fingers to "open the doors and show all the 'people'." George then realized that he had spontaneously given Ninochka the explanation of his finger manipulations in German, as he would have done for his daughter Inga, and that the Hawai'ian girl could not understand a word of what he was saying. But she giggled in response nevertheless. George's heart lightened and his recent travails seemed to disappear into the screening palm trees, which were swaying in a breeze-driven sprinkle of rain.

The sun at last penetrated through the low-scudding morning clouds and brightened the red earth outside Timofei's house. George and Timofei went outside, followed by Lara and the children. Across the valley to the west a brilliant rainbow arched fully across the sky, roundly framing a hill that sloped away toward the sea. It was a particularly glorious rainbow with a full spectrum of iridescent colors in its concentric bands. But in the very center of its span over the ground, coming across the hill in the distance, was a band of natives running toward them. George knew somehow from the purposeful way they were running, that they were coming to find him and bring him some news. What could it be?

In a few minutes, the men ran up to Timofei's house. They were warriors, unfamiliar to George, but a particularly fit lot. Timofei, who had already shooed his wife and children inside the house and armed himself with a pistol, muttered to George as the men approached, "This isn't good, Yegor."

George stepped forward to meet the warriors and they stopped a few feet from him. He noticed that two of the men were armed with muskets and European swords.

"What do you want?" he asked them in Hawai'ian. "Why have you come here?"

The leader of the band, a tall man with a head bare of hair except for a black ridge down the center that was paralleled by dark tattooing, said, "Five ships have arrived at Waimea and the foreigners are coming ashore without permission."

George looked at Timofei with a deep frown. "Whose ships are they?" he asked.

"We do not know this," replied the lead warrior.

"Are the cannons at the Fort firing at them?"

"'A'ole," said the man. "No, they are not firing at them."

"Why not?" asked George.

"I do not know this," said the man. "We are to bring you back to Waimea now."

Again George looked at Timofei. Then he told the man, "We will come back to Waimea today. You lead and we will follow as soon as we gather our things."

The head-tattooed leader thought for a moment and then agreed. He and his men turned away and, when they reached the edge of the clearing around Timofei's house, they began again to run in the same purposeful way they had before. Soon they had crossed the hill across the valley and were out of sight. The rainbow was gone.

As they hurried back toward Waimea in the late morning, George and Timofei discussed what they might do about the presence of the five ships and the unwanted foreigners coming ashore right under their silent guns.

"I wonder what Charles Fox-Bennick, Grigorii Terentev, and the others were doing," said George to Timofei. "Did they not see the ships and the men rowing ashore? And what about Kaumuali'i? Did he not send out canoes to tell the foreigners not to come ashore without permission? What do you make of it all?"

"I think we are in trouble, Yegor," answered Timofei. "It is the start of that time I have been dreading, that time that caused me to return to drink. My dread foresees a fight we can't win. We are likely to be killed."

"Nonsense," scoffed George. "We'll soon get the better of whomever it is…and we'll grow old together here in the sun with our families."

Timofei did not reply. By early evening they were in sight of the sea off Waimea as they approached it from the east. They could see the five ships on the horizon, far out from shore and out of cannon range. They could not see any flags or other identification.

"Can you tell what ships they are?" George asked.

"They're all three-masters and square-rigged, that's about all I can see," said Timofei. "They could have brought quite an army here."

"What if they're Spaniards, or Dutch, or…?" mused George. "We might have come here dreading the worst for nothing. Still, I think we should first try to get to Kaumuali'i's new Papa'ena'ena residence from the makai side. No one would expect us to approach in that way, and we will have a chance to speak with the King before anyone could intercept us."

"That's a good idea," answered Timofei, and the men turned toward the sea. In a half hour they were striding on the beach below the bluff on the east bank of the Waimea River on which Fort Elizaveta and the new Papa'ena'ena residence were located. Off shore, but much closer in than the five ships, they could see the *Ilmena*, the *Kadiak*, the *Lydia*, and the *Avon*. There were several canoes out beyond the surf, but the great majority of Kaumuali'i's fleet of canoes was beached across the river.

As George and Timofei broke up onto the top of the bluff through the dense brush that covered its sides, they got a quick view of the beach on the other side of the river from the higher elevation. There was a very large assembly of natives on the beach by the canoes. The disturbing sound of an agitated crowd came to them from there in waves of auditory assault…first loud, then fading away almost to silence, then loud again. George noticed the colorful capes and mahi'ole caps of several Chiefs in the mob. Then he noticed with unpleasant surprise that the Russian flag was not flying over the village. The flagpole was bare. Timofei noticed this at the same instant. "You see, Yegor," he said, "They've taken down our flag. We are in trouble, as I told you."

As George and Timofei tried to cross the bare ground between the bluff edge and the Papa'ena'ena residence, they found themselves surrounded by fifty to a hundred armed warriors. Among them was the head-tattooed man who had led the group of messengers to them earlier in Hanapepe. There was no chance of making a run to the residence or the Fort, and no chance of fighting. George feebly raised his hand and said in Hawai'ian, "Aloha. We have come back to Waimea as you desired. I wish to speak with King Kaumuali'i. He is my friend and he will speak with me."

"He is kapu to you," the man said. "You will come with me to the village."

There was no choice. George and Timofei were escorted down to the river and canoed across to the village side. In a few minutes they were being pushed through a thick mob of warriors…close to a thousand in number…onto the beach by the rows of canoes. Looking around, George saw several of the foreign sailors…Americans, he thought instantly, though he didn't recognize any of them personally. "You have no right to be here," he shouted at them in English. "This island is under the protection of Tsar Aleksander of Russia. King Kaumuali'i has signed agreements forbidding you to be here without my permission. I am the representative here of the Tsar and the Commissioner of the Russian-American Company."

One of the sailors, a robust young fellow in a striped jersey and tri-cornered hat, shouted back, "We know who you are, Dr. Sheffer. You are an interloper…and your days here are done."

The term "interloper" stung George sharply. He remembered the anger with which he had once used the term himself to refer to Archduke Ferdinand III of Tuscany, Napoleon Bonaparte's puppet ruler of Franconia in Würzburg. "Who are you?" he demanded to know. "What ship are you from?"

There was no answer from the sailors. George shouted then again in Hawai'ian that he wanted to speak with King Kaumuali'i. Catching sight of an Ali'i's mahi'ole cap at the land edge of the beach, he quickly stepped in that direction, encountering Chief Kaiawa, the rotund father of Queen Kekaiha'akulou, and several of his retainers. George instantly kneeled on the sand and bowed his head, asking the Chief loudly "Can I not speak with my friend, King Kaumuali'i? Does Kaumuali'i know what is happening here?"

"'Ae, he knows, Kepa," said Chief Kaiawa. "You can not speak with him. You are to leave or die."

"What about my men?" asked George.

"All Russians in Waimea are already on your ships waiting for you so they can depart," said Chief Kaiawa. "We are keeping only one man for sacrifice and he is not a Russian."

This confused George and he didn't know what to say. He could see that the warriors had seized Timofei and placed him into a canoe. They gave him a paddle, shoved the canoe out into the surf and told him to make for the *Kadiak*, which was the nearest Company ship. When he set frantically to paddling toward the ship, the warriors with muskets began to fire in his direction, laughing and shouting when the splashes of the balls came close to Timofei's canoe. Timofei's practiced paddling moved the canoe very rapidly, however, and in a few minutes he had put considerable distance between himself and the warriors' harsh amusement. The sunset visible behind his diminishing canoe and the *Kadiak* was a particularly spectacular one, vibrant with red, orange, and dusky-gray shades above the western horizon. George, however, did not appreciate it well through the continued loud and smoky fusillade of musket fire.

"The Tsar and the Governor will be very displeased if that man is hurt," shouted George.

"He will not be hurt," assured Chief Kaiawa. "And you will not be hurt, if you leave the same way."

"Yeah, Dr. Sheffer, we've got a canoe for you too," said one of the sailors, laughing drunkenly. "And it's a real fast one."

Several men then grabbed George and pulled him toward a canoe. They put him in it, gave him a paddle, and shoved him out toward the breaking surf. "Can you swim?" yelled one of the sailors in a sarcastic tone.

As he began to paddle, George steeled himself to be shot at as Timofei had been, but no shots were fired. He bent to his paddle strokes with all the strength he had, cresting the surf waves without difficulty and reaching calmer offshore waters on his way to the *Kadiak*. On the deck of the *Kadiak*, he could see a solid mass of people, including Captain George Young, who was shouting at him something he was still too far away to hear. He noticed then that the canoe was leaking badly through a large hole in its bottom that had apparently been filled with a plug made of salt block. The Americans had sabotaged the canoe so that it would sink. That is why the sailor had asked "Can you swim?" in such a sarcastic tone…he hoped that George would drown. George quickly removed his shoes and shoved one of his stockinged feet into the hole. He accelerated his paddling, which had relaxed some after he had cleared the surf and realized he was not to be the object of the warriors' target practice. The water kept coming into the bottom of the canoe, but more slowly. He would clearly be able to get quite close to the *Kadiak* before it sank under him and he had to swim for the ship. But he could swim. For that he was now most grateful.

The canoe sank within twenty yards of the *Kadiak* and George easily swam to the side of it. A rope ladder was passed down to him and he climbed aboard. A loud cheer of "URA!" from the men on deck greeted him. George saluted them and smiled while squeezing the seawater out of his beard and rubbing his bald head. His clothes were soaked and he had been left without shoes. But he was alive, and restored to his position of command.

At that moment cannon shots were fired from the village and from Fort Elizaveta almost simultaneously. The men cringed in anticipation of being struck by the cannon balls, but none came at them. It was a signal salvo, announcing the run-up of a new flag on the village flagpole. The growing dark limited the vision of the men on the *Kadiak*, but they could see that the flag was not one they had ever seen before. It was rectangular in shape, divided by two diagonals, with the top and bottom triangle formed by the diagonals colored white and the left and right triangles colored blue. In each triangle, in a cluster near the center of the flag, was a small black circle.

"We thought they might kill you, Yegor Nikolaevich," said Captain Young in Russian. "But by God's will you were spared. Slava Bogu…Glory to God. The Americans were inciting the savages, that's for sure."

"Who are they?" asked George. "I've never seen a flag like that one."

"I don't know for certain," said Captain Young. "I let our captive, William Wadsworth, put the glass to the ships and he says that it looks to him as if Captain Caleb Brintnell's *Zephyr* and Captain Dixey Wildes' *Paragon* are among the five…and perhaps Captain William Heath Davis' *Eagle*. But Wadsworth has been acting very strangely and I don't know if we can believe what he says at all. He claims he was bitten by a bat while below decks and that he's going rabid. He says that when he begins foaming at the mouth, he'll commence biting everyone who comes near him."

"Wadsworth is a liar and not to be trusted, but I wouldn't be surprised to see Brintnell's *Zephyr* among the ships," said George. "That damned Verol Madson gave him a letter I had written to Captain Kotsebue of the *Riurik*, of all the stupid things. Brintnell likely informed all the other American captains in Honolulu of the letter's contents…which were quite anti-American and negative toward John Young and Kamehameha. When they read it, they likely decided to band together and come here to cause us further trouble."

"Well, what shall we do?" asked Captain Young. "If we sail out of here now, we can expect no trouble from the five ships, since many of their men are ashore and they won't want to leave without them. If we wait, they may not let us leave. They outgun us and could easily sink us."

"It's getting late now, and we can wait until tomorrow," said George. "I don't think their men ashore would try to row that far out to those ships in the dark. And to do so in the daytime would take them right past our ships' guns. We still have some bargaining power. Tomorrow I'll try again to obtain a meeting with Kaumuali'i."

Then George thought of something else. "Who is the man they're planning to sacrifice?" he asked.

"It's Charles Fox-Bennick," answered Captain Young. "They came into the Fort as if friendly and seized him before any of us had even spotted the ships. Maybe the ships had already sent someone ashore elsewhere and communicated with Kaumuali'i and his chiefs, I don't know. After we saw the ships and the men rowing ashore in boats, we set about to fire on them as a warning. But Chief Kamaholelani suddenly appeared at the fort with a great number of warriors and threatened to kill Charles and all the rest of us if we did so. The next thing we knew, we were gathering on the beach for transportation out to the ships. Only Charles was not allowed to come."

"I'll wager that Charles' relationship with Queen Kekaiha'akulou had something to do with it," said George.

It was a long night, with George and his men sleeping in rows on the deck of the *Kadiak*. Every two hours another group of them were awakened to take their turns at the pumps, which were now siphoning more than thirty feet of water per day out of the ship's bottom. A count of the men indicated that a similar number were accommodated on the *Ilmena* about three hundred meters away. On the more distant *Lydia* were only three men who acted as a maintenance crew while the schooner was anchored. All in all, George had 92 men on the three ships…and still one ashore.

In the morning the strange flag was still flying over the Waimea village. No one on the ship could identify it. Timofei Tarakanov gave the opinion that it was a native flag…that King Kaumuali'i had likely decided to make a flag of his own in the European fashion and display it as a sign of his independence.

"But without us what independence will he have?" asked George bitterly. "He'll just be another of Kamehameha's chiefs."

Captain Young, who had been surveying the village with his telescope, pointed out a place on the shore where the natives had constructed a kind of scaffold with a raised platform floor and a high crossbeam. In a short while, a group of warriors led by a kapa-robed kahuna brought to the scaffold a captive European…it was Charles Fox-Bennick. Charles was struggling against them, but the warriors tightly tied his hands together behind his back. Using the same jute rope, they bound his feet together. Then they strung a noose over the crossbeam and tightened it around his neck. They pulled the noose rope so tightly that Charles, elevating to the tips of his toes, could only move a few inches in any direction without strangling. Then they left him alone on the platform.

"So they're not going to hang him straight away, then," said Captain Young. "They'll just leave him there until he can't stand any more and hangs himself. It might take him a day or more to die that way. It's a fiendish torture."

"And there are women and children throwing things at him, trying to move him to tighten the noose," said Grigorii Terentev, who had come up and borrowed the telescope from Captain Young.

"Damn them," said George. "I don't know what we can do."

"We might try to hit him with a cannon shot and put him out of his misery quickly," suggested Timofei Tarakanov grimly. "It's too far for a musket shot."

George and Grigorii Terentev and Captain Young looked at Timofei in shock. As they gaped at him, their ears picked up a gutteral anguished scream from shore. It was their friend and companion Charles Fox-Bennick, trying futilely to shriek in realization of his inevitable end. The men on the foredeck of the *Kadiak* looked at each other then and realized that Timofei's suggestion was the course of mercy.

"I don't have anybody on board who could hit him for certain," Captain Young admitted to George. "The *Ilmena* is closer and Verol Madson was once a first-rate cannonier. He could do it. He'd know what to use—shot, grape, a chain…what."

"Madson was a cannonier?" said George with surprise. "I didn't know that about him. But let's lower a boat right away. I'll go over to the *Ilmena* and ask him to do it. I really should advise him on what we're going to do, anyway."

Captain Young ordered that one of the *Kadiak's* boats be lowered. Six men turned the davits to it and hauled on the lines to lift it. They pushed it over the rail and loosed the lines until it was floating alongside the ship.

At this very instant, William Wadsworth sprang like a rabid dog up the stairway from the lower compartment and jumped across rows of men who were still lying on the deck. He was wearing only breeches and stockings. His hair was wildly disheveled and white foam like from soapsuds was dribbling out of his mouth. He growled like a beast, "AAARRRRRGGH!" and yelled "Stand avast or I'll bite you Russian bastards." Several of the sailors jumped away from him, but Filip Osipov, the young Russian-Aleut who had paddled with George in a baidarka back to Waimea from Ni'ihau the year before, leaped up and tried to seize the apparently crazed captive. Wadsworth, however, despite his bulk and apparent lack of athleticism, agilely slipped Osipov's grasp and, in a surprisingly graceful form, dived over the ship's rail into the ocean.

George and the others on the foredeck sprang to the side rail to see Wadsworth come to the surface and swim to the waiting boat. With an awkward climbing motion, he crawled up over the rear of the boat, almost capsizing it as he did so, and seated himself on the main bench. Placing the oars in the oarlocks, he threw off the davit lines and rowed away toward shore.

"I'll shoot the no-necked 'sukin syn'…son-of-a-bitch," shouted Timofei. He aimed his pistol and fired, but missed. "Bring me a musket," he yelled. But George stopped him, saying, "Let him go. We'll get him back, and the boat too, if I can just speak with the King."

"Something is happening on shore," reported Captain Young.

"One of the queens has come to the scaffold where they've hung Charles," said Grigorii Terentev, still using the telescope. "It's the young queen and her Mū."

George asked Terentev for the telescope and looked through it carefully for a time. "You're right, it's Kekaiha'akulou," he said. "Her men are cutting him down."

"Is he still alive?" asked Timofei.

"Yes, he is," answered George. "They're untying his hands and feet and he's apparently speaking with her."

"Slava Bogu," said Terentev.

Kekaiha'akulou and her men escorted Charles Fox-Bennick to the rows of beached canoes. They were apparently going to put him into one of the canoes when they spotted William Wadsworth rowing toward them in one of the *Kadiak's* small boats. One of them paddled a canoe out to escort Wadsworth in through the surf. The others waited for Wadsworth to beach the boat and get out of it. There was a scene of some confusion then, which George could not interpret clearly through the telescope. It looked like Wadsworth and Fox-Bennick had accosted each other so that Queen Kekaiha'akulou's Mū separated them by force. Two of them then put Charles into the rowboat and pushed it out into the surf. Two others sat on Wadsworth, whom they had knocked prostrate in the sand. Queen Kekaiha'akulou then motioned for them to bring Wadsworth along behind her as she walked back up into the village. It appeared that Wadsworth was now her captive instead of George's.

The men on the *Kadiak* cheered wildly when Charles Fox-Bennick came aboard. He was exhausted. George and Timofei gave him some water to drink, and then a dram of rum. "She saved my life, Yegor," he told George. "Kekaiha'akulou saved my life."

"I saw it all through the telescope, Charles," said George, smiling. "Before she arrived, we were ready to try to put you out of your misery with a cannon shot from the *Ilmena*. We couldn't stand your screaming any longer."

"You're joking, Yegor," said Charles inquisitively.

"Yes, just joking," George lied. Then he asked, "What did Wadsworth have to say?"

"He told Kekaiha'akulou she should have let me hang…that I was a traitor to my kind, helping the Russians steal Kaua'i from its rightful King," related Charles. "No matter how weak I was, I got angry and struck him. He struck me back and Kekaiha'akulou's Mū grabbed him. That was about it."

"Did you ever speak with King Kaumuali'i?" asked George.

"No, I never spoke with Kaumuali'i," Charles replied. "But Kekaiha'akulou told me that it is Kaumuali'i's will that Russians not be harmed. It's the Americans who mean you harm."

"So they are Americans for certain, then?" George asked. "Their ships have no flags and the sailors we saw, although they spoke English, wouldn't say who they are."

"Yes, they are Americans," said Charles. "There is no doubt about it."

Charles went below decks to rest. George and Timofei climbed down into the boat to row over to the *Ilmena*. On the way, Timofei asked George to consider his family in Hanapepe. "I don't think I can leave them, Yegor," he said. "If it looks like we'll be sailing away without them, I'll be jumping over the side like Wadsworth to take my chances with the savages."

"I understand," said George.

On the crowded *Ilmena*, they found Verol Madson in a state of nervous exhaustion. "What are we going to do?" he asked in fearful desperation. "Those ships will be coming in soon to sink us. We'll drown like rats."

"Get hold of yourself, man," said George in English. "If they planned to attack us by ship, they would have done so already. As it is, they're split in numbers and we're between them. For all they know, we could sail out and sink their ships as we go."

"I don't think so, Doctor Sheffer," said Madson. "I only saw a dozen or so of them ashore at most. There's likely plenty of crew still on the ships. They could easily move in here now that we're all on our ships and don't have the firepower of the fort and finish us off."

"Calm yourself, Mr. Madson," urged George. "I have good reason to think that they won't do this. King Kaumuali'i apparently wants us to leave, but he doesn't want us harmed. And the Americans will not disobey him in this. They know better."

"We should sail out of here, then," said Madson. "And we should sail now."

"I think that I can turn this situation to our favor if I can speak with the King," George stated firmly. "And so we will not leave here until I speak with him."

"But what if you don't speak with him?" asked Madson.

"Then we may have to leave. But I will make that decision. You are to stay anchored here and wait. You are only to sail if the *Kadiak* sails. Is that clear to you?"

"Yes, that is clear," answered Madson. "But if we have to go, where will we go…to Sitka?"

"Have you forgotten that we have Fyodor Leshchinskii and thirty men at the forts in Hanalei on the north shore?" asked George. "We'll sail there if we're forced to leave here."

"Of course," answered Madson. Then he repeated, "Of course."

As they were speaking, George noticed that a fleet of about twenty war canoes loaded with warriors had departed from the Waimea shore and were headed for the *Avon* and the schooner *Lydia*. On the lead canoe was Chief Kamaholelani, splendid in his cape and feathered cap and holding the slender barbed "laumeki" spear signifying the possibility of combat. By his side was Captain Isaac Whittemore, looking old and very feeble.

In a half hour Chief Kamaholelani and his warriors had occupied both the *Avon* and the schooner *Lydia* without opposition. Looking through Verol Madson's telescope, George could see the *Lydia*'s dinghy with three men aboard rowing toward him. Kaumuali'i had taken possession of these two ships, leaving him only the *Ilmena* and the leaky *Kadiak*.

George and Timofei decided to row out in the boat and try to intercept Chief Kamaholelani's war canoe as it returned to shore. Verol Madson thought they were mad to attempt this, saying, "He won't speak with you. He'll just have both of you killed." But George and Timofei were soon rowing on a course to cross the bow of Kamaholelani's war canoe.

As they came within hailing distance, George shouted out in Hawai'ian, "Aloha, Great Chief Kamaholelani! We greet you as friends. Will you speak with us?"

Chief Kamaholelani motioned for his warriors to cease paddling. The war canoe glided ahead, slowed, then stopped in the water only yards from George and Timofei.

"You must leave here, Friend George," said Kamaholelani. "If you come ashore here again, you will be killed."

"Am I not to speak with my friend, King George, again?" asked George.

"King Kaumuali'i is celebrating and saying prayers. He has been told that his son Humehume is alive in America and plans to return here. But Kaumuali'i will not speak with you again," answered Kamaholelani. "And he will not see you again. This makes him sad, but it is so."

"If that is true, and I must leave here," said George. "Then I ask a favor of you, Chief Kamaholelani, who has signed documents of agreement and friendship with me. This man with me, Timofei Osipovich Tarakanov, who was 'kahu' to the King's son Kahekili, who also signed these documents, smoking and drinking on it with you and your King, and who has done only good things for your people, has a wife and two children in Hanapepe. I beg you to allow him to come ashore, go to Hanapepe, and bring his family back here to leave with him. Do you agree to grant this favor?"

Kamaholelani answered, "He can have his family. I will send a canoe for him."

When George and Timofei were back on the *Ilmena*, they found Verol Madson considerably pacified. The fact that Kamaholelani and his warriors had not killed George and Timofei apparently convinced him that George was correct about King Kaumuali'i's desire that they not be harmed. He wanted to accompany them back to the *Kadiak* to speak with Captain Young. George appointed Filip Osipov to command the *Ilmena* in Madson's stead, and made room for Madson in the boat. He told Filip Osipov to muster some men in boats to tow the *Ilmena* closer to the *Kadiak* for communication purposes.

The two ships remained anchored off Waimea for more than a week. During that time Timofei Tarakanov was allowed to come ashore, not only to retrieve his family, but to retrieve certain negotiated items from Fort Elizaveta, including George's medical bag and a pair of shoes. Captain George Young and Verol Madson were allowed to come ashore also to negotiate for the return of William Wadsworth, who, they said, owed money both to the Russian-American Company and to them. They were not allowed to speak with King Kaumuali'i, but dealt with Chief Kupikēapio, or "Platov," instead. Kupikēapio insisted that Wadsworth be present during the negotiations, and he coarsely called Young and his former apprentice Madson liars, traitors, and "bootlicking Russian serfs." In the end Kupikēapio refused to return Wadsworth to the Russians, saying he would give him instead to the Americans.

Timofei Tarakanov was the only member of the Russian company who managed to gain an audience with King Kaumuali'i. While he was ashore he approached Chief Kamaholelani, requesting that he be allowed to present a letter George had written to the King. To his surprise, the request was granted. Kamaholelani escorted Timofei into the stone Papa'ena'ena residence to give the letter to Kaumuali'i, who had in his presence several American sailors. Since the letter was written in English, one of these sailors read it aloud to Kaumuali'i while Timofei listened. The letter read:

"Your Majesty, Friend George,

After a couple of days I hope to be in Hanalei, that you ceded to me and I renamed Shefferthal. At present you have a few days time to consider changing your opinion concerning us Russians, and everything may still be settled for the best for you, your people, and your island. I know very well that the revolution against the Russians was against your will and wishes, and you know very well that all my wishes were for the best for you and your people. If we go away from Hanalei, it will be too late to consider afterwards, and you and your island must expect the greatest ingratitude from the Russian Empire. The actions of certain bad chiefs will not excuse you from the consequences of the Russian Tsar assisting and demanding the rights of his chartered Company with which you signed many agreements for land and for provisions and for sandalwood. Now you are taking all our property and driving us off of the island—without paying for all the things you agreed to pay for. You asked for the protection of the Russian flag. I gave it to you and sent word to his Imperial Majesty in St. Petersburg that he should regard you as his loyal subject and even as a commander in his navy. Now you have taken down that flag. You promised that the Russian-American Company should have all the sandalwood on this island of Kaua'i in perpetuity forever. You and your chiefs granted that same Company and several of its agents tracts of land and the peasants on them. You granted to me the entire Province of Hanalei and all the people there. Don't forget! Don't forget! Don't forget! Don't forget that we have paid you and your chiefs for these lands and plantations. Don't forget that you have signed documents of agreement with me and with the Company and with our Tsar. Don't forget what bad fortune will come to you if you don't fulfill the promises in these agreements. Consider everything I have written here. If you wish to avoid the greatest shame that a man could be guilty of, and avoid the punishment that threatens you, I am ready to settle with you again in peace and friendship. Consider again everything. I will not stay in Hanalei longer than what is necessary to take what people and property belong to me. If in that time I receive an answer from you, I will stay and write to you again.

Your Friend, George Schaeffer

Waimea, 25 May, 1817."

Timofei reported to George that when the American sailor finished reading the letter, Kaumuali'i said, "This is true. This is also true that all the sandalwood belongs to the Russians. But I can do nothing now to change my course. Farewell, Tarakanov. Give my greetings to the Doctor."

Provisions on the *Kadiak* and the *Ilmena* had quickly been exhausted by the overload of people. Drinking water had to be tightly rationed. Personal privacy was difficult to maintain, especially for Timofei's wife Lara and the two children, even though they were given the Captain's compartment where William Wadsworth had been incarcerated. The people began to argue over petty matters, and the strain of this at last convinced George that it was time to sail for Hanalei. He gave the order at last on the 29th of May.

The Stand at Hanalei:

Out of immediate danger at Hanalei, and seeing again the inexpressible beauty of the place, George decided that he would not immediately leave it, but would try to defend it as his own province of Shefferthal. The industry of Shefferthal was to be the provisioning of the Russian-American Company and the shipping of sandalwood to China…a rich trade in which they would all share. And he told the men that Shefferthal was no less a protectorate of the Russian Tsar than Kaua'i itself. Other ships of the Russian-American Company and of the Russian Navy would eventually be coming to visit them, and, as these ships communicated their situation back to their homeports, the mens' security in Shefferthal would be assured. His plan, moreover, was to use Shefferthal as a base to take over the rest of Kaua'i in time, prevailing militarily over Kaumuali'i and his chiefs with the help of the Tsar's navy and the coming Company ships. The local natives in the population controlled by Chief Hanalei, he said, would be of immediate help to them in repelling any precipitous attacks from Kaumuali'i or others of his Chiefs.

George asked Timofei Tarakanov to take a party of men to visit with Chief Hanalei and to have Chief Hanalei reaffirm his loyalty to George and the Russians. Timofei came back the next day to report that Chief Hanalei was ready to commit his warriors to fight on their behalf against the warriors of the proximate Chief Kaela. He also agreed, to Timofei's surprise, to commit his warriors against his former superiors Kupikēapio, Kamaholelani, and even King Kaumuali'i himself. "He stated that his mana and the Russians' mana are now the same," reported Timofei.

George could not resist asking Timofei, "Did you see Queen Mi'ikina?"

"Yes, I saw her," grumbled Timofei. "We rubbed noses."

Emboldened by Chief Hanalei's pledge of support, George decided to write a document of commitment for his men to sign. He had the cannons at Fort Aleksandr fire a three-shot salute as the Russian flag was raised there and gave his assembled men a rousing speech. Then he read to them his document of commitment and asked them to sign it. The document read:

"Brothers!

The last hope of settling matters peacefully with the bandits of Kaua'i is lost. We have orders to leave here. If we stay, they threaten to attack us and our ships and refuse us provisions. We have already been subjected to barbarous and brutal treatment from them. Our ship, the *Kadiak*, is not in a condition to venture into the open sea, and we have not room for everyone here on the *Ilmena*. Consequently, I intend to show these savages what Russian honor is and that it cannot be treated lightly. Our Russian flag is not a toy, and the name of our great sovereign is not to be scorned or disregarded. Particularly, I will show these barbarians that a Russian commander can put down a rebellion. Who among you will join this good cause? Who is willing to follow me and fight in the face of privation and suffering? Let those shout 'Ura, Ura, Ura!'

Be assured that I shall always be with you and leading you and also that in a short time I expect large reinforcements from Sitka from our father Aleksandr Andreevich Baranov.

Signed:_____ Yegor Sheffer

Hanalei, 1st of June, 1817."

When he presented the document on a table for the mens' signatures, there was a disturbing murmur of reluctance among them. None of them had shouted "Ura!" at all. The independent-minded Stepan Likhachev, who had once argued against George's restrictions on fornicating with the women and girls of Kailua, stated forthrightly, "I won't sign it. I didn't sign on this trip as a soldier, and I don't want to fight with the natives here. I want to go home. We've been away too long."

The men looked to the leaders among them…the Aleuts to Grigorii Iskakov, the men who had been tending Forts Barclay and Fort Aleksandr to Fyodor Leshchinskii and Petr Kicherev, the few foreigners to Captain George Young and Charles Fox-Bennick. The hardy young Russian-Aleuts looked to Filip Osipov and Aleksei Odnoriadkin. But these men were silent and paused in their indecision. One of the foreigners, an Englishman named Francis Wallace who had an Aleut wife and five children in Novo-Arkhangelsk, looked to Timofei Tarakanov and asked, "Timo, are you going to sign this?"

George took a breath of anxiety. He knew that Timofei was aware that Governor Baranov had resolved not to help George with the extension of the intended outpost to Kaumuali'i's realm on Kaua'i at all. But he was an extraordinarily loyal man.

"I will sign it," said Timofei forcefully. "And I think that the rest of you should either sign or put your mark on it also. Yegor Nikolaevich has been a good leader on this mission, and he is indeed a 'brother' to us."

George dipped a quill into his bottle of ink...the same bottle of ink that had been in his medical bag retrieved from Fort Elizaveta by Timofei...and handed it to him. Timofei signed, followed by Captain George Young. Aleksei Odnoriadkin then announced that his signature would stand on the document for all the rest of them if they would merely shout "Ura!" A shout of "Ura!" immediately resounded over the bluff-top and out to sea. Aleksei then took the quill to sign. But Stepan Likhachev did not shout. He asked that his name be added to the document as a dissenter. Aleksei wrote "with the exception of Stepan Likhachev, who disagrees" on the document, and then signed it for the others, of whom there were 112 present at the ceremony. Another twelve men were on the *Ilmena* and the *Kadiak*, where the pumping was unabated.

Troubles began immediately. First, native runners came from Chief Hanalei to report skirmishes with warriors of Chief Kaela in which several men had been killed. It was clear that King Kaumuali'i's kapu against Chief Kaela trespassing onto George's territory had been lifted. Kaela's men stole many pigs, dogs, and chickens from the surroundings of Fort Barclay, and set fire again to the houses of the distillery. When George's men canoed up the Hanalei River, called by George the "Volga," they found their fish traps gone, and, coming back, they were fired upon from the jungle-like underbrush. The native laborers in the taro fields fled and could not be found.

George had taken command of Fort Aleksandr on the bluff-top personally. He left the former soldier, Fyodor Leshchinskii, in charge of Fort Barclay and the warehouse on the other side of the river below. But Fort Barclay was considerably more vulnerable to attack than Fort Aleksandr, and Leshchinskii advocated consolidating their positions into the one higher fort. George did not want to give up Fort Barclay, and he and Leshchinskii argued about this.

"I think they'll come in and burn our warehouse next, Yegor," Leshchinskii maintained. "We should move all our foodstuffs into Fort Aleksandr and make our stand there, lest we be starved."

But George was not convinced. "Just keep double guards on the warehouse...especially at night," he said. "The savages won't be able to get close enough to burn it."

This was a mistake. The very next night the warehouse was burned and everything in it was incinerated. But the worst was what happened to two of the guards, an older Russian named Ivan Chereglazov and an Aleut called "Gerasim." They had been killed with spears and warclubs, and their eyeballs had been cut out. It was a hard blow for George and the men. George was reminded of Governor Baranov's tale of his men who had been massacred by the Kolosh at Fort St. Michael…their heads displayed on poles. And this was, of course, a story with which Timofei Tarakanov was personally familiar.

"It's that damned Chief Kaela…taking revenge for having to give us the eyeballs of the earlier murderers," said George. "I can't believe I ever gave him the name Vorontsov. Vorontsov is too good a name for him!"

Two days later, after the funeral services for Ivan Chereglazov and Gerasim, Chief Hanalei, Queen Mi'ikina, with two servants and four of their children, came to Fort Barclay. Fyodor Leshchinskii escorted them up to Fort Aleksandr to see George.

"There was a large battle mauka from here yesterday," explained Chief Hanalei. "My men and I fought bravely, but we were outnumbered and many died. Kaela's men have taken many more for sacrifice and they will take us as well unless we can find sanctuary with you."

Are you defeated, then?" asked George, trying to digest this news as best he could. Fyodor Leshchinskii and Captain Young were standing by his side and had heard Chief Hanalei speak as well, but they did not understand Hawai'ian well enough to appreciate the severity of this news. Timofei Tarakanov, however, had heard it also.

"'Ae, Friend George, I am defeated," answered Chief Hanalei. "My villages are now Chief Kaela's villages, my people are his people. He seeks me now…and my wives and children for sacrifice to the Gods. I can not help you further, and only you can help me."

"You have been a good and brave friend, Chief Hanalei," said George. "Of course you and your wife and children can stay here with us. Here you will be safe."

"That is not true, Friend George," said Chief Hanalei. "Kaela will attack your forts very soon with many warriors. If he does not succeed in killing us all, then will come the warriors of all the other chiefs and of King Kaumuali'i. Here now on this island our deaths will surely come…sooner or later. We must leave on the ships. I have had a vision about this and I know that leaving on the ships is the only way to save our lives."

Timofei Tarakanov interjected a question in Hawai'ian into the discussion. He asked Chief Hanalei, "How many days do we have?"

"One day," answered the Chief.

"We've got to leave, Yegor," said Timofei. "And we must leave now."

George could see that Timofei was right. He would send Chief Hanalei and his family on the *Ilmena* with as many men as it could transport to Sitka. Captain George Young of the *Kadiak* would be given command of the *Ilmena* and Verol Madson would go as his first mate. He would take command of the

Kadiak himself and try, with a smaller cadre of his Aleuts and Russian volunteers, to make it to Honolulu on O'ahu.

The orders were given to abandon the forts and board the ships. In the interest of time, several of the forts' cannons were not transported, but they were spiked so that the natives could not use them. In only half a day, the ships were ready to sail. Attempts from the ships to row ashore to round up some pigs and sheep failed because of an attack by Kaela's warriors. The *Ilmena* was very crowded with seventy-four aboard, but Captain Young thought the task manageable, especially since the wind and the sea seemed very favorable. In parting, George commended Captain Young profusely and gave him a letter for Governor Baranov that he had very hastily written in Russian, adjusting the date back thirteen days for Sitka's reckoning:

"Your Honor, My Dear Sir, Aleksandr Andreevich,

This morning I sent about a dozen picked Russians by longboat to bring back from shore eight pigs and sixteen sheep, which belong to the Company. Six men had rifles. Our pigs had already been driven away by the savages, and, when our men started to chase the sheep, the savages attacked them and wounded the hand of one Aleut. Our men fired several shots. I ordered them to return because we could see a large crowd of enemy savages approaching. We sent three shells from the cannons over their heads. Although all our men returned to the ship safely, today the entire crew is resolved not to stay here any longer. After a council with Captain Young and our other leaders, we decided to go to the island of O'ahu, there to repair our ship as well as possible and wait for your further decisions concerning what we have left in the Hawai'ian islands. I am sending you Chief Hanalei and his wife Mi'ikina and their children. This was the native Chief of our province and always served us faithfully, whereas the other Chief is a great bandit.

Your Honor, etc. etc. etc.

Yegor Sheffer

Hanalei, June 16, 1817."

With George on the *Kadiak* were fifty-five men—forty Aleuts and fifteen others who had volunteered to accompany him to Honolulu. The others included Timofei Tarakanov, whose family accompanied him, Stepan Nikiforov, Ivan Bologov, Grigorii Iskakov, Petr Kicherev, Charles Fox-Bennick, Francis Wallace, Filip Osipov, Aleksei Odnoriadkin, Ivan Larionov, Nikolai Poliakov, Ivan Zholin, Ivan Felenin, Nikolai Ponomarev, Grigorii Terentev, and the dissenter Stepan Likhachev.

Crisis in Honolulu:

The leak along the *Kadiak's* keel worsened on the way to O'ahu. The pumps were no longer sufficient, even at peak effort, to expel the water. George organized the men into bailing lines, using even the kitchen implements to scoop the water below and pass it up to the deck and over the rails on both sides. The ship rode precariously low in the water, and it did not respond well to instruction from the helm or adjustments of sail. It took five days to get to O'ahu and drop anchor outside Honolulu Harbor. George then ordered a white flag to be flown from the foremast and the ship's Russian-American Company flag, with its crowned double-headed eagle on a large white field above narrower stripes of blue and red, run up to the top of the mizzenmast upside-down as a signal of distress. He had a cannon fired, and soon saw the Harbor Pilot's boat coming out toward them. In a half hour the Pilot, Englishman John Harbottle, was standing with George on the deck.

"Things have changed since you were last here, Dr. Sheffer," said Harbottle. "And none of the changes favor you. Kamehameha has replaced Governor Homa with Billy Pitt. He's revoked all your land and taken over your warehouse. He's planning together with the American captains to turn it into a fort. Your supercargoes and their men have taken to the village at Waikīkī, but they are very frightened. The natives there have abandoned them and run away. The captains want you to give yourself up to Billy Pitt. Some of them have recently returned from Kaua'i and they know all about your dealings there with King Kaumuali'i."

"I'll not be giving myself up to Billy Pitt," said George. "A civilized name for Kalanimoku does not mean that the man is civilized. That would mean a cruel death for me."

"If I were you, I'd sail on right now," suggested Harbottle.

"But I clearly cannot," answered George. "Without immediate serious repair, this ship will sink to the bottom in only a few days. I can go no further on her."

"I noticed how low she rides," said Harbottle. "Some of the captains thought your upside-down flag was a ruse, but I can see now that you are in real trouble. You can have her towed into the inner harbor. I'll bring the towing crews out as soon as I'm permitted to do so. I don't know if she can be careened over far enough to repair her. We might be salvaging her."

"Thank you, Mr. Harbottle," said George. "I won't leave the ship for now. But I ask you to convey to Billy Pitt and the American captains that there are fifty five people on board…Russians, Aleuts, and Englishmen too who need help. And these people are dear to the heart of Kamehameha's life-long friend, Russian-America's Governor Aleksandr Baranov. One of the Governor's oldest comrades, Timofei Tarakanov, is here accompanied by his Hawai'ian wife and two children. I assure you that Governor Baranov would not forgive any mistreatment of him. Even in times of war between countries, civilian citizens in emergency situations are given succour, is that not true?"

Harbottle did not answer directly. "I'll tell them what you've said, Dr. Sheffer," he replied. Then he climbed back down to his boat to return to shore.

The next day George sent Petr Kicherev, who had once commanded the O'ahu contingent for him, ashore to judge the situation there and to communicate with the Russians at Waikīkī. But Kicherev came back in only two hours, giving George the bad news that John Young was in Honolulu and that he was clearly "the man in charge," though he masqueraded as a mere advisor to Kalanimoku. Kicherev was not allowed to stay ashore or to contact the men at Waikīkī. He told George that Young was sending an inspection party out to the *Kadiak* to assess its condition. George then asked Timofei Tarakanov to go ashore, thinking that Timofei might have better luck, but, as soon as Timofei's boat was in the water, several approaching canoes were spotted and he returned to the ship.

In John Young's inspection crew were natives, Englishmen, and several Americans, including a man named George Beckley, a former seaman who was acting as an engineer to transform the Russians' Honolulu warehouse into a fort. Regarded as a construction expert, he was apparently the chief inspector and the others deferred to him. After he had looked all through the *Kadiak*, witnessing the continuing efforts of the pumpers and the bailers, he declared "She can't reach another harbor in her present condition. We'll have to tow her in here and try to make repairs." Then he asked George, "Can you pay for this?"

"Yes, I can pay," said George. "How much do you want?"

"Fifty-two piastres hard money and whatever trade goods you have aboard," answered Beckley. "And you'll have to pay in advance."

"I'll pay you right now," said George. "Just order the towing to begin immediately."

George went below to the Captain's compartment where Timofei's wife and children were quartered to open the cash box and retrieve the money. He asked Petr Kicherev to gather up the trade goods—2 wool blankets, 48 mirrors, 42 hand hatchets, 2 long-handled axes, and selected metal table knives, forks, and spoons. Before the inspection party left the ship he had given them what they asked for to accomplish the towing.

The next day the towing had still not begun, and there were no towing crews in sight. George decided to go ashore himself and try to settle things with John Young and the American captains. He asked Timofei Tarakanov to accompany him in the longboat. Filip Osipov, Aleksei Odnoriadkin, Ivan Larionov, and Nikolai Poliakov went also. These were his most formidable men, and they were well armed. In addition, Charles Fox-Bennick and Francis Wallace went along.

As the longboat approached the shore it was surrounded by a fleet of war canoes carrying fifty warriors or more. George counted the colorful caps of twelve chiefs among them. The American George Beckley was at the head of one of the canoes, and he shouted to them, telling them not to row ashore, but to go instead to the American ship *Paragon*, which was within easy rowing distance from where they were. There was clearly no choice but to follow this instruction. The men were frightened and clutched their weapons tightly. At any second they might be attacked by this overwhelming force.

On board the *Paragon*, George met Captain Dixey Wildes. He was a few years older than George—in appearance a tall and slender man who reminded George of his former Captain Iakov Anikievich Podushkin of the *Otkrytie*. He was wearing a tri-cornered hat like the one Podushkin often wore. Captain Wildes welcomed George and his men aboard in friendly fashion and began his conversation with George by asking about his birthplace and how he had come to Hawai'i. After listening to George's answer, he told George that he had been born in Massachusetts and had been at sea "all his life." George then asked him if he had ever been to Kaua'i, and Captain Wildes said, "Indeed I have. I was there when you left Waimea."

"So you're one of those who made trouble for me there, eh?" said George, turning his tone to anger. "No doubt you're taking orders from John Young then. I've no doubt that it was he who made up all that nonsense about Russia and the United States going to war...and he who sent you and the others to Kaua'i to scare King Kaumuali'i there into expelling us."

Captain Wildes did not deny anything that George said. He calmly turned to George Beckley who had also come aboard and was standing nearby and stated, "I think Mr. Beckley here will tell you that the reason you are standing here alive right now is because King Kamehameha wants to see you in person."

"That is correct," George Beckley said. "I am empowered to tell you, Dr. Sheffer, that if you will turn yourself in to Billy Pitt, you will be taken as a prisoner to Hawai'i to speak with Kamehameha and your fate will be in his hands. If all your people here, both on the *Kadiak* and ashore at Waikīkī, give up all their arms and ammunition, they will not be harmed. They can reside here until ships come from Sitka to get them."

"But what if I do not turn myself in?" asked George.

"Then your ship will sink untowed and you'll all drown," said Beckley. "And any Russians ashore will be hunted down and killed."

"That is an outrage!" exclaimed George. "I've already paid you for the towing. If I don't get it, all fifty-six of us will have no choice but to come ashore armed to fight to the death. And I don't think you're ready for such a fight as we will carry to you."

Beckley looked at George's men who were standing around him. They seemed resolute and all had their hands on their weapons. But he asked them,

"Do all you men feel the same way? Are you willing to fight to the death to protect this man?"

Timofei Tarakanov spoke up, saying, "With us, it's all for one and one for all. Whatever happens to Commissioner Sheffer happens to all of us."

"Does that mean you all want to go to Hawai'i as prisoners?" asked Beckley.

George's mind scrambled to defuse the explosiveness of this situation. He didn't want it to burst into violence right there on the deck of the *Paragon*.

"I would like to return to the *Kadiak* to discuss this offer with all my people there," said George conciliatorily. "If they want me to surrender so that they can reside here unharmed until ships come for them, then I will surrender. But you must agree to tow the ship into the inner harbor for repair."

George Beckley looked at Captain Wildes with a frown, and then agreed, "All right. You can return to the *Kadiak*. I'll tell John Young that you are considering the offer."

"Will you tow the ship in?" asked George. "We're out there in thirteen sazhens of depth. We need to get the sand a single sazhen or less beneath our keel immediately. The ship will be lost otherwise."

"It will be towed," answered Beckley.

As the men rowed back to the *Kadiak* they discussed John Young's offer. It was a clear choice—give up their leader or risk death. Filip Osipov and Ivan Larionov were fearless and wanted to fight anyway. "I think we should attack them before they expect anything from us," Filip said. "We could take quite a toll from them if we caught them by surprise. Maybe we could even kill John Young or Billy Pitt. That would hurt them mightily. And then we could run off into the hills where it would take them a long time to find us."

"There are too many of them," said Charles Fox-Bennick. "And we don't know precisely where to attack. Are they all at Don Marin's house? Are they at Kapapoko? Are they at the warehouse they're making into a fort? Who knows? And how can we prevent them from seeing us coming? They've got canoes paddling around us both day and night. A better course would be for us to make a surprise attack on one of the American ships…take it over while most of its crew is ashore, then sail it away. We'll need a fast one. I favor making a move on the *Paragon*, though it's not well armed."

"Are you all mad?" asked Francis Wallace. "I think Yegor Nikolaevich should turn himself in and go to Hawai'i to talk to Kamehameha. He will be all right. No one talks to these savage chiefs like he does. He'll soon have Kamehameha kissing his hand. And we won't have to attack anyone to preserve our lives."

George was surprised to hear Wallace make such a statement in his presence. "It's gratifying to see that you have such confidence in my powers of persuasion, Mr. Wallace," he said. "But I don't think that John Young would ever allow me to speak again with Kamehameha. If I turned myself in to Billy

Pitt here in Honolulu, as he wants, he would quickly see to it that I never get to Hawai'i. I would be killed…likely stuffed alive into that imu oven in Waikīkī where they burned up Kalanikūpule's chiefs."

When George and his men returned to the *Kadiak*, the discussion was widened to include the entire company. Francis Wallace continued to advocate that George turn himself in, even saying at one point that "It's the duty of a leader to sacrifice himself for his men." But Timofei and the majority of the others agreed that George was not to turn himself in. They favored considering other options, including those of preemptory attack. Even though he termed it an "act of piracy," George suggested that an attack on one of the American ships, as Charles Fox-Bennick proposed, would be easier if they waited until they were towed in closer to these ships. Besides, he said, the Americans would be celebrating their Independence Day in only two days time. The anticipated revelry and its associated drinking of spirits would render the American crews more vulnerable to their surprise attack.

The next morning, Pilot John Harbottle came aboard to announce that the towing was to commence using "Billy Pitt's men"—not the usual paddlers. The anchor was lifted, but a large part of it fell off as it was elevated above the water. It was an old anchor made of both iron and wood, and the wooden parts of it had been devoured by seaworms. Now just the smaller iron part would have to hold the ship in place in the inner harbor. Fortunately the weather was fine and the inner harbor was calmer so that the ship would likely stay in place. With the heavy jute lines attached to the tow canoes, the native teams began the job of towing the *Kadiak*.

Pilot Harbottle said he had been instructed to inform George that henceforth anyone on the *Kadiak* who tried to come ashore would be shot immediately. With Harbottle was a redheaded Irishman who was drunk. George asked his name but could not understand the response. Both men were friendly and commiserated with George and the others, saying that the Russians had been given a hard choice and blaming it all on "the Captains Ebbets, the Winships, and Hunt…all of whom were unscrupulous scoundrels."

In a few hours, George realized that Billy Pitts' paddlers who were supposed to be towing the ship into the inner harbor were instead towing the ship onto a coral reef, which rippled the surface of the water a short distance ahead of them. He yelled at the paddlers and motioned to them, pointing out a safer course, but they continued to pull the *Kadiak* toward the reef. Pilot Harbottle was angered by this and he also began shouting at the paddlers to change direction. But the ship was coming uncomfortably close to the reef.

"Cut the lines!" George shouted to his men. Filip Osipov and Ivan Larionov grabbed axes and quickly chopped through the thick towlines. When the lines fell off the ship into the water, the paddlers just continued on over the reef as if they had not been disconnected from the *Kadiak*. Soon they were beaching the tow canoes ashore and disappearing from sight. Likely they thought that the

Kadiak would now drift onto the reef by itself, driven by the inward running waves.

"Damn it, they tried to run us onto the reef," said George to Harbottle. "We'll have to get out in the boats and tow it in ourselves. I've got some Aleuts with me here who can pull a boat like no one else. All you have to do is point the direction."

"Get them out there," said Harbottle. "I'll point the way."

Timofei and Grigorii Iskakov hustled to muster all four boats of Aleuts who attached new lines and began to row with a rare fury until the *Kadiak* turned away from the reef and started toward the center of Honolulu's inner harbor. All the while the pumping and the bailing continued, but the ship's waterline was now only a yard or two beneath the level of the deck. The *Kadiak* was sinking. The only question was where…in what depth would it sink? If it came down centered in shallow enough water, there was hope of repair or significant salvage. But if it went down in deeper water, got turned by the waves and listed to one side or the other, it would be lost. Pilot Harbottle directed the Aleuts' efforts and brought the *Kadiak* into the ideal place…only a few feet of draft above a sandy bottom and centered perpendicularly to the direction of the waves.

Charles Fox-Bennick pointed out to George that their location was quite close to that of the *Paragon*, making an attack upon it a real possibility. When Harbottle and his Irish companion left the ship, they asked George what he planned to do…would he turn himself over to Billy Pitt or not? "I'm not a caught fish yet," George told them.

The next day was the 4th of July, 1817, on the Americans' calendar. In the morning, another American ship, a brig, arrived, anchoring in the outer harbor where the *Kadiak* had been. George did not recognize it, but he saw several boats from the ship rowing in to shore. Soon he noticed all the American ships in the harbor were running up their flags in honor of their Independence Day. At noon there began numerous rounds of cannon salutes, and loud cries of "Hurrah!" could be heard in the distance. Most of the ships were sending men ashore where a great bonfire was aflame, sending dark smoke high into the air. George ordered the Russian-American Company flag raised again on the *Kadiak*'s mizzenmast, but still upside-down. A party of American sailors in a boat came alongside. George Beckley was the leader of this party, and he shouted to George, "You can turn that flag right-side up now, Dr. Sheffer. The ship can't sink in its present position."

George shouted back, "Nevertheless, the ship is still in danger, Mr. Beckley! I'll keep the flag as it is."

"Have you decided to give yourself up?" yelled Beckley.

"I have not yet decided," answered George.

"Well, you had better hurry your decision. Mr. Young and Billy Pitt are growing impatient," Beckley shouted.

"Tell them they'll know tomorrow!" George replied.

Beckley and his men rowed back to shore. George and his companions on the *Kadiak* decided that they would make their attempt to take over the *Paragon* by force as soon as it became dark. They gathered their weapons and divided themselves into groups. The four dinghys would each hold eight men. These would spearhead the attack, with George, Timofei, Filip Osipov, and Charles Fox-Bennick in command. If the initial assault was successful, Grigorii Terentev and Grigorii Iskakov would commence using the two longboats to transport the others to the new ship. They imagined they could take the *Paragon's* maintenance crew captive and release them into a boat when they were underway…but deadly force was likely to be necessary, especially if the officers were aboard. George led the men in a prayer, calling upon God Almighty to "bless us and reward our righteousness with success."

As the sun approached the western horizon through crimson screening clouds, George noticed another rowboat approaching. "Who might this be?" he asked himself, but then, in a few minutes, he did recognize two of the men in the boat. They were Captain Isaiah Lewis and his first mate, John Marshall. The sight of them excited George. He did have some friends here, after all, he thought. He remembered climbing Mauna Kea on Hawai'i with John Marshall, the nephew of John Jacob Astor, and how he had treated Captain Lewis at Waikīkī for a bad tooth and an infected ear.

"Hello!" George shouted in English to the men as they came alongside. "Welcome to the *Kadiak*. Come aboard!"

Captain Lewis and his men tied up their boat and climbed aboard by merely stepping out of the boat and over the rail, so low was the ship in the water. George hugged both of his friends warmly, saying, "How good it is to see you…very good indeed."

Captain Lewis smiled and said, "We sailed in here today from Kailua, came ashore to celebrate our Independence Day…and found out that you are in a very bad situation. Old John Young and Kamehameha's Minister Billy Pitt want your head. It's as simple as that. I got myself into trouble arguing with the other captains that your Russian mission is a just one and that you are a good and honest man. But I didn't convince them. The American captains want your head also. You interfered with their prospects for profit. And here you are trapped among them like a fox in the kennel. But, like Daniel's lion, I don't forget how you doctored my ear and tooth. I was mad then with pain and likely would have died. John here and Don Marin brought me to you in Waikīkī, and you cured me, giving me back my life. So I talked it over with John, and we've come to offer you a way out. You can sail away tomorrow with us on the *Panther*. We're bound for China and we'll take you there. You can even share my cabin."

"So that ship is the *Panther*?" asked George, pointing to the newly arrived ship in the outer harbor. "I didn't recognize it when it sailed in and anchored. And so, you would depart from here without even coming in to the inner port?"

"I would and I will," answered Captain Lewis. "We don't need to provision here. We can still get provisions at Waimea."

"I can't go back to Waimea," protested George. "They'll kill me there too."

"But they wouldn't know you were on the ship," answered Lewis. "You would just stay out of sight in my compartment while we dealt with the chiefs there."

"What about my people here on the *Kadiak* and at Waikīkī?" asked George. "I can't abandon them. They've risked their lives by refusing to give me up."

Captain Lewis looked around at the men with George on the *Kadiak*. Only Charles Fox-Bennick and Francis Wallace had well understood the English conversation they had heard. "I suggest you talk it over with your men, Dr. Sheffer," said the Captain. "I don't think they will be harmed if you are taken away. They'll merely have to give up their guns and stay on until the next Russian ship comes from Sitka or Petropavlovsk."

John Marshall had allowed Captain Lewis to do the talking for some time, while he said nothing. But now he added, "You can go from China back home to St. Petersburg and try to convince the Tsar that he should send some armed ships to support your efforts here. Who will convince him if you do not?"

George talked the matter over thoroughly in Russian with his closest men, and particularly with Timofei Tarakanov. Timofei was of the opinion that George's escape on the *Panther* was the best course of action, the course of least possible danger to everyone concerned. The planned attack on the *Paragon* was a course necessitated by desperation. This was a better idea. Grigorii Terentev and Charles Fox-Bennick also strongly advocated this plan. And so it was agreed. George ordered that all hands come on deck to hear him.

"My dear friends and companions during many trials and adventures," he began. "I am taking my leave of you for your own good. I will depart here for China on the brig *Panther*. Captain Isaiah Lewis has given me his opinion that neither the natives nor the Americans will harm you after I am gone. You will wait here in Waikīkī for rescue from Sitka or Petropavlovsk…whichever Company ship comes first, and soon you will be safe and returned to your homes and families. I will sail from China to St. Petersburg and take up our cause with His Majesty, Tsar Aleksandr. When I return to the Pacific with Russian ships in support, we will return here and make these brigands pay dearly for the way they have treated us."

There was a rumble of support for this idea from the men. George continued, "I am appointing Company senior hunter and mission clerk Timofei Tarakanov, whom you all esteem, as Company Commissioner in my place. He will be your captain and commander beginning immediately. I hope that you will extend to him the same loyalty and obedience that you have given me. For this I thank you from the bottom of my heart. Now I say to you all not 'Proshchaite--Farewell,' but 'Do svidaniia—Good-bye until we meet again'."

Several men came up to hug George—Petr Kicherev, Ivan Larionov, and Aleksei Odnoriadkin among them. Then Timofei Tarakanov spoke up. "Now that I am in command, I am asking for volunteers who would accompany Yegor Nikolaevich to St. Petersburg, acting as aides and guards to assure his success. I ask you now—Who will accompany him?"

A host of hands sprang up and many shouted "I will, I will." Timofei thought for a moment and then chose, saying, "I think two of you should go…Filip Osipov, our toughest man, and Grigorii Iskakov, our oldest…and wisest…man." George wondered at the choice of Iskakov, but did not question Timofei's judgment. Instead, he turned to Captain Lewis and asked, "Is that all right?"

Lewis responded, "Yes, we've room for three. But we've got to get out to the ship tonight. I'll want to leave with the first breeze in the morning."

As George and his two volunteer companions got ready to leave the *Kadiak*, their things already stowed in the boat, Timofei came up and suggested that they all sit down for a moment before they left. This was a Russian superstition assuring a safe journey. While George was, in accordance with this suggestion, sitting on the rail, Timofei shook his hand and hugged him, saying "Idi s Bogom…Go with God! Uvidimsia naverkhu…we'll see each other up above, meaning 'in heaven'."

In a few minutes, George was looking back at the almost sunken *Kadiak* as it got smaller and smaller in the darkening night. The oars of the *Panther's* boat were pulling away from the island of O'ahu, away from his dreams of a glorious life in Hawai'i.

Hiding on the ship in Waimea:

When the *Panther* reached Waimea on its way westward on July 7th, Captain Lewis asked George to stay in the Captain's cabin and not show himself on deck. Before he retired to the cabin, George took a good look at the scene before him, the place of such memories for him. On shore the same blue and white flag with black circles that George had declared a "pirate" flag was still flying on the pole in the village. Fort Elizaveta, which George had had constructed on the bluff on the other side of the Waimea River above the village, looked impressively imposing. And the roof of King Kaumuali'i's new stone Papa'ena'ena residence could just be seen when the ship rolled to an apex in the waves.

John Marshall went ashore and came back with a party of natives, including Chief Kupikēapio and King Kaumuali'i's tall son Keali'iahonui. To the surprise of George's hidden eyes, Captain William Wadsworth was also with them.

"I'm the King's new fleet commander," said Wadsworth boastfully. "Of course the fleet's a mite small…only the schooner *Lydia* just now. Captain Whittemore is taking the *Avon* to Kamehameha…then quitting the islands. But I'll be taking charge of the Russians' sandalwood too, and it should bring a fortune when I can get it to Canton. I hope to see you there."

George was listening through the ventilation slats dividing the brig's captain's cabin from the main deck. He gritted his teeth in anger to hear of Wadsworth's new position and his plans for the sandalwood that he, George, had ordered amassed. He wanted to run out of the cabin and beat Wadsworth senseless…throw him over the side. But he remained quiet and hidden as he had been asked.

"What have you heard about Dr. Sheffer and his Russians on the *Kadiak*?" Wadsworth asked Captain Lewis. "Did they make it to Honolulu?"

"Yes, they did," answered Lewis. "And I saw them in the harbor there. John Young and Billy Pitt were demanding that Dr. Sheffer turn himself in to them in exchange for letting the others stay unarmed at Waikīkī to await rescue."

"That'll be the end of him, the son-of-a-bitch," said Wadsworth with a wry smile. "Hawai'i is better off without him."

BIBLIOGRAPHY

First, you should know that this bibliography is a list of the sources for the entire GEORGE ANTON SCHAEFFER trilogy…all three parts. It is given in each of the other two parts as well. This bibliography is meant primarily as a resource for those who wish to delve more deeply into any of the topics touched in this trilogy. I have tried to make it convenient and informative to use. That is why I include commentary on how the work cited relates to George Anton Schaeffer and various aspects of his peripatetic life. I realize that this bibliography may stray from canonical citation format in some places and I do not apologize for that. I include internet sites as well as printed texts, since this is the way of modern information exchange. I caution the reader about the dynamic nature of the internet. Sites that I accessed for information from 2000 to 2009 may have been taken down or altered. The reader may be able to retrieve them from the search-engine archives. Despite this seeming lack of permanence, however, the internet keeps adding more sources than it loses and remains in its dynamic state a most valuable resource. Indeed I have been impressed over and over again as I wrote this book with how much easier the internet, when used judiciously, of course, makes the search for needed facts. I began my scholarly career as a virtually perennial resident of libraries, typing my doctoral dissertation on a broken-down typewriter, hitting the keys with almost destructive force to make six copies through layers of carbon paper…no desktop computer, no word processor or printer, not even photocopy, which was too expensive for a poor graduate student per slick-paper sheet as late as 1972. Yet as easy as it might now be to find, you still have to help others find it too. So here it is:

Adam, Albrecht. Napoleon's Army in Russia: The Illustrated Memoirs of Albrecht Adam-1812. See North, Jonathan (below). Also see my review of this work at www.Amazon.com.

Adams, Alexander. "Extracts from an Ancient Log: Selections from the Logbook of Captain Alexander Adams in Connection with the Early History of Hawaii—Occurrences on Board the Brig *Forester*, of London, from Conception Towards the Hawaiian Islands." Hawaiian Almanac and Journal. 1906. pp. 66-74. Adams was Kamehameha's Captain of the *Forester* after it became the *Ka'ahumanu* in April 1816. These are selections from his logbook from January 16, 1816 to December 26, 1818.

Adams, John Quincy (1767-1848), sixth President of the United States (1825-1829) and, previously, Ambassador (1809-1815) to Russia. See primarily Claffey and Sikes below.

Aleksandrovskaia, O. "The Writings of Decembrist K. P. Torson, a Member of the First Russian Antarctic Expedition (1819-21)." This is about Konstantin

Petrovich Torson (1793-1851), exiled as a "Decembrist" in 1826, who participated as a watch officer on Captain Faddei Bellingshausen's flagship *Vostok*. This is published by the Museum of the World Ocean website on a 2002 Conference at http://vitiaz.ru/congress/en/thesis/72.html.

Alexander, W. D. "The Funeral Rites of Prince Kealiiahonui" in The 14th Annual Report of the Hawaiian Historical Society for the Year Ending December 31, 1906. Honolulu, Hawaiian Gazette Co, Ltd. Pp. 26-28. Accessed in 2009 also at http://www.horrormasters.com/Text/a0910.pdf. This concerns the tall son of Kaumuali'i, last King of Kaua'i who also was once married to Ka'ahumanu...mentions possible funereal sacrifices of humans as late as 1849.

Ancient Hawaiian Civilization: A Series of Lectures Delivered at the (Introduction by Glen Grant). Mutual Publishing. Honolulu, Hawaii. 1999. This is a reprint of a classic collection of studies of ancient Hawaiian life.

Antonson, Joan M. "Sitka." In Russian America: The Forgotten Frontier. Barbara Sweetland Smith and Redmond J. Barnett, eds. Tacoma: The Washington State Historical Press. 1990. pp. 165-175.

Arago, Jacques Etienne. Narrative of a Voyage Around the World, in the *Uranie* and *Physicienne* corvettes, commanded by Captain Freycinet, during the years 1817, 1818, 1819, and 1820. Treuttel & Wurtz, Treuttel, jun. & Richter. 1823. This is one of the primary artists depicting Hawaiian life in the early contact era. His life is a most fascinating one and his Wikipedia site at http://en.wikipedia.org/wiki/Jacques_Arago provides a link to a French work about curiosities in his travels he wrote while blind in 1853 without once using the French alphabet letter "a." Curious indeed.

Armitage, John (1807-1865). The History of Brazil from the Period of the Arrival of the Braganza Family in 1808, to the Abdication of Don Pedro the First in 1831. Compiled from State Documents and Other Original Sources. Forming a Continuation to Southey's History of That Country. Smith, Elder. London. 1836. (University Microfilms, Ann Arbor, Michigan, 1970). Appendix 1 by pre-1779 Portuguese Viceroy of Brazil the Marquis de Lavradio, mentions the situation of African Slaves.

Armstrong, Scott. Russian Snows: Coming of Age in Napoleon's Army. RedBarn Publications, Douglassville, PA. 2011. ISBN 978-1466331549. See http://www.RussianSnows.com and http://napoleon1812.wordpress.com. Also see my reviews of this book on www.Amazon.com and www.Shvoong.com.

Aroutunova, Bayara. Lives in Letters: Princess Zinaida Volkonskaya and her Correspondence. Slavica Publishers, Inc. Bloomington, IN. 1994. Includes letters from Tsar Alexander I (nothing about the balloon project at all) dating from 1812, and much cultural detail from Russian elite circles, 1812-50...includes salon activities in St. P. and Moscow prior to the 1825 Decembrist Revolt. The source here was most useful in informing activities of Barbara Schaeffer in St. Petersburg while her husband was away.

ASTOR, JOHN JACOB (1763-1848). "America's First Multimillionaire," Astor came to control the United States' fur trade in the first quarter of the 19th century. His ancestors have also been interesting characters in American history. See primarily the work by Axel Madsen (below).

Atherton, Gertrude. Rezanov. (With Introduction by William Marion Reedy). A Gutenberg Project e-publication, available at http://www.totse.com/en/ego/literary_genius/reznv10.html.

Austin, Paul Britten. 1812: Napoleon in Moscow. Greenhill Books. London (and Stackpole Books, Pennsylvania). 1995. There is a fine description of Rostopchin's estate at Voronovo and the hosting there of Mdme Germaine de Stael on pp. 124-30...also mention of how Rostopchin's daughter later marries "Phillipe de Segur" (nephew of Napoleon's aide and later historian, cf. the note by J. David Townsend on pp. 93 of Phillipe-Paul de Segur's Napoleon's Russian Campaign).

BARANOV, ALEXANDER ANDREEVICH (1746 or 1747-1819), Russian-American Company Manager and first Governor of Russian America (1791-1818). A modern comprehensive biography awaits (see Chevigny below, however, and Khlebnikov), but the National Endowment for the Humanities has given in 2003 a $75,000 grant to UC-Sacramento Prof. Kenneth Owens, with the collaboration of Russian scholar Alex Petrov, to complete one based on archival materials from both America and Russia. The project title is "Alexander Baranov and Russia's Multi-cultural Borderlands Empire in North America." See the online work through http://alexander-baranov.biography.ms/ or at www.bookrags.com (the biography on Baranov costs $6.99) and also through sites related to the history of Sitka, Alaska (see below). Baranov is treated peripherally but well by the site of the Congress of Russian Americans at www.russian-americans.org/CRA_History.htm. See also the citations below for Sitka, Fort Ross, Veniaminov. For a more negative portrayal of Baranov and his activities see the sources for Herman below. See the Rezanov citations for periphereal information.

Barratt, Glynn. The Russians at Port Jackson, 1814-1822. Australian Institute of Aboriginal Studies. Canberra, Australia. 1981. This work includes the memoirs of Russian sailors who visited Port Jackson (Sydney). Very thoroughly researched it includes a complete bibliography of archival sources.

Barratt, Glynn. Russia in Pacific Waters, 1725-1825: A Survey of the Origins of Russia's Naval Presence in the North and South Pacific. University of British

Columbia Press. Vancouver and London. 1981. The chapter of most interest here is entitled "The Company Under Attack" about the latter days of the Russian-American Company's operations. There is a fine illustrations section with the only known likeness of M.P. Lazarev and contemporary artists' views of the RAK settlement at Novo-Arkhangel'sk (Sitka, Alaska) in the early years of the nineteenth century.

Barratt, Glynn. The Russian Discovery of Hawai'i: The Ethnographic and Historic Record. Editions Limited. Honolulu, HI. 1987. Note: dedication to Pat Polansky (conferred with at U-Hawaii Hamilton Library, June 10, 2001). Translated documents of Hawaiian observers from the 1803-6 voyage of the Nadezhda (Ivan F.Kruzenshtern) and Neva (Iurii F. Lisianskii). Nikolai Rezanoff and Georg Heinrich Langsdorff were aboard. Mention of Hawaiian Kaneohe/Kenokhoia/adoption by Vasilii Fedorovich Moller...pp. 96 footnote, 102.

Barratt, Glynn. The Russian View of Honolulu: 1809-26. Carlton University Press. Toronto. 1988. A detailed scholarly work with a fine bibliography.

Barratt, Glynn. The Russians and Australia (Volume I of Russia and the South Pacific, 1696-1840). University of British Columbia Press. Vancouver. 1988. This is the most detailed treatment in English of the circumnavigation of the *Suvorov* and its consequences to Russian Pacific policy. Chapter 3, "The First Russian Visits to Port Jackson, 1807-14," explains the conflicts on the *Suvorov* between the "navy" men, including Captain Lazarev, and the "company" men, including Dr. George Anton Schaeffer and RAK supercargo Germann Molvo.

Bartholomew, Gail. (Photo research by Bren Bailey). Maui Remembers: A Local History. Mutual Publishing. Honolulu, Hawaii. 1994. Interesting is the brief treatment of "Kamehameha and Kahekili: Clash of Warriors" in chapter 3 and "Metcalfe and the Olawalu Massacre" in chapter 5.

Bass, Robert D. Gamecock: The Life and Campaigns of General Thomas Sumter. Holt, Rhinehart, and Winston. New York. 1961. See also www.virtualology.com/virtualwarmuseum.com/revolutionarywarhall/ThomasSumter.com. At the end of his active career in politics (U.S. Rep. and Senator), the U.S. Revolutionary War hero, General Thomas Sumter (1734-1832), was U.S. Minister to Brazil (1809-1811...notice that the title is not "Ambassador" really since Brazil at the time was still officially a Portuguese Colony). The story of how he, at the age of 76, pulled pistols on the guard-escorts of Brazil's eccentric Regent Consort Dona Carlota in Rio de Janeiro to prevent their forcing him to kneel in obeisance, is representative of his character. Fort Sumter in Charleston, South Carolina-the site of the first shots fired in the U.S. Civil War, is named after him. There is a city and a county in South Carolina that were given his name in 1800, even before he served as Minister to Brazil. Sumter (SC) High School and the University of South Carolina have given his nickname, the

"Gamecock," to their sports team, and he is one of the revolutionary war figures informing actor Mel Gibson's character, Benjamin Martin, in the popular movie, *The Patriot* (2002). When General Sumter died at the age of 98 in Statesburg, South Carolina, he was the last surviving general officer of the U.S. Revolutionary War.

Becher, Hans. <u>Georg Heinrich Freiherr Von Langsdorff in Brasilien: Forschungen eines deutschen Gelehrten im 19 Jahrhundert.</u> Dietrich Reimer Verlag. Berlin. 1987. See the mention of "Major" "Ritter Von Schaffer" on pp. 16-7 and the citation of Sheffer's book, pp. 89.

Beckwith, Martha Warren, ed. <u>Kepelino's Traditions of Hawai'i.</u> Bernice P. Bishop Museum Bulletin 95, Bishop Museum Press, Honolulu, HI, 2007 from a 1932 original publication.

Beeche, Arturo. "The Amazon Throne: The Orleans-Braganza of Brazil." Accessed in January, 2005 at http://www.eurohistory.com/braganza.html. This is a concise relation of the history of Brazil's royal family after the move from Portugal in 1807.

Bell, Susan N. <u>Unforgettable True Stories of the Kingdom of Hawaii.</u> Press Pacifica. Pacific Trade Group, P.O. Box 668, Pearl City, Hawaii 96782. This work has information about early Hawaiians who visited Europe soon after western contact and stories based on less well-known observers of post-contact cultural matters.

Berdnikov, Lev. "The Loud American," in <u>Russian Life</u>, Vol. 49, No. 5, (Sept./Oct. 2006), pp. 34-43 illustrated. This is a fine relation about the character of Fyodor Ivanovich Tolstoi, the "American." See also O. Vozdvizhenskaia and S. L. Tolstoi.

Berthels, D. E., Komissarov, B. N., Lysenko, T.I. (eds.) <u>Materialien Der Brasilien-Expedition 1821-1829 Des Akademiemitgliedes Georg Heinrich Freiherr Von Langsdorff (Grigorij Ivanovich Langsdorff).</u> Völkerkundliche Abhandlungen, Band VII: Publikationsreihe Der Volkerkunde-Abteilung Des Niedersächsischen Landesmuseums under Ethnologischen Gesellschaft Hannover E. V. VERLAG DIETRICH REIMER. Berlin, 1979. The English "Foreword" to this work describes it: "Vol. VII of the "Völkerkundliche Abhandlungen" presents, for the first time in German, the complete, immeasurably rich research material collected during the first Russian expedition to Brazil, 1821-1829, led by the German scholar Georg Heinrich Freiherr von Langsdorff." And, later in explanation: "During the above mentioned Brazil expedition, which had been beautifully organized, von Langsdorff unfortunately developed a severe psychological disorder as a result of malaria and other tropical diseases. Thus it was not possible for him to publish his scientific results."

Bezotosnyi, V. M. et. al. Otechestvennaia voina 1812 goda: Entsiklopediia. (The Great Patriotic War of 1812: and Encyclopedia). ROSSPEN. Moscow. 2004. 878 pp. ISBN 582430324X. This is a comprehensive reference work on the war between Russia and Napoleon's France in 1812. See the entry on "Leppich's Balloon" ("Vozdushnyi shar Leppikha," str. 141 and on "Tormasov," str. 707). I had no access to it while I was writing the chapter on Moscow and the war with Napoleon, but I fortunately found no substantive contradictions in the wok here and certainly recommend this outstanding work. See the review by Dominic Lieven in Kritika: Explorations in Russian and Eurasian History. 7, 1 (Winter 2006), pp. 133-35. Lieven terms it "the most valuable work on the history of the Napoleonic wars published in any language in recent years."

Binyon, T. J. Pushkin: A Biography. Vintage edition. Random House. New York. 2004 (reprint from London copyright, 2002). The most recent and detailed life of the great Russian Poet, Aleksandr Sergeevich Pushkin (1799-1837), this work includes a comprehensive depiction of life in Russia, particularly St. Petersburg, from 1812 to 1837. It includes many personal relationships in Pushkin's life...for example, Prince Repnin-Volkonskii, Prince Viazemskii, Nikolai and Ekaterina Karamzin and their children, and Fedor Ivanovich Tolstoi "the American," all of whom are characters in this book. It has a fine illustration section and is adorned throughout with Pushkin's own sketches of his acquaintances (e.g. Fedor Tolstoi). See also the review of this and three other recent biographical works on Pushkin by Caryl Emerson (below).

Birkett, Mary Ellen. "Hawai'i in 1819: An Account by Camille de Roquefeuil" in The Hawaiian Journal of History (A Publication of the Hawaiian Historical Society), Vol. XXXIV (2000), pp. 69-92. This account mentions Don Francisco de Paula Marin and precedes the better-known account of Freycinet (below) after the death, May 8, 1819, of Kamehameha.

Black, Lydia T. Russians in Alaska, 1732-1867. University of Alaska Press (PO Box 756240). Fairbanks, AK 99775-6240. ISBN 1-889963-05-4. 2004. This work has a most complete bibliography.

Black, Lydia T. "Native Artists of Russian America." In Russian America: The Forgotten Frontier. Barbara Sweetland Smith and Redmond J. Barnett, eds. Tacoma: The Washington State Historical Press. 1990. pp. 197-205.

Blinov, S. G., Voronin, S. D., Gorokhov, A. A., Mel'nikov, V. M., and Filii, M. D. et. al. 1812-1814: Reljatsii. Pis'ma. Dnevniki. Terra. Moskva. 1992. This is a compilation of letters and entries from journals and diaries taken from the collection of the Russian State Historical Museum, and copiously annotated. Here are secret correspondences of General Bagration, General Raevsky,

General Vorontsov, and other officers of the Russian army during the years 1812-4. One whole section is devoted to the correspondence between General Bagration and General Tormasov. Also prominent are the letters of Governor-General Rostopchin and Nikolai Karamzin. Letter 172 (pp. 173-5) from General Barclay-de-Tolly to General Bagration includes the ruminations of a scholar from Derpst University, Wilhelm Friederich Getsel', on the cabbalistic numerology of Napoleon's title and age (L'Empereur Napoleon and quarante deux=42), revealing Napoleon to be the beast, signified by the number 666 in St. John's vision of the Apocalypse in Revelations, 13.

Blond, Charles. La Grande Armée. (Translated by Marshall May). Arms and Armour Press. London. 1995. Mention is made of Napoleon's horse "Moscow" that he rode in the city during the Moscow fire (pp. 333).

Bobrova, Helene. "Russian Diplomats in Paris, 1791-1815." cf. www.museum.ru/artel of the project "1812 year," 1999-2000.

Boitsov, M. (red.). K chesti Rossii: iz chastnoi perepiski 1812 goda. Sovremennik. Moskva. 1988. This is a compilation of personal letters written by people who witnessed the events of Napoleon's invasion of Russia in 1812. It includes letters by Rostopchin, Batiushkov, Viazemskii, Konovnitsyn, Kutuzov, Karamzin, and others.

Bolkhovitinov, Nikolai N. The Beginnings of Russian-American Relations 1775-1815. Translated by Elena Levin. Harvard University Press, Cambridge, Massachusetts and London, England. 1975. This work has detailed information about the activities of Alexander Baranov on behalf of the Russian-American Company in Novo-Arkhangelsk (Sitka), Alaska.

Bolkhovitinov, N. N. "The Adventure of Doctor Schaeffer on Hawai'i, 1815-1819," in Hawaiian Journal of History, Vol. 7 (1973), pp. 55-70.

Bolkhovitinov, N.N. and Narochnitskii, A. L. red. Issledovaniia russkikh na Tikhom okeane v XVIII-pervoi polovine XIX v: Rossiisko-Amerikanskaia Kompaniia i izuchenie tikhookeanskogo severa 1799-1815: sbornik dokumentov. Nauka. Moskva. 1994. See document 167 by Lt. Unkovskii about the trip of the Suvorov from 11 November 1814 to 5 August 1815…and also note 115 (str. 256) which indicates that the Suvorov's route from Kronshtadt to Alaska went around the Cape of Good Hope (not Cape Horn), after provisioning in Rio de Janeiro, and spent time in August of 1814 in the Australian Port Jackson (Sydney). Documents 155 and 156 describe the staff and cargo of the ship, including "Doctor Collegiate Assessor Egor Anton Sheffer."

Bolkhovitinov, N. N. "Vydvizhenie i proval proektov Dobella," ("The Advancement and Failure of Dobell's Projects") in <u>Amerikanskii ezhegodnik</u>, Nauka, Moskva, 1976, str. 264-282.

Bolkhovitinov, N.N. <u>Istoriia Russkoi Ameriki, 1732-1867 v trekh tomakh</u>. Mezhdunarodnye otnosheniia. Moskva. 1997-9. Especially see volume 2, <u>Deiatel'nost' Rossiisko-amerikanskoi kompanii, 1799-1825.</u> This work is reviewed by Basil Dmytryshyn in <u>Slavic and East European Journal</u>, Vol. 61, No. 2 (Summer 2002), pp. 407-8.

Bondarenko, Viacheslav Vasilievich. <u>Kniaz Viazemskii: Zhizneopisanie</u>. ("Prince Vyazemsky: A Life Description"). Izdatelnyi tsentr "Ekonompress." Minsk. 2000. Prince Pyotr Andreevich Viazemskii (12/VI/1792-10/XI/1878) was the younger step-brother and ward of Nikolai Karamzin's second wife, Ekaterina. He inherited the Ostafievo estate near Moscow of the Vyazemskii family. Prince Pyotr, himself a significant poet, was a close friend of Aleksandr Sergeevich Pushkin and writes into the memoirs of his long life descriptions and characterizations of many contemporaries. In 1818 he wrote a poem entitled "To Tolstoy" portraying the character of Fedor Ivanovich Tolstoi, "the American." This work by Bondarenko includes a chronology of events in Vyazemskii's life, including his activities and political sympathies being reported to Tsar Nicholas' I's Third Section (Secret Police) by Faddei Bulgarin (see below under A. I. Reitblat, ed). See Viazemskii citations below.

Book, Martin. <u>Opium: A History</u>. Simon and Schuster. New York. 1996. This work mentions the importation of Turkish opium into European countries and China. In 1800 the British Levant Company purchased nearly one-half of all opium coming out of Smyrna, Turkey, for importation into Great Britain and the United States. In 1816 John Jacob Astor joined the opium smuggling trade when his American Fur Company purchased ten tons of opium in Smyrna, Turkey, and shipped the contraband (i.e. outlawed by the Chinese) narcotic to Canton, China on the ship *Macedonian*.

BORODINO, Battle of. (August 26/September 7, 1812). See Armstrong, Austin, Bezotosnyi, Blinov, Blonde, Bobrova, Boitsov, Brett-James, Cate, Chandler, Chuquet, DeCaulaincourt, Duffy, Duhem, Ezerskaya, Griess, Kulagin, Mikerabidze (2), Monakhov, Museum.ru, North (2), Olivier, Palmer, Porter (Robert), Putnam, Riehn, Rostopchin, de Segur, Smith, Tarle (2), Tolstoy, Uffindell, Zamoyski, and Zhilin. Note the "Virtual Battle of Borodino" by Brett Nolan, Shawn Murphy, and Natasha Sopevia for Prof. Frank Sciaca of Hamilton College's Russian Studies Dept. at http://hamilton.edu/academics/Russian/warandpeace/vb/. Also, a more recent and well-illustrated relation can be found at http://napoleonistyka.atspace.com/Borodino_battle.htm.

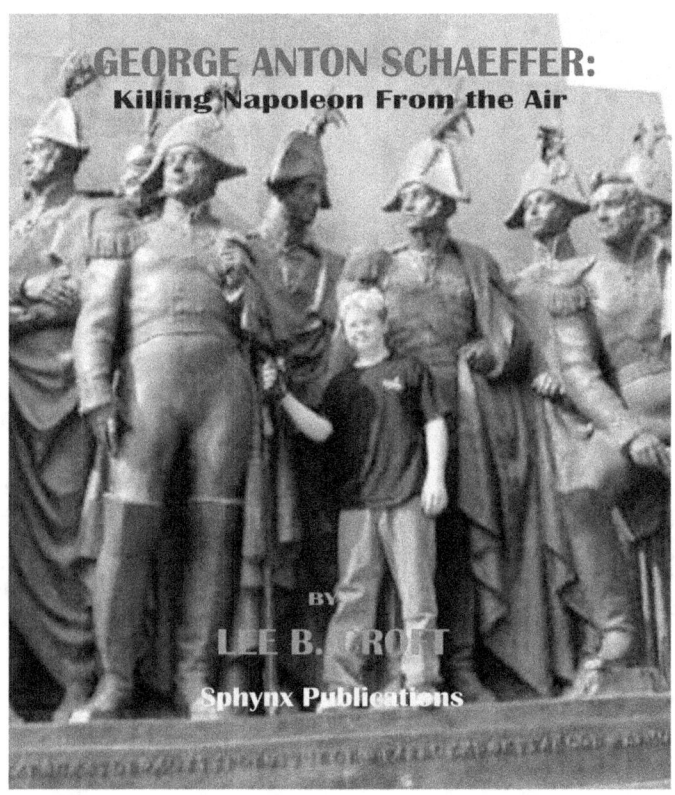

An unused draft of the First Book in the Trilogy's cover, showing the Author's son, Hayden L. Croft, among the statues of the Russian Generals at Moscow's Battle of Borodino Museum. Photo by Lesley Hoyt Croft, April 2002.

BRAZILIAN CURRENCY (MONEY). Useful websites here are http://www.v-brazil.com/information/ and http://en.wikipedia.org/wiki/Brazilian_real and http://www.gwu.edu/~ibi/statistics%20files/Brazilian%20currencies. Notice that the Brazilian Portuguese plural of "real" is "réis," so that "mil réis" is a thousand réis.

Brett-James, Anthony (Compiler, Editor, Translator). 1812: Eyewitness Accounts of Napoleon's Defeat in Russia. St. Martin's Press. New York. 1966. These memoirs are arranged chronologically as to the events of Napoleon's campaign in Russia. The index is one of the few that lists the first names of the figures involved wherever possible…much appreciated exactitude.

Buck, Sir Peter H. Arts and Crafts of Hawaii. See Hiroa, Te Rangi.

Burns, E. Bradford. A History of Brazil. Third Edition. Columbia University Press. New York. 1993. See chapters 2 and 3 on "The Colonial Experience" and "Nation Building," pp. 37-149.

Bushnell, O.A. (ed.) (Illustrations by Joseph Feher). The Illustrated Atlas of Hawaii, Including a Brief History of Hawaii by Gavan Daws. First Edition, Thirty-second Printing, 2003, from the 1970 copyright. An Island Heritage Book. Madden Corporation, 94-411 Ko'aki Street, Waipahu, Hawaii 96797. A fine simple resource.

Cahill, Emmett. The Life and Times of John Young: Confidant and Advisor to Kamehameha the Great. Island Heritage Publishing. Aiea, HI 96701. 1999. This recent work, with illustrations and art by Herb Kawainui Kane, has a chapter (14:pp. 111-7) entitled "The Russians are Coming" which treats Young's advice to Kamehameha concerning Schaeffer.

CALENDAR. For matching day with date in a "10,000 year Calendar" a very handy site is http://calendarhome.com. The site also has more information than needed about other calendars, rendering conversions between the old style (Julian) and new style (Gregorian) Russian dates. Also, to find out which day of the week any date of either Gregorian or Julian calendar is, see the Danish Perpetual Calendar schemes at www.Norbyhus.dk/calendar.html. Generally the Russians' calendar, the Julian, was 11 days behind the European/American Gregorian calendar in the eighteenth century, 12 days behind in the nineteenth century, and 13 days behind in the twentieth century until the Soviets changed to the Gregorian calendar Feb. 28/March 14, 1918. A complication is that, because there was no established dateline in a circumnavigation of the globe, the Russian-Americans in Alaska were, in Schaeffer's time, not 12 days behind as was Russia itself, but 13 days behind. Dates from personal logs or notes are sometimes confusing on this and one must be careful.

CARMINA BURANA. The translations here of the Carmina Burana are from http://www.classical.net/music/comp.1st/works/orff-cb/carbur1.html (carmlyr.html) (accessed 4 August 2003). See below the work by Frederic M. Wheelock.

Carrell, Jennifer Lee. The Speckled Monster: A Historical Tale of Battling Smallpox. Dutton: Penguin Group. New York. 2003. ISBN 0-525-94736-1. This is a historical novel, but with research and notes, detailing Lady Mary Wortley Montagu's life of struggle with smallpox, including early (late 17th and early 18th century) inoculations based on knowledge gained from Africa and Turkey.

Casey, Susan. "The Devil's Teeth." In Sports Illustrated. Vol. 102, No. 18 (May 2, 2005). Pp. 54-62. This article, with photography by Peter Pyle and illustrations of sharks by Ivy Rutzki, presages publication of Susan Casey's book (by Henry Holt and Company in June 2005) on the subject of the Farallon Islands off the California coast (the "Devil's Teeth"...10 very stark islets comprising 211 acres, now a wildlife refuge) and the studies done there of great white sharks. Timofei Tarakanov had seal hunted there with crews of Aleuts in baidarkas poaching on Spanish territory, which Casey now describes as "27 miles west of the Golden Gate Bridge."

Cassidy, Ed. (compiler). Hawaii Trivia. Rutledge Hill Press. Nashville, Tennessee. 1996. Diverse facts about Hawaii. "Scheffer" is mentioned twice on pp. 82.

Cate, Curtis. The War of the Two Emperors: The Duel Between Napoleon and Alexander: Russia, 1812. Random House. New York. 1985. See pp. 259-60 for the balloon episode.

Chamisso, Adelbert von. A Voyage Around the World with the Romanzov (sic) Exploring Expedition, 1815-1818. Edited and Translated by Henry Katz. University of Hawaii Press. Honolulu. 1986. Chamisso, a noted poet and prose writer in Germany, served as ship's scientist on the *Riurik* and was in Hawai'i in 1816. See Kotsebue and Choris and Schweizer (below).

Chandler, David G. The Campaigns of Napoleon: The Mind and Method of History's Greatest Soldier. Scribner. New York. 1966. This is a comprehensive and thorough description of Napoleon's military campaigns in chronological order by a distinguished military historian. It is 1172 pages in length but only mentions "balloons" in one illustration caption concerning the unrealized proposal to invade England by air. The indexing, however, is not completely thorough (cf. at least two mentions of the indexed Bavarian General Wrede are missed). The Moscow balloon project is not mentioned. Moscow Governor General Rostopchin is only mentioned once. But there are appendices listing the command structure of Napoleon's armies in 1808, 1809, 1812, and 1815...very useful.

CHANTS. "Church Singing." Russian Orthodox Church, Moscow. 1982. pp. 246-252. Translated into English from the Russian by Doris Bradbury.
See www.hello-online.ru/content.php?contid=1590. This is a brief history of church singing in the Russian Orthodox Church tradition…choral chants of male voices without musical instruments (znamennye chants, domestvennye chants, putevye chants and the introduction, in the sixteenth century, of polyphonic singing). Hawai'ians were also masters of chanting, though for other purposes.

Chapman, Don with William Kaihe'ekai Mai'oho. Mauna 'Ala: Hawai'i's Royal Mausoleum—Last Remnant of a Lost Kingdom. Foreword by Palani Vaughan. Mutual Publishing LLC, 1215 Center Street, Suite 210, Honolulu, HI 96816, 2004 (ISBN 1-56647-700-X). This 70-pp. book relates the history and lore associated with the burial place of Hawai'i's leading Ali'i and their relatives at Mauna 'Ala on Nu'uanu Street in Honolulu. It shows deep respect for these Ali'is' "mana," and the role of the Mauna 'Ala guardians. Interesting is the "Final Mystery" (Chapter 8) surrounding the fates of the Ka'ai covered Iwi of early big-island kings Liloa and Lonoikamakahiki. See also Klieger (below) on the Mau'i burial site, Moku'ula.

Charlot, Jean. Choris and Kamehameha. Bishop Museum Press. Honolulu. 1958. Charlot is a modern artist who created a mural in a Honolulu bank showing Ludwig Choris at work making a portrait of Kamehameha with Adelbert Chamisso looking on. Choris and Chamisso were on the Russian navy ship *Riurik* under Captain Otto von Kotzebue (Kotsebue) when it visited Hawai'i in late 1816. See Chamisso, Choris, Kotzebue, and Schweizer.

Chevigny, Hector. Lost Empire: The Life and Adventures of Nikolai Rezanov. Binfords and Mort. Portland, Oregon. 1937. This is a fictionalization (and romanticization) of Rezanov's life and his adventure in California.

Chevigny, Hector. Lord of Alaska: Baranov and the Russian Adventure. The Viking Press, New York. 1943. A popularized biography of Alexander Baranov, wonderfully written (especially the "Foreword") and without general sacrifice of historical accuracy…though Owens (see below) demonstrates how some of the relations therein are derived from stories fabricated by 1970's researcher and translator Ivan Petrov (Petroff).

Chevigny, Hector. Russian America: The Great Alaskan Adventure, 1741-1867. The Viking Press, New York. 1965. This is the story of Alaska, developed by the Russians and sold to the Americans, including tales of the major personalities involved. This is the work in which the assertion is made that Ivan Kuskov had a "peg-leg" (cf. pp. 88, 122). This assertion is not evidenced by any contemporary account I can find.

Choris, Louis (Ludwig or Liudovik). Voyage pittoresque autour du monde. Iles Sandwich. Paris. 1822. This work can be found in antiquarian shops on-line (expensive). Choris was the artist on Captain Kotsebue's ship *Riurik* and made likenesses of Kamehameha in 1816, which are our primary sources on Kamehameha's appearance late in his life. Choris was an adventurous young man and was shot and killed in 1828 by armed robbers in Mexico. See Kotsebue and Chamisso, Schweizer and Charlot.

Chuquet, Arthur. Human Voices from the Russian Campaign of 1812. Translated from "Etudes d'Histoire" by M. Harriet M. Capes. Andrew Melrose Publishers. London. 1913.

Claffey, Mary and Sara Sikes. "The First Ambassador: John Quincy Adams in St. Petersburg, 1809-1815," in Russian Life, Vol. 51, No. 5 (Number 526) (Sept./Oct. 2008), pp. 48-58. Authors Claffey and Sikes edit the Adams Papers for the Massachusetts Historical Society, and here they have produced a masterpiece of fascinating detail from John Quincy Adams' diaries about his service as U.S. Ambassador to Russia in St. Petersburg. Here can be found information about his salary, what he paid his servants, what gifts he purchased, his meetings, official and unofficial, with Tsar Alexander I, poignant relation of his family life, of the people he met, of his efforts to learn Russian, and, in fact, EVERYTHING he did EVERY DAY of his five-plus years of consequential service there. This is because John Quincy Adams meticulously kept a handwritten diary of his daily activities for **68 years**, from age 12 to his death at 81. The **fifty volumes** of this monumental work have been scanned and made available online at www.masshist.org/jqadiaries. There, for instance, I had little trouble finding in Diary number 29 John Quincy Adams' diary entries from February through April 1814 about meeting on more than one occasion with "an Irishman who spent time in Philadelphia" named Peter Dobell, including mention of Dobell's story about "being completely plundered" by Chinese pirates under the command of a woman. This conversation between Peter Dobell and John Quincy Adams I had earlier conjectured and included in the text, then, after the publication of the Claffey/Sikes article, I found the diary entry from John Quincy Adams that it had really happened...only did I have to change the venue.

Clark, Manning. A Short History of Australia. (Fourth revised edition). Penguin Books Australia, Ltd., 487 Maroondah Highway, P.O. Box 257, Ringwood, Victoria 3134, Australia. 1995. This is a classic work on Australian history, the focus here being on the status of things in Port Jackson and Sydney at the time Schaeffer passed through in 1814.

Cleeland, Hokulani. Olelo Oiwi Ke Kahua: He Puke A'o Olelo Hawai'i. Distributed by 'Aha Punana Leo, 1744 Kino'ole Street, Hilo, Hawai'i 96720. 1994. This is a modern pedagogical text for learning the Hawaiian language.

Connolly, James B. Master Mariner: The Life and Voyages of Amasa Delano. 1943. This is available at www.delanoye.org/Primary/AmasaXV.html. See also Delano, Amasa (below).

Cook, Chris (Editor and Contributor). A Kauai Reader: The Exotic Heritage of the Garden Island. Mutual Publishing, 1215 Center Street, Suite 210, Honolulu, HI 96816 (808-732-1709, fax 808-734-4094), ISBN 1-56647-006-8. This collection, typographically flawed for some reason (cf. pp. 47,8,9), includes useful mythology on Kauai's earlier Alii by King David Kalakaua (cf. pp. 40 for Mo'ikeha's contest recitation of his genealogical "kuauhau"), Chris Cook's article on "Kaumualii—Kauai's Last King," and Sheldon Dibble's 1838 version of "The Russian Incident."

Conrad, Agnes C. (ed.) The Letters and Journal of Francisco de Paula Marin. See entry under "Gast, Ross H."

Cordy, Ross H. A Study of Prehistoric Social Change: The Development of Complex Societies in the Hawaiian Islands. Academic Press (A Subsidiary of

Harcourt Brace Jovanovich Publishers. New York and elsewhere. 1981. In Chapter 7 (Epilogue) there is a section entitled "Hawaiian Oral Traditions and the Hypotheses" which lists the successions of Hawaiian rulers on the individual islands going back, by oral accounts, to the 13th century…see pp.200-15.

Cordy, Ross. Exalted Sits the Chief: The Ancient History of Hawai'i Island. Mutual Publishing. Honolulu, Hawaii. 2000. This is a wonderfully researched and detailed history of pre-contact Hawai'i Island…geneologies, family relationships, battles, heiaus, photos, site explanations…just amazing, and complete with copious sources and index.

Cordy, Ross. The Rise and Fall of the O'ahu Kingdom: A Brief Overview of O'ahu's History. Mutual Publishing, 1215 Center Street, Suite 210, Honolulu, HI 96816. 2002 (ISBN 1-56647-562-7). The detail of historical geographic description (e.g. moku and ahupua'a) here is valuable as is the table of rulers of O'ahu and the history itself.

Correa da Costa, Sergio. Every Inch a King: A Biography of Dom Pedro I, the First Emperor of Brazil. Translated from the Portuguese by Samuel Putnam. Robert Hale and Company. London. 1972 edition (reprinted from the original 1950 edition). This biography (230 pp.) is conventional in form in that it is chronological in narrative order, includes much valuable detail, and is equipped with a bibliography and an index. The author is a former Brazilian Ambassador to the Court of St. James (England) and, in November 1976, inscribed the copy I have to Zbigniew Brzezinski, U.S. Secretary of State during the tenure of President Jimmy Carter. Interesting is the contrast between this biography of Dom Pedro I and Gloria Kaiser's very different biography of Dom Pedro's wife, Dona Leopoldina (see below). It isn't so much a difference of fact…both biographies agree, for the most part, on the facts…but a difference of perspective and tone. Reading Kaiser's later work, I could not, in the absence of a bibliography, decide whether she had consulted the work by Correa da Costa. Correa da Costa mentions "Schaeffer" as a "devoted friend" of Leopoldina only twice, and the bibliography has no work specific to him or his activities in bringing Germans to Brazil. I also note that Correa da Costa's work is not included in the "bibliografia" of the 1973 work by Carlos H. Oberacker, Jr. on Schaeffer's bringing Germans to Brazil (see below). Only Oberacker cites Schaeffer's book, published in German in Altona (Hamburg) in 1824, on Brazil.

Craig, Robert. Captain Cook in the Pacific. Pamphlets Polynesia Series of the Institute for Polynesian Studies, Brigham Young University—Hawai'i Campus, Laie, HI 96762-1294. 1978. ISBN 0-939154-00-5. A 33-pp. overview, but accurate. Lacks a treatment of the disposition of the parts of Cook's body after his death.

Croft, Lee B. See my reviews on www.shvoong.com of: Daniel Harrington's www.hawaiianencyclopedia.com and Hanalei: A Kaua'i River Town; Bill Fernandez's Rainbows over Kapa'a; Donald Donohugh's The Story of Koloa: A Kaua'i Plantation Town; S. N. Hale'ole, et. al.'s La'eikawai; Neil Bernard Dukas' (below cited separately) A Pocket Guide to the Battle of Nu'uanu, 1795; Peter R. Mills' (cited below separately) Hawai'i's Russian Adventure: A New Look at Old History; Chuck Blay and Robert Siemers' Kaua'i's Geologic History: A Simplified Guide; and Raymond Massey's (cited separately below) Discovery of Hawai'i & Honolulu. Search shvoong under contiguous "LeeBCroft." Also reviews there, and on www.Amazon.com of North (2), and Armstrong.

Croft, Lee B. "A Chronology of George Anton Schaeffer's Life as Related by Lee B. Croft, Ph.D." A 10 pp. illustrated brochure, with recommended sources in English, Russian, and Portuguese, accompanying a lecture given at the Ship Store Gallery, 4-1379 Kuhio Hwy, Kapa'a, HI, on October 25th, 2011. See: http//www.shipstoregalleries.net.

Croft, Lee B. "George Anton Schaeffer: The Builder of Kaua'i's Russian Forts…And His Hawai'ian Fluency." Accepted in late 2010 for publication as a 4 pp. illustrated article in Pacific Journal (Tammi Andersland and John Lydgate, Editors), forthcoming.

Crosby, Alfred W., Jr. America, Russia, Hemp and Napoleon. Ohio State University Press. Columbus, Ohio. 1965. In Napoleon's time Russia produced most of the world's sailcloth fiber from its crops in Ukraine and elsewhere of hemp. The very word "canvas" is a contraction of "cannabis" from "Cannabis sativa," the Linnaeus designation for hemp. The Russian cognate is "kanoplia." The purpose here is to evidence Napoleon's desire to hamstring the British navy of its sail canvas by embargoing Russia's trade in hemp. See also the work of contemporary pot advocate Jack Herer, who calls Chapter 11 of his "The Emperor Wears No Clothes" "The Hemp War of 1812/Napoleon Invades Russia" at www.jackherer.com.

Cross, A.G. N.M.Karamzin: A Study of his Literary Career, 1783-1803. Southern Illinois University Press, Carbondale and Edwardsville/Feffer and Simons, Inc., London and Amsterdam. 1971. This study treats well Karamzin's involvement with freemasonry, but ceases its focus before the period of Napoleon's invasion.

Crouch, Tom D. The Eagle Aloft: Two Centuries of the Balloon in America. Smithsonian Institution Press. Washington, D.C. 1983. On pp. 120 is an illustration "The process of inflating a hydrogen balloon" ca. 1800.

Crowe, Ellie and William. Exploring Hawaii: Places of Power, History, Mystery, and Magic. Island Heritage Publishing. 94-411 Ko'aki Street,

Waipahu, Hawai'i 96797. First edition, second printing 2002. ISBN 0-89610-383-8. This work shows photographs of selected heiaus and other places on six of the Hawaiian islands with explanations of their historical significance and anecdotes about their spiritual power or "mana." A parenthesis in the introduction states, contrary to numerous other historical accounts, that "(Kamehameha I was over seven feet in height)," thus early establishing its primacy of mythology over a relation of objective reality...yet this is a work of value in its depiction of early Hawaiian life which was so dominated by concern for "mana" and mythology.

Currier, Dean P. "Adventures in Cybersound: Johann Wilhelm Ritter: 1776-1810." At http://www.acmi.net.au/AIC/RITTER_BIO.html, accessed May 16, 2002.

Damon, Ethel M. "George Prince Kaumualii," Fifty-fifth Annual Report of the Hawaiian Historical Society For the Year 1946. Honolulu Star Bulletin, Honolulu, 1948, pp. 10.

DauBach, Daniel Carl. Peter Dobell, 1775-1852: An American Opportunist in Russian Service in Early Nineteenth Century Siberia. University of Kansas Ph.D. dissertation, 1993. Available through University Microfilms International, 300 Zeeb Rd., Ann Arbor, MI 48106-1346 as order number 9425901. The internet presence of this work rephrases the title, replacing the word "opportunist" with "huckster." Dobell was from Philadelphia, but disavowed America and claimed to be an Irishman, being named Russian minister to the Philippines after trade activity in Canton. Dobell and Schaeffer never met, although their trails crossed several times...in Canton (Macao, Whampoa) and in St. Petersburg. Dobell's advice to the Russian government coincided with Schaeffer's as far as Hawai'i was concerned. He advocated a Russian annexation of the islands for trade purposes. See also Dobell (below).

Dauenhauer, Richard L. "Education in Russian America." In Russian America: The Forgotten Frontier. Barbara Sweetland Smith and Redmond J. Barnett, eds. Tacoma: The Washington State Historical Press. 1990. pp. 155-165.

Daws, Gavan. Shoal of Time: A History of the Hawaiian Islands. University of Hawaii Press. Honolulu, Hawaii. 1968 copyright, first printing in 1974. A most readable account, treating "Schaffer of Schafferthal" pages 49-53, foregrounding the sandalwood trade.

Day, A. Grove. "Georg Anton Scheffer: Russian Flags Over Hawaii" in Rogues of the South Seas. Foreword by James Michener. Mutual Publishing. Honolulu. 1986. An anecdotal treatment in a popular paperback, but accurate.

Day, A. Grove. Pacific Islands Literature: One Hundred Basic Books. University Press of Hawaii. Honolulu. 1971. In this collection of book synopses author A. Grove Day shares his vast knowledge of the literature of the Pacific Islands. Of particular interest to me here are the entries on William E. Giles "A Cruise in a Queensland Labour Vessel to the South Seas," describing an enterprise (called "blackbirding") which once involved my own Great Great Grandfather John Croft, who resided at his estate called "Mount Adelaide" on Darling Point in Sydney with wife Mary Stead Croft (died 7 March, 1857, interred with four children, who died in infancy, at Newtown's (Sydney) Camperdown Cemetery of Australian Pioneers) until returning to England with three surviving children in 1858, and Robert Dean Frisbie's "The Book of Puka-Puka" about life in the Cook Islands.

DEBRECEN. For city history, see http://www.debrecen.com/debrecen/angol/auth.html, accessed August 9, 2003. This is an outstanding city website, created by Editor-Systemorganiser Dr. Tamás Várhelyi and Web Constructor Dr. Laszló Szabó. The multipage site features streaming video of city and regional events. The text was written by Pál S. Varga and Pál Tóth, and is available in English. Copyright is held by OPTONET Co of Hadházi 38, Debrecen, Hungary 4028.

De Caulaincourt, General (Marquis) Armand, Duke of Vicenza. With Napoleon in Russia. The Universal Library. Grosset and Dunlap. New York. 1935 copyright by William Morrow and Company. These are the memoirs of an aide and confidant of Napoleon and a former French ambassador to the St. Petersburg court of Tsar Alexander I. It does not mention the balloon.

Delano, Amasa (1763-1823). A Narrative of Voyages and Travels in the Northern and Southern Hemispheres: Comprising Three Voyages Round the World; Together with a Voyage of Survey and Discovery in the Pacific Ocean and Oriental Islands. E. G. House. Boston. 1817. This work is the memoirs of American Revolutionary War hero and Boston "Master Mariner," Amasa Delano, who, after a visit to Hawai'i at Kealakekua Bay in 1801 on the *Perseverance,* carried away a son of Kamehameha's, calling himself Alexander Stewart (see text), together with four other Hawai'ian kanakas, to be trained as sailors and educated in the United States. Delano records innoculating the five kanakas with "kinepox" serum as they approached Canton, China, later that year. Thus a son of Kamehameha's was one of the first Hawai'ians vaccinated against smallpox. In Canton, this son transferred himself to a British Indiaman (trade ship) and was last heard of in London. See also the biography by James Connolly at www.delanoye.org/Primary/AmasaXV.html. Delano's adventures at sea inspired a short story by Herman Melville from 1855 entitled "Benito Cereno."

DERZHAVIN, GAVRIL ROMANOVICH. (1743-1816) Russian poet. See Glinka, and entries on Rezanov and especially Shelikhov, G.

Desha, Stephen L. Kamehameha and His Warrior Kekūhaupi'o. Translated by Frances N. Frazier. Kamehameha Schools Press. Honolulu, HI. 2000.

Dinklage, Karl Führer von. Münnerstadt mittelalterliches Kleinod. Würzburg. ca 1985. A history of Münnerstadt's position as the center of the Franconian catholic diocese.

Dobell, Peter. Travels in Kamchatka and Siberia: With a Narrative of a Residence in China. Arno Press Reprint. New York. 1970. Dobell wrote the original in 1828-30 based on articles he wrote in St. Petersburg's journal Syn Otechestva (Son of the Fatherland) in 1815-6 (cf. 1815, part 22, No. 25-6, str. 205; 1815, part 25, No. 45, str. 249; and 1815, part 26, No. 47, str.55) under the title "Otryvki iz zapisok puteshestvennika po Kamchatke i Sibiri" ("Excerpts from the Notes of a Traveler Through Kamchatka and Siberia"). As an advisor to the Russian-American Company, it is likely that he met Barbara Schaeffer while he was in St. Petersburg for the first time from 1814-1818 (he was there again later from 1827-1835, and yet again in 1852 where he died, after serving as Russian Consul to Helsingfors, Denmark, for 16 years) and that she likely read his notes. Peter Dobell traveled to Hawai'i not long after Schaeffer had left the islands, and later claimed to have acted to preserve Hawai'ian unity after the death of Kamehameha in 1819 by advising the successor Liholiho on how to deal with his father's leading chief, Kalanimoku. He is also the author of a pamphlet published in English in London in 1833 entitled "Russia as it is and not as it has been represented." Dobell is a character as colorful as Schaeffer...an American who disavowed his country, got involved in the opium trade in Canton, became a Consul for the Russian government...he was the uncle of Captain James Bennett of the wrecked *Bering* who accompanied Schaeffer to Hawai'i in 1815. Bennett, the son of Dobell's sister Ruth and her husband, Dobell's early partner, Samuel Bennett of Philadelphia, also had an adventurous life. In 1820 while with Dobell in Manila during a smallpox outbreak, he was captured and tortured by natives, but escaped. Dobell converted to Russian Orthodoxy and married a Russian woman, Dariia Andreevna, in Tobolsk in 1818, with whom he had children...but their fate is unknown. Peter and Dariia lived out their lives together, dying in the same year, 1852, in St. Petersburg...he at age 76, she at age 52. They were buried side-by-side in a catacomb beneath the floors of the Church of the Smolensk Mother of God in St. Petersburg. Part of their sepulcher was destroyed during the Soviet Civil War, ca. 1920, and reconstruction efforts in the 1990's did not include the preservation of their graves. See Bolkhovitinov and DauBach (above). Mention of Peter Dobell can be found as well in the diaries of John Quincy Adams (see Claffey and Sikes, above).

Dorrance, William H. O'ahu's Hidden History. Mutual Publishing, 1215 Center Street, Suite 210, Honolulu, HI 96816. Copyright 1998. Third Printing, March 2001 (ISBN 1-56647-211-3).

Dmytryshyn, Basil and E.A.P. Crownhart-Vaughan (translators and editors, with introduction and notes). <u>Colonial Russian America: Kyrill Khlebnikov's Reports, 1817-1832.</u> Oregon Historical Society, Portland. 1976. This is a great source of detail on the fur-trade values (appendix 1 has all furs taken by ship and captain from 1746-1797, and appendix 3 has all furs taken on Kodiak Island from 1803-1817 e.g.), the ships and their cargo and diverse other data defining life in Russia Alaska in this period…a very useful work by a personal acquaintance.

Duffy, Christopher. <u>Borodino and the War of 1812.</u> Charles Scribner's Sons. New York. 1973. Mention is made of Napoleon's horse, L'Embelli, ridden during the battle. Later, in other sources, two other horses are mentioned…L'Emir, on which he entered Moscow, and another (?) in addition to Blond's (passim) mention of the horse "Moscow." There is a chapter on "Borodino in History and Fiction," including synopses of the noted film treatments…e.g. the U.S. and USSR versions of <u>War and Peace.</u> For other works, including the "Virtual Battle of Borodino," see Ezerskaya, Kulagin, Mikherabidze and Monakhov below.

Duhem, Jules. "Le Ballon incendiaire de Moscou en 1812" in <u>Revue de l'Institute Napoleon.</u> Vol. 2, 2nd Quarter (1938), pp. 81-91. This article, a synopsis of the balloon project from French primary observers, confuses the parties but mentions a Würzburg physician 'nomme obscurement Sch...' (Schaeffer). There is also a sketch of the aerostat done by French officer de Segur, who investigated the Vorontsovo site after the balloon project's evacuation and interviewed local witnesses to it (see Napoleon, below, for a later 1876 German likeness from Tsar Alexander's archives).

Dukas, Neil Bernard. <u>A Military History of Sovereign Hawai'i.</u> Mutual Publishing. 1215 Center Street, Suite 210, Honolulu, HI 96816. First printing May 2004 (ISBN 1-56647-636-4). This is a fresh perspective on the Hawai'ian culture, characterizing the mana motivations for a warrior culture and its following military in the royal period of the 19th century.

Dukas, Neil Bernard. <u>A Pocket Guide to the Battle of Nu'uanu Pali: An Illustrated Guide to the O'ahu Battlefield.</u> Mutual Publishing, 1215 Center Street, Suite 210, Honolulu, HI 96816, First Printing May, 2010. ISBN 978-1-56647-922-6. I review this very fine work at http://www.shvoong.com/books/dictionary/2226308-pocket-guide-battle-nu-uanu/. It blazes new trails in the understanding of this important battle and features maps and site descriptions "then and now" with modern addresses given. Illustrators include Herb Kawainui Kane and Brook Kapukuniahi Parker.

Dwight, Edwin Welles, et. al. <u>Memoirs of Henry Obookiah, a Native of Owhyhee, and a Member of the Foreign Mission School, Who Died in Cornwall, Conn. Feb. 17, 1818, age 26 years.</u> Nathan Whiting, New Haven,

Conn., 1819. This book of memoirs is in the University of Hawai'i-Manoa's Hamilton Library's rare book collection at BV 3680.H4 O33 1819. Dwight is NOT directly related to the Rev. Timothy Dwight, President of Yale College. The collection includes an Inaugural Address (1817 formal opening of the Foreign Mission school where Obookiah and three other Hawai'ian youths (including Kaumuali'i's son Humehume or "George Prince Tomaree (see Warne below) were being 'christianized' and trained) by Governor John Treadwell of Connecticut, who is himself the author of A Narrative of Five Youths from the Sandwich Islands, J. Seymour, NY, 1816 (cited in Warne, below…I have not seen). The Obookiah memoirs are also published (and cited by Warne) as Memoirs of Henry Obookiah by the Kingsport Press of Kingsport, TN, 1968.

D'Wolf, John. A Voyage to the North Pacific. Ye Galleon Press. Fairfield, Washington. 1968. D'Wolf was an American trader who was the first to sell his ship to Aleksandr Baranov and the Russian-American Company. He then crossed Siberia to St. Petersburg on his way back to America, the first American to do so. The original version of this travelogue was published in Cambridge, Massachusetts in 1861.

EASTER ISLAND. For a description of Easter Island and its mysteries, see www.netaxs.com/trance/rapanui.html. The best starting place on the rapanui "hieroglyphics" is www.rongorongo.org. On the first page of this extremely rich website is mention of a link to the website by current Russian cryptanalyst Sergei Rjabchikov: www.openweb.ru/rongo, but, as is mentioned there, the link is very unreliable and the site almost never comes up. Instead, try it in the Google search field and then see it as stored in the Google cache…most of the links there also work.

Ebbets, John (New York Captain, 1775-1835, m. Sarah Woodward). See Steele, Edward E. below for a genealogical sketch of the Ebbets family.

Ellis, William. A Narrative of an 1823 Tour Through Hawai'i: With Remarks on the History, Traditions, Manners, Customs, and Language of the Inhabitants of the Sandwich Islands. Mutual Publishing, 1215 Center Street, Suite 210, Honolulu, HI 96816, 2004 edition (ISBN 1-56647-605-4). This is the journal, first published in 1825, of English-born missionary William Ellis (1794-1872) concerning his early days in Hawai'i. It is very interesting.

Emerson, Caryl. "Our Everything." In Slavic and East European Journal. Vol. 48, No. 1 (Spring 2004), pp. 79-98. This is a most comprehensive and detailed review of four recent biographies of Aleksandr Sergeevich Pushkin (1799-1837). Many of Pushkin's contemporaries and their relationships to him and to each other are discussed in this review. It gives its own picture of life in Russia after the expulsion of Napoleon and his army.

Engstrom, Elton and Allan Engstrom. Alexander Baranov and a Pacific Empire. Elton and Allan Engstrom, Box 723, Juneau, AK 99802. ISBN 0964570130.

Evatt, Herbert Vere (Justice of the High Court of Australia). Rum Rebellion: A Study of the Overthrow of Governor Bligh by John Macarthur and the New South Wales Corps. Includes the John Murtagh Macrossan Memorial lectures delivered at the University of Queensland, June 1937. Angus and Robertson Ltd. 89 Castelreigh Street. Sydney. 1938. This is a detailed and colorful treatment of the "Rum Rebellion" in the New South Wales Colony in 1808 against Governor William Bligh.

Ezerskaya, Irina. Frants Rubo I ego panorama 'Borodinskaja Bitva'. Izdatel'stvo gumanitarnoj literatury. Moskva. 2001. (ISBN 5-87121-011-2) The address of the Panorama Museum of the Battle of Borodino is 38 Kutuzovsky Prospect, 121170 Moscow, Russia. (telephone is 148-19-67, fax 148-94-89, e-mail b1812@online.ru). See "Borodino" above.

Faber du Faur (von), Christian Wilhelm. With Napoleon in Russia: The Illustrated Memoirs of Major Faber du Faur, 1812. See North, Jonathan (below). Also see my review of this work at www.Amazon.com.

Fenn, Elizabeth A. Pox Americana: The Great Smallpox Epidemic of 1775-82. Hill and Wang (Farrar, Straus and Giroux). New York. 2001. ISBN 0-8090-7821-X. This is a fine "personalized" historical treatment of the impact of smallpox.

FERDINAND III, GRAND DUKE OF TUSCANY and Archduke of Austria (Son of Holy Roman Emperor Leopold II and Princess Maria Luisa, infanta of Spain). For immediate family circumstances see http://www.wikipedia.org/w/wiki.phtml?title=Ferdinand_III%2C_Grand_Duke_Tuscany. Also very interesting, and including a fine color portrait of Ferdinand III is the genealogical work by Ingeborg Brigitte Gastel (1944-) at www.worldroots.com/brigitte/royal/habs-f.htm. This source is also definitive on the 13 children (by the first two wives, including the 12 with Elizabeth Wilhelmine Loise, Grand Duchess of Wurttemburg) of Franz Joseph II (Franz I), (1768-1835…Holy Roman Emperor Franz II until 1806, then Emperor Franz I of Austria until his death). See also mention of Ferdinand's role in Napoleon's marriage to Austrian Grand Duchess Marie Louise (Ferdinand's niece) at Fernwood, I. "Napoleon's Coronation as Emperor of the French," a 7-pp "E-article accessed January 15, 2002 at http://www.geocities.com/ifernwood/coronation/coronation.html.

FORT ROSS, CALIFORNIA. This was the southernmost outpost of the Russian-American Company, headed by Ivan Kuskov, a colorful character sent south from Sitka in 1811 by RAC Manager Alexander Baranov. See "History of the Russian Settlement at Fort Ross, California" at http://parks.sonoma.net/rosshist.html. See also www.basecamp.cnchost.com/fortross.htm. This latter site includes information from the Congress of Russian Americans that is also available at www.russian-americans.org/CRA_History.htm. This source is very good on both Alexander Baranov and Father Ioann Veniaminov (later Metropolitan and Saint Innokentii). On the character of Ivan Kuskov, I have tried to pin down the factuality from original sources of the occasionally published mention that Kuskov had a "peg-leg," and have been so far unable to do so. On this I note the museum in Tot'ma, Russia, Kuskov's home town to which he returned late in life with his wife, a native American. Sarah Gould of the guide staff at Fort Ross, who consulted with the producers of a recent television program on the Russian colonization of America (and which portrayed Kuskov with a peg-leg) has also been trying to identify the source of this allegation. I communicated and commiserated with her on it after finding her inquiry where I placed mine, at www.vologda-oblast.ru/chat.asp?Page=Object&Code=37&LNG=ENG.

So far (May 2005), there is no definitive original source. No contemporary of Kuskov's mentions any peg-leg (cf. e.g. Khlebnikov below). See also source by Watrous (below) and related "Role Play: Founding of Settlement Ross" at http://www.mcn.org/1/rrparks/fortross/Curriculum/roleplay.htm (accessed May 2005). This work includes much useful information about Fort Ross from Ivan Kuskov's 1821 census and reference to other works treating daily life in the settlement after its founding.

Fortuine, Robert, M.D. "Health and Medical Care in Russian America." In Russian America: The Forgotten Frontier. Barbara Sweetland Smith and Redmond J. Barnett, eds. Tacoma: The Washington State Historical Press. 1990. pp. 121-131.

Franchere, Gabriel. Narrative of a Voyage to Northwest Coast of America in the Years 1811, 1812, 1813, and 1814 of the First American Settlement on the Pacific. Translated and Edited by J. V. Huntington. Redfield. 110 and 112 Nassau Street. New York. 1854. The author, a Canadian working for John Jacob Astor's Pacific Fur Company, sailed on the *Tonquin* (Jonathan Thorn, Captain) from New York around Cape Horn to Hawaii and then the settlement called Astoria near the mouth of the Columbia River. His memoirs, which he wrote in 1819 and prepared for publication in the 1840's, provide historical accuracy to the related fiction of Washington Irving's novel Astoria (authored with Pierre Irving in 1836), which deals with some of the same dramatic events. The text here is a wonderful period piece with great detail concerning Kamehameha's Hawaii and western (coastal and inland) America during the time of the War of 1812 with England. It also gives a fine picture of life on a sailing ship at that time. The work is available completely online at http://roxen.xmission.com/~drudy/mrman/html/franchere/franchere.html. The story of how the *Tonquin*'s boatswain, John Anderson, a friend of character John Marshall in my relation, left the ship in Hawai'i, before its destruction, is in Chapter III, page 59.

FRANKENTHAL. The location in Brazil of George Schaeffer's initial plantation estate on that first square "legua" (2.5 km) of land was long a problem to me. I was mislead by the fact that modern maps show a "Leopoldina" and a reasonably nearby "Vila Vicosa" in the Minas Gerais State about 100 km north of Rio de Janeiro. I recall that Dr. Enrico Schaeffer, who, in 1959-60 described himself as a "collateral relative" of George Anton Schaeffer, wrote that he had tried to find the original estate of Frankenthal...and ostensibly George's grave... in the environs of Vila Vicosa and could not find any trace of it. The estate, he wrote, had "returned to the jungle." This may be true, but near which "Vila Vicosa" was he searching? My reading carefully through George Schaeffer's German book on Brazil and my search with internet advantage and Google Earth indicates to me that the site of the Frankenthal estate is inland along the Peruipe River from the modern extreme southern Bahia State city of Nova Vicosa...which in 1824 was named, as George writes, "Vila Vicosa." The site of Georg Wilhelm Freyreiss's colony, that George Schaeffer describes as being "downstream" from his Frankenthal estate, is to be found in the municipality of Helvecia...which in 1824 was named "Colonia Leopoldina." George's description includes the –18 degrees latitude, the River Peruipe's north bank overlooking the confluence of the tributary stream he calls "Jackarander," the downstream location of Freyreiss's colony, and the largest nearby city being "Vila Vicosa" that has needed things in abundance and from where agricultural products of his estate might easily be shipped to more populous markets. Thus, I am convinced that FRANKENTHAL is on this north bluff above the confluence of the Peruipe River and the Jackarander Stream about 25 KM upstream from the municipality of Helvecia (Colonia Leopoldina in George's time)which is 20 KM inland on the Peruipe from the substantial city of Nova Vicosa (Vila Vicosa in George's time) which is 750 km (i.e. five to seven weeks of overland mule travel in George's time, crossing a succession of rivers by ferry and ford, or a week's travel by ship if the wind is right) to Rio de Janeiro. The Minas Gerais sites called Leopoldina and Vila Vicosa are "red herrings" and do NOT meet George's detailed description of the location of his estate.

Freyreiss, G. Wilhelm. <u>Reisen in Brasilien.</u> The Ethnological Museum of Sweden Monograph Series, Publication number 13, Stockholm, 1968. Freyreiss (1789-1825) followed George Heinrich von Langsdorff to Brazil and led an exploratory expedition to the Minas Gerais area of Brazil in 1814-1815, previous to Langsdorff's own first expedition of 1816-17 mentioned in this book. Freyreiss was the leader of the "Leopoldina Colony" of Germans in the Vila Vicosa area, and is mentioned in Schaeffer's 1824 book. Freyreiss was a participant of Langsdorff's later expedition in the early 1820's and, like Schaeffer, wrote a book about Brazil in 1824 that was published in Germany the year before his death in 1825.

Frisbie, Robert Dean ("Ropati" in his works). <u>The Island of Desire</u>. Doubleday/Doran. New York. 1944. This work and others by Pacific island writer Frisbie inspired the residence of Tom Neale on Suvarov island…which was described to Neale by Frisbie as the most beautiful atoll in the Pacific. As Frisbie inspired Neale, so Frisbie was himself inspired by the writer James Norman Hall (1887-1951), co-author with Charles Nordhoff (1887-1947) of Mutiny on the Bounty. On these prolific authors on South Seas life, A. Grove Day recommends the biographical work by Paul L. Briand, Jr., In Search of Paradise: The Nordhoff-Hall Story (Duell, Sloan and Pearce, New York, 1966).

Gast, Ross H. Don Francisco de Paula Marin: A Biography; The Letters and Journal of Francisco de Paula Marin. Edited by Agnes C. Conrad. University of Hawai'i Press (2840 Kolowalu Street, Honolulu, HI 96822, www.uhpress.hawaii.edu) for the Hawaiian Historical Society, Honolulu, 1973, ISBN 0-945048-09-2. See Lee, Blanche (below) for a varying view about Marin's introduction of the pineapple to Hawai'i. Also Ten Bruggencate (below).

Gately, Iain. Tobacco: A Cultural History of How an Exotic Plant Seduced Civilization. Grove Press. New York. 2001. ISBN0-8021-3960-4. This interesting work informs the stance of Schaeffer and his wife towards tobacco.

Gibson, James R. Imperial Russia in Frontier America: The Changing Geography of Supply of Russian America, 1784-1867. With cartographer Miklos Pinther. Oxford University Press. New York. 1976. Table 7, pp. 78, has a log of supply ships' journeys, including the Suvorov under "Lt. M. P. Lazarev, 1813-6, value of cargo 246,476 rubles."

GIRARD, STEPHEN (1750-1831, Philadelphia magnate, philanthropist and early mentor of Peter Dobell…see above under Dobell, DauBach). Girard was wealthy enough by 1812 to bankroll the United States during its war with England and prevent its bankruptcy. He is a very eccentric character in American history and had an interesting personal life, involving a wife who was committed to a lunatic asylum, two long-term mistresses, and African-american slave named Hannah. See: www.ushistory.org/Girard or www.famousamericans.net/stephengirard. There is a feminist play by Laine Robertson entitled The Insanity of Mary Girard loosely based on Girard's relationship with his wife, Mary Lum Girard, and her life in the asylum. See http://students.washcoll.edu/Club-Pages/rsp/01_MaryGirard.html. There is even a man named Allen Hampton, an employee of the Pennsylvania Hospital in Philadelphia (endowed by Stephen Girard) who reports a 1999 dream about a "Sally (Bickham) Girard" at www.wirenot.net/X/Stories/Ghost/Ghost%20C-D/DreamofMaryandMistress.sthml.

Glinka, Natal'ia Ivanovna. Derzhavin v Peterburge. ("Derzhavin in Petersburg"). Leninizdat. Leningrad. 1985. This work describes the great poet Gavriil Romanovich Derzhavin's (1743-1816) activities in St. Petersburg and gives a list of his places of residence in the city and their more modern addresses. There is a floor plan and an illustration of his residence and garden on the fontanka near the Obukhov bridge. Derzhavin was once Nikolai Rezanov's superior. He wrote a poem characterizing M. S. Golikov and another memorializing Gregorii Ivanovich Shelikhov (see Shelikhov, below).

Glusing, Jean. "Brasilien Reproduktive Bauche" in Der Spiegel, Vol. 25 (2001), pp. 148. This article describes the selective breeding of African slaves in Brazil, particularly one "Santa Clara" estate of a Francisco Thereziano de Bustamente 250 kilometers west of Rio de Janeiro which masked its notorious slave breeding with coffee operations. The Bustamente operation began in 1824 and continued until his death in 1860. Glusing cites a "classic work" called "Herrenhaus und Sklavenhutte" by "Sociologist and Historian Gilberto Feyre Schildert" (undated) who describes how the slaves were considered "only reproductive vessels" and how the slave buyers were instructed to pay strict attention to the Negroes' sexual organs and reject any slaves who had undersized or misshapen organs. Despite several descriptions to the contrary (e.g. the early Brazilian Viceroy Lavradio or Wilhelm Humboldt), Schaeffer, in his 1824 work, describes the conditions of slave transport to be better than that for the transport of soldiers of the time.

Golovnin, Vasilii M. Around the World on the *Kamchatka*, 1817-1819. (Translated with introduction and notes by Ella Lury Wiswell (who once taught Russian to the parents of President Barack Obama, who met in her class)). University of Hawaii Press. Manoa. 1979. ISBN is 0-8248-0640-9.

Gomes, Dival da Costa. "Independence of Brazil: Expertise and Personalities of Maçonaria," at www.triplov.com/carbonaria/dival_gomes_costa/independencia_brasil/masonry.htm. This treats Schaeffer's contributions to founding the German Emigration to Brazil, listing the families' names of those brought to Brazil by ships Schaeffer chartered (see also Weissheimer below) and lamenting that this brother mason is not mentioned on any memorials thereby...no streets or plazas or cities named after him, etc. See also Weissheimer (below).

Govor, Elena. "Russian Ships in Australia During the First Half of the XIX Century," "Russian Convicts in Australia," "The Russian Odyssey of the Governor Macquarie," "The 'Otkrytie i Blagonamerennyi' in Australia," and (with Alexander Massov) "'Neva'—the First Russian Naval Ship in Australia." These wonderfully detailed articles, complete with tables and illustrations, are accessible at www.argo.net.au/andre/... adding final strings for each: russhipsbeforeCWENFIN.htm; RussianconvictsENFIN.htm; MacquarieENFIN.htm; OTKRYTIEenfin.htm; and nevaENFIN.htm. Since the *Neva* (under Lieutenant Leontii Andrianovich Gagemeister, 1807), the *Otkrytie* (Capt.-Lieutenant Mikhail Nikolaevich Vasiliev, 1820) and the *Blagonamerennyi* (Lieutenant Gleb Semyonovich Shishmarev, 1820) were Russian navy ships, the ships' logs and officers diaries became widely known public records, whereas the 1814 visit of the *Suvorov* was officially a venture of the Russian-American Company. The ship's log and the diaries of the parties involved were not public records and are therefore not as available to historians' examination. One specific memoir, that of "podshturman" Aleksei Ivanovich Rossiyskiy, and excerpts from Lieutenants Lazarev and Unkovskiy are included in the work, Russkie flotovodtsy: M.P.Lazarev: Dokumenty ("Russian Fleet Commanders: M.P. Lazarev: Documents") by Andrei A. Samarov (cf. below).

Grant, Glen. Waikiki Yesteryear. Mutual Publishing, 1215 Center Street, Suite 210, Honolulu, HI 96816. Copyright 1996. Third Printing, June 2002. (ISBN 1-56647-107-9). This work has many historical photographs of the Waikiki area and includes good topographical description of early Waikiki.

Grantham, Fred W. Did America Overthrow the Kingdom of Hawai'i & Steal the Hawaiian Islands? (For Those Who Want to Know!). Royal Designs, 44-106 BayView Haven Place, Kaneohe, HI 96744, copyright 2005 to F.W. Grantham. On page 14 of this work, author Grantham mentions the Russian presence in Honolulu during the reign of Kamehameha I. One particular detail of his narration caught my eye...a parenthesis saying "a memento of this action, we believe, is the Russian ship's cannon that is on display in Walker Park off Nimitz Hwy, right across from Honolulu Harbor and the Hawaiian Electric plant right on our waterfront." It took me awhile to find Walker Park mauka across Nimitz/Ala Moana from the Ewa side of the Aloha Tower Center...dedicated to the Mr. Walker who headed Amfac and was prominent in Hawaiian and Honolulu development...nice. There IS an old, looks to have been once submerged, cannon there on a wooden carriage that may have been added for purposes of land display later. It is a VERY heavy cast-iron cannon with no markings to be seen by the naked eye...it is a bit more than 10 feet in length, tapering from about 20" in diameter at the butt to 10" at the muzzle. The caliber is just a hair shy of 6". If author Grantham is correct (and I think he may well be), then *this is yet another physical memento that I have touched with my hands* that George Anton Schaeffer likely once touched (like the rocks of his Kaua'i forts, a copy of his 1824 book, the door of the Juliusspital in Würzburg...). He was in command of the Russian-American Company ship *Kadiak* when it came to Honolulu in the first days of July 1817 after he had been forcibly expelled

Author Lee B. Croft with the cannon alleged to be from the RAK ship *Kadiak* (sunk at Honolulu Harbor shoreline July 5-6, 1817). Photo by Lesley Hoyt Croft, September 2011.

from Kaua'i. It was leaking terribly...the men pumping twenty feet or more of water out of it daily. On 4 July 1817 George was rescued off it by Captain Isaiah Lewis of the *Panther* as George and his men were about to attack another ship and sail away on it in escape, since Kamehameha's advisor John Young and the British and American advisors wanted to kill George. After George was sailed away, the *Kadiak* sank on 5 and 6 July to the bottom of Honolulu harbor, very likely very close to the display position its cannon (if it IS a cannon from the *Kadiak*) now occupies, since the shoreline in 1817 was surprisingly inland of the current shoreline, as shown by an extent 1810 map. It was reportedly found during the excavation of the basement of the Amfac Building at a considerable depth of 15 feet below ground level. Grantham is correct that the rest of the Russians and Aleuts on the *Kadiak* were allowed to stay peacefully in their previous Waikiki settlement until Russian America Governor Alexander Baranov could send a ship to bring them back to Novo-Arkhangelsk (Sitka) in Alaska.

Gräter, Dr. Carlheinz (text), Elmar Hahn (photography) and Tina Neil (English Transl.). Würzburg: Tourist Guide. Elmar Hahn Verlag. Veitshöchheim. 4th revised ed. 2002. This guide book includes a table of "Important Dates in Würzburg's History."

Gray, Robert. Captain Robert Gray (1755-1806) is the namesake of Gray's Harbor on the northwest coast and the discoverer and namer of the Columbia River after his ship *Columbia* on which he, together with Captain John Kendrick (1745-1794, of the *Lady Washington*) explored and traded in the north Pacific in the 1780's and 1790's. See www.oregonpioneers.com/gray.htm. See also the entries on Kendrick, John and by Scofield, John (below). Also Ridley, Scott (below).

Greer, Richard A. "Memoirs of Thomas Hopo'o" in Hawaiian Journal of History (A Publication of the Hawaiian Historical Society), Vol. II (1968), pp. 42-54.

Greer, Richard A. "Along the Old Honolulu Waterfront" in Hawaiian Journal of History (A Publication of the Hawaiian Historical Society), Vol. XXXII (1998), pp. 25-66. Good detailed history, with included maps from 1810 and others, of Honolulu and environs, with relation of related events and historical developments.

GRIEB, BALTHASAR. The Brazilian family of descendents of this "Balthasar Grieb," whose last name has now changed to "Gripp," is responsible for relating online the tale of the "ill-fated journey of the ship *Argus*." See this at http://www.gripp.com.br/Historicofam.htm. I suggest "googling" "George Anton Schaeffer" and then, on page 3 of listed sites, clicking on the "translate this page" instruction. See also related genealogy at Weissheimer (below).

Griess, Thomas E. (Series Editor). West Point Atlas for the Wars of Napoleon. Square One Publishers. Garden City Park, New York, 11040. (telephone 516-535-2010...cf. www.squareonepublishers.com). 2003. This is a large-format compendium of military-style maps of troop movements, etc. There are six maps describing the stages of Napoleon's "Russian Campaign" (pp. 46-52).

Grimsted, Patricia K. The Foreign Ministers of Alexander I: Political Attitudes and the Conduct of Russian Diplomacy, 1801-1825. Berkeley, Ca. University of California Press. 1969.

Gusliarov, Evgenii. Vse dueli Pushkina. ("All the Duels of Pushkin"). Iantarnyi skaz. Kaliningrad. 2001. This work lists the circumstances of 21 conflicts the poet Aleksandr Sergeevich Pushkin (1799-1837) had over "points of honor" in which duels were mentioned, avoided, or took place. One of these (#14, pp. 72-75) concerns Pushkin's conflict with Count Fyodor Tolstoi, the American, and lists several memoirists' impressions of Tolstoi, including those of M. I. Semenovskii from conversation with Aleksei Vul'f, F. N. Luginin, Tolstoi's niece M. F. Kamenskaia, and Faddei Bulgarin. The artist A. Il'in provides a drawing of Tolstoi in his room, adorned as described by Kamenskaia with artifacts of Aleutian tribes and with the backs of his hands tattooed (pp. 75).

Gutmanis, June. Hawaiian Herbal Medicine. Translations by Theodore Kelsey. Illustrations by Susan G. Monden. Island Heritage Publishing.
94-411 Kō'aki Street, Waipahu, HI 96797. First edition, copyright 1976, fifteenth printing in 2004 (ISBN 0-89610-330-7). This work includes also a glossary of medical terms in Hawaiian.

Gutmanis, June. Na Pule Kahiko: Ancient Hawaiian Prayers. Drawings by Susanne Indich. An Editions Limited Book, P.O. Box 10150, Honolulu, HI 96816, 1983 (fourth printing, ISBN 0-9607938-6-0). Explanations and translations of native Hawai'ian prayers for a host of purposes. No mention, however, of Kaumuali'i's "Ane'ekapuahi" prayer, though "praying a person to death" is treated with a specific example of the prayer and the ritual (p. 27-8).

Handy, Willowdean Chatterson. Tattooing in the Marquesas. 2008 Dover Publications edition, Mineola, New York (ISBN 978-0-486-46612—5) from the original Bernice P. Bishop Museum Publication of 1922. Mentions Langsdorff's and Krusenstern's descriptions of tattoos from Nuku Hiva and elsewhere. See also Krutak and Kwiatkowski on tattoos.

Hartley, Janet M. Alexander I. Profiles in Power Series. Longman Group. London and New York. 1994. Here are the roles of Lord Castelreagh and George Canning as British Foreign Ministers in relations with Prince Clement Metternich in the chapter "Master of Europe: 1815-1825."

Haughton, Christine. Herb Profiles. Revised September 23, 2001. http://www.purplesage.org.uk/profiles. accessed April 11, 2002.

HAWAI"I…history of: For foreign ship contact see the list of "Ships to Hawaii Before 1819" at www.Hawaiian-roots.com/shipsB1880.htm. This is a very useful work, though not complete. See Howay (below). And, see these labors of love on Hawai'ian history: Daniel Harrington's http://www.hawaiianencyclopedia.com; and the new blogs: Peter T. Young's exciting and vital http://totakeresponsibility.blogspot.com/2012 and the related http://hookuleana.com; and the still unknown-to-me "Island Expat's" http://hawaiiantimemachine.blogspot.com/2011/.

Haycox, Stephen W. "Merchants and Diplomats: Russian America and the United States." In Russian America: The Forgotten Frontier. Barbara Sweetland Smith and Redmond J. Barnett, eds. Tacoma: The Washington State Historical Press. 1990. pp. 55-73.

Hellberg, Harry. Anders Ljungstedt och breven från Kina. Stalgarden Publishing House. Sweden. (undated…87 pp. 150 SEK, ISBN 91-87262-23-6). Hellberg, formerly Dean of Anders Ljungstedt College in Linköping, Sweden, is the author of this Swedish biography of Anders Ljungstedt. See Ljungstedt (below).

Helminger, Berhard. Mozart: His Life in Salzburg. Colorama. Salzburg. 2nd English edition of March 2002. An illustrated version of Mozart's life in Salzburg. Cf. portrait of Prince-bishop Hieronymus Graf von Colloredo, pp. 25 and entry under "1781."

Henry, Alexander (the Younger). (ca. 1765-1814) New Light on the Early History of the Greater Northwest: The Manuscript Journals of Alexander Henry and of David Thompson, 1799-1814. Elliot Coues, Ed. Ross and Haines. Minneapolis, MN. 1965, a republication of that by Francis P. Harper, New York, 1897. Three volumes, with three maps, 1027 pp. This is a treatment of interesting figures in the early fur trade. Also see: The Journal of Alexander Henry the Younger, 1799-1814. Barry Gough, Ed. Published by the Champlain Society and the University of Toronto Press. Toronto. 1988, and, about the interesting women (Jane Barnes, Isobell Gunn, and Anna Petrovna Bulygin) encountered by Henry, see the article by Alan Twigg for the BC Bookworld Author Bank at www.abcbookworld.com/?state=view_author&author_id=8484.

HERMAN, (Father or Elder, and later Saint, Herman of Alaska…1756-1837). The hermitic Father Herman (Elder Germann in the text), ministering on Kodiak Island and later at New Valaam on Spruce Island from 1794 on, opposed Manager Baranov and his policies because of perceived cruelty and exploitation of the Aleut population. On this see www.conciliarpress.com/again/content/view/55/31/9/9/ and also the explanation of an icon depicting Herman's activities at www.sspeterpaul.org/stherman.htm.

Hibberd, Isaac Norris. Sixteen Times Round Cape Horn: The Reminiscences of Captain Isaac Norris Hibberd. Foreword by Frederick H. Hibberd. Mystic Seaport Museum, Incorporated. Mystic, Connecticut. 1980. This is a valuable reminiscence of day to day details of life on a sailing ship going 'round the horn' in the later nineteenth century.

Hiroa, Te Rangi (Sir Peter H. Buck). Arts and Crafts of Hawaii. Bernice P. Bishop Museum Special Publication 45. Bishop Museum Press. Honolulu, HI. Copyright 1957. This is a classic treatment of Hawaiian arts and crafts with copious drawings and related historical anecdotes by a former (1936-1951) Director of the Bishop Museum. When it comes to pre-contact Hawaiian life and how things were done, what it doesn't have in it, you don't need. It's just amazingly comprehensive and detailed.

Hobbs, Christopher, L.Ac., A.H.G. Valerian and Other Anti-Hysterics in European and American Medicine (1733-1936). http://www.healthy.net/asp/templates/article.asp?PageType=Article&ID=961.

Ho'omāka'ika'i: Explorations! Compiled by the staff of the Kamehameha Schools Explorations Program (1968—summers). Fourth Edition. Kamehameha Publishing, 567 South King Street, Honolulu, HI 96813, 2007 (ISBN 978-0-87336-074-6). A wonderful illustrated textbook on the "foundations" of Hawai'ian culture.

Hopkins, Alberta Pualani. Ka Lei Ha'aheo: Beginning Hawaiian. University of Hawaii Press. Honolulu, Hawaii. 1992. This is a beginning Hawaiian language text.

Horwitz, Tony. Blue Latitudes: Boldly going Where Captain Cook Has Gone Before. Henry Holt and company. New York. 2002. This work provides most detailed descriptions of what it was like to sail long distances by sailing ship in the late 18th century. Horwitz describes a voyage on a replica of Captain James Cook's *Resolution*.

Howay, Frederic William, editor. The Voyage of the New Hazard, 1810-1813 (by Stephen Reynolds). Peabody Museum Publication, Salem, Mass., No. 49, pp. 148-9.

Howay, Frederic William. "The Last Days of the Atahualpa, Alias Bering," in The Forty-first Annual Report of the Hawaiian Historical Society for the Year 1932. Printshop Co., Honolulu, 1933, pp. 70-80.

Howay, Frederic William (Judge F.W. Howay, F.R.S.C., 1867-1943). "An Outline Sketch of the Maritime Fur Trade." Annual Meeting Presidential Address (see the entry below for information on the possible scholarly organizations to which Howay might have given a "presidential address"). Available at http://cha-shc.ca/bilingue/addresses/1932.htm.

Howay, Judge F. W., F.R.S.C. "A List of Trading Vessels in the Maritime Fur Trade, 1785-1794." Available at http://web.uvic.ca/~jlutz/courses/hist469/howay1.html. This work is also published posthumously with Richard Pierce as "A List of Trading Vessels in the Maritime Fur Trade, 1785-1794," Materials for the Study of Alaskan History, Limestone Press, Kingston, Ontario, 1973. Elsewhere online one can find Howay's expansion of the listing of ships to the year 1804, though this is not as complete. When you think you've done some historical digging and that the digging has gotten impressively comprehensive, then you encounter such work as this…the fruit of Howay's avocation for many years…and realize that you've only just begun. It is from this work, for example, that I discovered that "Alexander Stewart," the namesake of one of Kamehameha's sons, the one taken away by Captain Amasa Delano in 1801, was the master of the *Jackal* that had visited Hawai'i ten years before, when Kamehameha's son was ten years old. See also the essay on Howay entitled "Judge Howay—A Collector, the Student" at http://www.library.ubc.ca/spcoll/how_reid/howay.html. Another site for finding the whereabout of various ships in particular segments of time is www.Hawaiian-roots.com/shipsB1880.htm.

Hunsaker, Joyce Badgley. Sacagawea Speaks: Beyond the Shining Mountains with Lewis and Clark. A TwoDot Book of the Globe Pequot Press. P.O. Box 480 Guilford, Connecticut 06437. ISBN 1-58592-079-7. First edition/First printing. Copyright 2001. This is an edifying and valuable work on the "Corps of Discovery," treating Sacagewea's role from a first-person point of view. Much of the travel technology of the day is included, with specific illustrations…tea in cakes, sugar in cones, tobacco in braids and twists, the fire starter kit, the writing kit, the artist kit, the medical kit and its medicines, the muskets, including the calibers and the espontoon as a firing brace, the swivel-mounted blunderbuss and cannon. All of these things were part of George Schaeffer's life of travel also…as was the relationship between the Native and European American cultures.

Hunsche, Karl-Heinrich. Früheste Berichte über Schicksale deutscher Auswanderer nach Brasilien. Acht Todesurteile auf hoher see. Major von Schäffers "Seelenverkäuferey." Em: "Kalender fuer die Deutschen in Brasilien" (Rotermund-Kalender), 1937, p. 37 ss.

Hunsche, Karl-Heinrich. Major von Schäffers "Seelenverkäuferey." Eine "Unterthänigste Bittschrift" aus dem Jahre 1825. Em: "Kalender fuer die Deutschen in Brasilien" (Rotermund-Kalender), 1938, p. 38 ss.

Ii, John Papa. Fragments of Hawaiian History. Bishop Museum Press, 1525 Bernice Street, Honolulu, Hawaii. Copyright 1959. Sixth printing revised 1995. John Papa Ii was a personal witness to Hawaiian affairs since the time of Kamehameha I, having been attached to the Hawaiian royal household as a youth.

Iversen, Eve. The Romance of Nikolai Rezanov and Concepcion Arguello: A Literary Legend and its Effect of California History. Edited and with historical notes by Richard A. Pierce (see Pierce below). Alaska History No. 48. The Limestone Press. Kingston, Ontario and Fairbanks, Alaska. 1998.

James, Van. Ancient Sites of Kaua'i, Moloka'i and Lana'i. Mutual Publishing, 1215 Center Street, Suite 210, Honolulu, HI 96816. 2001. (ISBN 1-56647-529-5). A very concise work, with illustrations, photos, and sketched maps with the Hawaiian names.

James, Van. Ancient Sites of Hawai'i: Archaelogical Places of Interest on the Big Island. Mutual Publishing, 1215 Center Street, Suite 210, Honolulu, HI 96816. 1995. (ISBN 1-56647-200-8). An earlier volume in the series above…also one by James on O'ahu.

Joesting, Edward. Hawaii: An Uncommon History. W.W. Norton and Company, inc. New York. 1972. "Scheffer" is treated pages 60-64.

Joesting, Edward. Kauai: The Separate Kingdom. University of Hawaii Press and Kauai Museum Association, Ltd. Honolulu and Lihue, HI. 1984. A scholarly treatment, especially on King Kaumualii, with a fine bibliography.

Juliusspital. For information on the Juliusspital in Würzburg, Germany, consult: http://www.juliusspital.de. See below for "Würzburg" as well.

Kaeppler, Adrienne L. "Feather Cloaks, Ship Captains, and Lords." <u>Occasional Papers of Bernice P. Bishop Museum.</u> Vol. XXIV, No. 6 (July 8, 1970). Honolulu, HI. This is a treatment of the histories of notable particular feather cloaks, the 'ahu'ula of the Hawai'ian Ali'i, including the Kintore Cloak and the Elgin Cloak which wound up for a time in the hands of British lords. In this well illustrated monograph author Kaeppler states that "of the approximately 50 cloaks known today, 20 are still (1970, ostensibly) in the British isles."

Kaiser, Gloria. <u>Dona Leopoldina: The Habsburg Empress of Brazil</u>. Translated from the German by Lowell A. Bangerter with an Afterword by Ernestine Schlant. Ariadne Press. Riverside, California. 1998. The German work was published by Verlag Styria in Austria and Germany in 1994. The narrative is not chronological and incorporates dreams and hallucinations attributed to Dona Leopoldina as she is dying in 1826. The work is feminist in tone and elevates the role of Dona Leopoldina in establishing an independent Brazil over that of her husband, Dom Pedro I, who is portrayed quite negatively, especially as regards the issue of slavery. "Schäffer" is mentioned several times, but the description of him and his role in Leopoldina's life is seriously flawed (age, physical description, official position(s), apparent marital status and fidelity, personal wealth…all in error). Nevertheless, despite the lack of scholarly apparatus (e.g. no index), there is a great deal of useful detail about the lives of Dona Leopoldina and Dom Pedro I…and about European politics of the time…that can be gleaned from the "innovative" text here.

Kamakau, Samuel M. <u>Ruling Chiefs of Hawaii</u> (Revised edition). Kamehameha Schools Press. Honolulu, Hawaii. 1992 revision of the 1961 printing of this seminal history of the Hawaiian chiefs "from the time of 'Umi, eighteen generations before Kamehameha the Great, until the time of Kamehameha III in the 1840s" (when Kamakau wrote his original work).

Kamakau, Samuel Manaiakalani. <u>Ka Po'e Kahiko: The People of Old.</u> Translated from the Newspaper <u>Ke Au 'Oko'a</u> by Mary Kawena Pukui. Arranged and Edited by Dorothy B. Barrére. Illustrated by Joseph Feher. Bernice P. Bishop Museum Special Publication 51. Bishop Museum Press. Honolulu, HI. 1991. Tales of old Hawai'i by seminal historian Kamakau have good treatments of the family 'aumāku'a, medical practices and sorcery...e.g. "praying a person to death" and its consequences (cf. pp. 36-37 under "Kuni rituals").

Kame'eleihiwa, Lilikalā. <u>Native Land and Foreign Desires: Pehea Lā E Pono Ai?</u> (A History of Land Tenure Change in Hawai'i from Traditional Times until the 1848 Māhele, including an Analysis of Hawai'ian Ali'i Nui and American

Calvinists). Bishop Museum Press, Honolulu, HI. 2003 edition of 1992 copyright work (ISBN 0-930897-59-5). This is a very thoroughly researched and acute work on the concept of land ownership and its attribution in pre and post-contact times. Especially useful is the explanation of the Ali'i Nui's motivations, based on their endeavor to increase the "mana" of their place in the genealogy of rulers. The genealogies and the relationships of the Ali'i to the missionaries and their teaching are very detailed and insightful. This is a key work to understanding many philosophical and religious aspects of the European/Hawai'ian contact era.

KAMEHAMEHA I (The Great, (1758?-1819)), Sources here that touch on Kamehameha are many, but see: Adams, Barratt (3,4), Bartholomew, Birkett, Bolkhovitinob (1,2,3), Bushnell, Cahill, Charlot, Choris, Cordy (2,3), Crowe, Daws, Delano, Desha, Dorrance, Dukas (1,2), HAWAI'I, Ii, Joesting (1.2), Kamakau (1,2), Kane (2), Kotsebue, Kuykendahl, Levathes, Lundberg, Mahr, Malo, Mazour, Mehnert, Mills (2), Pierce (1,6), Pratt, Soboleski (1,2), Tregaskis, Warne (1,2), Wichman (2), Williams, Wisniewski, Withington.

Kane, Charlotte N. "Descendents of Kaumuali'i (1776-1824)" accessed in 2009 at http://familytreemaker.genealogy.com/users/k/a/n/Charlotte-Kane-HI/PDFGENE02.pdf.

Kane, Herb Kawainui. Voyagers: A Collection of Words and Images. WhaleSong, inc. (1-800-Whale-89). Bellevue, Washington. 1991. Kane, who has been elected a "Living Treasure of Hawaii," has read everything there is in print about Hawaiian-European contact history and gives his version of diverse aspects of it in this wonderful book. Prominent in this work is the treatment of the native Pacific sailing vessels and canoes. Schaeffer is not mentioned.

Kane, Herb Kawainui. Ancient Hawaii. The Kawainui Press. Captain Cook, Hawaii. 1997. A wonderfully illustrated, by Kane's art, relation of Hawaiian history and especially pre-contact customs. Kane is a resident of South Kona.

Kane, Herb Kawainui. Pele: Goddess of Hawaii's Volcanoes. The Kawainui Press. Captain Cook, Hawaii. Expanded edition, ninth printing, 2000. Here are stories and mythology associated with Pele. Kane includes some interesting personal experiences of a supernatural nature.

Karskens, Grace. The Rocks: Life in Early Sydney. Melbourne University Press. Carlton, Victoria. 1997. This is the definitive scholarly history of the "Rocks" area of Sydney. Author Karskens generally tries to refute or to explain away the stereotypic view of the Rocks as an uncivilized, wild and wooly place that preyed on visiting seamen. Nevertheless, the area's colorful history shines through, augmented by Karsken's very thorough scholarship. See also Messent's work below.

KAUA'I MUSEUM. There is an exhibit on "Russians on Kauai" at this museum, 4428 Rice Street, Lihue, HI 96766…see www.kauaimuseum.org (808-245-6931). Included is "Georg Anton Scheffer" with a concise but accurate recent rewriting of the information about him, including mention of the Russian balloon episode and the Brazilian emigration work. The only likeness of Schaeffer is represented by the oil painting there by Ardis Hertford, done in 1845, nine years after Schaeffer's death—meaning that it was done either from memory of a personal encounter (likely in his Brazil period) or by the description of others. It shows Schaeffer from the right side with bushy gray sideburns, beard and moustache. He is wearing a brown coat with medals and awards.

This is the Ardis Hertford portrait of Dr. "Georg Anton Schaffer" from 1845 that hangs in the Kaua'i Museum in Lihue, Hawaii. From: http://en.wikipedia.org/wiki/Georg_Anton_Schaffer.

The exhibit in the Kauai Museum discusses the lava-rock "Russian Fort Elisabeth" at Waimea and shows pictures of it from 1890 after its cannon had been removed and with no surrounding vegetation but with a "pili" grass house atop its west battlement, and an aerial photo from the sea side done in 1924 showing encroaching trees and bushes on the Waimea River side. I have visited the "Russian Fort" many times in the past two decades. It is a pleasant spot, but is not maintained in accord with its historical significance, in my opinion. The place where Kaumuali'i, the last king of Kauai, last resided on the island, just outside the walls to the east of the fort, is now covered with bushes and cast-off rusted cars and appliances. There is no mention on the signage that this was the site where the 1824 rebellion against the Oahu Ali'i placed in control of Kauai by Kamehameha's successors…a rebellion of Kaua'ians led by Kaumualii's son,

George Kaumuali'i, was put down and George Kaumuali'i captured (see Warne below). The earthen Fort Alexander, now featured at the entrance to the Princeville resort above Hanalei, is mentioned, but the other earthen Fort built by Schaeffer and his men, Fort Barclay, once examined by archeologists in the 1950s, is now gone. My wife and son and I found the hump that was left of it in 2001 just across from the parking lot at the Hanalei Pier. It was on private land. We crossed a wire fence to walk around it and photograph it. The circular earthen hump, fifty yards across, had been filled in with mature trees and bushes. But by 2003 the site had been bulldozed flat and a house constructed at 4911 Weke Road where it had been since 1816. There has been too much of this kind of destruction of historical sites in Hawaii. The golf course cutting across the sacred "Holua" slide and the burial ground of those who died in the conflict to eliminate the ancient kapus in the Kailua-Kona area of the big island of Hawaii is an egregious example. Another is in Lahaina, Maui, where a baseball field now surmounts the sacred "Moku'ula" burial ground of the ruling Ali'i's remains. Kaumuali'i's remains were interred there until the later years of the 19th century when Moku'ula was trammeled. His remains were transported (by the order of Bernice Pauahi Bishop) to the Waiola Congregational Church cemetery on Wainee Street and Shaw Street in Lahaina, Maui (he has never been returned to Kauai, apparently because of his stated desire to be buried "at the feet of Keōpūolani"). He is there with Keōpūolani, Nahi'ena'ena and Liliha. The white obelisk tombstone records his death in "1825," though he died May 26, 1824, and the epitaph after his name reads only "Kaahumanu was his wife, 1822." See Joesting, Soboleski, Warne, and Zambucka...also Pierce.

KAUMUALI'I, last King of Kaua'I (c. 1780-26 May, 1824). See Kane (Charlotte), Joesting, Lydgate, Mills, Pierce, Soboleski, Warne, Zambucka, and others. Also: http://en.wikipedia.org/wiki/Kaumualii, which is well done.

My thought here is to interpose a mini-article on aspects of Kaumuali'i's genealogy and family. I should start with his mother, Kamakahelei. The website http://en.wikipedia.org/wiki/Kamakahelei states Kamakahelei was "the 22nd ruling chiefess (Ali'i Aimoku) of Kaua'i, reigning from 1770-1794 and that her powerful mana derived primarily from her being the daughter of Peleioholani, 22nd Ali'i Aimoku of O'ahu and 21st Ali'i Aimoku of Kaua'i. These facts are repeated in the site http://www.guide2womenleaders.com/USA_Sub_States.htm (a very significant historical site, in my opinion), which adds the statement that "her daughter Kawalu married her half-brother George Kaumualii, King of Kauai (1794-1810)." This essentially adds a daughter to the conventional list of Kamakahelei's children, an addition my own research agrees with.

This daughter Kawalu is not the only recent scholarly addition to Kamakahelei's family. The consensus of current sources is that Kamakahelei was born about 1755 and that she had, in her life, two marriages, first to O'ahu Prince Kaneoneo in approximately 1770, and then, circa 1777, to Mau'i Federation King Kahekili's half-brother

Ka'eokulani (Ka'eo). But I was present at the November 12, 2011 lecture by former Kauai'i Mayor Maryanne Kusaka (see, of course, http://www.kauaihistoricalsociety.org and also http://www.remaxkauai.com/bio_maryanne-kusaka.htm) entitled "Kamakahelei as a 'Woman of Achievement'. In this lecture, Maryanne Kusaka added a husband to Kamakahelei's conventional list, this being Ni'ihau Prince "Kina" (or "Kuina"), with whom Kamakahelei ostensibly had her first children. This explains to me some of the temporal discordances my own research has found in the ages of her listed children, and the paternity of son Keawe when all is sorted out. The data in the splendid and useful site http://www.royalark.net/Hawaii/Kauai.htm adheres to the conventional two husbands consensus, but has resultant flaws in its accounts of Kaumuali'i's siblings, wives, and children.

Heeding all my sources, including George Anton Schaeffer's relation, and agreeing with both the www.guide2womenleaders.com website and with Maryanne Kusaka (and disagreeing some with www.royalark.net), I would move Kamakahelei's birth year back to ca. 1750 and list her children (Kaumuali'i's siblings, half and whole) as:

1. Daughter Lelemahoalani (with Kina…ca. 1765)
2. Daughter Kapua'amohu (with Kina…ca. 1773)
3. Daughter Kawalu (with Kaneoneo…ca. 1776)
4. Son Keawe (with Kaneoneo…ca. 1777)
5. Son Kaumuali'i (with Ka'eo…ca. 1780)
6. Daughter Kapiolani (with Ka'eo…ca. 1783)
7. Daughter Kaininoa (Naoa) (with Ka'eo…ca. 1785).

This order allows for the temporal plausibility of Kamakahelei's assenting to the offer (see Kamakau on this) of Lelemahoalani as a sexual partner for Captain Cook in 1778 (though barely), and of the regency of Inamo'o. Also, we must note that Kaumuali'i's wives include three of his sisters: Kawalu, Kapua'amohu, and Kaininoa (Naoa). Several of these wives are in George Anton Schaeffer's relation of events, but not all. Nevertheless, compiling from all sources, I get these (in approximate order of marriage):

1. Kapua'amohu (K's half-sister, m. ca. 1796)
2. Namahana (m. ca. 1798)
3. Kawalu (K's half-sister) (m. 1799)
4. Kaininoa (Naoa) (K's full-sister) (m. 1801)
5. Monalau (m. ca. 1802)
6. Naluahi (m. ca. 1803)
7. Makua (m. ca. 1806)
8. Kekaiha'akulou (later Deborah Kapule) (m. 1809)
9. Ka'ahumanu (by abduction), (m. 1821)

The list of Kaumuali'i's children includes, but is likely not limited to:

1. Son Humehume (Prince George Humehume, b. 1798, died 3 May, 1825 (see Warne below), mother listed as an unknown 'commoner')
2. Daughter Kekaulike Kinoiki (b. 1799 to Kapua'amohu)
3. Son Kelia'iahonui (b. 17 August, 1800 to Kapua'amohu, died 23 June, 1849)
4. Daughter Kapiolani (from Naoa, b. ca. 1802)
5. Son Kahekili (from Namahana, b. ca. 1808)

From these children of Kaumuali'i are drawn several of the current succession claims (see, of course, http://en.wikipedia.org/wiki/Kaumualii). Hawai'i and Kaua'i icon, Prince Jonah Kuhio Kalanianole (26 March, 1871-7 January, 1922) was Kaumuali'i's great grandson through daughter Kinoiki's marriage to a Prince Kalanianole. Kaumuali'i's line also figures into the Kawananakoa claims of succession. On these claims see: http://www.royalark.net/Hawaii/hawaii10.htm and http://en.wikipedia.org/wiki/Line_of_succession_to_the_former_Hawaiian_throne, and http://www.hawaiian-roots.com/chiefgen.htm. In addition, see the claim of Aleka Dayne Aipoalani, a "direct descendent of Kaumuali'i," to be the "Ali'i Nui of Modern Day Polynesia" at http://www.smokesignalsclothing.com/dayne-aipoalani.php.

This concludes my "mini-article" on Kaumuali'i's genealogy and family. ---Lee B. Croft.

Kendrick, John. Captain John Kendrick (1745-1794), together with Captain Robert Gray (1755-1806), were early traders on the northwest coast of America. Their ships, *Columbia* and its tender *Lady Washington*, later converted to a brig, made important journeys in the history of Pacific exploration and commerce. Gray in the *Columbia*, for example, discovered the river which now bears his ship's name. Kendrick was killed as a result of accidentally loaded salute fire from British ships at Pearl Harbor near Honolulu on December 7th, 1794 after involving himself in the battles between O'ahu's Chief Kalanikūpule and Kaumuali'i's father, Ka'eokulani. See www.Ladywashington.net/historyhawaii.php which also cites Scofield, John (below). See also the entry on Robert Gray. See also Scott Ridley (below).

Keneally, Thomas. A Commonwealth of Thieves: The Improbable Birth of Australia. Nan A. Talese: Doubleday. New York, London, Toronto, Sydney, and Auckland. 2006. ISBN 978-0-385-51459-0.

Khlebnikov, K. T. Baranov: Chief Manager of the Russian Colonies in America. (Translated by Colin Bearne and edited by Richard A. Pierce). The

Limestone Press. Kingston, Ontario, Canada. 1973. Kiril Timofeevich Khlebnikov (1776-1838) was a long-time employee of the RAK who, after 1817, helped assess Baranov's role in the development of Russian America. His relation of Baranov's life and career is the real key to all further work (e.g. Chevigny's biography and others), and the annotations and other scholarly work by Richard Pierce (see also below) make this a most valuable work. Kiril Khlebnikov's reports (1817-1832) on "Colonial Russian America" are included here also under Dmytryshyn, Basil and E.A.P. Crownhart-Vaughan…see above.

Klieger, P. Christiaan. Moku'ula: Maui's Sacred Island. Bishop Museum Press. Honolulu, Hawaii. 1998. This is a treatment of the island of Moku'ula in the fishpond of Loko o Mokuhinia—currently a Lahaina, Maui, public baseball field—which was a Hawaiian sacred site from which Kamehameha III ruled Hawaii in the first days of its royalty period. Several prominent Ali'i were interred, either originally or subsequently, in Moku'ula, including Keopuolani, Nahienaena, and Kaumualii, before their remains were transferred in the 1880s to the Wainee (now Waiola) churchyard in Lahaina by the Bishop estate. See also Chapman (above) on Ala Mauna…sacred burial place in Honolulu on O'ahu.

Kochetkova, Natalya. Nikolay Karamzin. Twayne Publishers World Authors Series (G.K. Hall and Co.). Boston. 1975. This is a concise biography of Karamzin...the best one in English for details of his family life. Best on this, however, is Lotman (below).

Komissarov, Boris Nikolaevich (B. N.) Grigorii Ivanovich Langsdorf, 1774-1852. Izdatel'stvo "Nauka," Leningradskoe otdelenie, Leningrad, 1975, 124 pp. with portrait frontispiece. This is the biography of Dr. Georg Heinrich von Langsdorff (see Langsdorff below). It has a useful chronology of Langsdorff's interesting life, and mentions family detail in text.

Kootz, Wolfgang (text) with photography by Willi Sauer, Ulrich Strauch and others. Frankfurt: An Illustrated Guide to the Metropolis on the Main. Kraichgau Verlag. Ubstadt-Weiher, Germany. 2001. This guidebook to Frankfurt has a table of dates on the history of Frankfurt and its surrounding area.

Kopp, Sebastian. Die Augustinerkirche in Münnerstadt. Karl Robert Langewiesche Verlag. Königstein. Undated. A pictorial treatment of the Augustine Church in Münnerstadt, site of one of the city's church schools founded before Schaeffer's time.

Kotzebue (Kotsebue), Otto von (Russian Sea Captain, born Dec. 30, 1787 in Revel (Tallin), Estonia, died also there Feb. 15, 1846). A Voyage of Discovery, 1815-1818, on the ship Rurick. Longman, Hurst, Rees, Orme and Brown. London. 1821 (also published by Da Capo Publishers, New York, 1967).

Kotzebue captained the Russian navy brig *Riurik* on world explorations from 1815-1818, including Hawai'i. He and his father, author, anti-Napoleon journalist (e.g. Die Biene and Die Grille) and diplomat August Friedrich Ferdinand von Kotzebue (5/3/1761-3/23/1819, stabbed to death in Mannheim by Karl Ludwig Sand who was executed, becoming a martyr for the cause of German nationalism). See the biographic entries on both father and son at www.en.wikipedia.org. See also entries on the *Rurik's* artist, Ludwig Choris (1795-1828), famous for his likeness of Kamehameha, and its noted author of Peter Schlemihl (1813) and scientist, Adelbert von Chamisso (1/30-1781-8/21/1838). On Chamisso see Niklaus R. Schweizer (below).

Krauss, Michael E. "Alaska Native Languages in Russian America." In Russian America: The Forgotten Frontier. Barbara Sweetland Smith and Redmond J. Barnett, eds. Tacoma: The Washington State Historical Press. 1990. pp. 205-215.

Krusenstern, Adam J. von (in Russian this is Ivan Fedorovich Kruzenshtern). Voyage Round the World in the years 1803, 1804, 1805, and 1806. Volumes 1 and 2. A republication of the English version of the original travel log of Captain Kruzenshtern of the *Nadezhda* originally published for John Murray in London in 1813. Now by The Gregg Press. Ridgewood, New Jersey. 1968. The scholarship available on this, the first Russian circumnavigation by the *Nadezhda* and the *Neva*, is unusually complete and offers diverse views, useful since the crews were badly factionalized by authority dispute and this colored the versions available. See Kruzenshtern, Lisianskii, Langsdorff and Löwenstern's contemporary views and the scholarship of Barratt, Becher, Chevigny, Iversen, and Pierce which include also parts of letters from Shemelin and Rezanov.

Krutak, Lars. "St. Lawrence Island Joint-Tattooing: Spiritual/Medicinal Functions and Intercontinental Possibilities." In Etudes/Inuit/Studies. 23 (1-2), 1999, pp.229-252. Krutak is a well published authority on native tattooing among the tribes with which Alexander Baranov had to deal: Yupiget, Aleut, Eskimo, Inuit, Kenaitze, Tlingit, and others. Baranov was given a captive Inuit girl as a gift by an Eskimo chief in the 1790's, and his wife, Anna Grigorievna, was from the woman-tattooing Kenaitze tribe.

Krutak, Lars. "Chapter 19: The Arctic." In A Source Book: Tattoo History. Edited and Introduced by Steve Gilbert with the collaboration of Cheralea Gilbert. Juno Books. New York. 2000. The methods and manners of native tattoo patterns are detailed in this work by a leading anthropological scholar of tattooing. See also Handy and Kwiatkowski on tattoos.

Krutak, Lars. "Many Stitches for Life: Traditional Tattooing on St. Lawrence Island (Sivuqaq), Alaska." In Skin and Ink, July 2001, pp. 37-43.

Kulagin, R. A. Borodino v vospominaniiakh sovremennikov. Izdatel'stvo "Skarabei." Sankt Peterburg. 2001. This work has appendices detailing the composition of both French and Russian armies at Borodino. The memoirs clarify many details of the battle. If one types "Battle of Borodino" into the Google search field, the first site seen will be the "Virtual Battle of Borodino" by Brett Nolan, Shawn Murphy, and Natasha Sopevia, done in 1996 for a Hamilton College Computer Sciences Seminar project for Prof. Frank Sciaca of the Hamilton College Russian Studies Department. This site is a marvel, with associated music, art, Tolstoy's text from War and Peace, and streaming video from the 1968 Russian version (Directed by and starring Sergei Bondarchuk) of the film, War and Peace. The site lets one follow either Napoleon or Kutuzov through the battle. See also Duffy and Ezerskaya above.

Kuykendall, Ralph S. The Hawaiian Kingdom: 1778-1854. 3 Vol., University of Hawaii Press. Honolulu, HI. 1938 but since reprinted at least five times. 462 pp. This is a fine work that is wonderful to read because it cites original logs and memoirs in the language as originally written.

Kwiatkowski, P. F. The Hawaiian Tattoo. Illustrated by Tom O'o Mehau. Halona, Inc. of Kohala, HI, 1996. (ISBN 0-9655756-0-8). This work is a bit rough (spelling and inclusion of a "Forward" (sic)), but is a good treatment of the unique aspects of Hawai'ian tattoos, both ancient and modern.

Langsdorff, George H. von. Voyages and Travels in Various Parts of the World During the Years 1803, 1804, 1805, 1806, and 1807. Volumes 1 and 2. (A facsimile of the English version printed for Henry Colburn in London in 1813) The Gregg Press. Ridgewood, New Jersey. 1968. This is a memoir truly wonderful to read. Langsdorff even includes musical notation to describe native songs from Nuku Hiva in the Marquesas. He makes no mention of the pranks of Count F. I. Tolstoi nor of his monkey (see Lowenstern and Rezanov below), but includes the amazing story of Frenchman Jean Baptiste Cabri (see the plate, pp. 96 of Volume 1, showing Cabri with his tattooing). Both Langsdorff and Lisiansii, in their memoirs describing the Marquesans and Hawaiians, marveled at their swimming ability and Lisianskii records timing one native's underwater dive at four minutes. Langsdorff lists the physical measurements of a Marquesan native, also an impressive swimmer and diver, named "Mufau" who, at "6 feet 2 inches high, Paris measure" caused Dr. Tilesius to remark that he had "never seen anyone so perfectly proportioned." Later a comparison of the measurements was made to the Apollo of Belvedere, one of the foremost masterpieces of Grecian art…and the measurements exactly coincided (pp. 109 of Vol. 1). Langsdorff writes that they were told of a neighboring island chieftain named Upoa who was of the same proportions as Mufau, but "a head taller…nearly seven Paris feet high."

Langsdorff, Georg Heinrich von. Remarks and Observations on a Voyage Around the World From 1803 to 1807. Vol. 1 "The Voyage From Copenhagen to Brazil, the South Sea, Kamtschatka and Japan; and Vol. 2 "The Voyage From Kamtschatka to the Island of St. Paul, Unalaska, Kodiak, Sitcha, New Albion, Kamtschatka, Ochotsk and Through Siberia to St. Petersburg." Translated and annotated by Victoria Joan Moessner. Edited by Richard A. Pierce. The Limestone Press. Kingston, Ontario and Fairbanks, Alaska. (Alaska History No. 41) 1993. This is a "new" and more accurate translation of the original text from the German with detailed notes and appendices, including one listing the original subscribers to Dr. Langsdorff's 1813 edition (see below for English facsimile edition in two volumes).

Langsdorff, Georg Heinrich von (Georg Heinrich/Grigorii Ivanovich Langsdorf (1774-1852). <u>Materialen der Brasilien-Expedition 1821-1829 des Akademiemitgliedes Georg Heinrich Freiherr von Langsdorff: Vollständige Wissenschaftliche Bescchreibung.</u> D. E. Berthels, B. N. Komissarov, and T. I. Lysenko, editors and compilers. Verlag Dietrich Reimer. Berlin. 1979. This work, also published by "Nauka" ("Science") Publishers in Leningrad in 1973, is a compilation of Langsdorff's reports to Russian Foreign Minister Karl Vasilievich Nesselrode concerning the findings of his Russian-government-funded (40,000 rubles plus 10,000 per year) naturalists' expedition to the Brazilian Amazon. For a biography of Langsdorff, see Komissarov above.

Langsdorff, Georg Heinrich von. <u>Bemerkungen über Brasilien. Mit gewissenhafter Belehrung für auswandernde Deutsche.</u> Verlag Karl Groos, Heidelberg, 1821. This work, cited by Oberacker (see below) evidences already by 1821 an awareness by Langsdorff, designated Russian Consul to Rio de Janeiro, that Post-Napoleonic Germans wanted to leave Germany and might be considering coming to Brazil. Ostensibly he wrote this and published it in Heidelberg after seeing George Anton Schaeffer in Rio de Janeiro in January of 1821 arriving with his family group from Germany looking to establish a plantation "colony." Langsdorff was on his way to St. Petersburg to gain financial support from Tsar Alexander I through the St. Petersburg Academy of Sciences to fund a more comprehensive expedition of prominent scientists to the Amazon. As a consequence of his persisting in the planning of this expedition (after his earlier, 1816-17 expedition-related "insanity"), his wife Friederike left him and remained in Europe with his two children. (See Komissarov above). See http://en.wikipedia.org/wiki/Grigory_Langsdorff, where a 24 February, 2010, study by Francisco Albuquerque is cited to state that "Langsdorff has 1,500 descendants in Brazil, among them the most famous is Luma de Oliveira, a Brazilian carnival queen."

LAPEROUSE, Jean-Francoise de Galaup de (1741-1787). Laperouse was an early French voyager who visited Mau'i for one day (29-30 May, 1786) with two ships, the 500-600-ton *Boussole* and *L'Astrolabe* (Captain Paul-Antoine-Marie Fleuriot de Langle). A Bay on the south shore of Mau'i is named for him. Later he discovered and named Necker Island after a French Minister of Finance. He and his ships were lost in the Solomons in 1787, though his memoirs were mailed before this and survive. His ships crossed paths off Mau'i in the Hawai'ian islands with the two British ships, the *King George* and *Queen Charlotte* (at Kealakekua Bay on Hawai'i 24 May, and O'ahu 28 May, 1786), under the command of Captain Nathanial Portlock, but did not sight each other. See http://pages.quicksilver.net.nz/jcr/~lap3. Also, one of the possible explanations for the presence on Nuku Hiva of Jean Cabri (see Chapter Nine: Barbara in St. Petersburg) is that Cabri (who claimed to have known young Napoleon Bonaparte, who also applied (but unsuccessfully) to participate in the Laperouse expedition) was a sailor on the *Boussole* who left the ship in Nuku Hiva.

LAZAREV, MIKHAIL PETROVICH (Nov. 3, 1788-either April 11 or May 10, 1851, depending on source). M. P. Lazarev (also spelled Lazareff in non-Russian sources) was one of three brothers, all of whom became prominent in the Russian Navy. From 1804 to 1808, Lazarev served in the British Navy to enhance his career, learning English as he did so. He captained the *Suvorov* on its circumnavigation of the globe in 1813-6, clashing with Governor Aleksander Baranov and with Russian-American Company representatives on his ship, including George Anton Schaeffer. He faced a naval board of inquiry when he returned to St. Petersburg in July 1816 without Dr. Schaeffer and RAK supercargo Molvo, and had to answer the complaints of the latter as well as those of Governor Baranov. But the naval board acquitted him of the charges against him and he went on to other important captaincies in exploring the Pacific and in Russia's subsequent naval campaigns. His name has been given to many public places in Russia, including, for example, one of the Neva embankments in St. Petersburg. According to www.philately.com/philately/biolala.htm, three Russian postage stamps have been issued with his likeness on them. He is reported to have died of unknown causes in Vienna, but www.findagrave.com reports that he is buried in Baykova Cemetery in Kiev, Ukraine…even showing the grave stone and its damage from WWII. Other sources, including www.sailingnavies.com state that he is interred in the crypt of St. Vladimir's Cathedral in Sevastopol. Some of Lazarev's journal from the 1813-6 circumnavigation are published in Samarov (below). Online biographical information is at www.navy.ru/history/hrn7-e.htm and at www.explore-biography.com/biographies/M/Mikhail_Petrovich_Lazarev. For a likeness, see Barratt, Glynn…Russia in Pacific Waters (above).

Lee, Blanche Kaualua Lolokukalani. Don Francisco de Paula Marin: The Unforgettable Spaniard Who Gave Hawaii the First Pineapple. Illustrated by Joseph Feher. Copyright by Banche Kaualua L. Lee. 2002. ISBN 1-052-027. Printed by Best Printing. Honolulu. Purchased at the Bishop Museum store, Honolulu, June 2005. This work has good family information about Don Marin as well as information about his residence in Honololu's "Kapu'ukolo" or waterfront area known as "America." See Gast (above) for an earlier and more conventional biography wherein Gast maintains that Marin was not the first to grow pineapples in Hawai'i. See also Ten Bruggencate (below).

Leichter als Luft: Zur Geschichte der Ballonfahrt. (compilers Bernard Korzus and Burkhard Leismann) Westfalisches Landesmuseum fur Kunst und Kulturgeschichte Munster Landschaftsverband Westfalen-Lippe. 1978. An Anthology of long, heavily illustrated articles by diverse authors on the history of ballooning...most relevant is that of Walter Locher, "Militarische Verwendung des Ballons," pp. 237-251. This book is a goldmine of illustrations of early balloon ascents and even inflation process and includes the most comprehensive time-table of early ascents...cf. "Zeittafel" pp. 284-291 (1670-1978 prominent ascents)". For online illustrations of the early balloon ascents, including one showing the "Ascent at Moorfields of Vincent Lunardi," having prototype "rotary wings" like those in Franz Leppich's later design, see: http://marinni.livejournal.com/501633.html?thread=5614977. This site also has a bawdy illustration of "love in the air."

Levathes, Louise E. "Kamehameha: Hawaii's Warrior King." Photographs by Steve Raymer and paintings by Herb Kawainui Kane. In National Geographic. Vol. 164, No. 5 (November 1983), pp. 558-599. This is such a fine article, and so well illustrated and accompanied by the National Geographic's high quality annotated map of the Hawaiian Islands, that it is definitely a "must read" for anyone interested in Kamehameha or Hawaiian history.

Lieven, Dominic. Review of V. M. Bezotosnyi, et. al. Otechestvennaia voina 1812 goda: Entsiklopediia (The Great Patriotic War of 1812: An Encyclopedia) (see above) in Kritika: Explorations in Russian and Eurasian History. 7, 1 (Winter 2006), pp. 133-135.

Lili'uokalani. Hawaii's Story by Hawaii's Queen. (intro. by Glen Grant). Mutual Publishing. Honolulu, Hawaii. 1990. Interesting here is Lili'uokalani's early discussion of her adoptive family upbringing as a Hawaiian "Ali'i."

OGIZ: gosudarstvennoe isdatel'stvo geografischeskoi literatury. Moskva. 1947. This is the republication of Captain Yurii Fedorovich Lisiansky's travel log, originally published in St. Petersburg in 1812.

Lisiansky, Urey (Iurii or Yurii...same as above). Voyage Round the World in the years 1803, 1804, 1805, and 1806. This, #42 in the Bibliotheca Australiana series, is a republication of the English version of Captain Lisianskii's (see source above) travel log from the Neva, which was published for John Booth in London in 1814. Now by Da Capo Press (a Division of Plenum Publishing Corp.). 227 West 17th St. New York. 1968.

Littke, Peter. Russian-American Bibliography: An English Guide to Literature About the History of Russian-America (1741-1867) (with a special emphasis on Russian and other non-English publications. Littlestone, UK, copyright Peter Littke, 2003. (ISBN 3-8330-0705-2) This work, dedicated "in admiration of the lifetime work of Professor Dr. Richard A. Pierce, Kingston, Ontario, Canada" (see Pierce below) was shown to me by U-Hawaii-Manoa's Hamilton Librarian Patricia Polansky, a most able Slavic bibliographer. On the back cover of Littke's work is mention of:

Littke, Peter. Vom Sarenadler sum Sternenbanner: Die Geschichte Russisch-Alaska" ("From the Czar's Eagle to the Stars and Stripes—the History of Russian Alaska"). Magnus Verlag, Essen, Germany, 2003 (ISBN 3-88400-019-5). I have not seen this. Peter Littke is at Peter@irah.org.

Littke, Peter. "Benedict Cramer (Venedikt Kramer), Director of the Russian-American Company" posted on www.IRAH.org in May 2003, accessed August 2008.

Ljungstedt, Anders (Sir) (1759-1835). An Historical Sketch of the Portuguese Settlements in China and of the Roman Catholic Church and Mission in China & Description of the City of Canton. Viking Hong Kong Publications. Hong Kong. 1992 (xvi + 280 pp, 3 maps, 200 HKD, ISBN 962-7650-01-3). Preface by Father Manual Teixeira, leading Macau historian. This is the republication of Ljungstedt's historical work on Macau, Canton, and the East India Trade, originally published in Boston in 1836. The fact that Ljungstedt was writing such a "sketch" was mentioned by George Schaeffer in his own notes, which commend Ljungstedt's work. Schaeffer stayed with Ljungstedt in Macau in 1817, appointing him China representative of the Russian-American Company. See also Hellberg (above) and http://runeberg.org/authors/ljungand.html and www.HawaiiHistory.com to "Russians in Hawai'i" wherein Ljungstedt is mentioned, as well as Peter Dobell.

Lotman, Yurii M. Karamzin. "Issskustvo-SPB." Sankt-Peterburg. 1997. This is a wonderfully detailed and insightful biographic work on Nikolai M. Karamzin and his times. It is divided into three parts: Karamzin's biography, treatments of his articles and researches, and discussion of his observations and reviews. The citations on F.V. Rostopchin are interesting...on pp. 178-80 is mention of Karamzin's visit to England in 1790, and of his encounter there, in the group of Russian Ambassador to England S. R. Vorontsov, with Fyodor V. Rostopchin, later Governor-General of Moscow during Napoleon's invasion. Rostopchin got lessons in boxing from "renowned boxer 'Rein' (likely Benjamin Brain...cf. Roberts and Skutt, below)," discovering the hard way that "battle with the fists involves the same degree of science as battle with rapiers." Lotman, a seminal scholar of both literary and linguistic semiotics, has a similarly detailed biography of Pushkin, but I have used the Binyon biography, which credits Lotman, more.

Löwenstern, Hermann Ludwig von. The First Russian Voyage Around the World: The Journal of Hermann Ludwig von Löwenstern (1803-1806). Translated by Victoria Joan Moessner. University of Alaska Press. Fairbanks,

AK. 2003. This is the diary of a member of the crew of Captain Kruzenshtern's *Nadezhda*. The account is more personal than that of Kruzenshtern or of Dr. Langsdorff, revealing more about the dissension aboard. The episode of Count Fyodor Tolstoy's monkey is related on pp. 106-7…see also Rezanov below.

Lucas, Lois. Plants of Old Hawaii. With Illustrations by Joan Fleming and Poems by Julie Williams. Bess Press, 3565 Harding Avenue, Honolulu, HI 96816. See www.besspress.com. 1982, ISBN 0-935848-11-8. 112 pp. This is an elementary treatment (English and Hawaiian Name; Poem about; Habitat; Description; Native Uses; Labeled Drawing) on each of the twenty plants brought by the Polynesian emigrants to Hawaii circa 450 AD, providing a guide to the plants in Hawai'i at the time of European contact (Arrowroot, Awa, Bamboo, Banana, Breadfruit, Candlenut, Coconut, Bottle Gourd, Hau, Indian Mulberry, True Kou, Milo, Mountain Apple, Paper Mulberry, Sugar Cane, Sweet Potato, Taro, Ti, Turmeric, and Yam).

Luebke, Frederick C. Germans in Brazil: A Comparative History of Cultural Conflict During World War I. Louisiana State University Press. Baton Rouge, LA and London. 1987. Chapter one on "A Century of German Settlement I Brazil: A Survey, 1818-1918" (pp. 7-35) mentions the activities of "Major Georg Schaffer" on pp. 8 and cites Brazilian sources from Porto Alegre.

Lundberg, Murray. "The Russian-American Company in Hawaii." Available at www.explorenorth.com/library/yafeatures/bl-RussAmCo.htm.

Lundy, Derek. The Way of a Ship: A Square-Rigger Voyage in the Last Days of Sail. First published by Knopf Canada in 2002, but now by HarperCollins Publishers Inc., 10 East 53rd Street, New York, NY 10022 (ISBN 0-06-621012-7). 2004. The idea of reading this book was to familiarize myself with life aboard a square-rigged ship in the age of sail. But I found the "Prologue," explaining author Lundy's personal connection to his character, part real relative and part fictional persona, both moving and inspirational. As to method, Lundy quotes Robert Foulke to say: "Usually (in historical and literary voyage narratives like The Odyssey and its descendents in Foulke's The Sea Voyage Narrative) no clear demarcation exists between fact and fiction, experience and imagination." He continues to describe his own method (and mine) "So a different kind of book, then: take the fragments of what I know about Benjamin, and the great deal that's known about square-riggers and life aboard them in his time and create a voyage. It will be typical in its incidents, suffering and accomplishment. Its officers and crew will be representative seamen of that time and of those ships. The ship itself: an imaginary one, the *Beara Head*—a name of an Irish promontory—but an actual sister to the big iron Cape Horners in all other respects. I will imagine the tale of Benjamin's voyage; not the voyage itself—that's unrecoverable—but as it might have been and emphatically, could have been."

Lydgate, Rev. John M. "Kaumuali'i: the Last King of Kaua'i," in Hawaiian Historical Society 24th Annual Report for the Year 1915 (1916), pp. 21-43.

Lyons, Jeffrey K. "Memoirs of Henry Obookiah: A Rhetorical History," in The Hawaiian Journal of History (A Publication of the Hawaiian Historical Society), Vol. XXXVIII (2004), pp. 35-57.

MACQUARIE, LACHLAN (1761-1824, Governor of New South Wales, Australia, 1810-1821). Macquarie is a large figure in Australian history and there are many biographical treatments. A concise treatment may be found on the internet at www.lib.mq.edu.au/lmr/biography.html. Schaeffer met Macquarie in Sydney during the August-September 1814 visit of the *Suvorov*.

Madsen, Axel. John Jacob Astor: America's First Multimillionaire. John Wiley & Sons. New York. 2001 (vii + 312 pp, ISBN 0-471-38503-4). See also the e-review of this work by Ann Harper Fender at http://www.eh.net/bookreviews/library/0392.shtml. In her review, Ann Fender points out that author Madsen "joins a long list of John Jacob Astor biographers." She also mentions that Astor's friend, noted American author Washington Irving, together with his brother Pierre (see Franchere, Gabriel, above), penned a "chronicle of Astoria, the failed venture on the Pacific coast that was published in 1836 as Astoria: Adventure in the Pacific Northwest." Astor was a major figure in the fur trade involving Governor Baranov and others, but my major investigation here concerns the character of John Marshall, who told George Schaeffer he was Astor's "nephew who had come to America from Germany with him" and was shipwrecked in Hawai'i on Astor's trading ship *Lark*. It is known that Astor did not come directly from Germany to America, but resided for some time in England, where he made contacts later important to him. So I was surveying the biographies of Astor for some mention of the name Marshall in order to establish the credibility of John Marshall's claim. The first place that the name turned up was in the work of Fritz Springmeier (real name Victor Earl Schoof, born in Garden City, Kansas, on Sept. 24, 1955 and currently resident in an Oregon prison). When you think you have been exposed to every kookball aspect of our culture's psychopathology (most, including this, drug induced, in my opinion), check out: www.thewatcherfiles.com/astor.htm or www.theforbiddenknowledge.com/hardtruth/the_astor_bloodline.htm or www.whale.to/b/sp/blood.htm for Springmeier's rambling indictment of "The Astor Bloodline" as "illuminati" in control of our economic/political realities. See also the article "Fritz Springmeier—Another Human Tragedy" by John Torell at www.eaec.org for the section entitled "Who is Fritz Springmeier?" This includes input by one of Springmeier's wives. Also interesting is the related material at www.sleazereport.com. Some people think that research is boring…nay!

Mahr, August C. The Visit of the *Rurik* to San Francisco in 1816. Stanford University Publications, University Series on History, Economics and Political Science, No. II:2, Stanford, Ca., 1932. This work contains extracts from the works, originally in German, of poet and scientist Adelbert von Chamisso (1781-1838), the artist Ludwig Choris (1795-1828) who were with Captain Otto A. von Kotzebue (Kotsebue, 1787-1846) on the *Rurik* when it visited Hawai'i in 1816.

Malo, David. Hawaiian Antiquities (Moolelo Hawaii). Bernice P. Bishop Museum Special Publication 2, Second edition (translated from the Hawaiian in 1898 by Dr. Nathaniel B. Emerson). Copyright 1951 by Bishop Museum, 1525 Bernice Street, Honolulu, Hawaii 96817. 7th reprinting 1997. This is a relation of Hawaiian history and customs by native Hawaiian David Malo (ca. 1793-1853), a long-time Lahaina, Maui, school agent.

MARIN, Don Francisco de Paula (Manini). See Conrad, Agnes C. (Letters and Journal), Gast, Ross H. (Biography), Lee, Blanche Kaualua Lolokukalani (family biographical treatment), and Ten Bruggencate, Jan K. (Introduction of Pineapple to Hawai'i).

Marion, Fulgence. Wonderful Balloon Ascents: or, The Conquest of the Skies. This is an "E-book" at http://www.bookrags.com/books/wonba/PART16.htm accessed January 15, 2002.

Massey, Raymond (with Editors Jean McGarry and Zelda Feldman). Discovery of Hawaii and Honolulu Harbor. Copyright 2009 by Raymond Massey, ISBN 978-1-60725-967-1. This is a self-published work featuring the art of prominent maritime artist Raymond Massey, whose historical acumen is here strikingly revealed. See my review at www.shvoong.com/books/historical-novel/1975654-discovery-hawaii-honolulu-harbor/. Relative to events related in this book is a fine treatment of the native Battle of Punahawale for control of Oahu in 1794, involving Kae'o and Kalanikupule and mentioning Mare Amara (pp. 96). Well related also are the deaths of Captains (John) Kendrick and (William) Brown. The bibliography is one of the best and is highly recommended. Massey's book may be ordered through www.masseymarineart.com or through Kapa'a, Kauai's SHIPSTORE GALLERY at www.shipstoregalleries.net. See also the novel by Scott Ridley.

MAU'I Historical Walking Guide. Joan D'A McKelvey, Publisher. Anaka Productions, 537 Kai Hele Ku St., Lahaina, Maui, Hawaii 96761. This pamphlet features maps, photos, and stories of Lahaina and Ka'anapali. It is published three times per year and distributed to tourists in the Lahaina/Ka'anapali area by resorts, hotels, and the Lahaina Center of the Lahaina Restoration Foundation. Volume V, Issue 1 is in Spring/Summer of 2003.

Mazour, Anatole G. "Doctor Yegor Scheffer: Dreamer of a Russian Empire in the Pacific." in Pacific Historical Review. No. 6 (March 1937). pp. 15-20.

McBride, Likeke R. Petroglyphs of Hawai'i. Second Revised Edition of 2004. Copyright by Andrew S. McBride from original Petroglyph Press edition of 1969 by his father who died in 1993. Petroglyph Press, Ltd. 160 Kamehameha Avenue, Hilo, HI 96720 (ISBN 0-912180-60-9). This is an illustrated treatment of the Petroglyphs on the big island of Hawai'i.

McClellan, Edwin North. "John M. Gamble," in the Thirty-fifth Annual Report of the Hawaiian Historical Society for the Year 1926. Honolulu Advertiser Publishing Co., Honolulu, 1927, pp. 44-58.

McDougal, Walter A. Let the Sea Make a Noise: four Hundred Years of Cataclysm, Conquest, War and folly in the North Pacific. Avon Books. New York. 1994. McDougal conjectures a colloquy involving diverse North Pacific historical characters, including Kaahumanu, Hirosi Saito, William Seward, and Sergey Witte, concerning conflicting colonial aspirations.

McRae, Robert J. "Ritter, Johann Wilhelm." in Dictionary of Scientific Biography. Charles Coulston Gillespie, Editor-in-Chief. Charles Scribner's Sons. New York. 1975. Vol. XI (of XV volumes and two supplemental volumes). pp. 473-5.

Mehnert, Klaus. "The Russians in Hawaii, 1804-1819." University of Hawaii Occasional Paper No. 38. University of Hawaii Bulletin, Vol. 18, No 6 (April 1939), pp. 6-9.

Mellen, Kathleen Dickenson. The Magnificent Matriarch: Kaahumanu, Queen of Hawaii. Hastings House. New York. 1952.

Melville, Herman. Moby-Dick. Edited and with introduction by Charles Child Walcutt. Bantam Books. This is the 1967 version of the 1851 original with a sampling of contemporary reviews, six modern essays, and a bibliography. Melville's depiction of 19th century sailors informs this account…in particular his definition of "Gam" on pp. 227.

Messent, David. The Rocks. ("Sydney's Birthplace"). David Messent Photography. Sydney, Australia. (telephone Sydney 971 5970). National Library of Australia ISBN 0 64623025 5. An illustrated characterization of the "Rocks" district of Sydney, including the time when Schaeffer was there while on the Suvorov. This work is a picture book for tourists, though it depicts the area's colorful history well. A more scholarly work is that of Karskens (above).

Mikaberidze, Alexander. "Reader's Articles: Politics and Government: Franco-Turkish Relationship..." cf. www.NapoleonSeries.org, parts I and II from November, 2000.

Mikaberidze, Alexander. "The Mutiny of the Generals" (in 11 parts with bibliography). cf. www.napoleon-series.org/military/battles/c_mutiny3.html from September 2001. Mikaberidze, the "Chairman of the Napoleonic Society of Georgia," is certainly a great master of detail and provides the most recent historical treatment of military aspects of Napoleon's campaign in Russia in 1812, being in complete command of all earlier sources. Note the frequent citation on http://www.napoleonistyka.atspace.com/Borodino_battle.htm. Recent English-language books by Alexander Mikaberidze include: The Battle of Borodino: Napoleon Against Kutuzov, and The Battle of the Berezina: Napoleon's Great Escape.

Mills, Peter R. "A New View of Kaua'i as 'The Separate Kingdom' after 1810" in The Hawaiian Journal of History (A Publication of the Hawaiian Historical Society), Vol. XXX (1996), pp. 91-104. In this article Mills contends with points made in Edward Joesting's Kaua'i: The Separate Kingdom about Kaumuali'i and the building of the "Russian Fort" at Waimea. An important point argued therein is that Kaumuali'i had already evidenced non-compliance with his 1810 agreement to function as a tributary chief subordinate to Kamehameha before George Schaeffer's arrival in 1816.

Mills, Peter R. Hawai'i's Russian Adventure: A New Look at Old History. University of Hawai'i Press. Honolulu. 2002. ISBN 0-8248-2404-0. This work focuses attention on the building and use of the "Russian Fort" near Waimea on Kauai, but also has very good biographical treatment of Kaumuali'i. Mills' bibliography is one of the very best...very useful and highly recommended. See my review of this work on www.shvoong.com.

Mitchell, Donald D. Kilolani. Resource Units in HAWAIIAN CULTURE. Book design and illustrations by Nancy Middlesworth. Third printing in 2007 of the Fourth Revised Edition of 1992, expanded in 1982 from the first edition of 1969. Kamehameha Schools Press, Honolulu. ISBN 978-0-87336-016-6. This is a key resource to illustrated information about the pre-contact Hawaiian culture...just a treasure.

Monakhov, A. L. Muzej-Panorama: Borodinskaja Bitva: 1812 god. Sorek-poligrafija. Moskva. 1997. A history of the Battle of Borodino, profusely illustrated with art. There is also an associated fold-out miniature reprint of the battle panorama by Franz Alekseevich Roubeau entitled Muzej-Panorama Borodinskaja Bitva (Izdatel'stvo gumanitarnoj literatury, Moskva, 2002...cf. Ezerskaja source for address) with explanatory text in Russian, English, French, and German. See "Borodino" above.

Mo'okini, Esther T. "Keōpuōlani: Sacred Wife, Queen Mother, 1778-1823," in Hawaiian Journal of History (A Publication of the Hawaiian Historical Society), Vol. XXXII (1998), pp. 1-24. A fine biographical treatment of Keōpuōlani...the most comprehensive on her and her impact on Hawai'ian society.

MOROSI, GIUSEPPE. For information on this Florentine "mechanic," and fabricator of his chess "automaton" for Ferdinand III of Tuscany, see http://www.galileo.imss.firenze.it/pubblic/e1998.html, accessed August 9, 2003.

Moser, Peter. Würzburg: Geschichte einer Stadt. Babenberg Verlag. Bamberg. 1999. This is a chronological table of dates, spelling out the history of Würzburg, capital of Franconia and seat of the Franconian Prince Bishop until Georg Karl von Fechenbach signed his assent to the secularization of 1802.

MUSEUM.RU. At www.museum.ru there is an "1812 Project" which includes a richly illustrated treasure trove of detailed information, more in the Russian version than the English version, about the events and the personalities involved in Napoleon's invasion of Russia in 1812. In addition, there are tables of generals, ministers, and essays on selected topics...for example, Helen Bobrova's article on "Russian Diplomats in Paris, 1791-1815 (see above)." There is also a very comprehensive illustrated genealogy of Tsar Alexander I's family with links to biographical data. This is a most helpful site. See also the "Virtual Battle of Borodino" at Duffy above.

NAPOLEON BONAPARTE. The site at www.Napoleon-series.org is a very valuable resource with its articles on diverse aspects of Napoleon's life and campaigns. On Napoleon during the Battle of Borodino, see http://www.napoleonistyka.atspace.com/Borodino_battle.htm. The Napoleon-series.org site has a sketch from tsarist archives of the Leppich aerostat's design. This

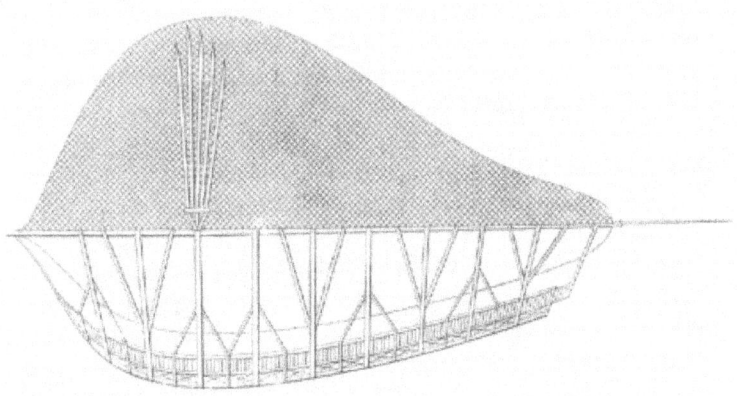

Kopie der Zeichnung des Luftballones von Franz Leppich, entnommen dem »Sammelband der historischen Unterlagen aus dem Archiv der Privatkanzlei Seiner Kaiserlichen Hoheit Alexanders I.«, St. Petersburg 1876.

sketch with its German caption ("A copy of a sketch of the airballoon of Franz Leppich, from historical notes in the private archive of his Imperial Majesty Alexander I—St. Petersburg, 1876") is very likely derived from a very similar one from French military archives drawn in 1812 by a French officer named de Segur (see Duhem, above, and de Segur, below) who inspected the Vorontsovo estate after the evacuation of the balloon project to Nizhnii Novgorod. The somewhat flawed explanation given on the napoleon-series site reads: "Franz Leppich (1776-1818) was a German inventor and musician. In 1811 he offered the idea of a hot air balloon to Napoleon, who turned it down, so Leppich went to Russia, where his offer was met with more success. Rastopchin (sic) hired him to build a military hot air balloon for the defence of Moscow. At this time ballooning was in its infancy. Leppich began work in a secret shipyard near Moscow, heavily defending the site against spies from France. But, during trials, the balloon failed to inflate, and Leppich left Russia in disgrace." These sketches only very roughly show the non-spherical "shark shape" of the aerostat's side view, and miss the rotary wings. Search also the site http://tywkiwdbi.blogspot.com under "killer-zeppelin-not-used-against-napoleon."

Neale, Tom. An Island to Myself. Introduction by Noel Barber. Holt Rinehart and Winston Co. New York. 1966. The first edition published in London by Collins the same year is entitled An Island to Oneself. This book is about Neale's solitary residence on Suvarov island from 1952 to 1954, then from 1960 to 1963. After the book was published he returned to the island and lived there from 1966 to 1972. He was originally inspired to go and live on the atoll by Robert Dean Frisbie (cf. above). The text of Neale's book is online at www.gutenberg.net.au/ebooks01/0100261.text. There is a very special "tribute" website to Tom Neale, with a remembrance article by Kenneth R. Vogel, a collection of photographs by Rhys Jones, photos of Tom Neale's gravesite in Rarotonga and his death certificate…contributions of photos by his daughter Stella and other information about his life and legacy at www.pacificislandsinfo.com.

Nebel, Henry M., Jr. N.M. Karamzin: A Russian Sentimentalist. Mouton and Co. The Hague and Paris. 1967. This is a literary treatment, but mentions the effects of freemasonry on Karamzin's thought and (cf. pp. 46) discusses political currents in the court of Tsar Alexander I.

Nickerson, Roy. Lahaina: Royal Capital of Hawaii. Hawaiian Service, P.O. Box 2835, Honolulu, Hawaii. 1978. A well illustrated treatment of Lahaina's history in its days "when kings and whalermen ruled the Sandwich isles."

Nicolson, Harold. The Congress of Vienna:A Study of Allied Unity: 1812-1822. A Harbinger Book. Harcourt, Brace, Jovanovich, Inc. New York. 1946. Here are the roles of Lord Castelreagh and Prince Klemens von Metternich in the post-Napoleonic situation in "the Italian and German Settlements" (pp. 182-199).

NINETEENTH CENTURY. The Illustrated History of the 19th Century: Month by Month, Year by Year. Text by Simon Adams, et. al. Hackberry Press on imprint of the Texas Bookman. Rebo International b.v., Lisse, Netherlands. ISBN 1-931104-001 X. An interesting illustrated compendium of prominent events in chronological order, as the title says, 'month by month, year by year.' Very useful to provide historical context for depicted events.

NEWSPAPERS, Hawaiian at www.nupepa.org, Ulukau Hawaiian Electronic Library. This source gives Hawaiian-language newspapers (e.g. Nupepa Kuokoa) published between 1834-1948 with word, title, and date searches possible.

North, Jonathan. With Napoleon In Russia: The Illustrated Memoirs of Major Faber du Faur, 1812. Greenhill Books, London, and Stackpole Books, Mechanicsburg, PA. 2001. ISBN 1-85367-454-0. North's presentation of Major Christian Wilhelm von Faber du Faur's (1780-1857) memoirs and sketches, with later prepared color plates is a real gem. See my review at the book's entry on www.Amazon.com.

North, Jonathan. Napoleon's Army in Russia: The illustrated Memoirs of Albrecht Adam-1812. Pen and Sword Books, South Yorkshire, UK. 2005. ISBN 1-84415-161-1. Another scholarly gem by prolific scholar of the Napoleonic Wars Jonathan North. See my review at www.Amazon.com.

Oberacker, Carlos H., Jr. Jorge Antonio Von Schaeffer: Criador Da Premeira Corrente Emigratoria Alema Para O Brasil. Editora Metropole. Instituto Estadual do Livro. Porto Alegre, Brasil. 1957 (reprinted in 1975). Includes much detail of Schaeffer's Brazilian emigration work in Europe, including a table of ships and the numbers of human cargo. See also http://www.brasilalemanhaonline.com.br/site/materias/1824_antesal.htm for a German article on the German emigration to Brazil mentioning the work of Jorge Antonio von Schaeffer, even giving the names of the first group of German émigrés to settle in the Rio Grande do Sul State. The terms of Schaeffer's offer to these émigrés is described in Portuguese at www.riogrande.com.br/historia/colonizacao4.htm. Both these latter two websites can be translated into rough English by accessing them through Google. For other sites on Schaeffer's role in the emigration of Germans to Brazil and yet more family detail, see http://www.es.beekeeping.wikia.com/wiki/Georg_Anton_von_Sch%C3%A4ffer and also Gomes (above), Sommer, Sawitzki, and Weissheimer (below) and the genealogical works on the families Grieb and Heuser.

Okun', Semen Bentsionovich. "Tsarskaia Rossia I Gavaiskie Ostrova" in Krasnyj arkhiv. Vol. 78 (1936): pp. 161-186. There are eight documents here of Sheffer's Russian correspondence, Russian-American Company Reports, and including King Kaumualii's (Sheffer's) signed proclamation of Kauai's Russian protectorateship. These are, specifically:

"1. A proclamation of May 21, 1816, signed by King Tomari (Kaumualii) of the two Sandwich Islands and acknowledging his willingness to accept a Russian Protectorate.
2. A report of a seven-man council of the Russian-American Company on the necessity for strengthening trade relations with the Sandwich Islands, March 26, 1818.
3. An extract from the journal of Dr. George Sheffer, representative of the Russian- American Company, describing his exploits in Hawaii in 1815-7.
4. A note from Sheffer to Alexander I on the political and commercial advantages of improving the Russian position in the Sandwich Islands, February 1819.
5. Comments on each of Sheffer's points by the Department of Manufacturing and Internal Trade, February 1819.
6. A supplement to Sheffer's note to Alexander I, March 2, 1819.
7. A note from the administrative officers of the Russian-American Company to the Department of Manufacturing and Internal Trade, March 18, 1819, concerning the Addition of the Sandwich Islands to the Russian possessions.
8. A letter from Count K. V. Nesselrode, Minister of Foreign Affairs, to O. P. Kozodavlev, Minister of Internal Affairs, June 24, 1819, revealing Alexander I's attitude toward the work of the Russian-American Company."

Okun', Semen Bentsionovich. The Russian-American Company. (Edited, with an introduction by B. D. Grekov, USSR Academy of Sciences, and with a preface by Robert J. Kerner, UC-Berkeley) (Translated by Carl Ginzburg, US Dept. of State). Harvard University Press, Cambridge, Mass. 1951.

Oleksa, Fr. Michael. "Intercessor and Defender of the Oppressed." This is an essay about the glorification of the Venerable Elder Herman of Alaska, presenting the reasons for his opposition to Alexander Baranov. See www.conciliarpress.com/again/index2. Undated.

Oleksa, Archpriest Michael J. "The Creoles and Their Contributions to the Development of Alaska." In Russian America: The Forgotten Frontier. Barbara Sweetland Smith and Redmond J. Barnett, eds. Tacoma: The Washington State Historical Press. 1990. pp. 185-197.

Olivier, Daria. The Burning of Moscow: 1812. (Translated by Michael Heron) Thomas Y. Crowell Company. New York. 1966. See pp. 29-30 for the balloon episode. There is also notice of French sources on pp. 216. This is a wonderful blend of detail and narrative on the topic…still unsurpassed.

O'Moore, Father Maurice M. The Concha Arguello Story: Memory Visits with Old Vinnie. Edited and with historical notes by Richard A. Pierce (see Pierce below). Published together in the Alaska History series No. 48 with the work by Eve Iversen (see Iversen above) by The Limestone Press. Kingston, Ontario and Fairbanks, Alaska. 1998.

Osetrov, Evgenii. Tri zhizni Karamzina: Roman-issledovanie. Izdatel'stvo "Moskovskii rabochii." Moskva. 1989. Here is considerable detail about Karamzin's life with illustrations and artwork on Russian history as related in Karamzin's History of the Russian State. Some of the pictures show various Moscow addresses and places as they were in the 1790s…as the Novikov typography site on pp. 43 and Prince Viazemskii's Ostafievo estate on pp. 204 and discussion of how Karamzin moved into Moscow Governor-General Rostopchin's Moscow home at the end of August 1812…before the fire destroyed his library.

Otto, Gerd (text) et. al. (English translation by Adrian Towersey). Munich. Schmid Verlag. Regensburg, Salzburg, Wien. Undated but recent. This is an English guidebook to Munich, profusely illustrated with an introductory history.

Owens, Kenneth N. (ed.) The Wreck of the Sv. Nikolai. Translated by Alton S. Donnelly. Lincoln and London: University of Nebraska Press (Bison Books). 2001. ISBN 0803286155. See the review by Dennis Reinhartz at the site of the Society for the History of Discoveries:
http://www.sochistdisc.org/2002_book_reviews/owens.htm (accessed May 2005). This work is ostensibly a re-issue of Owens, Kenneth N. (ed./intro.) The Wreck of the Sv. Nikolai: Two Narratives of the First Russian Expedition to the Oregon Country 1808-1810. Translated by Alton S. Donnelly and outstandingly illustrated with drawings by Karen Beyers. Portland: Western Imprints. The Press of the Oregon Historical Society. 1985. In this work historian Owens thoroughly evidences the case that one too-often consulted source on the events in "Tarakanov's" life is that of Ivan Petrov (Petroff), assistant and translator for earlier historian Hubert Howe Bancroft, who, in the late 1870's, fabricated a "Statement of my Captivity among the Californians by a Russian Fur-Hunter" purported to be the work of a "Vasilli Pyotrovitch Tarakanoff," with whom the actual Timofei Tarakanov was subsequently confused. In his introduction and annotations, Owens demonstrates how later treatments fall into falsehoods (e.g. Chevigny's Lord of Alaska on Alexander Baranov who includes mention of Timofei Tarakanov's period of captivity by the California Spaniards and also includes a relation from the monk Juvenal's diary…a Petrov fabrication) because of this work.

Pahinui, Chelle. "The Hawaiian Instrument of Love: The Story of the Ka Ūkēkē." In Kaua'i Traveler magazine, May-August 2008, pp. 82-85. See www.myhawaiitraveler.com and also www.humumoolelo.com since the article is an excerpt from Humu Mo'olelo: Journal of the Hula Arts, a "quarterly dedicated to all things hula."

Palmer, Alan. Napoleon in Russia. Simon and Schuster. New York. 1967. A well-detailed account of balloon mastermind Leppich's activities, pp. 89-90. Palmer is another author with a penchant for complete accuracy, including the full names of involved figures in his index.

Palmer, Colin (with photographs by Maggie Steber and paintings by Jerry Pinkney). "African Slave Trade: The Cruelest Commerce." In National Geographic. Vol. 182, No. 3 (September 1992), pp. 62-91. National Geographic has had other features on the African slave trade, but this article is particularly useful here for its mention of the slave routes to Brazil and for its inclusion of a diagram (pp. 78-9) of the inhumane close arrangement of the slaves in a ship unloaded in Rio de Janeiro as witnessed by George Anton Schaeffer and others from the *Suvorov* in 1814.

Pierce, Richard A. Russia's Hawaiian Adventure, 1815-1817. University of California Press. Berkeley, CA. 1965. This is the seminal scholarly work in English on the Russian actitivities in Hawaii and it includes a very useful bibliography. Pierce, together with Nikolai Rokitiansky, designed a gold-plated medal, minted in 1988, to commemorate Sheffer's founding of Fort Elizabeth on Kauai in 1816. I have one of these medals, very kindly sent to me by Pierce.

Pierce, Richard A. (Translator and introduction). The Russian-American Company: Correspondence of the Governors' Communications Sent: 1818. The Limestone Press, Kingston, Ontario, Canada. 1984. Efforts of Baranov's successor Hagemeister to cope with Hawaiian "damage" of Sheffer. See index.

Pierce, Richard A., ed. Documents on the History of the Russian-American Company. (Translated by Marina Ramsay). The Limestone Press. Kingston, Ontario, Canada. 1976. The documents here describe RAC activities 1795-1808…before Sheffer's involvement, but it has a list of RAC ships…see index pp. 217-8.

Pierce, Richard A., ed., with historical notes. Alaska History No. 48: The Romance of Nikolai Rezanov and Concepcion Arguello: A Literary Legend and Its Effect on California History, by Eve Iversen, and The Concha Arguello Story: Memory Visits With Old Vinnie, by Father Maurice M. O'Moore, O.P. The Limestone Press. Kingston, Ontario, Canada. 1998. An account of Rezanov's betrothal to Concepcion Arguello and all the fascinating historical and cultural ramifications of the story…see Russian literary elaborations, pp. 30-7. See also Rezanov, Nikolai below.

Pierce, Richard A. Russian America: A Biographical Dictionary. The Limestone Press. Kingston, Ontario. 1990.

Pierce, Richard A. "Georg Anton Schaffer, Russia's Man in Hawaii, 1815-1817." in Pacific Historical Review. Vol. XXXII, No. 4 (November 1963), pp. 3-23. A concise view, illustrated, of Sheffer's hawaiian activities. A personal letter from Richard Pierce (30 May, 2001) relates that Schaeffer impressed Captain Lazarev in a trip into London in 1813 with his ability to sing Latin songs...likely the Carmina Burana (cf. Carl Orff's modern versions) in addition to the "Gaudeamus igitur..." graduation ditty. These songs have an interesting history.

Pierce, Richard A. "Russian America and China" and "The Russian-American Company Currency." In Russian America: The Forgotten Frontier. Barbara Sweetland Smith and Redmond J. Barnett, eds. Tacoma: The Washington State Historical Press. 1990. pp. 73-81, pp. 145-155.

PITCAIRN ISLAND. See http://en.wikipedia.org/wiki/Fletcher_Christian for the history of its population by the *Bounty* mutineers. For a description of its absence of anchorage and its topography, see Hibberd (above), pp. 8.

Porter, Robert Kerr, Sir. A Narrative of the Campaign in Russian During the Year 1812. With an essay on subsequent events by William Dunlap. Hartford, Andrus, and Starr. 1815. This work is in ASU Hayden Library's special collections…a leatherbound volume.

Porter, Roy. "Chapter 7: The Eighteenth Century." This 105-pp essay is part of the Stanford University Medical Sciences Organization's history of medicine, available on-line at http:www.stanford.edu/dept/HPS/SciMedOrg/portereighteenthcentury.pdf.
(accessed 4 August, 2003). Porter mentions (pp. 469) the Juliusspital in Würzburg for having a "well planned operating theater" after 1789, mentions (pp. 426) electric shock as becoming common to treat lunatics, and includes (pp.448) a description of German medical education and licensing. Johann Wilhelm Ritter is not mentioned, but Franz Anton Mesmer, Johann Christian Reil, and Johann Peter Frank (prominent contemporary physicians in the area) are.

Postnikov, A. "The First Russian Round-the-World Voyage and its Influence on Exploration and Development of Russian America." At the website publishing the proceedings of a scholarly conference at the Museum of the World Ocean in 2002: http://vitiaz.ru/congress/en/thesis/10.html.

Postnikov, A. "New Source on the History of the First Russian Round-the-World Expedition." This reports the author's finding, in France, of the travel diary of Lt. Makarii Borisovich Ratmanov, Capt. Kruzenshtern's mate on the *Nadezhda*. At the website publishing the proceedings of a scholarly conference in 2002 at the Museum of the World Ocean: http://vitiaz.ru/congress/en/thesis/11.html.

Pratt, High Chiefess Elizabeth Kekaaniau Laanui. Keoua: Father of Kings. Kealii Publishing, 2637 Kuilei Street, Honolulu, Hawaii 96826. Copyright by David Castro. 1999. This is a republication of personal recollections by Keoua's great-great-granddaughter, originally published in 1920, by her great-great-great nephew. Keoua is generally considered the father of Kamehameha I, although Maui King Kahekili late in his life claimed to be Kamehameha's biological father.

Pritchard, Diane Spencer. "Joint Tenants of the Frontier: Russian-Hispanic Relationships in Alta California." In Russian America: The Forgotten Frontier. Barbara Sweetland Smith and Redmond J. Barnett, eds. Tacoma: The Washington State Historical Press. 1990. pp. 81-95.

Pukui, Margaret Kawena, Haertig, E. W., M.D., and Lee, Catherine A. Nana I Ke Kumu (Look to the Source). Volume II. Hu Hanai: Queen Lili'uokalani Children's Center. Honolulu, Hawaii. 1972. An annotated personal relation of Hawaiian personal and social customs.

Putnam, John J. (with photographs by Gordon W. Gahan). "Napoleon." In National Geographic. Vol. 161, No. 2 (February 1982), pp. 142-189. This is a wonderfully illustrated concise treatment of Napoleon and his legacy. Full-page spreads depict the French army's disastrous crossing of the Berezina River in 1812 (pp. 176-7) and the Battle of Waterloo (pp. 182-3).

Raeff, Marc. Michael Speransky. Martinus Nijhoff. The Hague. 1957. This work discusses the influence of francophile advisor Speransky on the government of Tsar Alexander I.

Reitblat, A. I., ed. Vidok Figliarin: Pis'ma i agenturnye zapiski F. V. Bulgarin v III Otdelenie. ("Vidocq Figliarin: Letters and agent notes of F. V. Bulgarin to the Third Section"). Novoe Literaturnoe Obozrenie. Moskva. 1998. Faddei Bulgarin (1789-1859) has a most interesting personal history. He was a soldier in Napoleon's army during the invasion of 1812, but, resettling after the campaign in St. Petersburg, he became an influential publisher and an innovative author of historical novels and fanciful stories. He clashed with Aleksandr Pushkin, and, after the Decembrist Revolt in 1825 began writing notes on the activities of diverse people to Tsar Nicholas I's secret police, the "Third Section." In these notes, using sometimes his pseudonym of "Vidocq Figliarin," (a renowned fictional former-criminal detective) he gives written expression to all manner of candid rumors about the leading personalities of the time. Reitblat's very thorough scholarship, listing and describing all the people mentioned in the thirty-year course of these notes in the indices, is very useful and much appreciated. The conflict with Pushkin is well described in Binyon (above).

Rempel, Gerhard. "Alexander the Sphinx." cf. www.mars.acnet.wnec.edu/~grempel/courses/russia/lectures/17alexander.html.

REZANOV, NIKOLAI PETROVICH (1764-1807) was a Russian court chamberlain, a founder of the Russian-American Company (1799) and first Russian ambassador to Japan (1804-5 incarcerated during the Russians' first circumnavigation on the *Nadezhda* (Captain Ivan Fyodorovich Kruzenshtern) and the *Neva* (Lieutenant Yurii Fedorovich Lisianskii) in 1803-7). He visited Alexander Baranov in Sitka in 1806 and sailed on the *Juno* to San Francisco where his famous "romance" with the daughter of the Presidio's commander, Conchita Arguello, took place (see under Richard Pierce above…work by Eve Iversen…and also the work by Gertrude Atherton above). "Commander Rezanov" has an impressive website devoted to him at http://rezanov.krasu.ru/eng/commander. This is a website created by Krasnoiarsk University in the city where Rezanov died and is buried. It is a particularly rich website, including the possibility for questions and answers by email. In one entry, from http://rezanov.krasu.ru/eng/meeting/index.php?book=rezanov&size=10&page=2, a woman named "Irina" contends with the Krasnoiarsk University website staff over their rights to certain information about Aleksandr Andreevich Baranov. She writes that she is the "pra-pra-pra-pravnuchka" ("great-great-great-great granddaughter") of Baranov…although other sources (see, for example, Hector Chevigny) state that Baranov has no remaining modern issue genealogically. Of interest is the story "Taina komandora" ("Secret of the Commander") by Ol'ga Arzhanykh, describing the moving of Rezanov's remains from Krasnoiarsk's Voskresensky Church, which was destroyed, to the Troitskii Church cemetery, and about the monuments on the sites. For the conflict on the *Nadezhda* see the citation for Fedor Ivanovich Tolstoi (below) also the citations of Postnikov and Sverdlov, as well as the citations for Baranov and Shelikhov. Memoirs by Kruzenshtern, Lisiansky, Shemelin, Lowenstern (best here), Ratmanov (cf. Postnikov), and von Langsdorff all bear on Rezanov as well, showing both positive and negative sides to his character. Rezanov's 16 August 1804 "Report to Tsar Alexander I about the voyage on the vessel *Nadezhda* from Brazil to Kamchatka and activities there prior to the departure for Japan" is document number 51 in Bolkhovitinov and Narochnitskii (1994, above). Rezanov is very diplomatic, trying to minimize the conflict in his report and suggesting that Count Tolstoi's bad behavior was due to youthful "enthusiasm." He requests the Tsar's "most merciful forgiveness" for Tolstoy and suggests that his being removed from participation in the "great exploit" was sufficient punishment (pp. 88, 90). The fact that Rezanov and poet Gavriil Romanovich Derzhavin (1743-1816) were both members of Tsar Paul's "Order of St. John of Jerusalem" is established at the website of the Russian Grand Priory:

http://www2.prestel.co.uk/church/oosj/osj.htm. Of interest also is the website of the Joseph Brodsky Museum in St. Petersburg: http://brodsky.spb.ru/eng/muzuri4.htm. This site gives the history of the "Muzuri House" on Liteinyi Prospect and Pantaleimonovskaia Street (formerly Pestel), nos. 24-7, in which the Nobel Laureate poet spent his youth. The house was located at the address where Nikolai Rezanov had previously built his own wooden mansion. The complete history of the address is given in the chapters by authors A. Kobak and L. Lurie.

Richter, Klaus. Das Leben des Physikers Johann Wilhelm Ritter: Ein Schicksal in der Zeit der Romantik. H. Böhlaus Nachf. Weimar. 2003. ISBN 3740011912. This 265-pp work is available through Amazon.de for Euro 49.95. The blurb mentions that the author, science scholar Klaus Richter, died in 2001, so this is a posthumous publication. See the other biography of Ritter by W. Wetzels (below) for the citation of some anonymous (as opposed to the internet biography by Dean P. Currier (above)) biographies of Ritter. None of the internet sites include any personal details about Ritter, but only synopses of his scientific achievements.

Ridley, Jasper. The Freemasons: A History of the World's Most Powerful Secret Society. Arcade Publishing. New York. 1999. There is a chapter devoted to "Napoleon" and freemasonry.

Ridley, Scott. Morning of Fire: John Kendrick's Daring American Odyssey in the Pacific. William Morrow, an imprint of HarperCollins Publishers, 10 East 53rd St, New York City, NY, 10022, copyright Scott Ridley, 2010. ISBN 978-0-06-170012-5. This work has a useful bibliography. See my review on Amazon at http://www.amazon.com/Morning-Fire-Kendricks-American-Odyssey/product-reviews/B0057DCJMM/ref=cm_cr_pr_btm_link_3?ie=UTF8&showViewpoints=0&pageNumber=3. See also the work by Raymond Massey.

Riehn, Richard K. Napoleon's Russian Campaign. McGraw-Hill. New York. 1990. This is a thorough work of over 500 pp.

Ritchie, John. Lachlan Macquarie: A Biography. Melbourne University Press. Carlton, Victoria. 1986. This is a comprehensive scholarly biography of the "Father of Australia."

RITTER, JOHANN WILHELM. See Currier, Dean P.; Richter, Klaus; and Wetzels, Walter D.

Roberts, James B. and Skutt, Alexander G. The Boxing Register. McBooks Press, London, 3rd ed. 2002. Accessed by excerpts on internet, key words "Boxing Hall of Fame Enshrinees," January 2004.

Rolt, L.T.C. The Aeronauts: A History of Ballooning, 1783-1903. Walker and Company. New York. 1966. A comprehensive and readable account of the history of ballooning...includes all the major figures (e.g. English balloon pioneer James Sadler, whose grave in the churchyard of St. Peter-in-the-east at Oxford University I visited in 2002), but does not mention the 1812 attempt on Napoleon. Napoleon's "pathological...dislike of balloons" is explained (pp. 108-9, 164-5) and an 1804 St. Petersburg ascent by Etienne Robertson and "Prof. Sakharoff of the Russian Academy" (pp. 185-6). From this it emerges that Schaeffer had a place-and-time opportunity to have witnessed the Garnerins' tethered ascent in Nürnburg in 1799. He may have read of others, notably those of Zambeccari (1752-1812). On pp. 161 is given, in a footnote, the "British recipe for balloon varnish" (to prevent permeation loss of hydrogen through the silk...a key limitation to hydrogen ascents). Includes a good timetable and bibliography.

Rostopchin, Fedor Vasilievich. Okh, Frantsuzy! Russkaia kniga (Sovietskaia Rossiia). Moskva. 1992. Published here are the "literary" works of Moscow Governor-General Fyodor V. Rostopchin (1763-1826) as well as 20 of his flyers (afishi) including No. 10 from August 22, 1812 mentioning the balloon project, and from "Notes about the Year 1812" (pp. 242-315...cf. especially pp. 263-4 where is the first person narration of his balloon project involvement and also pp. 301 and 309 about his evacuation of "the charlatan Schmidt" from Moscow). There is no mention of Schaeffer or Schaeffer's role in the communication between Rostopchin and "Shmidt," but notice that Rostopchin does not use the name Leppich in this memoir, written in French in 1825, rendering curious Tolstoy's use of "Leppich" in War and Peace. Curious also is Rostopchin's discussion of the failing "springs," the description of the large balloon as "taffeta," and the specific mention of how "This Shmidt cost us 320 thousand rubles."

Safaralieva, Diliara. "M. T. Tikhonov (1769-1862), Artist-Traveler." In Russian America: The Forgotten Frontier. Barbara Sweetland Smith and Redmond J. Barnett, eds. Tacoma: The Washington State Historical Press. 1990. pp. 33-41.

Samarov, Andrei A. Russkie flotovodtsy: M.P.Lazarev: dokumenty ("Russian Fleet Commanders: M. P. Lazarev: Documents"). Izdatel'stvo Istoriya. Moskva. 1952. Samarov's work, cited in the works of Glynn Barratt (cf. above), focuses on M. P. Lazarev, Captain of the Suvorov on its 1813-6 circumnavigation, but includes memoirs of second officer S. Ya Unkovskiy and assistant navigator Aleksei I. Rossiyskiy.

SAMBIR. For information on the city, see http://www.bohdanyurkiv.cityslide.com, accessed August 9, 2003.

Sawitzki, Sonja. "Die Erschiessung von acht 'Meuteren' an bord des Auswanderersleglers GERMANIA 1824: Bemerkungen zur offizielen Dokumentation." Deutsches Schiffahrtsarchiv (DSA), Bremerhaven, 28, 2005, pp. 267-281. See abstract at: http://www.dsm.museum/Pubs2/28_08.htm. Sawatzki examines documents on the "Germania incident" hearing and concludes that the execution of eight passengers was unjustified. See also Sommer and Weissheimer (below).

Schaeffer ("Ritter von Schäffer Dr./Major Der K. Brasilischen Khrengarde etc. etc. etc."), George Anton Aloysius. Brasilien als Unabhängiges Reich in Historischer, Mercantilischer und Politischer Beziehung. Altona (Hamburg, Germany) bei J. F. Hammerich. 1824. This is the 464-page book Schaeffer wrote and had printed in an edition of 100 copies. It is an important contemporary description of Brazil during the reign of Dom Pedro I. Schaeffer transported the copies himself around Germany and Austria in the late 1820's, giving copies to officials and to citizens in order to convince them of the virtues of emigrating to Brazil. He dedicates the work to "Ihrer Majestät Maria Leopoldine, Kaiserin von Brasilien." There is surprisingly little personal information about Schaeffer in it...no mention at all of his wife and daughter, for example. But there is interesting travelogue, social and political commentary, and laudatory descriptions of Brazil's natural resources and climate, and a copy of the Brazilian constitution. The copy I obtained by interlibrary loan from the St. Vincent Archabbey Library of Latrobe, Pennsylvania was apparently deposited there in 1846. As I first held the precariously aged paper-and-leather-bound book in my hands in 2001, I imagined that Schaeffer himself had also held it in his hands at some time as he distributed his copies in 1824, 177 years before. On Schaeffer, G. A. see: Barratt, Black, Bolkhovitinov, Gomes, Hunsche, the Kaua'i Museum, Oberacker, Mazour, Pierce, Schaeffer (Enrico), Sommer, Teilhet, Vasconcellos, Weissheimer, ...and others (above and below).

Schäffer, Georg Anton von. Brazilie, als onafhankelijk rijk, uit een geschied-koopandel-en staatkundig oogpunt: ook in betrekking tot Europa, beschouwd, in een historisch tafereel van deszelfs afscheiding van Portugal en verheffing tot zelfstandig keizzerijk: benevens een uitvoerig verslag der staatkundige gebeurtenissen in dit rijk, gedurende de jarn 1821, 1822, en 1823. C. L. Schleijer Editorial, Amsterdam, 1825. This is an abbreviated version of the above in Dutch translation.

Schaeffer, Enrico (Prof.). "De velhas Cronicas de Familias: O Cavalheiro George Antonio De Schaeffer (1779-1836) "Vendedor De Almas" e Confidante da Imperatriz D. Leopoldina." in Revista Genealogica Latina. No. 11 (1959). Pp. 157-161. This "Prof. Schaeffer" of Sao Paulo is described here as a "collateral relative" of "Cavalheiro George Antonio De Schaeffer." He had communicated with Richard Pierce in the 1970's, but I have been unable to find him (Richard Pierce sent me what contact information he had, but it was eventually to no avail, as Pierce advised me that he had also lost touch with the man). His photograph accompanying this article indicates, in 1959 or previous, a man of about fifty years of age, so that he is by now likely deceased. Since, according to this Prof. Schaeffer, George Anton Schaeffer left only a daughter behind (the "heiress of a considerable fortune"), the family connection of Prof. Enrico Schaeffer is not clear. Prof. Schaeffer mentions the above-described German book on Brazil by his relative and writes "this very rare book today is worth almost its weight in gold."

Schappelle, Benjamin, Ph.D. The German Element in Brazil: Colonies and Dialect. This 1917 book is available on Amazon.com, but was put online in 2005 by the Gutenberg project at http://www.gutenberg.org/17361/17361-8.txt. Schappelle lists the "founders of Frankenthal Colony" in Brazil's Bahia State as "Peter Weyll and Sauercrater." These were members of a group of Lutherans that George Anton Schaeffer invited into Frankenthal Colony in 1822, a year after its April 4, 1821 founding.

Schmitt, Robert C. (compiler) and Ronck, Ronn (ed.). Firsts and Almost Firsts in Hawaii. A Kolowalu Book. University of Hawaii Press. Honolulu, Hawaii. 1995. A listing of when all sorts of things first appeared or happened in Hawaii.

Schnell, Roland M. "A Short History about Alaska: Working Conditions in Sitka during the Baranov era (1791-1818)." This is a useful work, available at www.rollandinho.com/Rolland_the_artist/Essay_on_Alaska/essay_on_alaska.html.

Schom, Alan. Napoleon Bonaparte. HarperCollins Publishers. New York. 1997. A comprehensive biography of Napoleon, but no mention of balloons.

Schreiber, Peter (text) and Elmar Hahn (photography) and Tina Neil (English transl.). Würzburg: Scenes of a City. Elmar Hahn Verlag. Veitshöchheim. 3rd revised ed. 2001.   This is an illustrated guide book to Würzburg, including a table of "historical dates." There are pictures of the apothecary in the Juliusspital, where Schaeffer studied medicine.

Schütz, Albert J. Things Hawaiian: A Pocket Guide to the Hawaiian Language. Island Heritage Publishing. 99-880 Iwaena Street, Aiea, Hawaii 96701-7299. ISBN 0-89610-307-2.

Schweizer, Niklaus R. A Poet Among Explorers: Chamisso in the South Seas. Herbert Lang Verlag. Bern und Frankfurt. 1973. Illustrations here include a surrealist depiction by Jean Charlot from his Honolulu bank mural of artist Ludwig Choris painting a portrait of Kamehameha, with the poet and scientist Adelbert von Chamisso looking on. Comparing Charlot's Kamehameha (pp.10 and 11) with the from-life likeness by Choris (plate V on pp. 22) makes a person wonder about Charlot's creation, especially since the likeness on his depiction of Choris' easel (pp. 10) clearly resembles Choris' work…? See Charlot (above).

Scofield, John. Hail Columbia. Oregon Historical Society Press. Oregon. 1993. This work, part of the Pacific History Series, deals with the careers of Captains Robert Gray (1755-1806, master of the *Columbia* after which the river is named) and also John Kendrick (1745-1794, master of the *Lady Washington* which participated in internecine battles of the Hawai'ian chiefs).

De Segur, Count Philippe-Paul. Napoleon's Russian Campaign. Translated by J. David Townsend. Houghton Mifflin Company. Boston. 1958. Count de Segur, a French participant in Napoleon's campaign who recorded his experiences in popular memoirs, mentions the balloon project as meant specifically to kill Napoleon. He wrote, that "several attempts to raise it had been made, the wings breaking off each time." De Segur is an uncle of the man who marries Fyodor Rostopchin's daughter Sophia in Paris. Sophie de Segur becomes a prominent author of children's books. Count Phillpe-Paul de Segur's sketch of the "machine diabolique" from witnessing remnants at Vorontsovo and interviewing Russians who had peeped through the fence at the aerostat is apparently the basis for a copy with German caption from 1876 cited by http://www.napoleon-series.org as being in Tsar Alexander's personal historical archives (see Napoleon (Bonaparte), above).

Seiden, Allan. Waikīkī: Magic Beside the Sea. Island Heritage Publishing, 94-411 Kō'aki Street, Waipahu, HI 96797. 2001. ISBN 0-89610-363-3. This large-format coffee-table book has an especially strong author's relation of Waikīkī's pre-history and early days...the description most used to describe it in the time when George Schaeffer leased his agricultural outpost there from Ka'ahumanu. See also the general Waikīkī entry.

Shelikhov, Grigorii Ivanovich. A Voyage to America. Translated by Marina Ramsay with an introduction by Richard A. Pierce. The Limestone Press. Kingston, Ontario. 1981. Evidence of "Inscriptions on the Monument Erected in Memory of Grigorii Shekikhov in Rylsk by (Gavriil Romanovich) Derzhavin with copies, 1795" are given at the website of the US Library of Congress' Meeting of Frontiers Digital Library Project- http://frontiers.loc.gov/intldl/mtfhtml/mfdigcol/lists/mtfyumTitles2.html. The original of the poem *in Derzhavin's actual handwriting*, in which he states "Kolumb zdes' Rosskii pogreben" ("The Russian Columbus is here interred"), is here along with other letters of Shelikhov's and Rezanov's as part of the "Gennadii V. Yudin Collection of Russian-American Company Papers."

Sherwood, Zelie Duvauchelle. Beginners Hawaiian. Ku Pa'a Publishing Incorporated and Press Palcifica, Ltd. PO Box 37460, Honolulu, Hawaii. Fifth Printing, copyright, 1996. ISBN 0-914916-56-4.

SHIPS—whereabouts when. See Govor, Howay, and Pierce.

Silverman, Jane L. Kaahumanu: Molder of Change. Friends of the Judiciary History Center of Hawaii. Honolulu, Hawaii. 1987. A biography of Ka'ahumanu...fresh perspectives on Kaumualii.

Simpson, Alexander. The Sandwich Islands: Progress of Events Since their Discovery by Captain Cook. Smith and Elder. London. 1843.

Sinclair, Marjorie. Nahi'ena'ena: Sacred Daughter of Hawai'i: A Life Ensnared. Mutual Publishing. Honolulu, Hawaii. 1995. A biography of Kamehameha's sacred daughter, stressing the clash of diverse cultural values in her life.

Sinyukov, V. "Short Information about the Marquis de Traverse's Life." This article, about the life of Jean Francoise de Traverse (1754-1831), head of the Russian Navy Ministry during and after the Napoleonic wars, is available at the website of the Museum of the World Ocean in Moscow where is published the proceedings of a 2002 scholarly conference: http://vitiaz.ru/congress/en/thesis/81.html.

SITKA, ALASKA (the modern name for the city where the Russian settlement of Novo-Arkhangelsk was situated). There are many scenic websites for Sitka, but www.untraveledroad.com/USA/Alaska/Sitka/Sitkamap.htm has a useful "photo tour" included in its map giving views of the various sites. Clicking to Sitka through www.basecamp.cnchost.com/fortross.com gets a concise modern synopsis with a brief history. See also the work by Roland Schnell above entitled "A Short History about Alaska: Working Conditions in Sitka during the Baranov era (1799-1818)." See Antonson (above).

Skornjakova, N. N. Staraja Moskva glazami sovremennikov: Moskva pered Otechestvennoj vojnoj 1812 goda. Izobrazitel'noe iskusstvo. Moskva. 1996. An album of art works and essays about Moscow before the 1812 fire.

Smith, Barbara Sweetland and Redmond J. Barnett (editors). Russian America: The Forgotten Frontier. Washington State Historical Society, Tacoma, Washington. 1990. This is a well illustrated anthology of articles on various aspects of Russian American life. Most useful to me were the articles by Richard Pierce on "Russian America and China" and "The Russian American Company Currency," by Richard L. Dauenhauer on "Education in Russian America," by Michael Krauss on "Alaska Native Languages in Russian America," by Stephen W. Haycox on "Merchants and Diplomats: Russian America and the United States," and by Diane Spencer Pritchard on "Joint Tenants of the Frontier: Russian-Hispanic Relationships in Alta California."

Smith, Digby. Borodino. Great Battles Series of the Windrush Press. Gloucestershire. UK. 1998. A very concise treatment of the battle with elaborated command charts and maps.

Soboleski, Hank. Thirty-Nine Biographical Stories: HISTORY MAKERS OF KAUAI. Copyright Hank Soboleski, 2003. Printed in Hawaii (Purchased in Borders Bookstore, Lihue, HI in June 2005). These 2-5-page stories include entries on Kaumuali'i, George Anton Schaeffer, and Deborah Kapule (Kekaiha'akulou). The stories were published between Sept. 2000 and May 2002 as a series entitled "History Makers of Kauai" in Kaua'i's The Garden Island newspaper and there are copies of photographs serving as illustrations for most of the entries, including a rare artist's likeness of Kaumuali'i.

Soboleski, Hank. Twenty Biographical Stories: HISTORY MAKERS OF KAUAI, VOLUME TWO. Copyright Hank Soboleski, undated. This is a clone of the above work, except that the entries, except for six published from Sept. 2003 to July 2004 in the Kauai News Journal, have not been published before. This collection has Soboleski's entry on "Kamehameha I," focusing on Kamehameha's relations with Kaua'i.

Sommer, Friedrich. Major Georg Anton Schäffer und das Schicksal der deutschen Truppenteile in Brasilien 1824-1830. Em "Kalender fuer die Deutschen in Brasilien." (Rotermund-Kalender). S. Leopoldo, 1926, pp. 38 ss.

Sommer, Friedrich. Major G. A. Schäffer un seine Tätigkeit als brasilianischer Werber. Em: "Deutsche Zeitung" (jornol), vol. 48, n. 30 (July 31, 1926), S. Paulo.

Sommer, Friedrich. Wilhelm Ludwig von Eschwege. Das Lebensbild eines Auslanddeutshen mit kulturgeschichtlichen Erinnerungen dan Deutschland, Portugal, und Brasilien, 1777-1855. Em: "Schriften des Deutschen Ausland-Instituts," Stuttgart. Ausland und Heimat Verlags-Aktiengeseltschaft, Stuttgart, 1928. Sommer's view is the least sympathetic of Schaeffer's biographers, depicting the conditions on Schaeffer's transport ships as abominable...justifying the *Germania* mutiny in 1824...and maintaining that Schaeffer's promises to the emigrants were unconscienably inaccurate and that they suffered terribly in the new land as a result. Prof. Enrico Schaeffer contends with Sommer's work in his genealogical treatment of his "collateral relative."

Speakman, Jr., Cummins E. (and update by Jill Engleedow). Mowee: A History of Maui, The Magic Isle. Originally published by Peabody Museum of Salem, Massachusetts, in 1978 with copyright reserved to Mrs. Cummins Speakman. But now it is published by Mutual Publishing, 1215 Center Street, Suite 210, Honolulu, HI 96816 (phone: 808-732-1709 or fax at 734-4094, email at mutual@lava.net). (ISBN 1-56647-489-2). 2001.   Includes source notes and a comprehensive index.

Spoehr, Anne Harding. "Prince George Tamoree: Heir Apparent of Kaua'i and Ni'ihau." In The Hawai'ian Journal of History (A Publication of the Hawaiian Historical Society), Vol. XV (1981), pp. 31-49.

Stauder, Catherine. "George Prince of Hawai'i." In The Hawaiian Journal of History (A Publication of the Hawaiian Historical Society), Vol. VI (1972), pp. 28-44. This work includes the most published likeness of George Prince Kaumuali'i (Tamoree)...a portrait sketched by Samuel Finley Breese Morse, son of George's one-time caretaker Jedidiah Morse (a relative of Samuel F. B. Morse), and later painted, then made into an engraving in New Haven in 1822 by N. and S. S. Jocelyn...see Spoehr below for another derivative likeness and note pp. 43.

Steele, Edward E. Ebbets: The History and Genealogy of a New York Family. The internet site advertising this work includes an outline sketch of seven generations of the Ebbets family, from the seventeenth century through John (Sea Captain, 1775-1835, m. Sarah Woodward) and his younger brother Richard (Sea Captain, 1788-1824, m. Cornelia Wetmore) through Charles Ebbets, modern New York City sports magnate after whom Ebbets Field is named. See http://freepages.genealogy.rootsweb.com/Ebbets.

STORY OF LAHAINA. An excerpt from a report prepared for the County of Mau'i by Community Panning, inc. Published with the permission of the Mau'i Historic Commission by the Lahaina Restoration Foundation, Front Street at Dickenson, Lahaina, Mau'i. 1961. This booklet on Lahaina's history includes a chronological table of significant events in Mau'i's history from 1736 (Death of King Kekaulike) to 1959 (U.S. Statehood).

Strangford (Lord) (British Ambassador to Brazil, 1808-1815). Genealogical information on Percy Clinton Sydney Smythe (1780-1855) is to be found at www.stirnet.com/genealogy under "BE1883 'Smythe of Strangford and Penshurst." Lord Byron's mention of "Strangford" in his satiric poem "English Bards and Scotch Reviewers" can be found in the March 1809 Edinburgh Review. Lord Strangford's papers (e.g. correspondence with British Statesman George Canning (1770-1827)) are accessible at www.nra.nationalarchives.gov.uk/nra/searches/pidocs.asp?P=P26627. Lord Strangford, a "noted English lusophile" was the translator of Portuguese poet Luis de Camoes Poems, published in London in 1803 and in Philadelphia in 1805. A copy of the Philadelphia edition is currently (January 2005) for sale (for $585.00) at Philadelphia Rare Books and Manuscripts Company, Box 9536, Philadelphia, PA 19124 (cf. also www.prbm.com/interest/i.hrm?

Sumter, Thomas (Revolutionary War General and Minister to Brazil 1809-11). See above under Bass, R.D.

SUVOROV ISLAND…now most frequently spelled Suvarov (notice the "a" instead of the Russian stressed "o") or Suwarrow. This island has a colorful history. In the mid-19th century a salvage ship out of Tahiti unearthed a chest on one of Suvarov's islands containing $15,000 in coins dating from the 1740's, a period when the British navigator, George Anson, crossing the Pacific in a fleet led by the *HMS Centurion* lost five ships in a raid on Spanish shipping. In 1876 a New Zealander named Henry Mair discovered a cache of Spanish silver pieces-of-eight in a Suvarov island turtle nest, but reburied the treasure which remains unfound. See also the works by Robert Dean Frisbie (The Island of Desire) and Tom Neale (An Island to Myself) above. Online information is available with photographs and maps at: www.kiaorana.com/Suwarrow, www.janeresture.com/suvarov and at www.ck./suwarrow.htm. A Ukrainian "tall ship" called the *Batkivshchyna* visited Suvarov Island in October of 2003 and recorded that the atoll is now maintained as a preserve. A couple, "Papa" Ioane and Mareko Baker, are the wardens and only residents. They host ships in the inner harbor and entertain crews with tuna meals and shows of sharks for $50.00. See www.batkivshchyna.net/log2003.html.

Sverdlov, L. "Did Chamberlain Rezanov Have the Right to Consider Himself Chief of the Expedition?" At the website of the Museum of the World Ocean, Moscow, which in 2002 hosted a conference and published the proceedings at http://vitiaz.ru/congress/en/thesis/12.html.

Tabrah, Ruth M. Ni'ihau: The Last Hawaiian Island. Press Pacifica, P.O. Box 47, Kailua, Hawaii 96734. Copyright 1987. This is a history of Ni'ihau which includes mention of foreigners' contacts during Kaumualii's rule.

TAMBORA VOLCANO. The eruption of Tambora Volcano on Sumbawa Island in Indonesia in April of 1815 and its effect on worldwide weather is discussed at http://vulcan.wr.usgs.gov/Volcanoes/Indonesia/description_tambora_1815_eruption.htm.

TARAKANOV, TIMOFEI OSIPOVICH. "Calamity of the St. Nikolai: The Narrative of Timofei Tarakanov." Accessed May 2005 at http://www.corvalliscommunitypages.com/Europe/Russia_slavs/wreckofstnikolai.htm. See also Owens (above). The supposition that Tarakanov took a Hawai'ian wife on O'ahu derives from an entry of George Schaeffer's dated May 8, 1817 in his "Journal, January 1815-March 1818" (see Richard Pierce's Russia's Hawaiian Adventure, 1815-1817, University of California Press, Berkeley and Los Angeles, California, 1965, pp. 201 top) in which Schaeffer, expelled in a canoe to the *Kadiak* from Waimea, Kaua'i by Kaumuali'i's "thousand men," sent "our storekeeper Tarakanov" ashore to negotiate. Schaeffer writes that "At first they refused to let him ashore, but on his request to the King, that it was to get Company property, for which he was responsible, *and that he wanted to get his wife and children* (italics mine), they let him pass."

Since Tarakanov only arrived in the Hawai'ian Islands in May/June of 1816 on the *Ilmena* (on which he was most likely unaccompanied), having a "wife and children" to retrieve from Kaua'i by May of 1817 would imply his having taken a native wife who already had children. I believe there are Tarakanovs presently in Alaska who trace their genealogy to him. He could, of course, have had more than one wife.

Tarle, E. V. 1812 god. Izdatel'stvo akademii nauk SSSR. Moskva. 1961. This is the Russian version of the translation below...but is more complete. See str. 570-5 for the balloon episode and the episode of Rostopchin's ordering the execution of the merchant Vereshchagin (episode also depicted in Tolstoy's War and Peace).

Tarle, Eugene. Napoleon's Invasion of Russia, 1812. (Translated by "G.M.") Oxford University Press. New York. 1942. See pp. 217-19 for the balloon episode.

Teilhet, Darwin. Russian Flag Over Hawaii: The Mission of Jeffery Tolamy. Mutual Publishing. Honolulu, HI. 1986. This is an adventure novel about US President Jefferson's "secret agent" in Hawaii...and it includes a fictionalized "Dr. Scheffer" in command of a villainous band of Aleuts.

Ten Bruggencate, Jan K. Hawai'i's Pineapple Century: A History of the Crowned Fruit in the Hawaiian Islands. Mutual Publishing, 1215 Center Street, Suite 210, Honolulu, HI 96816. 2004 (ISBN 1-56647-667-4). This is a fine history of the Hawaiian pineapple industry, attributing the first cultivation of the pineapple in the islands to Don Francisco Marin. See Gast (above) and Lee (above).

Terras, Victor (ed.) Handbook of Russian Literature. Yale University Press. New Haven and London. 1985. This is a compendium of data on Russian literary figures, movements, and genres written by leading U.S. scholars.

Thompson, Scott. Russian Snows: Coming of Age in Napoleon's Army. 2010. See http://www.russiansnows.com. ISBN is 9781466331549. Thompson has a wonderfully educational blog on the 1812 campaign at http://napoleon1812.wordpress.com.

Tikhmenev, P. A. A History of the Russian-American Company. (Translated and edited by Richard A. Pierce and Alton S. Donnelly). University of Washington Press. Seattle and London. 1978. See pp. 120-5 for "Schaffer's" activities.

TOLSTOI, FYODOR IVANOVICH the "American" (1782-1846). On the Krasnoiarsk University website about Nikolai Petrovich Rezanov at http://rezanov.krasu.ru under "World Tour" is a brief article by Phillip Vigel entitled "They said about Count Tolstoy, F.I. that…" that includes an account of Tolstoi's unpleasant pranks on the *Nadezhda*. The "long-tailed macaque monkey" described by Lowenstern (see above) is described as an "orang-outang." Vigel points out that Alexander Pushkin later wrote one of his famous epigrams about Tolstoi, writing that he had "turned a new leaf in life," improving from abject dissipation to being a petty cheat. Pushkin tried to challenge Tolstoi to a duel at one point (ca. 1826-7), but later (1831) negotiated his marriage to Natalia Goncharova through him. Fyodor Ivanovich Tolstoi is mentioned in Aleksandr Griboedov's famous play, Woe From Wit, and described by his relative, Leo Nikolaevich Tolstoi, in his reminiscence, Childhood. The Wikipedia provides an essay on the Russian Tolstoy (Tolstoi) family, which mentions both Fyodor Ivanovich Tolstoi, the "American" and the famous author, Count Leo Nikolaevich Tolstoi (1828-1910) at www.answers.com/topic/tolstoy-1. A really comprehensive genealogy of the Tolstoi family, providing a decipherment of the exact relationship between Fyodor Ivanovich and Leo Nikolaevich (Leo's great grandfather and Fyodor's grandfather was Andrei Ivanovich Tolstoi (1721-1803) is made available by Alexandre Rozanov at http://gencircles.com/users/rozanov/1. See also L. Berdnikov, S. L. Tolstoi, and O. Vozdvizhenskaia.

Tolstoi, Sergei L'vovich. Fyodor Tolstoi-Amerikanets. Gosudarstvennaia Akademiia Khudozhestvennoi Nauki. Moskva. 1926. 96 str. with one frontispiece portrait. This is the seminal biography or memoir about Fyodor Ivanovich Tolstoi-the "American" by the son of the novelist Leo Tolstoy (see below), who was a first cousin, once removed, of Fyodor. See also Berdnikov and O. Vozdvizhenskaia.

Tolstoy, Leo Nikolaevich. War and Peace. (Translated by Louise and Aylmer Maude, edited by Henry Gifford). Oxford University Press. Oxford and New York. 1991 paperback edition. Tolstoy's great historical novel mentions the Russian balloon project in several places. Moscow Governor-General Fedor Vasilievich Rostopchin's "broadsheets" are best described on pp. 799-800. On pp. 805 protagonist Pierre Bezukhov drives, just prior to the battle of Borodino "to the village of Vorontsovo to see the great balloon Leppich was constructing" and records that the project was commissioned by Tsar Aleksandr I himself as evidenced by mentioned instructions in a letter to Rostopchin. In an explanatory note (pp. 1333), Tolstoy mentions facts about "Franz Leppich, a Dutchman," including Leppich's 1811 effort to sell the idea to Napoleon. He states that "Much time and government money were spent on this project," and that "At its trials in November 1812 (This date is curious, because it is after the battle at Borodino and after both Leppich and Schaeffer were in Nizhnii Novgorod and not yet in St. Petersburg) the balloon leaked gas and Leppich disappeared." On pp. 891-2 Tolstoy describes the September 1812 evacuation of Moscow, including Rostopchin's use of "one hundred and thirty six (carts which) removed the balloon that was being constructed by Leppich." Tolstoy's very use of the name "Leppich" is curious since "Leppich's" Russian contemporaries only knew him by his secret nom-de-guerre of "Schmidt," given to him by Tsar Aleksandr's command staff, and Rostopchin's memoirs (ostensibly a Tolstoy source on this) mention only "Schmidt" (cf. Rostopchin's memoirs, above).

Travers, B.H. The Captain-General: Being a Study of Lachlan Macquarie, Governor of New South Wales, 1809-1821. Shakespeare Head Press. Sydney. 1953. This biography of Macquarie focuses on his Governorship in Sydney. It is filled with details, charts, maps, and illustrations.

TRAVERSÉ, (Jean Francoise) (1754-1831)…French Marquis and Russian Admiral…see Sinyukov above.

Treadwell, John. Narrative of Five Youths from the Sandwich Islands. J. Seymour, NY, 1816. (see Dwight above and Warne below). This work is described by Anne Harding Spoehr as a "solid starting place" on the interesting character of George "Humehume" Prince Kaumuali'i (Tamoree). The Five youths are: Henry Obookiah ("Opuka'ia" see Dwight, Warne, Stauder), Thomas Hopoo (see Greer), William Tennooe (Keno'i...?), John Honooree (Honoli'i), and George Prince Tamoree. See Warne (below).

Tregaskis, Richard. The Warrior King: Hawaii's Kamehameha the Great. MacMillan Publishing Co., inc. New York. 1973. See the family chart before the preface including an indirect assertion by Maui King Kahekili that he was Kamehameha's real father.

Trei, Peter. An essay on the Bavarian "Illuminati," freemasons, and modern mythology. At http://a-albionic.com/a-albionic/gopher/conspiracy/illuminati/illuminati.txt, accessed August 6, 2003.

Troyat, Henri. Alexander of Russia: Napoleon's Conqueror. (Translated by Joan Pinkham). E.P. Dutton, Inc. New York. 1982. This treatment has no mention of the balloon episode, but has a most useful "Chronology" (pp. 312-22).

Ullman, Dana, M.P.H... A Condensed History of Homeopathy. An excerpt from Discovering Homeopathy: Medicine for the 21st Century. At http://www.healthy.net/asp/templates/article.asp?PageType=Article&ID=860 accessed April 11, 2002.

Uffindell, Andrew. Great Generals of the Napoleonic Wars and Their Battles, 1805-1815. Spellmount Ltd. The Old Rectory, Staplehouse, Kent, TN12 0AZ, UK. 2003. This work gives a new look, including recent research, at the lives and military achievements of Napoleon himself and eleven other leading Generals of his time: (French) de Beauharnais, Lasalle, (English) Moore, Wellington, Hill, (Austrian) Archduke Charles, (Prussian) Blücher, Gneisenau, and (Russian) Bagration, Barclay de Tolly, Kutusov.

Vasconcellos, Mario de e Andrä, Helmut. Weltumsegler, Naturforscher, Seelenverkäufer und Diplomat. Beitrage zum Lebensbild des Oberst-Leutnant Ritter Dr. G. Ant. Von Schäffer. Em: "Deutscher Morgen" (jornol), S. Paulo, 16 e 23. 2, 1940, 1.3. e 8.3.1940.

Vasconcellos, Mario de e Andrä. Schäffer e Mello Mattos nos Estados da Alemanha. Em: Archivo Diplomatico da Independencia, Vol. IV. Rio de Janeiro, 1922.

VENIAMINOV, FATHER IOANN ((1797-1879), born Ivan Popov in Siberia, later made Metropolitan and still later a Saint with the name of Innokentii). Fr. Veniaminov did not get to Alaska until 1823, but sources on him describe life in Alaska and in Sitka and deal with issues pertinent to the story here. See the Congress of Russian Americans' site at www.russian-americans.org/CRA_History.htm. For further elucidation of the relations between the Russian Orthodox priests and Russian-American Company Manager Alexander Baranov, see the citations on Elder Herman above.

Volkov, Genrikh. Mir Pushkina: Lichnost', Mirovozzrenie, Okruzhenie. ("The World of Pushkin: Personality, World View, Circle of Acquaintances"). Molodaia gvardiia. Moskva. 1989. This work treats Pushkin's personal relationships with several of the characters of this book…notably Fyodor Tolstoy (cf. pp. 77-80).

Von Faber du Faur, Christian Wilhelm. Napoleon's Army in Russia: The Illustrated Memoirs of Albrecht Adam-1812.

VORONTSOVO. Kratkii ekskurs v istoriiu Vorontsovo ("A Short Excursion into the History of Vorontsovo") Http://www.mmt.ru/vorontsovo.net/map/history.htm. This internet site, on the Moscow "microregion" of Vorontsovo, is very interesting and includes significant mention of the balloon project of 1812. It clarifies ownership of the estate before and after the conflict.

Vozdvizhenskaia, Ol'ga. "Tolstoi-Amerikanets," in Penthouse (The Russian version), Dekabr' 2007, str. 98-101 in the section entitled "Nravy" ("Morals"), illustrated feature.

Viazemskii, P. A. Stikhotvoreniia. ("Verse"). Vstupitel'naia stat'ia i premechaniia L. Ia. Ginzburg. (Introductory article and notes by L. Ia. Ginzburg). Biblioteka poeta. Sovietskii pisatel'. Leningrad. 1958. This is the volume on the poet and memoirist, Pyotr Andreevich Vyazemskii (1792-1878), of the renowned "Library of the Poet" series. It includes Vyazemskii's 1818 poem "To Tolstoy" about Fyodor Ivanovich Tolstoy, "the American."

Viazemskii, P. A. Zapisnye knizhki (1813-1848). ("Note books (1813-1848)"). V. S. Nechaeva, red. (ed.). Izdatel'stvo Akademii Nauk SSSR. Moskva. 1963. Here are Prince Vyazemskii's notebooks of all manner of personal, literary, and political observations. Editor Nechaeva's thorough listing and describing of the people mentioned in an index is very useful. When you want to know who is who when reading about events in early 19th century Russia (especially St. Petersburg around the time of the Decembrist Revolt in 1825), this is the place.

Waikīkī: Images of Yesteryear. A 48-pp. book of historical photographs by Mutual Publishing, 1215 Center Street, Suite 210, Honolulu, HI 96816. 2007. (ISBN 978-1-56647-824-3). See also White, Kai and Kraus, Jim, and Seiden, Allan.

Walker, Mack. Germany and the Emigration: 1816-1885. Harvard University Press. Cambridge, Massachusetts. 1964. PP. 38-41 lists the German recruitment activities of "Major Schaffer"...and "a certain Dr. Cretzshmar" from 1822-30, obtained from a US Library of Congress archive (LC PrAA 2-11...see pp. 253).

Wall, Bill. "The Chess Automatons by Bill Wall." An e-excerpt at http://www.geocities.com/siliconvalley/lab/7378/automat.htm, accessed August 9, 2003.

WAR OF 1812-4. US/Great Britain. See http://members.tripod.com/~war1812/intro or www.warof1812.ca/1812events.htm. Last accessed May 2005.

Warne, Douglas. "George Prince Kaumuali'i: The Forgotten Prince." In The Hawaiian Journal of History (A Publication of the Hawaiian Historical Society), Vol. XXXVI (2002), pp. 59-71.

Warne, Douglas. Humehume of Kaua'i: A Boy's Journey to America, an Ali'i's Return Home. Kamehameha Publishing, 567 South King Street, Honolulu, HI 96813, 2008 (ISBN 978-0-87336-151-4). A very positively impressive recent scholarly work on Kaumuali'i's son Humehume—his life in America and after his return to Kaua'i in 1820. It includes some great detail...for example part of Kaumuali'i's mele inoa chant, and the roster of the U.S. ship *Wasp* from 1813 showing "Geo. Prince" as a member of its Marine contingent. Good relation of events about Kaumuali'i, Kekaiha'akulou, Ka'ahumanu, Kalanimoku, Keali'iahonui and interisland politics after the 1819 death of Kamehameha and of Liholiho. 237 pp. with color ill. See also Dwight, Joesting, Lydgate, Mills, Soboleski, Treadwell, and Zambucka.

Watrous, Stephan. "The Cultural History of Fort Ross: Outpost of an Empire—Russian Expansion to America." Accessed May 2005 at http://www.mcn.org/1/rrparks/fortross/Russian%20American%20Company.htm.

Weissheimer, Egidio. "Imagração Alemã no RS." This work on the German Emigration of 1824- to the Rio Grande do Sul State of Brazil, expanding the information given by Oberacker *by listing the specific families brought to Brazil by George Schaeffer's expeditions*, was accessed in August of 2008 at www.marquardt.com.br/hist_imigr1.htm. See also Oberacker (above), Mack, Luebke, and http://heuser.pro.br/getperson.php?personID=O22239&tree=heusers. In this latter source (see also Gomez, Dival da Costa above, which has similar data in a relation from Hunsche and Oberacker) one can sleuth out of the genealogy of the Heuser family that a marriage took place (2 June, 1824) upon the later troubled ship *Germania* while it was waiting in the port of Glückstadt to depart for Brazil. This was the marriage, witnessed by ship's Captain Hans Voss and Schaeffer's Expedition Administrator Ferdinand von Kiesewetter and performed by later prominent pastor Johann Georg Ehlers, of Hanover-born 28-year-old mercenary Heinrich Hubertus Stock and Thüringen-born 30-year-old Dorothea Elisabeth Mentz, who was listed on board with her parents, Johann Liborious and Magdalena Ernestina (Lips) Mentz, as future settlers. From the Weissheimer source and others (e.g. Oberacker and the site http://www.es.beekeeping.wikia.com/wiki/Georg_Anton_von_Sch%C3%A4ffer) we can see the record that eight of the mercenaries mutinied against the ship's officers and the expedition's administration while in the Bay of Biscay in late August and early September of 1824. An initial quelling of the mutiny by force only led to another mutiny attempt in which the mutineers threatened to set the ship afire. By assent of the entire ship's company, according to the record of a subsequent investigation, these eight mutineers were then executed…most sources say shot, but one says hanged. Heinrich Stock was not listed among those who arrived in Brazil. His date of death in the family genealogy is listed as "Bef 6 Nov 1824" (the day of the *Germania's* arrival in Brazil)…ERGO, he must have been one of the eight executed mutineers. In the genealogy one notes also the interesting fact that Dorothea, who remarried in Brazil in 1848 and died in 1866, had a daughter named Ernestina who was 24 years old at the time of the second marriage, indicating that she was the mutineer Stock's biological daughter. My conclusion from these diverse facts is that Dorothea Mentz Stock (later Engelhaupt), then pregnant with Stock's child, and her parents gave assent to his execution. Another online source (July 2009 accessed) that has Weissheimer's excellent work is http://www.mluther.org.br/Imigracao/imigracao.ii.htm.
Also useful is the Wikipedia site: http://en.wikipedia.org/wiki/German_Brazilian See also the "contrary" 2005 article on this by Sonja Sawitzki (above) and also Sommers (above).

Wetzels, Walter D. Johann Wilhelm Ritter: Physik im Wirkungsfeld der deutschen Romanitk. Walter de Gruyter. Berlin and New York. 1973. This is a publication related to the topic of Prof. Wetzels' 1968 Princeton University doctoral dissertation. Wetzels is now, since 1996, a Professor Emeritus of

German Studies at the University of Texas. Some English-language internet sites on Ritter's scientific achievements include: http://www.voltaicpower.com/Biographies/RitterBio.htm; http://www.hao.ucar.edu/public/education/images.jwritter.html; and http://www.geocities.com/bioelectrochemistry/ritter.html. All, accessed July 25, 2003, include likenesses of Ritter.

Wheeler, Mary Elizabeth. "Empires in Conflict and Cooperation: the 'Bostonians' and the Russian-American Company." Pacific Historical Review. No. 40, 4 (November, 1971), pp. 419-441.

Wheeler, Mary Elizabeth. The Origins and Formation of the Russian-American Company. University of North Carolina at Chapel Hill Ph.D. Dissertation, History, 1965. Published by University Microfilms, Inc., 66-4735, Ann Arbor, Michigan, 1980.

Wheelock, Frederic M. Latin Literature: A Book of Readings from Cicero, Livy, Ovid, Pliny, the Vulgate, Bede, Caedmon, Medieval Poetry. Waveland Press, Inc. Prospect Heights, Illinois. 1969. ISBN 0-88133-721-8. Notes here describe the history of the Carmina Burana and include the Latin lyrics with accompanying glossary and notes.

White, Kai and Kraus, Jim. Waikīkī: Images of America. Arcadia Publishing. Charleston, South Carolina and elsewhere. 2007 (ISBN 978-0-7385-4880-7). This work, published by the leading local history publishers (see www.arcadiapublishing.com), is essentially 128 pages of historical photographs with the captions providing the informational text. But it is very well done and is a fine resource on the history of Waikīkī.

Whitworth, Robert. Flights of Fancy: A Short History, or Overview, of Ballooning during the Georgian and Regency eras: Together with Interesting Eye-witness Accounts, to which are Added Numerous Woodcuts and Descriptions of the Various Balloons. This is a 35-page "E-book" at http://www.printsgeorge.com/ArtEccles_Aeronauts1.htm accessed January 15, 2002.

Wichman, Frederick B. Kauai: Ancient Place Names and Their Stories. A Latitude 20 Book. University of Hawaii Press. Honolulu. 1998. This work includes stories of Kaumualii's personal history and of his parents and accession to rule.

Wichman, Frederick B. Na Pua Ali'i O Kaua'i: Ruling Chiefs of Kaua'i. A Latitude 20 Book. University of Hawaii Press. Honolulu. 2003. This is a historical tracing of the geneology of the Kaua'i chiefs and associated legends taken from the chants, which constitute the oral history. Geneologies are given in table form at the end.

Williams, Julie Stewart. Kamehameha the Great. (revised ed., illustrations by Robin Yoko Burningham). Kamehameha Schools/Bernice Pauahi Bishop Estate. Honolulu. 1993. A reader for young people ("Intermediate Reading Program") about Kamehameha's life, stressing his Hawaiian native upbringing.

Williams, Julie Stewart. From the Mountains to the Sea: Early Hawaiian Life. (Illustrated by Robin Yoko Racoma). Kamehameha Schools/Bernice Pauahi Bishop Estate. Honolulu. 1997. An attempt to portray Hawaiian life as it was 500 years ago, with explanations of Hawaiian terms, maps and drawings of various aspects of life.

Willmann, Josef. Münnerstadt: wie es einst war. Verlag T. A. Schachenmayer. Bad Kissingen. 2000. This is a local historian's work on Münnerstadt, complete with names and business registries and 236 historical illustrations, maps, and photographs. Several "Schäfers" are mentioned and there is a "Schäfergasschen" street in the town.

Wisniewski, Richard A. The Rise and Fall of the Hawaiian Kingdom: A Pictorial History. Pacific Basin Enterprises, P.O. Box 8924, Honolulu, Hawaii 96830. 1979.

Withington, Antoinette. The Golden Cloak: The Romantic Story of Hawaii's Monarchs. Mutual Publishing, 1215 Center Street, Suite 210, Honolulu, HI 96816 (cf. Cook, Chris for telephone and fax numbers). 1986. (ISBN 0-935180-26-5). www.mutualpublishing.com and email at mutual@lava.net. This work includes a wonderfully detailed telling of the story of Kamehameha's life and of Hawaii in the post-contact days. The Russian episode is treated primarily, but also by Captain Otto von Kotzebue's relation of Kamehameha's telling him about his problems with his "Russian predecessor in the islands," George Schaeffer.

Würzburg (Germany). Scenes and descriptions of Würzburg may be found on the internet. A useful site (accessed 4 August, 2003) is http://www.romanticroad.com/wurzsigh.htm.

Zambucka, Kristin. Princess Ka'iulani of Hawai'i: The Monarchy's Last Hope. Mutual Publishing, LLC, 1215 Center Street, Suite 210, Honolulu, HI 96816, ISBN 1-56647-710-7, March 205 printing, based on Kristin Zambucka copyright from 1998, originally published by Green Glass Productions. Cf. www.mutualpublishing.com.

Zambucka, Kristin (compiler). Kaumualii: King of Kauai: Excerpts from Early Writers (and a few later ones) on the Life and Times of Kaumualii, the King of Kauai. Published by Kawananakoa. 1999. This isn't so much a biography as a compilation of recorded impressions of Kaumualii and the associated events of his life. Schaeffer is substantially included, with texts of his documents and his likeness. The work I have has no table of contents, no foreword or prologue or textual commentary, and no list of sources or index, but still it is useful to have so many recorded impressions in one place. See also Warne above, Soboleski and Joesting.

Zambucka, Kristin. <u>Kalakaua: Hawaii's Last King</u>. Mana Publishing Co., Box 22525, Honolulu, HI 96823-2525, ISBN 0-931897-04-1, March 2006 second printing edition, from Kristin Zambucka copyright 2002.

Zamoyski, Adam. <u>Moscow 1812: Napoleon's Fatal March</u>. HarperCollins Publishers. London. 2004. I didn't see this work until I had completed the writing of my book's section on Napoleon's invasion of Russia in 1812. There was not much new to me in it, but I note that the author, in his introductory note, explains that his principal aim is to tell again the extraordinary story, surmounting the political and nationalistic bias of previous narrations and focusing on the individual human aspects of the struggle. In general I think he does this well. I notice the lack, however, of internet sources in the bibliography of sources at the end. I can only wonder what he would think if he were to click his way through the "1812" project of www.museum.ru with its wellspring of detail and illustration, or go through the articles by Alexander Mikerabidze in the www.Napoleon-series.org pages. Yet I applaud the rigor shown in his index, where he gives the full names of characters, including the Russian patronymics whenever possible, and confines himself to the rank of his characters at the time of the conflict, instead of citing them as holding the highest rank achieved in their lives. He does mention "Leppich" and the "aerostat" as a failed project of Governor-General Rostopchin's in a single paragraph on page 243. Also, the book's illustrations, especially the ones from contemporary artists, are very fine and well captioned. The caption under Rostopchin's likeness by Orest Adamovich Kiprensky labels Rostopchin as "the destroyer of Moscow" and says that he was "possibly mad."

Zhilin, P. A. <u>Otechestvennaia Voina 1812 Goda</u>. Izdatel'stvo "Nauka." Moskva. 1988.

I hope the readers are moved to give some thought to the large number of real historical figures that my "resurrection" of George Anton Schaeffer has brought into their awareness: Napoleon Bonaparte and several of his marshals, Archduke Ferdinand III of Tuscany, Johann Wilhelm Ritter, several prominent aerostiers including the Garnerins, the Blanchards and Count Zambeccari, Tsar Aleksandr I, the Grand Duke Konstantin, Tsar Nicholas I, Nikolai Rumyantsev, John Quincy Adams, Fyodor Rostopchin, Franz Leppich the balloon master, Russian Generals Platov, Tormasov, Bagration, Barclay de Tolley, Kutuzov, author and editor Nikolai Karamzin, the poet Gavril Derzhavin, Aleksandr Pushkin, Russian-American Company founder Grigorii Shelikhov, Nikolai Rezanoff, Georg Heinrich von Langsdorff, Count Fyodor Tolstoi the "American," Russian sea captains Krusenshtern, Kotsebue, Lazarev, Lisianskii and Hagemeister, Lachlan Macquarie, Aleksandr Baranov, Peter Dobell, John Jacob Astor, Stephen Girard, Kings Kamehameha and Kaumuali'i, Queens Ka'ahumanu, Keōpuōlani and Kekaiha'akulou (Deborah Kapule), Kalanimoku, Humehume, Governor Homa, Don Francisco de Paula Marin, John Elliot de Castro, Archibald Campbell, Isaac Davis, John Young, and a host of central pacific sea captains, Anders Ljungstedt, Apo-Tsy, Ching Shi the woman pirate, Dom João of Portugal and Brazil, Dom Pedro I, Dom Miguel I, Empress Leopoldina and her daughter who becomes Maria II of Portugal, Klemens von Metternich, Emperor Franz I, King Max I of Bavaria...the list goes on and on.

–Lee B. Croft

Illustrations in the Book:

1. A Likeness of George Anton Schaeffer at 34 years of age............page 11
2. The *Suvorov's* Captain Mikhail Petrovich Lazarev at 50.............page 12
3. The "Turk" Chess Automoton...page 15
4. Botofogo Bay, Rio de Janeiro, ca. 1814...............................page 24
5. Regent Dom João VI of Portugal..page 31
6. Regent Dom João and Dona Carlota......................................page 38
7. U.S. Minister to Brazil, General Thomas Sumter....................page 39
8. Herr Doctor Georg Heinrich von Langsdorff.........................page 42
9. A Single Unidentified Sky Object......................................page 55
10. The Formation of Unidentified Sky Objects.........................page 56
11. Australian Governor Lachlan Macquarie..............................page 59
12. Old Sitka, Alaska's, Castle Hill...page 81
13. Russian America's Governor Aleksandr Andreevich Baranov......page 82
14. Louis Glanzman's painting of the "Battle of Sitka"..................page 84
15. A Model of the Russian Navy Sloop *Neva*............................page 85
16. Russian Navy Lieutenant Yurii Fyodorovich Lisianskii.............page 86
17. Jacques Arago's "Execution of a Kapu Violator by Club"..........page 110
18. Jacques Arago's "Execution of a Kapu Violator by Strangling"...page 111
19. Jacques Arago's Sketch of John Young................................page 115
20. Hawai'ian King Kamehameha I, by Louis Choris in 1816..........page 121
21. Nathaniel Dance-Holland's Painting of Captain James Cook........page 131
22. Johann Zoffany's Painting of "The Death of Captain Cook".........page 132
23. A Sketch of Captain Amasa Delano....................................page 142
24. Hawai'ian Queen Ka'ahumanu by Louis Choris, 1816...............page 145
25. Hawai'ian "Sacred Queen," Keōpuōlani................................page 149
26. The "Black Rock" Leaping Place, Ka'anapali, Mau'i.................page 158
27. A Likeness of Don Francisco de Paula Marin........................page 162
28. Enoch Wood Perry's "Diamond Head From Waikīkī"...............page 165
29. The Nu'uanu Pali Battle Scene"...page 169
30. A Map of Kaua'i...page 185
31. John Webber's "A Heiau in Waimea"..................................page 187
32. John Webber's "An Inland View of Atooi (Kaua'i)"..................page 188
33. Brook Kapūkuniahi Parker's Portrait of Kaumuali'i..................page 194
34. Photograph of "Three Aleuts in a Baidarka".........................page 206
35. Photograph of the Na Pali Coast of Kaua'i...........................page 237
36. Photograph of Kaua'i's Hanalei Valley................................page 238
37. A Likeness of Waimea's Fort Elizaveta, ca. 1816...................page 241
38. Kaua'i's Chiefess Kamakahelei..page 243
39. Brook Kapūkuniahi Parker's "Spirit Leap From Wailua Falls".....page 245
40. Brook Kapūkuniahi Parker's "Dr. Schaeffer and Kekaiha'akulou"..page 261
41. Battle of Borodino Generals' Statues and Hayden L. Croft.........page 331
42. Author Lee B. Croft and RAK ship *Kadiak*'s cannon...............page 349
43. Ardis Hertford's 1845 Posthumous Portrait of Dr. Schaeffer........page 357
44. 1876 German Sketch of Leppich's Balloon to Kill Napoleon.........page 373